PROCEEDINGS OF THE
SIXTEENTH INTERNATIONAL CONGRESS
OF PAPYROLOGY

AMERICAN STUDIES IN PAPYROLOGY
VOLUME 23

PROCEEDINGS OF THE SIXTEENTH INTERNATIONAL
CONGRESS OF PAPYROLOGY

edited by
Roger S. Bagnall, Gerald M. Browne, Ann E. Hanson,
and Ludwig Koenen (Chairman)

PROCEEDINGS OF THE SIXTEENTH INTERNATIONAL CONGRESS OF PAPYROLOGY

New York, 24–31 July 1980

edited by

Roger S. Bagnall, Gerald M. Browne, Ann E. Hanson,
and Ludwig Koenen (Chairman)

SCHOLARS PRESS
1981

Distributed by
Scholars Press
101 Salem Street
P.O. Box 2268
Chico, CA 95927

PROCEEDINGS OF THE SIXTEENTH INTERNATIONAL CONGRESS OF PAPYROLOGY

edited by
Roger S. Bagnall, Gerald M. Browne, Ann E. Hanson,
and Ludwig Koenen (Chairman)

PA
3339
.I5
1981

Library of Congress Cataloging in Publication Data

International Congress of Papyrology (16th : 1980 :
    Columbia University)
    Proceedings of the Sixteenth International
Congress of Papyrology.

    (American studies in papyrology ; v. 23)
    English, French, and German.
    1. Manuscripts (Papyri) — Congresses. I. Bagnall,
Roger S. II. Title. III. Series.
PA3339.I5   1981   091   81–9025
ISBN 0–89130–516–5   AACR2

Printed in the United States of America
1   2   3   4   5   6
Edwards Brothers Inc.
Ann Arbor, Michigan 48104

PREFACE

The Sixteenth International Congress of Papyrology was held
at Columbia University in the City of New York from the 24th to the
31st of July 1980. The bulk of the papers presented to the Congress are published in this volume. Of those which are not, some
were preliminary sketches of work which appears elsewhere or presen-
tations of material which has appeared or will appear in book form.
A number of papers have been published elsewhere because the full
presentation of the subject required more space than could be allowed it in the *Proceedings*. Of these, the following have come to
my notice:

> R. Bogaert, "Les reçus d'impots en argent thébains de
> l'époque romaine et les banques," in *Chronique
> d'Egypte*;
> G. M. Browne, "Griffith's Old Nubian Lectionary," in
> the Acts of the First Nilo-Saharan Linguistics
> Colloquium (8-10 September 1980, Leiden);
> Helen M. Cockle, "Pottery Leases from Oxyrhynchus," in
> *Journal of Roman Studies*;
> W.E.H. Cockle, "A New Greek Glossary from Oxyrhynchos,"
> in *Bulletin of the Institute of Classical Studies*
> (London);
> Knut Kleve, "Lacunology: on the use of Computer Methods
> in Papyrology," in *Symbolae Osloenses* 56 (1981),
> with I. Fonnes;
> †H. C. Youtie, "Πράγματα μετέωρα, or Unfinished Business,"
> in *Scriptiunculae* IV.

It is a pleasure to be able to thank here all those who helped
to make the Congress possible: in the first place, all those who
assisted me with the work of preparing and carrying out the practical arrangements: Robert Brennan, Curtis Church, Elsa Gibson, Ralph
Keen, Lavinia Lorch, Geoffrey Mellor, Royce Morris, Michael Peachin,
Lin Welden, Stephen Wortman, and six members of my family: Alexander
Bagnall, my son; Catherine Bagnall and Anne Yardley, my sisters;
Robert Bagnall, my brother; Peggy and Roger Bagnall, my parents; and
Whitney Bagnall, my wife. Without their help, nothing would have
been possible. Bernard V. Bothmer and Robert Bianchi of the Brook-
lyn Museum, and Associate Provost Michael Mooney of Columbia Uni-
versity made many official operations run smoothly. The financial

Preface

assistance of various persons and agencies was also indispensable:
in the first place, the National Endowment for the Humanities
(through grant RD-0037-79-0443); and the American Society of Papyrologists, the Brooklyn Museum, Columbia University, the International Research and Exchanges Board, Meyer Reinhold, and the
Xerox Corporation. Much of the funds provided by these went for
travel assistance to participants in the Congress, and I know I
speak for them as well as for myself in renewing here our thanks.

Finally, I close by expressing my gratitude to the editorial
board of American Studies in Papyrology, especially to its chairman, Ludwig Koenen, for much hard work on this volume; and to our
typist, Joann Burnich, for coping so expertly with a manuscript of
such size and difficulty.

4 July 1981

Roger S. Bagnall
for the Organizing Committee

J. F. Gilliam, Chairman
Robert S. Bianchi, Co-Chairman
Roger S. Bagnall, Secretary
Whitney S. Bagnall
Alan Cameron
Lionel Casson
Ann E. Hanson
William V. Harris
Albert Henrichs
Ludwig Koenen
Naphtali Lewis
Timothy T. Renner
Morton Smith
Susan A. Stephens

TABLE OF CONTENTS

Table of Contents

Table of Contents

Table of Contents

-x-

Table of Contents

LIST OF PARTICIPANTS

ALLAM, Nimet I.
8 Saleh Ayoub Street, Apt. 103
Zamalek, Cairo
EGYPT

*ALY, Zaki
31 Sharieh Ismail Ramzy
Heliopolis, Cairo
EGYPT

ANDORLINI, Isabella
Via de' Baldovini 14
50126 Firenze
ITALY

+ Gabrielle Bogani Andorlini

ANGELI, Anna
Centro Internazionale per lo
  Studio dei Papiri Ercolanesi
Via Mezzocannone 16
80134 Napoli
ITALY

ARNOTT, W. G.
School of Classics
University of Leeds
Leeds LS2 9JT
ENGLAND

AURICCHIO, Francesca Longo
Piazza Donn' Anna 9
80123 Napoli
ITALY

+ Ferdinando Auricchio
  Alberto Auricchio

BAGNALL, Robert G.
125 Kellogg Street
Oyster Bay, New York 11771

BAGNALL, Roger S.
606 Hamilton Hall
Columbia University
New York, New York 10027

BAGNALL, Whitney S.
560 Riverside Drive, Apt. 18-J
New York, New York 10027

BEARZOT, Cinzia
Istituto di Papirologia
Università Cattolica del S. Cuore
Largo A. Gemelli, 1
20123 Milano
ITALY

BIANCHI, Robert S.
The Brooklyn Museum
Eastern Parkway
Brooklyn, New York 11238

BIEZUNSKA-MALOWIST, Iza
Brzozowa 10/4
00286 Warsaw
POLAND

BINGEN, Jean
97 avenue des Mimosas
1150 Bruxelles
BELGIUM

+ Marthe Bingen

BLANCHARD, Alain
17, avenue Jeanne d'Arc
92160 Antony
FRANCE

BOGAERT, R.
Koning Albertslaan 38
9000 Gent
BELGIUM

+ J. Bogaert-Heremans
  René Heremans
  Vera Heremans
  Dominique Heremans

BONNEAU, Danielle
17, rue Dantan
92210 Saint Cloud
FRANCE

+ Pierre-Arnand Grenade

---

* = Giving papers by title or in absentia

List of Participants

BORKOWSKI, Zbigniew
Institute of Papyrology
University of Warsaw
Warszawa 64
POLAND

BOWMAN, Alan K.
Christ Church
Oxford OX1 1 DP
ENGLAND

BRASHEAR, William
Staatliche Museen
Schloss-Str. 70
1 Berlin 19, Charlottenburg
GERMANY (BRD)

BROWNE, Gerald M.
4072 Foreign Languages Building
University of Illinois
Urbana, Illinois 61801

BÜLOW-JACOBSEN, Adam
Lundsgade 5, 4
2100 Kobenhavn
DENMARK

+ Berthe Bülow-Jacobsen

CAPASSO, Mario
Via Maglione 34
80144 Napoli
ITALY

+ Gabriella Caliman Capasso

CARRIÉ, Jean-Michael
Via Giulia 188
00186 Roma
ITALY

CASARICO CIGOLINI, Loisa
Via Cesariano 9
20155 Milano
ITALY

CLARYSSE, Willy
Lingestraat 17
2314 TG, Leiden
NETHERLANDS

+ Anny Clarysse

COCKLE, Helen M.
Department of Greek
University College London
Gower Street
London WC1E 6BT
ENGLAND

COCKLE, W.E.H.
Department of Greek
University College London
Gower Street
London WC1E 6BT
ENGLAND

COHEN, Getzel M.
Department of Classics
University of Cincinnati
Cincinnati, Ohio 45221

COLES, R. A.
Papyrology Rooms
Ashmolean Museum
Oxford
ENGLAND

COULTER, James A.
604 Hamilton Hall
Columbia University
New York, New York 10027

CRAWFORD, Dorothy
Girton College
Cambridge CB3 0JG
ENGLAND

CRISCUOLO, Lucia
Via B. Cesi 7
40135 Bologna
ITALY

CRUZ-URIBE, Eugene
Oriental Institute
1155 E. 58th Street
Chicago, Illinois 60637

CVETLER, Jiři
Botanicka 29
602 00 Brno
CZECHOSLOVAKIA

DARIS, Sergio
Piazza Sansovino 2/1
34131 Trieste
ITALY

List of Participants

DE LACY, Phillip
Box 64
Barnegat Light
New Jersey 08006

+ Estelle A. De Lacy

DORANDI, Tiziano
Centro Internazionale per lo
  Studio dei Papiri Ercolanesi
Via Mezzocannone 16
80134 Napoli
ITALY

DUNCAN-JONES, Richard
Caius College
Cambridge
ENGLAND

EL ABBADI, Mostafa
27 Abdel Hamid Badawi Street
Mazarita, Alexandria
EGYPT

+ Azza Kararah Abbadi
  Mohga el Abbadi

†ELIASSEN, Martha H.
Prof. Dahlsgate 46
Oslo 2
NORWAY

EL-MOSALLAMY, Abdalla Hassan
12 Dar-el-Sorour
Medinet Zahraa el-Helmia
Zeitoun, Cairo
EGYPT

ERLER, M.
Brühlstr. 9
7750 Konstanz 19
GERMANY (BRD)

FACKELMANN, Michael
3021 Pressbaum
Funkhgasse 25
AUSTRIA

FERRARIO, Matilde
c/o Omodeo
via Cacavallo 16
Napoli
ITALY

*FIKHMAN, I. F.
Institut Vostokovedenija
Dvorcovaja nab. 18
19241 Leningrad
U.S.S.R.

FORABOSCHI, Daniele
Soperga 39
Milano
ITALY

+ Luciana Foraboschi

FORSELV, Inger Louise
Odinsgt. 27
Oslo 2
NORWAY

FRANTZ-MURPHY, Gladys
Department of History
Loyola University
6525 N. Sheridan Road
Chicago, Illinois 60626

FRÖSÉN, Jaakko
Ruusulankatu 14 B 15
00250 Helsinki 25
FINLAND

GALLO, Italo
Corso Garibaldi 148
Salerno
ITALY

+ Luigi Gallo

GARA, Alessandra
Via S. Gregorio 25
20124 Milano
ITALY

GERACI, Giovanni
Istituto di Storia Antica
Università di Bologna
Via Zamboni 38
40126 Bologna
ITALY

+ Marta Carloni Geraci

GIBSON, Elsa
181 Summit Avenue
Upper Montclair, New Jersey 07043

List of Participants

GIGANTE, Marcello
Via G. D'Auria 3
80129 Napoli
ITALY

+ Valeria Lanzara Gigante

GIGNAC, Francis T.
Department of Biblical Studies
Catholic University of America
Washington, DC 20064

GILLIAM, J. F.
Institute for Advanced Study
Princeton, New Jersey 08540

GRUNEWALD, Winfried
Institut für Neutestamentliche
  Textforschung
Westfälische Wilhelms-Universität
Georgskommende 7
4400 Münster/Westf.
GERMANY (BRD)

GUERRA, Adele Tepedino
Via Cavalli di Bronzo 52
80046 S. Giorgio a Cremano (NA)
ITALY

+ Vincenzo Guerra

HAGEDORN, Dieter
Kirschblütenweg 6
5000 Köln 50
GERMANY (BRD)

HAGEDORN, Ursula
Kirschblütenweg 6
5000 Köln 50
GERMANY (BRD)

HANSON, Ann Ellis
176 Western Way
Princeton, New Jersey 08540

HARRAUER, Hermann
Buchfeldgasse 18a/11
1080 Wien
AUSTRIA

HARRIS, William V.
516 Fayerweather Hall
Columbia University
New York, New York 10027

HASLAM, Michael
Department of Classics
University of California
Los Angeles, California 90024

HAUBEN, Hans
Minnezang 3
3203 Linden
BELGIUM

+ Lutgart Hauben-Dewulf

HENGSTL, Joachim
Am Mehrdrusch 12
3551 Lahntal-Gossfelden
GERMANY (BRD)

HENRICHS, Albert
Department of the Classics
Boylston Hall
Harvard University
Cambridge, Massachusetts 02138

+ Ursula Henrichs

HUSSON, Geneviève
1 rue Gerson
76130 Mont-Saint-Aignan
FRANCE

+ Joëlle Husson

INDELLI, Giovanni
via Vernieri 119
84100 Salerno
ITALY

JOHNSON, Janet
Oriental Institute
1155 E. 58th Street
Chicago, Illinois 60637

JUDGE, E. A.
School of History
Macquarie University
North Ryde, N.S.W.
AUSTRALIA 2113

KAIMIO, Maarit
Helsinki University
Porthania
Hallituskatu 11-13
00100 Helsinki 10
FINLAND

List of Participants

KATZOFF, Ranon
Department of Classical Studies
Bar Ilan University
Ramat Gan
ISRAEL

KEEFE, John E.
Oriental Institute
Pusey Lane
Oxford
ENGLAND

KEEN, Ralph
54 Trumbull Street
New Haven, Connecticut 06510

KEENAN, James G.
Department of Classical Studies
Loyola University
6525 N. Sheridan Road
Chicago, Illinois 60626

KEULS, Eva
1776 Dupont Ave. S.
Minneapolis, Minnesota 55405

KLEVE, Knut
Klassisk Institutt
Universitetet i Oslo
Postboks 1026 Blindern
Oslo 3
NORWAY

KOENEN, Ludwig
1312 Culver
Ann Arbor, Michigan 48103

+ Margret Koenen

KRAFT, Robert A.
Box 36, College Hall
University of Pennsylvania
Philadelphia, Pennsylvania 19104

KRAMER, Johannes
Im Dau 12
5000 Köln 1
GERMANY (BRD)

KRAMER, Bärbel
Im Dau 12
5000 Köln 1
GERMANY (BRD)

KREK, Miroslav
805 Boston Post Road
Weston, Massachusetts 02193

LENGER, Marie-Thérèse
Rue Colonel Chaltin 32, Bte. 8
1180 Bruxelles
BELGIUM

LEWIS, Naphtali
51 Vista Drive
Easton, Connecticut 06612

LEWUILLON-BLUME, Marianne
Avenue Jean Volders 27, Bte. 2
1060 Bruxelles
BELGIUM

+ Serge Lewuillon

LEFKOWITZ, Mary
Wellesley College
Wellesley, Massachusetts 02181

LIVADARAS, Nicholas A.
Hippocratous 33
Athens 144
GREECE

LLOYD-JONES, Hugh
Christ Church
Oxford OX1 1DP
ENGLAND

ŁUKASZEWICZ, Adam
University of Warsaw
Institute of Papyrology
Krakowskie Przedmieście 26/28
00-927/1 Warszawa 64
POLAND

MACCOULL, Leslie S.B.
Society for Coptic Archaeology
222 Ramses Street
Cairo
EGYPT

MAEHLER, Herwig
Department of Greek
University College London
Gower Street
London WC1E 6BT
ENGLAND

List of Participants

MANDILARAS, Basil G.
10 Ioanninon Street
Philothei, Athens
GREECE

+ Athanasia Mandilaras
  George Mandilaras

MANFREDI, Manfredo
Via Gaspare Aselli 49
50141 Firenze
ITALY

+ Anna Maria Manfredi
  Galliani Belletti

*MARGANNE, Marie-Hélène
Rue Marcel Remy 14
4030 Grivegnée
BELGIUM

MCNAMEE, Kathleen
Department of Greek and Latin
Wayne State University
Detroit, Michigan 48202

MENCI, Giovanna
Istituto Papirologico
"G. Vitelli"
Via degli Alfani 46/48
50121 Firenze
ITALY

+ Elisabetta Menci Provvedi

MEYER, Béatrice
16 rue Saint-Maur
75011 Paris
FRANCE

MEYER-LAURIN, Harald
Hans-Thoma-Strasse 1
7815 Freiburg i. Br.
GERMANY (BRD)

+ Gred Meyer-Laurin

MONTEVECCHI, Orsolina
Via Goldoni 41
20129 Milano
ITALY

MOOREN, Leon
Minnezang 2
3202 Linden
BELGIUM

+ Magda Mooren

MORRIS, Royce L.B.
Emory and Henry College
Emory, Virginia 24327

+ Sue Ann Morris

NARDELLI, Maria Luisa
Via Guido de Ruggiero 37
80128 Napoli
ITALY

NELSON, C. A.
Department of Classics
Ballantine Hall
Indiana University
Bloomington, Indiana 47401

NUR-EL-DIN, M.A.A.
Faculty of Archaeology
Cairo University, Giza
EGYPT

OATES, John F.
Department of Classical Studies
Duke University
Durham, North Carolina 27708

+ Rosemary Oates
  Emily Oates
  Sarah Oates

O'DONNELL, Clifford R.
University of Hawaii
Honolulu, Hawaii 96825

OMAR, Sayed
El-Riad Str. 22
El-Muhandsin, Dokki
Cairo
EGYPT

ORLANDI, Tito
Via F. Civinini 24
00197 Roma
ITALY

+ Diamantina Orlandi
  Cristiana Orlandi

PARSONS, P. J.
Christ Church
Oxford OX1 1DP
ENGLAND

List of Participants

PASSONI DELL'ACQUA, Anna
Istituto di Glottologia
Università del S. Cuore
Largo Gemelli 1
20123 Milano
ITALY

+ Angelo Dell'Acqua

PATTIE, T. S.
Department of Manuscripts
The British Library
Great Russell Street
London WC1B 3DG
ENGLAND

+ D. H. Pattie

PEARL, O. M.
Department of Classical Studies
University of Michigan
Ann Arbor, Michigan 48109

+ Patricia M. Cobb

PESTMAN, P. W.
Brahmslaan 20
Voorschoten
NETHERLANDS

PINTAUDI, Rosario
Via Palazzo dei diavoli 70/A
50142 Firenze
ITALY

+ Mario Tesi

POETHKE, Günter
Staatliche Museen zu Berlin
Bodestr. 1-3
102 Berlin
GERMANY (DDR)

POLAČEK, Adalbert
Barkauer Strasse 32a
2300 Kiel 14
GERMANY (BRD)

+ Vera Polaček
  Vojtech Polaček

POMEROY, Sarah B.
Hunter College
695 Park Avenue
New York, New York 10021

QUAEGEBEUR, Jan
Bleydenberglaan 34
3010 Leuven-Wilsele
BELGIUM

+ Lieve Lesage

RATHBONE, Dominic
Jesus College
Cambridge CB5 8BL
ENGLAND

RAY, John D.
Faculty of Oriental Studies
University of Cambridge
Sidgwick Avenue
Cambridge CB3 9DA
ENGLAND

RENNER, Timothy
Department of Classics
Montclair State College
Montclair, New Jersey 07403

RISPOLI, Gioia Maria
Piazza Borsa 22
Napoli
ITALY

ROMEO, Costantina
Corso Italia, Parco dei Pini, 214
80063 Piano di Sorrento
(Napoli)
ITALY

RÖMER, Cornelia
Institut für Altertumskunde
Universität zu Köln
Albertus-Magnus-Platz
5000 Köln 41
GERMANY (BRD)

ROSENBAUM, Hans-Udo
Patristische Arbeitsstelle
Georgskommende 7
4400 Münster/Westf.
GERMANY (BRD)

ROWLANDSON, Jane
Queen's College
Oxford
ENGLAND

+ Michael F. Roberts

List of Participants

RUPPRECHT, Hans-Albert
In den Opfergärten 5
3557 Ebsdorfergrund 8
GERMANY (BRD)

RUSTEN, Jeffrey
Department of Classical Studies
703 Williams Hall CU
University of Pennsylvania
Philadelphia, Pennsylvania 19174

SAMUEL, Deborah H.
Division of Humanities
York University
4700 Keele Street
Downsview, Ontario M3J 1P3
CANADA

SANDY, D. Brent
Grace College
Winona Lake, Indiana 46590

SCATOZZA, Lucia
Viale Winspeare al Vomero 38
Napoli
ITALY

SCHÄFER, Wolfgang
Liebrechtstrasse 32
4130 Moers 1
GERMANY (BRD)

SCHERER, Jean
14 Boulevard Gambetta
94130 Nogent-sur-Marne
  (Val-de-Marne)
FRANCE

SHELTON, John C.
Institut für Altertumskunde
Neue Universität
2300 Kiel
GERMANY (BRD)

SIEGMANN, Ernst
Institut für Klassische
  Philologie
Residenzplatz 2
8700 Würzburg
GERMANY (BRD)

SIJPESTEIJN, P. J.
Wilhelminalaan 2
3743 DC Baarn
NETHERLANDS

SIOZIOS, George
Kassampa 35
Kaissariani, Athens
GREECE

+ Zaphiroula Sioziou

SMITH, Morton
Department of History
614 Fayerweather Hall
Columbia University
New York, New York 10027

SPEIDEL, Michael P.
Department of History
University of Hawaii
2530 Dole Street
Honolulu, Hawaii 96822

STEAD, Miriam
Egyptian Dept., British Museum
Great Russell Street
London WC1B 3DG, ENGLAND

STEPHENS, Susan A.
Department of Classics
Stanford University
Stanford, California 94305

STOHLER-ZIMMERMAN, Alice
Dietlikerstrasse 43
8302 Kloten
SWITZERLAND

TANNENBAUM, Robert F.
Sarah Lawrence College
Bronxville, New York 10708

TIBILETTI, Giuseppe
Istituto di Papirologia
Università Cattolica del S. Cuore
Largo A. Gemelli 1
20123 Milano
ITALY

TURNER, E. G.
Department of Greek
University College London
Gower Street
London WC1E 6BT
ENGLAND

+ Louise Turner

List of Participants

VAN HAELST, M. l'Abbé J.
3 Place St. Germain-des-Prés
75006 Paris
FRANCE

VAN RENGEN, Wilfried
Dennenlaan 7
3110 Rotselaar
BELGIUM

VAN 'T DACK, Edmond
de Grunnelaan 4
3030 Heverlee
BELGIUM

+ Yvonne Van 't Dack

VANDERSLEYEN, C.
Rue Baron Dhanis 31
1040 Bruxelles
BELGIUM

VLEEMING, Sven
Papyrologisch Instituut der
  Rijksuniversiteit
Breestraat 155A
2311 CN Leiden
NETHERLANDS

WAGNER, Guy
26 Avenue du Général de Gaulle
6700 Strasbourg
FRANCE

+ Liliane Wagner

WALL, E. W.
4072 Foreign Languages Building
University of Illinois
Urbana, Illinois 61801

+ Cheryl Anne Cox

WEHRLI, Claude
rue de Saint-Jean 34
1203 Geneva
SWITZERLAND

+ Clair-Live Wehrli

WHITEHORNE, J.E.G.
Department of Classics
University of Queensland
St. Lucia, Queensland 4067
AUSTRALIA

WILLIS, William H.
Box 4715, Duke Station
Durham, North Carolina 27706

+ Elizabeth H. Willis

WINNICKI, Krzysztof
Katedra Papirologii
Warsaw University
00927/1 Warszawa 64
POLAND

WIPSZYCKA, Ewa
Wlościańska 14/46
01-710 Warszawa
POLAND

WOLFF, Hans Julius
Schulhausstrasse 35
7815 Kirchzarten/Breisgau
GERMANY (BRD)

+ Mrs. Wolff

WORP, K. A.
Louise de Colignylaan 9
2082 BM Santpoort-Zuid
NETHERLANDS

YOUTIE, Louise C.
807 Hatcher Library
University of Michigan
Ann Arbor, Michigan 48109

ZAUZICH, Karl-Theodor
Westendallee 100 E
1000 Berlin 19
GERMANY (BRD)

PROGRAM OF THE CONGRESS

THURSDAY
24 July
9:00 a.m.

Session I: Opening of the Congress

Naphtali Lewis presiding

Greetings: George K. Fraenkel, Dean
Graduate School of Arts and Sciences

†H. C. Youtie: Πράγματα μετέωρα, *or Unfinished Business* (read by P. J. Parsons)

2:00 p.m.

Session IIa: *The Fourth Century, a Colloquium*

K. A. Worp presiding

Z. Borkowski, *Local Cults and Resistance to Christianity*
J.-M. Carrié, *L'Egypte au IVe siècle: Economie, fiscalité, monnaie*
M. Lewuillon-Blume, *Problèmes de la terre au IVe siècle après J.-C.*
A. K. Bowman (discussant), *Continuity and Change in Late Roman Egypt*

Session IIb: *Literary Papyri I*

M. W. Haslam presiding

H. Harrauer, *Die Neue Wiener Pinakesrolle: Ein Vorbericht*
H. Maehler, *Ein Fragment eines hellenistischen Epos*
T. T. Renner, *An Unidentified Michigan Verse (?) Text: Or, Who is being Eaten by Animals?*
A. Blanchard, *Les papyrus et la constitution des choix antiques d'auteurs dramatiques*
P. J. Parsons, *Euphorion's* Thrax: *Old Problems and New Readings*

7:00-9:00 p.m.

Reception given by Columbia University

FRIDAY
25 July
9:00 a.m.

Session IIIa: *The Interconnections of Greek and Demotic Documentation, a Colloquium*

P. W. Pestman presiding

K.-Th. Zauzich, *Vorschlag für eine demotische Berichtigungsliste*
J. Quaegebeur, *Demotic and Greek Ostraca Excavated at Elkab* (slides)

Program of the Congress

J. K. Winnicki, *Einige Bemerkungen zu dem griechischen und demotischen Briefen aus Pathyris*
S. Vleeming, *Maače, and Artabe*
K.-Th. Zauzich and E. G. Turner, discussants

Session IIIb: *Herculaneum Papyri I*

A. Henrichs presiding

M. Gigante, *Realtà nuove della papirologia ercolanese*
F. Auricchio and A. Guerra, *Aspetti e problemi della dissidenza epicurea*
G. Indelli, *Per l'interpretazione dell'opera filodemea 'Sull' ira' (P.Herc. 182, coll. XXXIV-L)*
M. Ferrario, *La concezione della retorica da Epicuro a Filodemo*

2:00 p.m.   Session IVa: *Social History: the Empire*

A. K. Bowman presiding

D. H. Samuel, *Greeks and Romans at Socnopaiou Nesos*
R. Morris, *Reflections of Citizen Attitudes in Petitions from Roman Oxyrhynchus*
J. Rowlandson, *Sales of Land in their Social Context*
A. E. Hanson, *Aspects of the Reign of Gaius in the Philadelphia Papyri*
D. Rathbone, *The Oxyrhynchite Estate of the Tiberii Julii Theones*
H. Cockle, *Pottery Leases from Oxyrhynchus* (slides)

Session IVb: *Herculaneum Papyri II*

P. H. DeLacy presiding

G. Rispoli, *Suono e articolazione nella teoria del linguaggio (PHerc. 994, 460 e 1073)*
M. L. Nardelli, *PHerc. 1676: contenuti di un libro dell' opera filodemea 'Sulla poetica'*
T. Dorandi, *Sulla trasmissione del testo dell' Index Academicorum Herculanensis (PHerc. 164-1021)*
A. Angeli, *Per una ricostruzione della biografia di Idomeneo di Lampsaco (PHerc. 1672, coll. X-XI e 463, col. IX)*
M. Capasso, *Il trattato etico epicureo del PHerc. 346*
C. Romeo, *Sofrone nei papiri ercolanesi (PHerc. 1014-1081)*

Program of the Congress

SATURDAY
26 July
9:00 a.m.
Excursion to the Brooklyn Museum, sponsored
by the Brooklyn Museum and the Xerox
Corporation

10:00-12:00   Admission to the collections on the third floor

12:00-1:00   Reception on the third floor

1:00 p.m.   Welcome to the Brooklyn Museum

Introductory remarks: Robert S. Bianchi

Session V: *Egyptian Elements in Greek and Roman Egypt*

Jean Bingen presiding

J. H. Johnson, *The Chicago Demotic Dictionary Project*
M. A. Nur-el-Din, *The Sign Heading Lists of Witnesses in Demotic Legal Documents*
L.S.B. MacCoull, *Greek and Coptic Papyrus Fragments from the Monastery of Phoebammon*
G. M. Browne, *Griffith's Old Nubian Lectionary*
T. Orlandi, *Two Coptic Papyrus Rolls by Horsiesi*
G. Husson, *A propos de quelques traditions pharaoniques dans l'architecture domestique de l'Egypte grecque, romaine et byzantine*
D. Bonneau, *La haute administration de l'irrigation dans l'Egypte grecque, romaine et byzantine*

4:45 p.m.   Closing Remarks

SUNDAY
27 July
FREE DAY

MONDAY
28 July
9:00 a.m.
Session VIa: *Christianity, Judaism and the Papyri*

Morton Smith presiding

A. Passoni dell'Acqua, *Note Lessicale sui papiri e la traduzione dei LXX*
W. Grunewald, *Das Neue Testament auf Papyrus*
E. A. Judge, *Fourth-century Monasticism in the Papyri*
E. Wipszycka, *Le christianisme et le degré d'alphabétisation dans l'Egypte byzantine*
H. Rosenbaum, *Patristik und Papyrologie*
A. Poláček, *Holocaust--two Millennia ago*

Program of the Congress

Session VIb: *Ptolemaic History*

L. Koenen presiding

E. Van 't Dack, *Le conflit syro-égyptien de
103/102 av. J.-C.*
D. J. Crawford, *Memphis: polis and necropolis*
J. F. Oates, *Arabs in Ptolemaic Egypt*
G. Geraci, *Da definire: sull' ὁ πρὸς τῆι συντάξει
tolemaico*
J. Frösén, *Documents from the Ptolemaic Period in
the Helsinki University Collections* (slides)
M. Kaimio, *On the Sureties of Tax Farmers in
Ptolemaic Egypt* (slides)
L. Mooren, *Ptolemaic Families*

2:00 p.m.

Session VIIa: *The Administration of Roman Egypt*

J. F. Oates presiding

M. Stead, *The High Priest of Alexandria and all
Egypt*
J.E.G. Whitehorne, *The Role of the Strategia in
Administrative Continuity in Roman Egypt*
R. Bogaert, *Les reçus d'impôts en argent thébains
de l'époque romaine et les banques*
D. Foraboschi and A. Gara, *Sulla differenza tra
tassi di interesse in moneta e natura*
M. Eliassen, *Pap.Osl. inv. 1518: an unknown
charis of Antoninus Pius?*
A. Łukaszewicz, *A Petition from Priests to
Hadrian with his Subscription*
M. P. Speidel, *The Prefect's Horse Guard* (Stud.
Pal. XXII 92)
O. M. Pearl, *Complex Arithmetic, Advantageous to
the Fisc*

Session VIIb: *Literary Papyri II*

W. H. Willis presiding

A. Bülow-Jacobsen, *A Ps.-Pythagorean Text in the
Copenhagen Collection* (slides)
M. Smith, *The Hymn to the Moon in the Paris
Magical Papyrus, B.N. s.g. 574 = P.G.M. IV
2242-2355*
J. Kramer, *Kommentar zum Folium Parisinum
(P.Louvre Eg. 2329)*
J. Van Haelst, *Réflexions sur la magie chrétienne
en Egypte: Commentaire de trois textes*

Program of the Congress

Program of the Congress

<table>
<tr><td>

WEDNESDAY
30 July
9:00 a.m.

</td><td>

Session Xa: *Apokrimata, a Colloquium*

Opening remarks by Arthur W. Murphy,
Vice-Dean, School of Law

N. Lewis presiding

R. Katzoff, *On the General Character of*
P.Col. 123
D. Nörr, *Aporemata apokrimaton* (summarized by
H. J. Wolff)

Session Xb: *Techniques of Preservation and*
Photography

H. Maehler presiding

K. Kleve, *Lacunology   a New Branch of Papyrology*
(slides, overhead)
A. Stohler-Zimmerman, *A Method to Save the Paint-*
ing from Papyrus Cartonnage to be Freed (slides)
M. Fackelmann, *Neuerungen in der Papyrusrestau-*
rierung
E. W. Wall, *Small-format Photography of*
Carbonized Papyri (slides)

</td></tr>
<tr><td>

2:00 p.m.

</td><td>

Session XIa: *Byzantine Egypt*

R. S. Bagnall presiding

H. Hauben, *On the Meletians in P.London VI*
(P.Jews)
J. G. Keenan, *On Village and Polis in Byzantine*
Egypt
G. Poethke, *Der Papyrus-Codex BGU 1024-1027*
R. Pintaudi, *I papiri Vaticani di Afrodito*
(slides)
C. Wehrli, *Un nouveau papyrus genevois des*
archives de Dioscoros (P.Gen. inv. 204)
M. el Abbadi, *Historians and the Papyri on the*
Finances of Egypt at the Arab Conquest
G. Frantz-Murphy, *Contract Law in the Arabic*
Papyri from Islamic Egypt

Session XIb: *Juristic Papyrology*

H. Meyer-Laurin presiding

H. J. Wolff, *The Political Background of the*
Plurality of Law in Ptolemaic Egypt
J. Hengstl, Λύειν, λύσις *und Verwandtes — Be-*
trachtungen zur Auflösung des Vertragsver-
hältnisses in den gräko-ägyptischen Papyri
H.-A. Rupprecht, *Die Ananeosis in den gräko-*
ägyptischen Papyri

</td></tr>
</table>

J. Shelton, *Court Proceeding on a Papyrus from the Bodleian Library*

Z. Aly, *A Petition for Restitutio in Integrum* (read by Ludwig Koenen)

THURSDAY
31 July
9:00 a.m.

Session XII: *Closing Lecture and AIP Business Meeting*

N. Lewis presiding

J. Bingen, *Les interactions culturelles, Thème de l'UNESCO et réponses de l'Egypte gréco-romaine*

10:00 a.m.

AIP Business Meeting

Papers Presented by Title Only:

I. F. Fikhman, *Les cautions pour coloni adscripticii*

M. Marganne *Un fragment du médecin Hérodote: P.Tebt. 2.271*

PART 1

GENERAL LECTURE

L'EGYPTE GRECO-ROMAINE ET LA PROBLEMATIQUE
DES INTERACTIONS CULTURELLES

[Le début de l'exposé fait à l'issue du XVIe Congrès a rappelé les liens de l'AIP et de l'Unesco. L'AIP est membre de la Fédération internationale des Associations d'Etudes classiques (FIEC), l'une des treize fédérations membres du Conseil international de la Philosophie et des Sciences humaines. Le CIPSH, à son tour, est une des organisations non-gouvernementales consultatives de l'Unesco.]

En décembre 1979, à la dernière assemblée du "Conseil international de la Philosophie et des Sciences humaines" à la Nouvelle Delhi, M. Conil-Lacoste, de la Division des Etudes et de la Diffusion des Cultures, a présenté les premiers résultats, essentiellement heuristiques et méthodologiques, des travaux qu'ont poursuivis depuis 1976, et un groupe de réflexion créé avec l'espoir d'élaborer un programme d'études interculturelles, et un Comité de coordination de ces mêmes études. Il a convié les Fédérations membres du CIPSH à participer à l'entreprise et à nourrir les différentes démarches qui se dégagent dès maintenant des premiers travaux du groupe de réflexion. Il ne m'appartient pas de m'étendre sur les perspectives très différentes que ces travaux ouvrent: depuis, par exemple, la préoccupation intimiste de juger notre mentalité dans la recherche, en descendant au plus profond de nous pour débusquer les restes d'un abord ethnocentrique de la culture "autre" (une de nos angoisses en papyrologie où, face à l'Egyptien, nous sommes des Janus ethnocentriques, à la fois Occidentaux du XXe siècle et Grecs de la suite d'Alexandre), jusqu'à la prospection d'applications pratiques plus conformes à l'esprit de l'Unesco, en dégageant des valeurs qu'on puisse rendre communes dans une sorte de "culture humaine" sans attenter aux spécificités créatrices de chacune des cultures des hommes. Une de ces perspectives, un de ces cheminements plutôt, serait de développer la connaissance des phénomènes associés dans le passé à la rencontre de deux cultures différentes. Ce volet historique ne comporterait pas seulement l'énumération et l'analyse des mécanismes de l'acculturation, perceptibles dans

l'Antiquité, mais aussi celles des attitudes négatives, qu'il
s'agisse de rejet ou simplement d'imperméabilité à l'apport
extérieur.

La FIEC peut présenter d'emblée à l'Unesco un premier acquis,
les travaux du VIe Congrès international des Etudes classiques ré-
uni à Madrid en 1974, avec l'aide de l'Unesco et du CIPSH. Ils
ont été publiés sous le titre d'"Assimilation et résistance à la
culture gréco-romaine dans le monde ancien" (Paris 1976). L'Orient
y est malheureusement peu étudié, l'Egypte gréco-romaine en est
même absente. Or, elle représente la plage géographique et chronologique qui joint à un beau dossier littéraire et documentaire grec
et latin, la documentation la plus riche, ou plus exactement la
moins pauvre, qui ait été fournie par une population d'accueil. On
a donc été tenté de combler cette lacune, avec la certitude de le
faire sans grands risques, car les papyrologues ont été attirés, et
même tiraillés dans des sens fort différents, par le problème de la
cohabitation de la culture grecque et des cultures orientales. Des
travaux récents ont affiné notre doctrine. Je songe, par exemple, au
Symposion de Berlin en 1976 (*Das ptolemäische Ägypten*, Mainz am
Rhein 1978) ou encore à bien des pages du *Monde hellénistique*
(Paris 1978) de Claire Préaux. La FIEC a proposé qu'une des contributions demandées au CIPSH fût un bref rapport sur le "cas" de
l'Egypte gréco-romaine. Malheureusement, les délais sont trop brefs
pour en faire le travail d'équipe envisagé à la Nouvelle Delhi.
Mon propos aujourd'hui n'est pas de faire ici ce rapport (les
termes vous en seraient trop familiers), mais d'aborder les pré-
alables structurels à toute étude descriptive des interactions
culturelles en Egypte, et les impératifs critiques que ces préa-
lables comportent.

Et d'abord ne faut-il pas circonscrire l'entité "culture,"
c'est-à-dire énumérer l'ensemble des valeurs selon lesquelles une
identité collective s'organise et se manifeste? D'autre part, on
nous demande d'analyser la culture dans sa double portée objective
et subjective: on peut décrire la création globale de cette collectivité, mais on peut aussi chercher la conscience qu'a ce groupe
(plus ou moins confusément) de son identité culturelle, que ce
soit la "conscience vécue" de la réalité particulière de ce groupe,

ou même la conscience mythologisée de son identité. Or, ce foi-
sonnement de démarches et d'enquêtes, il s'agit, pour nous papyrologues, de l'appliquer à la cohabitation d'une certaine grécité et
d'une certaine "égyptité," ou plutôt de les appliquer aux "Grecs"
et aux "Egyptiens" de nos documents, ainsi qu'aux "Egyptiens" que
démotisants et coptologues nous offrent d'après "leurs" documents.
Le caractère subjectif et relatif de la perception de ces groupes
que ne sépare aucune paroi étanche, est aggravé dans une enquête
d'ordre historique: le nombre des démarches possibles est limité
par le caractère lacunaire des sources littéraires, documentaires
et archéologiques dont nous disposons, même si nous pouvons les
situer dans un contexte historique et géographique exceptionnelle-
ment bien connu pour l'Antiquité. Ma première réaction à la tâche
qui m'est demandée est faite d'effroi: dès qu'on quitte le domaine
bien charpenté de la philologie du document ou celui de l'histoire
concrète avec ses méthodes et ses techniques pour aborder le monde
de la psychologie des groupes hétérogènes ou la sociologie de la
cohabitation culturelle, notre documentation n'apparaît plus que
comme un échantillonnage partiel et quelquefois peu significatif.

Notons cependant que le projet du groupe de réflexion s'est
orienté vers une conception très large de la culture "en y englo-
bant tous les domaines des comportements humains comme la technique,
l'art, la pensée, l'organisation sociale, l'économie." Et cela
nous rassure. Pour le papyrologue, le formulaire grec de la quit-
tance fiscale en Thébaïde, le temple purement égyptien d'Edfou, le
statut de la terre arable, la vis d'Archimède, voire le chameau
qu'on introduit dans le circuit rural, sont des paramètres de culture omniprésents et riches de sens autant que la place d'Homère
dans le livre de l'écolier grec du Fayoum ou les restes d'une littérature écrite en démotique. Encore faut-il ordonner ces paramètres, et en exploiter les données.

L'étude des interactions qui auraient pu se manifester en
Egypte même entre la culture grecque et la culture égyptienne autochtone depuis Alexandre le Grand jusqu'à la fin du Haut Empire,
porte sur un cas particulier: celui de la coexistence de deux
cultures fort différentes dans un même territoire. Ce cas se

présente à la fois sous la forme classique des rapports d'une minorité privilégiée et dominante et d'une majorité autochtone qui a
une moindre capacité d'organiser son devenir, majorité et minorité
correspondant approximativement aux deux groupes culturels envi-
sagés. Mais il présente aussi un caractère exceptionnel: cohabitent ici deux cultures évoluées et prestigieuses (quelle que soit
l'opinion qu'on ait sur une sorte de déclin qu'elles présenterai-
ent). Mais, en raison même de cette longue coexistence, nous au-
rons à être attentifs moins aux zones d'osmose des deux groupes
qu'à la note dominante que l'on a dégagée dans les rapports de ces
deux ensembles coexistants: une "opacité" marquée, qui va quelqe-
fois jusqu'au refus de l'"autre." Il ne faut pas rappeler ici les
conditions historiques qui ont créé en Egypte cette coexistence de
deux identités culturelles, le complexe culturel égyptien, qui est
le substrat autochtone de notre problème, et le complexe culturel
grec, qui est le facteur "étranger," le facteur "perturbant," minorité gréco-macédonienne qui organise le pouvoir dans le pays. Mais
aussitôt un détail ici va montrer que l'analyse historique peut
mettre en valeur des données purement formelles qui ont en réalité
peu de poids en regard des données psychologiques sous-jacentes. On
sait qu'Alexandre est entré en Egypte non en agresseur, mais en
libérateur de l'oppression achéménide. Ceci devrait simplifier à
première vue les rapports entre les deux groupes, en en excluant
un élément affectif qui eût pu être négatif pour les Egyptiens.
Ceux-ci ne se trouvent pas sous la domination gréco-macédonienne à
la suite d'une défaite; le Grec n'est donc pas un envahisseur
abhorré et par le fait même un sacrilège que la vengeance divine
frappera tôt ou tard. Une génération plus tard, Ptolémée prend le
diadème royal, un diadème qui est aussi la couronne de Haute et
Basse Egypte; et ceci va confirmer cette relation ambiguë du roi et
de l'Egypte, qui cesse d'être une satrapie subordonnée à un empire
étranger, même si le roi a sa capitale dans l'entité non-égyptienne
qu'est Alexandrie. Certes, les circonstances historiques ont permis de donner facilement de la consistance à la fiction admise dès
Alexandre le Grand que le roi macédonien est aussi le pharaon,
nécessaire aux dieux et aux hommes de la vallée du Nil; c'est un
élément important dans notre problème. Certes aussi, cela a

facilité des contacts, sinon de vrais échanges culturels, entre un milieu antique alexandrin curieux d'exotisme et le haut sacerdoce égyptien prêt à répondre à cet intérêt. Mais ces circonstances favorables, accueil du libérateur, devenu bientôt gage de l'indépendance, ne sont que des facteurs superficiels; elles peuvent sussusciter sur les parois des temples une mythologie du roi macédonien pourfendeur des sacrilèges perses, mais elles ont été incapables d'éliminer des sentiments profonds où prédomine chez les uns comme chez les autres ce qu'en jargon on appelle l'"étrangéité" de l'autre. Des difficultés entre les hommes sont nées très tôt à cause d'abus de pouvoir administratif ou économique. Elles sont souvent perçues par les Egyptiens comme un droit à l'oppression que s'arrogent les Grecs et comme une forme du mépris dans lequel on tient l'indigène. Lorsque l'affaiblissement de la monarchie fait éclore les premières révoltes à la fin du IIIe s. et au IIe s., les troubles prennent aisément le tour d'un clivage, où la dichotomie culturelle recouvre l'opposition entre privilégiés et exploités, encore que nous employions un peu trop facilement le terme de "nationaliste" pour les désigner. Et puis, le temple égyptien n'est-il pas le plus souvent interdit au Grec, malgré le mariage de raison de la dynastie macédonienne et de l'aristocratie sacerdotale?

Si l'"Ionien," même s'il a été un libérateur, reste l'étranger pour l'Egyptien, comment les Grecs ont-ils perçu leur pénétration en Egypte et l'installation de leur domination politique et économique permanente sur les autochtones?

Ici encore, il faut faire la part entre les schémas historiques et les mentalités. L'histoire nous fournit quelques paramètres que nous ne citons que trop facilement alors que leur incidence a été relativement faible. On a fait depuis longtemps un sort à l'idée que l'immigrant grec a eu le sentiment d'être dans la chôra par droit de conquête. La conquête n'a fait qu'accélérer l'immigration en Egypte, et le gros de cette immigration est même postérieure à la génération de la conquête. Même pour les Ptolémées, l'Egypte n'est "terre conquise à la pointe de la lance" que dans leur prétention de soutenir leurs droits face aux appétits des autres épigones d'Alexandre. En tout cas, notre analyse du fait grec en Egypte hellénistique ne doit pas se fonder sur une dialectique

juridique que le Grec utiliserait pour justifier sa présence ou ses
privilèges, mais elle tiendra compte du caractère purement "exis-
tentiel" du fait grec en Egypte: le Grec est là, et c'est parce
qu'il est présent qu'il se retrouve dans une structure grecque co-
hérente et légitimée par le pouvoir royal. N'oublions pas, d'autre
part, que l'immigration grecque en Egypte hellénistique, surtout si
l'immigré vient des îles, d'Asie Mineure ou de Chypre, s'inscrit
dans une antique tradition de passage de la mer: on rejoignait depuis longtemps Naucratis, Memphis, d'autres peuplements grecs, ou
simplement les pharaons nationaux ou les Achéménides, qui y utili-
saient des Grecs comme mercenaires. On a relevé des traces d'influence de ces immigrants dans la culture égyptienne préalexandrine,
par exemple, dans le domaine de l'art comme dans celui des techniques, mais ces traces sont limitées à des aspects trop spécifiques
pour qu'on puisse parler d'action culturelle. Inversément, on peut
se demander à ce propos jusqu'à quel point l'immigrant grec avait
en lui le sentiment de l'acquis culturel ancien emprunté par la
Grèce à l'Egypte, ou plutôt de l'image utopique qu'une certaine
intelligentsia grecque s'est faite de l'Egypte à l'époque archaïque
et classique. Christian Froidefond l'a appelée récemment le
"Mirage égyptien" (Aix-en-Provence 1971). Face à l'Egyptien fripon
du xénophobe Aristophane, il y a une Egypte et surtout une classe
sacerdotale égyptienne qui, pour les penseurs ioniens, puis d'Hérodote à Platon et Aristote, sont sources des sciences, de la sagesse
et de la philosophie, et même modèle incomparable de la piété et de
la morale. Certes, il y a au fond de tout cela, aux époques archaïque et classique, la perception par les Grecs de transferts
culturels, même si cette perception a débouché rapidement sur une
thématique d'Utopie littéraire. Ceci a pu marquer les rapports
entre Alexandre ou ses successeurs et le clergé égyptien et peut
expliquer la curiosité d'un milieu comme celui du Musée pour ce qui
est égyptien. Mais il est probable que l'immigrant grec moyen de
l'époque hellénistique ne doit avoir perçu que très confusément une
dette intellectuelle envers l'Egypte, si ce n'est peut-être sur le
plan religieux. Un tel sentiment n'expliquerait ni sa décision de
s'expatrier en Egypte, ni ses comportements dans le royaume lagide.

Lorsqu'on examine les deux groupes, lorsqu'on s'interroge sur le paradoxe de la longue coexistence des Egyptiens et des Grecs et du caractère superficiel des faits d'acculturation réciproque, il me faut d'abord émettre deux précautions oratoires: (a) chacun de ces groupes ne forme pas un ensemble homogène, Memphis n'est pas Thèbes. Soknopaiou Nèsos, restée profondément égyptienne n'est pas Arsinoè et ses notables grecs. Même dans un sous-groupe restreint, comme le sacerdoce égyptien ou le fonctionnariat grec, il y a des niveaux très différents. C'est dire qu'il est dangereux de simplifier nos propositions; (b) ces groupes ne sont pas étanches. Mais, en fait,les zones d'osmose sont secondaires: le mariage mixte, l'armée (le jour où elle s'ouvre aux Egyptiens), certaines branches de l'administration, le monde des femmes (celui des maîtresses et des servantes). Mais surtout,ces phénomènes mixtes sont souvent temporaires. Un mariage mixte finira probablement par inscrire la cellule familiale nouvelle dans un des deux groupes. Ou bien, la zone de mixité n'est pas significative sur le plan culturel: si l'on devine l'existence, à l'époque impériale surtout, de milieux urbains ou villageois qui semblent véritablement gréco-égyptiens, rien ne semble indiquer qu'ils aient eu en quoi que ce soit un rôle de transfert culturel. D'ailleurs, il faut se garder de donner une définition raciale à ces groupes.

Enfin, il faut souligner aussi qu'aucun des deux groupes n'a eu une vocation missionnaire, qui ait porté à persuader ou à contraindre sur le plan culturel. P. M. Fraser a montré que le rayonnement du culte de Sarapis, un culte alexandrin d'origine égyptienne, n'est pas dû à une volonté de convertir; en fait, la diffusion de Sarapis illustre un besoin religieux extérieur à combler. Notre analyse ne peut être biaisée par des comparaisons avec des mouvements missionnaires, comme le christianisme, l'Islam, le marxisme, etc.

La raison pour laquelle les deux grandes cultures qui ont coexisté en Egypte n'ont pas donné naissance à une culture mixte, c'est-à-dire à un processus d'acculturation réciproque profonde est dû à la fois aux structures et dynamiques différentes des deux groupes et au manque d'intérêt qu'il y avait (et ce dernier facteur est déterminant pour le groupe privilégié) à abandonner les signes

culturels fondamentaux de son groupe. Mais il y a surtout que chacun de ces deux groupes représente un système culturel intégré,
c'est-à-dire un système dans lequel les paramètres d'expression de
l'identité culturelle (langue, littérature, religion, etc.) sont
intimement liés aux structures juridiques, économiques, sociales,
ou plus généralement aux structures d'organisation du territoire du
groupe. Cette intégration du système égyptien ou du système grec
de la chôra égyptienne n'atteint pas l'omniprésence de l'Islam, par
exemple, mais ces systèmes n'en sont pas moins remarquables par
leur cohérence mais aussi par leurs incompatibilités réciproques.

A la haute époque hellénistique, le système culturel intégré
que représente la population de langue égyptienne semble être essentiellement fondé sur une structure cléricale. Cette population
se situe aisément et fonctionnellement dans un univers religieux,
riche d'explications du monde, de règles de vie, de modèles de
société, de promesses de survie du groupe et de l'homme. C'est ce
qui rend ce système jusqu'à un certain point monolithique. La pro-
lifération des divinités, le caractère local des cultes, la multi-
plicité et la concurrence des autorités religieuses, ne sont qu'une
apparence, d'ordre phénoménal, de dispersion ou d'unité. Ce qui
est fondamental, c'est l'unité de la piété profonde du peuple égyptien et c'est la cohérence de la réponse totale que lui fournissent
le système religieux et son clergé. La chose est particulièrement
précieuse dans une communauté qui s'estime lésée.

Au moment où Alexandre le Grand "libère" l'Egypte et rend aux
temples les trésors qui leur ont été arrachés, le clergé égyptien
n'a traversé qu'une courte période de persécution. En tout cas, au
début de l'époque hellénistique, il existe un réseau dense, hiér-
archisé, de sanctuaires, dont les principaux se trouvent dans les
métropoles des nomes et en forment un élément socio-économique
polyvalent. Le haut clergé est porteur de la tradition et de la
survie du groupe, il a le prestige de l'érudition, transmet les
enseignements théologiques, maintient les traditions scribales,
pratique les sciences, les mathématiques, la médecine. Mais ce
clergé a aussi le prestige que confère la richesse du sanctuaire.
Car celui-ci peut aussi être détenteur d'un domaine qui est considérable pour les grands sanctuaires. Les textes et les reliefs du
temple funéraire de Pétosiris à Hermoupolis sont les références

habituelles que nous utilisons pour décrire le domaine sacré égyptien au début de l'époque hellénistique, mais d'autres sources confirment l'image d'un ensemble où l'agriculture, l'élevage, l'arti-
sanat de l'or, du cuivre, des parfums et du bois, l'exploitation
des biens immobiliers, situent dans les grands domaines des communautés villageoises et urbaines. Mais, parallèlement à la gestion
directe qu'il assume pour le domaine sacré, le clergé a eu au départ certaines responsabilités sur le domaine royal. Pétosiris
n'était pas seulement prêtre et intendant des dieux, il était aussi
scribe royal, une fonction qui restera marquée par son origine
égyptienne quand les premiers Ptolémées la confieront souvent à des
Egyptiens. Et le cas de Pétosiris n'est pas isolé. Par sa double
vocation, le temple organise, à des degrés divers, la population de
langue égyptienne et lui propose, par la langue et par le culte,
les lignes fondamentales de son identité culturelle. Et l'Egyptien
les complétera d'instinct, comme ces paysans brimés qui défient le
Grec en déclarant qu'eux seuls connaissent bien leur terre. Ce
monde égyptien n'est ni homogène, ni exempt de tensions ou de cri-
antes inégalités, mais il nous paraît, dans le peu que nous connais-
sions de lui, former un ensemble équilibré. Hérodote déjà, en parlant d'une société de castes et de spécialistes, nous proposait en
fait l'image d'une société intégrée, stable et immobile.

La communauté de langue grecque installée dans la vallée du
Nil forme elle aussi un système culturel intégré, mais en fonction
de paramètres très différents.

Dans le système grec, par exemple, la religion n'est qu'un
élément adventice. L'immigrant grec provient d'un milieu qui a
fait sa mutation religieuse à l'époque classique: on est passé de
la religion du groupe à une religion de l'individu à rapports peu
contraignants entre le croyant, le clergé et la cité. C'est aussi
un milieu dont l'organisation cléricale est superficielle, même si
le pouvoir lagide va tenter d'asseoir des cultes dynastiques ou un
réseau dionysiaque structuré.

La communauté grecque qui nous intéresse ici, c'est la grécité
du Delta et de la vallée, et non Alexandrie. Certes Alexandrie,
siège du pouvoir, a été une source privilégiée d'influences culturelles sur l'Egypte, et particulièrement sur sa population grecque
à laquelle elle fournit une référence permanente sur le plan

intellectuel, sur le plan de l'administration et du droit, sur le
plan de l'économie.   Mais Alexandrie, l'Alexandrie de la cour royale, du Musée, du grand commerce, l'Alexandrie du néoplatonisme ou
des syncrétismes religieux, l'Alexandrie du paléo-christianisme,
c'est un autre monde: la communauté grecque s'y trouve majoritaire,
elle coexiste avec d'autres communautés importantes comme les Juifs,
elle est directement ouverte sur le monde méditerranéen oriental
avant de l'être sur Rome.

La grécité de la *chôra* a pu apparaître comme un ramassis de
Grecs, de Macédoniens ou de Thraces, mercenaires, fonctionnaires ou
affairistes, qui n'avaient comme dénominateur commun que le Roi.
Je crois que c'est une erreur et qu'on peut parler pour eux aussi
d'un système culturel intégré.   Ici également les paramètres d'expression culturelle, la langue, l'éducation traditionnelle grecque,
les comportements sociaux, rejoignent les paramètres de l'organisation du territoire, la volonté de lucre, le droit, l'administration
royale, la fiscalité, l'économie monétaire, qui sont tous fondés
sur une dialectique en langue grecque.   Particulièrement au début,
le milieu "prométhéen" grec de l'immigration se distancie des Egyptiens par ses comportements d'emprise intéressée sur le milieu naturel.   Mais même quand, au fil du temps et des contraintes du contexte géographique, ce monde grec s'usera, le système gardera sa
cohérence parce que le privilège de la minorité se justifie par la
culture grecque et se défend par cette même culture.   Et nous ver-
rons que cette cohérence sera institutionalisée par les Romains.

Certains aspects fondamentaux de l'Egypte hellénistique semblent mettre en doute l'imperméabilité relative des deux cultures.
On songe immédiatement au comportement des Grecs envers les dieux
égyptiens.   A vrai dire, nous nous représentons assez mal le sentiment religieux d'un Grec d'Egypte dont l'éducation est faite en
partie d'une formalisation littéraire de la religion ancestrale, et
pour qui le temple égyptien local est une réalité proche, où le
divin prend une forme exotique.   Jusqu'à quel point le Grec s'est-
il intégré dans cet exotisme religieux?   La réponse est d'autant
plus difficile à fournir qu'elle a dû varier de lieu en lieu.   E-
cartons le cas de Sarapis qui fut très tôt une divinité alexandrine
et qui, par exemple, n'a nourri que la seule onomastique grecque,
tandis qu'il est absent des parois décorées des temples égyptiens.

Le cas d'Isis est à peine plus significatif d'une acculturation du
milieu grec. Comme le culte de Zeus Ammon, celui d'Isis a connu
des formes hellénisées dès avant Alexandre le Grand. La polymor-
phie d'Isis aux 10.000 noms, avec sa théologie du divin omniprésent
et moteur de tout, créait des conditions de voisinage facile entre
fidèles grecs et égyptiens. Et pourtant nous nous imaginons mal la
place des croyants grecs dans le temple égyptien de Philae qu'ils
ont visité avec ardeur à en croire leurs proscynèmes. Isis tient
une place importante dans l'onomastique grecque. Mais un sondage
dans les couches privilégiées de la chôra à l'époque impériale
(même aussi tard, donc) tempère cette observation: parmi les gymnasiarques, on observe une fréquence élevée de théophores créés sur
Apollon, Dionysos et Sarapis, trop élevée pour qu'il puisse s'agir
d'une identification des deux premiers avec Horus et Osiris. Ce
n'est qu'en une deuxième zone de fréquence qu'apparaît Isis, au
même niveau qu'Alexandre, Héraklès, Zeus, Ammôn (la série grecque
d'Ammônios indépendante de la série égyptienne des Amounis et con-
sorts) ou simplement Πτολεμαῖος. Et Isis est donc favorisée par
rapport aux autres divinités égyptiennes absentes des fréquences
élevées. Même à Hermoupolis, un des lieux qui sont au départ du
prestige d'une science égyptienne patronnée par Thôt/Hermès, un des
lieux où se développera l'hermétisme gréco-égyptien, on constate
que les noms théophores d'Hermès n'apparaissent dans le groupe des
gymnasiarques, milieu grec fermé par excellence, qu'au IIIe siècle
de notre ère. Le réseau des temples égyptiens a dû répondre sans
trop de difficulté à des besoins religieux des Grecs que ne satis-
faisaient pas les survivances relativement rares de fêtes ou de
cultes grecs. L'assimilation des dieux égyptiens et des dieux grecs
était en effet une vieille tradition grecque que la lecture d'Hérodote pouvait entretenir. D'autre part, plus ou moins consciemment,
le Grec a toujours fait la part dans sa démarche religieuse entre
l'abord phénoménal de son polythéisme foisonnant et l'abord onto-
logique du divin sous-jacent. L'exotisme du culte pouvait n'être
perçu que comme une apparence locale à transcender. Il n'empêche
que si on reconnaît que le domaine religieux est celui où le Grec a
progressivement emprunté le plus à l'Egyptien, il faut bien constater que la religion égyptienne ne semble pas avoir eu une place

importante dans l'éducation des petits Grecs d'Egypte; que, d'autre
part, le Grec n'a pas toujours été accueilli dans le temple égyptien: un dévôt du Sérapéum de Memphis ne se plaint-il pas d'être
persécuté parce que Grec?

On pourrait examiner de même un domaine qui peut sembler avoir
été commun à nos deux systèmes intégrés et été par là porteur de
transferts culturels réciproques, le roi et le culte royal. Je ne
puis m'étendre ici sur ce sujet: mais là aussi il y a dichotomie.
Le roi-pharaon n'est pas le basileus, élément symbolique fondamental du système intégré grec et en même temps moteur concret de
l'organisation grecque du territoire. Winter a récemment montré
que le culte royal égyptien est purement fonctionnel: le roi est
le prêtre suprême, il doit, sinon lui-même, au moins sa représenta-
tion figurée ou son représentant, l'archiprêtre local, assurer la
pérennité du rituel. Les représentations du roi vivant le montrent
comme officiant ou comme roi consacré. Même à Memphis, qui a des
liens politiques privilégiés avec les Ptolémées, nous sommes en
tout cas loin des cultes royaux grecs d'Alexandrie ou de Ptolémaïs,
de tradition héroïque, sans autre théologie que la symbolique du
système intégré grec que je signalais plus haut. Même si le culte
royal égyptien a fait des concessions, comme celle de diviniser
Arsinoé Philadelphe, c'est que les rapports du clergé et de la
royauté alexandrine ont des aspects politiques et économiques qui
exigent une dialectique commune, mais on ne trouve que peu de
traces de concessions idéologiques du clergé. Il a fallu deux
siècles pour qu'il laissât introduire le 6e épagomène des années
bissextiles, et seulement dans le monde profane!

En fait, ce qui prédomine dans les paramètres classiques des
interactions culturelles, langue, éducation, littérature, religion,
etc., c'est plusieurs siècles d'opacité, d'impossibilité ou de
refus de l'emprunt. Et cela dépasse même ces paramètres classiques.
En 1979, H.-J. Wolff (*Das Problem der Konkurrenz von Rechtsordnungen
in der Antike*, p. 49) rappelait encore que le dualisme culturel de
l'Egypte ptolémaïque avait trouvé son expression la plus forte dans
le domaine juridique où droit grec et droit égyptien cohabitent
sans concession.

Cependant, dans les paramètres de l'organisation du territoire,
l'interaction culturelle va jouer, mais de manière si inégale entre

les deux groupes qu'il s'agit le plus souvent d'agression culturelle du groupe privilégié, là où le groupe envahi présente des
traces d'archaïsme.

J'ai montré ailleurs comment, en Egypte, l'économie monétaire,
familière aux Grecs, a été imposée par la force des choses aux
Egyptiens, et ce dans une double contrainte: d'abord, celle de
trouver de l'argent et des cautions, ne fût-ce que pour payer l'impôt ou les licences de fabrication ou de vente, celle aussi de
penser en termes d'argent l'estimation du produit futur. Certes,
l'économie nature, particulièrement au niveau de l'impôt et du
loyer en blé, garde un rôle important; elle est nécessaire dans une
économie rurale extensive, qui poursuit jusqu'à un certain point
l'économie de tribut de l'époque achéménide. Mais les versements
en nature au Trésor qui n'ont pas de contre-partie en argent, n'ont
fait qu'aggraver pour l'Egyptien la difficulté de disposer de li-
quidités et d'accéder au crédit. L'économie d'argent a accentué
la dépendance de l'Egyptien et a perturbé les rapports tradition-
nels dans la communauté égyptienne.

Envisageons un autre facteur, — et autre exemple d'une analyse
sociologique qui se place aux antipodes de l'interprétation historique. L'insuffisance du mercenariat venu d'outre mer, l'affaiblissement d'une royauté épuisée par les fastes coûteux de ce
qu'on appelle les grands règnes, et déforcée par les problèmes
dynastiques, vont contraindre les Ptolémées à enrôler des troupes
égyptiennes. C'est là la cause initiale, convenons-nous tous, des
concessions que les Ptolémées devront faire au IIe siècle au clergé
égyptien. Ce n'est pas ici l'endroit de revoir ce problème né de
la désagrégation de l'autorité royale; notons cependant qu'il se
manifestera tout autant par la régularisation des usurpations et
exactions des clérouques grecs et la reconnaissance d'une sorte de
féodalité militaire et administrative grecque dans la chôra, surtout en Haute Egypte. Notre point de vue est différent. L'installation des *machimoi* égyptiens, détachés de leur terroir natal, sur-
des champs qu'ils cultivent effectivement dans un système clérou-
chique de type grec, crée un milieu indigène nouveau plus ou moins
détaché de la société égyptienne traditionnelle. Le développement
parallèle d'un fonctionnariat égyptien de village, dont Menchès de
Kerkéosiris est un modèle, est une autre évolution centrifuge de

cette même société. L'émancipation de l'Egyptien se fait d'abord
au détriment du système intégré autochtone.   Les signes de l'affaiblissement de celui-ci, particulièrement
dans son armature cléricale, se multiplient. Au Ier siècle, la do-
cumentation épigraphique sur l'asylie du temple, en soulevant le
problème de l'autorité du roi (mais le roi, ce n'est pas la communauté grecque) et de l'autonomie du clergé égyptien, pousse l'historien à conclure à la faiblesse du premier et à la puissance du
second. Il y a là sans doute une illusion. La concession du droit
d'asylie par le Roi signifie en fait que le temple n'est plus protégé naturellement. D'ailleurs, détail révélateur, dans ces textes,
le temple a eu souvent besoin d'être reconstruit. D'autres muta-
tions en profondeur relevant à première vue du système culturel,
ont progressivement vidé le système intégré égyptien. Je ne cite-
rai brièvement que deux d'entre elles: la croissance de la propriété privée ou de la possession privée stable de terres concédées,
et, parallèlement, la tendance des Grecs à se concentrer dans les
centres urbains pour devenir une classe de notables vivant d'une
campagne plus ou moins lointaine. Il s'est créé là un réseau nouveau de relations entre les deux groupes, qui a modifié les deux
systèmes, en lésant un peu plus le système égyptien à fondement
clérical, mais en n'affaiblissant pratiquement pas le système grec,
qui conserve ses paramètres culturels d'expression, fondamentaux
pour lui: la langue du pouvoir et l'éducation grecque traditionnelle.

     Les Romains vont parfaire la destruction d'un système intégré
égyptien déjà durement touché par la ruine, sous Ptolémée Sôter II,
d'un centre religieux aussi important que Thèbes. Le culte impérial égyptien s'étiole dans le formalisme, sans avoir aucune part
aux cultes impériaux officiels, cultes qui, a bien des points de
vue, ont donné à la religiosité d'Etat l'échelle de l'Empire. Mais
l'attaque romaine contre ce qui reste du système clérical égyptien
a pris des formes beaucoup plus précises. La propriété sacrée,
mobilière, immobilière et foncière, est inventoriée, contrôlée,
quand elle n'est pas amputée au profit du domaine public. Les sta-
tuts personnels et fiscaux privilégiés des prêtres sont contestés.
Ainsi s'affaiblit progressivement la classe sacerdotale qui était à
la fois le guide et l'organisateur du système culturel égyptien.

Ce système entrait d'ailleurs difficilement dans l'ordre nouveau institué en Egypte par Auguste et ses successeurs: une société
hiérarchisée avec ses Romains, ses Alexandrins, les Grecs privilégiés de l'intérieur, et les non-privilégiés qui, pour la plus grande
part, sont de langue égyptienne. Le système culturel intégré des
Grecs, qui a évolué depuis le début de l'époque hellénistique, va,
dans les structures nouvelles de l'Egypte romaine, se simplifier
en une société de grands et petits notables de culture grecque traditionnelle, société fondée sur la propriété terrienne et vouée à
la gestion municipale. Cela se traduira par une étonnante conservation de la culture grecque jusque dans les métropoles de l'époque
byzantine. Les paramètres culturels d'expression, la langue grecque
et l'éducation du gymnase, loin d'être attaqués, deviennent (mais
pour une partie seulement des gens de langue grecque) des paramètres
culturels élitaires d'organisation du privilège, alors qu'avant cela
ils étaient seulement le mode d'expression des privilèges d'un système socio-politique. Mais, en fait, on ne peut plus parler d'un
système culturel grec intégré dans l'Egypte du Haut Empire. Le
haut fonctionnariat romain, l'armée romaine, l'intervention croissante du privilégié alexandrin dans l'économie de la chôra, plus
que les implantations de vétérans, sont autant d'éléments qui rom-
pent le caractère global de la structure culturelle. Le Grec de la
chôra n'a plus un basileus, il a un empereur.

Lorsqu'au Haut Empire, les deux ensembles culturels qui co-
existent en Egypte cessent chacun d'être un système intégré, ils
deviendront certainement plus perméables; cela se constate en de
nombreux domaines. En fait, les interactions culturelles seront
malgré tout freinées. Le clivage linguistique reste en grande partie un clivage social, avec les réactions d'autoprotection culturelle des privilégiés et de cristallisation culturelle des ran-
coeurs des non-privilégiés. Même le bouleversement culturel de la
tétrarchie et de l'époque protobyzantine n'y changeront pas grand-
chose. Mais surtout, cette perméabilité croissante des deux groupes
vient trop tard pour nous fournir un modèle d'interactions culturelles bilatérales. Les échanges culturels en dehors de l'Egypte
se font depuis tout un temps à l'échelle de l'Empire; Alexandrie a
très tôt été impliquée dans les nouveaux courants de la culture de
l'Orient romain. L'Egypte des empereurs, dans ses deux cultures,

s'ouvrira à ce brassage intellectuel et affectif. Comme ce n'est
plus mon sujet, je ne l'évoquerai ici, avec le risque de trop simplifier les choses, que par un signe symbolique de la désagrégation
du vieux système culturel global fondé sur la langue, la religion
et la tradition scribale des Egyptiens. Il s'agit de la création
et de la diffusion de l'alphabet copte, mais surtout de l'ouverture
de l'écrit copte, malgré des continuités égyptiennes évidentes, sur
de grands courants cosmopolites: le christianisme, le gnosticisme,
le manichéisme, etc. On est loin du monde égyptien fermé de
l'époque hellénistique, et que ce monde égyptien est déjà à se re-
fermer sur lui-même est un autre problème. L'Empire a créé les
conditions d'arrivée à Alexandrie des courants venus de l'Orient,
comme l'explosion gréco-macédonienne l'avait fait pour les cultures
venues du nord; ce qui a créé les conditions d'accueil dans le plat
pays des apports culturels extérieurs, particulièrement sur le plan
religieux et le plan artistique, c'est la disparition du caractère
intégré, c'est-à-dire de la fonction globale du système culturel
égyptien traditionnel. L'évolution du milieu grec, grâce à la référence alexandrine très présente dans sa culture, a précédé la
mutation copte, sans avoir été aussi radicale. Mais ce sont les
mêmes mécanismes qui ont joué dans les deux cas: non la concurrence
des aspects classiques de la culture, mais bien le travail de sape
des mécanismes culturels secondaires, ce que j'ai appelé les paramètres culturels d'organisation: l'organisation grecque du pays,
qui, à l'époque hellénistique, sape lentement les piliers cléricaux
du système culturel égyptien; la hiérarchisation romaine de l'Egypte,
qui a supprimé le caractère intégré de la culture d'expression
grecque et rend celle-ci plus disponible pour l'écoute du monde
égyptien et du monde extérieur.

Bruxelles   Jean Bingen

PART 2

LITERARY PAPYRI

Proceedings of the XVI Int. Congr. of Papyrology (Chico 1981) 21-30

LES PAPYRUS ET LA CONSTITUTION DES CHOIX ANTIQUES
D'AUTEURS DRAMATIQUES

Le problème des choix antiques d'oeuvres dramatiques est l'un des problèmes importants que pose l'étude de la tradition manuscrite médiévale d'Eschyle, Sophocle, Euripide et Aristophane.[1] Dans ces quatre cas, l'élément le plus assuré du choix est constitué par une triade: *Prométhée*, les *Sept*, les *Perses*, pour Eschyle; *Ajax*, *Electre*, *Oedipe Roi*, pour Sophocle; *Hécube*, *Oreste*, les *Phéniciennes*, pour Euripide; *Ploutos*, les *Nuées*, les *Grenouilles*, pour Aristophane. A cette triade initiale est attachée une tétrade: cela est certain pour les tragiques,[2] très probable pour Aristophane.[3] Pour deux auteurs enfin, Aristophane et Euripide, le choix comporte un troisième élément: dans le cas d'Aristophane, rien n'empêche de parler de seconde tétrade;[4] dans le cas d'Euripide, même si l'on admet que le choix comportait au total dix pièces,[5] il est dificile de parler de seconde triade. Récemment le problème des choix

---

1 Bibliographie fondamentale: U. von Wilamowitz, *Einleitung in die griechische Tragödie* (Berlin 1889); P. Boudreaux, *Le Texte d'Aristophane et ses commentateurs* (Paris 1919); A. Tuilier, *Recherches critiques sur la tradition du texte d'Euripide* (Paris 1968); A. Wartelle, *Histoire du texte d'Eschyle dans l'Antiquité* (Paris 1971).

2 Voir en particulier les analyses d'A. Tuilier, *Recherches*, 101-03.

3 La comparaison des deux grands manuscrits d'Aristophane, le *Ravennas* et le *Venetus*, révèle au moins les incertitudes de la tradition. Le *Venetus*, qui transmet sept pièces, présente, après la triade, les *Cavaliers*, les *Oiseaux*, la *Paix* et les *Guêpes*. Le *Ravennas*, qui transmet onze pièces, présente, après la triade, les *Oiseaux*, les *Cavaliers* (ordre inverse du *Venetus*), la *Paix*, *Lysistrata*, les *Acharniens*, les *Guêpes* (qui sont donc séparées de la *Paix* par deux pièces), les *Thesmophories* et l'*Assemblée des Femmes*.

4 Pour la marge d'incertitude, voir la note précédente.

5 Le problème est de savoir s'il faut mettre les *Bacchantes* d'une part, le *Rhésos* et les *Troyennes* d'autre part, en relation avec le Choix ou avec la série alphabétique.

antiques d'auteurs dramatiques a connu un développement nouveau
quand on a supposé que l'oeuvre de Ménandre--ignorée par la tradition manuscrite médiévale--avait fait, elle aussi, l'objet d'une
sélection dans l'antiquité.[6] On a suggéré que cette sélection
comportait 24 pièces.[7] A lui seul, Ménandre se serait donc trouvé
équilibrer les tragiques.[8]

Mais le problème posé par ces choix ne concerne pas seulement
leur étendue et leur nature. Les discussions les plus passionnées
ont porté sans aucun doute sur la date à laquelle il faut situer
leur apparition: Wilamowitz optait pour le IIe siècle de notre ère,
d'autres savants descendent maintenant jusqu'au Ve siècle.[9] C'est
à cette occasion surtout que l'on a invoqué le témoignage des
"papyrus," et il faut croire que son interprétation est délicate.
A vrai dire, l'exemple offert par les études sur la tradition
médiévale inciterait déjà à la plus grande prudence. C'est ainsi

------

6　Cf. D. Del Corno, "Selezioni Menandree," *Dioniso* 38 (1964)
130-81.

7　Ibid., 177. Pour les catalogues du XVIe siècle qui conservent le souvenir d'un ensemble de 24 pièces de Ménandre, voir
A. Dain, "La survie de Ménandre," *Maia* 15 (1963) 304-06.

8　Equilibre parfait si l'on admet qu'à un certain moment,
le Choix d'Euripide a comporté dix et non pas seulement sept ou
neuf pièces (mais voir ci-dessus, n. 5). Il pourrait alors répondre au désir de mettre en parallèle la poésie épique et la
poésie dramatique. *(Homerus) Iliadem ad instar tragoediae, Odyssiam
ad imaginem comoediae fecisse monstratur*, dit, au IVe siècle, le
grammairien Evanthius de Constantinople (Donat, *Comm. Ter.*, éd.
Wessner, I, p. 15). Aux 24 chants de l'*Iliade*, correspondrait donc
un choix de 24 tragédies, aux 24 chants de l'*Odyssée*, un choix de
24 comédies. En faveur d'une telle construction, on peut encore
citer Libanios, *Or.* LXIV (*Pro Saltatoribus*), §72 (éd. R. Förster,
t. IV, p. 466,7), qui résume l'essentiel de la poésie par les noms
d'Homère, Eschyle, Euripide, Sophocle et Ménandre. C'est aussi
admettre que l'on ne saurait descendre plus bas que le IVe siècle
pour situer la constitution des choix dramatiques, et même songer
à une date plus haute. L'érudition byzantine ne fait que transmettre les modèles forgés par l'érudition romaine. C'est ainsi
que très vite Ménandre est séparé des poètes de la Comédie Ancienne
(prototype de la satire latine pour Varron) et rejoint Eschyle,
Sophocle et Euripide; cf. Denys d'Halicarnasse, Περὶ μιμήσεως,
422-24, p. 206-07 U.-R., et Quintilien, *Inst. Or.*, XI 1.66-72.

9　Voir, en dernier lieu, A. Tuilier, *Recherches*, 99.

que l'on appelle "byzantine" la triade initiale des choix parce
qu'elle est seule transmise par certains manuscrits récents:[10]
cela ne doit pas faire oublier qu'elle est peut-être l'élément le
plus ancien.

En fait il se pourrait bien qu'ici comme ailleurs, tous les
problèmes soient liés et que la solution des uns facilite celle des
autres. Il convient donc de reprendre l'examen des papyrus sans
négliger aucune des voies d'approche qui peuvent s'offrir. Dans le
cadre de cette communication, on abordera successivement l'étude
des ensembles que forment certains papyrus complexes et celle de
l'ensemble que forme la catégorie des papyrus dramatiques. On
n'oubliera pas, pour terminer, de replacer la documentation dans
son contexte: celui de l'Egypte gréco-romaine.

Le hasard des découvertes a fait que les papyrus portant les
restes de deux pièces au moins d'un auteur dramatique sont peu
nombreux.

On n'en connaît aucun pour Eschyle ou pour Sophocle. Pour
Euripide, on peut citer seulement le *P. Oxy*. XI 1370, restes d'un
codex de papyrus du Ve ou du VIe siècle et qui transmet la fin
d'*Oreste* et le début de *Médée*, ce qui permet de déduire avec assez
de probabilité, mais non avec certitude, l'ordre des deux pièces
dans le manuscrit. Cet ordre *Oreste-Médée* fait se succéder la
pièce centrale de la triade et la deuxième pièce de la tétrade, du
moins si l'on suit la numérotation indiquée dans le *Laurentianus*
XXXII-2. Il est difficile d'aller au delà de cette constatation.

Pour Aristophane, deux papyrus sont à considerer. Le *P.
Berlin* 13231, restes d'un codex de papyrus du Ve-VIe siècle, transmet des fragments de trois comédies: les *Grenouilles*, pièce de la
triade, les *Oiseaux* et les *Acharniens*, pièces des tétrades; mais
l'ordre des pièces est inconnu et l'on ignore même si elles se
suivaient immédiatement dans le manuscrit. La situation est dif-
férente dans le *P. Oxy*. XI 1373, restes d'un codex de papyrus du
Ve siècle, où l'ordre des pièces est assuré avec la fin de la

---

10 Pour la dénomination de "Choix byzantin," voir A. Dain,
Les manuscrits[3] (1975) 152; éd. du théâtre de Sophocle, C. U. F.,
I, p. XXXVIII.

Paix sur une face et le début des *Cavaliers* sur l'autre face d'un
même folio. Il s'agit cette fois de deux pièces de la première
tétrade qui se présentent dans l'ordre inverse dans le *Ravennas* et
de plus à distance dans le *Venetus*. Le papyrus amplifie donc
l'idée que l'on pouvait avoir des flottements concernant les tétrades d'après la tradition médiévale. On peut en déduire ou bien
qu'au Ve siècle, l'ordre des pièces n'était pas encore définitivement fixé, ou bien qu'il était déjà incompris et bouleversé.

Finalement la documentation la plus riche concerne Ménandre,
mais l'ignorance où nous sommes du contenu du choix antique crée
des difficultés particulières. Comme pour Aristophane, il est des
cas où l'ordre et la proximité des pièces ne sont pas assurés.
Ainsi, dans le parchemin de Leningrad 388, restes d'un codex du
IVe siècle, qui transmet des fragments de l'*Arbitrage* et de l'*Apparition*, et dans le *P. Berlin* 13932 + *PSI* 126, restes d'un codex de
parchemin du Ve siècle, qui transmet des fragments du *Bouclier* et
du *Haï*, on ne peut guère que considérer l'alliance des titres et
déplorer l'incertitude du contexte. Plus important devrait être le
codex cu Caire qui, au Ve siècle, transmet, après une pièce non
identifiée, le *Héros*, l'*Arbitrage*, la *Tondue*, et, à une place non
parfaitement assurée, la *Samienne*. Là encore cependant, l'état du
manuscrit empêche de tirer des conclusions certaines. Reste le
codex Bodmer qui, au IVe siècle, transmet dans l'ordre la *Samienne*,
le *Bourru* et le *Bouclier*. C'est bien l'exemple unique pour nous
d'un codex antique dont nous ayons toutes les composantes et chacune d'elles dans un état de conservation tel qu'il permet d'en-
visager une interprétation de l'ensemble.

Il est d'abord évident que nous n'avons pas affaire à l'un
des 35 ou 36 tomes de l'oeuvre théâtrale de Ménandre classée dans
l'ordre alphabétique.[11]

Il est d'autre part peu vraisemblable que nous ayons affaire
à un tome de l'édition complète classée dans l'ordre

11 Suivant les témoignages, en effet, Ménandre a écrit 105
ou 108 comédies. Il est probable que les 21 comédies de Plaute
ont dû ainsi, à un moment donné, être réparties en sept tomes; cf.
A. Tuilier, *Recherches*, 113 n. 7. Dans le cas de Ménandre, on n'a
aucune preuve d'une telle opération.

chronologique.[12] S'agit-il alors d'un choix, classé dans l'ordre
chronologique, comme on l'a suggéré?[13] Cela n'est pas vraisemblable non plus: les parallèles manquent, et ce que révèle l'étude des
triades tragiques, c'est plutôt un classement de type logique.[14]

C'est également à un principe logique que paraît obéir la
triade Bodmer. Considérons, en effet, le jugement moral que le
poète, et après lui le spectateur, est amené à porter sur le prin-
cipal personnage de chaque pièce: ce jugement moral est une des
fonctions essentielles de la Comédie. A plusieurs reprises, le
Moschion de la *Samienne* est qualifié de κόσμιος, "correct": par
lui-même, au v. 18, mais aussi, aux v. 273 et 344, par son père,
qui, dans le dernier cas, ajoute le qualificatif de σώφρων,
"réservé." Bref, c'est un bon garçon, même si sa passion de
l'honneur lui fait provoquer des catastrophes imprévues. Très
différent est le Smicrinès du *Bouclier* que la déesse Tyché, au v.
140, dans le prologue, qualifie de πονηρός, "coquin," terme qui
sera repris par d'autres personnages. Et de fait, par une cupidité
qui le rend inhumain, le personnage est vraiment une incarnation
du mal. L'opposition de Moschion et de Smicrinès est d'autant plus
facile à percevoir que le jeune homme est paralysé par sa passion
tandis que le vieillard est rendu très actif par la sienne. La
tonalité des deux pièces s'en ressent: la *Samienne* est une pièce
rose et brillante, le *Bouclier* est une pièce noire et grinçante.

Entre ces deux types de comédie, le *Bourru* paraît représenter
une position médiane. Cnémon est un personnage aussi virulent que
Smicrinès, et, du moins dans la première partie de la pièce, aussi
fâcheux pour son entourage. Mais au fond, il est μισοπόνηρος,
c'est un "ennemi du mal," comme le reconnaît Sostrate au v. 388.

---

12 On ne saurait invoquer, en effet, le classement chronologique des six comédies de Térence présenté par le manuscrit le plus
ancien de ce poète, le *Bembinus*: il s'agit là d'une oeuvre de
faible étendue.

13 J.-M. Jacques, *Ménandre. La Samienne* (Paris, C. U. F.
1971) p. L.

14 C'est ainsi le cas de la triade de Sophocle, même si les
pièces qui la composent sont très proches chronologiquement.

Ainsi la trilogie Bodmer paraît avoir une structure très
marquée: elle présente deux extrêmes encadrant un moyen terme. Le
type de pensée qui a présidé à sa naissance n'est pas inconnu par
ailleurs. C'est lui qui, à l'époque hellénistique, a conduit à
diviser la Comédie en trois périodes, la Comédie Ancienne caracté-
risée par l'attaque personnelle et la Comédie Nouvelle dépourvue
de ces attaques encadrant la Comédie Moyenne où l'attaque personnelle est dissimulée.[15] C'est lui encore qui organise la triade
des poètes de la Comédie Ancienne, Cratinos, Aristophane et Eupolis, la violence amère du premier et la grâce du troisième trouvant
leur juste équilibre chez le second.[16]

Faut-il conclure que la triade Bodmer--et, avec elle, les
triades d'Eschyle, Sophocle, Euripide et Aristophane--a été insti-
tuée à l'époque hellénistique? Le problème n'est pas si simple.
A époque ancienne, en effet, triade et choix ne sont pas deux notions nécessairement liées. Que l'on songe à la tentative, avortée, d'Aristophane de Byzance pour organiser l'oeuvre de Platon en
trilogies.[17] Au moment de la constitution des choix (comportant
chaque fois, comme noyau immuable, une triade et une tétrade), la
ou les triades[18] peuvent avoir été simplement choisies dans un
stock préexistant ou peut-être composées à partir de plusieurs

---

15 Cf. R. Pfeiffer, *History of Classical Scholarship from the
beginnings to the end of the hellenistic age* (1968) 242. On trou-
vera les textes, tardifs, reflétant cette doctrine dans W. J. W.
Koster, *Scholia in Aristophanem*, IA: *Prolegomena de Comoedia*
(Groningue 1975) IV, 11-17; XIa I, 69-77, 97-104; XIc, 29-43; XVIIIa,
26-44.

16 Cf. Koster, *Scholia*, II, 14-17. Selon Pfeiffer (*History*,
160), l'auteur de la doctrine transmise ici par Platonius serait
Dionysiadès de Mallos qui vécut dans la première moitié du IIIe
siècle avant J.-C.

17 Cf. Diogène Laerce, III, 61-62.

18 Dans le cas de Ménandre, s'il y a eu un choix de 24 comédies (voir ci-dessus, nn. 7 et 8), trois possibilités se présentent: huit triades, ou six tétrades, ou bien encore, à l'image du
choix tragique, quatre triades et trois tétrades.

d'entre elles, l'opération étant rendue possible par l'identité de
structure des triades originelles.[19]

Le second point de cet exposé--l'analyse de l'ensemble que
forme la catégorie des papyrus dramatiques--se signale, au contraire du premier, par l'ampleur de la documentation et l'on peut en
espérer un élargissement notable des perspectives. Certes la
nature même de cette documentation, le fait qu'elle soit marquée
par le hasard des découvertes de papyrus, imposent une certaine prudence: on se gardera ainsi de fonder tout un raisonnement sur
l'absence d'attestation de tel auteur ou de telle oeuvre; on ris-
querait trop d'être un jour cruellement démenti. Cependant on peut
garder une certaine confiance. W. Willis, comparant, en 1958, le
catalogue d'Oldfather et le premier catalogue de Pack, reconnais-
sait l'existence d'une certaine constance dans la répartition des
auteurs transmis par les papyrus.[20] De son côté, B. Donovan, dans
le livre qu'il a consacré en 1970 aux papyrus d'Euripide trouvés à
Oxyrhynchos, remarquait que cet échantillon était assez représen-
tatif de l'ensemble des papyrus de ce poète trouvés dans toute
l'Egypte.[21] Autrement dit, les papyrus, dans leur masse actuelle,
offrent un élément de certitude. Leur grand avantage est alors
d'attirer l'attention sur des phénomènes connus par ailleurs, mais
dispersés: ces éléments connus, tout en contribuant à la solidité
de la démonstration, reçoivent eux-mêmes un nouvel intérêt de la
liaison que leur assurent les papyrus. Il ne saurait être question

---

19 Ce qui pourrait bien distinguer les triades du choix des
triades hellénistiques, c'est qu'elles répondraient à plusieurs
exigences à la fois: celle de la structure triadique "aristotéli-
cienne" (deux extrêmes encadrant un moyen terme), la complémenta-
rité des poètes (par exemple, Sophocle et Euripide), et enfin
l'ordre alphabétique, ordre alphabétique direct dans le cas des
triades tragiques (pour les titres d'Eschyle, il faut alors tenir
compte de l'article, cf. Tuilier, *Recherches*, 102), ordre alphabétique inversé dans le cas des triades comiques (Aristophane et
triade Bodmer).

20 W. H. Willis, "Greek Literary Papyri from Egypt and the
Classical Canon," *Harvard Library Bulletin* 12 (1958) 5-34, en
particulier 17.

21 B. E. Donovan, *Euripides Papyri. I: Texts from Oxyrhynchus*
(Toronto 1970), en particulier p. 4.

de tout exposer ici.[22] On retiendra seulement, comme particulièrement importantes, deux séries de faits.   .

D'abord les papyrus confirment l'existence de relations
binaires entre poètes et cela au profit de chacun d'eux.

Le couple essentiel est formé, depuis Aristophane de Byzance,
par Homère (poésie épique) et par Ménandre (poésie dramatique).
Les Latins ont imité en cela les Grecs et chez eux le couple formé
par Virgile et Térence symbolise aussi la poésie. On ne s'étonnera
pas de l'importance papyrologique de ces deux, de ces quatre
auteurs.

Dans le domaine grec, d'autres couples sont importants. Ainsi
Euripide symbolise la tragédie, tandis que Ménandre symbolise la
comédie; au sein de la tragédie Sophocle symbolise la noblesse
classique, Euripide une sorte de pathétique romanesque. La supré-
matie de ces poètes est définitive à l'époque dite byzantine (IVe-
VIIe siècles).

Parallèlement au renforcement constant des auteurs intégrés
dans des systèmes à deux éléments antithétiques, on observe la
régression de certains auteurs intégrés dans des systèmes à trois
éléments. On pourrait dire tout aussi bien que l'on assiste à une
régression des systèmes à trois éléments devant les systèmes à
deux éléments.

L'effacement le plus rapide a été celui du ou des poètes de
la Comédie Moyenne. On trouve encore un papyrus d'Antiphane au IIe
siècle de notre ère. Au sein de la triade tragique, on note l'effacement d'Eschyle à l'époque byzantine. De même dans la triade de
la Comédie Ancienne, on doit noter sans doute l'effacement de
Cratinos.

La netteté des tendances qui viennent d'être indiquées ne doit
cependant pas faire oublier que certaines d'entre elles seront
assez vite rectifiées. C'est ainsi qu'Eschyle aura une tradition
médiévale, mauvaise certes, mais réelle. Inversement des poètes

---

22 Une étude approfondie devrait évidemment comporter des
tableaux statistiques précis tenant compte des papyrus trouvés
depuis R. A. Pack, *The Greek and Latin Literary Texts from Greco-
Roman Egypt*[2] (Ann Arbor 1965) répertoire auquel je ne puis que
renvoyer ici.

jusque là favorisés, comme Ménandre, ou relativement épargnés,
comme Eupolis, ne survivront pas. Cela demande explication et il
ne sera pas inutile, pour terminer, de replacer les phénomènes
étudiés dans leur contexte historique et géographique.

Le contexte historique est donné par l'évolution de la critique littéraire dans l'antiquité.[23] Le contexte géographique,
c'est celui de l'Egypte d'où proviennent presque tous nos papyrus.[24]

A l'époque ptolémaïque, le centre le plus important de l'éru-
tion se situe précisément en Egypte, à Alexandrie, et l'on imagine
que les papyrus répercutent assez rapidement les orientations de
cette érudition. Mais si l'important, dans la perspective des
choix futurs, c'est l'organisation du corpus des textes dramatiques,
il est évident que ces papyrus, en tant que restes de *volumen*, ne
peuvent guère nous fournir de renseignements utiles.

Au Ier siècle avant J.-C., le centre vivant de l'érudition se
déplace: il se situe désormais à Rome. Grecs et Latins y travail-
lent. Varron, pour sa part, recueille l'héritage de l'érudition
alexandrine, mais il a des préoccupations nouvelles: il cherche
avant tout à donner ses lettres de noblesse à la littérature latine.
Avec lui, alors que Ménandre est naturellement le prototype de la
comédie latine, la triade de la Comédie Ancienne, Cratinos, Aristophane et Eupolis, devient le prototype de la satire. Etant donné
le petit nombre de pièces de ces trois poètes que les Grecs avaient
conservé, c'est le principe d'un véritable sauvetage. Mais les
idées de Varron n'auront leur plein effet que plusieurs générations
après, lorsque, la comédie mise à part, les nouveaux poètes auront
détrôné les anciens, essentiellement lorsque Virgile aura détrôné
Ennius. C'est alors que les systèmes binaires, qui n'étaient pas

---

23 C'est un contexte relativement limité. Pour une vision
plus large, on se reportera à A. Pertusi, "Selezione teatrale e
scelta erudita nella tradizione del testo di Euripide," *Dioniso* 19
(1956) 111-41; 195-216; 20 (1957) 18-37.

24 Ce problème n'a pas été oublié par M. Manfredi dans sa
communication au XIIe congrès de papyrologie à Ann Arbor, en 1968,
sur "I papiri e gli studi su Euripide negli ultimi decenni," *Proceedings* (Toronto 1970) 275.

inconnus des Grecs,[25] mais qui sont dominants en milieu latin,[26]
peuvent prendre leur forme définitive, toujours en intégrant les
éléments triadiques hérités de la pensée hellénistique. Est-ce
vers la fin du IIe siècle qu'à Rome la nouvelle poésie élimine
l'ancienne dans la tradition manuscrite?[27] En tout cas les papyrus
d'Egypte ne sauraient être si rapidement sensibles à ces changements importants, même s'ils ont eu des répercussions dans le domaine grec. Le IIIe siècle est un siècle incertain.

Au IVe siècle cependant, le centre vivant de l'érudition se
rapproche avec Constantinople. La nouvelle capitale est un instrument actif de romanisation et l'Egypte se trouve moins à l'écart.
L'histoire de cette époque, que la documentation papyrologique
éclaire alors assez bien, paraît se résumer en un double mouvement.
D'abord, bien évidemment, l'application des modèles latins: réap-
parition sensible d'Aristophane, déclin presque total d'Eschyle, en
particulier. Mais comme la littérature latine reste confinée en
Orient dans des cercles restreints et que l'essentiel de la culture
reste grec, l'on assiste bientôt, dans ce cadre même, à une sorte
de réaction qui prend la forme d'un retour aux sources et que les
papyrus ne font que suggérer: Eschyle n'est pas vraiment condamné,
et, alors que Ménandre va bientôt disparaître pour des raisons qui
lui sont propres, la survie du vieil Aristophane comme seul poète
comique est définitivement assurée.

Alain Blanchard

---

25 Cf. l'opposition d'Eschyle et d'Euripide dans les *Grenouilles* d'Aristophane ou le rapprochement d'Homère et de Ménandre par
Aristophane de Byzance, pour prendre deux époques différentes.

26 Cf., par exemple, le classement en tétralogies de l'oeuvre
de Platon (Diogène Laerce, III, 56, etc.).

27 Cf., pour Lucilius, F. Charpin, *Lucilius. Satires* I (Paris
C. U. F. 1978) 35.

Proceedings of the XVI Int. Congr. of Papyrology (Chico 1981) 31-41

A GREEK-LATIN VOCABULARY

P. Berol. 21246

Heracleopolis
late 1st c. B.C.

In the spring of 1975, the Deutsche Forschungsgemeinschaft
agreed to finance a six-year project researching the cartonnage
mummy cases from Abusir el-Melek now in the Ägyptisches Museum of
West Berlin. One mummy case produced documents dating to the reign
of Augustus[1] which will eventually appear in a *BGU* volume. In addition to these a fragment of Demosthenes *De Chersoneso* (to appear
in *ZPE*) and two subliterary texts came to light: a magical formulary (*P. Berol.* 21243) published in *ZPE* 33 ([1979] 261-78) and a
Greek-Latin word list written entirely in Greek letters,[2] the subject of the following pages.

I

Editors have traditionally assumed that transliterated vocabularies such as this were exercises created "für den Schulge-
brauch."[3] A. Wouters, however, in *Hermeneus* 48 ([1976] 188), takes
the tradition to task. In the first place, he argues, the pedagogical value of such an exercise is doubtful. In the second, no
ancient author ever mentions the practice. Lastly, he notes the
existence of bilingual word lists which have not been transliterated.

---

1 One exception is a document written in quadruplicate (*BGU*
XIV 2376, 2377) dating to 36/35 B.C.

2 Mentioned in *ZPE* 33 (1979) 261; *P. XV Congr.* 19 Anm. 2;
BGU XIV Einleitung, p. viii.

3 K. Preisendanz in F. Milkau, *Handbuch der Bibliotheks-
wissenschaft* (Wiesbaden 1952) I, 238. J. Rea, *P. Oxy.* XXXVI 2772
introd.; N. Priest, *ZPE* 27 (1977) 194-95; H. Marrou, *Histoire de
l'éducation dans l'antiquité* (Paris 1965⁶) 386-88; R. Gaebel, *BJRL*
52 (1969-70) 285; U. Wilcken, *Grundzüge* 138; P. Beudel, *Qua ratione
Graeci liberos docuerint, papyris, ostracis, tabulis in Aegypto
inventis illustratur* (Diss. Monast. 1911) 35 n. 2; A. Bataille,
RechPap 4 (1967) 165; G. Cuendet, *Mélanges Boisacq. Annuaire de
l'Institut de Philologie et d'Histoire Orientales et Slaves* 5 (1937)
221; and M. Leroy, *Byzantion* 13 (1938) 514 concur.

Differences in level of difficulty which might explain why some
vocabularies have been transliterated and others not are not readily apparent. He then suggests that transliterated word lists arose
from dictations to the students who wrote down what they heard as
best they could.

Albeit at first glance attractive, these arguments can be re-
futed and the traditional interpretation maintained--with certain
qualifications to be explained below.

Notwithstanding ancient authors' reticence on the methods of
acquiring a foreign language, the pedagogical value of transliterated texts in the initial phase of learning a language is obvious.
Any modern introductory grammar book contains phonetic transliterations in its first chapters--especially if the alphabet of the new
language is not the Roman one.

The crux of the matter lies in the necessary distinction between students' exercises, i.e. productions of the students themselves, and drills prepared by the teacher for the students' benefit. Students' exercises in transliteration in the first sense
never existed. Wouters is right: the pedagogical value of trans-
literating vocabulary words or a text is dubious. Bilingual transliterated glossaries[4] are not products of classroom dictation but
exercises in pronunciation and translation, prepared by the teach-
ers for the students. Solid evidence for this proposition are the
fine literary scripts in which some of them have been written (sometimes even on parchment, e.g. *ZPE* 27 [1977] 115).[5]

---

4   Whole transliterated documents, such as *PSI* VI 743, *P. Oxy.*
XXXVI 2772; *SB* III 6304 = *CPLat.* 193; *BGU* XI 2116.21-22, are the
products of bilinguals, illiterate in one or the other language
(Wouters, op. cit., 180-87; Lowe, *CLA Suppl.* [Oxford 1971] no.
1693).

5   Cf. W. Schubart's remark cited in n. 8. Worthy of note is
P. Ant. 1 (= H. Milne, *Greek Shorthand Manuals* [London 1934] pl.
IX); Lowe, *CLA* 1705), an elegantly written Roman alphabet. A hand
just as experienced has penned in above each letter the name in
Greek transliteration. The Roman alphabet in *P. Oxy.* 1315 (= Lowe,
CLA 1681) was written "by a beginner...or possibly by an aged
teacher." Above some of the Roman letters another, less experienced, hand (the student's ?) has written the corresponding Greek
letter. The purpose in both cases is to acquaint the beginner with
the sounds of the Roman alphabet. The exercise involves not the
transliteration but the pronunciation and memorization of the foreign alphabet.

The often peculiar, obscure and haphazard nature of the subject matter contained in these glossaries has also long demanded
an explanation. Lists of fishes (*ZPE* 27 [1977] 115-17; *ZPE* 29
[1978] 240) or vegetables (*P. Oxy.* XXXIII 2660) or birds, spices,
fishes, vegetables inter alia (*ZPE* 26 [1977] 231ff.) or parts of
the body (Pack[2] 2136) in transliteration seem very exotic study
material indeed for someone who is not yet even able to read the
new language. However, as postulated above, pronunciation, although perhaps the primary, was not necessarily the sole objective
of transliterated lists. If the student simultaneously picked up
some vocabulary words he would be that much further ahead in his
education, for the day would come when he would have to learn not
only these but many other words just as obscure. As M. Naoumides
(*Classical Studies presented in honor of B. E. Perry* [Urbana 1969]
185 n. 9) notes, "That memorization of the meaning of rare and obsolete words was part of the students' training in school is well
known from the famous fragment of Aristophanes' Δαιταλῆς."[6] S. F.
Bonner (*Education in Ancient Rome* [London 1977] 171) cites Varro
(*L.L.* IX 15): *et hi qui pueros in ludum mittunt ut discant quae
nesciunt verba quemadmodum scribant.* That the student soon memor-
ized his words not from transliterated but from normally written
vocabularies goes without saying.

Departing from the strict classroom situation and processes
of formal education[7] and broadening the scope of the word "student"
to include anyone learning to whatever extent and for whatever purpose a foreign language, one might consider these vocabularies as
forerunners of the modern "Polyglott-Sprachführer," a popular series in the German-speaking countries of Europe, which are not so
much grammars of the foreign languages as they are phrase-books,

---

6 A. Cassio, *Banchettanti* (ΔΑΙΤΑΛΗΣ) (Pisa 1977) 75:
πρὸς ταύταις δ' αὖ λέξον 'Ομήρου γλῶττας, τί καλοῦσι κόρυμβα;
                ... τί καλοῦσ' ἀμενηνὰ κάρηνα;
ὃ μὲν οὖν σός, ἐμὸς δ' οὗτος ἀδελφὸς φρασάτω τι καλοῦσιν ἰδυίους;

7 Bilingual transliterated vocabularies are not logically and
scientifically constructed grammar manuals, as are, for example, *P.
Iand.* 5.83; *P. Rein.* II 86-87 = Pack[2] 2659-2661, and 2738; *ZPE* 6
(1970) 133ff.

aids for the traveller or business man.[8]

With the date of the Berlin vocabulary in mind, it is easy to imagine why it was written. Soon after the battle at Actium some-one very eager to learn the language of the new rulers set out to study Latin even before he could properly read it. The economic and social advantages it would bring him were strong incentives.

II

The word list is written on the back of a register recording land holdings. Other fragments of the same land register have no writing on the back, while still others contain writing, but of an entirely different nature. The script is small and precisely writ-ten, very similar in appearance to *P. Hercul.* 1065, reproduced in Montevecchi, *La papirologia*, Tav. 26 (1st c. B.C.). Assuming that it is contemporaneous with the documents from the same mummy coffin the vocabulary would date to the late first century B.C., thus mak-ing it one of the oldest "Latin" papyri to date, predating the famous Giessen fragment of Cicero's *In Verrem* (= *P. Iand.* 90) by probably several decades (v. R. Seider, *Congr.* XIV 279 "spätaugust-eisch"; H. G. Gundel, *Kurzber. aus d. Papyrusslg.* 40 [1980] 402), and approximately contemporaneous with *CPLat.* 246 and 247.

The papyrus' condition is miserable. Breaks and tears, ripped-off fibers, cut edges and abrasions have all taken their share of letters. As if this were not enough, the phonetic rendition of the Latin words, the sometimes imprecise or incorrect translations coupled with the fact that any word in either entry might be a neo-logism, hence unattested in either normal or reverse lexica, have made the decipherment of these fragments particularly strenuous. Much still remains to be done.

Although most of the fragments break off to the right, the entries apparently consisted of no more than two or three words and extended little beyond the broken edge of the papyrus (v. lines 102, 104, 106, 118, 124, where there is ample space between the last word of the entry and the edge of the papyrus).

---

8   See W. Schubart on *P. Berol.* 10582, the famous Latin-Greek-Coptic conversation manual in which the Latin and Coptic are also written in Greek letters (*Berichte aus den Kgl. Kunstslg.* 31 [1909-10] 49-50); C. Préaux, *Cd'E* 14 (1939) 187 on Pack[2] 2136, a Greek conversation manual written in Armenian script.

Apart from isolated examples of verb conjugations (lines 5ff.,
23ff., 48ff.), the entries evidently follow in no order, alphabetical, contextual or categorical, but are rather thrown together
higgledy-piggledy, colloquial next to poetical, pedestrian and sub-
lime side by side. They consist of a Greek word or phrase, then
below and slightly indented the Latin translation in Greek letters.
Occasional paragraphoi (in one case a numeral--line 88) indicate
divisions. An obscure heading preserved on one fragment (line 1)
seems to be more an admonition to the student than a title.

Probably the most interesting aspect of this vocabulary is the
appearance of so many neologisms in both Greek and Latin (104
'Αμάλθαιος, 117 *improdest*, 124 ἀναλοία, 125 *apeps*). Were they
created just for the occasion of this word list or were they copied
from another manuscript, extracted from literary works unknown to
us?

Also worthy of note is the Greek proverb in line 74, σῦκον ἐφ'
'Ερμῇ, which is attested by Zenobius and Eustathios (v. n. ad loc.).

Both the Greek and Latin reveal sound classical traits. The
only example of itacism is in line 102. Latin quantities are generally faithfully rendered by the Greek, e.g. 4 δικτιωνης = dic-
tiōnēs, 69 ακητει = acētī, 103 κηναμ = cēnam, 117 ινπρωδεστ = im-
prōdest, 119 σινε = sĭnĕ - long i being rendered by -ει. However,
in line 119 ομο ≠ homō; 127 ουωουερε ≠ vŏvĕre.

Frg. 1 7.7 x 6.2 cm.		12	ρεδδιδει	[
(margin 1.2 cm.)			ἀποδέδωκεν	[
ε̣ 9̣ χαροντος ἀσχολία	[		ρεδδι̣[διτ	
ε̣ λατωνα οκκουπατι	[ωνε			
—			**Frg. 2 7.4 x 3.5 cm.**	
πτώσεις	[		ἰλαρό[ς	
4 δικτιωνης	[	16	ιλα̣[ρους	
ἁ]πόδος	[		ἵνα .ο[	
ρεδδε	[		ο̣υ̣[τ	
ἀποδώσω	[		ἀστή[ρ]	[
8 ρεδδαμ	[	20	[σ]τε̣[λλα	
ἀποδίδωμι	[		κ̣τη..[	
ρεδδω	[		[.].[	
ἀποδέδωκα	[		κρατ.[	

24 [τ]ε̣[ν-   ουην<ι>ηβατ [
    κρατε̣ι̣[(ται)?   ἡ φύσις   [
    τε[νετ(ουρ)   ινγεν[ι]ομ [
    κρατῆτ[αι   60   ἧτ[ει
28 τεν[εατουρ   -ποσκηβατ [
    (margin 1.4 cm.)   (margin 1.7 cm.)

    Frg. 3   5 x 3.5 cm.   Frg. 5   8.3 x 3.2 cm.
    διαμε[μυο̣[..]...[
      κου.[   ]α̣τα[
    διατη[64   ξένον διϛ[
32 κ<ο>υα[..]α[ο̣σπιτ[εμ
    δια[.]α̣.[..].[καμη̣λ̣κ̣ε[.].[
    [.].[ουε̣ι̣εριν[
    δι̣[α..]ε̣[68   δξους διαθε̣.[
36 [ακητει̣[
    επιμ[λιδος
    ι̣μ̣[ἀρτοπωδισε[
                                          πιστω̣ρ[ις
                                 72   εἰς οἶκον μὰ α[
    Frg. 4   12.4 x 4.6 cm.   δομι ειν [
      ].[σῦ]κον ἐφ᾿ ῾Ερμο̣ῦ[
40   ].[φε̣ι̣κ[ους Μερκουριω
      ].[
      ].ι[Frg. 6   12 x 4.6 cm.
      ]ωρη[76   ].[..] συν.[
44   ]αι[   ] [..]   [
      ]αιο[   ].[..] ἐπιμε̣[
      ]   [   ]   ι̣μ[
      ].εσ[80   ]   ἡμέραις [
48 ἦλ[θ]ετε   ]   ]   __ διη[βους
    [ο]υ̣ηνι[στ]ι̣ς[   ]   σῖτα̣ μο.ε[
    ἦ[λ]θο̣με̣ν̣ [   ].ϛ   [
    ουηγι̣μους [84   ]   ο̣ύρι[..].[.]δ[
52 ἦλθον   [   ].   σεκουγ[δ-
    ουηνει [   ]   γέροντος α..[
    ἦρχε[τ]ε̣ [   ].ι̣ω   σενε̣[ις
    ουην<ι>ηβα[τις   88   ]   λ̄ πλούσι[ο]ς δ̣α[
56 ηλθελεν [   ]   διο̣.[

]   ⁻.ọανα[.]σ[
]   .ο[
92]   ἡμιονικ[ὁ]ν [
]   μο[υλεινουμ
]   ἱερόν [
]   [τεμπλουμ
(margin 2 cm.)

ινσουλσους απεψ[
δ[ι]ὰ παντ[ὸς] εὔχεται .[
σεμπερ ουωουερε [
128 ......σις   [
μ.[.]φ[ο]υς μαιορ   [
(margin 2.2 cm.)

___

Frg. 7 19.4 x 5.5 cm.

96   ].α[
]   ].ιο[...]..[
traces
]   ].[..].ρ.ισ[
100 διὰ δακ[τυλίου] σφραγεί[ζων ?
ạγ[ουλω] οψιγναγ[ς ?
δ<ε>ίπνου κλῆσις [
αδ [κ]ηνα<μ> ουοκ[ατιω
104 Ἀμάλθαιος   [
κορ[ν]ου[κ]ωπι.[
.γ[.]φοοκ[.]πος
ιμ[..]να.ορσαμ[
108 ἀνήνυσ[το]ς δαπάνῃ [
ινετ ινσουμπ[τουμ
[γ]υνὴ πονηρά .   .[
..[...]ηκρυτρ[ιξ
112 εἰμὶ αικ[...]υς [
spatium
νύκτερ[ος] ἡμέρα [
νου[..]..νạσα[
116 ἀνωφελ[ὲς] .ενος [
                           ος
ινπρωδεστ ̣πρῶ[
[ἄ]θεος ἄνθ'ρ'ωπος [
σινε δειβους ομο [
120 του κόσμ[ο]υ σύνχυσις [
τερραι κοντουρβ[ατιω
πλουσίου [.]πατạτạ.ι [
διο.ειτιδηλ[.]κου[
124 ἀναλσία ἄπεπτος   [

___

Frg. 8 12 x 2.5 cm.

]ντ
]
].τ
]ν
]..ν.
]
]ωτε
]
].···   .[
]   θε[
]ρω   [
]   θ[
]···   [
]   ϑ.[
]βω   [
]   θε[
]βιτ   κ[
]   [
]του[ρ]   μα[
]   [
]τι   .ομ[
]
].τ[

___

Frg. 9 7.7 x 1.3 cm.

-ο]υη[ρο]υντ[
space of three lines
]τ
]
-ου]ντ

Frg. 10   4 x 2.8 cm.
traces

Frg. 11   2.5 x 1 cm.
].ων[

1 1. χαίροντος ?: Possible references here to Charon and in the
   next line to Latona seem in the context rather farfetched.

2 λατωνα: Probably something like *laetantis occupatione* was
   intended here, which would roughly correspond to the Greek of
   line 1. Taken together they exhorted the student to diligence
   in his new undertaking. The enigmatic signs to the left of
   lines 1 and 2 may form a sort of coronis.

3 πτώσεις: *Gloss.* (= *Corpus Glossariorum Latinorum*, ed. G. Goetz,
   [Leipzig-Berlin 1888ff., repr. Amsterdam 1965] πτῶσις: *casus*.
   Although most commonly applied to flexions of the noun, it can
   also be used for other parts of speech (v. LSJ s.v.) - among
   them the verb, as here and in Aristotle, *de Interpr.* 16 b 17:
   ὁμοίως δὲ καὶ τὸ ὑγίανεν ἢ τὸ ὑγιανεῖ οὐ ῥῆμα, ἀλλὰ πτῶσις
   ῥήματος.

4 δικτιωνης: *Gloss.*, *dictio*: ῥῆσις, λέξις.

5 *Gloss.* ἀπόδος: *redde*.

9 *Gloss.* ἀποδίδωμι: *absolvo, reddo, perhibeo, sarcio*.

12 ρεδδιδει: Cf. line 53 ουηνει. ει represents here the long i
   of the verb ending (cf. ZPE 27 [1977] 197: Λειβερα, Εισις; *P.
   Oxy.* 2660 Fr. 1: [λακ]ερτει, πεκτουνκ[ου]λει; here in line 69
   ακητει, where ει = ī).

15 *Gloss.* ἱλαρός: *hilaris, laetus*.

18 ου[τ: Mere dots are visible. *Gloss.* ἵνα: *ita ut, ut*. Regarding the difference between long and short u and their transliterations in Greek, s. W. Dittenberger, *Hermes* 6 (1872) 281,
   quoted in extenso in ZPE 26 (1977) 233.

19-20 *Gloss.*, *stella*: ἀστήρ, ἀκτῖναι; ἀστήρ: *aster, astrum, sidus,
   stella*.

23ff. *Gloss.* κρατῶ: *teneo*.

37-38 Cf. 78-79. The two fragments do not apparently join.

48 *Gloss.* ἔρχομαι: *venio*.

56-57 Either ἤρχετο = ουηνιηβατ or ἦλθεν = ουηνιτ are possible
emendations.

58 Gloss. φῦσις: sexus, natura, ingenium.

59 ινγεν[ι]ομ: ομ is a normal rendition of -um; see W. Dittenberger, Hermes 6 (1872) 281, quoted in ZPE 26 (1977) 233.

60-61 Gloss., poposci = ἤτησα.

66-67 The entries here defy interpretation. Other possible
readings include καπηα-, ουεισ-.

70-71 1. ἀρτοπῶλιδος πιστρικις or ἀρτοπῶλου πιστωρις. Gloss.
ἀρτοπῶλης: panarius; ἀρτοκόπος: pistor.

72-73 Gloss., domi: οἴκοι. P. Berol. 10582.143 (= CPLat. 281):
ιν δομουμ: εἰς τὴν οἰκίαν. If in line 73 the locative domi
is intended, then the corresponding Greek should be something
like κατ' οἴκον, ἐν οἴκῳ or οἴκοι. The rest of the entries are
enigmatic. ειν [δομω for in domo? The ī of the locative
domi is here mistakenly represented not by ει but by iota; cf.
88-89 n.

74-75 σῦ]κον ἐφ' Ἑρμοῦ (1. Ἑρμῇ): Cf. Zenobius 5.92: σῦκον ἐφ'
Ἑρμῇ· παροιμία ἐπὶ τῶν ἐκκειμένων ἐπ' ὠφελείᾳ τοῖς βουλομέ-
νοις· εἴ ποτε γὰρ φανείη σῦκον, τοῦτο τῷ Ἑρμῇ ἀνατιθέασι·
τοῦτο δὲ οἱ βουλόμενοι ἀνελάμβανον; Eustath. ad Od. 8.116:
σῦκον ἐφ' Ἑρμῇ ἤγουν ἕρμαιον καὶ εὕρημα ἐκκείμενον ἐπ'
ὠφελείᾳ τοῦ ἐντυχόντος. Hesychius, Photius and the Suda all
contain the phrase and almost identical explanations of it.
The Latin version is apparently unattested.

78-79 Gloss. ἐπιμένω: immaneo; ἐπιμερίζω: impertio; cf. lines
37-38.

82 σῖτα μορε[? A form of μείρομαι? However, rho and epsilon
are very uncertainly read.

84-85 Gloss., secundus: δεύτερος, οὔριος, δεξιός; secundus ventus
οὔριος ἄνεμος.

86-87 Gloss. γέρων evi maturus senex. σενε[ις ≠ senīs; cf. 72-73
n., 88-89 n.

88-89 πλοῦσι[ο]ς: A stroke slants from the middle of the left
side of omicron upwards to the left. Since it displays the
same curve as the left branch of the upsilon succeeding it,
it is probably a scribal error.
διου[ης ? If the scribe were consistent in his rendition of
the Latin quantities he would have to write δειουης = dīves.

90-91 προανα[ι]σ[ιμῶ, προανα[ι]σ[χυντῶ ?: Problematic is the
first letter of the Latin of which only the lower rightmost
corner remains. Two strokes, one not quite horizontal and
above it one diagonal, could belong to delta or beta.

94-95 *Gloss.*, *templum*: ἱερόν, ναός, σηκός, τέμενος.

100-101 *Gloss.*, *anulus*: δακτύλιος, δακτυλίδιν; *obsigno*: σφραγίζω,
κατασφραγίζω.
οψιγναγ[ς: E. Sturtevant, *The Pronunciation of Greek and Latin*
(Philadelphia 1940) 173-74, cites Quintilian 1.7.7, Terentius
Scaurus 7.27.11-17K and Velius Longus 7.61.5-9, who all discuss the discrepancy between the "p" sound one hears and its
rendition with "b" in such words as *plebs*, *urbs* and *obtinuit*.

102-103 *Gloss.*, δεῖπνον: *cena*; κλῆσις: *citatio*, *invitatus*, *vocatio*,
vocatus. There is between alpha and omicron either a vertical
stroke (iota ?) or a speck of dirt. *My* is definitely not
legible.

104 Ἀμάλθαιος: *addendum lexicis*. Ἀμαλθεῖον *aut sim.* is impossible.

105 *Gloss.*, *cornicupia*: κέρας Ἀμαλθέας τῆς θρεψάσης τὸν Δία αἰγός.

108-109 *Gloss.* δαπάνη: *expensa*, *sumptus*, *inpendium*, *inpensio*;
sumptus: ἀνάλωμα, δαπάνη. The letters preceding *insumptum* in
line 109 still defy interpretation.

114-115 *Gloss.*, *nocturnus*: νυκτερινός; ἡμέρα: *dies*, *aurora*.

115 l. νοχ[το]υρνα ?

116 *Gloss.* ἀνωφελής: *incommodus*, *infructuosus*, *inutilis*, *irritus*.
prosum: ὠφελῶ; *prodest*: ὠφέλιμόν ἐστιν.

117 ινπρωδεστ = *improdest*: *addendum lexicis*.

118 ἄθεος: *Gloss.* contain a number of words beginning with the
alpha privative and translated into Latin *sine*.... Ἄθεος =
sine dibus, however, is not among them. *Gloss.* ἄνθρωπος: *homo*.

119 δειβους = *dibus*. F. Neue, *Formenlehre der lateinischen Sprache*
(Leipzig 1902) I, 190: "In Inschr(iften) ist öfters *dibus*" e.g.
CIL VI 98, 224, 10217. He cites other heteroclitic forms like
filibus, *patronibus*, *amicibus*--all from inscriptions.

120-121 *Gloss.* κόσμος: *compositio*, *decus*, *mundus*; *terra*: γῆ, χθών.
τερραι: Roland Kent, *The Sounds of Latin* (Language Monographs
12, 1932) 48 (repr. 1966): "Greek transliterations of Latin *ae*
are consistently αι until 200 A.D. (after that date, regularly
αι, but occasionally ε)."

Gloss., *conturbo*: συνταράσσω.   Cf. *Thes. Ling. Gr.*, s.v.
σύγχυσις.

122-123 πλουσίου = διουειτι<ς> comes most readily to mind, but the
quantities dīvĭtīs militate against this; see, however, lines
87, 89 n.   Possible readings in line 122 include]παξαρκοη,
]παταγκον; in line 123 *dedecus*, *denique*, *deliquus*, *deliquium* ?

124 ἀναλσία: *addendum lexicis.*

125 απεψ: *addendum lexicis.*   Isolated ink traces after psi may
belong to a continuation of this word or to an interlinear
entry.   Why the scribe chose *apeps* instead of a good Latin
word like *incoctus* or *indigestus* (ἄπεπτος can mean both) is
inscrutable.

127 *Gloss.*, *vovere*: ἀνατίθημι, καθοσιῶ, εὔχομαι, καθιερῶ.   Regarding contemporary Greek renditions of the Latin consonantal v,
Roland Kent states that it was "ordinarily transliterated into
Greek by ου" (op. cit., 60); cf. Dittenberger, *Hermes* 6 (1872)
303 quoted in *ZPE* 26 (1977) 236.

128 *Gloss.*, *semper*: ἀεί, πάντοτε, διὰ παντός, διηνεκῶς.

West Berlin   William Brashear

Addendum:

ad n. 4: For an Arabic text in Coptic script, see H.G.E. White,
The Monasteries of the Wadi 'n Natrun I: *New Coptic Texts from the
Monastery of Saint Macarius*, 231ff.   For Egyptian in Greek letters,
see B. Boyaval, *CRIPEL* 3 (1975) 243, 247 (nos. 616, 632).

Proceedings of the XVI Int. Congr. of Papyrology (Chico 1981) 43-47

UN FRAMMENTO LETTERARIO DELL'UNIVERSITA' CATTOLICA DI MILANO

Il frammento di papiro P. Med. inv. 72.14 è uno dei pezzi entrati per acquisto nella collezione dell' Istituto di Papirologia dell' Università Cattolica di Milano, in epoca relativamente recente. Misura, nei tratti di massima estensione, cm. 6,5 di larghezza e cm. 8,5 di altezza; il materiale sembra essere stato di non buona qualità e mostra una coloritura bruna molto intensa.

Sul *verso* restano 17 righe di scrittura; la maggior parte di esse--con l'eccezione di quelle iniziali e finali--sono leggibili senza soverchia difficoltà. Quasi tutte conservano integro il loro inizio con il margine sinistro della colonna; al contrario sono lacunose a destra, ma, un calcolo attendibile alla riga 4, ci assicura che sono cadute quattro lettere e che, mediamente, nelle righe successive, tale lacuna non è di molto superiore alle sei lettere; la colonna quindi era costituita da righi che si estendevano per 18 lettere circa.

La scrittura libraria a contrasto modulare, con leggera inclinazione a destra, appartiene al secolo III d.C.; unico segno diacritico è la dieresi su *iota* iniziale (riga 11). Un errore di trascrizione alla riga 3 (τενομενοι per γενομενοι) è stato corretto dallo scriba medesimo (identico è l'inchiostro), con la collocazione della consonante giusta sopra quella sbagliata, nell' interlinea, a dimensioni ridotte.

Il *recto* è occupato da un testo di mano differente.

].[...]τε.ασϑ[

α[...]ταπεινοιδε..[
   γ
σειστενομενοιτρο[

4   εαυτουσαιχμαλω[

παραδιδοασινω[

τημενοικαιγε[

μενοιμηδεγ.[

8   τολμωντεσμη[

μεινετιδυναμ[

πολειδιατονεν[

ϊδρυμενοναη[

12   ϑεοναυτηεστι[

ωτεκνοναυτη[

.ογομιααυτη.[

].αουτ..[

16   ]ανϑρ[

]ε..[

La struttura espositiva del passo contenuto nelle prime dodici righe del frammento (cioè nella parte meglio leggibile) non può essere messa in discussione; al contrario, si deve constatare il respiro non limitato del brano, anche se non caratterizzato da particolari preziosismi lessicali. Alla tredicesima riga il discorso prosastico si interrompe con la presenza della apostrofe ὦ τέκνον: sino a che punto essa si prolungasse sarebbe arduo dire, perchè il papiro è danneggiato e non sempre quanto rimane può essere letto con sicurezza.

La sutura tra i due passi del testo e la loro intima connessione può essere recuperata in modo certo sanando la lacuna di riga 12 dove, con grande evidenza, si chiude la prima lunga frase. Materiali ragioni di spazio garantiscono la presenza della formula

con la quale abitualmente viene introdotta la citazione delle
parole iniziali di un componimento: αὕτη ἐστὶν ἡ ἀρχή. L'esatta
corrispondenza della parte formulare caduta con il guasto nel papiro permette di affermare che la citazione prende l'avvio solamente con l'inizio di riga 13 e non prima. La brevissima sequenza
iniziale ὦ τέκνον αυτη[, costituita da parole irrimediabilmente
generiche, coincide quasi con la metà di un trimetro giambico. Se,
come di solito avviene e come esplicitamente dichiara la formula
introduttiva, il verso che coincide con il primo dell'opera citata
era riportato nella sua interezza, doveva necessariamente concludersi con la parola o le parole (ora lacunose) della riga
seguente.

La situazione prospettata dalla prosa appare sufficientemente
chiara nei suoi tratti essenziali. I protagonisti della vicenda,
abbattuti e scoraggiati,[1] consegnano se stessi in prigionia,[2] forse
prima ancora di aver subito una sconfitta sul campo.[3] Ma non hanno
più né il coraggio né la forza di restare nella propria città.[4]
Mentre sinò a questo punto il racconto procede con buona linearità
e non pare difficoltosa una sua ricostruzione, esso diviene improv-
visamente oscuro e problematico proprio nel momento cruciale, quando
erano chiarite le ragioni che avevano portato i protagonisti alla
disperazione prima ed alla resa poi (righe 10-12).

A rendere malsicura la comprensione del passo, non mancano
perplessità di carattere lessicale e paleografico. Queste, in particolare, riguardano la penultima lettera di riga 11, nel nesso che
dava inizio ad una nuova parola. L'incertezza nasce dalla circo-
stanza che il papiro, in corrispondenza della lettera, è danneggiato

---

1 Se le quattro lettere iniziali di riga 3 -σεις appartengono
ad un aggettivo è naturale pensarlo correlato a ταπεινοί: alla
situazione descritta si adatta perfettamente ἀθαρσεῖς.

2 La lettura τρο[....] può essere considerata certa; tra le
numerose possibilita, è preferibile pensare ad un avverbio.

3 Righe 5-7 ὡ[ς ... ἡτ]τημένοι καὶ νε[νικη]μένοι.

4 Righe 8-10 μη[δὲ ἐπιδη]μεῖν ἔτι δυνάμ[ενοι ἐν τῇ] πόλει.
Non sono pochi i verbi che possono essere suggeriti per -μειν di
riga 9: il dativo seguente (πόλει r. 10) rende giustificabile
ἐπιδη]μεῖν.

quel tanto che basta a lasciare spazio alla duplice possibilità di
una lettura αη[oppure λη[; di maggior peso sembrano essere le
ragioni (ispessimento del tratto obliquo di sinistra alla base,
minima traccia di attacco della traversa sul tratto obliquo di
destra) che inducono a preferire la lettura αη[. Va fatto notare
che né l'una né l'altra[5] aiuta, in misura decisiva, a sgombrare le
incertezze poste dalla lacuna di fine riga.

Punto fermo di un possibile ragionamento è la convinzione che
l'articolo τόν di riga 10 sia riferito a θεόν di riga 12, con il
relativo participio ίδρύμενον. Resta incerto come tale participio
debba essere inteso[6] ma appare chiaro che la presenza (o anche la
non presenza) della divinità determina la risoluzione della resa.
Conclusa l'esposizione dei fatti, viene citato il primo verso del-
l'opera, la cui individuazione ed identificazione diviene il motivo
di primario interesse del papiro.

La traccia seguita porterebbe a ricostruire il frammento
secondo queste linee di ipotesi.

```
          ].[...]τε.ασθ[
        α[...] ταπεινοὶ δὲ κα[ὶ ἀθαρ-]
        σεῖς γενόμενοι τρο[....]
        ἑαυτοὺς αἰχμαλώ[τους]
5       παραδιδόασιν ὡ[ς ἤδη ἠτ-]
        τημένοι καὶ νε[νικη-]
        μένοι μηδὲ ν.[......]
        τολμῶντες μη[δὲ ἐπιδη-]
        μεῖν ἔτι δυνάμ[ενοι ἐν τῇ]
10      πόλει διὰ τὸν ἐν [τῇ αὐτῇ]
        ἱδρύμενον ἀή[ττητον]
        θεόν· αὕτη ἐστὶ[ν ἡ ἀρχή·
        ὦ τέκνον αυτη[
```

---

5 I vocaboli che incomincino per αη- o per λη-, adatti al
contesto, non sono molti.

6 Stabilito il legame τόν...θεόν, il participio può assumere:
un valore passivo (*a causa del dio...al quale era stato dedicato un
luogo sacro*), oppure intransitivo (*a causa del dio...che si trovava*),
oppure attivo (*a causa del dio...che poneva*). Scartata questa ipotesi (che non trova esempi probanti e che presenterebbe un giro di
frase molto faticoso), rimangono in discussione le prime due. Maggior credibilità va attribuita alla seconda. Anche nell'ambito di

Pensare ad una tragedia quale fonte del nostro frammento ed
alla citazione del primo verso del suo prologo, appare ipotesi ra-
gionevole, sia per la natura dell'argomento, così di scorcio conservato, sia per considerazioni di carattere prosodico.[7] Ma da
questo punto riesce molto arduo procedere e non si può non diventare esitanti sulla direzione da seguire. La tradizione mitologica
è avara di episodi che, in qualche modo, possano rientrare nella
tematica del frammento, né collegamenti di sorta possono essere
istituiti con il repertorio tragico noto. L'apparente novità di
contenuti potrebbe aprire spazio a miti e storie locali.

Rimane da definire la natura del frammento; da quanto è stato
detto sino a questo punto, emerge l'informazione erudita ed un sicuro possesso del testo teatrale; importante sarebbe stabilire se
il riassunto del dramma è innestato su un discorso di largo respiro
o se piuttosto la citazione si esaurisca in se stessa e sia esclusivamente destinata ad illustrare l'opera drammatica oggetto della
esposizione. L'insistenza su particolari risponde alle esigenze di
uno scritto di carattere tecnico e si adegua alla struttura di un
commentario in virtù di una elaborazione dei dati che supera il
rigido schematismo formale delle ipotesi tragiche o comiche tra-
mandate dai papiri.[8]

                                                    Sergio Daris

---

questa interpretazione, incerti rimangono i particolari, a causa
delle lacune di riga 10 e 11. In via di ipotesi, si potrebbe pensare ad una determinazione di luogo (riga 10) ed ad una aggettiva-
zione relativa al dio (riga 11). E' chiaro che, rifiutata l'ipotesi iniziale, altre soluzioni del tutto diverse potrebbero pro-
filarsi.

7 Τέκνον con sillaba iniziale lunga. La formula ὦ τέκνον
appare 29 volte in Sofocle; occupa la sede iniziale del verso 6
volte (*Oed. Col.* 81, 1102; *Tr.* 61; *Phil.* 249, 260, 875); 11 volte
in Euripide, 2 delle quali in prima sede (*Andr.* 413; fr. 504). In
entrambi i tragici prevale la collocazione nell'ambito delle due
prime sedi.

8 Per la tragedia v. *P. Oxy.* XXVII 2455, 2457; XXXI 2544;
PSI XII 1286; *P. Mil. Vogl.* II 44; per la commedia *P. Oxy.* X 1235.

EPIGRAMMINCIPIT AUF EINEM PAPYRUS AUS DEM 3. JH. V. CHR.

P. VINDOB G 40611   EIN VORBERICHT

Ein Charakteristikum der Papyrussammlung Erzherzog Rainer, die 1983 ihr Centennarium feiert, ist der überaus geringe Bestand an griechischen Papyri aus ptolemäischer Zeit. Die wenigen bedeutenden sind das euripideische Orestfragment mit Musiknoten (Pack[2] 411), eine stereometrische Aufgabensammlung (Pack[2] 2322), der Diogenes Kynikos-Papyrus (Pack[2] 1987)[1] und das Prostagma Ptolemaios' II. Philadelphos über Vieh- und Sklavendeklarationen ptolemäischer Besitzungen in Syrien und Phoinikien (*SB* V 8008). Die Klage der Artemisia (*UPZ* I 1) und die Zoispapyri (*UPZ* I 114) sind keine Erwerbungen Rainers; sie befinden sich schon seit dem 18. Jh. in der seinerzeitigen Hofbibliothek, der heutigen Österreichischen Nationalbibliothek.

Es ist nun das große Verdienst der Direktion von Frau Helene Loebenstein, daß in den letzten Jahren etwa 200 griechische Papyri aus ptolemäischer Epoche von der Republik Österreich angekauft wurden. Unter diesen wertvollen Texten beansprucht eine Rolle besonderes Interesse.

Diese Rolle ist 17 cm hoch und 70 cm lang; 5 Fragmente gehören dazu. Insgesamt sind 240 Zeilen darauf erkennbar. Etwa 130 Zeilen geben die Hoffnung, zur Gänze gelesen werden zu können.

Der Papyrus stammt aus Mumienkartonage, in die er, in mehr als 20 kleine und kleinste Teile zerrissen verarbeitet war. Die letzte und für die Lesbarkeit entscheidende Restaurierung verdanken wir dem vielfach bewährten Restaurator der Wiener Papyrussammlung, Michael Fackelmann.

Die Schrift auf dem Papyrus weist eine Buchstabenhöhe von 2-3 mm auf, so daß selbst bei einer nur geringfügiger Beschädigung des Papyrus die Lesbarkeit beeinträchtigt ist.

Nach der Schrift ist der Papyrus dem 3. Jh. v. Chr. zuzuweisen. Ein Vergleich mit *P. Mich.* 5, *P. Lit. Lond.* 54, *P. Stras.* WG 307

---

1 S. die Neuedition von I. Gallo, *Frammenti biografici da papiri* (Roma 1980) II, 253-309, Tav. XVII.

(s. *ZPE* 38 [1980] Taf. I) und *P. Sorb.* 1167 (s. E. G. Turner, *Greek Manuscripts of the Ancient World* [Oxford 1971] Nr. 53) stützt die Datierung. Im Zusammenhang damit ist zu erwähnen, daß in demselben Stück Kartonage Dokumente enthalten waren, die um 235 oder 210 v. Chr. zu datieren sind.

Der Titel der Rolle lautet:

1 τα επιζητουμενα των επι
2 γραμματων εν τηι ᾱ βυβλωι

Darauf folgen die ersten Wörter einzelner Epigramme und die Stichosangabe des vollständigen Epigrammes, z.B.

4 ευ Παρθενιος μοι κομψος απ Αρκαδιης η ⟦ς⟧
6   η γραυς η Τιμωνος απηγξατο της επιτ δ (δ ex β)

Die einzelnen Incipit sind durch Paragraphos voneinander getrennt. Kol. I endet mit Z. 23 (εισι) κ στιχο(ι) πη. Kol. II (ohne Titel) endet mit einer ähnlichen Addition wie Z. 23. Sie ist jedoch nur durch Spuren repräsentiert. Kol. III ist titellos; sie endet mit Z. 72 (εισι) κδ στιχο(ι) ρ. Kol. IV (ohne Titel) addiert 17 Zeilen der Kolumne (die Stichoszahl ist verloren) und in Z. 91 die Summe der aus Buch I verzeichneten Epigramme: (εισιν) επιγρ(αμματα) πγ στιχο(ι) τμδ (μδ sind sehr unsicher zu lesen; die spärlichen Spuren scheinen am ehesten zu μδ zu passen). Die ersten vier Kolumnen sind von einem Schreiber geschrieben. Ab Kol. V ist ein zweiter Schreiber zu erkennen, der kleinere Buchstaben schreibt und einen etwas dünneren Kalamos sowie tiefschwarze Tinte verwendet. Er ist auch der Schreiber der erhaltenen 5 Fragmente.

Kol. V führt als Titel, Z. 92 εν τηι β̄ βυβλωι. Von Kol. V-VII gibt es keine Additionen als Kolumnenschluß. Frg. c, Z. 173 überliefert einen weiteren Kolumnentitel εν τηι δ̄ βυβλωι.

Auf der Versoseite des 70 cm langen Teiles steht am linken Rand (= rechter Rand aus der Sicht des Rekto) eine etwa in der Zeilenmitte abgeschnittene Kolumne (die Rolle war also länger) und schließt mit Z. 213 λγ στιχοι σξδ. Der Schreiber dürfte jener von Kol. I-IV sein. Eine zweite Kolumne auf der Versoseite steht etwa in der Mitte der Rolle und ist in ihrem Ausmaß vollständig erhalten. Doch für die Zwecke der Kartonage fest aufgeriebener, grober Kalk hat die Schrift stark in Mitleidenschaft gezogen. Diese Kolumne

ist in flüchtiger, kleiner Kursivschrift geschrieben. Als Titel
ist mit etlicher Zuverläßlichkeit zu lesen bzw. zu rekonstruieren:

Z. 214   επιγραμ[μ]ατα

Z. 215   εν τ[η]ι . βυβ[λωι]

Die Buchzahl ist unbestimmbar, da von dieser Zahl (es dürfte sich
nur um einen Buchstaben handeln) nicht mehr als nur ein punktgroßer
Tintenrest erhalten geblieben ist. Unter der Kolumne gibt es auch
Spuren einer Additionszeile.

Von den Stichoszahlen sind 173 mit mehr oder weniger Sicherheit
lesbar. In 65 Zeilen sind diese Angaben nicht erhalten oder unles-
bar. Zu lesen sind: 13 mal "2", 106 mal "4", 20 mal "6", 9 mal "8",
1 mal "10", 2 mal "12" und "20" und je 1 mal "21,40, 52". Erwähnens-
wert ist in diesem Zusammenhang, daß die sonst schwer lesbare Zeile
225 (in der kursiv geschriebenen Kolumne auf dem Verso) mit κς (εστι)
ιγ endet, was in Anlehnung an Z. 23,72 und 91 als "26 Stichoi, das
sind 13 Epigramme" aufzufassen ist. Diese summarische Disticha-
Angabe ist zu den genannten 13 dazuzurechnen.

Gemäß dem Titel τὰ ἐπιζητούμενα τῶν ἐπιγραμμάτων ἐν τῆι ᾱ βύβ-
λωι sind auf der Rolle nicht alle Epigramme des ersten (zweiten und
vierten) Buches, sondern nur ἐπιζητούμενα verzeichnet, deren Anzahl
von einer (künftigen ?) Anthologie zu sprechen verlangt.[2] Die Papyri *P. Tebt.* I 3, *P. Petrie* II 49b, *P. Lit. Lond.* 60 und *P. Stras.*
WG 307[3] tradieren Epigramme verschiedener Autoren und stammen aus
der Zeit vor Meleager von Gadara, der die früheste, bekannte Epigrammanthologie schuf. Der vorliegende Papyrus ist für die Geschichte der Epigrammanthologie eine überaus wichtige Quelle, weil
er von wenigstens 200 Epigrammen Nachricht gibt und aus dem 3 Jh.
v. Chr. stammt.

Welche Kriterien für die Auswahl der Epigramme entscheidend
waren, läßt sich zur Zeit nicht sagen. Autor ist jedenfalls keiner
genannt. Das braucht nicht zu besagen, daß alle Epigramme von
einem Dichter stammen. Bisher konnte nur ein Epigramm (Z. 14) mit

---

2 Die Technik, nach der dieser Papyrus angelegt wurde, ist
die kallimacheische: Incipit und Zeilenzahl. Vgl. Athenaios,
Deipn. VI 244A, wo die kallimacheische Praxis beschrieben ist.

3 S. D. J. Mastronarde, *ZPE* 38 (1980) 1ff.

AP XII 46, Asklepiades von Samos identifiziert werden.[4]

An Testimonia konnten bisher festgestellt werden:

Z. 113: Ευφρων και Θ...ξ δυο αδελφεοι   δ. Vgl. *AP* V 161: Εὐφρὼ
καὶ Θαῖς καὶ Βοίδιον, αἱ Διομέδους.   Die Hss. nennen als Autor
Hedylos, Asklepiades von Samos oder "Simonides" (s. Gow-Page, *Commentary*, 143f. zu Z. 996f. [Asklepiades]; = 1516ff. Page [Hedylos]).

Z. 114 wird eine Kallistion genannt. Eine Hetäre dieses Namens begegnet in *AP* VI 148,1 (Kallimachos),[5] *AP* XII 131,3 (Poseidippos),[6]
1836 Gow-Page (= 1466ff. Page [Hedylos]).

An Jonismen begegnen: 'Αρκαδίης (4), 'Αστερίης (7), ιστίη (11),
ἀδελφέοι (113), πρηΰς (128), ἀριστίη (129) Dorisch ist εὖντα = ὄντα
(131; cf. Theokr. 2,3).

Ein offenes Problem stellt die insgesamt 17 mal (Kol. I-IV =
1. Schreiber: 15 mal; Kol. Vff. = 2. Schreiber: 2 mal) in margine
stehende Notiz ευ dar. Diese zwei Buchstaben scheinen von einem
Schreiber herzurühren. Es läßt sich nicht sagen, ob es einer der
beiden oder ein dritter Schreiber geschrieben hat. Es gibt keinen
Hinweis, daß das Wort abbreviiert ist. An abgekürzt geschriebenen
Wörtern gibt es auf diesem Papyrus in den Kolumnenschlüssen στιχ̥
und επιγρ (91); sie sind als Abbreviaturen deutlich. ευ könnte als
vollständiges Wort verstanden werden. Wenn es jedoch eine Abbreviatur ist, könnte als Auflösung εὖ(ρον) im Hinblick auf den Titel
(ἐπιζητούμενα) passend erscheinen. Grundsätzlich ist m.E. als Ein-
wand dagegen vorzubringen, daß ευ allein ein Wort ist und ohne
Markierung einer Abbreviatur mißverständlich sein kann. Freilich
ist in die Argumentation die Überlegung miteinzuschließen, ob diese
Marginalnotiz als Mitteilung für eine zweite Person gedacht war
oder nur für den, der sie schrieb, Bedeutung hatte. Zu beobachten

---

4 876ff. Gow-Page = 1031ff. Page. Die Identifizierung muß
jedoch mit einem gewissen Vorbehalt genannt werden. Man vergleiche
die ersten Worte der Epigramme *AP* VII 145 und 2666ff. Gow-Page
(see *Commentary*, p. 412) = 2646ff. Page. Das Incipit dieser beiden
Epigramme in der Praxis, wie sie auf diesem Papyrus anzutreffen
ist, ließe nicht bestimmen, von welchem Autor das Epigramm stammt.

5 LV Pfeiffer; = 1125ff. Gow-Page = 1230ff.

6 3084 Gow-Page = 1592 Page.

ist, daß ευ in margine steht, wenn in der betreffenden Zeile eine
Korrektur begegnet. Allerdings gibt es etliche Fälle, in denen die
Marginalnotiz geschrieben, die Zitatzeile jedoch nicht oder nur
teilweise erhalten ist, sodaß nicht mit völliger Sicherheit fest-
gehalten werden kann, daß ευ tatsächlich stets mit einer Textver-
besserung verbunden ist.

Die Edition wird in Zusammenarbeit mit Peter Parsons erfolgen.

Wien Hermann Harrauer

SPRACHLICHER KOMMENTAR ZUM FOLIUM PARISINUM
(P. LOUVRE EG. 2329)

Die auf Papyrus erhaltenen spätantiken lateinisch-griechischen
Glossare sind für uns eine wichtige Quelle für die Aussprache und
den Wortschatz der beiden klassischen Sprachen in ihrer volkstüm-
lichen, kaum von der literarischen Norm beeinflussten Form. Die
meisten Glossare sind offenbar von Griechischsprachigen für Grie-
chischsprachige verfasst, während nur recht wenige von Lateinisch-
sprachigen für Lateinischsprachige[1] zusammengestellt wurden.[2]
Eines dieser wenigen Glossare ist das um das Jahr 600[3] geschriebene
Folium Parisinum (P. Louvre Eg. 2329, früher *P. Louvre* 4 bis); es
scheint vollständig erhalten zu sein, jedenfalls stammt es nicht
aus einem Kodex.[4]   Die beiden Kommentare von F. Haase[5] und F.
Bücheler[6] sind heute veraltet; ein neuer Kommentar könnte also
nützlich sein.

---

1 A. Bataille, *Recherches de papyrologie* 4 (1967) 162: "Ad-
ministrateurs, commerçants et soldats, dépourvus le plus souvent de
culture héllenique, avaient interêt à connaître la langue usuelle
des habitants de la χώρα."

2 Ibid., 166 zählte 33 auf dem Griechischen und nur 6 auf dem
Lateinischen basierende Glossare; diese Liste ist inzwischen um
sechs gr.-lat. zu erweitern: *P. Oxy.* 2660, 2660a, 3315; Chester
Beatty Library Dublin Ac 1499 (vgl. A. Wouters, *Ancient Society* 3
[1972] 259-62); P. Mich. Inv. 2458 (vgl. N. Priest, *ZPE* 27 [1977]
193-200); ausserdem ein von W. Brashear auf dem 16. Papyrologenkongress vorgestellter Westberliner Papyrus und ein lat.-gr. Glossar (*CGL* 2,559-561 aus Göttingen; fehlt bei Pack² ; *P. Sorb.* I 8 ist
hingegen als Pack² 3008 erfasst). Vgl. *ZPE* 40 (1980) 161-79.

3 R. Seider, *Paläographie der lateinischen Papyri* II 1
(Stuttgart 1978) 165; E. A. Lowe, *CLA* 5 (Oxford 1950) Nr. 696.

4 Seider, op. cit., 165.

5 L. Brunet de Presles/F. Haase, *Notices et extraits des
manuscrits de la Bibliothèque Impériale* 18 (2) (Paris 1865) 125-26.

6 F. Bücheler, *Jahrbücher für Philologie* 111 (1875) 309-13.

1	*pane*	*binu*	*oleu*	
	oxomin	*enari*	*eladi*	
	carne	*pisce*		
4	*creas*	*opxarin*		
	ubepass	*aput*	*eces*	
	focu	*lanbron*		
	laguna	*paucali*		
8	*aqua*	*nero*		
	calice	*poterin*		
	poru	*praston*		
	iscaria	*seris*	*misce*	*cera'su'*
12	*damesa*	*parates*	*aparai*	*leba*
	adelfos	*fratres*	*ospiti'u'*	
		nonis		
	cibitas	*polis*	*aceta*	
	olera	*lacana*	*caput*	
16	*cefalen*	*linguia*	*closa*	
	manos	*ceras*	*pedes*	*potes*
	bentre	*cilia*	*culcita*	*piloto'n'*
	barba	*pogoni*	*oculos*	*optalmo's'*
20	*buca*	*istoma*	*bile*	*utelo*
	iana	*tira*	*sela*	*sifrin*
	tunica	*isticarin*		
	iscio	*eddam*	*sutipola*	*cinido*
24	*coclia*	*miaci*	*cacabu*	*cetra*
	labamanos	*nibson*	[[*manus*]]	*'ceras'*
	colonbu	*peristeri*	*cubicla*	*cli'n'di*
	secure	*axnari*	*bilosa*	*maloton*
28	*ficu*	*suca*	*aleu*	*iscorda*
	inple	*cemmiso*	*bacula*	*arafi'cen'*

Textausgaben (außer Brunet de Presles/Haase und Bücheler [s. Anm. 5-6]): G. Loewe/G. Goetz, *Corpus Glossariorum Latinorum* (Leipzig 1888) II, 563 (*CGL*); R. Cavenaile, *Corpus Papyrorum Latinarum* (Wiesbaden 1956-58) 384-85; R. Seider (s. Anm. 3) (dort S. XL auch die beste Photographie).

1 Dem Text geht ein Kreuzzeichen voran (Seider, Lowe); man kann es nicht als *t* (*toxomin*) interpretieren (Brunet, Bücheler, *CGL*, *CPL*), obwohl das sprachlich gut passen würde (τὸ ψωμίν) *binu* Brunet, Bücheler, *CGL*, *CPL* : *bina* Seider

5   *ubepass* Bücheler : *ubepais* Brunet, *CGL*, *CPL*, Seider
    aput Brunet, *CGL*, *CPL*, Seider : *aspat* Bücheler

7   *laguna* Seider : *lagona* Bücheler, *CGL*, *CPL* : *lagena* Brunet

9   *calice* Brunet, *CGL*, *CPL*, Seider : *calicē* Bücheler

12 *aparai* Brunet, *CGL*, *CPL*, Seider : *aparon* Bücheler zögernd
    nonis interlinear an der angegebenen Stelle

16 *linguia* Brunet, *CGL*, *CPL*, Seider : *lingua* Bücheler

23 *eddam* Bücheler, *CGL*, *CPL*, Seider : *oiddam* Brunet
    satipola Brunet, *CGL*, *CPL*, Seider : *sagirola* Bücheler. Das
    t ist aus einem anderen Buchstaben, vielleicht *g*, verbessert.

25 *ceras* ist über ein durchgestrichenes *manus*, das der Schreiber
    aus Unachtsamkeit widderholt hatte, verbessert.

26 *colonbu* Bücheler, *CGL*, *CPL*, Seider : *colonba* Brunet
    cubicla Bücheler : *cabicola CGL*, *CPL*, Seider : *cubiclu* Brunet

Es handelt sich um ein Glossar, das für den täglichen Bedarf
von Römern, die überhaupt kein Griechisch konnten, bestimmt war.
Um 600 n. Chr. ist die für die römische Kaiserzeit charakteristische griechisch-lateinische Zweisprachigkeit,[7] die keineswegs ausschliesslich auf die Oberschicht beschränkt war,[8] bereits wieder
rückläufig,[9] was das verstärkte Auftreten von Glossaren in Ägypten
erklärt,[10] das zwar zum Ostreich gehörte, aber noch viele Bindungen
zum lateinischen Westen hatte.[11] Als Zielpublikum des vorliegenden
Glossars kommen vor allem aus dem Westen stammende Soldaten niedri-
gen Ranges[12] und Händler in Frage. Dafür spricht auch der Wortschatz: Speisen, Getränke, Körperteile, Aufforderungen an Gastwirte,

---

7   G. Devoto, *Geschichte der Sprache Roms* (Heidelberg 1968)
211-12.

8   J. Kramer, *Studii clasice* 18 (1979) 126-35.

9   H. Zilliacus, *Zum Kampf der Weltsprachen im oströmischen
Reich* (Helsinki 1935) 126-32.

10 Eine Liste bei Pack[2] 2119-2137 (Basis gr.) und 3003-3008
(Basis lat.); vgl. auch Anm. 2.

11 A. Ch. Johnson/L. C. West, *Byzantine Egypt: Economic
Studies* (Princeton 1949, repr. Amsterdam 1967) 137 (Handel) und 216
(Soldaten aus den lateinischen Provinzen).

12 Bataille, op. cit., 167.

auch zumindest ein Wort aus der Bordellsphäre (Z. 23).

Eine strenge Ordnung der Wörter lässt sich nicht feststellen;
von Z. 1-15 geht es vor allem um Speisen, Getränke und Aufforderungen an Gastwirte, von Z. 15-20 stehen Körperteile im Mittelpunkt
des Interesses, von Z. 21 bis zum Schluss scheint wieder die Gast-
haussphäre in den Vordergrund zu treten; überall jedoch finden sich
Wörter eingestreut, die nicht zum Generalthema passen (etwa Z. 13
"Bruder," Z. 18 "Kissen," Z. 27 "haarig"). In den ersten beiden
Zeilen sind die lateinischen Wörter in etwas kleinerer Schrift über
ihre griechischen Entsprechungen geschrieben worden; von da ab stehen, wie es der Tradition der Glossare entspricht,[13] links die lateinischen und rechts die griechischen Wörter, wobei diese Reihenfolge jedoch gelegentlich nicht beachtet wird (Z. 12 *aparai = leba*,
Z. 13 *adelfos = fratres*, Z. 15 steht *caput, cefalen* folgt erst Z.
16).

Das lateinische Lemma wird meist nicht im Nominativ, sondern
in der für das späte gesprochene Latein typischen Obliquusform,
also dem Akkusativ Singular ohne Schluss-*m*,[14] zitiert, obwohl auch
einige Nominative (Z. 14 *cibitas*; Z. 15 *caput*; Z. 23 *cinido*) und
Pluralformen (Z. 5 *ubepass<e>*; Z. 13 *fratres*; Z. 15 *olera*; Z. 17
manos, pedes; Z. 19 *oculos*; Z. 26 *cubicla*), die ihrerseits wider
im Obliquus (Akkusativ) stehen, vorkommen.

Bei den griechischen Lemmata finden sich auffällig viele Formen auf -ι bzw. -ιν: die Kontraktion der alten Diminutivendung -ιον
zu -ιν ist uns seit dem 3. Jh. v. Chr. sporadisch belegt,[15] der
Abfall des Schluss-ν ist in der römischen und byzantinischen Peri-
ode ebenfalls ausgesprochen häufig.[16] Die im Neugriechischen so
häufigen Neutra auf -ι waren also nach dem Ausweis des Folium Parisinum bereits im gesprochenen Griechisch des 6. Jh. ganz geläufig.

Es seien im folgenden die einzelnen Wörter, die eines Kommen-
tars bedürfen, erklärt.

---

13 Bataille, op. cit., 165.

14 V. Väänänen, *Introduction au latin vulgaire* (Paris[2] 1967)
122-24.

15 E. Schwyzer, *Griechische Grammatik* (München 1953) I, 472.

16 F. Th. Gignac, *A Grammar of the Greek Papyri of the Roman
and Byzantine Periods* (Milano 1976) I, 111.

z. 1/2   *oxomin:* Gemeint ist ψωμίν.[17] Anstelle des alten ἄρτος
hatte sich für "Brot" immer mehr das ursprünglich "Stück, Bis-
sen" bedeutende ψωμίον durchgesetzt (in diesem Sinne zuerst Joh.
13,26 belegt),[18] das heute im neugriechischen ψωμί weiterlebt.
Der Wortanfang im Folium Parisinum ist wohl daraus zu erklären,
dass dem Verfasser der dem Lateinischen ja fremde Anlaut *ps-*
ungeläufig war. Er hat das *ps* durch das ähnlich klingende *x*
ersetzt,[19] ausserdem durch die Prothese des *o*, das wohl seine
Qualität der Wirkung des nachfolgenden *o* verdankt,[20] vermieden,
dass das *x* am Wortanfang steht. Die an sich naheliegende Lesung
τὸ ψωμίν ist paläographisch ausgeschlossen, weil das früher als
t gedeutete Kreuz, das am Anfang der Wörterliste steht, die übliche Einleitung der Urkunden dieser Zeit ist und niemals einen
Lautwert hat.[21]

binu = enari: Das lateinische Wort ist *vinum.* Die Vertauschung
von *v* und *b* "zeigen die Inschriften der Kaiserzeit in weitem Umfang; man mag die Erscheinung als vulgärlateinische betrachten."[22]
Das Fehlen des Auslaut-*m* ist ebenfalls typisch für das gesprochene
Latein;[23] nach Quintilian (inst. 9,4,40) wurde es ja sogar in den
gebildeten Kreisen nur ganz schwach angedeutet. Als griechische
Entsprechung von *vinum* ist *enari* gegeben, was den umgangssprach-
lich für οἶνος übliche gewordene Diminutiv οἰνάρι meint, welcher
in der Spätantike und im frühen Mittelalter noch ausgiebig bezeugt ist,[24] jedoch auf dem Weg zum Neugriechischen vor dem

---

17 Büchelers Form ψῶμιν ist sprachlich unmöglich.

18 H. Eideneier, *Sogenannte christliche Tabuwörter im Griechischen* (Diss. München 1966) 7-30.

19 Ersatz von *ps* durch *x* ist auch sonst belegt, vgl. etwa
Suet., *Aug.* 88, wo von einer Verwechselung von *ipsi* mit *ixi* die
Rede ist.

20 Die Umformung des normalen Prothese-Vokals *i* in *o* vor
dunklem Tonvokal ist durchaus möglich, vgl. Schwyzer, op. cit., 412.

21 Lowe, op. cit., Nr. 696; Seider, op. cit., 165.

22 M. Leumann, *Lateinische Laut- und Formenlehre* (München
1977) 159.

23 Väänänen, op. cit., 68-70.

24 LSJ 1206: "colloquial for οἶνος"; seit Theophrast belegt.

anschaulicheren κρασί zurücktreten musste.[25] Die Wiedergabe des
damals sicher als [ü] ausgesprochenen οι durch e ist zunächst
verwunderlich, denn man würde ja i erwarten; es gibt jedoch
Parallelfälle (z.B. Oribas. 923,25 celefia < κοιλοφυῆς). Hier
spielt wohl die alte Gewohnheit mit, οι durch oe wiederzugeben,[26]
das ja im späteren Umgangslatein zu e wurde.[27]

eladi: In der Kaiserzeit wurde ἐλαία durch ἐλάδιον verdrängt;
hier der älteste Beleg für ἐλάδι, Vorstufe zu neugr. λάδι.[28]

Z. 3/4   opxarin: Das griechische Wort ist als ὀψάριν zu lesen;
für x ist der Lautwert [s] anzusetzen.[29] Das Wort ἰχθύς "Fisch"
wurde in der Spätantike mehr und mehr durch ὀψάριον ersetzt, was
ein Diminutiv von ὄψον "Zukost" ist;[30] das neugriechische ψάρι
geht darauf zurück.

Z. 5   ubepass<e> = aputeces: Die von Bücheler vorgeschlagene Lesung ubepass ist der von den anderen Editoren festgehaltenen
Lesung ubepais vorzuziehen; der als i gelesene Buchstabe ist als
erster s aufzufassen, denn bei Doppel-s wird in der lateinischen
Kursive beim ersten s der Aufstrich sehr dünn und flüchtig angedeutet;[31] am Original ist eine ganz schwache Spur zu erkennen.
Gemeint sein muss das in Glossaren häufig vorkommende[32] uvae
passae "Rosinen"; durch ein Versehen des Schreibers ist das
letzte e weggeblieben.

   Das mit einem Punkt und einem Punkt und einem deutlichen
Spatium voneinander getrennte aput eces bietet grössere Probleme.

---

25 Eideneier, op. cit., 31-84.

26 Leumann, op. cit., 77; Väänänen, op. cit., 39.

27 Die ersten Beispiele stammen aus Pompei, vgl. V. Väänänen,
Le latin vulgaire des inscriptions pompéiennes (Helsinki 1937) 40.

28 N. Π. Ἀνδριώτης, Ἐτυμολογικὸ λεξικὸ τῆς κοινῆς νεοελ-
ληνικῆς (Thessaloniki² 1967) 178.

29 Leumann, op. cit., 204.

30 Eideneier, op. cit., 85-101.

31 Beispiele in den Schrifttafeln von E. M. Thompson, An Introduction to Greek and Latin Paleography (Oxford 1912) 336-37.

32 J. Kramer, ZPE 26 (1977) 237.

Bücheler hatte fälschlicherweise die Unterlänge des *x* von *opxa-rin* für ein *s* in Rasur gehalten und ausserdem das *u* als *a* ge-lesen, so dass er zu *aspateces* kam, worin er eine Verballhornung von ἀσταφίδες, also ἀσταπίδες oder gar ἀσπατίδες, zu erkennen glaubte. Abgesehen davon, dass die sprachliche Wahrscheinlich-keit dieser Lösung gering ist, lässt sie sich paläographisch nicht halten. Wahrscheinlicher ist, dass man ἀποθήκης lesen muss, was dann als ἀποθήκης σταφύλια "Lagertrauben" aufzufassen wäre. Offen bleibt nur die Frage, was der Punkt und das Spatium sollen. Vielleicht könnte man sich zumindest fragen, ob dadurch nicht die Aspiration des *th* angedeutet werden sollte.

Z. 6   *focu = lanbron:*   Das klassische lateinische Wort *ignis* ist im Umgangslatein durch das konkretere *focus* (ursprünglich "Herd des Hauses," "heilige Feuerstätte") ersetzt worden.[33] Im Grie-chischen ist λαμπρόν eines der Ersatzwörter für das wegen seinen vielen Nebenbedeutungen (z.B. "Leidenschaft" oder "Fieber") un-beliebt gewordene πῦρ; es konnte sich nicht bis ins Neugriechi-sche, wo wir heute φωτιά finden, halten, ist aber in der Spätan-tike und im Mittelalter gut belegt.[34] Phonetisch ist zu bemer-ken, dass die für das Neugriechische Sonorisierung der stimm-losen Verschlusslaute nach Nasal bereits eingetreten ist.[35]

Z. 7   *laguna = paucali:*   Für "Flasche" ist in lateinischen In-schriften *laguna* ebenso wie *lagona* belegt, während Formen wie *lagena, lagoena, laguina* oder *laguena* nur in Handschriften vor-kommen.[36] Der Papyrus bietet also hier einen weiteren Beleg für die unentstellte lateinische Form dieses früh aus griech. λάγυ-νος entlehnten Wortes.

---

33   C. Tagliavini, *Einführung in die romanische Philologie* (München 1973) 168; W. von Wartburg, *Französisches etymologisches Wörterbuch* (Leipzig 1934) III, 658.

34   E. A. Sophocles, *Greek Lexicon* (Cambridge 1914) 705; C. Du Cange, *Glossarium* (Lyon 1688) I, 786-87.

35   Die ersten Belege sind zusammengestellt bei F. Th. Gignac, op. cit., 83-85.

36   U. Knoche, *Hermes* 63 (1928) 350 (Anm. 1).

Griechisch *paucali* ist als βαυκάλι zu interpretieren. Der
Wechsel zwischen stimmhaften und stimmlosen Verschlusslauten ist
sowohl im Griechischen Ägyptens[37] als auch im späteren Latein[38]
gut bezeugt (vgl. auch Z. 16 *closa*, Z. 17 *potes*).

Z. 8   *nero*: Das neugriechische Wort für Wasser, νερό, ist bekanntlich aus dem Adjektiv νεαρός "frisch" (νεαρὸ ὕδωρ) entstanden;
die Form νηρό ist seit dem 6. Jh. häufig belegt[39] und dürfte
wohl auch hier gemeint sein.

Z. 10   *poru = praston*: Dem lateinischen *porrum* "Lauch" entspricht
in den Glossaren πράσον,[40] das auch hier gemeint sein muss. Das
Auftreten des *t* erklärt sich entweder als Anklang an *pransitare*
"frühstücken" (das ja volkssprachlich **prastare* lautete) oder
ist dem im Griechischen normalen Schwanken zwischen σ / σσ / στ
zuzuschreiben.[41]

Z. 11   *iscaria = seris*: Das lateinische Wort ist als *escaria* zu
verstehen, was vom Adjektiv *escarius* "essbar" kommt. Die griechische Entsprechung σέρις lässt vermuten, dass die Bedeutung
des lateinischen Wortes ebenfalls "Endivie" sein muss.[42] Diese
Vermutung wird durch die Tatsache zur Gewissheit, dass eine Ab-
leitung von *escaria*, nämlich *escariola*, in den romanischen
Sprachen in der Bedeutung "Endivie" weiterlebt.[43] Der Anlaut
des lateinischen Wortes erklärt sich daraus, dass im kaiserzeit-
lichen Latein der normale Prothesevokal vor *s* impurum ein *i* war,

---

37   Gignac, op. cit., 63-64.

38   Väänänen, op. cit. (Anm. 14), 59; U. L. Figge, *Die romanische Anlautsonorisation* (Bonn 1966).

39   Eideneier, op. cit., 104-19.

40   *CGL* 7,108 (Index s.v. *porrum*).

41   Zum Schwund der Vortonsilbe und des *n* vor *s* im Vulgär-
lateinischen, vgl. Väänänen op. cit. (Anm. 14), 41 und 66-67. Zum
Wechsel zwischen σ(σ) und στ, vgl. Gignac, op. cit., 66.

42   *ThLL* kennt neben unserer Stelle nur Garg. Mart. med. 39,
p. 177, 9-10 in vergleichbarer Bedeutung. Die Glossare haben
escaria = τρώξιμα (*CGL* 3,88,60; 359,71).

43   von Wartburg, op. cit., 245.

während ein *e* in der entsprechenden Fuktion als weniger korrekt empfunden wurde und auch seltener vorkam.[44] An der vorliegenden Stelle wurde das *e* von *escaria* fälschlicherweise als Prothesevokal aufgefasst und durch die "vornehmere" Variante *i* ersetzt.

misce = *cerasu:* Das griechische Wort *cerasu* ist mit Bücheler als κέρασον aufzufassen: die Labilität der lateinischen Auslautnasale trifft sich hier mit der Labilität der griechischen Auslautnasale.[45]

Z. 12 *da mesa* = *parates:* In *mensa* hat der für das gesprochene Latein charakteristische Ausfall des *n* vor *s* stattgefunden.[46] Auch das griechische παράθες bedeutet "tische auf!"

aparai = *leba:* Die übliche Reihenfolge lateinisch-griechisch ist umgekehrt. Die griechische Infinitivform ἀπᾶραι ist als kräfiger infinitivaler Imperativ zu verstehen: "abtragen!"[47] Im Lateinischen ist wieder wie in Z. 1 *b* für *v* eingetreten.

Z. 13 *adelfos* = *fratres:* Warum dem griechischen Singular ἀδελφός (oder etwa ἀδελφούς zu lesen?) ein lateinischer Plural gegenübersteht, ist nicht einsichtig.

nonis: Bücheler äusserte die Vermutung, dass diese Interlinearglosse *non est* bedeuten soll; in der Tat ist *ospitium* ein lateinisches Lehnwort im Griechischen (ὁσπίτιον, neugr. σπίτι),[48] so dass keine "Entsprechung" auftaucht.

Z. 14 *cibitas* = *polis:* Zu allen Zeiten stand *civitas* (zum *b/v*-Wechsel, vgl. Z. 1 *binu*), das ja eigentlich die Bürgerschaft als Gesamtheit der Bürger bezeichnete, in der Bedeutung "Stadt" neben

---

44 Leumann, op. cit., 104-05.

45 S. oben, Anm. 14 und 16.

46 Väänänen, op. cit. (Anm. 14), 65-66.

47 E. Schwyzer, *Griechische Grammatik* (München 1950) II, 380; E. Mayser, *Grammatik* II 1 (Berlin 1926) 150-51 und 303-05; B. Mandilaras, *The Verb in the Greek Non-Literary Papyri* (Athens 1973) 316-20.

48 A. Carnoy, *Mélanges H. Grégoire* (Bruxelles 1949) I, 109-13.

den literarischeren Wörtern *urbs* und *oppidum*,[49] so dass die
Gleichsetzung mit πόλις als völlig normal zu betrachten ist.[50]

aceta: Es taucht keine griechische Entsprechung auf, so dass
man *nonis = non est* mit Bücheler auch auf dieses Wort beziehen
wird. Seine Erklärung "ceterum plurali numero non utebantur in
aceto, itaque cum λάχανα subsequantur, fortasse *acetaria* scrip-
tor cogitarat" erklärt das Fehlen einer griechischen Entsprechung jedoch nicht, denn λάχανα ist ja die übliche Glosse zu
olera.[51] Man wird vielmehr bei *aceta* nicht an *acetum* "Essig,"
sondern an *acetum* "Jungfernhonig" denken, das tatsächlich aus
griechisch ἄκοιτον entlehnt ist,[52] weswegen das Fehlen einer
griechischen Entsprechung eine gewisse Berechtigung hat.

Z. 14/15 *caput = cefalen:* Das Auftreten dieser Glosse an der
Stelle, wo nach der Behandlung von Kohl Körperteile folgen, ist
vielleicht nicht rein zufällig: *caput* und κεφαλή können ja sowohl "Kohlkopf" als auch "Kopf" als Körperteil bedeuten. Bei
cefalen tritt wieder das ν mobile auf.[53]

Z. 15 *linguia = closa:* Das in *linguia* auftretende *i* scheint
einer hyperkorrekten Tendenz zu verdanken zu sein: der Neigung,
das halbvokalische Element von *gu* verschwinden zu lassen,[54] wird
dadurch entgegengewirkt, dass der Halbvokal als Vollvokal ausgesprochen wird (also *lingu-a* statt *lingu̯a*): der dann entste-
hende Hiat bewirkt das Auftreten des Hiattilgers *i*.[55] Bei *closa*

---

49 *ThLL* 3,1232-1234; W. von Wartburg, *Französisches etymologisches Wörterbuch* (Leipzig/Berlin 1940) II, 725; E. Löfstedt, *Phi-
lologischer Kommentar zur Peregrinatio Aetheriae* (Uppsala 1911) 174-
75.

50 Vgl. auch *CGL* 6,218 (Index).

51 Sehr häufig in den Glossaren (*CGL* 6,525 Index).

52 *ThLL* 1,419 (*acoetum*). Bedeutung nach K. E. Georges, *Aus-
führliches lateinisch-deutsches Handwörterbuch* (Hannover[10] 1959) I,
78.

53 S. oben, Anm. 16.

54 C. Battisti, *Avviamento allo studio del latino volgare*
(Bari 1950) 161-62.

55 Väänänen, op. cit. (Anm. 14), 46.

für γλῶσσα tritt der häufig bezeugte Wechsel zwischen γ und κ auf;[56] die Degeminierung des *ss* ist ganz üblich.[57]

Z. 17 *manos = ceras*: Beide Wörter stehen im Akkusativ Plural. Die Wiedergabe des χ von χεῖρας durch *c* ist nicht erstaunlich, denn dem gesprochenen Latein der ungebildeten Schichten fehlt ja die Aspirata, die im Normlatein mit *ch* geschrieben wird.[58]

pedes = potes: Im griechischen Wort πόδες, das im Nom. Plural steht, wieder Wechsel zwischen stimmhaftem und stimmlosem Konsonanten.[59]

Z. 18 *bentre = cilia*: Zu *b* statt *v* in *ventre*, vgl. Z. 1. Das griechische Wort κοιλία, eigentlich "Magengrube," wird oft für "Magen," "Bauch" verwendet,[60] was neugriechisch κοιλιά noch heute bedeutet.[61] Die Wiedergabe des vortonigen οι, das damals ja als [ü] ausgesprochen wurde, mit *i* ist normal.[62]

culcita = piloton: Das lateinische Wort *culcita* "Kissen" wird durch πιλωτόν wiedergegeben, das "aus Filz gefertigt" bedeutet. Dieses Wort wird jedoch auch kurz statt πιλωτὸν προσκεφαλαῖον verwendet, was völlig eindeutig durch das *Etymologicum Magnum* (p. 672,2) bestätigt wird: πῖλος, τὸ ἐξ ἐρίων εἰργασμένον πρὸς τὸ κοιμᾶσθαι ἐπιτήδειον, ὃ πιλωτὸν φαμὲν ἡμεῖς.[63]

Z. 19 *oculos = optalmo's'*: Während das lateinische Wort im Akkusativ Plural steht, scheint das griechische Wort im Nominativ Singular zu stehen. Bemerkenswert ist die Wiedergabe des φ von ὀφθαλμός als *p* und nicht als *f* (wie Z. 13 *adelfos*). Die

---

56 Gignac, op. cit., 77-78.

57 Ibid., 158-60.

58 Leumann, op. cit., 160-61; auch das Gotische gibt χ noch im 6. Jh. mit *k* wieder, vgl. Battisti, op. cit., 178-79.

59 Gignac, op. cit., 80-83: "most frequent."

60 LSJ 966-67.

61 Ἀνδριώτης, op. cit., 160.

62 Gignac, op. cit., 199.

63 H. Stephanus, *ThLGr* s.v.

Wiedergabe von φ als *f* wird seit den pompejanischen Inschriften,
wo sie zum ersten Male belegt ist, immer häufiger;[64] es kommen
jedoch in den Papyri auch im 6. Jh. noch Verwechslungen von π
und φ vor, ausserdem auch sporadisch Wiedergaben von φ als lateinisches *p*,[65] so dass man wohl annehmen muss, dass die Aussprache des φ sich immer mehr von einer Aspirata zu einer Frikative verändert hatte, jedoch noch keine völlige Identität mit
der lateinischen Frikative *f* erreicht war: nur so lässt sich das
Schwanken zwischen *p* und *f* erklären.

Z. 20 *buca = istoma*: Bei *buca* statt *bucca*, welches im volkstüm-
lichen Latein *os* vollkommen ersetzt hatte,[66] ist die nicht gen-
erelle, aber häufige Reduktion der Doppelkonsonanten zu einfachen Konsonanten zu beobachten.[67] Bei στόμα tritt ein Prothesevokal auf, was wohl nicht aus dem Griechischen,[68] sondern
aus den Sprechgewohnheiten des lateinischen Schreibers zu erklären ist: im Vulgärlatein ist *i* ja der übliche Prothesevokal
vor *s* impurum.[69]

bile = utelo: Mit dem lateinischen Wort ist *vile* gemeint; die
griechische Entsprechung ist in den Glossaren εὐτελῶς.[70] Aus
einigen Beispielen kennen wir die Ersetzung eines griechischen
εὐ durch lateinisches *u*, doch gehören diese alle in eine wesentlich frühere Zeit;[71] man wird daher eher annehmen, dass im Griechischen die häufig belegte Zerdehnung von εὐ zu εου vorliegt[72]
und dass dann der lateinische Schreiber den Anlaut weggelassen

---

64 Väänänen, op. cit. (Anm. 14), 57.

65 Gignac, op. cit., 99-100.

66 Väänänen, op. cit. (Anm. 14), 80.

67 Ibid., 60.

68 Schwyzer, op. cit. (Anm. 14), 413 kennt nur Beispiele aus
Kleinasien.

69 S. oben, Anm. 44.

70 *CGL* 2,319,54-56.

71 Leumann, op. cit., 71 und 77.

72 Gignac, op. cit., 230-31.

hat. Das Fehlen des Auslaut-*s* hat wohl eher graphische als lautliche Gründe: auch in den beiden vorhergehenden Zeilen war der letzte Konsonant in Rasur geschrieben, hier wurde das wohl vergessen.

Z. 21 *iana = tira:* Im lateinischen *ianua* ist der Halbvokal weg-gefallen, was für das Vulgärlatein typisch ist;[73] das griechi-sche ϑύρα bietet keine Besonderheit.

sela = sifrin: Im Lateinischen liegt wieder Geminatenreduktion vor.[67] Als griechische Entsprechung kennen die Glossare δίφρος,[74] was auch hier gemeint sein muss. Der Ersatz von δ durch *s* ist nicht als ungewöhnlich zu bezeichnen, denn die dentale Aussprache war wohl schon zu einer frikativen wie im Neugriechischen gewor-den,[75] wofür auch die Wiedergabe von δ durch z im sahidischen Dialekt des Koptischen spricht;[76] andere lateinische Belege feh-len allerdings. Im Auslaut ist das *i* statt des zu erwartenden *o* wohl durch einen Hörfehler zu erklären; διφρίς "sellularius, qui ita effeminatus est, ut lecticaria sella gestari semper ve-lit" (H. Stephanus, *ThLGr* s.v.) kann nicht gemeint sein.

Z. 22 *tunica = isticarin:* Gemeint ist das griechische Wort στι-χάριον, eine in den Papyri häufig, in literarischen Quellen je-doch überhaupt nicht vorkommendes[77] Diminutiv zu στίχη "Tunica." Im christlichen Bereich, wo das Wort gut bezeugt ist, bedeutet στιχάριον "Chorhemd";[78] in dieser Bedeutung lebt es auch im Neu-griechischen noch als στιχάρι.[79] Zum anlautenden *i-* vgl. Z. 20 *istoma.*

---

73 Väänänen, op. cit. (Anm. 14) 48.

74 *CGL* 7,252 (Index).

75 Gignac, op. cit., 75.

76 C. Wessely, *Die griechischen Lehnwörter der sahidischen und boheirischen Psalmenversion* (Wien 1910) 8.

77 LSJ 1646; F. Preisigke, *Wörterbuch* (Berlin 1927) II, 489.

78 G. W. H. Lampe, *A Patristic Greek Lexicon* (Oxford 1961) 1260.

79 ʼΑνδριώτης, op. cit., 342.

Z. 23 *iscio* = *eddam:* Das lateinische, mit *s* impurum anlautende
Wort ist mit dem üblichen Prothese-Vokal *i* versehen worden. In
eddam ist ohne Zweifel mit Bücheler οἶδα zu erkennen (zu *e* für
οι, vgl. Z. 1/2 *enari*). Das auslautende *m* dürfte sich daraus
erklären, dass dies für den Lateiner ein Charakteristikum der
1. Ps. Sg. bei Verben war (vgl. *amabam, amem, amarem* etc.),
welches jedoch nur geschrieben, nicht gesprochen wurde; diese
Verhältnisse wurden aufs Griechische übertragen. Die Doppelung
des *d* ist nicht erstaunlich: sowohl im Lateinischen als auch im
Griechischen wurden Geminaten weitgehend mit den einfachen Konsonanten identifiziert.[80]

sutipola = *cinido:* Das zweite Wort ist eindeutig als lat.
cinaedus bzw. griech. κίναιδος "Lustknabe" zu interpretieren;
Schwierigkeiten bereitet die im ersten Worte liegenden Entsprechung. Büchelers *sagirola* ist paläographisch nicht möglich,
seine Erklärung *sargirola* führt auch nicht weiter; das von den
anderen Editoren gelesene *satipola* bietet keinen Sinn. Nun kann
man als zweiten Buchstaben statt *a* auch *u* lesen, was zu *sutipola*
führt, das man als ζυτοπώλης "Bierverkäufer, Kellner" interpretieren kann;[81] wenn man bedenkt, welche Funktion Kellnerinnen in
Bars und Hafenkneipen heute oft haben, wird einen die antike
Gleichsetzung *cinaedus* = ζυτοπώλης nicht wundern. Falls diese
Interpretation richtig ist, geht natürlich auch in dieser Glosse
das griechische Wort dem lateinischen voraus.

Z. 24 *coclia* = *miaci:* Das lateinische Wort ist als *coclea*
"Schnecke" zu interpretieren; *e* und *i* vor anderen Vokalen sind
seit dem 1. Jh. n. Chr. zum Halbvokal *i̯* geworden, haben also

---

80 Vgl. Anm. 57 und Anm. 67.

81 Das Eintreten eines lateinischen *s* für griechisches ζ ist
in nichtliterarischer Sprache vollkommen normal, vgl. Leumann, op.
cit., 180; auch für das Griechische Ägyptens gilt "/s/ and /z/ were
undifferentiated and identified in /s/ by many speakers through
bilingual interference" (Gignac, op. cit., 120). Zur Wiedergabe
von υ durch *u* vgl. Z. 28 *suca*. Das *-i-* statt eines zu erwartenden
-o- in der Kompositionsfuge erklärt sich wohl daraus, dass die lateinische Gewohnheit, Komposita mit *-i-* zu bilden (*pedisequus,
munidator, agricola* [vgl. Leumann, op. cit., 394-95]), auf das
griechische Wort übertragen wurde.

ihren Silbenwert verloren;[82] dieser Halbvokal verband sich dann mit einem vorangehenden *l* zum Palatalkonsonanten *l*.[83] Das griechische Wort ist als μυάκιν zu interpretieren, was ein nur in Glossaren belegter Diminutiv von μύαξ ist (= μυάκιον),[84] womit allerdings ein anderes Weichtier, nämlich die "Miesmuschel," bezeichnet wird (neugriech. μύδι).

cacabu = cetra: Dem lateinischen Wort *caccabus* entspricht das griechische χύτρα "Kochtopf." Der Ersatz von χ durch unaspiriertes *c* ist normal (vgl. Z. 15 *lacana*, Z. 17 *ceras*). Erstaunlicher ist das Eintreten von *e* für υ: die zahlreichen Beispiele von Vertauschung von η und υ[85] können wegen des sicher schon im Vormarsch begriffenen Jotazismus nicht als Parallelfälle herangezogen werden. Jedoch gibt es auch einige Fälle von Vertauschung von ε und υ, wenn auch meistens in unbetonter Silbe;[86] ausserdem gibt es einige andere Belege für Wiedergabe eines griechischen υ durch lateinisches *e*.[87] Die Begründung dafür dürfte wohl darin zu sehen sein, dass das griechische υ in der Kaiserzeit in Kleinasien, Syrien und Ägypten eine Aussprache hatte, die von *u* etwas abwich.[88]

Z. 25   *laba manos = nibson ceras:* Natürlich zu interpretieren als *lava manos* = νίψον χεῖρας.

Z. 26   *colonbu = peristeri:* Dieselbe Gleichung findet sich im Londoner Glossar (*P. Lond.* II 481),[89] wo bemerkenswerterweise ebenfalls *n* und nicht *m* verwendet ist (κολουνβος). Das

---

82   H. Lausberg, *Romanische Sprachwissenschaft* (Berlin 1969) I, 195.

83   Väänänen, op. cit. (Anm. 14), 47.

84   *CGL* 2,373,42; 521,39.

85   Gignac, op. cit., 262-65.

86   Ibid., 273-75.

87   Leumann, op. cit., 76 (§85 B 3 γ).

88   J. Kramer, *ZPE* 26 (1977) 233.

89   J. Kramer, *ZPE* 26 (1977) 233, Z. 2.

Maskulinum *columbus* ist selten, kommt aber vor.[90] Im folgenden
Wortpaar ist ohne jeden Zweifel *cubicla*, die übliche vulgärlateinische Form[91] statt *cubicula*, zu lesen, wie Bücheler vorschlägt; der zweite Buchstabe ist nämlich ein *u* mit enger oberer
Öffnung, und das *o*, das einige Editoren zwischen *c* und *l* lesen,
ist nur der Anstrich des *c* in Verbindung mit einer Materialbe-
schädigung. Die griechische Entsprechung *clindi* ist mit Bücheler als κλινίδι zu interpretieren.

Z. 27 *secure = axnari:* Das griechische Wort ist mit Bücheler als
άξινάρι zu deuten.

bilosa = maloton: Dem lateinischen Adjektiv *villosus* "zottig"
entspricht im Griechischen μαλλωτός.[92] Das substantivierte Neu-
trum μαλλωτόν bedeutet nun im Griechischen "Wollkleidungsstück,"
und eine vergleichbare Bedeutung wird auch für lateinisch *villo-
sa* sc. *vestis* anzusetzen sein.

Z. 28 *ficu = suca:* Das griechische Wort ist völlig eindeutig als
σῦκα, Plural von σῦκον "Feige," zu interpretieren. Bemerkenswert ist dabei die Entsprechung griechisch υ = lateinisch *u*. Im
allgemeinen kann man sagen, dass in der republikanischen Zeit
der den Römern unbekannte Vokal υ mit *u* wiedergegeben wurde und
dass in der Kaiserzeit die dem Griechischen entsprechende Aussprache mit *y* die Norm war, während Leute, die diesen Laut nicht
auszusprechen vermochten, *i* sagten;[93] jedoch gibt es, wie etwa
vier Glossen der Appendix Probi beweisen (1: *porphireticum marmor*, non *purpureticum marmor*; 17: *Marsias*, non *Marsuas*; 191:
tymum, non *tumum*; 195: *myrta*, non *murta*), auch in der Spätantike
offenbar im Latein der niedrigsten Schichten immer noch die Neigung, υ durch *u* wiederzugeben.[94]

---

90 *ThLL* s.v.

91 Väänänen, op. cit. (Anm. 14), 43-44.

92 E. Leopold, *Lexicon graeco-latinum* (Leipzig 1874) 518.

93 J. Kramer, *Studii clasice* 18 (1979) 133.

94 Väänänen, op. cit. (Anm. 14), 38.

aleu = iscorda: Dem lateinischen *allium*[95] entspricht griechisch σκόρδον (hier im Plural σκόρδα).[96]

Z. 29 *inple = cemmiso:* Dem lateinischen *imple* sc. *aquam* muss, wie Bücheler richtig erkannte, γέμισον entsprechen (zum Wechsel γ/κ vgl. Anm. 56; zur Endung vgl. κέρασον Z. 11).

bacula = araficen: Bücheler interpretiert diese unklare Glosse als "bacula ex spina Arabica facta." Der Ersatz von -*b*- durch -*f*- ist sonst allerdings nur als italische Dialekteigenheit bekannt[97] und daher hier auffällig.

Siegen   Johannes Kramer

---

95 Vgl. zum hier auftretenden palatalen *l* Z. 24 *coclia.*

96 Zum Prothesevokal, vgl. Z. 20 *istoma.*

97 Leumann, op. cit., 169-70.

UN FRAGMENT DU MEDECIN HERODOTE: P. TEBT. II 272

En histoire de la médecine antique, les informations que l'on tire des grandes oeuvres éditées peuvent avantageusement se compléter par le témoignage de sources négligées, les papyrus grecs d'Egypte. Cette abondante littérature de première main, qui comprend une trentaine de papyrus d'auteurs et plus de 150 textes anonymes, recouvre une période remarquablement longue (du IIIème s. avant au VIIème s. de notre ère) et présente une grande variété (exposés théoriques, définitions, questionnaires, prescriptions, materia medica, encyclopédies byzantines, etc.). Pour en tirer parti, une étude d'ensemble est nécessaire.[1] Leur corpus, dont l'achèvement est proche, nous a notamment permis de restituer certains papyrus,[2] d'apporter des lumières nouvelles sur des problèmes de sources (Dioscoride)[3] et de transmission de textes, et d'identifier plusieurs fragments d'auteurs (par exemple, Héras).[4] A ce propos, le cas de *P. Tebt.* II 272 est exemplaire.

Daté de la fin du deuxième siècle de notre ère, *P. Tebt.* II 272[5] contient deux colonnes écrites en petite onciale au verso de comptes. De la première restent 21 lignes sur le traitement de la soif dans les fièvres et de la seconde, quelques lettres. Considéré comme anonyme par ses éditeurs Hunt et Goodspeed, ainsi que

---

1 Voir notre article, "En préparant un corpus des papyrus grecs de médecine," à paraître dans les *Acta de la XVIIème Session des Journées des Orientalistes Belges (28-31 mai 1979)*.

2 Par exemple, *P. Aberd.* 11 (= Pack[2] 2342): voir notre article "Deux questionnaires d'ophtalmologie: *P. Aberdeen* 11 et *P. Ross. Georg.* 1.20," dans *Cd'E* 53 (1978) 313-20.

3 Voir notre communication au *XXVII Congreso Internacional de Historia de la Medicina (Barcelona, 31 août-6 septembre 1980)*.

4 Voir notre article, "Une étape dans la transmission d'une prescription médicale: *P. Berlin Möller* 13," dans *Miscellanea Papyrologica* (Firenze 1980) 179-83.

5 = Pack[2] 2365. Nous remercions vivement Monsieur le Professeur Mertens de nous avoir communiqué la photo du papyrus.

par Körte,[6] le papyrus est en réalité un fragment du médecin Hérodote, conservé presque textuellement par Oribase (*Collectiones
medicae*, V, 30, 6-7) dans un chapitre intitulé Περὶ ποτοῦ, ἐκ τῶν
Ἡροδότου, καὶ ποίῳ καιρῷ παροξυσμοῦ τούτῳ χρηστέον.
La vie d'Hérodote[7] est mal connue: d'après Galien, ce pneumatiste,[8] élève d'Agathinos,[9] a exercé la médecine à Rome vers 100 de
notre ère.[10] De son oeuvre aujourd'hui perdue, il ne subsiste
guère que deux titres, Ἰατρός et Περὶ βοηθημάτων,[11] auxquels on
peut tenter de raccrocher un certain nombre de fragments. Ainsi,
selon les démonstrations de Wellmann et de Gossen,[12] le chapitre

---

6 *Archiv* 6 (1913) 262, n° 502.

7 Voir surtout H. Gossen, "Herodotos" (12), *RE* 8,1 (1912)
990-91; J. Steudel, "Die physikalische Therapie des Pneumatikers
Herodot," *Gesnerus* 19 (1962) 75-82; F. Kudlien, "Herodotos" (3),
Der kleine Pauly (1969) III, 1103.

8 Galien, *De simpl. medic. temp. ac fac.*, I 29 (XI, 432
Kühn); M. Wellmann, "Die pneumatische Schule bis auf Archigenes,"
Philologische Untersuchungen 14 (1895) 14-16.

9 Galien, *De pulsuum differentiis*, IV 11 (VIII, 750-51).
Sur le pneumatiste Agathinos de Lacédémone, voir M. Wellmann, "Agathinos" (8), *RE* 1 (1894) 745; idem, "Die pneumatische Schule," 8,
11-12.

10 Galien, *De pulsuum differentiis*, IV 11 (VIII, 751), déjà
cité.

11 Sur l'oeuvre d'Hérodote, voir Wellmann, "Die pneumatische
Schule," 15; Gossen, "Herodotos." Sur la polémique autour de
l'attribution à Hérodote du Περὶ τῶν ὀξέων καὶ χρονίων νοσημάτων
(traité anonyme conservé par plusieurs manuscrits), voir surtout R.
Fuchs, "Anecdota medica Graeca," *RhM* 49 (1894) 532-58 et 50 (1895)
576-99; idem, "Aus Themisons Werk über die acuten und chronischen
Krankheiten," *RhM* 58 (1903) 67-114; M. Wellmann, "Zu Herodots
Schrift Περὶ τῶν ὀξέων καὶ χρονίων νοσημάτων," *Hermes* 40 (1905)
580-604 et 48 (1913) 141-43; H. A. Diels, *Die Handschriften der
antiken Ärzte* (Berlin 1906, réimpr. Leipzig-Amsterdam 1970) II, 48;
W. Schmid, *Wilhelm von Christs Geschichte der griechischen Literatur* (München 1920) II,1, 452; Kudlien, "Herodotos." Alors que
Fuchs attribue ce traité à Thémison de Laodicée, Wellmann conjecture qu'il appartient à Hérodote. Pour Kudlien, cette hypothèse
n'est pas démontrée.

12 Wellmann, "Die pneumatische Schule," 15; Gossen,
"Herodotos."

cité par Oribase et conservé en partie dans *P. Tebt.* proviendrait
de la première section du Περὶ βοηθημάτων, intitulée Περὶ κενου-
μένων βοηθημάτων.

Dans ce chapitre, Hérodote énumère les circonstances qui ré-
clament l'administration de boisson lors des quatre phases d'un
accès de fièvre (ἐπισημασία), c'est-à-dire au commencement (ἀρχή),
à l'augment (ἐπίδοσις), à l'acmé (ἀκμή) et au déclin (παρακμή).[13]
C'est la théorie relative à l'augment qui se trouve dans la première colonne de *P. Tebt.*, dont voici le texte:

```
1    [. .] χάριν ἀλλὰ καὶ [τ]ῆς διαθέσε-

     [ω]ς· γένοιτο γὰρ ἂν πως ἐντεῦθεν

     [ἐπ]ὶ πολὺ ἕως ἂν μεταβάλῃ· ἐν δὲ
     ─────────
4    [τοῖ]ς τῆς ἐπιδόσεως χρόνοις πλεί-
              .των.    .ρῶν.
     [ου]ς αἰτίαι τῆς προσφορᾶς εἰσιν· εἰ

     [γο]ῦν τισιν ἐν τοῖς παροξυσμοῖς δί-

     [ψο]ς συνεισβάλοι σφοδρὸν καὶ δύσ-

8    [[. ].]οιστ[α]ον οὐ διὰ [α] πονηρίαν καὶ ϙυν-

     [αὔ]ξησιν τῶν νόσων, ἀλλὰ διὰ τι-

     [ν]α τοῦ πάθους ἰδιότητα, πᾶσα

     [ἀ]νάγκη ὡς σύμπτωμα ἀποδε-

12   [ξ]αμένους παρηγορεῖν κἂν τὴν
```

---

13 Hérodote *ap.* Orib., *Coll. med.*, V 30,1: διαιρουμένης τῆς
ὅλης ἐπισημασίας κατὰ τὴν ὁλοσχερεστέραν τομὴν εἴς τε ἀρχὴν καὶ
ἐπίδοσιν καὶ ἀκμὴν καὶ παρακμήν, πᾶν μέρος ἀναγκαῖον πρὸς ποτοῦ
παράθεσιν εὑρίσκομεν.

Nous avons adopté le texte de l'édition de Bussemaker-Daremberg,
fondé sur les manuscrits C²Dg, et nous rejetons la leçon choisie
par Raeder, qui omet καὶ ἐπίδοσιν. En effet, la deuxième phase
(augment) est clairement étudiée par Hérodote aux §6-7: ἐν δὲ τοῖς
τῆς ἐπιδόσεως χρόνοις... Du reste, cette division en quatre
phases est également adoptée par Galien, *De optima secta ad Thrasy-
bulum*, 36 (I, 198): τῶν μὲν νοσημάτων τέσσαρές ἐστι καιροί, ἀρχή,
ἐπίδοσις, ἀκμή, καὶ παρακμή.

[τ]οιαύτην θεράπειαν μὴ ἀπαι-

[τ]ῶσι οἱ καιροί· κριθήσεται δὲ

[ο]ὔτως ἔχον ἐὰν τοῦ κατὰ τὸν

16 [π]υρετὸν μεγέθους μᾶλλον

[π]αραύξηται τὸ δίψος. Δεῖ δὲ καὶ

[τ]ὴν φύσιν τοῦ νοσο[ῦ]ντος ἐπιθε-

[ω]ρεῖν· εἰ γὰρ ἀνεξ[ί]κακος ἐν τοῖς

20 [λ]οιποῖς ὧν μὴ ὑπομένοι τὸ διψ[εῖν]

[ἐπιτήδειος ἂν εἴη πρὸ]ς [τὸ] πί[νειν].

(...) mais aussi à cause de l'état de santé. En effet, désormais, (cela) pourrait durer longtemps, jusqu'à une évolution. Dans les moments de l'augment, les raisons de |⁵ donner à boire sont plus nombreuses: si, par exemple, dans certains paroxysmes, s'abattait une soif violente et difficile à supporter, non pas à cause d'une malignité et d'une aggravation des maladies, mais à cause |¹⁰ d'une particularité de l'affection, il serait tout à fait néces- saire de l'accepter comme symptôme et de la calmer, même si les circonstances ne réclament pas un tel traitement. Il en sera jugé |¹⁵ ainsi si la soif s'aggrave trop en proportion de la fièvre. Il faut aussi considérer la nature du malade; car si, endurant dans le reste, |²⁰ il ne supportait pas la soif, il serait dans les dispositions pour boire.

1-3 Comme l'indique la paragraphos (3), ces lignes, omises par Oribase, représentent la fin du paragraphe précédent sur l'adminis- tration de boisson au commencement (ἀρχή) de l'accès.

4-5 Nous lisons et restituons πλεί|[ου]ς αἰτίαι, qui correspond au texte d'Oribase, au lieu de πλεῖ|[σ]ται <αἱ>τίαι des éditeurs du papyrus. Dans la suite, προσφορᾶς désigne, non pas l'"*increase*," comme le suggèrent Hunt et Goodspeed, mais l'"administration de boisson" (ce substantif est également attesté aux §9, 11, 15, 18, 20, 24 du chapitre 30 d'Oribase). L'hésitation du scribe entre

le singulier et le pluriel n'apparaît pas dans les manuscrits
d'Oribase.

6 D'après Oribase, nous restituons [γο]ῦν plutôt que [ο]ῦν des
éditeurs.

7 Légère variante chez Oribase: δίψος σφοδρὸν συνεισβάλλοι καὶ
δύσοιστον au lieu de δί|[ψο]ς συνεισβάλοι σφοδρὸν καὶ
δύσ|[[.].]οιστ[α]ον de *P. Tebt.*

8-9 Par référence à Oribase, nous restituons ςυν[αύ]ξησιν au lieu
de ςυν[άρ]τησιν, que les éditeurs jugeaient d'ailleurs peu satis-
faisant.

10-14 On observe que, dans cette phrase, Oribase omet le participe
ἀποδε|[ξα]μένους et la proposition concessive κἂν τὴν | [τ]οιαύτην
θεράπειαν μὴ ἀπαι|[τ]ῶσι οἱ καιροί. Contrairement à la traduction
des éditeurs (*mischance*), σύμπτωμα doit être pris dans son sens
médical (comparer, au §15: παρηγοροῦντες τὸ σύμπτωμα). A la ligne
12, nous déchiffrons κἂν (καὶ pour Hunt et Goodspeed).

15 Variante chez Oribase: εἰ οὕτως ἔχοι; on remarquera toutefois
que εἰ est omis par les manuscrits AC¹N¹.

20-21 διψ[εῖν]... πί[νειν]. Ces lignes ont pu être restituées
grâce au texte d'Oribase.

On ne peut rien tirer de la col. II de *P. Tebt.*, dont il ne reste
que quelques lettres initiales.

   P. Tebt. II 272 apporte des informations utiles, tant sur
Hérodote que sur Oribase. Non seulement il représente le seul
papyrus conservé d'Hérodote, mais, fournissant sur lui un témoignage qui lui est de peu postérieur, il atteste la diffusion rapide
de sa doctrine. Or, il ne semble pas que ce médecin célèbre à
Rome[14] ait jamais séjourné en Egypte. Quant à Oribase, la comparaison entre *P. Tebt.* et les *Collectiones medicae* révèle que le
compilateur, fidèle à sa source, ne s'en écarte que sur des points
de détail.

---

   14 Galien, *De pulsuum differentiis*, IV 9 (VIII, 751), déjà
cité: πάνυ δ' ἐπιφανῶς ἰατρεύσαντι κατὰ τὴν τῶν Ῥωμαίων πόλιν.

Au terme de cette étude, il paraît intéressant d'analyser les problèmes méthodologiques que pose à l'historien de la médecine l'identification de tels fragments. Quand les papyrus citent des noms d'auteurs ou d'oeuvres, leurs sources peuvent être déterminées. Mais il arrive que l'oeuvre en question soit perdue, inédite ou inconnue. Parfois, des textes mentionnent seulement les courants auxquels ils se rattachent (atomistique, humoral, méthodique, empirique, etc.). Les tentatives d'identification plus précise s'avèrent alors hasardeuses.[15] Lorsque le papyrus ne contient aucune référence, on recourt à l'étude lexicale des mots rares (par exemple, ἀνεξίκακος pour *P. Tebt.*) et, dans tous les cas, à la comparaison avec les oeuvres des grands médecins de l'antiquité. Toutefois, il serait illusoire de vouloir identifier tous les papyrus médicaux. Le naufrage de la littérature médicale antique a été tel qu'en dépit des recherches, la plupart restent malheureusement anonymes. L'examen approfondi de tels témoins n'en revêt que plus d'importance.

Liège   Marie-Hélène Marganne

---

15 Ainsi, il paraît téméraire d'attribuer à Soranus d'Ephèse tout fragment de gynécologie (Pack[2] 2347) et à Héliodore tout fragment de chirurgie (Pack[2] 2374 et *P. Ryl.* III 529 = Pack[2] 2376).

Proceedings of the XVI Int. Congr. of Papyrology (Chico 1981) 79-91

GREEK LITERARY PAPYRI REVISED BY TWO OR MORE HANDS

One of E. G. Turner's criteria for identifying a scholar's text is that it should contain clear signs of revisions, particularly revisions copied from a manuscript different from the original scribe's antigraph.[1] In search of such texts I have compiled a list of about 150 literary papyri[2] in which critical alterations have been made by two or more revisers.[3] In general, editors' judgments about the number of hands at work have been accepted; where useful and possible, photographs have been consulted. But certainty in this matter is hard to come by: it is difficult and sometimes impossible to distinguish between revisers' hands. Some editors conventionally have attempted to do so, but others have limited themselves to reporting the number of hands they believe are at work, and have avoided assigning responsibility for individual revisions. Where an editor was uncertain about how many revisers worked on a text, or about the kind of revisions each one made, it seemed best for this study to adopt his more conservative judgment.

How can we determine which papyri actually have been collated with an exemplar different from that used by the original scribe? The simple fact that text has been revised by two hands is not sufficient proof. In about a third of the 150 papyri collected, for example, all the surviving revisions are corrections of error and were apparently added by the original scribe and a second hand. In cases like these it is likely that the original scribe added corrections as he copied, whenever he happened to notice a mistake.

---

1 E. G. Turner, *Greek Papyri* (hereafter *GP*; Oxford 1968) 94.

2 Texts have been compiled from the listings in the catalogue of Pack (second edition) and its supplement by F. Uebel (*APF* 21 [1971] 167ff.), and by a search through papyrological publications after 1971.

3 Later hands working on a text will be referred to here as revisers' hands. The term *diorthotes* is reserved to refer only to the professional reviser whose job it was to eliminate errors from a newly written manuscript, very likely by collating it with its exemplar.

The second corrector was presumably the *diorthotes*; because his revisions import no new readings into the text we deduce that they are probably the result of collation with the first scribe's exemplar. In any case, such a papyrus has not been formally revised twice. If our understanding of the process of ancient book production is accurate, in fact, such a text received no more than the single *diorthosis* to which books were supposedly submitted before leaving the copying house.[4] Papyri of this description do not qualify as "scholars' texts" on the strength of their corrections alone, and therefore will not receive further attention here.

The papyri in the remaining group, however, have stronger claim to distinction. In each of them at least one reviser has added critical notes, sigla or variant readings deriving from traditions independent of that in the original scribe's antigraph.[5] These papyri are presented in the accompanying table (pp. 86-90). A few (group A) were worked over by three or more hands; thirteen of these (nos. 1-13) contain variant readings or critical notes-- not simply corrections--which come from at least two pens. (Usually the other hand is that of the original scribe who contributed corrections, presumably in the course of copying.) In group B are listed those papyri in which additions were made by two revisers, neither of whom was the original scribe. Four of these (nos. 20-23) are of special interest, since in each case two revisers contributed variants or critical notes--an indication that each may have been collating with an independent exemplar. These texts, along with nos. 1-13 in group A, have *prima facie* a better claim than others to be called scholars' texts. In group C are listed the papyri in which only two scribes, one of whom was the original scribe, have made alterations. As in groups A and B, the papyri in which both the revisers contributed variants and the like (nos.

---

4 *GP* 93, with n. 51.

5 A working assumption here is that all variants are the result of collation, but this assumption is fallible: some variants may be conjectures by ancient revisers; some may have been present in a scribe's antigraph and then faithfully copied by him into the margin of a new text. The variants in *P. Köln* I 12, for example, were written neatly in the hand of the original scribe, and may have been present in the antigraph.

29-38) are of greatest interest to this study. For the balance of
the papyri in the table (group D) there is some question either
about who was responsible for critical additions (nos. 74-86) or
about whether variant readings and the like are present at all
(nos. 87-103).

Which of these texts were most certainly collated with manuscripts other than their antigraphs? The most impressive evidence
for this is the presence of variants attributed to individual
scholars or to copies of a work. Such specific references occur
in more than a dozen of these papyri. For present purposes it
does not matter whether individuals cited were the owners of the
books used for comparison or their annotators or their scribes.
What is significant is that their versions were authoritative
enough for them to be cited by name in support of readings. Among
the authorities named in this group are Theon (nos. 3, 10, 13, 57,
58), Apion (nos. 7, 32) and Ptolemy (nos. 8, 60). ἡ κοινή, αἱ
ἀρχαῖαι and perhaps τινές are cited in two or three other texts
(nos. 30, 82, 84?). Personal attributions cannot always be identified with certainty, however. Perhaps Aristonicus is to be recognized in the abbreviation ΑΡΙ which accompanies some revisions
(nos. 3, 8, 13, 57),[6] and Nicanor in the monogram Ν written beside
others (nos. 3, 9, 32, 33, 58, 59).[7] The correct expansion of
other abbreviations can hardly even be guessed.[8] Even amid this
uncertainty, an interesting feature of these attributions presents
itself. Theon, Ptolemy and Aristonicus (who lived about the time
of Augustus), Apion (who worked at the time of Tiberius), and the
Hadrianic Nicanor[9]--if these are the persons to be recognized in

---

  6 For the expansion see E. Lobel, n. *ad P. Oxy.* XXIV 2387
fr. 1 margin.

  7 Νί(κανδρος) has also been suggested. The monogram is problematic, for in different contexts it had different meanings. For
the most recent discussion see H. C. Youtie, "Πράγματα Μετέωρα, or
Unfinished Business," *ZPE* forthcoming.

  8 Αν( ) (Appendix, 2 & 6); Ερω( ) (Appendix, 1); Αμ( ) [or
αμ( )?] (ibid.).

  9 Theon: *RE* 5A (1934) 2054ff.; Ptolemy: *RE* 23 (1959) 1863
(Ptolemy 79); Aristonicus: *RE* 2 (1895) 944-66 (Aristonicus 17);
Apion: *RE* 1 (1894) 2803-06 (Apion 3); Nicanor: *RE* 17 (1936) 274ff.
(Nicanor 27).

these notes--were scholars prominent in Alexandria. Since they are
cited, in some cases, in papyri copied as much as two centuries
after their lifetimes, we deduce that their influence among some at
least of the literate population of Greek Egypt was enduring.

Eleven of the papyri just discussed (nos. 3, 7, 8, 10, 30, 32,
33, 57, 58, 82, 84) plus eight others (nos. 11, 12, 23, 34, 44, 65,
67, 81) contain marginal notes in which the technical language employed by the revisers shows that they probably gave scrupulous attention to textual detail. A reviser indicates that he collated
with two separate manuscripts, for example, when he records that a
reading occurred in "both" exemplars [ἀμ(φοτερ-?); nos. 23, 32] or
"only" in one [μό(ν-); nos. 8, 57, 58]. More often, his language
implies careful comparison with only one copy: οὐκ ἦ(ν) ἐν τ(ῷ)
ἀγτιγ(ράφῳ) is written beside a line of text in no. 11; ἡ ἀκριβ(εία)
is cited as authority in no. 10. In several other cases, suspected
readings have been checked and verified by the addition of οὔ(τως)
in the margin, and occasionally a reviser explicitly states οὔ(τως)
ἦν or οὔ(τως) γέγρ(απται). In cases of lingering doubt he sometimes
records that doubt by writing an abbreviation of ζήτει in the margin
(nos. 3, 11, 33, 44?, 57). In each case the language he uses implies his careful scrutiny of the text in question and is another
sign that it probably belonged to a scholar.[10]

Critical sigla may indicate that a book had some connection
with a scholarly commentary and therefore are also of interest in
this study. Although nearly a third of the texts in the accompanying table are marked with sigla of one sort or another, the mere
presence of signs does not identify a papyrus as a scholar's text.
Certain ones simply articulate the text, and may have been added by
the first scribe, a *diorthotes* or a reader.[11] Others accompany

---

10 The monogram ⳨, standing for δι(ώρθωται) (no. 67) and
δι(ορθωτέον) (no. 34) confirms that a text has been revised by a
diorthotes, but does not necessarily guarantee that he did a careful job. It is worth noting too that even if the reviser of a papyrus was using the original scribe's antigraph for comparison [and
this is likely when notes like οὔ(τως) and οὔ(τως) ἦν occur: see
93 on the meaning of οὔ(τως)], notes like those just quoted indicate a special interest in textual accuracy.

11 No. 27: ʃ; no. 29: /, ⌐, Χ.

revisions or mark the place for their insertion.[12] These will usually have been added by a *diorthotes*, and are of no special interest here. In more than thirty-five texts, however, the function of
sigla is different, although not always obvious.[13] They may, like
the monogram ℟,[14] mark notable portions of text; others were perhaps used as reference marks beside passages which the ancient
reader could find discussed in a separate commentary. Aristarchus
and later Homeric critics used the *diple* (>) in this way as an all-
purpose sign whose full significance was not obvious without commentary.[15] Perhaps in non-Homeric papyri the same sign and others
(χ and / are the most common) served the same function. If so,
they are indeed marks of a scholar's text, since the ordinary reader would have had little use for commentaries.

Up to this point the discussion has centered only on forty to
fifty papyri which can be identified with more or less certainty as
scholars' texts. It is not possible to claim the same distinction
for all the other entries in the table, although some probably
qualify. The best candidates are those in which variants--without
specific attribution--have been added by two or more hands. It is

---

12 Nos. 27, 31, 39, 52, 53, 67, 69, 85, 95; the signs encountered here are the *ancora* (⌐, ⌡), *antisigma* (ͻ) and marks of
similar shape (ᒐ, ᑎ), and the diagonal stroke (/).

13 Nos. 2, 3, 7, 8, 9, 10, 12, 13(?), 22, 23, 25, 26, 30, 32,
33, 37, 40, 41, 42, 44, 46, 47, 48, 49, 57, 58, 60, 74, 75, 79, 81,
82, 83, 94, 97, 103. The function of the Aristarchan sigla in two
texts of Homer (nos. 30, 82) is familiar from the scholia in the
manuscript of the *Iliad* known as *Venetus* A (Venice, Bibl. Marciana
Ms. gr. 454).

14 χρ(ηστόν, -ῆσις, -ήσιμον?); see E. G. Turner, *Greek Manuscripts of the Ancient World* (Oxford 1971) 17 and ibid., no. 27.

15 *P. Oxy.* VIII 1086 (1st cent. B.C.; Aristarchan comm. on
Hom. *Il.* 2): > ἐρχομένων· μάλα δ' ὦκα διέπρησσον πεδίοιο (*Il.* 2.785)·
ἡ διπλῆ ὅτι ἐλλείπε[ι] ἡ διὰ πρόθεσις...; [πᾶσαι δ' ὠίγνυντο πύλαι,
ἐκ] δ' ἔσσυτο λαός (*Il.* 2.809)· τὸ σημεῖον πρὸς τοῦτο ὅτι τὴν πύλην
π[ληθυντικῶς εἴρηκεν. Cf. Schol. A, ed. Erbse passim, e.g. *ad* Hom.
Il. 5.245 (ἵν' ἀπέλεθρον ἔχοντας): ἡ διπλῆ πρὸς τὴν ἰδιότητα τῆς
φράσεως.... See also T. W. Allen, *Homeri Ilias* (Oxford 1931, repr.
New York 1979) 198; *GP*, 115-18 (on sigla in non-Homeric papyri);
and S. West's cautionary remarks à propos the unconventional use of
the *diple* and other sigla in a papyrus of Homer (*The Ptolemaic Papyri of Homer* [Cologne/Opladen 1967] 132-33).

possible, of course, that these were occasional additions made by
readers as they read their books, and were not the result of
methodical collation. If twofold collation *has* been practiced
here, however, it is worth noting as something extraordinary; and
it should perhaps be taken as a sign of a book prepared for a
scholar, since the high proportion of error and the absence of
variants in the vast majority of literary papyri indicates that
most of the reading public had no such scrupulous regard for the
text tradition of ancient authors.

There remain several papyri in the table in which only one
reviser has added variant readings. The scholarly quality of these
must be examined case by case. Perhaps those with extensive marginal annotation (no. 18, e.g.) should be given most weight. In some
of these, however (no. 74, e.g.), the poor condition of the text
and the elementary or misguided nature of many marginal comments
make them easy to exclude from consideration. In other papyri so
little of the text remains that the overall quality of the whole
original book cannot really be judged. In still others (nos. 14
and 15, for example), variants are very rare although the length
of the surviving text is considerable.[16] How or why variants found
their way into their margins is not obvious, but it is likely that
they were occasional additions, perhaps made by readers. The small
ratio of variants to corrections in these texts leaves the impression that these were not books that were methodically collated with
independent witnesses.

A few general observations about the character of the papyri
assembled here will conclude this survey. *First:* They are predict-
ably few in number, relative to the number of literary papyri published to date. Most (about seventy-five) are texts of poetry,
often by authors whose dialect or style present special problems
and who would therefore be likely subjects of scholarly research.
Homer, Pindar and Lesbian lyric are each represented by at least
seven papyri. *Second:* The date of a plurality of these papyri
(about fifty) has been set or assigned to between the end of the
first and the beginning of the third centuries of our era, the
period that has produced the most literary papyri overall.

---

16 No. 14: twenty-five complete columns, nineteen fragmentary;
no. 15: more than forty columns.

Noteworthy exceptions, however, are three Ptolemaic texts of Homer
(nos. 1, 38, 73) dated to the third or second century B.C. *Third:*
Marginal comments and glosses are not uncommon. They occur in more
than forty of the texts of this table and almost always, when it
can be determined, are the work of someone other than the original
scribe. *Fourth:* It is most unusual, in any of the texts in the
table, to find the original scribe adding variant readings. He has
done so certainly in only sixteen to eighteen cases.[17] No doubt in
some texts he simply copied readings which he found in the margins
of his antigraph. *Fifth:* Texts from Oxyrhynchus predominate, probably partly because of the chance and the richness of the finds
there, but probably also because, as Turner has argued,[18] Oxyrhynchus
was the abode of professional scholars associated with the Museum at
Alexandria. It is possible, moreover, to recognize among these
Oxyrhynchus papyri the hands of four different scribes who each
copied two or three texts listed in the table.[19] *Sixth*, and last:
The table presented here does not incorporate all the papyri which
may be considered scholars' texts. For a list of them to be complete it must be augmented by scholarly commentaries and by papyri
in which all revisions are the work of a single hand but include
critical additions. A tentative list of such papyri is given in
the Appendix to the table, where an attempt has been made to separate out the more likely examples of scholars' books by listing
first those in which annotators identified their sources (with more
or less exactitude), and by giving in a second group those papyri
in which the language or symbols employed by revisers indicate that
they worked with care.

---

17 Nos. 3, 4, 7, 29, 31, 32, 33, 35, 36, 37, 38, 39, 43, 44?,
45, 83, 85, 95?

18 E. G. Turner, *MPER* N.S. V, 141-46.

19 Nos. 5 (Pind.), 12 (Pind.) and 75 (Alc.) are the work of
one scribe (see also E. Lobel, introduction to *P. Oxy.* XXVI 2445);
nos. 84 (Hdt.), 86 (Euphorion) and 97 (Alc.) are the work of
another (Turner's scribe #5, op. cit. supra n. 18); nos. 32 (elegy)
and 77 (comm. on Alcm.) are by a third; nos. 57 and 58 (Soph.) are
the work of a fourth.

TABLE: Papyri showing revisions by two or more hands and containing
variant readings, critical notes or sigla.[20]

A. Texts with three or more revisers

Two or more hands make critical additions:

1. *P. Grenf.* II 4 + *P. Hib.* I 22 + *P. Heid.* IV 2, Hom. *Il.*
   21-23 (3)
2. *P. Oxy.* II 223, Hom. *Il.* 5 (III; written on verso of a
   petition; S)
3. *P. Oxy.* V 841, Pind. *Paeans* [II; written on verso of documents; 4-5 revisers; reference to ?Aristonicus, ?Nicanor,
   Theon, Chrysippus, Aris( ), Ar( ); ζή(τει) and γρ(άφεται)
   added in marg.; M, S]
4. *P. Oxy.* XI 1376, Thuc. 7 (II/III)
5. *P. Oxy.* XIII 1604, Pind. *Dith.* (II, M; text written by the
   same scribe as nos. 12, 75)
6. *P. Oxy.* XX 2256, Aesch. hypotheses & frr. of plays (II/III?;
   critical additions occur only in the text of the plays)
7. *P. Oxy.* XXI 2295, Alc. (I; 3-6 revisers; ref. to Apion in
   marginal notes; S)
8. *P. Oxy.* XXIV 2387, Alcm. *Parthenia* [1/I; additions by 3-5
   hands; ref. to ?Aristonicus, Ptolemy in notes; ?ού(τως),
   μό(νος) Π(τολεμαῖος) in marg.; S]
9. *P. Oxy.* XXIV 2394, choral lyric (Alcm.?) (II/III; 3-4 revisers; ref. to ?Nicanor; M, S)
10. *P. Oxy.* XXV 2427, Epich. frr. [II/III; ref. to Theon,
    ἢ ἀκριβ(εία?); οὔ(τως) added in marg.; S]
11. *P. Oxy.* XXV 2430, choral lyric (Simon.?) [I/II; οὐκ ἦ(ν) ἐν
    τ(ῷ) ἀγτιγ(ράφῳ), ὀΰ(τως) ἦν, ζή(τει) added in marg.; M]
12. *P. Oxy.* XXVI 2445, Pind. *Dith.*(?) [II; ref. to Didymus in
    marginal comment; οὔ(τως) γέγρ(απται) written in marg.; S;
    text by the same scribe as #5, 75]
13. *P. Oxy.* XXXVII 2803, Stesich.? (1; 3-4 revisers; ref. to
    ?Aristonicus, Theon; M, S?)

One hand makes critical additions:

14. Br. Mus. inv. 132 (Pack[2] 1272), Isoc. *De Pace* (I/II)
15. Br. Mus. inv. 135 (Pack[2] 485), Herondas *Mimes* (I; M; vari-
    ants possibly by more than one hand)
16. Br. Mus. inv. 732 (Pack[2] 899), Hom. *Il.* 13, 14 (I)
17. *P. Oxy.* XI 1370, Eur. *Med.*, *Or.* (V; *Or.* revised by 2-3 hands,
    one of which added variants; *Med.* corrected by a still dif-
    ferent hand; M)
18. *P. Oxy.* XXIII 2372, Boeotian lyric (II; M; variants possibly
    by 2 or 3 hands)
19. Univ.-Bibl. Leipzig inv. 613 (Pack[2] 1303), Men. *Pk.* (III;
    variants perhaps by 2 hands)

---

20 After the author and title in each entry the date is given,
with Arabic numerals referring to centuries B.C. and Roman numerals
to centuries of our era. "M" and "S" mean that marginal comments
or critical sigla are present.

B. Texts with two revisers, neither of whom is the original scribe

Both hands make critical additions:

20. *P. Oxy.* VII 1017, Pl. *Phdr.* (II/III)
21. *P. Oxy.* VIII 1082, Cerc. Meliambi (II)
22. *P. Oxy.* X 1247, Thuc. 8 (II; S)
23. *P. Oxy.* XXXII 2617, Stesich. *Geryoneis* [collation with two exemplars indicated by ref. to ἀμ(φότερ-)?; M, S; corrections perhaps by a third hand]

One hand makes critical additions:

24. *P. Köln* I 17, Dem. *De Falsa Leg.* (I)
25. *P. Oxy.* II 212, Ar. *Thesm. Secundae*(?) (II/III; revisers make corrections only; one added a siglum)
26. *P. Oxy.* VII 1011, Callim. *Aet.*, *Iambi* (IV; revisers make corrections only; one or both add sigla)
27. *P. Oxy.* XV 1820, Hom. *Od.* 18 (VI/VII; M; S accompany revisions and articulate the text; revisions perh. by 3 hands)
28. *P. Oxy.* XIX 2214, Callim. *Aet.* (1/I; M)

C. Texts with two revisers, one of whom is the original scribe

Both hands add variant readings

29. *P. Harr.* 38, Eur. *Med.* (II; M?; S articulate text)
30. *P. Oxy.* III 445, Hom. *Il.* 6 [II/III; ref. to ἡ κο(ινή), Aristarchus; M; Aristarchan sigla are the contribution of the original scribe]
31. *P. Oxy.* XIII 1620, Thuc. 1 (II/III; S accompany variants)
32. *P. Oxy.* XXII 2327, elegy (Simon.?) [II; ref. to Apion, ?Nicanor, ἀμ(φότεροι?); M, S] text written by the same scribe as no. 77]
33. *P. Oxy.* XXVI 2442, Pind. *Hymns*, *Paeans* [III; ref. to ?Nicanor; ζή(τει) added in marg.; M, S]
34. *P. Oxy.* XXVI 2450, Pind. frr. [I/II; ↑, i.e. δι(ορθωτέον?) written in a lacunose marginal note; the original scribe contributes sigla only; M]
35. *P. Oxy.* XXXIV 2693, Ap. Rhod. *Argon.* 3 (II; M)
36. *P. Oxy.* XXXV 2735, Choral lyric (Stesich. *Helen*?) (II; M)
37. *P. Ross. Georg.* I 2, Hom. *Il.* 2 (II/III; S)
38. P. Sorbonne inv. 2245A (Pack[2] 1081), Hom. *Od.* 9, 10 (3; S used for stichometry)

Only the original scribe makes critical additions:

39. *P. Amh.* II 24, Dem. *In Phil.* 2 (IV; S accompany corrections)
40. *P. Lond. Lit.* 6, Hom. *Il.* 2 (I; revisers make corrections only; orig. scribe [?] added one siglum)
41. *P. Oxy.* X 1233 + XVII 2081d + XVIII 2166b, Alc. (II; revisers made corrections only, but one siglum was added, perhaps by the original scribe)
42. *P. Oxy.* XVII 2100, Thuc. 4, 5, 8 (II; all revisions are corrections of error; orig. scribe adds a siglum)
43. *P. Oxy.* XVII 2101, Xen. *Cyr.* (III; some variants added by a 2nd hand?)
44. *P. Oxy.* XVIII 2165, Alc. [II; ζ(ήτει?) added with variant; S]

45. *P. Oxy.* XIX 2208, Callim. *Aet.* (III; some variants added by a 2nd hand?)
46. *P. Oxy.* XXII 2310, Archilochus? (II; revisers made corrections only, but one siglum was added by the original scribe)
47. *P. Oxy.* XXXVII 2812, commentary on tragedy? (I; revisers made corrections only, but one siglum was added by the original scribe)

Only the second hand makes critical additions:

48. Brit. Mus. inv. 136 (Pack² 697), Hom. *Il.* 3, 4 (III?; revisers made corrections only, but one [not the original scribe?] has added a siglum)
49. *P. Ant.* III 158, Hom. *Il.* 8-16 (parts) (III; revisers made corrections only, but one [not the original scribe?] has added a siglum)
50. *P. Fay.* 8, Dem. *In Phil.* 3 (II)
51. P. Mich. inv. 918 (Pack² 266), Dem. *In Phil.* 3 (IV)
52. "*P. Morgan*" (Pack² 870), Hom. *Il.* 11-16 (IV; only *Il.* 11 contains revisions by 2 hands; S at omissions in the text)
53. *P. Oxy.* I 12, chronological work (III; sigla added by 2nd hand at errors, omissions)
54. *P. Oxy.* III 459, Dem. *In Aristocr.* (III)
55. *P. Oxy.* IV 700, Dem. *De Cor.* (II)
56. *P. Oxy.* VI 852, Eur. *Hyps.* (II/III; written on verso of an account; M; S accompany revisions)
57. *P. Oxy.* IX 1174 + XVII 2081a, Soph. *Ichneutai* [II; ref. to Theon, ?Aristonicus, Ari( ); οὔ(τως) ἦν ἐν τ(ῷ) Θέω(νος), ζή(τει) in marg.; γρ(άφεται), μό(νος, -νον) accompany revisions in the margin; M, S; text by the same scribe as no. 58; possibly revised by more than 2 hands]
58. *P. Oxy.* IX 1175 + XVII 2081b, Soph. *Eurypylus* [II; ref. to Theon, ?Nicanor; οὔ(τως) ἦν μό(νον) ἐν ἐτ(έρῳ) added in marg.; M, S; by the same hand as no. 57; possibly revised by more than 2 hands]
59. *P. Oxy.* X 1234 + XI 1360 + XVIII 2166c + XXI pp. 130-34, Alc. (II; ref. to ?Nicanor; M)
60. *P. Oxy.* XI 1361 + XVII 2081e, Bacchyl. *Scolia*? (I; M, S; ref. to Ptolemy in marginal note; possibly 2 hands have added variants)
61. *P. Oxy.* XV 1807, Arat. *Phaenom.* (II; M)
62. *P. Oxy.* XXVI 2447, Pind. *Threnoi*(?) (II; M)
63. *P. Oxy.* XXIV 2404, Aesch. *In Ctes.* (II)
64. *P. Oxy.* XXX 2518, Antimachus *Thebais* (II; M?)
65. *P. Oxy.* XXX 2526, Euphorion? [II; οὔ(τως) added in margin; M]
66. *P. Oxy.* XXXIX 2883, Rhianus *Messianica* (III; original scribe may also have added variants)
67. *P. Ross. Georg.* I 4, Hom. *Il.* 17 (III; *diorthotes* signed off ✝; M; S accompany revisions)
68. *P. Ryl.* I 47, Hom. *Il.* 5 (II; original scribe may also have added variants)
69. *P. Ryl.* I 53, Hom. *Od.* 12-24 (parts) (III; revisers made corrections only; sigla mark omissions)
70. *PSI* I 11, Hom. *Il.* 4 (IV/V; M?)
71. *PSI* VI 721, Dem. *De Cor. Trierarch.* (II; revisers made corrections only; siglum accompanies explanatory marginal note)

72. *PSI* IX 1091, mythographic text [I/II; οὕ(τως) ἦν written in margin by 2nd hand]
73. *P. Tebt.* III 697, Hom. *Od.* 4, 5 (2; text written by 2 scribes, one of whom made corr.; a third hand added variants)

D. Doubtful cases

Additions perhaps the work of both the original scribe and a 2nd hand:

74. The Antinoe Theocritus (Pack^2 1487) (V/VI; M, S)
75. *P. Oxy.* XV 1788, Alc. (II; a lengthy comment in the margin quotes Didymus; S; text written by the same scribe as nos. 5, 12)
76. *P. Oxy.* XXIII 2370, Corinna *Veroia* with prose arguments(?) (ca. A.D. 200)
77. *P. Oxy.* XXIV 2389, comm. on Alcm. (I; two revisers made corrections; one or both added a variety of sigla; M; text written by the same scribe as no. 32)
78. *P. Oxy.* XXVI 2448, Pind. frr. (II/III)

Critical additions present, but the activity of 2 hands not certain:

79. *Berl. Klas. Texte* III 10-19 + *P. Ryl.* I 21 + *P. Rein.* I 2, treatise on physiology (1; S)
80. P. Col. inv. 414 (Pack^2 918), Hom. *Il.* 14 (III)
81. *MPER* VI 81-97, Xen. *Cyr.* [II; reviser wrote οὕ(τως) ἦ(ν) in margin and referred to another source (or sources) as ἀλ(λ-); S]
82. *P. Hawara* 24-28, Hom. *Il.* 1, 2 [II?; ref. to Aristarchus, ἡ κο(ινή), τι(νές); οὕ(τως) added in margin; M, Aristarchan sigla; additions perhaps by more than 1 hand]
83. *P. Oxy.* I 16 + IV 696, Thuc. 4 (I; activity of 2 hands proposed by editors in I 16, doubted by them in 696; S)
84. *P. Oxy.* VIII 1092, Hdt. 2 [II; οὕ(τως) ἐν τ(ῷ) ἄ[λλῳ or οὕ(τως) ἐν τ(ισιν) ἄ[λλοις, e.g.; added in M by reviser; text written by the same scribe as nos. 86, 97]
85. *P. Oxy.* X 1232, Sappho (III; S accompany revisions)
86. *PSI* XIV 1390, Euphorion *Thrax* and *Hippomedon Maior* (II; M; text written by the same scribe as nos. 84, 97)

Two revisers at work but presence of critical additions not certain:

87. *P. Ant.* I 15 + *P. Schub.* 23, new comedy (Men.? Apollodorus?) (III/IV)
88. *P. Ant.* III 164, Hom. *Il.* 17 (IV; S marks omission)
89. *P. Oxy.* II 218, historical text (III; M?)
90. *P. Oxy.* III 454 + *PSI* II 119, Pl. *Gorg.* (II)
91. *P. Oxy.* V 843, Pl. *Symp.* (II; M)
92. *P. Oxy.* XI 1369, Soph. *OT* (V/VI)
93. *P. Oxy.* XV 1790 + XVII 2081f, Ibycus (1; M accompanied by S)
94. *P. Oxy.* XV 1792, Pind. *Paeans* (II; S)
95. *P. Oxy.* 2064 (Pack^2 1489), Theocr. (II; M; S mark omissions)
96. *P. Oxy.* XVII 2095, Hdt. 1 (II)

97. *P. Oxy.* XXI 2297, Alc. (II; M, S; text written by the same
    scribe as nos. 84, 86)
98. *P. Oxy.* XXIII 2377, Callim. *Hecale* (III/IV)
99. *P. Oxy.* XXXII 2624r, choral lyric (Simon.?) (II)
100. *PSI Omaggio* 1 (*SIFC* N.S. 38 [1966] 63-69), mime (I; M)
101. P. Soc. Pap. Alex. inv. 242 (Pack² 765), Hom. *Il.* 5 (II)
102. P. Stras. inv. Gr. 31+32 (Pack² 591), Hom. *Il.* 1 (II;
     written on the verso of documents)
103. *P. Tebt.* III 692, Soph. *Inachus* (2; S)

APPENDIX: Papyri revised by only one hand which show evidence of
          careful collation with sources other than the original
          scribe's antigraph.

A. Texts in which the sources of variant readings are identified
   1. Br. Mus. inv. 271 (Pack² 1039), Hom. *Od.* 3 [I; ref. to Apion,
      Ερω( ), Αμ( )?, τι(νές), Γλωσσογρ(άφοι); ζή(τει) added in
      margin; M, S]
   2. *P. Bodm.* XXVIII (Turner, *Mus. Helv.* 33 [1976] 1-23), satyr
      play [II; ref. to An( )?; S accompany revisions]
   3. *P. Oxy.* IV 671, epideictic epigrams (III; ?Nicanor cited)
   4. *P. Oxy.* IV 685, Hom. *Il.* 17 [II; ἡ κο(ινή) cited]
   5. *P. Oxy.* XXVII 2452, Soph. *Theseus* [II; οὔ(τως) ἐν ἐτ(έρῳ),
      οὔ(τως) ἐν β' μό(ν-), χρ(ηστόν?) written; Aristophanes or
      Aristarchus (?) cited]
   6. P. Oxy. inv. 16 2B.52, new comedy [E. W. Handley, *Proc.* XIV
      Int. Congr. 133-48; II; ref. to Αν( )]
   7. *P. Par.* 71, Alcm. *Parth.* (I; ref. to Aristophanes, Pamphi-
      lus, ?Aristarchus; M, S)
   8. *PSI* II 123, Sappho (II/III; ref. to ?Nicanor; S)

B. Others
   9. *Berl. Klass. Texte* II, commentary on Pl. *Tht.* [II; ⸓, i.e.
      δι(ορθωτέον) written beside a correction]
  10. *P. Flor.* II 112, comm. on lost comedy of Aristophanes (II/
      III; Didymus quoted in marginal note)
  11. *P. Oxy.* II 221, comm. on Hom. *Il.* 21 (II; signed in margin:
      Ἀμμώνιος τοῦ Ἀμμωνίου ἐσημειωσάμην)
  12. *P. Oxy.* VI 874, Ap. Rhod. *Argon.* 3 [III; ἕν τι(σι) οὔ(τως)
      φέρεται added in margin]
  13. *P. Oxy.* XVII 2080, Callim. *Aet.* [II; οὔ(τως) added in marg.]
  14. *P. Oxy.* XVIII 2181, Pl. *Phd.* [II; οὔ(τως) α· added in marg.]
  15. *P. Oxy.* XXII 2333, Aesch. *Sept.* [II; ζ(ήτει?) accompanies
      variant]
  16. *P. Oxy.* XXV 2429, comm. on Epich. *Odysseus Automolos* [II;
      ζή(τει) in margin]
  17. *P. Oxy.* XXVI 2441, Pind. *Prosodia*? [II; οὐ̈(τως) τιν(ές) ac-
      accompanies variant; M, S]
  18. *P. Oxy.* XXVII 2468, Pl. *Pol.* [II; οὔ(τως) ἥν in margin; S]
  19. *P. Oxy.* XXXIV 2694, Ap. Rhod. *Argon.* 2, 4 on recto; comm.
      on *Argon.* 4 on verso [II; ζ(ήτει) added in margin of comm.;
      M (on recto), S accompany revisions (recto)]

20. *P. Oxy.* XXXV 2741, comm. on Eup. *Maricas* [II/III; ζή(τει),
    χρ(ηστόν?) written in margin; S]
21. *P. Oxy.* XXXVII 2806, old comedy [II; ἐν τ(ισι) written with
    variant; M]
22. *P. Oxy.* XLV 3224, Hes. *Op.* (II; a variety of critical sigla
    written beside a short passage of text)

(See Turner, *GP*, 116-17 for additional texts containing
 critical sigla.)

Wayne State University   K. McNamee

A COMPOSITION CONCERNING PAMPHILUS AND EURYDICE

P. Mich. inv. 3793, reported to have come from Oxyrhynchus, contains portions of two columns of a text which mentions among other things a love affair, events connected with a spring, and devouring by beasts. The goddess Aphrodite probably is mentioned early in the fragment, and two names of mortal persons, Pamphilus and Eurydice, can be read with certainty. The greater part of what survives is apparently narrative in the third person, but instances of the first person and of direct address do occur.

Some peculiarities of the format call for comment (see plate). The hand, although the work of a practiced writer, shows a unique blend of characteristics, including both cursive and noncursive elements, which are topped with a hint of somewhat pretentious mannerism. It is consequently difficult to find close palaeographical parallels, but taken as a whole the writing suggests a date in the third or perhaps the early fourth century of the Christian era.[1]

The writer did not concern himself with keeping the line ends in Column I even; they vary in alignment by as much as eight letter-widths and rarely, possibly never, fall within a word. Insofar as they are preserved, several lines in both columns could be scanned as iambic. However, our initial impression that the text may be in verse is surely misleading--at least if one is speaking of verse in the normal sense--since a discernible metrical scheme is not adhered to throughout.[2] Further, nothing in the surviving

---

1 The writer's use of linking strokes varies greatly, and the frequent appearance of separately made letters of basically cursive shape gives the text an air of exaggerated carefulness. The following show many points of similarity: Schubart, *P. Gr. Berol.* 32a (219/20), 32b (ca. 200), 34a (202/3), Seider, *Pal.* I 38 (301/2), 46 (259), II 53 (third/fourth cent., assigned), *P. Oxy.* XXXVIII 2847 (first half of third cent., assigned).

2 I 1,4-5, possibly 6-7 (assuming crasis in the last), II 1, 3-6, 10-11 could be read as iambic. Spondees impermissible in iambic trimeters appear in I 2 and 8-9. I 9 when scanned yields anapaests, II 13 anapaests or choriambs. The "scansion" of II 9 (possibly iambic with synizesis) and 12 is questionable. Hiatus seems to be frequent throughout. To satisfy all criteria in the fragment,

vocabulary compellingly suggests poetry. Lastly, while such a degree of unevenness in the right edge of a column of prose is rare
in literary papyri of the period, it can be paralleled, especially
in subliterary papyri.[3]

There are no accents, punctuation marks, or other aids to the
reader. The orthography appears to be free of major faults. Some
letters in a thinner ink were evidently written in the margin before line II 1. The writing is with the fibers, and the back is
blank. There is no certain clue as to the original width of the
columns, or the number of lines lost between I 14 and II 1.

P. Mich. inv. 3793   Third/early fourth cent. A.D.
12.5 x 11.5 cm.   Provenance: Oxyrhynchus?

Column I

margin

←→   ]ǫδειτης θεᾶς

              ].. καρπῶν

     ].ω.[±7   ]ν

4   ]δ̣ι̣τ̣η̣θ̣[±6   ]νον ὁ Πάμφιλος

     ].α̣τ̣αλ.[±6   ]ην ῷχετο

     ].παλη.α̣ρ[±3   ].[.].ναϙου.ασ

     ].η ξενια τῆι̣ πο̣θουμένηι

---

a metrical scheme would have to be as flexible as the "iambic senarii" for which H. W. Prescott argued in P. Oxy. II 219 (cf.
Class. Phil. 5 [1910] 158ff.). In any case, chances are that the
lines of writing in our papyrus were somewhat longer than trimeters
or senarii. On iambic patterns in prose, see Aristotle's well-
known observation in Poet. 1449a 27.

3 For comparably "free" treatment of the right margin (coupled
with the tendency to end the lines with complete words) in prose
texts, see P. Oxy. XXV 2435 (Acta Alexandrinorum; early first cent.),
especially the portion illustrated as Turner, Gr. Manuscripts no. 57,
and P. Oslo I 1 (magical; fourth cent.). The Oxyrhynchus mimes (P.
Oxy. III 413; second cent.; plates I-II in Bull. Ac. Roy. d. Sc. et
d. Let. d. Danemark, 1915), although the presence of dialogue and
occasionally of metre vitiates the comparison somewhat, provide
another parallel--as do of course a number of documents. Parallels
from Ptolemaic literary texts, beginning with the Derveni papyrus,
are somewhat more numerous.

8   ].πρου κάλλιστον καὶ βελτίονα ἀποβλέπ˙ω˙

    ]. κάλλιστον καὶ βελτίονα

      ]πρῶτα ἀπορ<ρ>ίπτων .....

    ]. ὁδοιπορίας κεκονι<ο>ρτωμένηι

12].α σύ<γ>κοπος ἀνελύσατο

    ]].μα καὶ ἐξεδύσατο

      ]..[   ]...[

    — — — — — — — — — — — — — —

                Column II

                margin

←→ κα   κατη.[

          τοδεει[

          κατασφα[

4   ἀπεδρα.[μ-

          παρην[

          παντοι.[   ].[

          ανθε[.]α[.]εφερε με.[

8   ἐπὶ τὴν κρηνὴν ἐκ τῳ[

          θεωρεῖ τὰ ενκυκ..ι...[

          καὶ τοὺς καλοὺς χιτῶν[ας

          ὅδε, ἄγε καὶ σάρκας ὁ.[

12   διανοηθει Εὐρυδ[ί]κη[

          θηριόβρωτον γεγον[

    — — — — — — — — — — —

     Col. I   1.]ọ: or ω   3.]των[?   4.]δ̣: or α   5.].:
prob. ν, η, or π (κ, υ also poss.)   τ̣: could be υ   6. η.αρ[: or
ηαρ[   ]. before να: prob. α or ε   . before ασ: κ or ρ   7.].:
prob. α, δ, κ, λ, μ, or χ   8.].: σ or υ   αποβλεπ̂ pap.   9.].:
end of horiz. in mid-line   βελτείονα pap.   10. απορ̣ιπτων pap.;
next letter α, δ, or λ   11.].: prob. γ, η, π, or τ

κεκονιαρτωμενηι pap.   12. σύνκοποσ pap.

    Col. II   1. ҳα in marg.: lighter ink than main text   .[:
ι, π, or τ   7. second [.]: see comm.   .[: γ, ν, or π
9. .. after κυκ: λ(?) written over cancelled letter (o?); then α,
o, or ω   11. σάρκας: or σάρκες   12. διανοηθει: see comm.
]ҳ: top right missing   η[: the left upright

Column I:

1. E.g. 'Αφρ]οδείτης (read -δίτης), θεᾶς | [οὔσης.
3. Perhaps the unusual amount of space at the end of this line
    was left to mark a section break.
4. E.g. 'Αφρο]δίτη, θ[εά.
5. E.g.]να τὰ λ.[;]κατὰ λ.[. If αταλ.[begins a word, the
    choices are limited: ἀταλα[ίπωρος, several not particularly
    frequent words confined to poetry, and]ἡ 'Αταλά[ντη. E.g.
    πρώ]ην ᾤχετο.
6. E.g.]ἀπαλὴ γάρ[;]. πάλη γάρ[. The end of the line may have
    broken a word: e.g. -μ]ένας οὐκ ἀσ-|[κεῖ; a form of ἀσκέω
    could tie in with πάλη, "wrestling" (possibly a sexual meta-
    phor as in the Lucianic *Onos* 8-11). Such an approach to the
    problem might be preferable to -μ]ένας οὐράς or -μ]ένα Σούρας.
    (For towns called Σούρα, cf. Pape-Benseler, s.v. The most in-
    teresting one was in Lycia and was noted for its oracular pool
    with carnivorous fish, described in Plut., *Soll. an.* 23.976c,
    Athen. 8.333d-f, etc. I once toyed with the possibility that
    the spring, pieces of flesh, and devouring by beasts which are
    mentioned in Column II below might be part of a scene at this
    locality. Polycharmus of Naucratis, whose Λυκιακά is quoted
    by Athen. on the subject of Σούρα, according to Athen. 15.675f
    also wrote a work on Aphrodite.)
7. Either ἡ ξενία ("hospitality, lodging"; cf. Lampe, *Patr. Gr.
    Lex.*) or ξένια ("gifts") might fit well with τῆι ποθουμένηι,
    "to/for the one longed for."
8. The first word is probably Κ]ύπρου. E.g. τὸν ἄνδρα τὸν πάντων
    τῶν ἐκ τῆς Κ]ύπρου κάλλιστον καὶ βελτίονα ἀποβλέπω. The com-
    bination of the comparative and superlative is noteworthy.
10. ἀπορ<ρ>ίπτων: The verb can denote throwing aside or casting
    away figuratively as well as literally. However, the form

here may be the genitive plural of ἀπόρριπτος -ον.

11. E.g. αὐτῆι κα]τ᾽ (or με]τ᾽ or ἐ]π᾽) ὁδοιπορίας κεκονι<ο>ρτω-
μένηι, "to/for her, covered with dust in the course of the
journey"--with failure to aspirate the stop, as often in papyrus documents (cf. Gignac, *A Grammar of the Greek Papyri of
the Roman and Byzantine Periods* I, 134).

12-13. σύ<γ>κοπος is attested only in Diod. Sic. 3.57. It is the
adjective from συγκοπή, a medical term describing a sudden
loss of strength and consciousness accompanied by sweating
and chilliness of the body (extensive references in Stephanus,
Thes. Gr. Ling., s.v.).

ἀνελύσατο: "loosened, took off," probably with something
worn as the object (cf. Stephanus for parallels). The verb
would then be almost a synonym for ἐξεδύσατο, "stripped off,"
which should have an item of clothing as object. E.g. ἀνελύ-
σατο | [. . . τὸ ζ]ῶμα καὶ ἐξεδύσατο | [τὴν ἐσθῆτα (of course,
one might also have ἀνέλυσα τό . . . ἐξέδυσα τό).

Column II:

3. E.g. κατασφα[γέντος; κατασφα[γή.

4. E.g. ἀπέδρα[με.

5. E.g. παρῆν; παρ᾽ ἦν.

6. E.g. παντοῖ[α.

7. The second [ ] in the line may in fact have been a blank
space; the broken remains of this area along with the fibers
carrying the preceding α have been lost since the photograph
was made. E.g. ῎Ανθε[ι]α ἔφερε; -αν θε[ῖ]αν ἔφερε (or perhaps
we have an imperative φέρε similar to ἄγε in line 11 below).

8. E.g. ἐκ τῶ[ν.

9. E.g. τὰ ἐν κύκλωι; τὰ ἔνκυκλα (read ἔ<γ>κυκλα). ἐγκυκλα,
"women's upper garments" (many references in the lexicographers;
cf. Stephanus) would tie in well with the next line.

11. σάρκας (or σάρκες): Probably "pieces of flesh."

12. διανοηθει: Perhaps δι<ε>νοήθ<η> (cf. Gignac, *Grammar* I, 283;
Mayser, *Grammatik* I.2, 101) or διανοηθ<ῇ> is to be read--unless
this is not a form of διανοέομαι but a present form of an
otherwise unattested verb διανοήθω (on the pattern of ἀλήθω,
νήθω and the like; cf. in general Chantraine, *Morph. hist. du*

grec 264, Schwyzer, *Gr. Grammatik* I, 703). Cf. next note.

13. θηριόβρωτον: This adjective is attested elsewhere only in
Diod. Sic. 18.36.3 and three times in Christian writers of
the fourth century (references in Lampe).
If we take δι<ε>νοήθ<η> in 12 as meaning "think" and as
patterning with the accusative and infinitive (as in Plato,
Prot. 324c), these two lines may have run something like
δι<ε>νοήθ<η> Εὑρυδ[ί]κη [αὐτὸν . . .] | θηριόβρωτον γεγον[έναι
or δι<ε>νοήθ<η> Εὑρυδ[ί]κη[ν . . .] | θηριόβρωτον γεγον[έναι.
But perhaps the verb was used in its more usual sense of "have
in mind": e.g. δι<ε>νοήθ<η> Εὑρυδ[ί]κη[ν . . .] | θηριόβρωτον
γεγον[υῖαν.

To recapitulate and to try to get some feeling for the narrative overall: The name Aphrodite occurs in all likelihood in I 1
and possibly again in I 4, although we cannot tell what her role is.
Fruits, often associated with the goddess in myth and cult, are
mentioned in I 2. A human character, Pamphilus, appears at the end
of I 4; and he or someone else departs by the conclusion of I 5.
While line I 6 yields nothing that is certain, we seem to be on
firmer ground in what follows. There is talk in I 7 probably of
hospitality or gifts for a woman who is "longed for." By I 8 someone is speaking in the first person: "I gaze upon (or admire) the
fairest and one who is better" (presumably, better than someone
else who is understood from the context): κάλλιστον καὶ βελτίονα
ἀποβλέπω. "The fairest" is masculine and is apparently connected
with Cyprus; κάλλιστον καὶ βελτίονα is repeated as if for emphasis
in the following line. ἀποβλέπω and κάλλιστον point to love and
the doings of Aphrodite; is the "I" of ἀποβλέπω the woman who is
ποθουμένηι in line 7, now speaking directly and rejecting one of
her admirers--perhaps his gifts or hospitality--in favor of another?
In I 10 something--gifts, words, or advice, perhaps--is being
thrown away or rejected--by a male, if ἀπορ<ρ>ίπτων is a present
participle. A reference to a woman (unless κεκονι<ο>ρτωμένηι is
instrumental) who is dust-covered with traveling follows in I 11.
The next two lines appear to describe someone disrobing. Unless a
sentence break prevents this, the subject seems to be someone who
is σύ<γ>κοπος; but since this adjective elsewhere describes a state

of shock or unconsciousness, one must ask how a person who is
σύ<γ>κοπος can be disrobing! Perhaps the adjective is used here in
an exaggerated sense similar to English "dead with exhaustion" or
the like. If this is the case, the dust and travel alluded to in
line 11 might serve as motivation for weariness and disrobing
(σύ<γ>κοπος could be feminine, and κεκονι<ο>ρτωμένηι above might
modify the subject of the same sentence if the final *iota* is a
superfluous one, as frequently happens in papyri).

In the opening lines of Column II, violence must have taken
place before the reader's eyes or been described by someone: note
the probable form of κατασφάττειν, "to slaughter," or a related
word in line 3 followed by someone running away in the next line
(perhaps ἀπέδρα[με). Perhaps someone new then comes on the scene
(παρῆν, line 5); possibly this is "Ανθε[ι]α, who if my supplement
is correct is named in line 7. Antheia apparently was carrying
something (ἔφερε), probably to a spring from somewhere (ἐπὶ τὴν
κρηνὴν ἐκ τῶ[ν, line 8). Perhaps it also is she who in line 9 observes either some items in a circle or some women's garments (τὰ
ἔ<γ>κυκλα) and then, in line 10, τοὺς καλοὺς χιτῶν[ας. A command
is then given to someone: ὅδε, ἄγε καί . . . --"You there, come
and . . ." (line 11). The following word σάρκας (or σάρκες) may
have a link with the slaughter of line 3; in any case, presumably
someone is now telling another person to do something with (or to
look at) these pieces of flesh. That something gruesome has occurred would seem to follow from this and from θηριόβρωτον, "eaten
by beasts," in line 13. In the meantime a certain Eurydice has
appeared in line 12. As suggested in the commentary, one tempting
reconstruction of 12-13 involves someone thinking--perhaps mis-
takenly--that someone else (possibly Eurydice) has been eaten by
beasts. When coupled with the mention of the clothing (lines 9-10)
this hints at a sequence of events similar to the tale of Pyramus
and Thisbe (Ovid, *Met.* 4.55ff.), where Pyramus sees Thisbe's
bloodied clothing scattered about and thinks that she has been de-
voured by a lioness (a spring is present in the setting of the
story).

The sham or supposed death of a heroine is of course easily
paralleled from Greek romance; incidents in Achilles Tatius, Chari-
ton, and Iamblichus come especially to mind. Actual or threatened

devouring by beasts is also part of the common cloth of romance.[4]
To speculate a bit further where the papyrus is concerned, we might
imagine someone (say Eurydice) disrobing, alone or in company with
someone else, after a dusty journey (I 11-13) and perhaps near a
spring. She is then described as witnessing a slaughter of some
sort (II 3) and running away (II 4) in fright, perhaps abandoning
her clothing. Another person (perhaps Antheia) happens upon the
scene and the spring and sees the clothing and some pieces of flesh,
about the latter of which she speaks to someone else (II 5-11). In
the absence of Eurydice and the presence of evidence of violence
along with her clothing, the conclusion of one of the other parties
is that she has been eaten by beasts (which lurk in or around the
spring and which were probably responsible for the earlier slaughter
and the pieces of flesh). Such may have been the story line.

In general, although certainty about specific details of the
plot usually eludes us, the density with which incidents involving
Aphrodite, love, travel, wild beasts, and acts of violence appear
to be packed into this scanty fragment points clearly to romance as
the genre to which the work belongs. The general time period fits
the great age of Greek romance well--although the language of our
text suggests that it is part of a rather bald and pedestrian narrative rather than a particularly elevated or rhetorical one. Persons named Pamphilus and Eurydice do not occur in extant romances
(Pamphilus is frequent enough in comedy and elsewhere in Greek
civilization over many centuries), but they would be suitable in a
work of this kind.[5] Moreover, the name Antheia seems to have a

---

4 For another mistaken belief in death by beasts, cf. the
incident of Sinonis and the dog in Iamblichus' *Babyloniaka*, 18.

5 If the name Ἀταλάντη is present in I 5 (see comm.), this
would give us another character name with a mythological flavor.
A number of individual details in Column I (e.g. Aphrodite, the
fruits, the love affair, the casting away of something) might be
taken as suggestive of the story of Atalanta and Hippomenes (complete references in *RE*, s.v.). However, in that case finding a
suitable link between this material and that in Column II would be
difficult. A similar problem arises if we try to see the events of
Column II as those involving Hypsipyle, Archemorus (whose mother
was named Eurydice), and the serpent at the Nemean spring (see e.g.
Apollod. 3.6.4; full references in Bond, *Euripides' Hypsipyle* [Ox-
ford 1963]). Of course, it is conceivable that we are dealing with
(possibly reworked) mythological material rather than straight
romance.

particularly close connection with this genre: an Antheia is the
heroine in Xenophon of Ephesus, and a similarly named woman is a
character in the so-called Antheia Romance, a fragmentary work
represented by *PSI* VI 726. Such, then, is the literary background
against which this tantalizing fragment should be viewed.

Montclair, New Jersey   Timothy T. Renner

PART 3

HERCULANEUM PAPYRI

NUOVE REALTA' DELLA PAPIROLOGIA ERCOLANESE

Per riferire brevemente sull'attuale momento della ricerca sui papiri della Biblioteca ercolanese prenderò l'avvio dagli Atti del XV Congresso Internazionale di Papirologia che ebbe luogo a Bruxelles nel settembre del 1977. Nella seduta dedicata ai papiri ercolanesi, che già di per sé indicava il progresso degli studi rispetto a Congressi precedenti, ebbi l'onore di presentare il *Glossarium Epicureum* di Hermann Usener pubblicato da me e da Wolfgang Schmid, uscito appena allora a Roma, frutto della collaborazione organizzativa del Centro Internazionale per lo Studio dei Papiri Ercolanesi con l'Istituto del Lessico Europeo. Esposi che cosa il *Glossarium* abbia rappresentato sia nella storia degli studi su Epicuro sia nella storia della filologia classica tedesca della seconda metà dell'Ottocento: inoltre, il *Glossarium* ci rendeva accessibile una personalità ricca di umori e ci lasciava prefigurare la progettazione di un completo e moderno vocabolario epicureo.[1]

La pubblicazione del *Glossarium Epicureum* ha anche un altro significato, non meno importante: la ripresa a Napoli di una coscienza della tradizione europea di studi sui papiri ercolanesi, stabilitasi specialmente in seguito alla pubblicazione degli 11 volumi della cosiddetta *Herculanensium Voluminum Collectio Altera* avvenuta dopo l'Unità d' Italia. Per rinverdire tale coscienza abbiamo anche promosso a Napoli la pubblicazione degli *Studi Ercolanesi* di Wilhelm Crönert già nel 1975: un volume che rende accessibili ricerche fondamentali da una parte sulla conservazione e il trattamento dei rotoli ercolanesi, sugli apografi e sulle abbreviazioni e, dall'altra, sull'epicureo Filonide, sui *Loghikà Zetemata* di

---

1 Le intenzioni degli editori del *Glossarium Epicureum* sono state intese nel senso giusto dalla maggior parte degli studiosi: vorrei citare la favorevcle accoglienza dell'Arrighetti in *Gnomon* 51 (1979) 645-61, del Sedley in *Prudentia* 10 (1978) 54-56 e del De Lacy, *AJP* 100 (1979) 468-72.

Anche al Mette, che ha dedicato nel *Lustrum* 21 (1979) il rapporto bibliografico alla ricerca di Epicuro negli anni 1963-1978, non è sfuggita l' importanza dell'opera: egli stesso poi munisce la via alla costituzione di un nuovo lessico epicureo, dando un elenco di citazioni aggiornate.

Crisippo, su testi relativi alla storiografia epicurea su Socrate e
sulla tradizione di una parte cospicua della *Syntaxis ton philoso-
phon*, vale a dire dell'*Index Academicorum*.

Questa raccolta di studi ercolanesi fu promossa a prescindere
da particolari che ora possono risultare non più validi; abbiamo
contribuito a rendere più esatta la fisionomia di uno studioso
originale quale fu il Crönert e a completare il profilo dell'autore
delle due opere più conosciute, la *Memoria Graeca Herculanensis* e
il *Kolotes und Menedemos*. Nessuno ignora che specialmente il *Kolotes* suscitò riserve da parte di autorevoli filologi come il Koerte,
ma d'altra parte nessuno ignora che il Crönert, pur con le sue biz-
zarrie e le sue incongruenze, ebbe, in quanto uomo probo e geniale,
la stima del Wilamowitz.

Ancora nel 1979, in occasione del XIX Centenario dell'eruzione
del Vesuvio del 79, abbiamo messo insieme un'altra raccolta di contributi, i *Saggi* di papirologia ercolanese di C. Jensen, di W.
Schmid e di me stesso. Anche questo volume, che schiarisce la
storia del passato bisecolare dei papiri epicurei, vuole accentuare
la coscienza internazionale che presiede, a Napoli, alle iniziative
papirologiche. È appena necessario ricordare la dimensione straordinaria che le edizioni ercolanesi di Christian Jensen prima
nella serie Teubneriana poi nella serie Weidmanniana hanno acquisita nel tempo e l'esemplarità del suo lavoro scientifico specialmente nell'interpretazione del celebre V libro della *Poetica* di
Filodemo del 1923: non a torto W. Schmid ha scritto un saggio che
prende le mosse dai contributi del grande storico della filosofia
greca Theodor Gomperz per concludersi con la figura del Jensen.

Il tentativo di riconsiderare il contributo europeo alla ricerca ercolanese non ha fatto dimenticare l'esigenza di esplorare
la storia più propriamente locale dei nostri papiri nella Officina,
una volta del Museo ercolanese di Portici poi del Museo Nazionale
ed ora della Biblioteca Nazionale di Napoli. Così in occasione di
questo Congresso ho il piacere e l'onore di presentare il volume
ora pubblicato di contributi alla storia della Officina dei Papiri
Ercolanesi: le figure di Antonio Piaggio, il famoso inventore della
prodigiosa macchina, e del suo collaboratore Vincenzo Merli riemer-
gono sulla base di documenti inediti in tutto il loro autentico

valore: così pure ai nomi di svolgitori e disegnatori dei papiri o
di studiosi come il Baffi e il Rosini si uniscono i grandi nomi
della cultura europea (ricordo per tutti il Winckelmann con i suoi
Sendschreiben e John Hayter di cui viene pubblicato in italiano il
famoso *Report*). Altri documenti consentono di penetrare nella vita
bisecolare della Officina non solo nei suoi successi ma anche nelle
sue miserie. Quel che conta è che pur tracciando una storia locale
della Officina ci imbattiamo in personaggi della civiltà europea
sia del Settecento che salutò nel grande Re Carlo III di Borbone lo
scopritore di Pompei ed Ercolano sia dell'Ottocento che registra
l'accorrere a Napoli di grandi filologi, specialmente tedeschi, a
verificare coi propri occhi i testi che erano stati divulgati nelle
incisioni della Seconda serie degli *Herculanensia Volumina*.

Ma nel Congresso di Bruxelles l'*équipe* del nostro Centro Internazionale per lo Studio dei Papiri Ercolanesi diede anche notizia dell'imminente pubblicazione del primo catalogo completo e
moderno dei papiri ercolanesi. Il *Catalogo dei Papiri Ercolanesi*
apparso nel 1979 che ancora mancava agli studi di Papirologia, porta a compimento gli sporadici, sia pure insigni, tentativi di Emi-
dio Martini, Domenico Comparetti, Domenico Bassi, Francesco Castaldi.
Di ogni papiro sono forniti non solo i dati tecnici sulla condizione
attuale, sul quoziente di leggibilità, sul numero delle colonne e
dei frammenti, ma soprattutto i dati bibliografici.

Ma la realtà più consistente della papirologia ercolanese
nell'ultimo decennio è costituita dal rinnovato studio dei testi
papiracei quale viene perseguito nelle *Cronache Ercolanesi* che è
l'organo annuale del Centro Internazionale per lo Studio dei
Papiri Ercolanesi e nella serie La Scuola di Epicuro i cui primi
due volumi sono apparsi nel 1978.

Nelle *Cronache Ercolanesi* sono stati esaminati, integralmente
o parzialmente, numerosi papiri. Richiamerò l'attenzione soprattutto sulle edizioni integrali cominciando dai testi di Epicuro.
Tutti sappiamo che, dopo la grande opera innovatrice di Achille
Vogliano, la ricerca sull'opera capitale di Epicuro *Della natura*
ha trovato esito nella edizione di G. Arrighetti (1960, 1973[2]).
Alla revisione testuale dei papiri *Sulla natura* di Epicuro, dopo
l'edizione del papiro 1413 *Sul tempo*, curata nel 1972 dal compianto

Raffaele Cantarella e dallo stesso Arrighetti, le *Cronache Ercola-nesi* contribuiscono in modo decisivo col XXVIII libro curato da D. Sedley e col XV libro curato da C. Millot: qua e là nei dieci volu-mi della nostra rivista sono stati esaminati luoghi isolati di al-tri papiri di Epicuro. I risultati conseguiti dal Sedley o dalla Millot hanno segnato un notevole progresso sulle edizioni pur bene-merite di Vogliano e Arrighetti e consentono di porre in modo chia-ro i libri *Della natura* accanto alle *Lettere a Erodoto* e *a Pitocle* nella ricostruzione della fisica epicurea: il rapporto tra l'opera *Della natura* e le grandi *Lettere* è stato chiarito dallo stesso Arrighetti nel V volume delle nostre *Cronache*. I ristudiati papiri *Della natura* concernono le questioni epistemologiche sul linguaggio, le categorie epicuree del procedimento logico, la visione della na-tura degli atomi e della composizione degli aggregati. Le nuove letture dimostrano che in parte il successo è dovuto all'uso dei microscopi binoculari introdotti nella Officina dei Papiri Ercola-nesi in seguito a una visita di E. Turner a Napoli, il quale volle inaugurare con un suo articolo il primo numero della nostra rivi-sta. Naturalmente, il microscopio non sostituisce l'intelligenza del lettore così come le fotografie di cui si è riusciti a dotare la nostra Officina ottenute col grande impegno della tecnica mo-derna non sostituiscono gli originali: sia il microscopio sia le fotografie sono però un prezioso aiuto alla faticosa decifrazione dei nostri testi anneriti. Anche gli immediati successori di Epi-curo, i *catheghemones*, sono stati rivisitati sulle colonne di *Cronache Ercolanesi*. Così gli opuscoli polemici di Colote *Contro il Liside* e *Contro l'Eutidemo di Platone* hanno ricevuto attento esame nel sesto volume delle *Cronache*. Di Metrodoro è stato indi-viduato lo scritto *Sulla ricchezza* nel papiro 200, erroneamente ritenuto di Filodemo. Il valore di tale scoperta comunicata al Congresso di Bruxelles è divenuto chiaro con l'edizione del papiro 163 *Della ricchezza* di Filodemo nell'VIII volume delle nostre *Cronache*: si è potuto conseguire un progresso decisivo nell'accer-tamento della concezione epicurea della povertà e della ricchezza o dei mezzi di sostentamento del sapiente epicureo: anche per tale tramite è riuscita convalidata la compattezza del sistema epicureo dal maestro fondatore fino a Filodemo.

Ma anche sulle testimonianze degli altri *catheghemones* come
Ermarco e Polieno si è cominciato ad indagare: finora è stata ap-
prestata una silloge di testimonianze in cui i *catheghemones* sono
chiamati *andres*, ma è stata progettata una raccolta completa delle
testimonianze relative al periodo eroico della storia del Giardino,
di cui vengono esplorati, per quanto sia possibile, i momenti di
sviluppo.

Del terzo scolarca, Polistrato, sono state studiate le due
opere superstiti: il *Disprezzo irrazionale delle opinioni popolari*
e *La filosofia*. Una scrupolosa indagine ha chiarito l'obbiettivo
polemico di Polistrato negli Scettici (oltre che negli Stoici) e
ha restituito una chiara personalità a Polistrato che riesprime in
una vibrata forma stilistica la sua fedeltà alla dottrina del
maestro. Vano risulta il tentativo del Vogliano di arricchire
l'eredità di Polistrato con un' altra opera protrettica.

Ma l'*équipe* del nostro Centro non poteva trascurare Demetrio
Lacone, l'epicureo fiorito nel secondo secolo a.C. in un intreccio,
ancora da chiarire, con Zenone Sidonio. Dopo il volume d'assieme
del De Falco pubblicato nel 1923, i papiri demetriaci non erano
stati più studiati. Lo sforzo del De Falco fu notevole ma gli
esiti della sua ricerca meritavano di essere sottoposti a nuovo
esame. I risultati finora conseguiti sono brillanti: i papiri
Sulla poesia, del cui II libro il Wilamowitz avrebbe voluto essere
editore, e altre opere incerte danno nuova materia di riflessione
sulla filologia epicurea e su questioni di geometria o astronomia,
ma soprattutto viene arricchita la nostra conoscenza della poesia
greca.

Per la prima volta sono state raccolte insieme e sistemate le
testimonianze di Zenone Sidonio. Anzi tutto si è potuto assodare
che il nostro Zenone, scolarca nel periodo 110-75, rivide a livello
sia grammaticale sia contenutistico i testi della scuola epicurea.
Di Zenone viene confermata l'ortodossia, generalmente finora negata, e insieme individuato un tentativo evolutivo della dottrina
epicurea. Si può dire che in una visione di sviluppo nella difesa
dei dogmi fondamentali della dottrina epicurea va inquadrata anche
l'attività molteplice di Filodemo.

Appunto a Filodemo il nostro Centro ha potuto dedicare la
maggiore porzione di ricerca. Non solo si sono curate nuove edizioni di papiri come l'873 *Sulla conversazione* o il 1414 *Sulla
gratitudine* o il 163 *Sulla ricchezza* e particolarmente il 1418 *Su
Epicuro e gli Epicurei* (le note *Pragmateiai*), ma si può dire che
tutte le opere di Filodemo sono state parzialmente riconsiderate:
Su Epicuro, l'*Etica Comparetti*, *Gli dèi*, *I vizi*, *Il buon re secondo
Omero*, *I metodi inferenziali*, *L'adulazione*, *L'economia*, *L'ira*, *La
libertà di parola*, *La musica*, *La poesia*, *La provvidenza*, *La reli-
giosità*, *La retorica*. Lo studio di tali testi ha come traguardo
la ricostruzione del ruolo che ebbe Filodemo in Italia quale arte-
fice della diffusione dell'epicureismo e dell' adeguamento della
dottrina alle esigenze della società del tempo. Lo stadio della
valutazione di questo epicureo, le cui opere rappresentano la parte
preminente della Biblioteca Ercolanese, lascia ancora a desiderare:
un grave pregiudizio domina sulla sua figura ritenuta quella di uno
stanco, puntiglioso, polemico ripetitore della dottrina epicurea.
Ma saggi parziali di intelligenza delle sue opere, su poesia o
musica, sulla libertà di parola o sulla morte mostrano la inconsi-
stenza di un giudizio malfondato e impongono la necessità di una
severa ricerca nel vasto àmbito della sua produzione per determi-
narne con sicurezza anche il ruolo creativo. Al di là degli sche-
matismi di scuola o del tributo che egli deve a tendenze comuni
della sua epoca, Filodemo rappresenta certamente qualcosa di più
che una mera adesione alla dottrina epicurea. Soprattutto gli va
riconosciuta l'ambizione di inserire, a Roma, l'epicureismo fra le
altre vittoriose filosofie ellenistiche riproposte da Cicerone.
D'altra parte, il ruolo di Filodemo nei confronti di Lucrezio e di
tutta la cultura della tarda repubblica e del primissimo impero
romano dev'essere ancora chiarito. Le revisioni autoptiche e er-
meneutiche dei papiri di Filodemo su grandi temi culturali possono
donare a questo pensatore la sua autentica fisionomia.

Si sa che nella Biblioteca Ercolanese non mancano resti di
opere latine, come di un carme sulla battaglia di Azio: anche su
questi papiri è ritornata l'attenzione degli studiosi. Ma la nostra rivista non poteva trascurare gli altri problemi che pongono i
papiri ercolanesi. I sia pur magri risultati della nuova tecnica

di svolgimento del Fackelmann, che troppo ottimisticamente al Congresso Parigino dell'Association Budè nel 1968 lo Schmid salutava come l'inizio di un'età dell'oro della ricerca ercolanese, sono stati esposti sulle pagine di *Cronache Ercolanesi*; lo studio della scrittura è stato avviato con saggi storici e metodologici in attesa di un'opera complessiva sulla paleografia ercolanese inquadrata nella storia della paleografia grecolatina; monumenti ed iscrizioni di Ercolano sono oggetto di studio per tener viva la coscienza dell'ambiente in cui si svilupparono gli interessi per l'epicureismo; infine sono stati riproposti momenti culminanti della storia della papirologia ercolanese.

Come dimostra anche il decimo volume delle *Cronache*, apparso in questi giorni, tendiamo a una riproposizione dei papiri ercolanesi come testimoni della cultura antica e, in particolare, dell'epicureismo e dei suoi rappresentanti. In tale tendenza riteniamo produttivo lo studio anche dei frammenti minori di un'opera trascurati finora dagli editori: frammenti della *Retorica* trascurati dal Sudhaus o *Sulla libertà di parola* trascurati dall'Olivieri hanno dimostrato la loro validità per la ricostruzione del pensiero epicureo e dello stile di Filodemo non meno delle parti meglio conservate.

Un'altra tendenza che si cerca di far fruttificare sulla base della autopsia dei papiri è la utilizzazione dei nostri testi per la storia delle filosofie antiche, non solo ellenistiche.

Come dicevo prima, oltre alle *Cronache Ercolanesi* il nostro Centro ha voluto creare una serie di volumi dal titolo augurale La Scuola di Epicuro. Si tratta di riproporre i testi meglio conservati in edizioni fornite non solo di testo con relativi apparati (critico e papirologico), ma anche di traduzione in una lingua della cultura moderna e di adeguato commento. Questa serie vuole togliere agli storici della filosofia antica l'alibi di essere costretti a ignorare i papiri ercolanesi. Abbiamo ritenuto necessario liberare i nostri testi da un dannoso e sterile specialismo e portarli allo stesso livello di chiarezza grafica e disponibilità scientifica degli autori che ci sono stati trasmessi dai codici medievali, intendendo tale disponibilità come l'esito della cooperazione di una tecnica esperta con una matura coscienza storiografica.

Così, oltre alla consueta esatta informazione tecnica su un papiro,
viene dato adeguato spazio al contenuto dell'opera e alla personalità dell'autore: siamo orgogliosi di aver potuto sostituire a pe-
disseque versioni latine moderne traduzioni in inglese o in italiano. La novità più appariscente è che il testo greco viene dato in
modo continuo e non per colonne. Le colonne sono indicate, ma il
testo viene diviso in capitoli in base al contenuto. Il primo
volume della Scuola di Epicuro è dovuto a due studiosi americani,
Phillip ed Estelle De Lacy, ed è una nuova edizione del papiro 1065
Perì semeion, *On Methods of Inference*. Il secondo volume è relativo al papiro 336/1150, l'opera di Polistrato *Sul disprezzo irrazionale delle opinioni popolari* curata da G. Indelli, un giovane
borsista del Centro. Impostata sui medesimi criteri, l'edizione
ripropone la complessa valenza di Polistrato quale testimone del-
l'epicureismo nel III secolo.

   Questo è il rapido bilancio dell'attività papirologica a Napoli dodici anni dopo il Congresso Parigino dell'Association Budé
dedicato all'epicureismo greco e romano, dove i papiri ercolanesi
fecero solo una fugace apparizione. Da allora ad oggi è stato compiuto un notevole passo avanti nella ricerca. Tuttavia questo bilancio non può non chiudersi con una connotazione negativa. Fin
dal 1969 il nostro Centro ha fatto presente l'opportunità, se non
la necessità, di riportare alla luce l'insigne monumento della
Villa Ercolanese dei Pisoni, della cui biblioteca facevano parte i
nostri papiri epicurei. Per rendere sempre più chiara tale nozione,
ripubblicavamo nel 1972 il non ancora sostituito volume di D. Comparetti e G. De Petra, *La Villa Ercolanese dei Pisoni. I suoi monumenti e la sua biblioteca*. Nel Congresso Internazionale di Papirologia di Oxford del 1974 fu approvata all'unanimità una proposta
per la creazione di un fondo internazionale finanziario per conseguire tale scopo, alla cui realizzazione purtroppo le autorità ufficiali dell'archeologia napoletana non hanno voluto contribuire.
Tuttavia ritengo ancora una volta necessario ribadire la validità
del progetto di riportare alla luce la Villa dei Papiri in questo
Congresso Internazionale, fiducioso nella solidarietà dei papirolo-
gi di tutto il mondo. Forse si riuscirà a riprendere lo scavo
della Villa dei Papiri anche contro l'opposizione delle autorità

archeologiche locali; forse il nuovo Ministero italiano dei Beni
culturali e ambientali e una commissione per programmi finalizzati
del Consiglio Nazionale delle Ricerche riusciranno a rimuovere
l'attuale ristagno. Ritengo mio dovere riaffermare in questa sede
l'importanza dell'impresa nella coscienza della necessità di una
collaborazione internazionale al compimento dell'opera, che fu già
sognata dal Waldstein e Shoobridge nel 1904. È giusto che qui,
negli Stati Uniti, venga ricordato il programma (solo parzialmente
eseguito più tardi dal Maiuri) della ripresa dello scavo a Ercolano
perché esso non fu il miraggio di due visionari, ma il progetto di
due competenti archeologi. D'altra parte, nel momento attuale, per
rinnovare le basi stesse della conoscenza della civiltà antica già
conosciuta non abbiamo una città, oltre Ercolano, da cui possano
venire nuovi testi specialmente in lingua latina o di letteratura
greca non epicurea: come fu affermato solennemente dal Maiuri, le
possibilità della Villa dei Pisoni non furono esaurite dallo scavo
borbonico.

Possa partire anche da questo Congresso un voto per la ripresa
dello scavo della Villa Ercolanese dei Papiri sia per l'importanza
del monumento sia specialmente per la restituzione dell'intera
Biblioteca della Villa al mondo della cultura.

Napoli   Marcello Gigante

PER UNA RICOSTRUZIONE DELLA BIOGRAFIA DI IDOMENEO DI LAMPSACO
(P. HERC. 463 COL. IX, 1672 COLL. X 21-XI 13)

Nel 310/309 Epicuro si recò da Mitilene a Lampsaco, dove tenne scuola per cinque anni,[1] e dove, secondo Strabone,[2] strinse rapporti con gli ἄριστοι del luogo, Idomeneo e Leonteo.[3] Poiché dalla lettera degli ultimi giorni[4] e dal passo di Teone[5] risulta che Idomeneo seguì Epicuro sin da giovane, il suo primo incontro col filosofo di Samo dové avvenire all'età di quindici anni, per cui la sua nascita va posta intorno al 325.

Di tutti i suoi compagni di filosofia[6] fu l'unico a partecipare alla vita politica della sua città tanto da destare vive apprensioni nel Maestro, come testimonia in primo luogo Seneca:

---

1 Secondo la *Cronologia* di Apollodoro presso D.L. 15 Epicuro giunse a Lampsaco all'età di trentadue anni e vi rimase per cinque anni: sarebbe tornato ad Atene nel 304. Invece, secondo D.L. X 2, egli rientrò in Grecia sotto l'arcontato di Anassicrate, nel 307-306.

2 XIII 389: "Di Lampsaco (furono) Carone lo storico e Adimanto e Anassimene il retore e Metrodoro, l'amico di Epicuro; e lo stesso Epicuro fu in un certo modo lampsaceno, giacché si trattenne a Lampsaco e si servì dei nobili in questa città, Idomeneo e Leonteo." L'espressione τοῖς περὶ 'Ιδομενέα καὶ Λεοντέα, può indicare, secondo l'uso più comune, l'appartenenza o la frequentazione di una scuola, oppure può essere intesa col semplice valore di "Idomeneo e Leonteo," se il passo straboniano si riferisce ad un periodo antecedente alla fondazione della scuola a Lampsaco.

3 Leonteo di Lampsaco fu, insieme con Idomeneo, direttore del centro epicureo di Lampsaco ed in quanto tale è spesso citato in Filodemo accanto all'altro: cf. Philod., *Epic. II* (*P. Herc.* 1289) fr. 6 col. III Vogliano, su cui cf. A. Angeli, "Eterodossia a Lampsaco?" di prossima pubblicazione negli *Atti del Convegno Intern.: La regione sotterrata dal Vesuvio: studi e prospettive* (Napoli 11-15 Novembre 1979).

4 D.L. X 22 (= fr. 138 Us. = 52 Arr.).

5 *Prog.* 169 II p. 71, 12 Spengel (= fr. 131 Us. = 57 Arr.).

6 Nella storia dell'Epicureismo un caso simile si registra per Aristione su cui cf. Angeli-Colaizzo, "I frammenti di Zenone Sidonio," *CErc* 9 (1979) 87 s.

questi chiama Idomeneo *rigidae tunc potentiae ministrum*[7] e cita
alcuni *excerpta* di epistole a lui indirizzate da Epicuro che lo
richiama "da una vita fastosa ad una gloria durevole e stabile."[8]
Analoghe esortazioni si possono leggere in un altro frammento di
lettera conservato in Plutarco: "non vivere asservendoti alle leggi
e alle false opinioni, fino al punto almeno in cui esse non pro-
curano paura del turbamento dalla punizione del vicino."[9]

In nessun luogo tràdito, comunque, è specificata l' *aula regia*
presso la quale Idomeneo visse, né il *titulus* conferitogli. La
critica moderna ha accolto generalmente la tesi dell'Usener[10] sulla

---

7 *Ep.* XXI 3-4 (= fr. 132 Us. = 55 Arr.).

8 Ibid., cf. Sen., *Ep.* XXII 5-6 (= fr. 133 Us. = 56 Arr.).

9 *Adv. Col.* 1127 d (= fr. 134 Us. = 61 Arr.): μὴ νόμοις καὶ
δόξαις δουλεύοντα ζῆν ἐφ' ὅσον ἂν μὴ τὴν διὰ τοῦ πέλας ἐκ πληγῆς ὄχλη-
σιν παρασκευάζωσιν. L'espressione sottintende la distinzione tra
l'osservanza delle leggi, condizione indispensaile perché gli uomini vivano in società, e l'asservimento ad esse, inevitabile conseguenza per chi partecipa alla vita statale.

10 *Epicurea* (Lipsiae 1887) 408: *versatur in rebus politicis,
fortasse in aula Lysimachi.* Cf. F. Jacoby, *RE* IX (1914) 910 (s.v.
Idomeneus), il quale tuttavia in *FGrHist* 338 (III b Komm., p. 84 e
n. 4) superò l'iniziale indecisione e parlò di una tirannide simile
a quella esercitata in Atarneo da Ermia o a Scepsi dai platonici
Erasto e Corisco (su questi cf. M. Isnardi Parente, *Studi sull'
Accademia platonica antica* [Firenze 1979] 283-89). Si espressero
in favore di un potere personale Christ-Schmid, *GGrLit* VI 1, 99 ed
A. Vogliano, *RFIC* 54 (1926) 319, che pose Idomeneo alla corte di
Lisimaco, così come C. Jensen, *Ein neuer Brief Epikurs*, AGWG
philol.-hist. Kl., dritte Folge, 5 (1933) 37 ss., R. Philippson,
RE XI (1936) 1266 (s.v. Timokrates). Ad un generico potere politico presso Lisimaco accennano G. Arrighetti, *Epicuro. Opere* (Torino[2]
1973) 673 e M. Isnardi Parente, *Opere di Epicuro* (Torino 1974) 76.
Quanto alla ricostruzione tentata da N. W. De Witt, *Epicurus and
his Philosophy* (Minneapolis[2] 1964) 80 ss. degli avvenimenti che
segnarono il primo soggiorno di Epicuro a Lampsaco, a mostrarne la
infondatezza basterebbe far notare che, ponendo nel 310 il primo
incontro tra Epicuro e Mitre, poiché quest'ultimo avrebbe presen-
tato Idomeneo al filosofo, il Lampsaceno avrebbe dovuto occupare
la sua carica presso Lisimaco all'età di quindici anni. Meno az-
zardate sono le obbiezioni mosse da H. Steckel, *RE* Suppl. XI (1968)
582-84 (s.v. Epikuros) contro l'ipotesi della datazione alta, sebbene anche esse urtino con la situazione politica di Lampsaco nel
periodo 310-294.

collocazione di Idomeneo alla corte di Lisimaco, a volte radicaliz-
zandola al punto che si è parlato di una tirannide instaurata dall'
Epicureo a Lampsaco (cf. *FHG* II, p. 489) ed a questa è stata riferita la stesura dell'opera *Sui demagoghi in Atene*, quasi un sigillo
che Idomeneo avrebbe posto al suo trascorso non epicureo.[11]

Una disamina dei frammenti relativi al parziale distacco dalla
linea ideologica dell'Epicureismo e degli altri di contenuto
storico-biografico, ha condotto da un lato alla rivalutazione dell'
ipotesi del Momigliano,[12] secondo la quale Idomeneo ottenne la sua
carica di ministro da Antigono Monoftalmo, dall'altro alla inatten-
dibilità della attribuzione ad una autore epicureo dello scritto
sopra citato.

In primo luogo, l'affermazione di un potere conferito ad Idomeneo dagli Antigonidi e non già da Lisimaco è in perfetto accordo
col quadro politico delle città della Frigia Ellespontica dal 310
in poi: nel corso del 310-309 Polemeo, nipote di Antigono e satrapo
della Frigia Minore, passava dalla parte di Cassandro, sottraendo
Lampsaco dal dominio dello zio sino agli inizi del 308; da questo

---

11 L'attribuzione ad Idomeneo di Lampsaco è stata giustificata in vari modi: o è stato ipotizzato l'intento puramente etico
di mettere in risalto la degenerazione degli ἔνδοξοι ἄνδρες (Luzac,
Lect. att., 113, Hermann, *Index lectt.* [Marburg 1836] p. VII,
Westermann, *Quaest. Dem.* I 4, 30 s., Vossius, *Hist. gr.*, 105) oppure la stesura è stata collegata al ritiro di Idomeneo dalla vita
politica: in quest'ultimo caso egli avrebbe maturato il suo disegno
"als Folie für sein eigenes einwandfreies Leben als τύραννος"
(Christ-Schmid, *GGrLit* VI 1, 99 e n. 3) oppure per dare una base di
autorevolezza alla sua decisione di ritornare alla vita contempla-
tiva (Wilamowitz, *Aristoteles und Athen* [Berlin 1893] I, 183).

12 A. Momigliano, *RFIC* 63 (1935) 302-16. Tale contributo,
tuttavia, è valido solo parzialmente, giacché lo storico subordinò
gran parte della sua ricerca agli ipotetici risultati raggiunti da
E. Bignone, *L'Aristotele perduto e la formazione filosofica di
Epicuro* (Firenze 1936, 1973²) I, 473-501, nella definizione dei
rapporti di Epicuro, Idomeneo e Timocrate con Mitre da un lato e
gli Antigonidi dall'altro. Il Momigliano accetta quanto il Bignone
sostenne riguardo alla cronologia dell'apostasia di Timocrate, i
cui primi contrasti con Epicuro furono fatti erroneamente risalire
al 309-308. Cf. per questo problema W. Liebich, *Aufbau, Absicht
und Form der Pragmateiai Philodems* (Berlin 1960) 13 s.

momento fino al 303, il potere degli Antigonidi restava incontra-
stato nell'Asia Minore; esso avrebbe subìto un momentaneo contrac-
colpo con l'intervento di Lisimaco nella coalizione di Seleuco,
Tolemeo e Cassandro contro Demetrio Poliorcete, intervento che si
concluse con la conquista da parte di Lisimaco di Lampsaco, Pario,
Clazomene e le città giacenti ἐπὶ τὸ στόμα τοῦ Πόντου.[13] Nell'
estate o autunno del 302 Demetrio riuscì a riprendere Lampsaco e
gli altri centri asiatici e a tenerli saldamente in suo potere sino
al 294.

Ora, quando il Momigliano[14] avverte che per un Lampsaceno
essere dignitario di Lisimaco porterebbe ad un periodo successivo
al 301, non è pienamente nel vero, giacché, pur se dopo Ipso la
nuova spartizione delle province dette a Lisimaco la Frigia Ellespontica, questi entrò praticamente in possesso delle città ricon-
quistate nel 302 da Demetrio, soltanto dopo il 294. Ciò torna,
comunque, a riconferma della ipotesi del Momigliano, per il fatto
che Idomeneo poteva divenire ministro di Lisimaco o tra il 303-302
o, più verisimilmente, dopo il 294. Incontrovertibile è, invece,
quanto asserisce il Momigliano (art. cit. [n. 12] 307) a proposito
del passo plutarcheo sul viaggio di alcuni Epicurei in Asia per
allontanare dalla corte Timocrate.[15] La βασιλικὴ αὐλή di cui parla
Plutarco colloca tale avvenimento negli anni successivi al 306,
quando Antigono e Demetrio assunsero il titolo regio e si collega
alla figura di questi due monarchi, poiché essi e non Lisimaco ebbero in Asia una residenza regia. Del resto, i buoni rapporti
stretti da Epicuro con la corte di Lisimaco sono di ostacolo alla
presenza di Timocrate presso questo sovrano. Ma anche se si
volesse ammettere ciò, Epicuro, potendo disporre dell'aiuto di
Idomeneo e Mitre, non avrebbe certo organizzato un viaggio da Atene

---

13 Cf. Geyer, *RE* XIV 1 (1928) 9.

14 Art. cit. (n. 12) 306 s. Tuttavia poco convincente è
quanto afferma il Momigliano sull'uso della forma ἄριστοι in
Strab., XIII 589 che attesterebbe che Idomeneo era una persona
autorevole già durante la residenza di Epicuro a Lampsaco. Molto
più probabile è invece un semplice riferimento all'appartenenza
del giovane all'aristocrazia del luogo, tanto è vero che ἄριστος e
detto anche Leonteo.

15 Plut., *Adv. Col.* 1126 c (= p. 123, 22 Us.).

in Asia per difendersi dalle calunnie del transfuga. Poiché il
limite *post quem* per l'apostasia di Timocrate è il 305,[16] si deve
dedurre che il fratello di Metrodoro agì alla corte degli Antigonidi, presso la quale Epicuro non ebbe un seguito particolare.
Idomeneo poteva intercedere in suo favore, ma probabilmente l'esito
di tale intervento rese opportuno inviare a discolpa dell'intera
scuola una rappresentanza ateniese.

Ed ancora, posto pure che il *rex* cui accenna Seneca sia Lisimaco, Idomeneo sarebbe divenuto ministro dopo il 294, vale a dire:
dopo aver conosciuto Epicuro nel 310, sarebbe stato membro della
scuola per sedici anni, distaccandosene poi all'età di circa trenta.
Poiché la fase politica di Idomeneo urta con le motivazioni etiche
del λάθε βιώσας epicureo, essa diviene ancora più problematica se
si pensa che quegli non fu un semplice adepto, ma diresse insieme
con Leonteo la comunità epicurea di Lampsaco. Ed Epicuro si pre-
occupò troppo della compattezza della sua scuola (D.L. X 17) perché
avesse potuto affidare un simile compito di responsabilità a chi
non avesse assimilato fedelmente il suo insegnamento. La ipotesi
della datazione alta trova un ulteriore riscontro nella col. IX del
P. Herc. 463,[17] dove alcuni avversari contestano agli Epicurei la
assoluta mancanza di obbiettività dal momento che essi, se da un
lato rinnegano la partecipazione del sapiente alla vita dello Stato,
dall'altro salvano da questa condanna il loro discepolo Idomeneo,

---

16 Cf. Liebich, *Aufbau* (n. 12) 14.

17 La colonna è stata di recente pubblicata da F. Longo Auricchio, "Nausifane nei papiri ercolanesi," in F. Sbordone, *Ricerche
sui Papiri Ercolanesi* I (Napoli 1969) 18 s. Ecco il testo: ταύτην]
θαυμαστὴν | [ἐπα]γγελίαν ἂν ἀκρο|[ασάμε]νοι, μετὰ ταῦ|[τα] πρὸς τὴν
τέχνην |[5] [τί δ]ὴ λέγουσιν ἀλλ' ἢ | ["φιλ]όσοφος ἀνὴρ [οὐ | πολ]ειτεύ-
σεται"; δι[ό|περ] ἄρχονται μακρῶς |ἢ πρὸς τὸν Δημοκρίτ[ει]|[10]ον
Ναυσιφάνην διαμά | χονται, πρὸς δὲ τού | τοις μάλα πιστῶς | μειρακίσκον
ὄντα{ι} | τὸν ἑαυτῶν 'Ιδομενέ|[15]α μαθητὴν παρεισά|[γ]ουσιν ἐν τοῖς
χα[ύ|νο]ις οὕτω περιγεινόμε[νον.
      1 supplevi   7 sq. Gigante, δί [ὃ | δὴ edd.   14 ἑαυτῶν
legi θ' αὐτῶν edd.   _ 17 sq. Usener et Philippson
"...i quali avrebbero udito questa straordinaria notizia; dopo di
ciò, che mai dicono contro l'arte (retorica) se non che 'il saggio
non governerà lo Stato'? Perciò esordiscono a lungo o combattono
contro il democriteo Nausifane ed inoltre rappresentano del tutto
in buona fede Idomeneo, loro discepolo, il quale da giovane si
aggira in tal modo tra cose vane...."

il quale, secondo la loro opinione, fu attirato ad essa μειρακίσκος,
quando non poteva agire che in buona fede, senza essere sorretto
nella sua scelta di vita da una profonda presa di coscienza.
Possiamo pertanto ricostruire questa prima fase della vita di
Idomeneo collocandone l'attività politica negli anni immediatamente
successivi al 306, non oltre il 301: dopo aver ascoltato le lezioni
di Epicuro a Lampsaco, Idomeneo fu attratto dalla personalità del
filosofo divenendone seguace. La partenza di Epicuro per Atene
coincise pressappoco con una fase di smarrimento della scuola, per
cui il giovane aristocratico entrò a far parte della corte degli
Antigonidi in qualità di ministro. Questa sua carica non dové,
comunque, durare a lungo: la assidua corrispondenza con Epicuro si
concluse col ritorno alla scuola, accolto dal Maestro quasi come
una propria vittoria: "Per nulla ritenesti volgari--gli scrisse
Epicuro--le forme di vita che conducono alla felicità,"[18] ed ancora:
"Per gli dèi, ti dimostrasti con tutto il tuo carattere degno a noi
di una libertà diversa da quella sancita dalle leggi."[19]
        Tra gli altri riconoscimenti fatti da Epicuro ad Idomeneo
merita particolare menzione il ruolo che gli fu assegnato nel *Simposio*: esso rivela un significativo legame con la precedente esperienza di attivismo politico di Idomeneo, il quale in nome di
essa viene introdotto nella trattazione a difesa della tesi epicurea della condanna degli studi di retorica politica. Il frammento, riportato da Filodemo nel secondo libro della *Retorica*,[20]

---

18 Philod., *Tract.* (*P. Herc.* 1418) col. XXXII 2-5 Spina,
CErc 7 (1977) 63 s.

19 Ibid., 5-8. Le due citazioni, inserite nella sezione
dell'opera dedicata a Mitre, anche se non contengono espressamente
il nome di Idomeneo, sono con ogni probabilità estratte da epistole
di Epicuro al discepolo. Infatti Filodemo inizia a parlare dello
scambio epistolare tra Epicuro e Mitre, relativamente al tema delle
forme di vita, solo alla fine della col. XXXII e pertanto il personaggio al quale sono rivolti i due *excerpta* non può non essere
che Idomeneo, l'unico tra gli Epicurei vicino a Mitre per esperienza di vita politica.

20 Philod., *Rh.* II (*P. Herc.* 1672) col. 21-XI 13 Longo, pp.
171-75. Il testo proposto dalla Longo ha indubbiamente superato
alcune delle difficoltà testuali presentate dalla precedente edizione del Sudhaus; quanto al contenuto, tuttavia, bisogna notare
che, integrando alla l. 32 della col. X σ]υνάπτοντά τι|ν᾽ α[ὐτῶ]ν

rappresenta una scena simposiaca di cui i protagonisti sono due,
entrambi giovani: il primo, identificato dal von Arnim[21] con Anassimene, celebre sofista di Lampsaco, vantandosi di eccellere, non
ostante la giovane età, nella capacità retorica, riconosce indiret-
tamente che non esiste una distinzione oggettiva tra retorica propriamente detta e sofistica, quindi tra retorica politica e pane-
girica, e che non esistono studi diversi che conducono ad una spe-
cializzazione nelle singole aree dell'*ars dicendi*. Epicuro confuta
questa argomentazione attraverso Idomeneo, il quale, dopo aver riportato ironicamente le testuali parole dell'avversario, definisce
cosa sia la retorica e cosa invece la *physiologia*, precisando di
ciascuna di esse le rispettive aree di competenza. Si scorge qui
un Idomeneo fedele alle opinioni del Maestro non solo nella distinzione tra attività metodica e scienza e, pertanto, nella ribadita
specificità dell'indagine filosofica, ma anche ad un livello meno
concettuale: alla boria del giovane sofista Epicuro ha volutamente
contrapposto la modestia dell'allievo, il quale, in quel consesso
di uomini saggi, chiede scusa se il permesso che gli si concede di
parlare liberamente, lo porterà a dire cose ardite a causa della
giovane età.

Questo ruolo di difensore della comune condanna della retorica
politica è attestato anche in alcuni frammenti che ci sono giunti

---

ed intendendo: "(Epicuro cita) uno d'essi--di quelli cioè che con-
futano il giovane sofista, cf. ἐλεγχομένους alla col. X 22--mentre
si esprime con siffatte testuali parole," si pongono in bocca a
tale personaggio le parole che sembrerebbe aver pronunziato Idomeneo, giacché lo stesso Filodemo, poco più avanti (col. XIV 10-19)
afferma: "Esitare a dire la verità...per un riguardo al sofista
non è nelle abitudini del giovane quando è intento a discutere né
di Epicuro in quanto autore del dialogo" (cito secondo la traduzione della Longo, 187). Accettando, pertanto, alla l. 2 [ἤ]ιπερ
in luogo di ọῦπερ, per l'altro passo si potrebbe proporre σ]υνάπ-
τοντά τι|ν᾽ ᾱ[ὑτοῖς, intendendo il verbo col suo comune valore di
'aggiungere' e considerandolo un participio coordinato rispetto
ad αἰτούμενον, come il precedente ἐλεγχόμενον (col. X 30).

21 *De restituendo Philodemi de Rhetorica lib. II*, Rostock.
Progr. (1893) 9.

da un'opera *Sui Socratici*,[22] particolarmente quello nel quale
l'Epicureo riconosce a Socrate e a Eschine il primato nell'insegnamento della retorica (D.L. II 20). Un'analisi delle cinque testimonianze superstiti ha consentito un ridimensionamento dello sfavo-
revole giudizio espresso a riguardo dalla critica, mettendo in evidenza le più complesse motivazioni dell'antisocratismo di Idomeneo.

Ugualmente una disamina delle testimonianze storiografiche in
Plutarco ed altre fonti sull'opera *Sui demagoghi in Atene*[23] di Idomeneo, a causa delle difformità con le linee generali dell'etica
epicurea, ha messo in discussione quanto è stato sinora sostenuto
dagli storici moderni: certi atteggiamenti propri di una morale
aristocratica antica, quali la condanna di Temistocle per aver
avuto rapporti con etère,[24] l'uso eccessivo ed irresponsabile del
materiale aneddotico fine a se stesso, la tendenza a mettere in
cattiva luce, attraverso pettegolezzi e storielle facete, l'operato
di uomini come Temistocle e Pericle,[25] su cui l'Epicureismo si
espresse in modo ben diverso,[26] sono alcune delle motivazioni che

---

22 Quattro frammenti sono conservati in Diogene Laerzio, uno
in Ateneo: essi soltanto con H. Sauppe, *RhM* 2 (1843) 450-52 furono
rivendicati ad un'opera sui βίοι Σωκρατικοί, dopo che il Sintenis,
Plut. Pericl. Exc. V, 313 ss. aveva riportato sia queste che le
testimonianze storiografiche conservate in Plutarco ed in altri
autori, ad un solo trattato *Sui Socratici*.

23 Di questo trattato disponiamo di diciassette frammenti
tramandati in massima parte da Plutarco. Il titolo fu congetturato
dal Sauppe, art. cit. (n. 22) 451 sulla base di una corruttela in
Lex. Rhet. 249, 32 Becker (= *FHG* II 493 = *FGrHist* 338 F 2): qui
l'espressione 'Ιδομένης φησὶ δημαφωγόν fu intesa dallo studioso
come 'Ιδομενεύς φησι περὶ δημαγωγῶν. La congettura Περὶ τῶν 'Αθή-
νησιν Δημαγωγῶν fu del Jacoby.

24 Athen. XIII 576 c (= *FGrHist* 338 F 4 a), XII 533 d (=
FGrHist 338 F 4 b).

25 Plut., *Pericl.* X 6-7 (= *FGrHist* 338 F 8).

26 Filodemo accoglie la *communis opinio* dell'assennatezza e
delle valenti qualità di stratega di Temistocle, nominandolo accanto a Pericle, Epicuro e Metrodoro come esempio di quanti com-
pirono illustri azioni (*Mor.* col. XXIX fr. 17 Kuiper). Temistocle,
Aristide e Pericle sono presentati come campioni di virtù politica
in *Rh.* II 212 Sudhaus e di essi soprattutto Pericle, che seppe mettere a frutto gli insegnamenti ricevuti dai filosofi grazie alla
predisposizione del suo animo--lo stesso non accadde ad Alcibiade e

consentono di credere che l'Idomeneo autore di questi βίοι non è
l'Idomeneo di Lampsaco, discepolo di Epicuro, bensì l'omonimo
ἱστορικός citato da Suida quale autore di un trattato *Sulla
Samotracia*.[27]

Anna Angeli

Crizia, sebbene avessero avuto come maestro Socrate--(*Rh.* I 350 s.
Sudhaus), divenendo così il modello della politica, come "la giustizia è nell'imitazione di Aristide e la probità in quella di
Focione e la saggezza in quella di Epicuro" (*Poem.* V col. XXXI 3-10
Jensen). Naturalmente simili giudizi, talvolta topici, non esclu-
dono la generale condanna del βίος πρακτικός propria dell'etica
epicurea.

27 S.v. Ἰδομενεύς, ἱστορικός, ἔγραψεν ἱστορίαν κατὰ Σα-
μοθράκην (= *FHG* II 494 = *FGrHist* 547 T 1). Resta ancora aperto
comunque il problema della cronologia e della eventuale collocazione filosofica di questo autore: per la prima il Jacoby, *FGrHist*
III b Komm., p. 470 proponeva l'età ellenistica, per la seconda si
potrebbe prospettare come ipotesi di lavoro una appartenenza alla
scuola peripatetica.

ASPETTI E PROBLEMI DELLA DISSIDENZA EPICUREA

Finora la ricerca epicurea è stata orientata verso la individuazione di avversari appartenenti ad altre scuole filosofiche. Dall'esame dell'opera di Filodemo si è appreso molto sul contenuto delle polemiche, ad esempio, tra la scuola del Giardino e la Stoa riguardo a problemi di logica (*De signis*), di teologia (*De pietate*) e di musica (*De musica*). Altrettanto è risultato dallo studio dei rapporti con la scuola peripatetica nell'ambito della morale (*De ira, De adulatione*), della poetica (*De poematis V*) e con la scuola cinica su problemi concernenti l'economia (*De oeconomia, De divitiis*). Inoltre sappiamo da Polistrato che molto viva era la polemica con gli scettici (*De contemptu*). E' stato invece trascurato il problema dei contrasti che sorsero all'interno della stessa scuola epicurea.

Fin dai primi decenni di vita, nel Giardino, quando ancora erano attivi Epicuro ed i primi maestri,[1] non mancarono spunti polemici ed atteggiamenti, sia pure larvati, di dissenso. Testimonianza ne sono la nutrita corrispondenza di Epicuro con le scuole di Mitilene e Lampsaco,[2] ed i suoi viaggi, gli unici, in Asia Minore (D.L. X 10), dopo la fondazione della scuola ateniese. Certamente maggiore pensiamo che fosse la fioritura dei contrasti nel periodo successivo alla professione filosofica dei *catheghemones*, nel quale l'atteggiamento del pensiero epicureo e la sua evoluzione furono caratterizzati anche dall'approfondimento e dall'affinamento delle polemiche contro le altre scuole.[3] Si può considerare una

---

1 Cf. F. Longo Auricchio, "La scuola di Epicuro," *CErc* 8 (1978) 21-37.

2 Cf. *P. Herc.* 1418 e 176, editi rispettivamente da L. Spina, *CErc* 7 (1977) 43-83 e A. Vogliano, *Epicuri et Epicureorum scripta in Herculanensibus papyris servata* (Berolini 1928) 23-55. Cf. anche A. Angeli, "Eterodossia a Lampsaco?" in corso di stampa negli *Atti del Convegno Internazionale: Pompei e la regione sotterrata dal Vesuvio.*

3 Cf. M. Isnardi Parente, *Opere di Epicuro* (Torino 1974) 67 ss.

testimonianza della dissidenza il noto passo di Diogene Laerzio in
cui gli epicurei genuini sono opposti ai sofisti.[4] Non abbiamo
ulteriori nuovi elementi che ne risolvano l'interpretazione; tuttavia vorremmo, in primo luogo, soffermarci sul reale significato
del termine *sophistes*.

Il vocabolo assume nei testi epicurei due accezioni che rappresentano il punto di arrivo della sua evoluzione semantica.[5]
Nella *Retorica* di Filodemo il *sophistes* è il "maestro di retorica
a pagamento."[6] Accanto a questo valore, il vocabolo ricorre nel
senso di "filosofo" riferito a rappresentanti di altre scuole.
Potrebbe darsi che con tale termine si designassero coloro che si
facevano portatori, nell'ambito della dottrina epicurea, di concezioni divergenti da quelle della scuola-madre, così come diverse
erano le idee dei filosofi di altre correnti.[7] D'altra parte, nei
testi epicurei superstiti, ercolanesi e non, il vocabolo non sembra
ricorrere mai nell'accezione così specificamente definita di "spuri"
in contrapposizione a "genuini," come attesta Diogene Laerzio.

Sui *sophistai*--epicurei dissidenti--apprendiamo dall'opera
filodemea e, soprattutto, dal *P. Herc.* 1005.[8]

---

4   X 26; cf. R. Hirzel, *Untersuchungen zu Ciceros philosophischen Schriften* I (Leipzig 1877) 180; R. Philippson, "Philodems
Buch über den Zorn," *RhM* 71 (1916) 439. Diversamente intendono E.
Zeller, *Die Philosophie der Griechen in ihrer geschichtlichen Entwicklung* III³ (Leipzig 1865) 548 n. 6; H. Usener, *Epicurea* (Lipsiae
1887) 417; A. Koerte, "Metrodori Epicurei fragmenta," *JCPh* suppl.
17 (1890) 552 s. ed altri, tra cui, recentemente, A. Laks, *Etudes
sur l'Epicurisme antique* (Cahiers de Philologie 1; Lille 1976) 25,
97.

5   Cf. per la storia dell'evoluzione semantica del termine,
W. K. Guthrie, *A History of Greek Philosophy* III (Cambridge 1969)
27-54, 176-81.

6   Come ha dimostrato C. Brandstaetter, *Leipz. St. zur Class.
Philol.* 15 (1893) 215 ss.

7   Cf. Usener, loc. cit. (n. 4). In questo luogo sono elencati i passi in cui *sophistes* equivale a *philosophus*. Cf. anche
Epic., *Nat. XIV* fr. [29. 29] 19 s. Arrighetti; Philod., *Epic. II*
fr. 6 col. V Vogliano, ed. cit. (n. 2) p. 61.

8   Ed. F. Sbordone, *Philodemi Adversus [sophistas]. E papyro
Herculanensi 1005* (Neapoli 1947), il quale, XII s., propone di
pensare ai *sophistai* come ad avversari filosofici.

Da questo scritto sono evidenti alcuni atteggiamenti assunti[9] in generale dalla dissidenza e che sono poi riscontrabili nei singoli personaggi: scarsa e superficiale preparazione filosofica (coll. III-IV, pp. 85-87 Sbordone), mancato adeguamento alle concezioni della scuola (col. VI, p. 91 Sbordone), falsificazione delle opere dei *catheghemones*.[10] Da altri trattati filodemei ricaviamo notizie più precise e particolareggiate sui singoli epicurei o sulle scuole e qualche informazione, sia pure lacunosa, circa il loro pensiero: è evidente comunque l'esasperazione e l'estrema radicalizzazione di problemi particolari rispetto alle concezioni ufficiali della scuola-madre.

Al tempo di Zenone Sidonio[11] centri vitali della dissidenza erano Cos e soprattutto Rodi, da cui partivano vive polemiche contro la scuola ateniese guidata dallo stesso Zenone. D' altra parte che a Rodi l' epicureismo fosse variamente e lungamente professato, apprendiamo da Diogene di Enoanda, anche se è forse ardito pensare che la scuola dissidente, di cui è testimone Filodemo, sia rimasta attiva fin nel II sec. d.C.[12]

Contro questi dissidenti è diretta la chiusa del I libro della *Retorica* filodemea, che è un'invettiva ed insieme una dichiarazione programmatica: "Bisognerebbe poi biasimare i nostri e specialmente coloro i quali hanno stabilito che la retorica sofistica non sia arte ed hanno composto trattati a conferma di ciò. Infatti, se Epicuro e Metrodoro ed inoltre Ermarco dichiarano che essa è arte, come ricorderemo nei libri che seguono, non si sono tenuti in certo

---

9 Secondo lo Sbordone in alcuni luoghi sarebbero da ravvisare le preoccupazioni di Epicuro circa i possibili sbandamenti dei discepoli lontani (fr. d[1] col. II, p. 27; fr. f[2], p. 42; fr. f[10], p. 48). Cf. anche Sbordone, "Per la storia dell'espistolario di Epicuro" in *Miscellanea Rostagni* (Torino 1963) 26 s.

10 Col. VIII, p. 95 Sbordone; cf. A. Angeli-M. Colaizzo, "I frammenti di Zenone Sidonio," *CErc* 9 (1979) fr. 25, pp. 80, 118 s.

11 Cf. T. Dorandi, G. Indelli, A. Tepedino Guerra, *CErc* 9 (1979) 141 s.

12 Frr. 16, 51 Chilton; e N. F. 10 ed. M. F. Smith, *AJA* 75 (1971) 373-75, N. F. 58, *Anatolian Studies* 28 (1978) 53 s. e N. F. 107, *Anatolian Studies* 29 (1979) 70-74.

senso molto lontani dalla colpa di parricidio coloro i quali
scrivono in contrasto con essi."[13]

Ed infatti le scuole di Rodi e Cos svolgono il loro insegnamento basandolo sulla convinzione che la retorica sofistica non sia
un'arte, contrariamente al pensiero epicureo genuino di Zenone e
Filodemo.[14] Ed è proprio di Rodi l'avversario, per noi difficile
da identificare, autore di un'opera contro Zenone, nella quale sostiene che nessuna delle tre parti della retorica sussista come
tecnica.[15]

Riguardo al medesimo argomento e nell'ambito della stessa dissidenza, è possibile cogliere anche altre sfumature, molteplici e
varie, che si possono così schematizzare: (1) esasperazione della
concezione epicurea, secondo cui la retorica sofistica è una *techne*,
fino a non ammettere l'esistenza della retorica alla base dell'
attività giudiziaria e forense;[16] (2) affermazione da parte di
alcuni che la retorica indistintamente sia una *techne*,[17] da parte
di altri che lo sia la politica,[18] da parte di altri ancora che lo
siano ambedue.[19]

Questo era chiaramente in netto contrasto con i primi maestri
e gli epicurei ortodossi più recenti.

Un caso a sé è rappresentato da Bromio, il quale, mentre da un
lato è per Filodemo un valido punto di riferimento nella confuta-
zione delle obbiezioni mosse alla logica epicurea dagli stoici,[20]

---

13 *Rh. I* VII 9 ss., p. 21 Longo [= Sudhaus I, p. 12].

14 Coll. LII 11-34, p. 151; LVI 18-LVII 4, pp. 159-61 Longo
[= Sudhaus I, pp. 89 s., 95 s.].

15 Col. LIII 7-LVI 17, pp. 153-59 Longo [= Sudhaus I, pp.
90-95].

16 Coll. XXI 17-30, p. 87; XXII 6-34, pp. 89-91; XXIII 7-XXIV
9, pp. 93-95 Longo [= Sudhaus I, pp. 47-49].

17 Coll. XXII 34-XXIII 7, pp. 91-93; XXVI 23-28, p. 99 Longo
[= Sudhaus I, pp. 49, 53].

18 Coll. XXIV 9-15, p. 95; XXVI 28-35, p. 99 Longo [= Sudhaus
I, pp. 50, 53 s.].

19 Col. XXIX 23-25, p. 105 Longo [= Sudhaus I, p. 57].

20 Cf. P. H.-E. A. De Lacy, *Philodemus On Methods of Inference*
(La Scuola di Epicuro, collezione di testi ercolanesi diretta da
M. Gigante 1, Napoli 1978) 54 ss.

dall'altro, a proposito della retorica, presenta incertezze che Filodemo si preoccupa di chiarire.[21] Bromio, cioè, ha inteso scrivere un'opera sulle *technai* e, nelle sue ricerche, ha omesso la sofistica, concentrando l'indagine sulla politica e privilegiandola dal punto di vista tecnico.

A capo della scuola di Rodi[22] pare fosse Nicasicrate, che trattò svariati punti della dottrina epicurea, in contrasto con la *pragmateia* ufficiale, soprattutto per quanto riguarda l'ira e l'adulazione. Infatti è troppo mutilo il contesto del passo del III libro *Perì theon*, in cui egli è in disaccordo con Filodemo riguardo all'origine degli *eidola* divini (fr. 65, p. 63 Diels).

Riguardo all'ira egli rigetta per il saggio la *physike orghe* (*Ir.* coll. XXXVIII 28-XXXIX 7, p. 78 Wilke), ammessa invece da Filodemo (col. XLV, p. 89 Wilke). Inoltre, trattando dell'adulazione, Nicasicrate, sulla scia di Democrito, non accetta il concetto, del quale Filodemo si compiace, di rendersi gradito ai vicini, cioè ai compagni di dottrina.[23]

Ancora, il suo accordo con il peripatetico Aristone di Ceo nell'indagine sulle affinità in amore (ibid., col. XII, p. 55 Kondo), è beffeggiato aspramente da Filodemo, così come riguardo alla caratterizzazione dei vari tipi di adulatore, sono per lui di scarsa entità elementi che, invece, per Filodemo sono importanti.[24]

Probabilmente rodio fu anche Timasagora, il cui atteggiamento di "contraffattore"[25] della dottrina epicurea, soprattutto per quanto riguarda la vista, è attestato non solo da Filodemo,[26] ma anche da Cicerone (*Acad.* II 80) ed Aezio (IV 13,6, p. 403 Diels).

---

21   Col. XXXIV 15, p. 115 Longo [= Sudhaus I, p. 64].

22   *P. Herc.* 1746 fr. II b, ed. W. Crönert, *Kolotes und Menedemos* (Leipzig 1906, Amsterdam 1965) 92 ss.

23   *P. Herc.* 1457 col. X 6-12, ed. Kondo, *CErc* 4 (1974) 54.

24   *P. Herc.* 1457 col. IV, p. 50 Kondo, che interpreta diversamente; cf. Crönert, *Kolotes*, 182, col quale siamo d'accordo, pur proponendo qualche modifica.

25   *P. Herc.* 19/698 col. XIX, ed. W. Scott, *Fragmenta Herculanensia* (Oxford 1885) 275.

26   A Filodemo è forse da attribuire la paternità di questo papiro in cui si tratta dei sensi e delle sensazioni.

Comunque, non si può stabilire se il disaccordo con Filodemo sia di carattere strettamente linguistico--uso di *aporroia* invece di *eidolon*--o se vi sia un ritorno da parte di Timasagora alla dottrina di Democrito e soprattutto di Empedocle, con i quali Epicuro stesso sembrerebbe polemizzare (*Epist.* I 49). Inoltre il dissidente sembra non solo rifiutare l'ira (*Ir.*, col. VII 7, pp. 24 s. Wilke), ma anche essere completamente scettico nei riguardi di una critica a tale *pathos*, che, in quanto inevitabile, andrebbe prevenuto più che biasimato *a posteriori*.[27]

Infine dell'ultimo dissidente di cui conosciamo il nome, Antifane, ben poco possiamo dire sul contenuto del pensiero. Oltre che a rimproveri da parte di Filodemo per la mancanza di considerazione per le opere scritte,[28] esistono riferimenti ad una sua trattazione estesa di problemi riguardardanti la divinità ed in particolare la teoria antropomorfica del *quasi corpus quasi sanguis*.[29] La sua concezione si colloca, secondo il nostro punto di vista, in posizione intermedia tra Filodemo, che esclude la possibilità che gli dei vadano soggetti al sonno, come inconciliabile con la loro natura divina--esente da tutte le condizioni che ne postulano la necessità per gli uomini--l'avversario, forse uno stoico, il quale non lo esclude e, comunque, non lo considera un elemento limitante per la divina *aphtharsia*, come, al contrario, ritiene Filodemo. A ciò che Antifane dice, nell'avanzare la possibilità di ammettere una "certa qual specie di sonno" un dormiveglia, collegato all'ingestione del cibo, Filodemo risponde postulando per gli dei soltanto una lieve quiete, il che non muta le caratteristiche della funzione del sonno.

Da quanto è stato detto, poiché consideriamo Filodemo epicureo ortodosso, fedele seguace e interprete della dottrina degli *andres* pur nell'inevitabile adeguamento ai tempi, è chiaro che i dissidenti sono compagni di dottrina, che però, in misura maggiore o minore, fraintendono o rimaneggiano i dogmi dei maestri fondatori.

Francesca Longo Auricchio
Adele Tepedino Guerra

---

27 Cf. Philippson, "Philodems Buch" (n. 4) 437 s.

28 *P. Herc.* 1044 fr. 24, p. 52 Crönert, *Studi Ercolanesi* (Napoli 1975); per altre interpretazioni cf. *CErc* 6 (1976) 57 s.

29 Philod., *D. III* col. XIII 5, ed. G. Arrighetti, *SCO* 10 (1961) 112-21.

P. HERC. 346: UN TRATTATO ETICO EPICUREO

In memoria di Domenico Bassi

...ὑμνεῖν | καὶ τὸν σωτ[ῆ]ρα τὸν ἡμέτερον | καὶ κτίσαι...

Sono le parole più famose del *P. Herc.* 346 (col. IV b 6-8),
contenente un trattato etico epicureo, nel quale l'autore tesse le
lodi della ἀγωγή del Giardino sul registro di una celebrazione en-
tusiastica della figura del fondatore, definito ancora in col. VII
b 5s. καθηγεμὼν καὶ σωτήρ.

Il papiro, credo, non ha avuto la diffusione che merita. Fu
pubblicato per la prima volta nel 1907[1] da D. Bassi, da poco nominato Direttore dell'Officina dei Papiri Ercolanesi. Era il primo
volumen della raccolta che il Bassi studiava: la scarsa esperienza,
l'insufficienza degli strumenti critici di cui allora lo studioso
disponeva e, infine, lo stato di conservazione del rotolo, certamente non tra i migliori dell'intera biblioteca, fecero sí che egli
fornisse un'edizione assolutamente insufficiente: quasi mai il
Bassi si rese esatto conto dell'estensione delle lacune e non di
rado lesse male il papiro. Il testo da lui fornito è estremamente
frammentario e quasi mai continuo. Il commentario naturalmente ri-
sente di ciò. Forse la sua prima esperienza di studioso dei papiri
di Ercolano sarebbe stata meno infelice se il Bassi avesse cominciato con un rotolo meglio conservato.[2]

---

1 *RFIC* 35 (1907) 257-309.

2 In questa sede mi piace, comunque, rilevare come il Bassi,
che W. Schmid non considera nel suo lavoro "Zur Geschichte der
Herculanischen Studien," *PdP* 45 (1955) 478-99 (= C. Jensen, W.
Schmid, M. Gigante, *Saggi di papirologia ercolanese* [Napoli 1979]
29-44), si riscatti ampiamente grazie ad alcune qualità positive,
che contraddistinsero la sua direzione dell'Officina dei Papiri, da
lui proficuamente retta dal 1906 al 1927 più o meno da solo, qualità che già in questo suo primo lavoro ercolanese rivela di possedere: grande interesse per i *volumina*, una non superficiale conoscenza della loro problematica, una costante prudenza e, almeno in
tale edizione, una sicura modestia. Non credo di sminuire l'importanza degli altri Direttori--peraltro assai meritevoli--che hanno
retto nella sua storia l'Officina, se dico che forse la conservazione della preziosa raccolta presenterebbe oggi meno problemi, se

L'edizione del Bassi, che G. Pasquali salutò con benevolenza,[3]
fu assai severamente, se non impietosamente, giudicata da A. Vogliano,[4] solitamente non tenero nei suoi giudizi sull'editore della
Collectio tertia.[5] Il Vogliano pubblicò una seconda edizione del
papiro nel suo importante volume *Epicuri et Epicureorum scripta in
Herculanensibus papyris servata* (pp. 77-89). È senz'altro un lavoro
migliore di quello dell'*editor princeps*. Lo studioso lesse ed in-
tegrò spesso bene, fornendo un testo innanzitutto abbastanza continuo e, per lo più, sufficientemente attendibile. Tuttavia l'uso
del microscopio bioculare mi ha permesso di rilevare l'inesattezza
di numerose letture del Vogliano. Inoltre molte integrazioni sue e
di R. Philippson, che collaborò al volume del Vogliano, sono risul-
tate chiaramente inaccettabili. Credo doveroso notare che in qualche caso[6] fu il Bassi, non il Vogliano a leggere bene il papiro. Il
fatto poi che quest'ultimo ignori volutamente l'edizione precedente
fa sí che attribuisca a sé integrazioni che si trovano nel Bassi.
Il commentario del Vogliano è estremamente sintetico e non sempre è
possibile sapere come lo studioso intenda il testo. Il volume ber-
linese del Vogliano è caratterizzato da alcuni aspetti negativi,
come la non sempre esatta lettura dell'originale, l'infelice collaborazione col suo contubernale Philippson--che, è noto, non ha mai
visto un papiro ercolanese[7]--e quel costante disamore per l'esegesi
del testo che, di recente, G. Arrighetti nella splendida introduzione

---

fosse stata affidata sempre a una figura come il Bassi. Aveva visto
giusto il giovane W. Crönert, che, dopo di avere denunciata nel suo
Kolotes und Menedemos (Leipzig 1906; Amsterdam 1965) 36 la grave
approssimazione con cui i papiri erano allora custoditi nel Museo
Archeologico di Napoli, salutò con entusiasmo dalle colonne della
Wochenschrift für klassische Philologie 23 (1906) 831s. la nomina
del Bassi a Direttore, convinto che con lui si aprisse una nuova
era della papirologia ercolanese.

3 *Ausonia* 2 (1908) 162.

4 *Epicuri et Epicureorum scripta in Herculanensibus papyris
servata* (Berolini 1928).

5 *Acme* 1 (1948) 399s. e *Prolegomena* 2 (1953) 128-30.

6 Alla col. IX b 3, ad esempio.

7 Cf. Schmid, art. cit. (n. 2), 495 = *Saggi*, 43.

al suo *Epicuro*[8] ha ricondotto alla vera natura del Vogliano, che fu
"troppo papirologo" per sobbarcarsi al commento esegetico e storico-
filosofico dei testi ercolanesi. A questi limiti complessivi del
pur fondamentale volume Weidmanniano--a suo tempo accolto in generale positivamente[9]--va aggiunta, nel caso del *P. Herc.* 346, una
certa fretta, con cui il Vogliano confessa di avere letto e commen-
tato le ultime colonne: spinto dalla necessità di andare in stampa,
lo studioso in alcuni punti dà ciò che presenta il disegno, senza
controllare l'originale.

Intendo fornire alcuni esempi dei progressi consentitimi nella
comprensione del testo da una nuova autopsia del *volumen*.

Inaccettabile è la tesi del Vogliano relativa alla paternità
della nostra opera. Egli ritiene che si tratti di uno scritto sicuramente di Polistrato. Infatti afferma che quando nel 1912 per
la prima volta si imbatté in esso vide: "statim illius viri [i.e.
Polystrati] certa quasi vestigia." Una convinzione che in lui andò
radicandosi negli anni e che sarebbe stata illustrata, a suo dire,
in alcune pagine lasciate inedite. Nel 1927, ritornato a leggere
il papiro, egli scoprí con grande soddisfazione e con bruciante
rammarico di non avere pubblicato le osservazioni precedenti, che
sotto l'ultima colonna (XIII) c'erano tracce di titolo, sfuggite,
secondo lui, sia al disegnatore che al Bassi. Cosí il Vogliano
leggeva: Π[|] ΥÇ[. Π era per lui l'inizio del nome del terzo sco-
larca del Giardino; ΥÇ apparteneva al titolo dell'opera, per cui
integrava Π[ολυστράτου | Πρὸς το]ὺ̣ς [. A sostegno della
paternità polistratea il Vogliano, oltre a quella paleografica,
adduceva prove interne: (1) un certo andamento diatribico; (2) il
color rhetoricus; (3) le *laudes physiologiae*, caratteristiche che
avvicinerebbero il nostro scritto al libello polistrateo *Sul disprezzo irrazionale delle opinioni popolari*.[10] Per la verità non

---

8 *Epicuro, Opere* (Torino 1973[2]) p. XXVI.

9 Cf. le recensioni citate in *Catalogo dei Papiri Ercolanesi*,
sotto la direzione di M. Gigante (Napoli 1979) 40s.

10 Sulla presenza di questi caratteri nel libello dello scolarca rimando a G. Indelli, "Polistrato, Sul disprezzo irrazionale
delle opinioni popolari," *La Scuola di Epicuro, Collezione di testi
ercolanesi* diretta da M. Gigante, II (Napoli 1978) 28-82.

ho ravvisato con sicurezza nessuno di questi tre motivi. Della diatriba sono assenti alcuni caratteri fondamentali, quali l'introduzione di avversari fittizi e l'accesa e viva polemica, presenti nel *Disprezzo*. Significativo mi pare, a questo proposito, il fatto che Philippson, recensendo l'edizione del Vogliano, pur lodando il lavoro del suo sodale, ravvisava nel *P. Herc.* 346 i segni non già della diatriba, bensí quelli di un trattato protrettico.[11] Quanto al colorito retorico dirò che c'è piuttosto spesso iato e che, tutt'al piú, si nota, talvolta, una certa ridondanza espressiva, che collegherei con la particolare *Stimmung* dell'autore, impegnato di continuo ad elogiare la dottrina epicurea. Non trovo strano, infine, che in uno scritto come il nostro, che è un inno ad Epicuro e alla capacità che la sua filosofia ha di guadagnare l' ἀγαθόν, si sottolinei l'importanza della φυσιολογία base indiscutibile della dottrina epicurea e oggetto di esaltazione in tutti i filosofi del Giardino, dal fondatore[12] a Diogene di Enoanda (frr. 3-4 Chilton).

L'autopsia ha, infine, eliminato la prova principale della paternità polistratea sostenuta dal Vogliano. In quella che egli riteneva alla fine della col. XIII la *subscriptio* il papiro mostra]ΙϹ[|]ΥϹΤ[e non Π[|]ΥϹ[: impossibile quindi la sua ricostruzione;[13] non solo, ma queste tracce non appartengono al titolo, bensí costituiscono la parte finale della colonna. Già il Bassi aveva dato queste due linee come ultime di col. XIII.[14] In un papiro ercolanese è impossibile che la *subscriptio* si trovi

---

11 *RFIC* 57 (1929) 108s.

12 *Ep.*, *Ep. I* 37,76-83, *Ep. II* 85-87, *RS* XI-XIII, *GV* 29, fr. [198] e [259] ARR.

13 Rilevo che l'integrazione del Vogliano Π[ολυστράτου | Πρὸς το]ὺς [lasciava perplessi, perché non teneva conto del fatto che gli scribi ercolanesi iniziano e terminano le lineee per lo piú simmetricamente, cf. F. Sbordone, *Philodemi Adversus* [*sophistas*] (Neapoli 1947) p. XII. Ci sarebbe cioè troppo spazio tra il presunto Π del rigo superiore e ΥϹ di quello inferiore, nel senso che il titolo Πρὸς τοὺς [starebbe eccessivamente spostato a sinistra rispetto al nome dell'autore Πολυστράτου. Di là da una certa oggettiva inverosimiglianza la ricotruzione del Vogliano ancora oggi pare trovare credito, cf. Indelli, ed. cit. (n. 10), 26s.

14 Cf. Bassi, ed. cit. (n. 1), 297.

immediatamente sotto l'ultima colonna, dopo lo spazio di appena 2
linee, come invece capiterebbe nel nostro papiro secondo l'interpretazione del Vogliano. Della relazione spaziale esistente tra
l'ultima colonna del testo e il titolo finale nei *volumina* ercolanesi si occupò il Crönert nel suo studio sulla tradizione dell'
Index Academicorum (*P. Herc.* 1021).[15] Egli notò alla fine dei rotoli conservanti il titolo la presenza di un ἄγραφον, cioè una
parte non scritta di varia estensione, nella quale si trovava la
subscriptio. Un esame diretto su una quindicina di papiri forniti
di titolo lo portò alla conclusione che: "...i rotoli ercolanesi
finora studiati presentano dopo l'ultimo foglio di testo uno spazio
bianco di 1-3 fogli, su cui poi è annotato il titolo in ordine
variabile, e non c'è nessun motivo per contestare che questa sia la
regola, per tutti i rotoli." Ho allargato questo tipo di ispezione
a tutti i papiri che conservano ancora il titolo. Tale esame ha
dimostrato innanzitutto che non è vero quello che dice il Crönert,
che cioè nei nostri *volumina* non sia mai possibile "che il titolo
venga apposto all'ultima colonna del testo." Risulta invece che
questo si verifica qualche volta. L'altro dato paleografico certo
è che la *subscriptio* non si rinviene mai immediatamente sotto l'ultima colonna, vale a dire dopo uno spazio di sole 2 linee. Nei 69
papiri che conservano il titolo o tracce di esso 63 hanno la *subscriptio* alla destra dell'ultima colonna;[16] 1 (*P. Herc.* 1497) ha
due titoli, a lato della parte finale del testo;[17] 5 (*P. Herc.* 362,
697, 1007/1673, 1497/1417, 1675) hanno il titolo sotto l'ultima
colonna: di essi è il *P. Herc.* 1007/1673 soltanto ad avere la *subscriptio* piuttosto vicina alla fine del testo, ma ad uno spazio di
circa 5 linee di scrittura. Insomma anche nei casi, come vediamo
non numerosi, in cui il titolo è sotto la colonna di chiusura, c'è

---

15 *Hermes* 38 (1903) 398-405 = *Studi ercolanesi*, a c. di E.
Livrea (Napoli 1975) 195-202; cf. dello stesso Crönert l'articolo
in *Hermes* 36 (1901) 551 n. 2 = *Studi*, 66 n. 5.

16 In 21 di essi lo scriba disponeva di uno spazio sufficiente
per apporlo sotto questa stessa colonna.

17 Il primo è a destra della colonna di chiusura, dopo cm 2,5;
il secondo, in caratteri più grandi, è a lato del primo, dopo cm
11,5 ca.

un certo intervallo che separa l'ultima linea dal titolo stesso.
Le poche lettere, quindi, leggibili alla fine della col. XIII sono
quasi certamente le ultime di questa colonna. La *subscriptio* si
sarà trovata verisimilmente più a destra nel rotolo, in una parte
del *volumen* ora perduta.

Quanto al contenuto dell'opera, il Vogliano sulla base della
sua ricostruzione della 1.2 del presunto titolo (Πρὸς το]ὺς [ )
riteneva il libello scritto contro determinati avversari. Ma la
sua ipotesi urta sia nell'assenza di una qualsiasi polemica contro
filosofi rivali,[18] sia nello spirito essenziale dell'opera, che
sembra essere una παραίνεσις del tipo di vita condotto nel Giardino.
Siamo, insomma, in presenza di quel genere di composizione
encomiastico-esortativa che non fu rara nella produzione epicurea.
Quanto all'autore, avanzerei, con cautela, l'ipotesi di una paternità filodemea, soprattutto basandomi su singolari simiglianze tra
l'*usus scribendi* del Nostro e quello del Gadarese. Ho il conforto,
in questo senso, dell'opinione del Crönert, che nel suo approccio
al rotolo pensò ad un *tractatus moralis* di Filodemo.[19]

Presento alcuni esempi di *novae lectiones* che il controllo
dell'originale mi ha consentito rispetto all'edizione del Vogliano.

Alla col. I b 1-5 quella che già all'illustre studioso apparve
una formulazione epicurea del "carpe diem" oggi appare più completa:
il Vogliano infatti lesse: καὶ [τ]ῆς νῦν | καθηκούσης ἡμέρας [πρὸς]
τ[ε]λεί|ωσιν τοῦ [ἀγαθοῦ τὴν κ]υριω|τάτην αἰτίαν προσφε[ρομέ]νης |⁵
αὐτῆς---, il papiro mostra: καὶ [τ]ῆς νῦν | καθηκούσης ἡμέρας ἐς
[τὴν τε]λεί|ωσιν τοῦ ὅλου β[[ο]υ [τὴν κ]υριω|τάτην αἰτίαν προσ-
φερ[ομ]ένης |⁵ αὐτῆς---. "---ed essendo ora il giorno adatto al
perfetto compimento della vita, dal momento che esso presenta il
motivo principale---."

Alla col. II b 3-6 credo si possa recuperare l'accenno alla
necessità di fruire nella condotta di vita degli εἰκότα; così il
Vogliano: ὅθ[εν] οὐδεί[ς ...]ι̣δη καὶ οἰκείωμα [δ]ι᾽ ἐ|λάτ[τ]ον[ος

_____

    18 Certe prese di posizione assunte dall'autore nelle coll.
III, XI, XII, sono genericamente riferite ai πολλοί, alla massa dei
non epicurei.

    19 *RhM* 56 (1901) 625 = *Studi*, 123.

....με]νος τῶν ἐο[ικό]|⁵τωγ μορφῆς σοφίας ἀληθινὸς [ἐρ]ασ|τῆς
εὑρεθ[ήσε]τ[αι]---, cosí il papiro: ὅθεν οὐδεί[ς .].δη καὶ
οἰκειώματι ἐ|λάτ[τ]ονῐ κ͇[χρημέ]νος τῶν ἐο[ικό]|⁵τωγ μορφῆς ἢ
σοφίας ἀληθινὸς ἐρασ|τῆς εὑρεθήσͺετα[ι]---. "Per cui nessuno---che
abbia esercitato possesso inferiore al plausibile, si scoprirà
verace innamorato di bellezza o saggezza---."

Qualche recupero in col. IV b 4-8, dove il Vogliano restitui-
va: σ[υν]όλως ἢ τῆι |⁵κατὰ μέρο[ς] καὶ ͺς[πανίαι(?)] ἢ τῆι γε
ἀθρό|αι ἐπιβολῆ[ι] χρωμένοͺυ[ς ὑ]μνεῖν | καὶ τὸν σωτ[ῆ]ρα τὸν
ἡμ[έ]τερον | καὶ κτίστη[ν---, ho potuto leggere: σ[υν]όλως ἢ τῆι |⁵
κατὰ μέρος ἀρθρͺω[δῶς] ἢ τῆι γε ἀθρό|αι ἐπιβολῆ[ι] χρωμένοͺυς ὑμνεῖν |
καὶ τὸν σωτ[ῆ]ρα τὸν ἡμέτερον | καὶ κτίσαι---.²⁰ "---complessiva-
mente servendosi dell'atto apprensivo delle singole parti, in modo
ben articolato, o dell'atto apprensivo dell'insieme, celebrano sia
la figura del nostro salvatore sia che abbia fondato---." A 1.5 si
può forse pensare anche a ἀρθρͺῳ[δει].

Novità anche in col. VI a 9-12, dove il Vogliano lesse: αὐ|¹⁰τοῖς
ἐπ[ὶ τ]ὸ ἐν αἰτίοις γω[.... κ]αὶ | φόβου καὶ δυσελπιστίας ἀμ[αύρω|μα]
γίνεται---, il papiro ha: αὐ|¹⁰τοῖς ἔξωθεν αἰτίοις αͺἰω[νίου] | φόβου
καὶ δυσελπιστίας ἄμ[α ταρα]|χͺὴ γίνεται.²¹

L'accenno ai benefici che la *physiologia* dà al saggio nel
Vogliano suonava (col. VIII a 1-5): ἐξ ὅ[ν π]ροσευ|[ρεθή]σεται
ͺἀ[ληθῶς κτ]ησά|μενος ὃ αὐτ[ὴ] ἐπ[ε]σημ[ήν]ατο ἡ | φύσις, καὶ ἀπ[ὸ
τ]ῶν πρώτων καὶ |⁵ἀρχ[όν]των ὁρμῆσαι---, ho letto invece ἐξ ὅ[ν
π]ροσευ|ρͺε[θή]ͺςετα<ι> κ[ριτήριον κτ]ησά|μενος ὃ αὐτ[ὴ] ἐπεσημͺήνατο
ἡ | φύσις καὶ ἀπὸ [τ]ῶν πρώτων καὶ |⁵ἀρχηγῶν ὁ[ρ]μͺήσας---.
"---grazie alle quali cose si troverà a possedere il criterio che
la natura stessa ha segnalato e ad essere partito dai principi e
dalle cause prime---." Nella *physiologia* epicurea il κριτήριον è
un valido strumento di conoscenza, che ha il potere di guidare
l'uomo verso scelte positive e rasserenanti, cf., *ex. gr.*, D.L. X
30 e 31.

---

20 La lettura κτίσαι è di F. Longo Auricchio, *CErc* 8 (1978)
32.

21 La congettura αͺἰω[νίου] è di M. Gigante.

In col. IX b 3-5 si esprime il travaglio in cui versano coloro
che non si dedicano allo studio della natura; il Vogliano leggeva:
ἀπατωμένο[υ]ς εἰς <δυσχερεῖς> (?) | καὶ ἀλυσ[ι]τελεῖς ὁ[ρ]μὰς κα[ὶ]
ἐπιθυ|⁵μίας ἐμπίπτειν, ἐξ ὧν πολλα|πλασί[ως] τ[ὸ ὀχλη]ρὸν ἀπο[β]αί-
νει | τῆι φύ[σ]ει, [πολ]λὺς δὲ καὶ πα[ν]|τοδα[πὰς---, il papiro
mostra: ἀπατωμέ{με}νο[υ]ς εἰς δεινὰς μὲν | καὶ ἀλυσιτελεῖς ὁρμὰς καὶ
ἐπιθυ|⁵μίας ἐμπίπτειν, ἐξ ὧν πολλα|πλασίως τὸ [ὀ]χ[λη]ρὸν ἀπο[β]αί-
νει | τῆι φύ[σ]ει [ποικί]λας δὲ κα[ὶ] πα[ν]τοδα[πὰς---. "---ingan-
nati cadono in impulsi e desideri angosciosi e nocivi, dai quali
nasce per natura, in molteplici modi, il fastidio---."
        Concludo nel segno di una elevata celebrazione del magistero
di Epicuro, quale diverse mie fortunate letture e alcune felici
congetture di Marcello Gigante hanno consentito di leggere alla
col. V a 5-14. Il luogo era così restituito dal Vogliano: πᾶν | γὰρ
τὸ τοιοῦτο καὶ τὸ ὁμοειδὲς | τούτων πλήρωμα καὶ σ[....]ύ|[·]ημα τῆς
ἡμ[ετέ]ρας διαγ[ωγῆς, τὸ] | γινόμενόν τε καὶ ἐσόμενον ἐκ [τῆς] |¹⁰
περὶ ἐκεῖνον ὀρθῆς διαλογίσεως | καὶ πρὸ ὀμμά[τ]ων θέσεως ἀπάν|των
τῶν ἐκε[ί]γου †λαθηι† 'ἀγαθῶν καὶ ἀπὸ τῆς' [φ]ύσεως | γεννω[ω]μέ-
νων[.........]εκτι|κοῖς αυ[...]νουτα[......]τω[.]λω, oggi leggiamo:
πᾶν | γὰρ τὸ τοιοῦτο καὶ τὸ ὁμοειδὲς | τούτων ἐπιλόγ[ι]σμα καὶ
σ[υ]γαύ|ξημα τῆς ἡμετέρας διαγ[ωγῆς τὸ] | γινόμενόν τε καὶ ἐσόμενον
ἐκ [τ]ῆς |¹⁰ περὶ ἐκεῖνον ὀρθῆς διαλογίσεως | καὶ πρὸ ὀμμάτων θέσεως
ἀπάν|των τῶν ἐκε[ί]νου 'τε ἀγαθῶν καὶ ἀπὸ τῆς' καθηγήσεως | γεννω-
μένων [ἀνδράσι δ]εκτι|κοῖς αὐτ[ῶ]ν οὕτ' ἀ[γαθῶν] τῶν λώ|¹⁵[ιων---.²²
"Infatti ogni siffatta e simile considerazione di queste cose e il
rinsaldarsi della nostra condotta di vita, ciò che ci deriva e ci
deriverà in futuro dalla retta riflessione intorno a lui Epicuro e
dal porre davanti ai nostri occhi tutti i beni che vengono da lui
Epicuro e che sono generati dal suo magistero per uomini disposti
a riceverli...."

                                                Mario Capasso

_____

22 Le integrazioni delle 11.13-15 sono del Gigante.

SULLA TRASMISSIONE DEL TESTO DELL' "INDEX ACADEMICORUM PHILOSOPHORUM HERCULANENSIS" (P. HERC. 1021 E 164)

Che il rotolo 1021 della Biblioteca di Ercolano tramandi il testo dell' *Index Academicorum philosophorum Herculanensis*[1] con profonde alterazioni e grande disordine era già stato intuito dal Mekler[2] ed è divenuta una acquisizione generalmente accolta dopo il fondamentale contributo del Crönert: "Die Überlieferung des Index Academicorum."[3] È un merito del Crönert aver individuato la confusione con cui si succedono in quel testimone le colonne di scrittura e le più o meno palesi incongruenze che rendono oscuro e saltuario il testo almeno nella prima parte (coll. I-XXII).

Di *P. Herc.* 1021 si conservano otto pezzi distribuiti in altrettante cornici per un totale di trentasei colonne di scrittura; a queste si aggiungono altre dodici colonne, indicate con le lettere dell'alfabeto da M a Z (esclusa U) e conosciute solo attraverso l'apografo oxoniense per la perdita dell' originale: esse dovevano occupare tre cornici.[4] La confusione che ha sconvolto l'ordine delle colonne era imputata dal Crönert a tre persone distinte: l'autore, lo scriba e l' incollatore (*glutinator*). L'autore avrebbe consegnato il suo manoscritto ancora in forma di una serie di schede allo scriba. Questi lo copia su singoli fogli di papiro di ineguale larghezza, e, scrivendo in fretta commette molti errori che poi corregge; qualche volta fa confusione fra i fogli dell' originale salvo

---

1 Dopo F. Bücheler, *Ind. Schol. hib. Griphysw.* 1869, 3-24, l'opera venne edita da S. Mekler (Berolini 1902, 1958).

2 Mekler, ed. cit., xxii ss.

3 W. Crönert, *Hermes* 38 (1903) 357-405 (= *Studi Ercolanesi*, tr. it. a c. di E. Livrea, Collana di Filologia Classica diretta da M. Gigante, 3 [Napoli 1975] 155-202); d'ora innanzi solo Crönert e la pagina.

4 Crönert, 358 ss. (= *Studi*, 156 ss.). Le giustificazioni addotte dal Crönert per spiegare questa perdita non sono confermate dalla realtà oggettiva dei fatti.

poi annotare la svista con un segno angolare posto in basso, a destra della colonna di scrittura. Il *glutinator* avrebbe sconvolto ulteriormente l'ordine dei fogli incollandoli talvolta fuori posto: questo almeno fino alla col. XXII.

Un sommario di tutto lo scritto venne approntato dal Crönert con l'ausilio del *P. Herc.* 164, che contiene una seconda copia di quell'opera, non turbata, a quanto pare, da disordine nella successione delle colonne.[5] La ricostruzione proposta dal Crönert presupponeva un rotolo compòsito risultante da un determinato numero di *kollemata*,[6] ognuno dei quali conteneva un numero di colonne variabile da 1 a 5. Il Crönert intravedeva lucidamente una controprova del suo calcolo nella individuazione delle *kolleseis* (di esse non aveva potuto tenere conto nella stesura dell'articolo), e risolveva il problema in maniera sbrigativa alcuni anni dopo in una breve annotazione nel *Kolotes und Menedemos*.[7] Sull'argomento il Crönert ritornava nella risposta a un' aspra recensione del Körte al *Kolotes*,[8] ricorrendo a una soluzione ancor più sofisticata che lo costringeva ad ammettere l'intervento diretto dello stesso Filodemo--è la dibattuta questione della cosí detta *manus Philodemi*, esclusa, a ragione, nella precedente ricerca.[9] Il Crönert cosí schematizzava il processo compositivo del rotolo 1021: (1) Filodemo detta il testo allo scriba oppure glielo consegna, indicandogli i manoscritti dei passi citati che vuole riprodotti alla lettera. (2) Lo scriba sbaglia due volte e si corregge. (3) Filodemo appone nel testo e nel margine le correzioni e le aggiunte. (4) I singoli fogli con tre o cinque colonne di scrittura vengono incollati a formare un rotolo in ordine sbagliato, corretto poi con segni.

─────────────

5 Su *P. Herc.* 164 cf. Crönert, 370 ss. (= *Studi*, 168 ss.).

6 Per la terminologia (*kollema, kollesis*) mi uniformo alle indicazioni di E. G. Turner, *The Terms Recto and Verso. The Anatomy of Papyrus Roll* (Pap. Brux. 16; Bruxelles 1978).

7 W. Crönert, *Kolotes und Menedemos* (Leipzig 1906; Amsterdam 1965) 183.

8 A. Körte, *GGA* 169 (1907) 264.

9 W. Crönert, *RhM* 62 (1907) 624 s. (= *Studi*, 221 s.). La *manus Philodemi* è negata con buoni argomenti da B. Hemmerdinger, *REG* 78 (1965) 327-29. Un resoconto della questione in G. Cavallo, *CErc* 1 (1971) 16 n. 41.

L'abbandono, ormai da tutti accolto, della postulata *manus*
Philodemi e una autopsia dei *P. Herc.* 1021 e 164 (d'ora innanzi da
me indicati con P e P[1]) mi ha permesso di prospettare una diversa
soluzione che qui propongo come mia ipotesi di lavoro, che sarà al-
altrove più largamente documentata.

Secondo la ricostruzione prospettata dal Crönert avrei dovuto
riscontrare tracce di *kolleseis* dopo le coll. I, II, III, IV, V,
VIII, XII, XVI, XVII e XX dell'attuale rotolo e la scrittura non
avrebbe mai dovuto passare sopra le eventuali *kolleseis*. L'autopsia di P ha dato risultati negativi: sono riuscito a individuare
tracce di *kolleseis* a livello delle colonne II/III; della col. VII;
delle coll. XII/XIII, XV/XVI e XX (le ultime due meno sicure). Di
queste la *kollesis* a livello della col. VII e, forse, quella a
livello della col. XX sono coperte dalla scrittura delle rispettive
selides. Se ne deduce che lo scriba copiava su un rotolo normalmente fabbricato, non su singoli *kollemata*: perde così valore la
tesi del Crönert. Ecco come penso possa esser ricostruita la vicenda del rotolo 1021: (1) Filodemo scrive la sua opera su singole
schede (possono essere stati *kollemata* o tavolette cerate). (2)
Passa le schede allo scriba che ne altera la successione, copia il
testo, e, solo dopo, resosi conto degli errori, appone dei segni di
richiamo e così corregge. Questo spiega anche la ripetizione di
alcuni versi della *Cronologia* di Apollodoro (col. XXIX 6-17 = XXXVI
33-44).[10] La distrazione dello scriba è palesata anche dai molti
errori e correzioni. La genesi delle alterazioni, a mio avviso, va
pertanto imputata al solo scriba. Il *glutinator* ne è estraneo.[11]
Presuppongo, come già in parte il Crönert,[12] che peraltro rifiutò
in séguito questa via interpretativa,[13] una confusione ancora più
diffusa di quanto sia stata prospettata. Anche uno studio del

---

10 Cf. T. Dorandi, *Versi della* Cronologia *di Apollodoro di
Atene nell'* Index Academicorum Herculanensis, in corso di stampa.

11 Che un rotolo di papiro uscisse dalla bottega del fabbri-
cante già composto, è ribadito da N. Lewis, *Papyrus in Classical
Antiquity* (Oxford 1974) 71 n. 2 e dal Turner, op. cit. (n. 6) 15 e 17.

12 397 n. 2 (= *Studi*, 194 n. 83).

13 Crönert, *RhM* 62 (1907) 625 n. 1 (= *Studi*, 222 n. 5).

contenuto dell'opera porta una conferma in tale direzione. Cito
soltanto due casi: la col. T andrà attribuita col Mekler e col Gigante all'ambiente dell'Academia al tempo dei successori di Arce-
silao e non al *bios* di Polemone con il Crönert;[14] cosí la col. P
ha poche probabilità di appartenere al *bios* di Carneade. Se l'ipotesi del Crönert si fosse verificata avrebbe rappresentato un caso
unico di grande interesse. Sarebbe rimasto, pur sempre, impossibile il suo tentativo di estendere questa singolarità a tutta la
problematica connessa con l' *Antike Buchwesen*.[15] Nel caso specifico di P lo scriba ha copiato da schede sparse su un rotolo di papiro compiuto. P rappresenta, a mio parere, l'unico esemplare, di
ragguardevole antichità, che contenga tracce evidenti di questo
processo, non solo nello svolgimento e nella composizione dell'
opera in esso contenuta, ma anche e soprattutto come manufatto. Il
rotolo 1021 è un importante documento che lascia ancora trasparire,
come testimone originale, l'evoluzione di un processo compòsito
finora sempre postulato, ma mai tangibilmente provato.[16]

Rimane infine da accennare alla sistemazione delle cornici
conservate dal solo apografo di Oxford, alle aggiunte o integrazioni testuali e ai rapporti fra P e P[1]. Del *P. Herc.* 1021 vennero
eseguite due serie di disegni, una conservata a Napoli (*N*) e una
nella Bodleian Library di Oxford (*O*). I disegni Oxoniensi, oltre a

_____

14 Cf. M. Gigante, *Polemonis Academici Fragmenta* (Napoli
1977) 15; Crönert, 377, 385 s. (= *Studi*, 175, 183 s.).

15 Crönert, 397 s. (= *Studi*, 194 s.).

16 È stato postulato, come è noto, per Aristofane (*Rane* e
Vespe), Demostene (*III Filippica*), Lucrezio, Platone (*La Repubblica*),
Tucidide ecc. Cf., p. es., rispettivamente: C. F. Russo, *Storia
delle Rane di Aristofane* (Padova 1961) 93 e *Aristofane autore di
teatro* (Firenze 1962) 316 ss.; C. F. Russo, *Belfagor* 23 (1968) 317-
24 e G. Mastromarco, *Storia di una commedia di Atene* (Firenze 1974);
L. Canfora, *Belfagor* 22 (1967) 152-65 e *RFIC* 100 (1972) 129-31;
Id., ibid. 28 (1973) 161-67; F. Solmsen, *Philologus* 109 (1965) 182-
85; W. K. Prentice, *CP* 25 (1930) 117-27 e L. Canfora, *Tucidide con-
tinuato* (Padova 1970) 9 s. Cf., in gen., anche A. Carlini, *Studi
sulla tradizione antica e medievale del Fedone* (Roma 1972) 5 s.,
n. 11. Non in tutti i casi sopra accennati e in molti altri, che
parte della critica recente viene mettendo in risalto, si può parlare con uguale sicurezza e rigore. C'è forse la tendenza a gene-
ralizzare un po' troppo il fenomeno. Il caso del *P. Herc.* 1021
rappresenta, pur sempre, a mio avviso, un caso unico, e, come tale,
deve essere considerato.

essere più accurati, riproducono tre cornici di papiro, per un totale di dodici colonne, andate perdute durante il trasporto dei
papiri a Palermo nel 1801-1802: questi apografi assumono, per noi,
il valore di originali. Le colonne contenute in quelle cornici
vennero indicate con le lettere dell'alfabeto e, nella serie dei
disegni oxoniensi sono poste prima delle copie delle colonne conservate. La mancanza assoluta di elementi che possano chiarire la
loro originaria sistemazione all'interno del rotolo, costringe gli
studiosi a ricorrere a supposizioni basate esclusivamente sull'
esame di dati interni di carattere codicologico. Il Crönert così
supponeva l'inserimento delle tre cornici oxoniensi (da me indicate
a, b, c): a (coll. M-P), prima della cr. 1; b (coll. Q-T), dopo la
cr. 3; c (coll. V-Z), dopo la cr. 4; cioè i pezzi di papiro contenuti nelle cr. 3-4 e 4-5 non dovrebbero combaciare: la situazione
si verifica soltanto tra le cr. 4 e 5.[17]

Un esame delle sezioni di papiro ha fatto sì che potessi prospettare la seguente successione: a+1+b+2+3+4+c+5 ecc., cioè la cr.
b va inserita fra la cr. 1 e la cr. 2, sistemazione avallata dallo
scarto nell'ampiezza delle sezioni fra i due pezzi di papiro contenuti in quelle cornici. Il problema delle aggiunte o integrazioni testuali e quello dei rapporti fra P e P[1] sono strettamente connessi. La mano di scrittura di queste aggiunte è diversa da quella
che ha scritto il testo di P: esclusa la possibilità che questa sia
la *manus Philodemi* si può pensare all'intervento di un revisore o
di un lettore dotto.[18] I rapporti fra i due mss. non possono essere quelli indicati dal Crönert, che parla di P come "brutta
copia," cioè la prima redazione dell'opera, corretta da Filodemo
stesso e di P[1] come "bella copia" da esso derivata.[19] Se P[1] ha
ripristinato la successione giusta delle colonne deve averlo fatto

---

17 Cf. Crönert, 397 s. (= *Studi*, 194 s.).

18 La cosa si riscontra, p. es., in *P. Herc.* 1148, XV (Epicuro, *La natura XIV*). L'intervento di un dotto nel *P. Herc.* 1021
fu prospettato dal Crönert, 386 s. (= *Studi*, 166 s., ma vedi già
qualche dubbio, ibid. 400 s., n. 1 = *Studi* 196 s., n. 87) e poi
rifiutato ("Telesstelle") con l'acquisita convinzione dell'esistenza della *manus Philodemi*.

19 *RhM* 62 (1907) 624 s. (= *Studi*, 221 s.).

indipendentemente da P, quindi, data la recenziorità di P^1, accer-
tabile paleograficamente (P è databile ai primi decenni, intorno
al 70 ca, del I^a; mentre con P^1 si deve scendere alla fine del I^a),
sembra plausibile postulare un ms. β, ora perduto, fratello indi-
pendente e corretto di P, da cui sia disceso, per filiazione diretta, P^1. Avremmo pertanto una tradizione bipartita in cui α rappresenta le schede di Filodemo, capostipite corretto di tutta la tradizione, P e β i due discendenti, più o meno coevi. La necessità
di esemplare un nuovo testimone e il problema connesso con l'ulteriore derivazione da questo di P^1, invece che da α, può essere
spiegato con la probabile perdita o distruzione di α sùbito o poco
dopo la copia di β:

Dobbiamo altresí supporre una probabile collazione di P su β per
spiegare alcune correzioni di P: l'aggiunta marginale apposta nell'
intercolumnio destro a livello di col. VI 12 di P, che in P^1 è
inserita nel testo e cosí doveva essere necessariamente in β, e una
significativa correzione di nomi propri nella col. IX 3 di P (*Hera-
kleídes* in *Herákleitos*). Poiché P era quasi inservibile, deturpato
da una infinità di errori e distrazioni, possiamo pensare sia stato
necessario approntare una seconda copia, β, esemplata sulle medesime schede, questa volta ordinate oppure dettate di persona dall'
autore per garantirsi dagli errori precedentemente verificatisi.
Di qui P^1, la cui importanza per la costituzione del testo è di
prim'ordine. *Recentiores non deteriores*.

Tiziano Dorandi

LA CONCEZIONE DELLA RETORICA DA EPICURO A FILODEMO

La concezione di Epicuro riguardo alla retorica ed una eventuale modificazione di essa nei suoi successori appaiono ancora
molto incerte a causa soprattutto della scarsità e della poca chiarezza delle testimonianze, che si riducono alle esigue informazioni
degli autori antichi e al trattato Περὶ ῥητορικῆς di Filodemo. Da
quest'ultimo, da Diogene Laerzio e da uno scolio ad Ermogene abbiamo la notizia che Epicuro abbia scritto un trattato intorno alla
retorica.[1] Tuttavia esso non compare nell'elenco che Diogene stesso
fa delle opere del filosofo (egli dice di citare τὰ βέλτιστα); Quintiliano accenna soltanto al fatto che Epicuro scrisse contro la retorica (II 17,15) e Sesto Empirico, che pure nell'opera sua lo nomina
spesso, nel libro contro i retori, dove informa puntualmente sulle
concezioni delle varie scuole filosofiche ed ha pure occasione di
menzionare gli epicurei per altri motivi (relativamente cioè alle
persecuzioni che subì la loro setta), non fa neppure parola delle
idee del fondatore.

Soprattutto questo silenzio di Sesto, che complessivamente non
mostra per Epicuro maggiore antipatia che per gli altri filosofi,
potrebbe indicare che egli non abbia composto uno scritto apposito
sulla retorica, sia pure nella forma di libello polemico, ma abbia
parlato di tale argomento soltanto in altra sede oppure che comunque
la trattazione della materia era giudicata inferiore per complessità
ed importanza a quella dei rappresentanti delle altre scuole.

Del resto anche gli epicurei di Rodi e di Cos, con i quali
Filodemo polemizza, citano l'opinione del maestro richiamandosi al
Simposio del medesimo o ad uno scritto Περὶ βίων (Philod., *Rh.* II
151 Longo). O forse la *Retorica* di Epicuro era un'opera giovanile
del tempo in cui egli doveva ancora concorrere con uomini come Nausifane o Prassifane di Mitilene (H. Steckel, *RE* Suppl. XI [1968]
629-630).

---

1 Philod., *Rh.* II 135 et al. Longo; D.L. X 13; *schol.* Hermog.
t. V 440,25 W. (= fr. 55 Usener).

Le testimonianze degli autori antichi sono abbastanza concordi
nel presentare la figura del filosofo come dissuadente i discepoli
dal seguire le varie discipline che costituiscono la παιδεία, dalla
matematica alla poesia, ad eccezione forse della grammatica elemen-
tare che reputa indispensabile, perchè inutili e dannose per la
formazione del sapiente, ponendosi in questo modo in contrasto con
le varie scuole filosofiche, se si esclude lo scetticismo pirron-
iano.[2]

In un frammento di epistola a Pitocle tramandatoci da Diogene
Laerzio Epicuro esorta il discepolo a prendere il largo con una
navicella, fuggendo da tutta la cultura.[3] Lo stesso Diogene ci
informa del fatto che gli epicurei rifiutavano la dialettica come
superflua (nell'elenco dei titoli delle opere di Epicuro della *Vita*
laerziana compare un Πρὸς τοὺς Μεγαρικούς ed in quello degli scritti
di Metrodoro un Πρὸς τοὺς διαλεκτικούς) e con lui concordano Cicerone e Sesto Empirico.[4] Se si considera il legame che la dialettica
ha con la retorica nel sistema di Aristotele e soprattutto in quello degli stoici, si può sospettare anche soltanto per questo un atteggiamento negativo di Epicuro nei riguardi della retorica stessa.[5]

Per tutto ciò è facile da parte degli avversari passare all'
accusa di ignoranza ed "incultura" nei riguardi di Epicuro, critica
abbastanza diffusa presso esponenti o simpatizzanti di altre correnti filosofiche: quasi una eccezione è rappresentata da Seneca
che mostra di apprezzare Epicuro nelle *Epistulae morales* (e forse
lo ha tenuto presente come modello) e Tacito nel *Dialogus*.[6] Ma
entrambi sono rappresentanti di quella latinità non più "classica"
che aveva smesso di nutrire gli ideali letterari di Cicerone.

---

2 Cic., *de fin.* II 4,12; Quint. XII 2,24; Plut., *non posse
suav. viv.* 11 1093 c; 12,1094 d; Athen. XIII 53,588 a; Sext., *adv.
math.* I 2-3,49.

3 D.L. X 6; cf. Plut., *de aud. poet.* 1 15 d.

4 D.L. X 31; Cic., *de fin.* I 7,22; II 2,4; *de nat. deor.* I
25,69; *de fato* 37; Sext., *adv. math.* VII 22.

5 Cic., *de fin.* II 6,17; cf. R. Philippson, *Rh. Mus.* 71
(1916) 439.

6 Cic., *de fin.* I 11,26; *de nat. deor.* I 26,72; Plut., *quaest.
conv.* III 6,1,653 b; Tac., *dial.* XXXI; Sext., *adv. math.* I 1; cf.
H. Mutschmann, *Hermes* 50 (1915) 321 ss.

Venendo ora in particolare all'ostilità di Epicuro nei riguardi della retorica, abbiamo anzitutto la testimonianza di uno
scolio scivolato nel testo della *Vita* laerziana nel l'intervallo
fra la seconda e la terza *Epistola*, in cui è detto che il sapiente
non praticherà l'oratoria con gli artifici del bello stile (D.L.
X 118). Altre testimonianze abbiamo in Quintiliano, Plutarco e
Sesto Empirico, il quale ultimo sottolinea l'avversione di Epicuro
per il maestro Nausifane che fra gli altri μαθήματα si dedicava
soprattutto alla retorica.[7]

Ci si potrebbe chiedere come questo atteggiamento si accordi
con lo stile accurato delle *Epistole*, in particolare della terza
(in contrasto tuttavia con quello dell'opera Περὶ φύσεως, per quel
che appare dai frammenti, e in genere degli scritti filodemei), che
non disdegna certi procedimenti retorici. Che non sappiamo se
siano da porre in relazione con il biasimo che il retore Elio Teone
all'inizio dei suoi *Proginnasmi* riserva allo stile di Epicuro (egli
cita due frammenti di epistole) definito "asiano" in quanto usa le
misure del linguaggio poetico (λέξις ἔμμετρος καὶ ἔνρυθμος).[8]
L'Usener spiega l'accuratezza dello stile delle *Epistole* (in contrasto con i giudizi negativi su Epicuro scrittore espressi generalmente dagli autori greci e latini) come necessaria in opere des-
tinate al pubblico diversamente dagli ὑπομνήματα letti soltanto
all'interno della scuola.[9]

Il De Lacy osserva che l'ideale epicureo di un linguaggio
filosofico che poneva regole e limitazioni troppo severe nei riguardi degli artifici retorici non poteva essere sempre mantenuto
coerentemente (*AJP* 60 [1939] 92). E notiamo in Sesto Empirico
(*adv. math.* I 272-73) una testimonianza del divario per così dire
fra teoria e pratica nel filosofo che, per quanto nemico delle lettere (γραμματικῆς κατήγορος), si fa scoprire tuttavia a prendere
dai poeti le più significative fra le sue sentenze. Leggiamo in

---

7 Quint. II 17,15; Plut., *adv. Col.* 33,1127 a; Sext., *adv.*
math. I 1.

8 *Progymn.* 2 in E. Spengel, *Rhetores Graeci* (Lipsiae 1854) II,
71; cf. U. v. Wilamowitz-Moellendorff, *Hermes* 35 (1900) 6.

9 *Epicurea* (Lipsiae 1887, Roma[2] 1963) XLII, 88-90.

Diogene Laerzio (X 13) che Epicuro nel trattato Περὶ ῥητορικῆς per noi perduto sosteneva che la sola norma cui deve ispirarsi lo stile (e quindi la prosa filosofica) è la chiarezza (σαφήνεια): egli stesso era chiaro nella esposizione, virtù che gli è riconosciuta anche da Cicerone, che pure per altri versi lo critica,[10] ed aveva una proprietà di linguaggio che viene tuttavia censurata dal grammatico Aristofane di Bisanzio come troppo "personale" (e quindi forse di non immediata comprensibilità) — "inquinata da idiotismi" secondo l'interpretazione dello Hirzel,[11] per il quale invece l'idioma di Epicuro è soltanto comune e non scientifico, un esempio della βιωτικὴ ἀφελὴς συνήθεια τῶν ἰδιωτῶν secondo la definizione che Sesto Empirico dà del linguaggio ordinario e parlato in contrapposizione a quello tecnico (adv. math. I 232).

E se Filodemo rispecchia fedelmente le linee del pensiero del maestro a questo proposito, è espresso l'ideale della prosa come stile "naturalmente bello" (φυσικῶς καλὸς λόγος) nel quarto libro del Περὶ ῥητορικῆς, dove lo stile sobrio e razionale dei filosofi è contrapposto a quello dei retori esorbitante di artifici e di metafore.[12] Riguardo alle quali ultime non è escluso che la sua critica sia diretta anche agli stoici e ai peripatetici che mostravano di apprezzarle in modo particolare.[13]

Quanto ai motivi precisi della ostilità di Epicuro per la retorica, motivi che si possono cogliere quasi soltanto dal trattato di Filodemo, sempre che esso, come si è detto, sia un riflesso attendibile del pensiero più antico, essi sembrano derivare, oltre che dagli eccessi di un certo stile, come appare dal già nominato

---

10 Cic., de fin. I 5,15; Quint. XII 14; Tac., dial. XXXI.

11 Untersuchungen zu Ciceros philosophischen Schriften (Leipzig 1877) II, 380 n. 1; cf. A. Laks, Vie d'Epicure, Cahiers de philologie, 1: Etudes sur l'épicurisme antique (Lille 1976) 71-73.

12 Philod., Rh. I 151 Sudhaus; cf. L. Radermacher, Rh. Mus. 54 (1899) 364 ss.; P. H. De Lacy, AJP 60 (1939) 87.

13 Cf. A. Plebe, Studi sulla retorica stoica (Torino 1963) 36 ss. Si veda in particolare Strabone (I 2,6) che ripete il punto di vista stoico (posidoniano?) secondo il quale la prosa è una derivazione del linguaggio poetico.

libro quarto, anche e soprattutto dall'uso che della retorica medesima facevano i suoi sostenitori, come di una "summa" di tutta la
sapienza (*Rh.* I 223 s. Sudhaus), considerata indispensabile anche
all'arte di governare lo stato o addirittura identificantesi con
essa. E' questa una tendenza ben nota nei sofisti e in Isocrate e
seguaci fino a Cicerone e Dionisio di Alicarnasso (che scrisse una
πολιτικὴ φιλοσοφία = "ars rhetorica" attaccata dagli epicurei) e,
per quanto con una diversa origine, anche in Nausifane di Teo,[14]
con il quale Filodemo polemizza soprattutto nel libro VI del suo
trattato. Infine nello ὑπομνηματικόν in particolare viene soste-
nuta contro gli isocratei l'autonomia della politica e del πολιτι-
κὸς λόγος dalla retorica sofistica.[15]

Quando Cicerone accenna agli epicurei più in vista dei tempi
recenti, Zenone e Fedro soprattutto, il suo giudizio diventa più
positivo riguardo alla cultura ed egli ha perfino parole di lode
per la chiarezza e la bellezza dello stile.[16] Le nuove generazioni
di epicurei sotto l'influsso delle altre scuole filosofiche, specialmente della Nuova Accademia, avrebbero rotto l'antico isola-
mento e si sarebbero aperte alla cultura, accogliendo anche la dialettica. Oltre a ciò altri aspetti del pensiero epicureo hanno
diviso gli studiosi intorno alla dibattuta questione della "stabil-
ità" ed immobilismo del "Kepos", di cui come tale appunto avevano
ricevuto l'immagine in genere gli autori antichi.[17]

Una di queste differenze tra il vecchio e il nuovo potrebbe
forse apparire nella concezione della retorica e precisamente a
proposito della questione se la retorica sia arte o meno, che è

---

14 S. Sudhaus, *Rh. Mus.* 48 (1893) 334 ss.; H. v. Arnim, *Leben
und Werke des Dio von Prusa* (Berlin 1898) 43 ss.; K. v. Fritz, *RE*
XVI 2 (1935) 2023-24.

15 Philod., *Rh.* II 239-50 et al. Sudhaus. Cf. H. M. Hubbell,
CP 11 (1916) 405 ss.

16 Cic., *acad.* I 12,46; *de fin.* I 15,16; II 26,86; *de nat.
deor.* I 21,58; *in Pis.* 68,70; cf. Hirzel, op. cit. (n. 11) I, 170-
71.

17 Cic., *Tusc.* III 17,38; Eus., *praep. ev.* XIV 5; cf. Hirzel,
op. cit. (n. 11) I, 98 ss.; E. Zeller, *Die Philosophie der Griechen*
(Leipzig 1923) III[1], 498 ss.; Philippson, loc. cit. (n. 5) 439; W.
Schmid, *RAC* (1961) 755.

stata oggetto di acceso dibattito soprattutto nel secondo secolo
a.c. e sulla quale gli epicurei del primo secolo a.c. si presentano
divisi. Filodemo ne tratta nei primi due libri del trattato Περί
ῥητορικῆς e sostiene che, secondo il suo maestro Zenone che inseg-
nava ad Atene ed il cui pensiero egli condivide, per Epicuro, Metrodoro ed Ermarco la retorica sofistica ovvero epidittica è arte,
mentre non lo sono la retorica deliberativa e quella giudiziaria,
prodotte soltanto dalla pratica e dall'esercizio.[18] A questo proposito Filodemo polemizza con altri epicurei — la cui identità ci
è ignota — che egli dice insegnavano a Rodi e Cos, i quali soste-
nevano il contrario, che cioè secondo i capiscuola la retorica sofistica non è arte (Rh. II 151 Longo).

Ciascuno di questi due gruppi accusava dunque l'altro di
eterodossia e si riteneva depositario delle parole di Epicuro. Una
terza opinione è rappresentata da un certo Bromio che attribuisce
la prerogativa di arte alla retorica politica (ovvero deliberativa)
e di cui non sappiamo se invocasse per questo l'autorità del
maestro.[19] Il Sudhaus in un articolo del 1895 (Philologus 54 [1895]
85) afferma che Epicuro non doveva essersi posto la domanda se la
retorica sia arte o meno; ma fra gli epicurei delle generazioni
successive la contesa a tale proposito risulta insanabile, poichè
cercavano una risposta negli scritti del fondatore.

Similmente il von Arnim ritiene che questa distinzione fra due
generi di retorica e l'attribuzione della qualità di τέχνη al genere epidittico siano caratteristiche più del tempo di Filodemo che
di quello di Epicuro; nè può valere come prova quanto adduce Filodemo, che cioè Epicuro parlava sempre delle "scuole dei retori",
di "coloro che provengono dalle scuole di retorica", delle "facoltà" di tali scuole e simili. Gli epicurei si divisero più
avanti in una parte ostile alla retorica e in un'altra relativamente amica, alla quale apparteneva Zenone Sidonio maestro di Filodemo.[20] Infine secondo H. M. Hubbell il fatto che Filodemo non

_____

18 Philod., Rh. II 115, 121, 145, 161, 215 Longo.

19 Philod., Rh. II 115 Longo. Tralasciamo di parlare qui di
due gruppi minori di eterodossi che il Sudhaus indica a p. XXIV
della sua edizione.

20 V. Arnim, loc. cit. (n. 14) 74, 75, 89. Cf. Philippson,
AGPh 23 (1910) 306.

faccia al riguardo una precisa citazione da Epicuro indica che negli scritti di quest'ultimo non si trovava nessuna dichiarazione esplicita.[21] A queste argomentazioni si può aggiungere che, da quel poco che dell'atteggiamento di Epicuro si sa o si presume di sapere, come si è visto, attraverso la tradizione indiretta e il trattamento che lo stesso Filodemo, se è portavoce del maestro, riserva alla retorica sofistica, connotandola in maniera alquanto negativa, sia nel libro quarto a proposito dello stile sia nel quinto nel confronto con la filosofia sia nello ὑπομνηματικόν nel confronto con la politica, si ricava un'immagine della sofistica stessa che è, per così dire, quasi in opposizione con certe altre affermazioni, che cioè secondo Epicuro essa è arte. Volendo prospettare una soluzione diversa da quella del Sudhaus e degli altri studiosi citati sopra e mantenere al tempo stesso una certa coerenza nell'insieme del quadro, si potrebbe formulare l'ipotesi che Epicuro riconoscesse nella retorica sofistica o epidittica una serie di elementi fissi o principii che possono essere assunti ed appresi come regole, utili o indispensabili per un certo genere di elaborazione letteraria, a cui nel rispetto della logica non si può disconoscere il rigore formale e l'organicità della τέχνη o della ἐπιστήμη o della μέθοδος--termini che in questo caso dal testo di Filodemo appaiono in certo modo sinonimi--per evidenti analogie di struttura con altri complessi apprendibili dal punto di vista conoscitivo, cui spettano a pieno titolo tali denominazioni. Tra i quali complessi di norme tuttavia ve ne possono essere alcuni - come l'arte del medico e quella del timoniere - di contenuto tale da non meritare la massima considerazione da parte di un filosofo, entrando nel cerchio della sua attenzione soltanto per esigenze di esemplificazione o di classificazione. A questo livello forse - o poco più - Epicuro vede la retorica, quasi declassata al rango di ciò che noi intendiamo come "arti e mestieri": riconoscimento dell'appartenenza di essa alla categoria delle τέχναι, ma valutazione assai

---

21 H. M. Hubbell, *The Rhetorica of Philodemus* (Trans. of the Connecticut Academy of Arts and Sciences 1920) 256; cf. G. M. Grube, *Greek and Roman Critics* (London 1965) 194.

limitata del suo contenuto soprattutto in vista dell'utilità per la
vita del singolo ed il bene dello stato.[22]

Così questa, che non lascia certamente senza perplessità, è
forse l'unica ipotesi — fino a quando nuove interpretazioni di
testi non imporranno di rivederla — che permetta di conciliare le
immagini contrastanti sulla concezione della retorica che di Epicuro ci ha tramandato Filodemo, senza peraltro che si ritenga di
poter prendere posizione sulla autenticità delle medesime.

Matilde Ferrario

22 Cf. M. Isnardi Parente, *Techne. Momenti del pensiero greco
da Platone a Epicuro* (Firenze 1966) 388; idem, *La cultura* 7 (1969)
80-81.

PER L'INTERPRETAZIONE DELL'OPERA FILODEMEA
SULL'IRA (P. HERC. 182, COLL. XXXIV-L)

Il *P. Herc.* 182[1] conserva, in discrete condizioni, buona parte
dell'opera filodemea *Sull'ira*, la cui lettura presenta molteplici
motivi di interesse; tuttavia, tranne qualche eccezione,[2] essa non
è stata ancora studiata a fondo.[3] L'importanza maggiore è costituita dal fatto che ci permette di conoscere la posizione degli
Epicurei su questo πάθος, un argomento che non risulta trattato nei
resti degli scritti di Epicuro a noi pervenuti: è il tema della
seconda parte del papiro, che, come sempre accade per i rotoli ercolanesi, è la meglio conservata. Espongo le grandi linee della
trattazione, facendo qualche considerazione su alcuni punti salienti.

Filodemo, che nella prima parte descrive estesamente il comportamento dell'irato e le conseguenze dell'ira, non astenendosi dal
polemizzare con gli avversari,[4] nella sezione finale del libro
espone il punto di vista della sua scuola,[5] che non si riduce ad
una astratta affermazione di principio, ma è fondato su due cardini

---

1 L'edizione seguita è quella di K. Wilke (Lipsiae 1914), ma
tutti i passi sono stati da me controllati sull'originale.

2 Mi riferisco all'Introduzione del Wilke, dove ampio spazio
è dedicato all'interpretazione dell'opera (pp. xiii-xxi), agli avversari in essa combattuti (pp. xxi-xxvi) e alle fonti utilizzate
(pp. xxvi-liv); e al contributo di R. Philippson, "Philodems Buch
über den Zorn," *RhM* 71 (1916) 425-60, che sarebbe dovuto essere
solo una parte di una più ampia ricerca sulla psicologia dell'ira,
mai pubblicata.

3 In studi sulle teorie antiche dei πάθη, l'attenzione a
Filodemo è minima, rispetto agli altri autori; v. il volume di P.
Rabbow, *Antike Schriften über Seelenheilung und Seelenleitung. I:
Die Therapie des Zorns* (Leipzig 1914) 100-105 e 184 s., e la dis-
sertazione di H. Ringeltaube, *Quaestiones ad veterum philosophorum
de affectibus doctrinam pertinentes* (Gottingae 1913) 38-50, in cui
si punta soprattutto ad individuare gli avversari di Filodemo.

4 Soprattutto in coll. I-VII e XXXI 31-XXXIV 7.

5 Anche in queste colonne non vengono risparmiati gli attac-
chi, soprattutto contro Nicasicrate.

della filosofia epicurea, l'osservazione della natura delle cose[6]
e l'assenza di false opinioni--in questo caso, "relativamente al
calcolo degli svantaggi e alle punizioni di coloro che arrecano
danno."[7] È una posizione articolata, come dichiara lo stesso Filodemo (col. XXXVII 15-19) contrapponendosi alle affermazioni estre-
mistiche dei Peripatetici e degli Stoici che si limitavano a dire
che l'ira è un bene o un male: "Noi invece non facciamo una semplice affermazione, poiché un falso ragionamento interviene anche
relativamente ad una espressione." Se gli Epicurei respingono, con
motivazioni analoghe a quelle stoiche, la concezione peripatetica
della indispensabilità dell'ira, vi si avvicinano quando ammettono
l'esistenza dell'ira naturale, definita inevitabile e non dannosa.
La tesi basilare è che si deve distinguere l'ira come πάθος in sé
dall'ira come stato d'animo provocato da cause esterne: della prima
non bisogna cadere preda, perché è motivo di turbamento dell'equi-
librio psichico dell'uomo; la seconda, quando le ragioni per adirarsi siano fondate, va accolta, perché è connaturata all'indole
umana (col. XXXVIII 14-28). Tale specie, chiamata φυσικὴ ὀργή, è
caratterizzata dalla breve durata e dalla moderata intensità: ad
essa può andare soggetto anche il sapiente, come sostennero i primi
Maestri della Scuola epicurea. Il secondo tipo, il θυμός (intendendo con questo termine l'ira furiosa e immotivata, che fa provare
piacere nella vendetta e nella punizione), è da condannare, perché
arreca danno non solo agli altri, ma anche a chi ne è preda.[8]
    Filodemo distingue, innanzi tutto, l'ira dall'irascibilità,
cioè il πάθος vero e proprio dall'inclinazione a caderne preda:
anche gli uomini non proclivi all'ira possono talvolta trasformarsi
in iracondi, ma certamente non per molto tempo daranno l'immagine

_____

6 Col. XXXVII 27-30; anche Polistrato aveva affermato che un
modo di vivere tranquillo e conforme a natura è prodotto dalla ὀρθὴ
φυσιολογία di chi esamina com'è la natura delle cose (De contemptu,
col. XIX 1-8 Indelli).

7 Col. XXXVII 30-34; cf. Polystr., De cont., coll. XV 24-27
e XVI 1-7.

8 Fondamentale, nel discorso filodemeo, è la διάθεσις: se è
παμπόνηρος, il sentimento che può nascere è la κενὴ ὀργή, da considerare un male; se, invece, è σπουδαία, ci troviamo in presenza
dell'ira naturale, che non è un male, ma un bene (coll. XXXVII 34-
XXXVIII 13).

di ὀργίλοι, poiché il loro è uno stato d'animo momentaneo, che maschera l'autentica indole (col. XXXIV 8-29). L'Epicureo si scaglia poi contro Nicasicrate, che respinge anche l'ira naturale; del suo ragionamento è messa in rilievo l'incoerenza: infatti, poiché parla di una φυσικὴ ὀργή, Nicasicrate non può definirla causa di mali, dal momento che ciò che è naturale deve essere un bene; d'altra parte, se condanna anche questa specie d'ira non può chiamarla φυσικὴ (col. XXXIX 21-33). A proposito dell'ira il medesimo discorso può adattarsi sia all'uomo comune sia al sapiente, purché si tenga presente che il σοφός non può mai essere preso da violento turbamento, quindi neppure da ira intensa, anche se βλάπτεται ὑπό τινων εἰς τὰ μέγιστα, perché non tiene in grande considerazione nessuna delle circostanze esterne (coll. XLI 27-XLII 12). Dopo aver sottolineato la differenza tra ira e sentimento di vendetta,[9] Filodemo analizza il diverso valore semantico di ὀργή e θυμός (col. XLIII 40 ss.), prima di sferrare l'attacco conclusivo contro gli avversari che sembrano aver forzato il significato di alcuni ἐπιλογισμοί impiegati dagli Epicurei (coll. XLVI 16-L).

Più di una volta, in momenti importanti della sua trattazione, l'Epicureo si richiama al pensiero e al comportamento dei καθηγεμόνες per trovare un sostegno alle sue asserzioni: è un dato di fatto molto significativo, un contributo a favore della sua ortodossia, talvolta messa in dubbio. Né questa è la sola opera nella quale Filodemo mette l'accento sulla necessità di attenersi all'insegnamento dei fondatori; oltre che nell'*Economia*[10] e nella *Retorica*,[11] soprattutto nell'opera *Sulla libertà di parola*[12] viene riaffermata "la catena ininterrotta dei *leaders* della Scuola":[13] "Con molta fiducia ammoniremo gli altri e da tempo e ora dopo aver

---

9   Col. XLII 20 ss.; l'argomento è ripreso in col. XLIV 15-34.

10   *P. Herc.* 1424, col. XII 18-22 Jensen.

11   *P. Herc.* 1674, col. XXIII 14-24 Longo-Auricchio.

12   *P. Herc.* 1471, fr. 45, 1-6 (il testo di Olivieri è stato modificato, con l'inserimento di πάλαι prima di καὶ νῦν, da M. Gigante, *Ricerche Filodemee* [Napoli 1969] 51).

13   Gigante, *Ricerche*; sua è la traduzione del passo.

acquistato una posizione preminente, cresciuti nell'orma dei fondatori quasi fossimo nati dal loro grembo."

Tornando allo scritto *Sull'ira*, Filodemo, quando discute della differenza tra ira e irascibilità, porta come esempio Epicuro, il sapiente che, pur essendo per natura ἀόργητος, "dette ad alcuni l'immagine dell'uomo iracondo" (col. XXXV 2-5) per svariati motivi. Alcuni di essi potrebbero essere stati quelli che sùbito dopo sono riferiti ad un generico σοφός,[14] cioè "il rimprovero frequente e intenso, a causa dell'amore, per tutti i discepoli o per la maggior parte" (col. XXXV 12-15) e la franchezza nel parlare che ha provocato il suo abbandono da parte di alcuni amici.[15] Infatti dall'opera *Sulla libertà di parola* sappiamo che "l'ἐπιτίμησις, il rimprovero, è parte integrante della παρρησία esercitata dal maestro"[16] e nella concezione epicurea non può disgiungersi dal φιλεῖν, poiché ha sempre valore correttivo, tende al miglioramento dei discepoli. Riguardo, poi, all'impiego della παρρησία, non va dimenticato che per Epicuro essa era un attributo fondamentale del vero filosofo, che non avrebbe mai dovuto tradirla, anche a costo di perdere i suoi seguaci, come si legge nella *Sentenza Vaticana* 29.[17]

---

14 Mi sembra che non esattamente Chr. Jensen, *Ein neuer Brief Epikurs*, AGWG philol.-hist. Kl., dritte Folge, 5 (1933) 58 n. 2 e 72 n. 8, abbia affermato che anche in coll. XXXV 11-XXXVI 6 ci si riferisca ad Epicuro; all'ipotesi del Jensen si oppongono considerazioni logiche e la stessa struttura del discorso filodemeo di coll. XXXIV 30-XXXV 5: φαί[νο]νται δ' [οὖ]ν πρὸς τό|σον καὶ τὴν [ἐν]αντιωτά̣ | [τη]ν ἔχοντες διάθεσιν, | ὥστε κἂν σοφὸς καθάπερ | ἀμέ[λει] καὶ 'Επίκουρος | ἀπ[έ]δωκεν ἐ]νίοις τοιού|του̣ [φαντασ]ίαν.

15 Col. XXXV 31-33; si allude a Timocrate?

16 M. Gigante, "Per l'interpretazione dell'opera filodemea 'Sulla libertà di parola,'" *CErc* 2 (1972) 64 n. 58.

17 Già i discepoli più immediati avevano insistito sulla necessità di essere sempre franchi nel parlare; Polistrato, criticando quei filosofi che, incuranti della coerenza, stravolgevano il loro autentico pensiero per compiacere il prossimo e guadagnarne il favore, aveva dichiarato che era necessario servirsi della παρρησία e della ἀκόλουθος καὶ ἀληθὴς φιλοσοφία per portare a compimento con piena consapevolezza τὸ τῆς ἀληθινῆς φιλοσοφίας ἔργον (*De cont.*, coll. XVI 33-XVII 7). Filodemo, poi, nell'opera Περὶ παρρησίας "espone il punto di vista della scuola epicurea sulla libertà di parola, concepita come tecnica per l'acquisto della sapienza e della felicità" (Gigante, *Ricerche*, 45 s.).

Il nucleo della col. XLIII è costituito dalla difesa delle
Κύριαι Δόξαι attuata da Filodemo. Nella prima *Massima* Epicuro,
riferendosi alla divinità, essere beato e incorruttibile, aveva
voluto sottolinearne le differenze con l'essere umano, designato
con l'aggettivo ἀσθενής. Gli avversari, travisando--forse di
proposito--il significato della *Massima*, ritennero πάνδεινον che
Epicuro avesse potuto "definire nell'àmbito della debolezza l'ira,
la gratitudine e sentimenti siffatti, dal momento che Alessandro,
di gran lunga il più potente di tutti, non solo era andato soggetto a numerosi moti d'ira, ma anche si era mostrato grato a moltis-
sime persone" (col. XLIII 22-28). A costoro Filodemo replica che
con ἀσθένεια Epicuro intendeva non "la costituzione fisica che si
contrappone a quella degli atleti e dei re, ma quella che può andare incontro a dolori e morte," cioè la costituzione fisica del-
l'uomo, imperfetta e corruttibile, della quale ovviamente fu parte-
cipe Alessandro (col. XLIII 28-40): ne consegue che l'ira può essere
un sentimento tipico anche del sapiente, perché costui è un uomo
come tutti gli altri e, in quanto tale, è ἀσθενής.[18] Da questo
luogo pare risulti che Filodemo fu un corretto interprete dei testi
dottrinari e si allineò con i primi maestri contro quella parte
della Scuola schierata su posizioni deviazionistiche per quanto
riguarda non solo l'ira ma anche la retorica e altri problemi.

Ne riceviamo la conferma dalla lettura di uno dei più importanti passi dell'intero libro, quello di coll. XLIV 40-XLV 22:
Filodemo, per dare una base più solida alla sua affermazione che
anche il sapiente può essere preda del θυμός--se si usa questo termine con un significato analogo a ὀργή--, ricorre ai tre antichi
Maestri, insistendo ripetutamente, con citazioni anche letterali,
sul medesimo concetto e dimostrando che gli avversari, che pure si
vantano di essere gli autentici depositari del pensiero dei καθηγεμόνες, lo hanno frainteso. Dice Filodemo: "Anche ai maestri piace
che il sapiente vada incontro al θυμός non secondo questa prolessi,[19]

---

18 Col. XLIII 14-18. Dell'ἀσθένεια, carattere tipico della
condizione umana e causa principale della morte, Filodemo parla
anche nell'opera *Sulla morte*, col. XXXVII 31 (v. Gigante, *Ricerche*,
70 e 93).

19 Cioè nel senso di ira furiosa, che spinge alla vendetta
come a un godimento (v. col. XLIV 5 ss.).

ma secondo quella più comune.[20] E infatti Epicuro nelle *Enuncia-
zioni*[21] chiarisce che cosa sia il sopraggiungere del θυμός e il
caderne preda con moderazione; e Metrodoro, se propriamente dice
'il θυμός del sapiente,'[22] mostra insieme che (l'infuriarsi) è di
assai breve durata;[23] anche ad Ermarco non sembra da rifiutare che
il sapiente andrà soggetto al θυμός, ma solo l'ira intensa:[24] così
che provoca meraviglia, in uomini che vogliono essere accurati let-
tori dei libri della Scuola, che, avendo trascurato queste cose e
quanto è stato in precedenza segnalato, conseguentemente mostravano
il fatto che, secondo i maestri,[25] il sapiente sarà preda dell'ira
furiosa."

---

20   Cioè, θυμός = όργή (v. coll. XLIII 40-XLIV 5).

21   È l'unica testimonianza su quest'opera di Epicuro. Secondo il Philippson ("Die Κύριαι Δόξαι," *PhW* 40 [1920] 1031 s.), essa
coinciderebbe con la raccolta delle *Sentenze Vaticane*; il Sedley,
invece ("Epicurus, On Nature Book XXVIII," *CErc* 3 [1973] 59), ba-
sandosi sul significato del termine άναφώνησις in *Epist. ad Herod.*
76 e in Dem. Lac., *P. Herc.* 1012, col. XLV 9-12 De Falco, la considera un'opera nella quale forse venivano studiati i significati
naturali delle parole (cf. *Epist. ad Herod.* 72, in cui ricorre il
verbo άναφωνέω): da Filodemo apprendiamo che in questo scritto Epicuro si occupava dei gradi di intensità del θυμός e della sua ef-
fettiva natura, e questo potrebbe coesistere con una discussione
sui significati originali delle parole, che per Epicuro risalivano
in parte ai πάθη degli uomini che per primi le pronunziarono
(*Epist. ad Herod.* 75).

22   L'integrazione τ[οῦ δὲ] σοφοῦ (1. 10), che mi sembra la
più convincente tra le tante proposte (Wilke aveva lasciato lacuna),
è del Gigante, *CErc* 8 (1978) 25; brutta la proposta quasi uguale di
J. Hayter, nella inedita trascrizione manoscritta con traduzione
latina conservata nella Bodleian Library di Oxford: λέγει τ[ό, ό
τοῦ] σοφοῦ.

23   Interpreto in questo modo l'espressione συνεμφα[ίνε]ι τὸ
λίαν βραχέως (1. 11 s.) per ragioni di carattere logico e grammaticale: Filodemo cita Metrodoro per dimostrare che il θυμός di cui
egli parla dura poco, corrisponde all' όργή; con questa traduzione,
inoltre, si giustifica la presenza del neutro τό, che richiama [τό]
τε θυμωθήσεσθαι καί [τὸ] μετρίως della 1. 7 s.

24   Alla 1. 14 dell'edizione del Wilke si legge άλλά .]ην,
seguito da una lacuna di una linea; il Philippson, *RhM* 71 (1916)
457, congetturò άλλά τ]ὴν | [σύντονον όργήν].

25   L. 20 s. κατὰ | τοὺς ἄνδρας; cf. F. Longo Auricchio, "La
scuola di Epicuro," *CErc* 8 (1978) 21-37, sp. 26-30 e relativo
commento.

Il costante riferirsi all'autorità dei capi del Giardino non
si spiegherebbe se si ammettesse un distacco di Filodemo dalla
dottrina di Epicuro; al contrario, per due volte egli addebita
un'errata interpretazione del pensiero epicureo agli avversari,[26]
i quali, pur leggendo i testi canonici della Scuola, di cui preten-
dono di essere profondi conoscitori--questo mi pare possa essere il
valore di βυβλιακός--,[27] non ne traggono le giuste conclusioni.
Essi infatti utilizzavano affermazioni dei capiscuola avendole de-
liberatamente estrapolate da un contesto più ampio e senza preoccu-
parsi di inserirle nel complesso della dottrina, in modo da at-
tribuirvi un significato non autentico ma che fosse il più conveniente per loro (come nel caso della prima *Massima Capitale*); oppure
ricavavano da ragionamenti usati dai maestri conclusioni che per
niente rispecchiavano il punto di vista di coloro che originariamente li avevano formulati:[28] è il caso dei tre ἐπιλογισμοί[29] fina-
li, dei quali gli avversari si servono per far sostenere ad Epicuro
e ai suoi discepoli che il sapiente non solo può adirarsi μετρίως,
ma potrà andare soggetto anche all'ira furiosa (coll. XLVII 39-
XLVIII 3); ma, dice Filodemo (col. XLV 22-39), sono argomentazioni

---

26 Il problema della loro individuazione è complesso, poiché
la polemica di Filodemo non si indirizza in una sola direzione.
Sono propenso a credere che in queste ultime colonne siano presi di
mira seguaci non ortodossi della filosofia epicurea, ma nella parte
precedente sono attaccati anche i Peripatetici (coll. XXXI 31-
XXXIV 7) e gli Stoici (col. XXXV 22-24).

27 Parola poco usata (ricorre in Plut., *Rom.* 12; Polyb. XII
25⁹, 2.25ʰ, 3; Timo, fr. 12 Diels) e, in questo caso, non priva di
una sfumatura ironica (cf. Philippson, *RhM* 71 [1916] 458). Una
situazione analoga è rappresentata in *P. Herc.* 1005, col. V 7-10
Sbordone, in cui si parla di un avversario che ἐ[π]ιδεῖ|[κνυ]ται
δὲ τὴν κατοχὴν | [ἔχειν ἐν το]ῖς βυβλίοις τα| [ράττων (alla l. 7 s.
l'integrazione è del Crönert; la congettura della l. 9 è di A.
Angeli, che ringrazio).

28 Penso che questo sia il senso delle parole di Filodemo
in col. XLIV 34-40: ἔξεσ|τιν δὲ καὶ τῶν προενεχθη|σομένων εἰς τὴν
παραμυ|θίαν ἐνίοις χρήσασθαι (gli avversari) λό|γοις ἐπιλογιστι-
κοῖς (dei maestri) τοῦ προ|κειμένου χειρισμῶι διαλ|λάξαντας.

29 Sull'ἐπιλογισμός, tipica forma di ragionamento adottata
dagli Epicurei, molto si è scritto; accolgo la spiegazione del
Sedley (*CErc* 3 [1973] 27-34), in parte già del De Lacy ("Epicurean
ἐπιλογισμός," *AJP* 79 [1958] 179-83).

che non reggono, poiché nella discussione su ὀργή e θυμός non sono
stati da loro ben valutati i dati empirici.

La dottrina epicurea ammetteva (primo ἐπιλογισμός) che se il
sapiente si mostra grato a chi gli ha fatto del bene si adirerà con
chi gli arreca danno di proposito e viceversa--secondo altri, si
potrebbe parlare di istinto naturale all'ira e alla gratitudine per
opposti motivi (col. XLVI 18-40). Gli avversari deducono da questo
ragionamento che "se per natura tendiamo a mostrarci molto grati
verso coloro che ci hanno di propria volontà beneficato, per natura
siamo provocati anche ad adirarci intensamente verso chi ci ha
danneggiato per sua scelta" (col. XLVIII 5-12). La replica di
Filodemo comincia in una parte lacunosa, ma il senso generale è
chiaro: poiché il sapiente non tiene in gran conto né i beni né i
mali che gli possono derivare dall'esterno, conseguentemente né
proverà profondi sentimenti di gratitudine né sarà preso da grandi
moti d'ira (col. XLVIII 14-28). Con il secondo ἐπιλογισμός gli
Epicurei affermavano che come l'ubriachezza non si riscontra solo
negli stolti ma anche nei sapienti, così all'ira può andare soggetto chiunque (coll. XLVI 40-XLVII 16). Una lacuna nella parte
centrale della col. XLIX non ci permette di comprendere con assoluta sicurezza la risposta di Filodemo all'errata conclusione tratta
dagli avversari, ma è possibile intendere che costoro avessero de-
dotto dal fatto che il sapiente più facilmente può ubriacarsi[30] un
analogo comportamento di fronte all'ira, e il Gadareno abbia con-
testato questa interpretazione in modo energico,[31] asserendo che il
σοφός è soltanto più incline all'ira, ma non per questo è maggior-
mente preda di essa. Con il terzo ἐπιλογισμός si sostiene che
anche il sapiente si adira se ha ricevuto un danno, perché com-
prende di essere stato danneggiato, ma la sua è un'ira breve e
moderata (col. XLVII 16-39); questo non significa, come vogliono
gli avversari, che la semplice ὑπόληψις τοῦ βεβλάφθαι sia δραστικὸν
αἴτιον dell'adirarsi, ma solo che può condizionare l'ira, nel senso

---

30 Non ne conosciamo i motivi; forse erano esposti nelle
linee mancanti.

31 Coll. XLVIII 29-XLIX 22 (l'argomentazione degli avversari
è definita ἄθλιον).

che "neppure lo stolto, quando è colpito da un fulmine, è preso da
vani moti d'ira, ma (si adira) secondo le supposizioni antece-
denti."[32] Per dimostrare ciò Filodemo si serve di un esempio semplice, ma nello stesso tempo probante, con il quale conclude il suo
trattato (col. XLIX 29-L): "Come infatti senza imparare le lettere
non è possibile diventare sapienti, ma, se qualcuno imparò le lettere, non si concluderà che sia anche sapiente, così, adducendo che
l'ira segue alla supposizione di essere stato danneggiato, altrimenti è impossibile, neppure (si concluderà che) assolutamente si
adirerà chi abbia ricevuto l'impressione di un danno, a meno che
non si dimostri che la supposizione del danno sia anche causa ef-
ficiente dell'ira."

Da questo sguardo d'assieme risulta evidente l'interesse suscitato dallo scritto *Sull'ira*, che illustra, con argomentazioni
chiare e con vivacità di stile, l'opinione degli Epicurei su una
delle peggiori affezioni dell'anima.

Giovanni Indelli

---

32 Col. XLVII 16-21; attribuisco all'aggettivo προηγούμενος
valore logico, seguendo il Philippson (*RhM* 71 [1916] 458), non
cronologico, come spiegava il Wilke nella sua edizione (p. xxi).

P. HERC. 1676: CONTENUTI DI UN LIBRO DELL'OPERA FILODEMEA "SULLA POETICA"

Tra i non molti papiri ercolanesi che, pur se privi alla fine dell'indicazione del titolo e del nome dell'autore, vengono comunemente assegnati all'opera Περὶ ποιημάτων di Filodemo,[1] un posto di particolare rilievo occupa il *P. Herc.* 1676 e per le buone condizioni in cui ci sono pervenuti gli 11 frammenti e le 13 colonne superstiti e, soprattutto, per l'interesse che presenta la discussione ivi contenuta.[2]

Punto chiave intorno al quale ruota tutto il papiro è il rapporto intercorrente, in un'opera d'arte, tra forma e contenuto, problema fondamentale dell'estetica antica e che si trova al centro di tutte le polemiche che Filodemo, nel corso del V libro Περὶ ποιημάτων, svolge contro avversari delle più diverse tendenze filosofiche.

L'antagonista col quale si polemizza nel nostro caso è Eracleodoro, visto come rappresentante di quel gruppo di critici letterari che vanno sotto il nome di *kritikoi*[3] dei quali si fa menzione, solo fugacemente, anche in alcune colonne del V libro "Sulla

---

1 Cf. F. Sbordone, *RAAN* 31 (1956) 161-71.

2 **Edd.:** *Herculanensium Voluminum quae supersunt. Collectio Altera* (Neapoli 1876) XI, 147-66; T. Gomperz, "Philodem und die ästhetischen Schriften der Herculanischen Bibliothek," *SAWW* philos. hist.Cl. 123 (1890) 51-68; J. Heidmann, *Der Papyrus 1676 der herculanensischen Bibliothek. Philodemos über die Gedichte* (Bonn 1937) = *CErc* 1 (1971) 90-111; F. Sbordone, *Ricerche sui Papiri Ercolanesi* (Napoli 1976) II, 189-267 (= *Tr.C.* Nelle citazioni dei frammenti e delle colonne del papiro mi rifaccio a quest'ultima edizione).

3 Sulla dottrina di Eracleodoro e dei *kritikoi* cf. C. Jensen, *Philodemos über die Gedichte fünftes Buch* (Berlin 1923) (rist. 1973) 137 s., 147 ss.; M. Pohlenz, *NGG* 16 (1933) 77 ss. = *Kleine Schriften* (Hildesheim 1965) I, 124 ss.; H. Gomoll, *Philologus* 91 (1937) 373-84; F. Sbordone, *RAAN* 30 (1955) 25-51; idem, *RAAN* 32 (1957) 173-80; D. M. Schenkeveld, *Mnemosyne* 4 ser. 21 (1968) 176-215; F. Sbordone, *Contributo alla Poetica degli antichi* (Napoli² 1969) 76 ss.; idem, *CErc* 2 (1972) 47-58; idem, *Mus. Philol. Lond.* 2 (1977) 255-82. Dell'appartenenza di Eracleodoro ai *kritikoi* dubita Kroll (*RE* Suppl. 3 s.v. Herakleodoros) che lo ritiene un "Epikureer strengerer Richtung."

poetica."[4] Costoro, accentuando l'importanza della σύνθεσις τῶν
λέξεων[5] nonché dell'eufonia che si manifesta tramite essa ed asse-
gnando la valutazione di tale eufonia alla sola ἀκοή,[6] negavano che
il contenuto potesse giocare un ruolo nella κρίσις τῶν ποιημάτων;[7]
l'ἀγαθὸν ποιητικόν, pertanto, che essi identificavano con l'influenza che il poeta esercita sull'animo del lettore, cioè con la
psicagogia, finiva per essere realizzato unicamente dalla *synthesis*
(*Tr.C* XV 20 ss., XVIII 12 ss.).

Nell'àmbito di tale dottrina viene introdotta, nel nostro papiro, l'antitesi ἴδιον-κοινόν: ciò che è peculiare dell'opera
d'arte, la *synthesis* e l'eufonia da essa prodotta, è nettamente
distinto da ciò che è caratterizzante, i λόγου διανοήματα καὶ
λέξεις, vale a dire il materiale poetico (*Tr.C* XVII 1 ss.). A tal
uopo, assumendo come base comune la mìmesi,[8] ci si avvale dell'usuale confronto con le arti plastiche[9] e lo si articola in molteplici
esempi, diversi ma sfocianti in un'identica conclusione: come nelle
arti plastiche la ὕλη impiegata è indifferente mentre quel che conta è l'uso che di tale ὕλη fa il τεχνίτης, allo stesso modo nella
κρίσις τῶν ποιημάτων non sono determinanti i διανοήματα o le singole λέξεις bensì il modo in cui il poeta individualizza questo
materiale mercé la *synthesis*.[10]

---

4 Phld., *Po.V* XVIII 7 ss., XXIV 3 ss.

5 Sul diverso significato che la formula σύνθεσις τῶν λέξεων
(equivalente a σύνθεσις τῶν ὀνομάτων) ha in Filodemo rispetto a
σύνθεσις (o σύνθεσις λέξεως) cf. A. Ardizzoni, ΠΟΙΗΜΑ (Bari 1953)
80 ss. n. 5.

6 Cf. Phld., *Po.V* XX 21-XXI 11, XXIV 9-11.

7 Cf. in particolare *Tr.C* n 6 ss.

8 *Tr.C* e I 12 ss., i 6 ss., XV 4 ss., XVI 7 ss.

9 *Tr.C* a I 8 ss., e I 20 ss., l 1 ss., VII 3 ss., XIV-XVI.

10 L'opinione che nella poesia gli ὀνόματα, come i φάρμακα
per il pittore, siano qualcosa di comune mentre la particolarità
dell'opera d'arte risieda nella *synthesis*, ritorna in D.H., *de comp.*
21 (p. 95 Us.-R.). Cf. altresì Phld., *Po.V* XXI 11 ss. ove Aristone
istituisce un confronto tra l'arte dello scrivere e quella del di-
pingere sulla base della corrispondenza che vi è tra l'udire ed il
vedere.

Una siffatta concezione estetica la quale, bandito qualsiasi
criterio razionale, fa appello, per raggiungere le sue valutazioni,
solo all'irrazionale funzione dell'ἀκοή,[11] porta seco importanti
conseguenze che investono sia la scelta del materiale poetico--se
l'ἴδιον ποιητικόν si attua unicamente attraverso la *synthesis* non
sarà necessario che il poeta usi sempre materia nuova ma egli potrà
rilevare da altri διανοήματα e λέξεις--sia l'impiego delle tradi-
zionali *virtutes dicendi* che subiscono una completa svalutazione.[12]
Non ci stupisce, quindi, di trovare nel *P. Herc.* 1676 un riferimento alle lungaggini di alcune narrazioni di Euripide (*Tr.C* VI 23 ss.)
i cui prologhi sono citati, in alcuni trattati di retorica, in connessione con l'assenza di συντομία (Ps. Cornutus, *Rh.* 65, p. 365 H.)
né la duplice affermazione che la σαφήνεια è irrilevante per conseguire la psicagogia (*Tr.C* III 22 ss.) e che l'ἴδιον ποιητικόν può
realizzarsi anche se il poeta non ha impiegato διανοήματ' οἰκεῖα
καὶ λέξεις προσηκούσας (*Tr.C* XV 9 ss.). Nello stesso ordine di
idee rientra altresì il riferimento ai πράγματα οὐκ ἄγνωστα καὶ
λέξεις οὐκ ἀρεσταί delle arti matematiche (*Tr.C* XI 27-XII 5) che,
nei trattati retorici, troviamo citate in connessione con l'ἀσάφεια
(Ps. Cornutus, *Rh.* 81, p. 367 H.). La menzione di Protagora,
d'altra parte, e della sua opposizione alle arti tecniche,[13] che
accompagna tale riferimento, doveva servire ad Eracleodoro per in-
ferire un colpo basso agli epicurei il cui disprezzo per le diverse
scienze, in particolare per i platonici ed aristotelici studi mate-
matici, era fin troppo noto.[14]

---

11 Indicazioni di una simile posizione estetica si ritrovano
in Dionigi d'Alicarnasso che, in non pochi passi, definisce irrazionale il criterio dello stile (cf. soprattutto *de comp.* 23 [p.
119 Us.-R.] ove l'ἄλογον τῆς ἀκοῆς πάθος è chiamato a testimoniare
del pregio della *synthesis* di un passo isocrateo).

12 Cf. J. Stroux, *De Theophrasti virtutibus dicendi* (Lipsiae
1912) 43-54.

13 Cf. Plato, *Protag.* 318E; Ar., *Metaph.* B 997b 32 ss. (= 80A
5, B 7 D.-K.).

14 Su tale polemica che rientra nell'attacco generale che gli
epicurei sferravano ai metodi *a priori* di ragionamento cf. E. Bignone,
L'Aristotele perduto e la formazione filosofica di Epicuro (Firenze[2]
1973) I, 110 s., 134 s., 451 ss.; M. Isnardi Parente, *Techne. Momenti
del pensiero greco da Platone ad Epicuro* (Firenze 1966) 367 ss.;
idem, "A proposito di physis e techne in alcuni passi epicurei,"
La cultura 7 (1969) 71 ss.

Il punto di vista di Filodemo diverge totalmente da Eracleodoro e, pur se espresso in modo non sempre coerente e del tutto
chiaro, mira, di fronte all'eccessiva valutazione dell'elemento
formale fatta dall'avversario, ad affermare l'unità di pensiero e
forma.[15] Non che l'epicureo non creda nel valore della *synthesis*
ché anzi conviene spesso con l'avversario nel riconoscerne l'importanza (*Tr.C* XII 9 ss., m 5 ss.), nega che l'ἴδιον e l'ἀγαθὸν ποιητικόν debbano realizzarsi solo con essa e che, quindi, il poeta
possa esercitare la psicagogia senza l'intervento di διανοήματα e
λέξεις (*Tr.C* XVIII 12 ss.). A tal fine Filodemo si serve, come al
solito, delle argomentazioni dell'avversario per scardinarne le
tesi; l'espediente della metatesi, ad esempio, che Eracleodoro usa,
al pari di Dionigi d'Alicarnasso,[16] per mettere in luce il pregio
della *synthesis*, viene utilizzato per esaltare il valore del contenuto: la metatesi influisce sul significato del passo nel quale
viene impiegata, per non parlare del ῥυθμός, del μέτρον, della προ-
φορά che risentono, inevitabilmente, dello spostamento (*Tr.C* XIX 2
ss.). Eguale adattamento subisce il confronto tra poesia ed arti
plastiche:

> Come, infatti, un incisore di anelli la cui peculiarità
> consista non già nel produrre la simiglianza, il che
> sarebbe comune al pittore ed allo scultore, bensì
> nel realizzare mercé l'incisione nel ferro e nella pietra
> preziosa, si trova ad avere il suo pregio non in questo
> bensì nel produrre la simiglianza, cosa che è comune a
> tutti gli artisti, allo stesso modo anche dal poeta si
> richiede che egli voglia far consistere la sua peculiarità
> nella *synthesis* ma cerchi di realizzare il pregio in modo
> comune a tutti attraverso i concetti e le espressioni,
> cosa che, a suo dire, non arrecherebbe affatto né van-
> taggio né danno.[17]

---

15 Cf. Phld., *Po.V*, passim e, in particolare, X 32-XI 4,
XXVI 4-7.

16 Cf. D.H., *de comp.* 4 ss. (p. 15 ss. Us.-R.) e N. A. Green-
berg, *TAPA* 89 (1958) 262-70.

17 *Tr.C* XVI 7-23: ὡ[ς] γὰρ [δ]ακτυλιογλύ|φ[ο]ς ἴδιον ἔχων οὐ
τὸ ποι|εῖν ὅμο[ι]ον – κοινὸν γὰρ ἦν|καὶ πλ[ά]στου καὶ ζωγρ[ά]|φου –
[τὸ δ'] ἐν σιδήρω<ι> καὶ λι|θαρίωι διὰ τῆς ἐγ[γ]λυφῆς, |'τἀγ[αθὸ]ν
οὐκ ἐν τούτωι | κεί[με]νον, ἀλλ' ἐν τῶι ποι|εῖν ὁμ[ο]ιον, ὃ πάντων
κοι|νόν, ἔχει, παραπλησί|ως ἀξιοῦτα[ι] καὶ ὁ ποιητὴς | τὸ μὲ[ν ἴδι]ον
ἐν [τῆι συ]ν|θέσει β[ούλε]σθαι, τὸ δ' ἀγα|θὸν δι[αν]οία[ι καὶ]
λέ[ξει] κοι|νῶ[ς] θηρεύε̣ιν, ὃ φησιν οὗ|τος ἀπλῶς μηδὲ ἐν ὠφε|λεῖν
ἢ βλάπτειν.

Non c'è chi non veda la forzatura alla quale Filodemo ha co-
stretto il paragone giungendo, pur di convalidare la sua tesi, ad
ammettere sia il carattere κοινόν di διανοήματα e λέξεις che l'ec-
cellenza del processo mimetico.

Nel complesso, comunque, la posizione dell'epicureo appare
molto più aperta di quella dell'avversario in quanto, di fronte al
rigore di questi nell'accettare il risultato eufonico come unico
criterio reale per giudicare di poesia, egli proclama l'esigenza
che anche altri elementi vengano presi in considerazione, ἐκλογή
(*Tr.C* XII 19 ss.), συνήθεια (*Tr.C* IX 22 ss., XXII 1 ss.), caratteristiche dei singoli generi letterari (*Tr.C* XX 23-XXI 4), voce ed
abilità declamatoria dell'attore,[18] elementi tutti che, per il nostro, hanno non minore importanza né più scarsa efficacia della *synthesis*. Insomma né la *synthesis* può arrogarsi il diritto di determinare essa sola la κρίσις né l'eufonia deve considerarsi suo risultato esclusivo;[19] la διάνοια è, quindi, pienamente rivalutata nel
P. Herc. 1676 oltre che come momento fondamentale del processo della
conoscenza, come elemento primario, non separabile dalla λέξις,
dell'opera di poesia.[20]

Queste le linee generali del trattato contenuto nel *P. Herc.*
1676. Vorrei ora fermare l'attenzione su alcuni punti fondamentali:

(a) Eracleodoro è il principale avversario col quale polemizza
Filodemo. La presenza di altri antagonisti, come ad esempio Cratete, è secondaria e rispecchia l'opposizione Cratete-Eracleodoro
quale troviamo nel V libro "Sulla poetica" (XXI 27 ss.): come in
questo, nel trattare della dottrina del filosofo di Pergamo, occa-
sionale appare il richiamo ad Eracleodoro, così nel *P. Herc.* 1676,
nell'esporre le teorie estetiche di Eracleodoro, solo casualmente
si fa menzione di Cratete.

---

18 *Tr.C* XX 3-17. Sul significato che in questo passo assume
il vocabolo διάθεσις cf. Longin., *Rh.* p. 194 H. Sull'importanza
della φωνή dell'attore cf. Phld., *Po.IV* IX 12 ss. Sbordone (*Ricerche sui Papiri Ercolanesi* [Napoli 1969] I, 333).

19 Cf. *Tr.C* XVIII 7 ss. ove il πάθος è chiamato a testimoniare della mancata eufonia di un verso euripideo (fr. 330b Snell).

20 Sulla teoria linguistica di Epicuro cf., tra gli altri, P.
H. De Lacy, *AJP* 60 (1939) 85-92; A. A. Long, *BICS* 18 (1971) 114-33.

(b) Il problema del rapporto pensiero-espressione formale è l'argomento di tutto il papiro, anche di quei primi frammenti che, privi purtroppo della parte superiore, si ritenne contenessero un testo non molto coerente. Nell'àmbito di questo problema rientra il contrasto tra Cratete ed Eracleodoro, il primo citato con riferimento al suo metodo allegorico,[21] il secondo attaccato in quanto sostenitore dell'ἀσάφεια (*Tr.C* I 20 ss., III 22 ss.). I due λόγοι posti a confronto da Filodemo (*Tr.C* III 22 ss.) riflettono, attraverso l'opposizione σαφήνεια/ἀσάφεια--sostenuta la prima da Cratete la seconda da Eracleodoro--, la ben più profonda antitesi tra due posizioni estetiche che, partendo da punti di vista diversi, finiscono entrambe per umiliare il materiale poetico, la prima in quanto postula al di là del contenuto vero e proprio un significato allegorico che solo il poeta può cogliere, la seconda in quanto arresta il processo critico al giudizio formulato dall'ἀκοή.

(c) La maggior parte dei frammenti di *P. Herc.* 1074 + 1081 (tipo *b* Hausrath = tipo γ Crönert)[22] rientra nell'àmbito delle idee dei *kritikoi* e presenta corrispondenze e riferimenti al *P. Herc.* 1676. Anche quei passi nei quali la moralità o immoralità del contenuto è vista in funzione della buona o cattiva forma, passi sui quali Schenkeveld sembra avanzare delle riserve, sono, io credo, perfettamente in armonia coll'affermazione di Eracleodoro sull'irrilevanza del contenuto nella κρίσις τῶν ποιημάτων.[23] Tale discussione ritorna anche in un altro papiro ercolanese, il 444, nel quale non pochi elementi ci inducono a ritenere che proprio i *kritikoi* fossero oggetto di polemica,[24] per non parlare del *de compositione* di Dionigi d'Alicarnasso ove l'episodio erodoteo di Gige e Candaule è introdotto a testimoniare del pregio della *synthesis* nonostante il πρᾶγμα sia esplicitamente definito: οὐχ.......σεμνὸν

---

21 *Tr.C* II 18-III 14. Sul metodo allegorico di Cratete cf. H. J. Mette, *Sphairopoiia. Untersuchungen zur Kosmologie des Krates von Pergamon* (München 1936).

22 Sui rapporti tra *P. Herc.* 1074 + 1081 e 1676 cf. M. L. Nardelli, "Papiri 'della poetica' di Filodemo," *CErc* 9 (1979) 137 ss.

23 *Tr.C* f II 11-III 26. Cf. Schenkeveld, 196.

24 *P. Herc.* 444 Sbordone (*RAAN* 35 [1961] 99-110).

ἢ καλλιλογεῖσθαι ἐπιτήδειον, ἀλλὰ καὶ παιδικὸν καὶ ἐπικίνδυνον καὶ
τοῦ αἰσχροῦ μᾶλλον ἢ τοῦ καλοῦ ἐγγυτέρωι.[25]

(d) Il papiro richiama, in non pochi punti, l'*Ars* oraziana.
Già Gomperz aveva posto in relazione il passo filodemeo nel quale
si tratta dei proemi omerici (*Tr.C* V 22 ss.) con *Ars* 140, confronto
ripreso, in tempi più recenti, da Brink che, tuttavia, si dichiara
non molto sicuro dell'accostamento.[26] Né l'uno né l'altro studioso
han notato, però, come la discussione sui proemi sia strettamente
connessa, anche nel nostro papiro, con quella delle *virtutes dicendi* e cioè come essa, in Filodemo come in Orazio, apra la strada
alla tecnica narrativa.[27] L'unica differenza è rappresentata dal
fatto che, mentre in Orazio i proemi omerici vengono contrapposti
ai ciclici, in Filodemo la contrapposizione è fatta coi prologhi
euripidei. Ma l'esempio, anche se meno comune, non era sconosciuto,
si è visto, ai trattati retorici.

Ad Orazio ci riportano altresì due frammenti conservatici da
P. Herc. 1074 + 1081:

> Pur tuttavia, come riguardo a coloro che praticano le arti
> manuali non giudichiamo inferiore un artista in quanto,
> fatta sua la materia di un altro, ha saputo ben elaborarla,
> così neppure il poeta qualora, avendo assunto una trama
> grezza, vi applichi il proprio ingegno, lo riteniamo in-
> feriore e ci comportiamo in tal modo non solo riguardo
> ai piccoli componimenti ma neppure se, avendo tratto da
> un altro una trama di pubblico dominio concernente le
> vicende di Ilio o di Tebe, venga come a dissolverla e,
> avendola in qualche modo ricomposta, la rivesta della
> propria personale elaborazione.[28]

---

25 D.H., *de comp.* 3 (p. 12 Us.-R.). Diversa la posizione di
Filodemo il quale nega che il giudizio estetico possa influenzare
quello etico (cf. *Tr.C* h 13 ss. e soprattutto XI 17 ss. ove l'epicureo, pur riconoscendo e lodando l'abilità tecnica del cuoco, bia-
sima il suo comportamento immorale qualora questi giaccia con
l'etèra).

26 Gomperz, "Philodem," 53 s.; C. O. Brink, *Horace on Poetry*
(Cambridge 1971) II, 213.

27 W. Steidle, *Studien zur Ars Poetica des Horaz: Interpretation des auf Dichtkunst und Gedicht bezüglichen Hauptteils (1-294)*
(Würzburg 1939) 85; Brink II, 212 ss.

28 *Tr.C* e I 20-II 9: ἀλλ' ὅμως κα|θάπερ ἐπὶ τῶν κατὰ τὰς | χει-
ρουργίας οὐχ ἡγούμε|θα χείρω{ι} παρ' ὅσον ὑφέ{μ}|μενος ὕλην ἑτέρου
τε|χνείτου, καλῶς ἠργάσα|το, οὕτως οὐδὲ ποιητὴν ἐ|ὰν ἀπόητον ὑπόθε-
σιν λα|βὼν προσθῇ<ι> τὸν <ἴ>διον νο[ῦν], ‖ χείρω νομίζομεν, καὶ | οὐκ

...è necessario che vi sia una radicale differenza nell'àmbito della poetica. L'una, infatti (= una qualsiasi delle arti tecniche), non si deve creare la materia, mentre si ritiene che la poetica debba talvolta dar forma personale anche ad una trama generale e sia questa che quella tradizionale suddividere e, per ogni singola parte, inventare pensieri e parole....[29]

I due passi la cui corrispondenza con l'*Ars* (v. 131 il primo, v. 119 e 128 il secondo) pur se non precisa è indubbia,[30] consentono alcune riflessioni:

--κοινόν è usato da Filodemo con duplice significato, corrispondendo nel primo frammento al *publicum* (131) nel secondo al *commune* (128) oraziano;

--κοινὴν ὑπόθεσιν πλάττειν nel secondo passo conferma il rapporto esistente nell'*Ars* tra il v. 119 e il v. 128 e cioè che *communia* (128) esprime il contenuto di *finge* (119);[31]

--la contrapposizione κοινήν-δεδομένην, presente nel secondo frammento, prova che l'interpretazione del v. 128 dell'*Ars* data da Rostagni è sostanzialmente esatta: *communia* non indica gli argomenti di dominio pubblico ma quelli "non contrassegnati dalla tradizione e dalla storia," cioè quelli mai trattati prima;[32]

ἐπὶ τῶν μεικρῶν | μόνον οὕτως ἔχομεν, | ἀλλ᾽ οὐδ᾽ ἂν τὰ κατ᾽ Εἴλιον | [ἢ] Θήβας κοινῶς παρ᾽ ἐτέ|ρου λαβὼν ὥσπερ διαλύ|σηι, καί πως πάλι συντά|ξας ἰδίαν κατασκευὴν περιθῆ<ι>.

29 *Tr.C* VII 1-12: ε[ἶναι] | δ[εῖ] παραλλάττον ὅλως | ἐν ποιητικῆι. τὴν μὲν | γὰρ οὐθὲν δεῖ τῆς ὕλης | ἑαυτῆ<ι> γεννᾶν, τὴν δὲ ποη|τικὴν ἀξιοῦσι καὶ τὴν | κοινὴν ὑπόθεσιν ἔστιν | ὅτε πλάττειν αὐτῆ<ι>, καὶ | μερ[ί]ζειν ταύτην τε καὶ | τὴν δεδομένην, καὶ τὰ | κατὰ μέρος εὑρίσκειν δι|ανοήματα καὶ λέξεις....

30 Citato da Heinze nel suo commento ad *Ars* 130, il primo passo è stato ampiamente studiato da A. Rostagni (*AR* N.S. 1 [1920] 52 = *Scritti minori* [Torino 1955] I, 364 s.; *Arte poetica di Orazio* [Torino 1930] 40) e, da ultimo, da Brink che lo ha messo a confronto con *Ars* 129-31 (II 209 e 441 s.). Il secondo passo, pubblicato da Sbordone (*AAPN* N.S. 9 [1960] 245; *Ricerche* II, 233), è ignorato da Brink.

31 Cf. C. O. Brink, *Horace on Poetry* (Cambridge 1963) I, 107; II, 196 ss., 204.

32 Sulle possibili interpretazioni di questo assai tormentato verso cf., oltre la rassegna presente in Brink II, 432-40; E. Pasoli, *AAT* 106 (1972) 39-54; G. Grosso, *AAT* 106 (1972) 589-92.

--μερίζειν e κατὰ μέρος del secondo passo mostrano come la nuova triade retorica (*inventio-dispositio-elocutio*) sia stata applicata alle vecchie *partes orationis*;[33]

--i passi attestano come sia diverso per Filodemo rispetto ad Eracleodoro il concetto di materiale poetico: ai διανοήματα καὶ λέξεις dell'avversario egli sostituisce la semplice ὑπόθεσις. Su tale ὕλη, ancora ἀπόητος, opera il poeta, per Eracleodoro mercé la sola *elocutio*, per Filodemo attraverso *inventio, dispositio, elocutio*;[34]

--tutta la sezione centrale dell'*Ars* manca nel V libro "Sulla poetica" di Filodemo e solo ipoteticamente si fa risalire a Neottolemo.[35] Non so se sia troppo azzardato concludere che Orazio può averla trovata in questi preziosi frammenti relativi alla polemica contro Eracleodoro e i *kritikoi*.

Maria Luisa Nardelli

---

33 Cf. F. Solmsen, *AJP* 62 (1941) 35-50 e 169-90; Brink I, 81 ss.; II, 127 ss. L'espressione μέρη τῆς ὑποθέσεως (con la susseguente divisione in προοίμιον, διηγήσεις, πίστεις, ἐπίλογος) si ritrova in D.H., *Rh*. 12 e 19 (p. 367 e 374 Us.-R.).

34 Conservo, pertanto, ἀπόητον nel primo passo, a differenza di Brink (II, 441) che, sulla scia di Immisch, lo corregge, ritenendolo "nonsensical." L'aggettivo ritorna in numerosi passi (cf. *Tr.C* f I 12 ss., h 22 s., m 10 s., n 1 ss.).

35 Cf. Brink I, 100 ss.

SUONO ED ARTICOLAZIONE NELLA TEORIA EPICUREA DEL LINGUAGGIO

Lo studio dei problemi linguistici, sia da un punto di vista
genetico che da un punto di vista storico, ha in occidente un'antica tradizione che affonda le sue radici nella cultura greca; questa,
infatti, fin dai tempi più remoti si pose il problema del rapporto
intercorrente fra il pensiero e la sua veste sonora, e avviò conseguentemente l'indagine sulla natura della parola e sul suo valore
conoscitivo. L'importanza degli studi antichi sulle teorie del
linguaggio appare oggi sempre più evidente, ad opera soprattutto
delle ricerche svolte dai linguisti contemporanei. Tuttavia molto
rimane ancora da esplorare; tra gli aspetti più interessanti e non
sufficientemente indagati particolare rilievo riveste quello articolatorio, nei suoi risvolti fonologici e nelle sue implicazioni
epistemologiche. Abbastanza sviluppato negli studi di Platone, di
Aristotele e della Stoa, esso appariva estraneo alle riflessioni
del Giardino;[1] a colmare questa lacuna un contributo può venire da
alcuni luoghi filodemei, non considerati finora sotto questo
profilo: *TrA* VI[2] e *TrB* 23 II[3]:

TrA VI 1-VII 1:

...βαρβαριζόντων ἕτερος | [αὐ]τῶν, τοῦ μὲν ἡδέως | [ἡ]μᾶς

---

1 Cic., *Fin.*, I 7, 22, escludeva positivamente che Epicuro
si fosse interessato della questione, come d'altra parte escludeva
altri aspetti che sappiamo non estranei alla scuola epicurea.

2 *TrA* = P. *Herc.* 994, pubblicato integralmente per la prima
volta da F. Sbordone, *Ricerche sui papiri ercolanesi* II (Napoli 1976)
sotto il nome di *Tractatus A* (1-113). Al testo di questa edizione
mi attengo, anche per il *TrB*. La col. VI era già stata edita da F.
Buecheler, *RhM* 25 (1870) 623-24 (parzialmente); A. Hausrath, "Philodemi περὶ ποιημάτων libri secundi quae videntur fragmenta," *JCP*
Suppl. 17 (1889) 218-19; T. Gomperz, "Philodem und die ästhetischen
Schriften der Herculanischen Bibliothek," *SAWW*, philos. hist. cl.
123 (1890) 27-28; F. Sbordone, *PP* 44 (1955) 390-403.

3 *TrB* = P. *Herc.* 460+1073, pubblicato da Hausrath, è stato
ripubblicato da Sbordone, *Ricerche*, 115-87, sotto il nome di "*Tractatus* B," tenendo conto anche di alcuni disegni tralasciati da Hausrath. Sul nesso fra *TrA* VI e *TrB* 23 II, cfr. Hausrath, 218-19;
Gomperz, 27-28; Sbordone, *PP* 44 (1955) 401-02; idem, *Atti XI Congr.
Int. Pap.* (Milano 1966) 312-24, in particolare 320ss.; idem, *Mus.
Phil. Lond.* 2 (1977) 255-82, in particolare 272-73.

ἀκρύειγ, τοῦ δὲ τά|ναντ[ί]α, κἄν διὰ μηδὲν | ἕτερον ἤ διὰ
τὸ(ν) ἦχογ γεί|νηται καὶ ἐ[πὶ] τῆς ἀηδό|νος καὶ τῶν ἄ[λ]λων
ὀρ|νέων, πῶς ἀ[πο]δεικτι|κόν ἐστι τοῦ τὸν ἐκ τῆς | ἀρθρώσεως
ἦχον ἀπ[ο]|τελεῖν τινα χάριν, περιρ|[π]ᾶσθαι δ' ὑπ' [ἄ]λ[λ]ων
τι̣[νῶν; λέ|γει γ]ὰρ ἐπὶ [τ]ῶν βαρβαριζόν|[τ]ων ὑπ[ὸ] τοῦ διὰ
τὴν ἀρ|[θρ]ωσ[ιν ἦχ]ου τῇ[ν] ἡδο|[ν]ὴν ἔξω χεῖν, καὶ τὴν |
[ἀλ]λοτριότη[τ]α συμβαί|[ν]ειν. ἀλλ' [ἡ] ἀρθ[ρω]σις [τῆς |
ἀλ]λοτριότητ[ος α]ὑτῆ[ς]| οὐκ [ἐ]στιν [αἰ]τία, καὶ | συμφορὰν
[ἐ]δειμνύ|ομεν καὶ διὰ τὰς ἀρθρώ|[σ]εις λέγειγ παρακολου|-
θεῖγ, καὶ ταύτηι δυσχερ|[ἐ]ς εἶνα[ι] λαμβάν[ειν τι ἡδο]|νῶν,
οὐδ' εἶναι πρός (τι) | κακῶς.[4]

TrB 23 II 1-15:

... ἀρθρώ]σεως [δὲ ψεύ]|δετ' ἀναλ[όγως, λέγων] | ἕτερον δι'
[αὑτῆς εἶναι] | τὸν ἦχον, ᾧ[ς γίνεται] | ἐπὶ τῆς ἀη[δόνος καὶ
ἐ]|πὶ τῶν ἄλλων ὀρνέων. | οὕτω τοίνυν καὶ ἐπὶ | τῶν ἑλληνι-
ζόντων ὁ | μὲν ἦχος ἀποτελεῖ τὸ | ἴδιον κατὰ τὴν δ[ι]ά[λεκτον] |
--ἤ δεινὸν ἄν εἴη [τὰ ἴ]δι|α τὸν ἑλληνισμὸν ἀπο|στερεῖσθαι--
περισπᾶ|ται δ'ἴσως ὑπὸ ἄλλων | [τ]ινῶν....[5]

---

4 "...di chi parla commettendo *barbarismi* diverso (è il
suono), sicché l'uno lo ascoltiamo con piacere, l'altro provoca
effetto contrario; anche se ciò non avvenisse per nessun'altra
causa che per il suono, e nel caso dell'usignuolo e nel caso degli
altri uccelli, come potrebbe servire a dimostrare che il suono
proveniente da articolazione produca un qualche godimento, ma venga
deviato da altri elementi? Dice infatti che per coloro che parlano
commettendo *barbarismi*, ad effetto del suono che ha luogo mediante
articolazione, il piacere si dilegua e il disagio sopraggiunge.
Eppure l'articolazione non è causa del disagio stesso, e abbiamo
mostrato che (questo) è un caso accidentale, e che attraverso le
articolazioni ha luogo la parola, e pertanto è difficile ricavarne
qualche diletto, e non trovarsi male sotto qualche aspetto."

5 "Quanto all'articolazione, mente in maniera analoga, di-
cendo che per suo mezzo il suono diviene diverso, come avviene per
l'usignuolo e per gli altri uccelli. Così anche per coloro che
parlano greco correttamente il suono attua la propria specificità
secondo la lingua--sarebbe altrimenti strano che l'*ellenismo*
venisse privato della sua specificità--ma viene forse deviato da
altri elementi...." Ritengo che a 1.10, al δ[ι]ά[νοιαν] di
Hausrath-Sbordone, vada preferito δ[ι]ά[λεκτον]--suggerito indiret-
tamente dal Gomperz (p. 28)--sulla base di un confronto con Diog.
Bab., *SVF* III 213, 10ss.: διάλεκτος δὲ ἐστι λέξις κεχαραγμένη
ἐθνικῶς τε καὶ Ἑλληνικῶς...; cfr. *Schol. Lond. (AE) Dion. Thr.*,
GG, I III, 446, 12-17 Hilgard.

E' stato da tempo individuato un rapporto fra i due passi, ai
quali va aggiunto *TrB* 26 I-II, connesso ai primi due dal tema
ἦχος/ἄρθρωσις e dal discorso sulle capacità articolatorie degli
uccelli. Questi frammenti, riconducibili nell'àmbito più generale
della trattatistica *poetica*, ampiamente rappresentata nei papiri
ercolanesi, lasciano emergere stralci di una teoria secondo cui la
produttività linguistica, nel suo aspetto materiale, è riservata
alla sola articolazione, rimanendo separati l'àmbito del suono in
quanto tale e quello propriamente linguistico-epistemologico.[6]
Queste evidenze sono molto importanti per chiarire, attraverso
Filodemo, due questioni: (a) presenza nella teoria epicurea del
linguaggio di un aspetto assai poco investigato,[7] anzi pressocché
ignorato: l'aspetto tecnico-articolatorio; (b) valutazione della
parola, ma anche e soprattutto della musica, sotto il profilo del
suono che, nella sua materialità, si rapporta unicamente alla per-
cezione sensoriale, né può, pertanto, influenzare in alcun modo
l'animo umano. Di (b), in particolare per ciò che concerne la
musica, mi sono occupata ed intendo ancora occuparmi in altra sede;
(a) costituisce invece l'oggetto di questa comunicazione.

Come giustamente osservava Gomperz (loc. cit. [n. 2] 8), a
differenza di quanto avviene per la maggior parte dei testi teorici
trasmessici dalla tradizione antica, nei quali si parte dalla conoscenza dell'autore per illuminare l'opera, per i papiri ercolanesi
siamo per lo più costretti a risalire, dalla comprensione dei testi
e dal loro inquadramento nelle nostre ulteriori conoscenze

---

6 Sul valore epistemologico che il linguaggio riveste per
Epicuro cfr. A. Long, *BICS* 18 (1971) 114-33; D. Sedley, *CErc* 3
(1973) 5-87, in particolare, 13-23.

7 Sulla teoria linguistica di Epicuro nel suo complesso cfr.
Sedley e la letteratura ivi richiamata (n. 3). Ricordiamo che per
Epicuro il dare nomi alle cose, e quindi il parlare, era attività
connessa strutturalmente alla natura dell'uomo, e aveva origine
direttamente nelle sensazioni, senza mediazione--a questo livello--
del pensiero (cfr. frr. 334-335 Us); la diversità delle lingue era
motivata da differenziazioni fisiche connesse alle differenziazioni
etniche. All'opposto, per la Stoa non si dava linguaggio se non
ἀπὸ διανοίας. I suoni, che pure si organizzavano in catena sonora
nei bambini e in taluni animali, sia emessi ἐκ μιμήσεως sia ὑπὸ
ὁρμῆς, non potevano essere considerati altro che λέξις (*SVF*, I 40,
30; II 43, 18ss.; 44, 8ss.; 45, 12ss.; 24, 11ss.; III 213 passim).

filosofiche, all'attribuzione delle dottrine ivi contenute ai singoli filosofi o alle singole scuole. Dalla critica svolta in termini schiettamente epicurei in *TrA* VI[8] è possibile enucleare il
punto di vista di Filodemo e dell'avversario sulla tematica in
esame. L'avversario afferma che il pronunziare commettendo *barbarismi*[9] provoca un'alterazione dei suoni, la quale suscita una sensazione sgradevole all'udito (1-4); che quest'alterazione fonica avviene mediante l'articolazione, che è responsabile anche di sensa-
sioni piacevoli, e che di ciò sono dimostrazione gli usignuoli ed
altri uccelli, evidentemente ritenuti in grado di articolare la
voce e di produrre quindi una λέξις; che pertanto la causa effet-
tiva del mancato piacere o del senso di disagio avvertito dall'as-
coltatore è l'articolazione stessa (5-18). Le prime linee di
questo frammento, attraverso la contrapposizione τοῦ μὲν ἡδέως |
[ἡ]μᾶς ἀκούειν, τοῦ δὲ τἀ|ναντ[ί]α, istituiscono un'opposizione tra
il fastidio che deriverebbe dal suono emesso da chi nel parlare
commette *barbarismi*, ed il piacere che invece scaturirebbe dai
suoni di chi parla greco in maniera corretta.[10] A ciò Filodemo
obietta vigorosamente: non è possibile dimostrare che il suono

---

8 I dubbi sollevati da Hausrath, 213ss., circa la paternità
di *P. Herc*. 994 ed i rapporti intercorrenti tra questo e *P. Herc*.
460+1073, su cui problematicamente torna Ph. De Lacy, *AJP* 98 (1978)
203, mi sembra siano stati convincentemente chiariti da Gomperz,
1-8. La consuetudine con i testi filodemei, il loro linguaggio, lo
stile della polemica (cfr. ad es. i continui riscontri fra il primo
ed i successivi libri del trattato di Filodemo sulla musica) induce
alla persuasione che entrambi i papiri siano da attribuire all'epicureo: in uno egli espone le teorie di uno o più avversari, non
senza sporadiche osservazioni critiche, nell'altro procede ad una
analisi minuziosa dello stesso testo, sottoponendolo ad una critica
più serrata. Siffatta procedura rende complesso determinare a prima
vista il rapporto tra sezione espositiva e sezione dedicata al con-
traddittorio; questo rapporto però emerge da un esame più approfon-
dito, che tenga conto dei contenuti, del lessico e di quegli elementi di tecnica precedentemente accennati; così il famoso esempio
tratto dalla citazione sofoclea è introdotto in *TrA* V 5 da φησί,
ma il corrispondente luogo in *TrB* 23 II 15-III 2 è seguito da un
λέγει δ' ...; in entrambi i casi ci troviamo nell'àmbito di una
citazione fatta dallo stesso Filodemo.

9 Sul *barbarismo* inteso come cambiamento della composizione
sonora del corpo della parola cfr. H. Lausberg, *Handbuch der literarischen Rhetorik* (München 1973[2]) I, 59. Questioni di pronunzia
sono largamente trattate in *TrA* e *TrB*.

10 Su τὸ ἑλληνίζειν, ἑλληνισμός cfr. Lausberg, 249ss.

susciti sensazioni di disagio se alterato da *barbarismi* (12ss.), o provochi una sensazione acustica gradevole all'udito (2-3) se prodotto da ἑλληνίζοντες,[11] né che di per sé possa produrre un qualche godimento, ed essere successivamente deviato rispetto ai suoi effetti fisici dall'intervento di altri elementi.[12] L'epicureo muove quindi una critica di fondo: ammettendo pure che un linguaggio alterato da *barbarismi* produca sensazioni sgradevoli all'ascolto e che, al contrario, la lingua greca correttamente pronunziata susciti sensazioni di piacere, in che modo ciò potrebbe dimostrare che sia proprio il momento articolatorio a determinare sensazioni sgradevoli o senso di disagio, anche se la difformità delle sensazioni dipendesse dal suono, come si verifica per gli uccelli? L'ἄρθρωσις --afferma l'epicureo--ha infatti come specifico, positivo prodotto, il *parlare* (*TrA*, VI 22-24) e non può di per sé generare ἡδονή né ἀλλοτριότης.

Emerge qui il rapporto univoco che Filodemo pone fra articolazione e linguaggio; questo rapporto si rivela ortodosso rispetto all'insegnamento epicureo mediante il confronto con alcuni luoghi lucreziani; in essi l'articolazione del suono ad opera della lingua, presentandosi come una possibilità fisiologicamente connaturata alla sola natura umana, evidenzia una teoria linguistica che fa del momento articolatorio premessa necessaria, anche se non sufficiente, del linguaggio degli umani. In Lucrezio *vox* e *sonitus* appaiono infatti usati con valori distinti: mentre *vox* abbraccia uno spazio semantico che include tutte le emissioni sonore prodotte da esseri animati[13] (IV 527ss.), *sonitus* indica esclusivamente il suono articolato dalla lingua (V 1028-1044). Lucrezio ha inoltre avvertito

---

11 *TrB* 23 II 7-13; 26 I 7-10; in tal caso l' ἦχος riuscirebbe ad effettuare ciò che gli è proprio, l' ἑλληνισμός.

12 *TrA* VI 11-12; *TrB* 23 II 14-15; 26 I 6ss.; gli "altri elementi" sono identificati nel pensiero in numerosi frammenti di queste due serie, ad es.: *TrA* IV 19-20; V 1-4; XIV 22-24; XVII 15-16; *TrB* 23 I 16-18.

13 Per analogia vengono designati con questo termine anche i suoni emessi da strumenti musicali (IV 542ss.).

l'esigenza di coniare un neologismo, il verbo *articulo*[14] (che designa l'attività della *daedala lingua* finalizzata all'articolazione
della voce, IV 549) allo scopo di rendere il greco ἀρθρόω, che fa
parte del lessico tecnico-linguistico dell'antichità, ma che non
compariva nel passo dell'*epistola ad Erodoto* concernente le origini
del linguaggio--né avrebbe potuto comparirvi dato l'orientamento
storico, non tecnico, del passo stesso--e tanto meno nei passi
greci di tradizione epicurea ad esso direttamente collegati.[15]

Il λέγειν, che nella sua materialità fonetica si attua negli
ἦχοι, che scaturiscono dall'articolazione, è consentito poi, in
quanto operazione epistemologico-logica, dalla conoscenza dei si-
gnificati concettuali sottesi ai suoni (τὴν δ' ὑπο|[τετα]γμένην
ἔνγ[οιαν], *TrB* 26,1-2; [ὑ]ποτεταγμένον, *TrB* 26 I 13; τὰ ὑποτεταγ-
μένα τοῖς φθόγγοις, Ep., *Hdt.* 37; παντὶ οὖν ὀνόματι τὸ πρώτως ὑπο-
τεταγμένον, D.L. X 33,[16] significati che, essi soli, possono agire
sull'animo umano.

E' possibile identificare la scuola di cui è portavoce il
filosofo che Filodemo critica contrapponendo l'ἄρθρωσις come momento tecnico-fonatorio che consente il λέγειν all'ἄρθρωσις, concepita
come produttrice di suoni piacevoli o spiacevoli? Il tema della
capacità articolatoria degli uccelli riappare in *TrB* 26 I-II, dove
fra due battute filodemee è incastonato un frammento da tempo riconosciuto come stoico.[17] Filodemo lo riporta, e dalla mancanza

---

14 Cfr. C. Bailey, *T. Lucretii Cari, De rerum natura* (Oxford
1972) II, 1248; cfr. inoltre Cic., *Nat. deor.*, II, 59, 149, *in ore
sita lingua est...ea vocem immoderate profusam fingit et terminat
atque sonos vocis distinctos et pressos efficit* dove *sonus vocis
distinctos et pressos* designa il suono articolato ed è equivalente
al *sonitus* lucreziano.

15 Ep., *Hdt.* 76; Dem. Lac., *P. Herc.* 1012 XLV 9-12 in V. De
Falco, *L'epicureo Demetrio Lacone* (Napoli 1923) 48-49 (su questo
passo cfr. Sedley, 18 n. 89); D. Oen., 10 II-IV.

16 Cfr. inoltre Ep., *Nat.*, XXVIII 6 I 11; 10 Ib; 13 VII 4
Sedley; Philod., *Rh.*, II 190, 6 Sudhaus; *Oec.*, XII 14 Jensen.

17 Qui viene riportata la teoria del filosofo cui Filodemo si
oppone, come dimostra una battuta in prima persona, e perciò filodemea, che tiene dietro immediatamente alle linee in cui questa
teoria articolatoria è esposta e che, attraverso una preterizione
(τὴν δ' ὑπο[τετα]|γμένην ἔνγ[οιαν ἅ]|φῶμεν νῦν), introduce la criti-
ca dell'epicureo, purtroppo mutila nella parte che per noi sarebbe
stata la più interessante.

di tono polemico nel modo della citazione, sembra non negare, in
questa sede, la possibilità che alcuni uccelli, come l'usignuolo,
emettano qualcosa di simile ad un'ἔναρθρος φωνή. Purtroppo la
parte conclusiva del ragionamento di Filodemo, in cui la critica
veniva svolta compiutamente, è caduta; ma è evidente che l'epicureo
non poteva accettare lo sdoppiamento stoico fra λέξις e λόγος, in
base al quale λέξις poteva designare una catena di suoni non si-
gnificanti, ma anche la vera e propria parola, presa nel suo aspetto
fonatorio, nella sola veste esteriore, scissa dal significato: alla
luce delle ultime linee di *TrA* VI egli doveva affermare che, anche
se i suoni emessi da un uccello possono in qualche caso assomiglia-
re a suoni emessi dagli umani, di articolazione vera e propria è
impossibile parlare, essendo questa univocamente collegata al
λέγειν, che è dote dell'uomo.

TrB 26 I 19-II 1: ὅτι δ' ἀρχεγὸν ἡ φωνή | καὶ ἐκ τῶν ὀρνέων
ἐσ|τὶν ἰδεῖν, καὶ γὰρ ἐπ' ἐ|κείνων χωρὶς τοῦ ἐκ|πίπτοντος ἤχου
ἀπο|τελεῖταί τις καὶ ἔναρ|θρος φωνή, καθάπερ | καὶ ἐπὶ τῆ[ς ἀηδόν]ος |
φέρεται.[18] Queste poche righe, che si inseriscono appieno nella
tradizione stoica, suggeriscono l'appartenenza a questa scuola[19]
del filosofo a cui Filodemo è debitore dell'asserzione.

Tale asserto si muove in un àmbito teorico analogo a quello
profilatosi in *TrA* VI e *TrB* 23 II, in piena coerenza con quanto
traspare da tutti i luoghi dei papiri ercolanesi riguardanti problemi *poetici* ed attribuibili agli stoici: valorizzazione assoluta

---

18   "Che la voce sia il punto di partenza è possibile consta-
tarlo anche dagli uccelli, ed infatti nel loro caso, oltre l'emis-
sione del suono, si realizza anche qualcosa di analogo ad una voce
articolata, come si produce per l'usignuolo."

19   Su questo punto della dottrina linguistica stoica cfr. M.
Pohlenz, *NGG* Fachgruppe I.N.F. III 6 (1939) 151-98, in particolare
l'*Anhang*, 191-98 ora in M. Pohlenz, *Kleine Schriften* (Hildesheim
1965) I, 39-86; idem, *La Stoa*, tr. it. (Firenze 1967) I, 61-65; J.
Stroux in *Antidoron, Festschrift Wackernagel* (Göttingen 1923) 309-
25, in particolare 309-13; H. Dahlmann, *Varro und die hellenistische
Sprachtheorie* (Berlin 1932) 41; L. Melazzo, *Lingua e Stile* 5
(1975) 199-230.   Del fatto che il filosofo criticato da Filodemo
appartenesse alla Stoa era già convinto Jensen (apud Stroux 312 n.
3), il quale aveva pensato a Cratete.   Più che a Cratete pensa invece ad un crateteo (Andromenide), Sbordone, "Eufonia," 282.

del suono e della sua capacità psicagogica, e quindi tendenza a
considerare le composizioni poetiche preminentemente dal punto di
vista della λέξις, senza tener conto, in sede di esame *poetico*,
degli aspetti contenutistici; posizione a cui sempre Filodemo oppone il primato del pensiero, del contenuto concettuale.[20] La risposta di Filodemo alla sopravvalutazione del momento articolatorio
ai fini della produzione di un suono piacevole, e quindi di una
sensazione di piacere, è ricavabile ancora una volta da quanto
Filodemo stesso afferma già alla fine di *TrA* VI: l'articolazione è
matrice del parlare, e unicamente sotto questo profilo va considerata.

L'appartenenza dell'avversario alla scuola stoica è inoltre
confermata dal fatto che il materiale che egli utilizza nella discussione non è originale: proviene da un'antica disputa fra academici e stoici, apertasi nel 2° secolo a.c. sull'individuazione di
parametri differenziali tra uomo e animale, alla luce di una ri-
lettura in termini continuistici dell'universo (specularità
macrocosmo-microcosmo, messa in crisi da Aristotele ma ripristinata
da Teofrasto): momento non secondario della polemica fu infatti la
possibilità che gli animali, a guisa degli umani, articolassero il
linguaggio,[21] possibilità accettata in toto dall'Academia, parzialmente dalla Stoa che, dei due λόγοι individuati--il λόγος προφορι-
κός e il λόγος ένδιάθετος--attribuiva agli animali, e in modo particolare ad alcuni tipi di uccelli, solo il primo. Temi di questa
discussione furono gli uccelli, la loro capacità articolatoria,

---

20 Polemica sulla λέξις considerata come φωνὴ ἔναρθρος è già
in Dem. Lac., *P. Herc.* 1014, XXXVI, C. Romeo, *CErc* 8 (1978) 104-23,
in particolare 117; notiamo inoltre che in XIV 8-9, compare un'interessante τ[ὴ]ν βαρβάρα[ν γλῶτ]τ[αν].

21 G. Tappe, *De Philonis libro qui inscribitur* 'Αλέξανδρος ἢ
περὶ τοῦ λόγον ἔχειν τὰ ἄλογα ζῷα *quaestiones selectae* (Göttingen
1912) 25ss., 54ss., sulla base di un confronto tra Porph., *Abst.*
III 2,1-18,2, S.E., *Hyp. Pyrr.* I 62-77 e l''Αλέξανδρος attraverso
la versione armena congetturò l'esistenza di un testo academico del
II secolo a.c., nato nell'àmbito della polemica apertasi fra Academia e Stoa sulla differenze/identità fra gli uomini e gli altri esseri animati. Esso costituirebbe la fonte dei tre luoghi citati e
di numerosi altri dallo stesso Tappe individuati. Cfr. Pohlenz,
Kleine Schriften, 81; idem, *Stoa*, 61; J. Bouffartigue-M. Patillon,
in Porph., *Abst.* (Paris 1975) 138-42, 231-36.

l'argomentazione che la loro lingua, pur essendo articolata, poteva
presentarsi a chi non fosse in grado di comprenderla, alla stregua
di quella dei barbari, ἄναρθρος e ἀγράμματος (Porph., *Abst.* III 3,
4), μονοειδής (S.E., *Hyp. Pyrrh.* I 74), e la contrapposizione fra
βάρβαροι/"Ελληνες e le loro lingue, elementi che ritroviamo tutti--
seppur trasposti dal terreno della comunicazione a quello della
fonazione--nella discussione di cui ci tramandano il ricordo questi
frammenti ercolanesi. Nasce allora il suggestivo sospetto di trovarsi qui di fronte ad una singolare operazione: il trasferimento
di materiale proveniente da un dibattito filosofico-ontologico--che
per altro ebbe una sua vita autonoma durante l'arco di alcuni
secoli--su un terreno critico letterario, dove esso finì per essere
considerato soltanto nelle sue implicazioni fonetiche.

                                        Gioia Maria Rispoli

SOFRONE NEI PAPIRI ERCOLANESI (P. HERC. 1081 E 1014)

Mancava una raccolta complessiva dei testi ercolanesi che
trattano di Sofrone; alcuni passi di Filodemo hanno ricevuto le
cure di studiosi come il Gomperz, l'Hausrath, il Radermacher, il
Sudhaus; due luoghi di Demetrio Lacone hanno suscitato l'attenzione
del Kaibel, ma nessuno ha sinora considerato in un'analisi organica
e globale le testimonianze di Demetrio Lacone e Filodemo su Sofrone
né ha indagato sul motivo dell'interesse destato negli epicurei dal
mimografo siciliano. Di qui la necessità di riconsiderare questi
passi sulla base di una nuova autopsia degli originali e delle più
recenti acquisizioni sia dell'estetica epicurea sia degli studi
sofronei.

I due Epicurei si occupano del mimografo unicamente nelle loro
opere *Sulla poesia*, il nome di Sofrone infatti ricorre tre volte
nei papiri ercolanesi: due volte nei frammenti 53 e 72 del *P. Herc.*
1081, che presumibilmente conteneva il secondo libro della *Poetica*
di Filodemo,[1] e una volta alla col. LX del *P. Herc.* 1014, che contiene il secondo libro dell'opera *Sulla poesia* di Demetrio Lacone;[2]
ma c'è anche un altro passo di Demetrio, che deve essere sicuramente riferito a Sofrone anche se il nome non compare. Filodemo e
Demetrio citano Sofrone per due motivi diversi: Filodemo quando
tratta il problema se i mimi e altri componimenti affini, non
ostante la forma, possano essere considerati buona poesia, Demetrio
invece utilizza Sofrone per illustrare la figura dell'*onomatopea*.

I due luoghi di Filodemo, che sopravvivono nelle sole trascri-
zioni napoletane,[3] sia per le numerose lacune sia per il consueto

---

1 A. Hausrath, "Philodemi περὶ ποιημάτων libri secundi quae
videntur fragmenta," *JCPh* Suppl. 17 (1889) 213-76.

2 *Poem.* II (*P. Herc.* 1014) col. LX in C. Romeo, "Nuove letture
nei libri Sulla poesia di Demetrio Lacone," *CErc* 8 (1978) 121.

3 Del *P. Herc.* 1081 rimane soltanto la scorza, restaurata nel
1965 da A. Fackelmann, e 45 disegni eseguiti da F. Casanova nel 1835,
per cui cf. *Catalogo dei Papiri Ercolanesi*, sotto la direzione di M.
Gigante (Napoli 1979) 260 s. Trattandosi di un papiro "scorzato,"
la successione dei frammenti va probabilmente invertita (prima fr.
29 *N* e poi 27 *N*); ciò sembra confermato anche dal contenuto dei passi.

impeto polemico dell'autore, indussero gli studiosi a interpretazioni contrastanti:[4]

P. Herc. 1081 fr. 29 *N* (= 72 Hausrath, *VH*[2] VII 106)

ὁμογλώττω[ν καὶ....] | ζων καὶ αὐτὸς εἶν[αι ἐ]|κεῖνα ποήματα ἔ[φη
καὶ] | μὴ μόνα· καὶ γὰρ [τὰ τοῦ] |⁵ Σώφρονος καὶ τὰ [τῶν] ἄλλων
μιμογρ[άφων] | εἴποτε ποήμα[τα λέ]|γεται· καὶ μηγ[......] | οἱ
συντιθέν[τες τὰ τῶν] |¹⁰ μίμων ποη[ται...

   Ante 1.1 καταγελάστως δὲ καὶ Σώφρονι, οἶμαι Sudhaus; καίτοι
   λέξεων ὄντων Schaechter   1 ([λέξεων]) | ὁμογλώττων [τε καὶ
   πε] | ζῶν Radermacher, Schaechter   1 sq. [καὶ νομί] | ζων
   Hausrath; ὁμογλωττῶν [καὶ σικελί] | ζων Sudhaus   2 sqq.
   suppl. Hausrath; εἰ ν[ὴ Δι' ἐ] | κεῖνα Gomperz   3 ε[ἶπε καὶ]
   Sudhaus   4 [εἰ τὰ] Sudhaus   5 [τῶν] Gomperz: [πολλῶν]
   Hausrath, Schaechter   6 μιμογρ[άφων· καὶ] Sudhaus
   7 suppl. Gomperz; ποήμα[τα ὀρθῶς λέ] | γεται Hausrath: ποήματα
   ταῦ[τα λέ] | γεται Sudhaus; ἁ] | εἰ ποτε ποήμα[τ' ἐπιλέ] | γεται
   Schaechter   8 μὴ [μόνοι] Gomperz: μὴ μ[όνα, καί] Sudhaus:
   μὴ[ν εἴπερ] Schaechter   8 sqq. λέγ] | οι συντιθέν[αι λέξεις
   καὶ] | μίμων ποη[τάς dubitanter Hausrath   9 suppl. Gomperz;
   παίγνια] Radermacher, Schaechter   10 ποη[ται δικαίως ἂν
   λέγοιντο καὶ ἄλλοι πολλοί] Sudhaus; ποη[ται νομίζον | ται
   Schaechter; ποή[ματα Gomperz

P. Herc. 1081 fr. 27 *N* (= 53 Hausrath, *VH*[2] VII 104)

[....]ονεν δε[..]ιτα[...] | καὶ κατὰ τοῦτο δηπο[..|...... το]ιαῦτα
τέρπε[ιν | τε καὶ] ποήματ' εἶναι· καὶ |⁵ [τὰ] κρούματα γὰρ οὐ|[κ
ἁ]ν φθάνοιεν οὕτω | ποήματα λέγοντες· ὑ|πὲρ γὰρ τοῦ διὰ μηδὲν |
ἕτερον ἡδὺ πόημα τὸ |¹⁰ [το]ῦ Σώφρονος [εἰ]ρηκέ|[ναι...

---

    4 R. Schächter, "De finibus poeseos et pedestris locutionis
quae videntur opiniones," *Eos* 27 (1924) 13-18, in polemica col Gomperz, "Philodem und die ästhetischen Schriften der Herculanischen
Bibliothek," *SAWW* philos.-hist. Cl. 123 (1890) 77 ritenne che Filodemo volesse difendere il valore poetico dei mimi di Sofrone e di
altri componimenti che, privi, come i mimi sofronei, dell'elemento
metrico, potevano tuttavia essere considerati poesia in quanto
imitazione della realtà.

Ante l.l [τὸ δὲ καλῶς με|μιμημένον εἶναι τὸ πο|ητικ]ὸν
ἐνδέ[χο]ιτ' ἄ[ν τις] Schaechter   1 sq. ἀνάλογ]ον ἐνδέ[χο]ιτ'
ἄ[ν εἶ]ναι Radermacher   2 sq. καὶ κατὰ τοῦτο δῆπο[υθεν τὰ
το]ιαῦτα rest. Usener (apud Hausrath); δῆπο[υθεν οὐχὶ
τ]αὐτὰ Gomperz: δὴ πο[ητι|κὸν τὰ το]ιαῦτα Schaechter
4 τε καὶ] Usener, Gomperz, Hausrath: [ἀλλὰ] Radermacher:
καὶ] Schaechter   4 sq. κα|[τὰ τὰ] Hausrath: καὶ | [κατὰ τὰ]
Schaechter   9 ποηματος N, corr. Hausrath   10 sqq.
[εἰ]ρηκέν|[αι ἢ διὰ τὸ καλῶς μιμεῖ|σθαι πολλὰ ἤδη γέγραπται
Schaechter.

Il Sudhaus, a mio giudizio, avviò alla corretta intelligenza
dei passi:[5] Filodemo, connazionale e contemporaneo di Publilio
Siro, critica l'inclusione da parte dell'avversario, identificato
da alcuni in Eracleodoro,[6] dei mimi di Sofrone nel novero dei
ποιήματα, obbiettando che in base allo stesso criterio dovrebbero
essere considerati poesia anche gli scritti degli altri mimografi e
dovrebbero essere definiti poeti anche οἱ συντιθέν[τες τὰ τῶν]
μίμων cioè coloro che compongono pezzi per l'uso quotidiano del
mimo. Nella distinzione filodemea tra μιμογράφοι e οἱ συντιθέν[τες
τὰ τῶν] μίμων si intravedono due diverse categorie, che al tempo di
Filodemo, in Roma, potevano essere rappresentate da Laberio, puro
scrittore di mimi, e Publilio Siro, autore di semplici canovacci
mimici, che prendevano corpo proprio nella rappresentazione scenica.[7]
   Il motivo per cui l'avversario considerava poesia il mimo sofroneo, a mio parere, è ravvisabile nei *cola* poetici, nelle

---

5 S. Sudhaus, "Der Mimus von Oxyrhynchos," *Hermes* 41 (1906)
275 s. L'interpretazione del Sudhaus è seguita da A. Olivieri,
*Frammenti della Commedia Greca e del mimo nella Sicilia e nella
Magna Grecia* (Napoli 1947) II², 62 s. e da F. Giancotti, *Mimo e
gnome. Studio su Decimo Laberio e Publilio Siro* (Firenze 1967) 37 s.

6 La supposizione del Sudhaus, "Der Mimus," 275 che Eracleodoro fosse siciliano non convinse C. Jensen, *Philodemos über die Gedichte Fünftes Buch* (Berlin 1923) 148 n. 2. Lo Sbordone, "Filodemo
e la teorica dell'eufonia," *RAAN* 30 (1955) 47 n. 1 non esclude che
potesse essere milesio.

7 Cf. Giancotti, *Mimo e gnome*, 38 n. 19, il quale confronta
οἱ συντιθέν[τες di Filodemo con la frase di Macrobio, *Sat.* II 7, 7
cum mimos componeret.

antitesi, negli omeoteleuti, negli omeoptoti, nelle anafore, nelle
assonanze, di cui danno notizia le fonti antiche e che si riscon-
trano nei pochi frammenti superstiti di Sofrone.[8] Tutti questi
mezzi espressivi, senza dubbio, contribuivano a rendere piacevoli i
componimenti anche all'udito. Ma il fatto che i mimi dilettino e
siano piacevoli non sembra sufficiente a Filodemo perché siano
considerati poesia; procedendo in questo modo gli avversari non
esiterebbero a dire poesia le semplici note.[9]

Anche in questo caso il procedimento del Gadareno è quello
consueto: egli esaspera, polemizzando, le affermazioni degli avversari, fino a giungere all'assurdo, proprio per dimostrarne la fu-
tilità. La conclusione cui perviene Filodemo, cioè che il mimo,
anche quello sofroneo, non può essere considerato poesia, è in contrasto con la posizione di Aristotele, il quale, nella *Poetica* I
1447 b e nel dialogo *Sui poeti* fr. 3 Ross, aveva ritenuto che i
mimi di Sofrone e di suo figlio Senarco e i dialoghi socratici di
Alessameno di Teo, pur scritti in prosa e non in versi, devono tuttavia essere considerati arte, in quanto attuano la μίμησις.[10]

La mia interpretazione del pensiero filodemeo riguardo al mimo,
che diverge dalla Schächter, è confermata da un passo del più famoso V libro della *Poetica*, col. IX 10-24 Jensen:[11]

τῶν το[ί]νυν παρὰ τῶι Φι|λομήλ[ωι] γεγραμμέ|νων οἱ μὲν
οἰόμενοι | τὸν ἐν τοῖς μύθοις καὶ | ταῖς ἄλλαις ἠθοποιίαις |[15]
κἄν τῆι λέξει παραπλη|σίως ὁμαλ[ίζο]ντα ποη|τὴν ἄριστον
εἶναι λέ|[γου]σι μὲν ἴσ[ω]ς ἀληθές | τι, τὸν δὲ ποιητὴν τὸν

---

8 Demetr., *De eloc.* 128 accenna alla grazia dei mimi sofronei e lo scoliasta al λόγος πρὸς παρθένον παραινετικός di Gregorio
Nazianzeno si riferisce espressamente a κῶλα e ritmi poetici presenti nei componimenti di Sofrone. Isocola e omeoteleuti sono rav-
visabili, per esempio, nei frr. 6, 24, 30 Kaibel.

9 Diversamente intese la Schächter, "De finibus poeseos," 15.

10 La Schachter, ibid., che completò il pensiero filodemeo:
διὰ μηδὲν | ἕτερον ἡδὺ πόημα τὸ | [το]ῦ Σώφρονος [εἰ]ρηκέν ||αι ἢ διὰ τὸ
καλῶς μιμεῖ|σθαι ritenne che Filodemo concordasse con Aristotele.

11 L'ispezione dell'originale, che conferma le congetture di
Jensen, permette di scrivere a 1.16 ὁμαλ[ίζο]ντα con maggiore certezza e di togliere le parentesi a ἐκθεῖτο di 1.23 s.

ἀ|²⁰γαϑὸν οὐ διορίζουσι· καὶ | γὰρ μιμογράφου καὶ ἀρε|ταλό-
γου [ἢ ἄλλ]ου συγγρα|φέως ἀρετὴν ἄν τις ἐκ|ϑεῖτο ταύτην·

Sottolineando la distinzione tra "colui che compone bene" e il
"buon poeta" Filodemo, in polemica con i seguaci di Filomelo, afferma che i racconti (μῦϑοι), le descrizioni di caratteri (ἠϑοποι-
ίαι) e l'espressione (λέξις) non fanno ancora il buon poeta, perché
sono comuni anche al mimografo e agli altri scrittori. Il mimo
dunque non è poesia. Le riserve filodemee nei confronti del mimo
trovano riscontro, a mio parere, anche in Cicerone (ad fam. XII 18,
2) e in Orazio (Sat. I 10,5 s.).¹²

Demetrio Lacone non si pronuncia sulla questione se i mimi
sofronei potessero essere considerati poesia, o comunque non ne
rimane traccia nella parte superstite dell'opera Sulla poesia,
nella quale invece accenna all'uso dell'onomatopea da parte di Sofrone. Dopo aver illustrato altre figure poetiche, come la cata-
cresi e l'allegoria, il Lacone si soffermava anche sull'onomatopea,
di cui probabilmente dava prima una definizione, ora non più leggibile, e poi osservava:¹³

.αυιν· τα[δο|κ]ιμάζειν ωουσ⸱· κα[ὶ τὴν] | ἀλήϑηαν τ[ο]ῦ
λεχϑέ[ντος] | ὑφ' ἡμῶν ῥάδιόν ἐστ[ιν] |⁵ συνιδεῖν ἐπι[βάλλον]|-
τας τοῖς προεκκειμέ[νοις] | ὑπὸ τῆς εἰσαγομένη[ς] | γυναικός·
Κοικόαν μὲν | γὰρ ὠνοματοπόησεν |¹⁰ [τὴ]ν ϑούλην ξενίζ[ου|σαν]
κτλ.

Manca il soggetto del verbo ὠνοματοπόησεν, ma è evidente che deve
essere Sofrone, perché il nome Κοικόα compare in altri frammenti
(frr. 15-18 Kaibel) di un mimo sofroneo intitolato dal Wilamowitz
Ταὶ Συναριστῶσαι. In questo mimo era riprodotta la situazione,
divenuta poi frequente nella Commedia Nuova,¹⁴ nei mimiambi di

---

12 Manifestazioni di disistima nei confronti del mimo non
sono limitate a quelle di Cicerone e Orazio; si veda anche Quintil.
I 10,17 che dalla generica condanna salva solo Sofrone, per l'ammi-
razione che Platone nutrì nei suoi confronti, di cui dà notizia
anche Diog. Laert. III 18.

13 Cf. Poem. II col. LI, 120 Romeo.

14 Per la moderna interpretazione del mosaico di Dioscuride
di Samo, rinvenuto nella "Casa di Cicerone" a Pompei, che rappresenta l'inizio delle Synaristosae di Menandro cf. M. Gigante, Civiltà delle forme letterarie nell'antica Pompei (Napoli 1979) 139.

Eroda[15] e negli idilli mimici di Teocrito, della padrona, che fa
colazione con amiche, alle prese con la serva Κοικόα, che nel fr.
16 Kaibel viene chiamata disgraziata (τάλαινα Κοικόα), grulla e
scimunita, lenta ad eseguire gli ordini che le vengono impartiti.
Demetrio Lacone, che certo poteva ancora leggere integralmente
il mimo sofroneo, osserva che la donna si manifestava nel suo modo
di essere già dalla prima comparsa in scena e che il nome coniato
per lei da Sofrone è onomatopeico e adatto all'ottusità della mente
e alla condizione di serva straniera. Pape e Benseler si erano
orientati verso una interpretazione onomatopeica del nome Κοικόα,
ritenendolo derivato da κοᾶ, che Esichio spiega come ἀκούει, πεύθε-
ται; e cosí pure l'Hauler,[16] che lo considerò derivato da κοᾶξ, il
verso onomatopeico delle rane (Ar., *Ra* 209) e il Führ[17] da κοΐζειν,
il grugnito del porco. Il nostro Demetrio Lacone garantisce del
valore onomatopeico del nome Κοικόα, che Sofrone inventò per designare la stupidità della serva e la sua incapacità, in quanto
straniera, di parlare in maniera comprensibile o, comunque, per
richiamare l'attenzione sullo strano accento di lei, che sembrava
riprodurre il grugnito (κοΐ κοΐ) del maiale (Ar., *Ach.* 746.780).
    Non bisogna dimenticare, infatti, che i Greci avvertivano par-
ticolare molestia nell'udire la lingua dei barbari.[18] Il contegno
grossolano degli schiavi stranieri, in particolare degli Sciti, la
loro cattiva pronuncia greca, mancante di aspirazioni e spesso ten-
dente a deformare addirittura le parole,[19] e la loro stupidaggine
in genere davano luogo alla derisione,(Ar., *Lys.* 424 ss.), e offri-
rono anche ad Aristofane facile materia ai suoi scherzi.[20]

---

15   Cf. A. D. Knox e W. Headlam, *Herondas. The Mimes and
Fragments* (Cambridge 1922) LVI n. 2.

16   "Über Sophron, Theocrit und Herondas" in *Verhandlungen der
zweiundvierzigsten Versammlung deutscher Philologen und Schulmanner
in Wien* (1893) 257.

17   Cf. Olivieri, *Frammenti della Commedia Greca*, 89.

18   Philod., *Poem.* I col. VI in F. Sbordone, *Ricerche sui
Papiri Ercolanesi* (Napoli 1976) II, 49.

19   Ar., *Thesm.* 1001 ss., 1082 ss., 1176 ss.

20   Cf. V. Ehrenberg, *The People of Aristophanes* (Oxford 1951)
175 s.

In corrispondenza del nome Κοικόα Sofrone escogitò anche il
verbo κοικύλλειν, riferendolo particolarmente agli ὀψιμαθεῖς; ce
ne dà notizia Demetrio, il quale più oltre nella sua opera afferma:[21]

[κοι]|κύ[λλ]ειν [γ]ὰρ ἐν προφοραῖς | ταῖς ἐκ τῶν Σώ[φρ]ονος
μείμων τοῖς ὀψιμαθέσιν |[10] [.....]ρείσθω· κτλ.

La parola ὀψιμαθέσιν, che ora scrivo in luogo della congettura
[π]άθεσιν del De Falco, rende il testo intellegibile. Il papiro in
questo punto, dopo una lacuna di quattro lettere, conserva soltanto
αθεσιν, ma il disegno oxoniense riporta in margine un frammentino,
recante le lettere οψιμ, che si inserisce perfettamente nella lacuna.

Demetrio ha avvertito la necessità di precisare che il verbo
κοικύλλειν nelle espressioni tratte dai mimi di Sofrone va riferito
a quelli che imparano tardi. Infatti Eliano (v.h. XIII 15) tramanda
che un tale di nome Κοικυλίων, ovviamente derivato da κοικύλλειν,
era tanto stupido da contare le onde del mare. L'osservazione del
Lacone è interessante e preziosa, perché fa pensare che κοικύλλειν,
per noi attestato in un solo luogo di Aristofane (Thesm. 852), in-
terpretato nei modi più vari dagli scoliasti,[22] fosse usato da Sofrone con un significato diverso da quello che ebbe in altri autori.

In conclusione, la figura di Sofrone[23] esercitò il suo fascino
anche sugli epicurei, i quali lo citano nell'àmbito specifico di

---

21 Cf. Poem. II col. LX, 121 Romeo. Il Kaibel, pur ravvisando
tra le parole del disegno oxoniense il nome di Sofrone, annotava:
"quae quo pertineant non video." Neppure nell'edizione del De Falco,
L'epicureo Demetrio Lacone (Napoli 1923) 92 col. LXI, il passo appariva più comprensibile.

22 Cf. schol. ad Ar., Thesm. 852, Hesych. e Phot. s.v. κοικύλλειν, Suid. κ 2534.

23 Il mimografo ha destato l'interesse anche dei filologi
moderni; tra i numerosi contributi sull'autore si vedano: M. Norsa-
G. Vitelli, "Da un mimo di Sophron," SIFC 10 (1933) 119-24; Iidem,
"Ancora frammenti di Sophron," SIFC 10 (1933) 247-53; N. Festa,
"Sofrone e Teocrito (A proposito di una recente scoperta)," Il Mondo
Classico 3 (1933) 476-84; C. Gallavotti, "Per il nuovo Sofrone,"
RFIC 61 (1933) 459-76; A.S.F. Gow, "Sophron and Theocritus," CR 47
(1933) 113-15; K. Latte, "Zu dem neuen Sophronfragment," Philologus
88 N.F. 42 (1933) 259-64; P. E. Legrand, "A propos d'un nouveau
fragment de Sophron," REA 36 (1934) 25-31; M. Pinto Colombo, Il Mimo
di Sofrone e di Senarco (Firenze 1934); C. Kerény, "Sofrone ovvero
il naturalismo greco," RFIC 63 (1935) 1-19; B. Lavagnini, "Virgilio,
Teocrito e Sofrone," AC 4 (1935) 153-55; G. Perrotta, "Sofrone poeta
in versi," SIFC 21 (1946) 93-100; U. Albini, "Il frammento 24 Kaibel

trattazioni sulla poesia: Filodemo infatti lo introduce per dimostrare che i mimi non sono poesia e per ribadire, contro gli avversari, la posizione epicurea sull'estetica; Demetrio invece cita
Sofrone in un contesto meno generale, limitato alle figure poetiche
e qui riconosce a Sofrone il merito di aver escogitato un nome,
Κοικόα, che già nel suono rivela il carattere della serva straniera.

Costantina Romeo

---

di Sofrone," *Maia* 13 (1961) 126-30; P. Chantraine, "Le fragment 26
de Sophron et les noms grecs de la crevette," *Maia* 15 (1963) 136-42;
Q. Cataudella, "Mimo e romanzo (Sofrone, 22, 30, 145b, 39, 01),"
RCCM 8 (1966) 3-11; R. Cantarella, "Aspetti sociali e politici
della commedia greca antica," *Dioniso* 43 (1969) 321-23; M. W. Haslam, "Plato, Sophron and the Dramatic Dialogue," *BICS* 19 (1972)
17-38.

PART 4

DOCUMENTARY TEXTS AND LANGUAGE

Proceedings of the XVI Int. Congr. of Papyrology (Chico 1981) 193-197

A QUADRILINGUAL CURIOSITY IN THE
BODLEIAN LIBRARY IN OXFORD

This paper is a preliminary publication of a Bodleian Library papyrus, inventory number MS.Gr.class.f.126(P), a previously-unpublished fragment of accounts from the time of Augustus. It is hoped that in due course the text will be taken up into the new catalogue of Bodleian papyri of which the first volume is currently in preparation by Dr. R. P. Salomons and is scheduled to appear as *Studia Amstelodamensia* XXVI. Meantime the text poses several problems and this provisional airing will, I hope, bring solutions for some of them. I am grateful to the Curators of the Library for permission to publish the papyrus, and to the many who in conversation or correspondence have endeavoured to elucidate its difficulties, especially Sebastian Brock, Walter Cockle, John Ray, John Rea, Colin Roberts and John Tait.

The provenance of the papyrus is not certain but it was probably purchased by Flinders Petrie, possibly at Oxyrhynchus in 1922. It was subsequently presented to A. S. Hunt and later by Mrs. Hunt to the Bodleian.

The text measures 16 x 12.5 cm., and below a heading contains two columns of items with their quantities or prices. The first of these is broken off at the foot, but the second column is only half-height and the papyrus may be almost complete. The text has entries in Greek, Latin and Demotic and an unidentified section, possibly all by the same hand. I make no attempt to transcribe the Demotic and the unidentified parts for which the reader is referred to the plate. Written along the fibres; along the fibres on the back, a Latin docket.

ἔτους ιη Καίσαρος, Χοιάκ.
ἃ δεῖ ἀγορ(άσαι)·

(col. i)   (4 lines unidentified and not transcribed; see plate)

        αμβ( ) εχιν( )   (notation not transcribed)
        σιρικ( )   ' '
        δακτ( ) σφρ( )   ' '
    10   ὁμ(οίως) ιβαρια   ' '
        panes   as(sibus)   x
        olio   as(sibus)   v
        [   ]..

        .   .   .   .   .   .

(col. ii)   (A line partially Demotic and 5 further lines of
            Demotic not transcribed; see plate)

Back, along the fibres:

    20   rationes C.Calpur(nii) Ptol(emaei).

    2 αγορ^L 7 αμβ' εχι^v 8 σιρι^κ 9 δακ^τ σφρ^L
10 ο^μ 11 panes· as·   12 olio· as· l. oleum
20 rationes· c· calpur· ptol·

1   Year 18 of Caesar (= Augustus), Choiak = November/December,
        13 B.C.
3-6   Cf. the plate. I have not identified the script used in
        these lines. A priori we would expect entries in this posi-
        tion to be read from left to right. The script is clearly
        different from the Latin, Greek and Demotic. It does not
        appear to be Greek or Latin shorthand. Dr. Sebastian Brock
        assures me that it is neither Hebrew nor Aramaic and is
        inclined to say that it is not Semitic at all. The first
        part of line 14 (the top of col. ii; or is it a continuation
        of line 3?) appears to be in the same script. There are two
        sets of notations following the main entries in 3-6: the
        notations of the first set are identical except for the
        placing of a dot in 6. The second set may be figures, since

signs from the main entries on the left reappear and may be
being used numerically here. We get an impression here and
there that earlier writing may have been washed off, especially in 6 *init*.

7   αμβ( ) εχιν( ): expansion and meaning uncertain. A combina-
           tion of LSJ[9] s.v. ἄμβιξ and ἐχῖνος suggests some kind of
           beaker or jar.

7-10   The notations ending these lines are not obviously Greek,
           and the different elements all recur in the unidentified
           lines 3-6. Presumably quantities are indicated, not prices
           as in 11-12.

8   σιριχ( ): a reference to silk? For silk in Egypt, see M. G.
           Raschke, *Aufstieg und Niedergang der römischen Welt* II 9.2,
           625 with notes.

9   δαχτ(ύλια) σφρ( ), signet-rings? Expansion of σφρ( ) un-
           certain.

10   ιβαρια: = Latin *eburea*, i.e., ivory rings [δαχτ(ύλια) sc.
           from 9]?

11-12   On an as: obol ratio of 2:3, price-comparisons suggest that
           the amounts involved might be 15-30 loaves and half a litre
           of oil. Cf. A. C. Johnson, *Roman Egypt* (*ESAR* II) 316.
           Pleasingly Italianate *olio* shows an unwarranted change of
           case. The presence of *asses* is curious, and I have no
           answer yet for the circumstances in which in Egypt a quan-
           tity of a commodity would be measured in terms of a quantity
           of *asses*.

14   Cf. the note on 3-6 above.

14-19   Do the Demotic entries contain a medical recipe? The nota-
           tions on the right may possibly be reconcilable with Demotic
           fractions. I owe this and the following notes to John Ray.

14-15   Entries begin *š*ỉ (*n*) "lake of..." and the word following this
           in 15 looks like *Pa-DN*, where DN is a god's name, possibly
           Ophois. The whole group would be a man's name.

16   *t₃ pn₃*, with an evil or violent determinative, followed by a
           fraction, perhaps 1/4.

18   This line deals with linen. The opening word might be *f'*
           "hair."

20   "Accounts of Gaius Calpurnius Ptolemaeus," who has not been
        identified in any other source. Other ink marks on this
        side are blots.

        The only explanation I have thought of for this polyglot shop-
ping list is that the items are given in the language of the stall-
holders or shopkeepers who sold them. Nevertheless in that case we
might expect a unified currency system, and apart from the problem
with *asses* (see 11-12 n. above) it is further odd that the Greek
items in 7-10 are followed by apparently non-Greek notation. Oxyrhynchus may have been the modern provenance of the papyrus, but
the seeming cosmopolitan milieu suggests the possibility that it
was written in Alexandria or one of the Red Sea ports. Bilingual
papyri are not uncommon, and *CPLat*. 281 is an example of a tri-
lingual papyrus, a Latin-Greek-Coptic conversation-manual, but the
Latin there is transliterated into Greek characters. Is this the
only known quadrilingual papyrus?
        If any readers can throw light on the problems of the text
and so contribute to a definitive publication of it in due course
in the new catalogue of Bodleian papyri, they are urged to write
to me.

Oxford   Revel Coles

SOME INTERESTING MORPHOLOGICAL PHENOMENA IN THE LANGUAGE OF THE PAPYRI

This paper is a preview of some of the more interesting dis-
coveries made in the preparation of the second volume of my *Grammar
of the Greek Papyri of the Roman and Byzantine Periods*,[1] scheduled
for publication later this year.

In the declension of nouns, as is well known, there is much
analogical levelling within each declension and among the various
declensional types. In the first declension in particular, feminine nouns in -ρᾰ very frequently have -ρης, -ρῃ instead of -ρας,
-ρᾳ in the genitive and dative. The word ἄρουρα is almost always
declined this way;[2] other nouns have these forms competing with the
classical Attic forms in -ρας, -ρᾳ.[3] These new forms in -ρης, -ρῃ
are not Ionicisms in the Koine,[4] because nouns in -ρᾱ are not so
affected. They are the result of levelling of this declensional
system with that of other nouns in -ᾰ whose stem ends in a conso-
nant, as δόξα or γλῶσσα. This declensional pattern, attested already in the Ptolemaic papyri from the middle of the third century
B.C. on,[5] became established before the loss of quantitative distinction, when -ρᾰ could still be distinguished from -ρᾱ.

---

1 Vol. II: *Morphology* (Milano: Istituto Editoriale Cisalpino-
La Goliardica, 1981). [The numbers in brackets at the end of the
following footnotes are references to the page(s) of Vol. II where
more data and interpretation may be found.]

2 An exception is ἑκάστης ἀρούρας *P. Oxy.* I 102.12 (A.D. 306);
P. Ross. Georg. III 32.8 (A.D. 504); *P. Cair. Masp.* III 67329 i.11,
12 (A.D. 524/525: *BL* IV 15); etc. [4].

3 E.g., σπείρης *P. Mich.* IX 569.6 (A.D. 90?), but σπίρας *P.
Lond.* II 256a (p. 99) = *Chrest. Wilck.* 443.3 (A.D. 15); λείτρης *BGU*
III 781 ii.8,13,16; vi.12, but λείτρας iii.1,16,19; v.7,9,11,14;
vi.1,2,16 (1st cent.); μοίρης *P. Mil. Vogl.* II 99.10 (A.D. 119),
but μοίρας *P. Monac.* 6.64 (A.D. 583); etc. [5].

4 As was held by Schweizer, *Grammatik der pergamenischen Inschriften* (Berlin 1898) 40-42, and Thumb, *Die griechische Sprache im
Zeitalter des Hellenismus* (Strassburg 1901) 70-72.

5 Mayser, *Grammatik* I[2], 1 11-12.

Some feminine Latin loanwords of the first declension in -α
are declined -α, -ης, -ῃ, -αν, as *ala* and *tabella*;[6] others are declined -α, -ας, -ᾳ, -αν, as *matrōna* and *porta*;[7] but most fluctuate
between the two declensional types, as *cella* and *annōna*;[8] only a
few appear in -η, -ης, -ῃ, -ην, as *cortīna*, *scala*, and the Latin
third declension military term *cohors*.[9] Some first declension
Latin loanwords also have second declension by-forms or are declined exclusively according to the second declension, as *tabula*
and *dalmatica*.[10]

In the third declension, the nominative plural ending -ες is
occasionally used for the accusative plural of masculine and feminine nouns.[11] This reflects a middle stage in the process by which
the nominative supplanted the accusative in the plural. The process began with numerals and designations of quantity in various
ancient dialects,[12] spread to *i*-stems in early Attic and then to

---

6 E.g., ἄλης *P. Hamb.* I 1.8 (A.D. 57); ἄλαν *BGU* II 623.5
(2nd/3rd cent.); ταβέλλη *P. Oxy.* II 273 = *Chrest. Mitt.* 221.7 (A.D.
95); ταβέλλαν *SB* I 5217.16 (A.D. 148); etc. [6].

7 E.g., ματρώνας *P. Stras.* I 8.11 (A.D. 271-76); ματρώνᾳ *P.
Ryl.* II 165.9 (A.D. 266); πώρτας *O. Petr.* 417.5 (n.d.) [7].

8 E.g., κέλλα *P. Erl.* 40.9,11 (2nd cent.), κέλλη *SB* I 5168.
26 (A.D. 138-61), κέλλης *P. Oxy.* VIII 1144.16 (late 1st/early 2nd
cent.), κέλλας (gen.) *P. Petaus* 36.5 (ca. A.D. 185), κέλλη *BGU* I
98.14 (A.D. 211), κέλλαν *P. Oxy.* VIII 1128.15 (A.D. 173), etc.;
ἀννώνης *P. Berl. Leihg.* 9.3 (A.D. 240/41), ἀννώνας (gen.) *P. Mich.*
VI 390.4 (A.D. 215), *SB* VI 9429.4-5 (A.D. 247) [7-8].

9 E.g., κορτίνην *P. Cair. Masp.* I 6 V.48 (ca. A.D. 567);
σκάλη *P. Oxy.* XVI 1925.42 (7th cent.); χώρτη *SB* I 4591.3-4, inscr.
(Rom.), χώρτης *P. Panop. Beatty* 2.292 (A.D. 300), χώρτη, χώρτην
Chrest. Mitt. 372 v.16, iv.5 (2nd cent.) [8].

10 τάβλα *BGU* IV 1079 = *Chrest. Wilck.* 60.29 (A.D. 41),
τάβλη[ς] *BGU* III 847 = *Chrest. Wilck.* 460.15 (A.D. 182/83), τάβλαν
P. Paris 18b = *Chrest. Wilck.* 499.5 (2nd/3rd cent.), τάβλου *SB* I
4924.2 (Byz.), neut. pl. τάβλα *BGU* I 338.8 (2nd/3rd cent.); δαλμα-
τική *CPR* 21 = *Stud. Pal.* XX 31.16 (A.D. 230), δαλματικόν *PSI* VIII
900.7 (3rd/4th cent.) [8-9].

11 E.g., τοὺς δέκα στατῆρες *PSI* XIV 1432.5-6 (1st half 1st
cent.), εἰς ἄνδρες *P. Erl.* 43.5,8,11 (2nd cent.), τὰς γυναῖκες *P.
Oxy.* III 465.146,153, astrological text (late 2nd cent.) [46-47].

12 Cf. 5th cent. B.C. Delphian δεκατέτορες, Phthian τοὺς
δεκαπέντε στατῆρες, etc.; acc. γυναῖκες also occurs in late Lesbian
(Schwyzer, *Grammatik* I, 563; Buck, *Greek Dialects* §107.4).

diphthongal and consonantal stems, and resulted eventually in the
adoption of the ending -ες as the nominative and accusative plural
ending of the first declension in Modern Greek with the shift of
consonantal stems to the α-stem declension.[13]

Many adjectives of the first and second declensions which in
classical Greek are adjectives of only two terminations -ος, -ον,
or fluctuate between two and three terminations, tend to have a
distinct feminine.[14] This reflects a general tendency which reached
its final stage in Modern Greek, in which all adjectives have three
terminations.[15] Greek adjectives of the first and second declensions adopted as loanwords in Coptic tended to retain their distinction of gender while losing their case and number, but the feminine
occurs less frequently and is often replaced by the masculine and
sometimes also by the neuter.[16]

Material adjectives normally contracted in classical Attic are
usually contracted in the papyri, but open forms sometimes occur in
ἀργύρεος, χάλκεος, and χρύσεος, as well as in the new σμάλλεος.[17]
These open forms could be an Ionic legacy in the Koine.[18] Neither
the contracted nor the open forms have survived in Modern Greek.

---

13 Cf. Schwyzer, *Grammatik* I, 563-64, with literature; for
Modern Greek (ἡ)μέρες, etc., see Thumb, *A Handbook of the Modern
Greek Language*, §80-90; Mirambel, *Langue Grecque*, 112; idem, *Gram-
maire du Grec Moderne*, 48-60.

14 E.g., αἰωνία P. *Grenf.* II 71 = *Chrest. Mitt.* 190 i.11 (A.D.
244-48); βεβαία P. *Amh.* II 85 = *Chrest. Mitt.* 274.21 (A.D. 78);
σπορίμη P. *Oxy.* XVI 1915.4 (ca. A.D. 560) [105-12].

15 Thumb, *Handbook*, §108. See further Jannaris, *An Historical Greek Grammar*, §308-10; Dieterich, *Untersuchungen zur Geschichte
der griechischen Sprache*, 178-79; W. Kastner, *Die griechischen Adjective zweier Endungen auf* -ος (Heidelberg, 1967).

16 For examples, see Böhlig, *Die griechischen Lehnwörter im
sahidischen und bohairischen Neuen Testament*, 123-28. There are
comparatively few true adjectives native to Coptic; adjectival relationship is normally expressed by an adnominal genitive. Coptic
adjectives are usually used without distinction of gender and in-
declinably.

17 E.g., ἀργύρεα, ἀργύρεον, ἀργυρέων P. *Lond.* III 1007 (pp.
262-64).3,4,7 etc., with ἀργυρᾶ (neut. pl.) 26 (ca. A.D. 558);
χρύσεα, χρυσέων SB VIII 9763.6,16 (A.D. 457-74); σμάλλεα (neut. pl.)
P. *Oxy.* VI 921.6 (3rd cent.) [116-20].

18 So Kretschmer, *Entstehung der Koine*, 22-25.

Despite the simplification of comparison and the gradual decline of the superlative in Koine Greek,[19] the formation of the
comparative and superlative degrees of adjectives is still very
much a living feature of the language of the whole period of the
papyri. More than seventy-five formations of the superlative
alone, which occurs considerably less frequently than the comparative grade, are attested in the Roman and Byzantine papyri. The
primary comparative suffixes -ίων, -ιστος, never as common in Greek
as the secondary comparative suffixes -τερος, -τατος, are no longer
productive in the Roman and Byzantine periods. But they are retained in the most common adjectives, though sometimes in competi-
tion with the secondary comparative suffixes.[20] Both long and
short forms occur, but the long forms predominate, except in stereo-
typed expressions.[21] Double comparison is also found in various
forms, including πρεσβυτερωτέρα,[22] καλλιότεραι,[23] μειζότερος (both
as an adjective[24] and as a title[25]), μεγιστότατος,[26] and the periphrastic μᾶλλον λεπτοτέραν.[27]

The declension of numerals, like that of pronouns, shows some
morphological changes which are further advanced along the line of
development from ancient to Modern Greek than those observed in the
declension of nouns and adjectives. In particular, the formation

---

19 See especially Blass-Debrunner-Funk, *A Greek Grammar of
the New Testament and Other Early Christian Literature* (Chicago
1961) §60.

20 Comparatives in -ίων, -ιστος became rarer elsewhere in the
Koine, as in the New Testament (Blass-Debrunner-Funk, *Grammar*, §61).
In Modern Greek, only κάλλιο is retained in certain usages (Schwy-
zer, *Griechische Grammatik* I, 537 n. 4; Mirambel, *Grammaire*, 88).

21 E.g., τὰ πλείω P. *Lond.* II 359 (p. 150).3 (1st/2nd cent.);
πλέω ἔλαττον P. *Lond.* V 1770.7 (6th cent.); etc. [151-55].

22 P. *Lond.* II 177 (pp. 167-69) = *Chrest. Mitt.* 57.15 (A.D.
40/41) [157].

23 P. *Oxy.* XIV 1672.6,8 (A.D. 37-41) [157].

24 P. *Lips.* 28 = *Chrest. Mitt.* 363.8-9 (A.D. 381), etc. [158].

25 P. *Oxy.* VI 943.3 (6th cent.), etc. [158].

26 P. *Lond.* I 130 (pp. 132-39).49, horoscope (1st/2nd cent.) [158].

27 P. *Oxy.* VII 1066.5 (3rd cent.) [159].

of the compound numerals, ordinals, and fractions anticipates the
Modern Greek method of computation. Numerals above twelve are
normally so formed that the larger number precedes and the unit
follows.[28] This late mode of formation developed concomitantly
with a change in the word order of substantive and numeral. The
classical forms τρεῖς καὶ δέκα, etc., usually preceded the substantive, so that there was a logical progression from the smaller number to the larger and then to the substantive. With the change in
the order of the formative elements of these numerals in later
Greek, the place of the substantive is also changed, so that the
substantive is written first, followed by the numeral, with the
result that the larger number remains next to the substantive, and
there is now a logical progression from the substantive to the
larger number and then to the smaller. δεκατρεῖς and δεκαπέντε are
already found following the substantive in Attic inscriptions from
ca. 400 B.C. on, and are normal in the Ptolemaic papyri and elsewhere in the Koine.[29] But the number eleven, normally δεκαεὶς in
the Ptolemaic papyri, reverts to its classical form ἕνδεκα in the
early Roman period,[30] to be followed in Byzantine times by the
number twelve, which fluctuates between δώδεκα and δεκαδύο in Roman
times.[31] The numbers from twenty on are similarly so formed that
the larger numbers precede the smaller without an intervening καί;
again the substantive normally precedes the entire numeral.[32]

Various new formations of fractions developed from the regular
formation of compound ordinals in quite different ways. The

----

28 E.g., δεκατρεῖς P. Hamb. I 10.14 (2nd cent.), δεκατέσσαρες
P. Flor. II 143.12 (A.D. 264), δεκαπέντε PSI XIII 1324.9 (A.D. 173)
[195-96].

29 Meisterhans-Schwyzer, Grammatik der attischen Inschriften
(Berlin[3] 1900) 160-61; Mayser, Grammatik I[2], 2, 75-76; Blass-
Debrunner-Funk, Grammar, §63.1.

30 E.g., P. Mich. V 347.6 (A.D. 21), P. Rein. II 143.4 (A.D.
228/29), SB VI 9154.17 (6th/7th cent.) [194].

31 E.g., δώδεκα P. Bad. II 25.11 (1st cent.), BGU III 744.9,11
(A.D. 261/62), P. Monac. 6.77 (A.D. 583), etc.; δεκαδύο SB IV 7344.
11 (A.D. 8/9), P. Mert. I 19.5-6 (A.D. 173), P. Flor. II 211.6 (A.D.
255) [195].

32 E.g., ἀρουρῶν εἴκοσι μιᾶς P. Flor. III 325.12 (A.D. 488)
[196].

classical compound ordinal formation retained in the papyri consists of ordinal + καί + ordinal, as ὄγδοος καί τεσσαρακοστός. The
new forms of ordinals used as fractions evolved from the regular
compound ordinals and became proper compounds, either by transpos-
ing the composite elements and dropping καί, as τεσσαρακοσθόγδον,[33]
or by changing the first element either to a combinative form
(sometimes with loss of καί), as τετρακαιεικοστόν[34] or τετραεικοσ-
τόν,[35] or to a cardinal with loss of καί and sometimes with trans-
position, as δυτριακοστόν[36] or ἑβδομηκοστοδύο.[37]

In conjugation, the augment, both syllabic and temporal, is
occasionally omitted in past tenses of the indicative or transferred to other moods and tenses.[38] Reduplication is likewise occasionally omitted or replaced by the syllabic augment.[39] This
occasional loss and converse transfer of the augment, paralleled
in great part elsewhere in the Koine,[40] is a step toward a more
restricted use of the augment in Modern Greek. Since the past
tenses of the indicative were already sufficiently characterized
in most verbs by the endings and/or the stem, the augment was
largely a superfluous morpheme,[41] making it particularly subject

---

33 *SB* I 4325 i.13 partly restored, ii.10,11, iii.4,12,
v.8-9,12, etc. (3rd cent.) [208].

34 E.g., *P. Ryl.* II 156.10 (1st cent.) [208].

35 *SB* I 4325 xi.4, with τετρακαιεικοστόν ix.8, etc. (3rd
cent.) [208].

36 *P. Mich.* V 322a.23 (A.D. 46), etc. [207].

37 *P. Oxy.* I 46.25-26 (A.D. 100) [209].

38 E.g., διάγραψεν *PSI* 181.3 (A.D. 91), ἐρώτησα *P. Herm.* 50.7
(6th cent.), ἐδέδωκας *O. Bodl.* II 2139.2 (5th/6th cent.) [223-42].

39 E.g., ἐπίδωκα (for ἐπιδέδωκα) *Chrest. Wilck.* 26 ii.34
(A.D. 156), μίσθωκα (for μεμίσθωκα) *P. Amh.* 87 = *P. Sarap.* 27.3
(A.D. 125), ἐπλήρωκα *P. Oxy.* XXXIV 2729.21-22 (4th cent.) [242-48].

40 E.g., in the Attic inscriptions, Asia Minor inscriptions,
Ptolemaic papyri, New Testament (Meisterhans-Schwyzer, *Grammatik*,
170, 172-74; Schweizer, *Grammatik*, 169-70; Mayser, *Grammatik* I², 2,
98; Blass-Debrunner-Funk, *Grammar*, §66.1).

41 The augment, originally facultative, remained largely optional in poetry but became regular in prose (Schwyzer, *Grammatik* I,
651-52; Chantraine, *Morphologie historique du grec* [Paris² 1973]
§358).

to phonological tendencies. In particular, the reduction of diph-
thongs to simple vowels[42] and the loss of all quantitative distinction[43] made temporal augment and reduplication solely a qualitative
rather than a quantitative change and consequently no longer
lengthening.

Considerable variation is found in the formation of various
tense systems, especially in the perfect stem of individual verbs
with competing -κ- and root perfects, aspirated perfects, and perfects formed by Attic reduplication. There is also a tendency for
the simple perfect to be replaced by periphrastic constructions.
Thus, a late Greek -κ- perfect is used more frequently than the
older aspirated perfect in γράφω,[44] and several older, partially
dialectal, -κ- perfects are found along with the root perfect in
τυγχάνω,[45] δείδω,[46] πείθω,[47] ἀκούω,[48] and ἀπόλλυμι.[49] Examples of
periphrastic construction with a form of εἰμί and the perfect participle, especially passive, represent a middle stage in the gradual replacement of the perfect system by periphrasis. Periphrasis
in the perfect tense, found early in Greek (e.g., Homeric τετελεσ-
μένον ἐστί) was originally expressive, but became merely an equivalent substitute for the corresponding simple forms.

The language of the papyri follows the preference of the Koine

---

42 Gignac, *Grammar* I, 183-234.

43 Ibid., 325.

44 E.g., διαγεγράφηκεν *O. Bodl.* II 450.1 (A.D. 19), γεγράφη-
κα *P. Fuad Crawford* 6.22 (3rd cent.?), καταγεγραφηκέναι *P. Cair.
Goodsp.* 13.3 (A.D. 341) [297-98].

45 τετεύχηκα *P. Oxy.* XXII 2343.9 (ca. A.D. 288), *P. Lond.* II
412 (pp. 318-19) = *P. Abinn.* 55.15 partly restored (A.D. 351) [298].

46 δεδοικώ[ς] *BGU* I 361 iii.6 (A.D. 184) [299].

47 πέπε[ι]κας *SB* I 5231.2 (A.D. 11), similarly *SB* I 5247.3
partly restored (A.D. 47) [299].

48 ἤκ[ου]κα *P. Giss. Bibl.* III 31.21-22 (4th cent.) [299].

49 ἀπολωλεκέναι *P. Lips.* 35, above line 15 (ca. A.D. 275)
[299-300].

in general for second aorist passive forms.[50] There is little
increase in this tendency, however, and in Byzantine documents,
many first aorist passive forms reappear.[51] Some variation also
occurs in the formation of the aorist passive stem of δύναμαι, which
which has both the Attic[52] and Ionic[53] forms of the first aorist
passive in the papyri of the Roman and Byzantine periods, with occasional hybrid forms arising from a confusion of the two.[54]

There is much analogical levelling in the interchange of endings of the various tense systems of thematic verbs. The endings
of the first aorist are used for those of the second aorist,[55] perfect,[56] and imperfect;[57] those of the present, imperfect, and second aorist for those of the first aorist[58] and perfect.[59] The

---

50 E.g., ἐγράφη BGU III 891 R.25 (A.D. 135/36), ἐβλάβην P.
Mich. VIII 473.31,33 (early 2nd cent.), παραγγελῆναι P. Oxy. XIX
2235.23 (ca. A.D. 346), ἐσκύλην P. Osl. II 162.6-7 (4th cent.) [308-16].

51 E.g., γραφθέντα Stud. Pal. XX 223.1 (6th/7th cent.), ἀπαλ-
λαχθῆναι PSI 47.7 (6th cent.?), παρεγγέλθην sic P. Cair. Masp. I
67076.8 (Byz.).

52 E.g., ἠδυνήθην P. Mich. VIII 486.5 (2nd cent.), δυνηθῶ P.
Mert. II 91.18 (A.D. 316), δυνηθῆναι P. Oxy. I 71 i = Chrest. Mitt.
62.21 (A.D. 303) [317-18].

53 E.g., ἠδυνάσθην P. Oxy. IV 743.36 (2 B.C.), δυνασθῶ PSI
967.11-12 (1st/2nd cent.), δυνασθῆναι P. Mich. V 226.32-33 (A.D.
37) [318-19].

54 δυνησθῆ P. Mich. VIII 464.21-22 (A.D. 99), δυναθῆ P. Mich.
VIII 518.5 (1st half 4th cent.) [319].

55 E.g., ἦλθα BGU III 814.13 (3rd cent.), ἔλαβα P. Athen.
61.11 (1st cent.), ἔσχαμεν P. Cair. Isid. 41.60 (A.D. 302-5) [335-45].

56 E.g., ἀναδέδωκαν SB VI 9369 = PSI XIII 1324.19 (A.D. 173),
εἴληφαν P. Mich. V 333-4.11 (A.D. 52), οἶδαν P. Iand. II 23.13
(6th/7th cent.) [354-55].

57 E.g., εἶχα P. Cair. Isid. 65.5 (A.D. 298/99), ἔλεγας BGU
II 595.9 (ca. A.D. 70-80), ἐχαρίζατο P. Lond. V 1674.3 (ca. A.D.
570); cf. also προεγάμουσαν BGU I 183 = Chrest. Mitt. 313.6 (A.D.
85), etc. [331-32].

58 E.g., ἔπεμψες SB IV 7356 = P. Mich. III 203.4 (A.D. 98-117),
ἐκομίσου P. Oxy. II 300.6 (late 1st cent.), imperative ὑπόμεινε P.
Giss. 19.16 (A.D. 115: BL V 34) [348-53].

59 E.g., οἶδες BGU III 923.11 (1st/2nd cent.), τεθελήκουσι P.
Amh. II 130.16-17 (A.D. 70), εἴληφον (1 sg.) P. Select. 18.26 (4th
cent.) [253-56].

present, future, and aorist are sometimes confused, especially in the infinitive[60] and imperative.[61] In addition, the subjunctive is often confused with the indicative,[62] the imperative with the infinitive,[63] and less regular endings tend to be replaced by more regular ones.

This evidence for morphological development in the papyri of the Roman and Byzantine periods shows the language in a transitional stage. The morphemic systems are still basically those of classical Attic, but forms from other dialects have been incorporated and very many analogical formations have sprung up, serving to level the greater irregularities of the classical systems and anticipate many Modern Greek morphological systems.

The Romans of Imperial times had a proverb which ran, "Ex Aegypto semper aliquid novi." I hope that my organization of grammatical phenomena in the language of the papyri of the Roman and Byzantine periods from Egypt will be yet another fulfillment of this adage and will prove useful to you in your work.

The Catholic University of America   F. T. Gignac

---

60 E.g., ἐπελεύσασθαι *SB* I 5275.18 (A.D. 11), παρέξασθαι *PSI* VIII 897.29 (A.D. 93), ἔσασθαι P. *Flor*. III 370.2 (A.D. 132) [332-33].

61 E.g., πέμψε P. *Meyer* 22.7 (3rd/4th cent.), ἀλλαξέτω *BGU* II 597.10-11 (A.D. 75), σπουδασέτωσαν P. *Fay*. 112.18 (A.D. 99) [349-53].

62 E.g., ἐὰν οὖν θέλεις P. *Oxy*. XIV 1668.20-21 (3rd cent.), εἰ δὲ ἴδῃς P. *Lond*. III 1032 (p. 283).6 (6th/7th cent.) [358-59].

63 E.g., imperative πέμψαι P. *Fay*. 127.14-15 (2nd/3rd cent.), infinitive πέμψεν P. *Mich*. VIII 520.5 (4th cent.) [349-53].

Λούειν-λοῦσις DANS LE VOCABULAIRE DES BAINS
(PAPYRUS ET INSCRIPTIONS)

Dans le grec littéraire, λούειν est un mot qui ne pose pas de problème. Son sens est à la fois précis et limité: il signifie *baigner*, *laver*, mais uniquement en parlant du *corps* (corps d'un homme, corps d'un dieu, corps vivant ou cadavre), --se distinguant par là de νίζειν, qui signifie *nettoyer en frottant* et s'applique notamment aux pieds et aux mains ou à un objet, et de πλύνειν, qui s'applique aux étoffes et aux vêtements.[1] Comme son sens, sa construction est simple et constante: à la forme active, λούειν a normalement pour sujet un nom de personne, et aussi un nom de personne comme complément d'objet direct: λούει τίς τινα. Si je rappelle ces banalités, c'est pour rendre plus sensible ce qu'il y a de singulier, de non conforme au schéma traditionnel, dans le fait que, dans les documents papyrologiques, λούειν est parfois associé à βαλανεῖον (établissement de bain) pour former expression avec lui, et cela de deux façons différentes: dans l'une, βαλανεῖον est complément, --λούει τις τὸ βαλανεῖον (ou ποιεῖταί τις τὴν λοῦσιν τοῦ βαλανείου), dans l'autre, βαλανεῖον est sujet, --τὸ βαλανεῖον λούει, le verbe étant intransitif. Je voudrais examiner ces deux types d'expression, en fixer le sens, et montrer que le sens est le même dans les inscriptions où ces expressions apparaissent.

Le *P. Mich.* V 312, de 34 après J.C., est un contrat de location d'un établissement de bain, situé à Théogonis, dans le Fayoum. La première obligation à laquelle doivent satisfaire les locataires est exprimée ligne 17: ἐφ' ὧι λούσωσι τὸ βαλανῖον κατὰ μῆνα ἕκαστον μίαν παρὰ μίαν...καὶ ταῖς ἑορταῖς: ils devront "λούειν l'établissement de bain chaque mois, un jour sur deux, et aux jours de fête." Comment interpréter λούειν? L'éditeur a pensé qu'il s'agissait de "nettoyer" ("wash out") le bain. Interprétation peu vraisemblable: on s'étonne que la principale préoccupation des bailleurs ait été la propreté de leur établissement, et qu'ils aient jugé nécessaire

---

1 Voir P. Chantraine, *Dictionnaire étymologique de la langue grecque* (Paris 1974) III, 647, 754 et 918.

de consigner dans le contrat à quelles dates ces travaux de nettoyage devaient être exécutés. On s'attend plutôt à trouver indiquées ici les conditions dans lesquelles cet établissement, dont
il a été dit trois lignes plus haut qu'il était "en état de marche"
(ἐνεργόν), doit *fonctionner*. Il semble que λούειν ait ici une
valeur causative: les preneurs doivent *faire* que l'établissement
λούει, donne des bains, fonctionne comme bain. Il est alors naturel que soient fixées avec précision les modalités d'ouverture du
bain: toute l'année, un jour sur deux, et aux jours de fête.[2]

Que pour λούειν τὸ βαλανεῖον le sens de *nettoyer* doive être
écarté pour retenir celui de *faire fonctionner le bain*, c'est ce
qui apparaît dans le *P. Flor.* III 384 (V° siècle?), qui est lui
aussi un contrat de location des deux-tiers d'un grand établissement de bain d'Hermoupolis.[3] Les obligations des preneurs sont
stipulées aux lignes 23-31: elles consistent à assurer la λοῦσις du
bain (ποιεῖσθαι τὴν λοῦσιν τῶ[ν] δύο μερῶν τοῦ αὐτοῦ βαλανείου), le
chauffage (ὑπόκαυσις), le nettoyage (φιλοκαλία) et l'arrosage des
sols (ἀρδεία τῶν πάτων). Puisque les opérations de nettoyage sont
désignées par φιλοκαλία,[4] force est de donner un autre sens à
ποιεῖσθαι τὴν λοῦσιν: la formule exprime *la mise en activité du
bain*, et si on avait besoin d'une preuve supplémentaire, on la
trouverait à la fin du paragraphe (lignes 29-31), où il est répété

----

2 De même, dans un contrat de location d'un pigeonnier (*SB* V
7814), le bailleur se préoccupe de la manière dont sera traité le
pigeonnier par les locataires, et la première obligation de ceux-ci
est de "prendre soin des pigeons et de leur procurer la nourriture
convenable": lignes 9-11: ὥστε τοὺς μεμισθωμένους τὴν τούτων ἐπι-
μέλειαν ποιήσασθαι, [π]αραβάλλοντας τὰς ἐνχρηζούσας τροφάς....

3 L'éditeur du *P. Mich.* 312, A. E. Boak, n'a pas manqué de
faire le rapprochement avec le *P. Flor.* 384, mais en proposant la
même interprétation ("similar provisions for *cleaning* the baths").
Le sens exact est donné par le *LSJ*, "washing, bathing," avec référence au papyrus de Florence.

4 Φιλοκαλία n'est pas attesté dans les papyrus avant l'époque
byzantine. On ignore quel mot était employé, à l'époque romaine,
pour le nettoyage d'un bâtiment: sans doute κάθαρσις ou un mot de
la famille de κάθαρσις. On lit dans un papyrus de Brême, publié
par H. Maehler dans *CdE* 41 (1966) 349 (= *SB* X 10278): χρείαν ἔχουσι
(scil. οἱ τόποι) καθαρεοσύνης. La "saleté" se disait ἀκαθαρσία (*P.
Mert.* II 76.25; *P. Yale* 69.19).

que les preneurs ne doivent "mettre aucun empêchement au fonctionnement des deux-tiers du bain en question," <μὴ>[5] ἐνεδρεῦσαι λούειν
τὰ δύο μέρη τοῦ αὐτοῦ βαλανίου, mais, au contraire, "faire en sorte
que le bain fonctionne chaque jour, sans interruption," τα[ῦτα]
ἐφ᾽ ἑκάστης ἡμέρας ἀδιαλίπτως λούειν.

Dans cette dernière formule il est probable que nous avons
affaire au second type de construction, où λούειν est pris intran-
sitivement, et a pour sujet, exprimé ou non, τὸ βαλανεῖον.[6] Cet
emploi apparaît dans deux autres documents. Dans le *P. Lond.* III
1177 (p. 180) 32, de 113 après J.C. (partiellement reproduit dans
Sel. Pap. II 406), qui concerne la fourniture d'eau au Bain de
Sévère à Arsinoé, il est dit que cette fourniture fut interrompue
durant la deuxième quinzaine de Mésorè διὰ τὸ ἀπὸ ις ἕως λ μὴ λελου-
κέναι, "parce que, du 16 au 30, le bain n'a pas fonctionné" (Hunt
et Edgar traduisent très exactement "no baths"). De même, dans le
P. Giss. 50, de 259 après J.C., qui est une proposition de prendre
à ferme deux vestiaires municipaux aux Thermes du gymnase d'Oxyrhynchos, il est fait allusion à la redevance (φόρος) que doivent
payer les *capsarii* qui ont obtenu le marché: τοῦ τελουμένου φόρου
ὑπὸ τῶν καψαρίων τοῦ λούοντος βαλανείου (lignes 13-16). On a été
embarrassé par τοῦ λούοντος βαλανείου, génitif objectif de φόρου:
c'est le φόρος payé pour le λοῦον βαλανεῖον. L'éditeur traduit:
"hinsichtlich der von den Garderobiers für jede Benutzung des Bades
zu leistenden Abgabe," suivant une suggestion de Wilcken: "des
badenden Bades, des zur Zeit benutzten Bades." Cependant on ne
saurait dire que l'idée d'*utilisation* de l'établissement de bain
soit dans les mots grecs. Le λοῦον βαλανεῖον "l'établissement de
bain *baignant*," c'est l'établissement quand il *fonctionne comme
bain*; le φόρος payé par les *capsarii* ne l'est pas pour chaque
utilisation du bain, mais pour les périodes où l'établissement est
en activité, est ouvert.

---

5 Pour la clarté du sens, nous tirons ce μή de μηδεμίαν de
la ligne 28.

6 L'expression τα[ῦτα] ἐφ᾽ἑκάστης ἡμέρας ἀδιαλίπτως λούειν
est susceptible de deux constructions: ou bien λούειν étant tran-
sitif et ταῦτα complément "que les preneurs le fassent fonctionner,"
ou bien λούειν étant intransitif, avec ταῦτα pour sujet" que ce
bain fonctionne." La seconde construction nous semble plus
probable.

Si ces remarques sont exactes, elles peuvent contribuer à dissiper quelques incertitudes de sens dans les inscriptions où figurent λούειν et λοῦσις. Ces inscriptions ne sont pas nombreuses.
Dans sa dissertation de 1960, *Die Verwaltung und Finanzierung der
öffentlichen Bäder zur römischen Kaiserzeit*, H. Meusel en cite
quatre (p. 106)--les mêmes qui avaient été rassemblées par J. et
L. Robert, *Bull. Epigr.* 1954, 146. Dans l'une d'elles, une inscription de Kys, en Carie (*BCH* 11 [1887] 306 n. 1), un gymnasiarque est loué en tant que λοῦσας δὲ καὶ τὸ βαλανεῖον: c'est la
même construction que dans le *P. Mich.* 312 pré-cité, et le même
sens: *il avait assuré le fonctionnement de l'établissement de bain.*
Plus intéressant encore pour nous est le décret des démiurges de
Delphes (319 après J.C.), publié par E. Bourguet,[7] commentée par le
juriste E. Cuq (*RevPhil* [1911] 182-93 et 347-48), reprise en 1907
dans *Syll.*[3] 901, enfin republiée par J. Bousquet dans *BCH* 76 (1952)
653-60. Il y est question d'une donation de 500.000 drachmes
d'argent, faite εἰς τὴν λοῦσιν τῶν βα[λανείων]. Le premier éditeur
avait pensé qu'il s'agissait du nettoyage de l'établissement, *ut
lavarentur balnea*, --interprétation admise par *LSJ*, qui donne le
sens de *cleaning*, avec référence à ce texte. Explication qui
heurte le bon sens, comme l'a bien marqué Cuq, car il est inconcevable qu'une somme aussi importante (un demi-million de drachmes)
ait été affectée à de simples travaux de nettoiement. Il n'est pas
possible non plus de donner à λοῦσις, avec J. Bousquet, le sens
d'*embellissement*,[8] par trop éloigné du sens étymologique. B. Laum
(*Stiftungen*, 11 n. 30) était plus près de la vérité, quand il tra-
duisait par "Wasserversorgung der Bäder," et E. Cuq en donnant à
λοῦσις un sens en quelque sorte juridique[9] "le droit de se baigner

---

7 Dans sa thèse latine (Paris 1905), *De rebus Delphicis
imperatoriae aetatis*, 45.

8 Loc. cit., 659, J. Bousquet se réfère au *P. Flor.* 384, où
il traduit λοῦσις par "entretien du bain."

9 E. Cuq appuie cette opinion sur les expressions parallèles
d'inscriptions latines: *in hujus balinei lavationem* (*CIL* XI 720),
ad lavacrum balnearum publicarum (*CIL* X 3678). Le parallélisme des
expressions incite à se demander si *lavatio* n'a pas le sens que
nous proposons pour λοῦσις: le fonctionnement du bain.

dans un établissement de bain," rangeait cette donation parmi les
"dons et legs destinés à permettre aux habitants d'une ville ou à
certaines catégories de personnes de se baigner gratuitement aux
bains publics." Cependant, ni la "fourniture d'eau," ni le "droit
de se baigner" ne peuvent être considérés comme des traductions
exactes de λοῦσις, et la comparaison avec le *P. Flor.* 384 permet de
dire que cette donation εἰς τὴν λοῦσιν τῶν βαλανείων[10] a été faite
pour le *fonctionnement* des bains.

La λοῦσις, associée à la fourniture d'huile au gymnase, était
une libéralité dont on faisait honneur au gymnasiarque.[11] Dans une
inscription de Beroia de Macédoine (Dimitsas, *Makedonia*, 51), un
gymnasiarque est remercié pour avoir procuré huile et bains du ma-
tin au soir, pour tout le peuple (τὸν γυμνασίαρχον ἀλείψαντα καὶ
λούσαντα δι᾽ ὅλης τῆς ἡμέρας πανδημεί. De même, une inscription
d'Ancyre de l'Abbaïtide (*IGR* IV 555), reprise partiellement par L.
Robert (*Gladiateurs*, n. 133), honore Ménélas pour avoir procuré au
peuple l'huile que les gens puisaient dans les "louters," et assuré
le service du bain, sur sa fortune personnelle (καὶ ἀλείψαντα τὸν
δῆμον ἐγ λουτήρων καὶ λούσαντα ἐκ τῶν ἰδίων.[12] Sur ces deux textes,
je voudrais présenter deux remarques; le *Supplement* du *LSJ* s'appuie
sur l'inscription d'Ancyre pour proposer la traduction "fournir des
bains gratuits" ("provide free baths"). En réalité, la notion de
gratuité n'est pas plus dans λούσαντα qu'elle n'est dans ἀλείψαντα
(ou dans λούσας τὸ βαλανεῖον). Si elle est exprimée par des mots,
c'est par ἐκ τῶν ἰδίων. Mais elle réside essentiellement dans la

10   D'où l'heureuse restitution de J. Bousquet, ligne 9: ἐφ᾽[ᾧ
τε λοῦσαι τὰ βαλανεῖα].

11   La libéralité des évergètes prenait souvent pour objet les
bains publics: à Kenamos, deux époux, ἀρχιερατεύοντες offrent à la
cité un bain public (I. Lévy, "Etudes sur la vie municipale," *REG*
12 [1899] 262); ailleurs, un particulier restaure les exèdres d'un
bain public (ibid., 355 n. 4). A Lindos, un prêtre d'Athana Lindia
s'est illustré pendant sa prêtrise, entre autres choses, en procu-
rant une utilisation des bains qui a été louée, "παρασχόντα...τὰν
τῶν λουτρῶν ἐπαινομέναν χρῆσιν (*IG* XII 832). Voir aussi *P. Oxy.*
III 473.

12   De même, à Sidyma, en Lycie (*IGR* III 584, *TAM* II 189), on
lit: τελέσασαν τῇ πατρίδι ἱερωσύνην Σεβαστῶν καὶ τὰς [δύ]ο τῶν νέων
γυμνασιαρχίας καὶ τὰ[ς] λούσεις.

nature des documents où ces expressions apparaissent. C'est le
caractère évergétique de l'inscription qui ajoute aux mots cette
notion de gratuité.

Ma seconde remarque sera pour noter que λούσαντα, dans ces
deux inscriptions, est pris absolument, sans complément exprimé.
J. Marquardt (*Das Privatleben der Römer* I, 273 n. 5), suivi par H.
Meusel (loc. cit.), s'appuyant sur *IGR* IV 555 (ἀλίψαντα τὸν δῆμον...
καὶ λούσαντα), dit que la formule grecque pour une telle libéralité
est λούειν τὸν δῆμον. C'est affirmer plus que ne le permet le
texte, car τὸν δῆμον se présente dans la phrase comme le complément
dû seul ἀλίψαντα, non comme le complément commun de ἀλίψαντα et
λούσαντα. Λούειν τὸν δῆμον se lira peut-être un jour dans un document; l'expression n'aurait rien que de très naturel, de même que
ἀλείψαντα peut être (comme dans *IGR* IV 555), ou n'être pas (comme
dans l'inscription de Beroia), suivi de τὸν δῆμον. Mais dans
l'état actuel de la documentation, on est, semble-t-il, autorisé à
parler d'un emploi absolu, sans complément exprimé, de λούειν, toujours avec un sujet de personne, et il est oiseux de se demander
s'il faut entendre λούσαντα comme "ayant assuré le fonctionnement
du bain" (λούσας τὸ βαλανεῖον), ou comme "ayant fourni des bains au
peuple" (λούσας <τὸν δῆμον>, non encore attesté), car cela revient
pratiquement au même.

Ainsi, dans les documents papyrologiques et épigraphiques,
λούειν garde son sens précis de "baigner, laver," tel qu'il est attesté dans les textes littéraires; dans l'expression λούειν τὸ βαλανεῖον, il a une valeur causative,[13] "faire que le bain baigne," ce
qui, du point de vue de la langue, est aussi normal que γεύειν τινά
"faire que quelqu'un goûte." Λοῦσις n'est rien d'autre, quant à sa
forme et son sens, que le substantif verbal de λούειν, et ποιεῖσθαι
τὴν λοῦσιν est l'exact équivalent de λούειν. Le sens de "nettoyer"
doit être éliminé.

Béatrice Meyer

---

13 Voir Schwyzer-Debrunner, *Griechische Grammatik*, II, 233:
"Seit dem Beginn der Überlieferung ist produktiv das Nebeneinander
eines kausativen Aktives und eines intransitiven Mediums, wobei das
Aktiv gewöhnlich jünger ist." Parmi les exemples cités: γεύομαι/
γεύω.

PUBLIC NOTICES CONCERNING EPITĒRĒSIS OF THE ŌNĒ ZYTĒRAS[*]

Pap. Eg. Mus. inv. 43   29.3 x 24.4 cm.   A.D. 135/6
Arsinoe

Although the margins of the papyrus have been preserved on all sides, it is difficult to read at many points because of holes, abrasions on the surface, and faded ink. The document consists of two columns, each containing a πρόγραμμα; this gives the impression that the scribe copied from a *tomos synkollesimos*. Kollesis appears at the beginning of the intercolumnium; in col. I, the scribe generally kept his writing within the left kollema and only occasionally (lines 9-11, 13, 16 and 17) continued the lines beyond the kollesis. Parallels for the professional, skilful, neat hand are Schubart, *Griech. Pal.* 37 and *P. Leit.* 5.

The two "public notices" were issued by Vegetus alias Sarapion and Herakleides, two successive strategoi of the Themistes, on August 26 of 135 A.D. and in July/August of 136 A.D. (posted between August 24 and 29) respectively. The first πρόγραμμα announces the appointment of liturgical supervisors (ἐπιτηρηταί) of farmed taxes (τελωνικαὶ ὠναὶ καὶ ἄλλαι)[1] for the 20th year of Hadrian (135/136). The present excerpt, however, presents only four names (lines 20-24) for the supervision of farming the beer-tax (19 ζυτηρά; 36 ἐπιτήρησις ὠνῆς ζυτηρᾶς). Among them is Gaius Antonius Gallicus who is appointed for the village of Theadelphia (line 37). The second πρόγραμμα releases him from that liturgy by appointing Apion son of Ammonios as his replacement (line 35). The present excerpts from the files of the public archives (βιβλιοθήκη δημοσίων

---

* In preparing the final version of this paper I made use of many suggestions which Professors A. E. Hanson, L. Koenen, N. Lewis, P. J. Sijpesteijn, and L. C. Youtie offered me for readings and interpretations. Unfortunately, I myself was absent from Egypt and could not consult the original at this stage. Hence a number of readings are based on the photograph.

1 Cf. *P. Mert.* II 70 of 159 A.D. (ἐπιτηρηταὶ ὠνῆς πλύνου γναφέων [H. C. Youtie, *TAPA* 92 (1961) 562f. = *Script.* I 368f. and in *BL* V 66; J. Bingen, *JEA* 48 (1962) 179]).

λόγων) were prepared in the interest of Antonius Gallicus. After
his original appointment by the first πρόγραμμα he appealed to the
epistrategos, Gellius Bassus (cf. lines 27-31; see 27 n.) who,
though he had not been in charge of the original appointments,[2]
had clearly the authority over appeals (cf. *P. Leit.* 5 of 180 A.D.
[= *SB* 10196]) and wrote to the strategos Herakleides, the successor of Vegetus alias Sarapion, ordering that Antonius Gallicus
be released because of physical disability due to old age (lines
27-31; see 29 n.). Herakleides then obtained the nomination of
Apion and, sometime in Mesore (July 25-August 23) of 136 A.D., he
issued the second πρόγραμμα, releasing Antonius Gallicus and appointing Apion.

The process of appeal was slow and inefficient. "Physical
disability due to old age" (line 29), the reason for which Antonius Gallicus was finally discharged, is not likely to have been a
condition which developed during the year of service. He must have
appealed as soon as he heard of his appointment (shortly after
August 26, 135 A.D.), but his release and the appointment of Apion
was not posted before August 24, 136 A.D. (see above), less than 6
days before his term would have been completed. This did not provide much relief, except for the fact that a precedent was set
which could prevent future nomination to liturgies.[3] His successor
was ordered to continue his service through the following 21st
year of Hadrian (136/137 A.D.; lines 40f.). In a similar case (*P.
Brux.* 21.37f.), an ἐπιτηρητής of a 14th year is replaced on Dec. 7,
and his successor served for the remainder of the 14th and the entire 15th year (see *P. Brux.* I 21, p. 61). In our present papyrus,
Herakleides the strategos refers to the nominations made "by the
komogrammateis of the division and--in villages where there are no

---

2   On the restricted role of the epistrategos in liturgical
appointments, see N. Lewis, *Cd'E* 44 (1969) 339ff.

3   The belated success of Antonius Gallicus' appeal and the
appointment of Apion for the remainder of the 20th and the entire
21st year invite consideration of whether Antonius Gallicus was
actually serving a term of two years, though admittedly the language in line 7 limits his term to the 20th year. Terms of more
than one year occurred (*PSI* XII 1245 mentions three years), and the
ἐπιτήρησις was renewable; see N. Lewis, *Invent. of Comp. Serv.*
(Am. Stud. Pap. 3), s.v. (revised sheet of 1975) and idem in *Atti
dell'XI Congr. Intern. di Pap.* (Milan 1966) 514 and 539.

komogrammateis--by the presbyteroi performing the duties of the
office of komogrammateis" (lines 31-34). This phrase hardly ap-
plies to the nomination of a single replacement. We may understand
that Apion's name was selected from the nominations for the 21st
year and that he, therefore, had to serve for both the remainder of
the 20th year and all of the 21st year.

Gaius Antonius Gallicus was a veteran (see line 20 n.), but
this did not constitute a reason for his release from the liturgy.
It emerges that, already in 135 A.D., veterans no longer enjoyed
total and permanent exemptions from liturgies. At that time their
exemption was probably restricted to the first five years after
service, as we know was the case by 172 A.D. (*W. Chr.* 396).[4]

In the course of his πρόγραμμα (col. I), the strategos Vegetus
alias Sarapion specified some of the responsibilities which the
liturgy of supervising tax farming entailed: first, to submit the
usual reports, every five days, of amounts collected for the tax
(lines 11-13),[5] and second, apparently, to collect and deposit outstanding (?) revenues in the public bank;[6] if reading and restoration are correct, the supervisors are to be assisted in this by the
πράκτορες (lines 13-17; cf. 37-39). ἐπιτηρηταί occur as collectors
of both taxes which were farmed (side by side with the tax farmers
[τελῶναι, μισθωταί, ἐγλήπτορες, ἐξειληφότες etc.]) and those which
were directly collected by the state (along with πράκτορες, ἀπαιτηταί, πρεσβύτεροι).[7] If, according to the regulations of the

---

4 N. Lewis in *Actes du Xe Congr. Intern. de Pap.* (Breslau-
Warsaw-Cracow 1964) 72f.; idem, *Atti* (see n. 3), 539.

5 See below, 11 n. For example, *P. Mich.* IX 544, *P. Oslo* III
92, and P. Giess. Univ. inv. no. 331 (= *Le monde grec. Homm. à C.
Préaux* [Brussels 1975] 596) are monthly reports by supervisors
(cf. also *P. Brux.* 21.39ff.).

6 See, for example, *P. Mert.* III 102 (report of ἐπιτηρηταί;
line 8: payment into the public bank) and *O. Heid.* N.F. III 274 and
275: receipts for τιμή φοινίκων γενήματος with the additional statement καὶ διαγρ(άψομεν) ἐπὶ τὴν δ(ημοσίαν) τράπ(εζαν). For payments
of the beer tax to the public bank, see nn. 11 and 13.

7 See already U. Wilcken, *Griech. Ostraka* (Leipzig-Berlin
1899) I, 575ff. and 599ff.; S. L. Wallace, *Taxation* (Princeton
1938) 288. For the πρεσβύτεροι, see n. 13; for the ἐκλήμπτορες,
cf. Wallace, loc. cit.; E. Wipszycka, *JJP* 16/17 (1971) 127; N.
Lewis, *Papyrus in Classical Antiquity* (Oxford² 1974) 106; D. Crawford in note to *P. Oxy.* XXXVIII 2837.1; G. Casanova, *Aegyptus* 55

present papyrus, ἐπιτηρηταί and πράκτορες collaborate within the
system of farmed taxes,[8] it is tempting to conclude that they were
collecting taxes which the tax farmers had failed to collect and,
therefore, had to be gathered directly by the supervisors together
with the appropriate public collectors;[9] elsewhere ἀπαιτηταί are
seen performing the same function.[10] This argument seems to confirm the interpretation of ἐλλε{ι}λε<ι>μμένα (line 13) as arrears.

πράκτορες are known to have collected the beer-tax and to have
paid the amounts into the public bank,[11] but the ἐπιτηρηταί of
these particular tax farming contracts appear here for the first
time. In the Ptolemaic period, production and sale of beer had
been a state monopoly, and the ζυτηρά was levied by contractors
(ἐξειληφότες τὴν ζυτηράν) as a tax on the concessions (φόρος ζυτηρᾶς) and probably also as a capitation tax based on consumption
(τέλος τῆς ζυτηρᾶς).[12] Under the Roman administration brewing

---

(1965) 111; for the μισθωταί ἱερατικῶν ὠνῶν, cf. E. Wipszycka, *JJP*
15 (1965) 165ff.; and for receipts issued by tax farmers διὰ ἐπι-
τηρητῶν, see, for example, *O. Bodl.* II 709, *O. Wilb.* 46 and Wilcken,
loc. cit., 599f. According to H. C. Youtie, even tax farmers could
be called ἐπιτηρηταί (*TAPA* 92 [1961] 562f. [= *Script.* I 368f.] on
P. Mert. II 70, hardly correct; in *Class. Weekly* 35 [1941] 184 [=
Script. II 860] the same scholar regarded the ἐπιτηρηταί as "obviously liturgical officials").

8   In *W. Chr.* 392 i 3 a person holds both offices simultaneously: πράκτωρ καὶ ἐπιτηρητ(ἧς) ἐνκυκλίο(υ).

9   The arrears could result from the failure of individuals to
pay the taxes in question, or of the administration to find tax
farmers. At times the latter situation may have caused temporary
substitution of tax farmers by ἐπιτηρηταί.

10   For example, *O. Strasb.* 244.1 ἀπαιτηταί μερισμοῦ ὠνίων
ἐν(λείματος) τελωνικ(ῶν); *O. Wilb.* 21.1f. (see C. Préaux's note);
WO 558 etc. (see Wilcken I, 577); cf. *O. Strasb.* 253.1; *O. Ashm.*
(Tait I) 39.1 and 40.1; Wallace, loc. cit. (see n. 7) and, for
ἔνλειμα, below, 12-13 n.

11   *P. Oxy.* XII 1433 (238 A.D.) where πράκτορες ἀργυρικῶν report to the strategos that two payments for ζυτηρά were made into
the public bank; cf. C. A. Nelson, *Cd'E* 51 (1976) 125.

12   See, for example, *P. Tebt.* I 40 (117 B.C.); *P. Fay.* 13 (170
B.C.?); *P. Rev. Law* fr. 6a 13 and h 3; M. Rostovtzeff, *SEHHW* I 308f.
and III 1390; F. Heichelheim in *RE* 31,170ff.; C. Préaux, *L'écon.
roy. des Lagides* (Brussels 1939) 152ff., particularly 157f.; C.
Gallazzi in the introduction to *O. Teb.* 28-53 (p. 47).

became a private trade and home brewing was permitted. Under the names of ζυτηρά κατ᾽ ἄνδρα or simply ζυτηρά, the tax was levied per capita, though the details of the assessment and organisation of the collection remain uncertain. The administrative responsibility was shared by the strategos and the nomarches, and we see πρεσβύτε- ροι of a village collect the amounts and deliver them to a μισθωτής ἱερατικῶν ὠνῶν Τεβτύνεως; in other cases the payment was made into the public bank.[13] As is attested by the present papyrus, the su- pervision, the obligation of reporting to the strategos and other officials, fiscal liability (lines 15-17) and, it seems, also the responsibility for collecting arrears (see above) rested with the ἐπιτηρηταί. In addition we may conclude from analogies of other trades that the supervisors were also in charge of leasing the privilege of brewing beer to contractors.[14]

---

13 For the ζυτηρά (κατ᾽ ἄνδρα) and a full discussion of earlier theories, see C. Gallazzi, loc. cit. (see n. 12), 47-57. Payments by tax collectors were made εἰς τὸν τῆς νομαρχίας λόγον (*Stud. Pal.* XXII 183.40f.; cf. *P. Mich.* IV 2, 362.28; *P. Ryl.* II 196; *SB* III 7166 [cf. *BL* II 2.128, U. Wilcken]; Gallazzi, loc. cit., 47); and financial reports were written to the nomarches (*SB* I 5982; incomplete draft by a komogrammateus) and strategos (*P. Mich.* II 123 r. vii 33f.; *P. Oxy.* XII 1433; the reports on collections over five-day periods were primarily directed to the strategos [cf. 12- 13 n.]). For collection by the πρεσβύτεροι and payment to the μισθωτής ἱερατικῶν ὠνῶν, see *P. Giss. Univ.* 48 (224/25 A.D.); in *P. Lond.* II 255 (p. 117 [136 A.D.]) a πρεσβύτερος who was appointed by his colleagues as their deputy for the collection of beer- and sheep-taxes paid the former into the δημοσία τράπεζα. Cf. Nelson, loc. cit. (see n. 11), 124f.; A. Tomsin, "Et. sur les πρεσβύτεροι des villages" II, *Acad. Roy. de Belg.*, *Bull. de la Cl. des Lettres et des Sc. Mor. et Pol.*, 5e s., 38.10 (1952) 489f.

14 Cf., for example, *P. Oxy.* XLVI 3268 (lease of fishing rights) and the lists of applications for various concessions and rights, partly directed to ἐπιτηρηταί and ἐκλήμπτορες, which G. M. Browne provided in his edition of *P. Mich.* Inv. no. 178 (applica- tion to ἐπιτηρηταί ὑικῆς for the right to sell and pickle meat; *Proc. XII Intern. Congr. of Pap.*, Am. Stud. Pap. 7 [Toronto 1970] 64f.). *P. Tebt.* II 359 is a receipt for payments made by fishermen(?) to a former ἐπιτηρητής ἰχθυ<η>ρᾶς δρυμῶν Τεβέτνυ καὶ Κερκήσεως (cf. S. Eitrem and L. Amundsen in the introduction to *P. Oslo* III 89/90), whereas *P. Tebt.* II 329, a petition to a strategos, mentions a pay- ment for the concession of collecting the τέλη ἰχθυ[ηρᾶς δρυμῶν Τε- βέτνεως] καὶ Κερκήσεως. This payment was made into the public bank [εἰς νομάρχο]υ λόγον (cf. n. 13); see *P. Tebt.* 308.4 n.

In the first πρόγραμμα, four persons were appointed for the
ἐπιτήρησις of the (ὠνή) ζυτηρᾶς (see above). Four is a conventional number for a board of ἐπιτηρηταί though in certain ἐπιτηρήσεις
larger numbers are not uncommon: twenty-five in *P. Brux.* 21 (presumably for the collection of revenues on a large estate); eleven
in *P. Mert.* III 102.6; ten in *BGU* I 277 i 19ff. (large) and *P. Ryl.*
II 98.1 (?; μισθοῦ βαφικῆς); and eight (plus μέτοχοι) in *P. Oslo*
III 89 (νομῶν καί δρυμοῦ).[15] There are indications that occasionally the labor was divided into areas of competence and possibly
also fixed periods of time.[16] Moreover, the larger the number of
persons the Roman government could keep liable for any loss of
revenues, the more certain it was that the state would receive full
payment. Thus the ἐπιτηρηταί served in boards or collegia.[17] The
office is first attested in 88 A.D.,[18] and it disappeared during

---

15 Cf. Lewis's inventory (see n. 3).

16 For a cautious discussion of possible divisions of labor
among ἐπιτηρηταί, see N. Lewis in his introduction to *P. Leit.* 14
(p. 29f.). The reporting periods of five days seem not to have
corresponded to five-day shifts of the ἐπιτηρηταί. In *BGU* XIII
2275 and P. Freib. glass 18 (R. W. Daniel, *Greek Papyri from the
Collections of Freiburg, Vienna, and Michigan* [Diss. Univ. of Mich.
1981] I, 5 [to be republished in a forthcoming volume of Freiburg
Papyri]), the same named members of the board of ἐπιτηρηταί (Neilos
and μέτοχοι in *BGU* 2275; Heroninos and Zoilos in P. Freib. gl. 18)
report the revenues of two subsequent periods of five days. *P.
Coll. Youtie* 31.6-9 λόγος τῶν περιγενομ(ένων) ἀπὸ τῆς [προκ(ειμέ-
νης)] | ἐπιτηρήσεως τῶν ἀπὸ κα⁻ ἕως | κε⁻, ἧς ἡμέρας κατεστάθην
ἐπι[τ(ηρητής),] τοῦ Θὼθ μηνὸς τοῦ ἐνεστ(ῶτος) η (ἔτους) ˙seems not
to indicate that "die Epiteretai umschichtig das Amt versahen und
Didymos als der diensttuende Epiteretes des 21.9.199 den Bericht
über die verflossenen fünf Tage verfasste" (thus the first editors),
but that Didymos, the ἐπιτηρητής in charge, was appointed to his
office on Thoth 25 (on καθίστημι, see below, 29 n.), obviously as a
replacement for a predecessor who had served through Thoth 24. If
ἐπι[τ(ηρητής] is correctly restored (the first editors call it
"sehr fraglich"), Didymos reported the revenues of a five-day period which included the last four days before he took office.

17 μέτοχοι: e.g. *W. Chr.* 412; *P. Oslo* III 89-91; *P. IFAO* I 3
(P. Soc. Pap. inv. no. 82 I-III and 31); *P. Leit.* 14 (= *SB* 10206);
also cf. n. 16. καί οἱ λοιποί: e.g. *P. Köln* II 84.18; *SB* I 5670
and IV 7342; *P. Amh.* II 119. καί οἱ σὺν αὐτῷ ἐπιτηρηταί: e.g. *BGU*
III 697; *P. Phil.* 11.23; *P. Oxy.* XLVI 3268.

18 *P. Oxy.* I 174 ὁ καθεστάμενος (cf. n. 16) ἐπιτηρητής καί
χειριστής καταλοχισμῶν 'Οξυρυγχείτου (cf. Lewis' invent. [see n.
3]).

the second half of the third century.[19]

The description of the duties of the supervisors in the new papyrus serves to remind us that a comprehensive study of their functions remains a desideratum.[20] Further, the two προγράμματα together illuminate the administrative reform in the year 136/37 A.D., which resulted in a merger of the Themistes and Polemon divisions. At the end of the preceding year, the 20th year of Hadrian, the Herakleides of the present papyrus was strategos of the Themistes (attested for a date between July 25 and August 29 of 136 A.D.; cf. lines 26 and 44ff.). He must have taken office after April 17, 136 A.D. (see below). On July 9, August 6, and probably on September 12 of 137 A.D., an official of the same name was serving as strategos of the two divisions which had now been merged.[21] For 136/37 A.D. (i.e. the 21st year ending on August 28, 137), another strategos of the two divisions is believed to have been in office: Hierax alias Hermoapollonios.[22] If this is correct, then Herakleides was replaced by Hierax for part of 136/37 A.D. when the

---

19 Cf. Lewis's inventory (see n. 3).

20 In the meantime, cf. F. Oertel, *Die Liturgie* (Leipzig 1917) 237ff.; *P. Oxy.* XXXVIII 2856.2 n. The title ἐπιτηρητής is so general that our perception of the liturgical service of ἐπιτήρησις could be distorted by our inability to distinguish the liturgical officials from other persons using the same title in every instance.

21 *PSI* VIII 883: July 9, 137 A.D.; *SPP* XXII 184.48 and 53f. (lines 50 and 55f. of P. J. Sijpesteijn's new edition in a forthcoming volume of *ZPE* 1981): August 6, 137. With the help of a new fragment, P. J. Sijpesteijn was also able to recognize a letter written on September 12, 137 A.D., and addressed to the strategos of the two divisions (lines 86-99). In the initial formula of address (line 86), the space does not suit the names of Hierax alias Hermoapollonios or Aelius Numisianus, the next strategos. The name of Herakleides, however, fits well.

22 *P. Leit.* 11 (= *SB* 10203). If Herakleides continued in office at least into the 22nd year of Hadrian, then Hierax, serving in the 21st year, must have preceded him (cf. N. Lewis in the introduction to *P. Leit.* 11; G. Bastianini, *Gli strateghi dell' Arsinoites*, Pap. Brux. 11 [Brussels 1972] 50). If, however, the restoration of Herakleides' name in line 86 of *SPP* XXII 184 (see n. 21) should be wrong, Hierax could have replaced Herakleides during the last days of the 21st year; in this case Herakleides, the last strategos of the separate Themistes, would have become the first strategos of the combined Themistes and Polemon divisions. See also n. 23.

two divisions were merged, but, after a brief interruption, returned
to the office of strategos of what had become the Themistes and Polemon divisions.[23] From lines 2 and 18 of the present document (as
well as from *P. Berl. Leihg.* II 46 iii 37f.) we also learn that
Vegetus alias Sarapion was the predecessor of Herakleides as head
of the administration of the Themistes and was in office on August
26 of 135 A.D. He is also attested on January 25, 135 A.D. in that
post,[24] and he continued in it until after April 17, 136 A.D. (*P.
Berl. Leihg.* II 46 iii 35). By January 28, 137 A.D., however, he
was strategos of the Herakleides division (see 2 n.). We might
assume that in 136 A.D., sometime after April 17th, when Vegetus
was succeeded in the Themistes by Herakleides, he was transferred
to the Herakleides division either immediately, or after a short
lapse of time. In any case, before May 14, 138 A.D., Vegetus
himself was replaced by Tiberius Claudius Cerealis, the new strategos of the Herakleides division.[25]

COL. I

   [ἀντίγρα(φον)] πρ[ο]γράμματος ἐξειλη[μ(μένον) ἐκ βιβλι]οθή-
                        [κ(ης) δη]μοσίω(ν) λόγων.
   Ο[ὐέ]γ[ετ]ος ὁ καὶ Σαραπίων στρατηγὸ[ς Ἀρσι]νοΐτου Θεμίστου
     μ[ερ]ίδος
4 τοῖς ὑπογεγραμ[μέ]νοις ἀναδο[θ]εῖσί μοι ὑπὸ τῶν τῆς
   μ[ε]ρ[ίδος πραγ]ματικῶν ὡς εὔποροι καὶ ἐπιτήδειοι
   ε[ἰς τὴν ἐπιτήρ]ησιν τῶν ὑπογεγραμμένων ἐν τῇ
   μ[ε]ρίδι τε[λ]ωνικῶν ὠνῶν καὶ ἄλλω(ν) τοῦ κ (ἔτους)

---

23 The assumption that Herakleides took office as strategos
of the Themistes after April 17, 136 A.D., then, on the occasion of
the merger of the two divisions, was replaced by Hierax alias Hermoapollonios before the end of year 21st of Hadrian (August 28, 137
A.D.) but assumed the office of strategos of the merged divisions
before July 9, 137, might seem suspicious; and the dating of *P.
Leit.* 11 and, therefore, the attestation of Hierax for 136/137 is
not beyond doubt. D. Hagedorn will deal with these problems in a
forthcoming article in *ZPE.*

24 See A. Tomsin in his introduction to *P. Berl. Leihg.* II 46
p. 150.

25 *P. Lond.* III 1222 (p. 126); Bastianini, loc. cit. (see n.
22), 37.

8   Αὐτοκράτορος Καίσαρος Τραϊανοῦ Ἀδρια[νοῦ] Σεβαστοῦ
    παραγγέλλω ἀντιλαμβάνεσθαι τῆς ἐπιτηρήσεως
    μετὰ πάσης πίστεως καὶ ἐπιμελείας καὶ τοὺς
    λόγους τῶν προσπειπτόντων διὰ πενθημέρου
12 καταχωρίζειν, ὡς ἐκελεύσθη, ἐμοί τε καὶ
    οἷς δέον ἐστιν, τά τε ἐλ...λ..μεν[α] διαγράφειν
    ἐπὶ τὴν δημοσίαν τράπεζαν μετ[ὰ τ]ῶν πρακτόρων
    κινδύνου πρὸς τούτους ὄντος, ἐάν τ[ι] τῷ φίσκῳ
16 ἐμπέσῃ ἢ παρὰ τὸ δέον γενῆται ἢ οὗτινος συκαμε
    .[..]ου.[.]ς (ἔτους) ιθ Αὐτοκράτορος Καίσαρος Τραϊανοῦ
    Ἀ[δρ]ιανοῦ Σεβαστοῦ Μεσορὴ ἐπαγομ(ένων) γ.
    ζυτηρᾶς   ἔστι δέ·
20 Γάιος Ἀντώνιος Γαλλικὸς ἀπολύσιμος ἀπὸ
    ....[.]..[..... ..]..... ας
    Πτολεμαῖος Σωπάτρου τοῦ Διδύμου ἀπὸ μητρο(πόλεως)
    Ἀρποκρατίων Θέωνος ἀπὸ Μακεδόνων
24 Ζωίλο(ς) τοῦ Χάρητος ἀπὸ [Ἱ]ερακίο[υ]

COL. II

    [ἀντί]γρα(φον) προγράμματος .[...].( ) .ομ..[]
    [Ἡ]ρακλείδης στρατη[γὸ]ς Ἀρσινοΐτου Θεμίστ[ου μ]ερίδος.
    [Γ]ελλίου Βάσσου τοῦ κρατίστου ἐπι[σ]τρατήγου
28 γράψαντός μοι ἀντὶ Γαΐου Ἀντωνίου Γαλλικοῦ
    διὰ γήρα[ς] ἀσθένους τῷ σώματι καταστῆσαι
    ἕτερον εἰς τὴν ἐπιτήρησιν ἐν ᾗ ἐδήλωσεν
    ὁ Γαλλικὸς εἶναι, ἀνεδόθη ὑπὸ τῶν τῆς μερίδος
32 κωμογραμματέων ὧν δὲ κωμῶν μή εἰσιν
    κωμογραμματε[ῖ]ς πρεσβυτέρων διαδεχομένων
    τὰ κατὰ τὰς κωμογραμματείας
    Ἀπίων Ἀμμωνίου τοῦ Μύσθου ἀπὸ Χηνοβοσκ(ῶν)
36 εἰς τὴν ἐ[πι]τήρησιν ὠνῆς ζυτηρᾶς κώμης
    Θεαδελφία[ς.] παραγγέλλ[ο]μεν αὐτῷ πιστῶς καὶ
    ἐπι[μελῶς] τ[ὴ]ν ἐπιτήρη[σ]ιν ποιεῖσθαι καὶ [τ]οὺς
    λόγο[υς] καταχωρί[ζειν] ἐμοί τε καὶ οἷς δέον ἐστὶν
40 τῶν περιουσῶν ἡμερῶν τοῦ ἐνεστῶτος
    ἔτους κ[α]ὶ [το]ῦ ἰσιόντος κα (ἔτους) Ἀδριανοῦ Καίσαρος τοῦ
    κυρίο[υ ....]υ με...δηλον [ἀν]τὶ τοῦ Γαλλικοῦ

...πρ....[.... τ]ὴν χρείαν.   σεσημ(ειωμαι)
44 (ἔτους) κ Αὐτοκράτορος Καίσαρος Τραιανοῦ ᾽Αδριανοῦ
        σε[β]αστοῦ Μεσορὴ.
    Σαρα[....] ..... .κλ..ων ὑπηρέτης προθεὶς κατε(χώρησα).
    (ἔτους) κ Αὐτοκράτορος Καίσαρος Τραιανοῦ ᾽Αδριανοῦ
    [σεβαστοῦ] Μεσορὴ ἐπαγο(μένων).

1]μοσιω   7 αλλω   11 read προσπιπτόντων   18 επαγο
22 μητροπο)   24 Ζωιλο   25]γρ· (see note)   35 Χηνοβοσκ
41 read εἰσιόντος   43 σεση⌢   48 επαγο

                        Translation
COL. I

[Copy] of a public notice, excerpted from the public archives.

Vegetus alias Sarapion, strategos of the division of Themistes in the Arsinoite nome.

To those listed below who were nominated to me by the local officials of the division as being propertied and suitable for the superintendency in this division of the following tax-farming contracts and other concessions of the 20th year of the Emperor Caesar Trajan Hadrian Augustus, I give instructions to take over the superintendency with all faithfulness and care, to submit, as ordered, the accounts of collections in each five-day period to me and the appropriate officials, and, together with the praktores (?), to pay the outstanding (?) amounts into the public bank, the risk being theirs if any loss falls to the fiscus or anything is done improperly or ---. Year 19 of the Emperor Caesar Trajan Hadrian Augustus, Mesore, on the 3rd intercalary day.

For the beer tax:

Gaius Antonius Gallicus, veteran (?), of ---.

Ptolemaios son of Sopatros, grandson of Didymos, of the metropolis.

Harpokration son of Theon, of the amphodon of the Macedonians.

Zoilos son of Chares, of the amphodon of Hierakeios.

COL. II

[Copy] of a public notice, ---.

Herakleides, strategos of the division of Themistes in the Arsinoite nome.

After his excellency Gellius Bassus, the epistrategos, had written to me to appoint, instead of Gaius Antonius Gallicus, who is physically disabled owing to old age, another person to the superintendency in which Gallicus (in his petition) stated himself to be, there was nominated by the komogrammateis of the division and--in villages where there are no komogrammateis--by the presbyteroi performing the duties of the office of komogrammateus

Apion son of Ammonios, grandson of Mystes, of the amphodon of Chenoboskia

for the superintendency over the farming of the beer-tax of the village of Theadelphia. We instruct him to carry out the superintendency faithfully and [carefully] and to submit the accounts to me and the appropriate officials for the remaining days of the present year and coming 21st year of Hadrian Caesar the lord --- the liturgy instead of Gallicus. I have signed, year 20 of the Emperor Caesar Trajan Hadrian Augustus, Mesore, on the xth of the intercalary days.

1: [ἀντίγρα(φον)] πρ[ο]γράμματος: thus by reason of space (as, for example, in *BGU* I 18). The following text, however, is an excerpt from a πρόγραμμα. With indention for the space of three letters, [ἐκ] πρ[ο]γράμματος (as, e.g., in *P. Leit.* 11.1 [= *SB* 10203]) would be possible, but the heading of col. II was, as it seems, slightly exdented (see 25 n.). There the phrase [ἀντί]γρα(φον) προγράμματος is appropriately used since in col. II the full text of the πρόγραμμα is given.

   For the βιβλιοθήκη δημοσίων λόγων and its particular competence in filing all documents concerning revenues and their collection, see H. J. Wolff, *Das Recht der griech. Papyri Ägyptens* (Handbuch V 2 [München 1978]) II, 51, 53ff. and 221.

2: Cf. introd. p. 222. Vegetus alias Sarapion is here attested as strategos of the Themistes on Aug. 26, 135 A.D. (see line 18; H. Henne referred already to our present papyrus [then unpublished]: *Liste des stratèges*, M. IFAO 56 [Cairo 1935] *8). For his subsequent career as strategos of the Herakleides in 136/37 A.D. (*BGU* I 352 [Jan. 28, 137]; *P. Grenf.* II 45a; *P. Phil.* 8.2 etc.), see G. Bastianini, *Strateghi* (see n. 22), 37.

3:   πραγ]ματικῶν: sc. the kommogrammateis and the presbyteroi who, in villages where there was no komogrammateus, performed the duties of the office of komogrammateus; see lines 31-34 and, for example, *P. Leit.* 15 = *SB* 10207: παρὰ ʾΑμόιτος καὶ ʿΩρίω-νος καὶ ʾΑλεξάνδρου καὶ τῶν σὺν α(ὐτοῖς) πρεσβ(υτέρων) [κώ]μης ʾΙσίου ʿΑνω καὶ ἄλ(λων) τόπ(ων) --- διαδεχομένων [τὰ κ]ατὰ τὴν κωμογραμματίαν.

7:   καὶ ἄλλω(ν): Cf., for example, *PSI* V 459.3 καὶ ἄλλων ὠνῶν.

11   διὰ πενθημέρου: For a list of such reports and updates, see the introductions to *P. Fouad* 17, *P. Leit.* 14; P. IFAO I 3 + *P. Köln* II 84; *P. Köln* II 83; C. A. Nelson, *Mus. Philol. Lond.* II (1977) 233ff. and 244, and finally, R. Daniel, *Greek Papyri* (see n. 16) I 5. *SB* IV 7342 mentions a receipt for a penthemeral report. See also n. 5.

12-13: These reports are mostly addressed to the strategos; in addition the matter concerned the basilikogrammateus (*PSI* III 160; cf. J. Schwartz in the introd. to *P. IFAO* 3), the βιβλιο-θήκη δημοσίων λόγων (*BGU* II 478; cf. S. Eitrem and L. Amundsen on *P. Oslo* III 89 and above, 1 n.), the nomarches (cf. *P. Oslo* III 92 and above, n. 13), and the komogrammateus (cf. Eitrem and Amundsen on *P. Oslo* III 91).

        ελ . . λ . μεν[α]: The traces seem to suit ελλειλεμμενα (i.e. ἐλλελειμμένα), though, on the photograph (see n. *), the sequence λει and the third ε are difficult readings and the scribe's spelling is in general correct (except for προσπειπ-τοντων [line 11] and ἴσιοντος [line 41]). The word would be synonymous with the noun ἐλλείματα, which is frequently used to denote arrears (*O. Edfu* 174.1 and 178.2; see n. 10 and *WB* IV s.v.). In *BGU* IX 1895, the heading προσόδ(ων) ὑπαρχ(όντων) [ἐλ]λειμμά(των) introduces a list of names and arrears, possibly (pace the editor) of arrears which were entered into this list as they were finally paid. For the general interpretation, see the introduction.

13-14: For such payments to the public banks see, for example, nn. 6, 11, and 13.

14:   μετ[ὰ τ]ῶν πρακτόρων: their activity is not expected in tax-farming but may be explained, if they assisted in collecting outstanding taxes (see lines 12-13 n. and above, n. 8).

15:   In the context, τούτους refers, at least primarily, to the ἐπιτηρηταί.

16:   ουκ: perhaps ουκ or ου κ--though the photograph may be misleading (see n. *).

19:   ζυτηρᾶς: In light of line 36 (cf. line 7), this is to be understood in the meaning of ὠνῆς ζυτηρᾶς.

20-24: For the physical arrangement of the list, see 33-34 n.

20: Gallicus may be the same person who appears in *BGU* IX 1893.211
(Γάιος Ἀντώνιος Γαλλικός; 149 A.D.).

21: Insignificant traces, possibly (20) ἀπολύσιμος ἀπὸ | στρα[τ]εί-
[ας ἀπὸ Θε]αδελφίας. See the introduction for a discussion of
the fact that Gaius Antonius Gallicus could not claim exemption from liturgies on the basis of being a veteran.

23: ἀπὸ Μακεδόνων: referring to the amphodon of that name in Arsinoe (cf. C. Wessely, "Die Stadt Arsinoe in griechischer Zeit,"
Sb. Wien, phil.-hist. Kl. 145 (1902) 31; *WB* III 412 and IV
444.

24: For the amphodon Ἱερακείου (or with its full name ἀ. Ἀπολλωνίου Ἱερακείου), see Wessely, loc. cit. (see 23 n.), 28f.;
Diz. geogr. et topogr. I 2,153; *WB* III 411 and IV 443.

25: [ἀντί]γρα(φον): At the beginning of the line, most of the papyrus disappeared in holes, except for a little piece with a
horizontal stroke, slightly curved and, if the photograph can
be trusted, thicker at its right edge; this trace is apparently followed by the remnant of a raised diagonal stroke. All
this suits]γρα() very well while it precludes the reading of
ἐκ. The word was obviously exdented by the space of about one
letter. Cf. the note on line 1.

The text after προγράμματος does not follow the pattern
of line 1, and it is almost impossible to differentiate between blanks left by the scribe and abraded ink. The raised
letter looks like α or μ, deformed as is usual when indicating
an abbreviation. After a blank of the size of one or two letters, there follows what could be read as τόμου (ομ rather than
ακ [cf. ακ in line 24]). If this is correct, we might expect:
κ[ολλή]μ(ατος) (number), τόμου (number).

26: This Herakleides is probably to be identified with Herakleides,
strategos of the Themistes and Polemon divisions in 137 (Bastianini, *Strateghi* [see n. 22], 50 and note 3; also see above,
introduction).

27: Gellius Bassus was known to have been epistrategos of the Heptanomia and Arsinoite at least from Dec. 134 to July 12, 135
A.D. (M. Vandoni, *Gli epistrategi nell'Egitto greco-romano*,
Testi e doc. per lo stud. dell'antichità XXXIII [1970] 24).
Since Herakleides does not refer to him as a *former* epistrategos, we may assume that he was in office when Herakleides wrote
his πρόγραμμα. Hence Gellius Bassus continued in office at
least till the middle of August of 136 A.D.

29: Cf. *P. Leit.* 5.7-9 (= *SB* 10196) μὴ δυνάμενος ἀντιλαβέσθαι τῆς
λιτο[υ]ργίας μεγίστης οὔσης καὶ ὑπὲρ ἐμὲ καὶ ὑπονο[σ]ήσαντα.
Apokr. 36-49 (H. C. Youtie, *Cd'E* 30 [1955] 32ff. [= *Script.* II
661ff.]) αἱ πρόσκαιροι νόσοι τῶν πολιτικῶν οὐκ ἀπαλλάσουσιν
λιτουργιῶν, καὶ οἱ ἀσθενεῖς δὲ τῷ σώματι λιτουρ[γ]οῦσιν, ἐὰν
τῇ φροντίδι τῶν οἰκίων πραγμάτων ἐξαρκῖν δύνωνται. See N.
Lewis, *Symb. R. Taubenschlag ded. I, Eos* 48,1 (1956) 216ff.;
idem in *Atti* (see n. 3), 518ff.; idem in *Actes* (see n. 4), 69f.

For καθίστημι ("appoint") in liturgical context, see,
e.g., *P. Oxy.* XXXVIII 2856.1-2 n.; *P. Brux.* 21.6 n.; N. Lewis,
Cd'E 44 (1969) 339f.; and above, nn. 16-18.

31: ὁ Γαλλικὸς: the trace of the first letter is not very distinct,
but the letter is needed for reasons of space. Without it, the
line would be indented, for which there is no reason.

33-34: The scribe left the last part of line 34 blank in order to
begin a new line with the name of the nominee (similarly in
lines 19 and 21; cf. the same arrangement for other reasons in
lines 18, 25[?], 43 and 46). In line 35, the name is indented
by the space of one letter (as in lines 20 [also 21(?)] and
22-24, though there the indentation is a little larger [about
two letters]), and the initial letter is written in an enlarged
version (as in lines 20, 22, 23, and 24). The name fills the
entire line. The following lines 35-37 and probably line 38
continue at the indented space as if they were part of a list
of nominees (cf. lines 20-24). Between lines 38 and 44, each
line begins slightly more to the left until line 44 reaches
the original left edge of the column.

32-34: The komogrammateus nominated the liturgical officers; see,
e.g., *P. Petaus* 75-77 (nomination of ἐπιτηρηταί); 46f.; 52-53;
55-56; 59; 60; 62; 65-66; and 68. For the elder of the village acting in place of the komogrammateus, see *P. Leit.* 5.40-
42 (= *SB* 10196) and 15 (see N. Lewis's introd.; *SB* 10207); A.
Tomsin, loc. cit. [see n. 13], 505ff.; for the use of this
general formula in the context of a single nomination, see
introduction (p. 216).

35: Χηνοβοσκ(ῶν) or Χηνοβοσκ(ίων). There were two amphoda of this
name in Arsinoe (see Wessely, loc. cit. [see 23 n.], 37f.; *WB*
III 415 and IV 445, also *P. Petaus* 125.7.

38: ἐπι[μελῶς]: The traces are extremely faint and ambiguous (cf.
P. Lond. II 301 (p. 256) regarding a transportation of cargo:
ἀντιλήμψασθαι τῆς χρείας πιστῶς καὶ ἐπιμελῶς, and also see
line 10 of Vegetus' πρόγραμμα); more common is the phrase ὑγιῶς
καὶ πιστῶς (see, for example, *BGU* 18.15; *P. Oslo* III 93.7; *P.
Vindob. Sijp.* 2 i 10 and ii 13; *P. Oxy.* 2721.35 and *WB* II 310.

39: See 12-13 n.

40-41: See introd., p. 220.

43: ...πρ....[....: Palaeographically διαπράττε[σθαι is possible,
but idiomatically suspect.

46: Probably Σαρα[πίων] followed by his alias. For this notation,
cf., e.g., *P. Leit.* 5.37f. (= *SB* 10196): Σεραπάμμων ὁ καὶ
Ἰσίδωρος ὑπηρέτης προθεὶς κατεχώρησ(α).

48: ἐπαγο(μένων) : Possibly ἐπαγο(μένων) β (August 25, 136).

Cairo   A.H.S. El Mosallamy

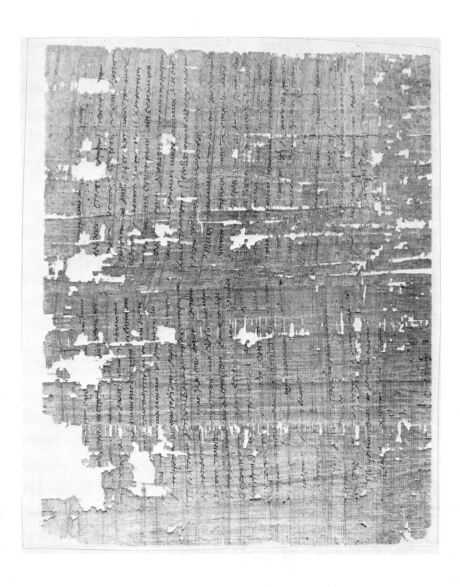

PART OF TOMOS SYGKOLLESIMOS OF HYPOMNEMATA
(P. CAIRO SR 3049,36-39)

In 1973 a team of the International Photographic Archive
photographed a large group of papyri which had been brought to the
Egyptian Museum on June 26, 1927. Most of these texts were found
in Theadelphia, a few in Karanis and Oxyrhynchos. A number of
these papyri have been recently published.[1] I am at present editing a group of seven leases from the same find. The seven texts
were pasted together to form part of a roll which looks like a
tomos sygkollesimos. The preserved part of the tomos is 63 cm. in
width and 21 cm. in height, this being separated into four pieces
with the following respective widths: 26, 17, 10, 10 cm.

All the leases are in the form of *hypomnemata*. The format is
that characteristic of the Arsinoite nome: τῷ δεῖνι παρὰ τοῦ δεῖνος,
βούλομαι μισθώσασθαι after which are stated the object and the duration of the lease, the amount of the rent and the payment dates, the
usual terms of work, and ἐὰν φαίνηται μισθῶσαι.[2]

The seven *hypomnemata* belong to five different contracts written in the 7th year of Antoninus Pius. The first contract is represented by the first *hypomnema* which was written on August 1, 144 AD.
The object of the lease is a house and a yard. A part of the house
had collapsed and was to be rebuilt by the owners with the help of
the new tenant: ἐμοῦ τοῦ Πασίωνος συνυπουργοῦντος.

The second and the third *hypomnemata* of the series are both
for the second contract. They are copies of the same lease for a
parcel of cleruchic land for three years (144-47 AD). Both copies
were left incomplete by the scribe, though they lack only personal
descriptions and the date.[3]

---

1   *P. Soterichos*; *P. Col.* VII 175 (by R. S. Bagnall); *Stud Pap*
15 (1976) 52ff. (by L. Koenen); an additional papyrus, edited by L.
Koenen and myself, is *P. Turner* 21.

2   On this form of lease, see H. J. Wolff, *Das Recht der Griechischen Papyri Ägyptens* (München 1978) 114-22 and the literature
cited in n. 26.

3   On this text, see below, pp. 234ff.

The third contract is also extant in two *hypomnemata*, the
fourth and fifth of the series. Here two farmers offer to sublease
two thirds of one year's harvest of dates and olives from a lessee:
κοινωνήσειν σοι ἕκαστος ἡμῶν κατὰ τὸ τρίτον μέρος. Their install-
ments for the rent were due at the same time that the original
lessee had contracted to pay the rent for the whole harvest. It
should also be noted that the scribe began, but failed, to complete
the personal description of the lessor in the first copy; also he
wrote no date. But the contract was written on June 4, 144 AD as
we learn from the second copy.

The fourth contract, or the sixth *hypomnema* in the series, is
a lease of land for three years (144-47 AD). The personal description of the lessee and most of the dating formula are broken off.

The last or seventh document belongs to the fifth contract.
Written on July 25, 144 AD, it concerns the lease of a house for
one year. Only this document has the lessor's endorsement.[4]

None of the parties in the five contracts are identical. The
lessees in all the contracts, except the last one which is broken
off, and the lessor of the third contract were registered in Arsinoe. Moreover, the houses to be rented under the first and last
contracts were also located in Arsinoe. Hence it seems that the
contracting parties and the objects of leases were all from or
around Arsinoe. The second contract concerns a parcel of land located near the village Persyai in the Heraklides division. We may
conclude that this village was also relatively close to Arsinoe
(see line 14f. note).

In this connection it is appropriate to remark on the back of
the roll. It contains seven columns (nos. 16-22) of a list of
taxes on land: ναύβιον κατοίκων, γεωμετρία, ἀριθμητικὸν κατοίκων.
The entire list is written by one hand which is different from
those of the recto. Nine of these taxpayers seem to be identical
with persons named in taxlists of Theadelphia: *P. Col.* V (160-61 AD);
BGU IX (166-67 AD). Our texts contain three infrequent names which

---

4 Personal descriptions of lessor (4th *hypomnema*) and lessees
(1st, 5th, and 6th *hypomnemata*) fulfill the same function; cf. G.
Hübsch, *Die Personalangaben als Identifizierungsvermerk im Recht
der gräko-ägyptischen Papyri* (Berlin 1968) 55; A.E.R. Boak, *P. Mich.*
III 184 introd.

occur elsewhere only in the Theadelphia taxlists: Πᾶπος κοσμητ(ής)
(col. 17.1), Στατίλλις (col. 18.4), Φλαβία ᾿Αντωνίνα (col. 19.19);
cf. *P. Col.* V lb.61, 67, 77 respectively. Three other names in col.
17 (Χαρίτιον Χαιρᾶ [7], Χαρίτιον ᾿Αφροδ() [9], Σεύθης Πᾶπου [10])
occur together in line 42 of *BGU* IX 1896. In all likelihood, then,
the taxpayers in the new list paid their taxes in Theadelphia,
which accords with the fact that most papyri in this mixed group
were found in this town. Hence papyri which were originally written in offices of scribes of Arsinoe were reused by a tax official
at Theadelphia. The tax list may provisorily be assigned to the
years after 155 AD, since the texts on the recto which are all from
144 AD probably became obsolete in a relatively short time.[5]

To sum up: contracts written in the office of private scribes
in Arsinoe ended up in the hands of tax officials at Theadelphia;
they wrote on the back of those documents after they had been pasted
together into a roll. It is difficult to determine whether the roll
was made from waste paper precisely for the purpose of recycling or
the scribes in Arsinoe already pasted the roll together in order to
keep a convenient record, thus imitating the practice of the public
notary's offices (*grapheion, agoranomeion, mnemoneion*) where copies
of all contracts were collected into *tomoi sygkollesimoi*.[6] The
latter explanation is indicated by the following facts.

(1) The extant first copies of all five contracts were written
by a single scribe. Only the second copies of the second and third
contracts were written by another scribe. Since neither the persons taking part in the transactions, nor the transactions themselves are connected with each other, the only link between them is
the fact that they all were written in the same office and represent the same type of document.

(2) The seven documents were pasted together so that all *hypomnemata* remain clearly readable. Each document has a left margin,
though next to no right margin. The right side of each document
was pasted on the empty left margin of the following document.

---

5 The longest period of lease mentioned in the preserved
contracts is 6 years, though there may have been longer periods in
the lost *hypomnemata* of the same roll. Nevertheless, after 10 or
15 years, such a *tomos* would be ready for recycling.

6 The practice of filing by pasting the relevant documents
into a roll occurs also elsewhere; cf. *P. Köln* I 52 and 53.

The waste basket even of a single scribe is not likely to contain always the same type of documents, particularly when these
documents were written over a period of at least seven and a half
weeks: the earliest contract is dated June 4, 144 AD (no. 3) and
the latest July 25th of the same year (no. 5). According to these
facts I am inclined to assume that the present roll indeed served
the purpose of record keeping. On the other hand, there are also
grounds for the opposite assumption that the roll was made from
waste paper either by the scribes who sold them to the tax officials in Theadelphia or by the tax officials themselves. The following reasons point in this direction. (1) The *hypomnemata* are
not arranged in a strictly chronological order. All from 144 AD,
the first is dated to August 1, the third to June 4 and the last to
July 25. (2) Two contracts are preserved in two copies.[7]

The disorderliness may, however, be explained if we suppose
that, in the absence of the parties, the scribe prepared routinely
the number of copies he expected would be needed by the parties.
All copies in excess of those needs were then filed into separate
rolls according to their subject matter so that documents of the
same type would end up in the same roll. Chronological order may
generally have been helpful for purpose of later reference, but
firm consistency was not needed. Since the names of the parties
were written on the top of the *hypomnemata*, it would have been easy
to find any contract. For the purpose of record keeping the personal description may have been of little importance. The omission
of the date on copies filed in the tomes may be pure negligence.

As an example of these *hypomnemata* I present the second which
belongs to the second contract. The application is addressed to
Thermoutharion daughter of Didas appearing with her guardian and
husband Harpochras son of Harpocration; it came from a certain Heron son of Sarapion, grandchild of Heron, who was registered in the
quarter of Tharapia in Arsinoe and appears to be identified as the
socially weaker party by being described as Πέρσης τῆς ἐπιγονῆς
(see note on line 7). He wanted to lease two arourae of a cleros

---

7 Personal descriptions of the lessees in the 1st, 5th, and
6th *hypomnemata* suggest that these documents were designed for the
purpose of the lessor, whereas the 4th *hypomnema* (a duplicate of
the 5th *hypomnema*) with the personal description of the lessor and
the 7th with the lessor's endorsement were composed from the view-
point of the lessee.

near the village Persyai (see note on lines 14f.) for three years
from the eighth year of Antoninus Pius at a yearly rent of nine
artabae barley, repayment of seed not included. The lessee was to
perform all the appropriate agricultural operations at his own expense and without causing any damage (see note on lines 20ff.). He
was free to choose the crops for the first two years except safflower (see note on line 27), but in the last year of the lease he
had to sow barley. The rent was to be paid in the month of Pauni
(see note on line 31) on the threshing floor of the arourae in new,
pure and unadulterated barley. At the expiration of the lease, the
lessee was to return the land in a clean state. The lessor, on the
other hand, had to guarantee the lease and to pay all the public
dues except the public freightage, which was to be borne by the
lessee (see note on lines 38ff.).

Θερμ[ουϑ]αρίωι   Διδᾶτ(ος)
μετ[ὰ] κυρίο(υ) τοῦ ἀνδρὸς
Ἀρποχ[ρ]ᾶτ(ος) τοῦ Ἀρποκρατ(ίωνος)

4 παρὰ Ἥρωνος τοῦ Σαρα-
πίων[ο]ς τοῦ Ἥρωνος
ἀναγρα(φομένου) ἐπ' ἀμφόδ[ο]υ Θαρα-
πίας Πέρσου τῆς ἐπιγονῆς.

8 βούλομαι μισθώσασθαι
παρὰ σοῦ εἰς ἔτη τρε[ί]α
καρποὺ[ς] τρεῖς ἀπὸ τ[ο]ῦ
ἰσιόντ[ο]ς η (ἔτους) Ἀντω[νίνο]υ

12 Καίσαρος τοῦ κυρί[ου τὰς]
ὑπαρχούσας συ [περὶ κώ-]
μην Περσύ[ας] κλῆρο(υ)
ἀρούρας δύο ἢ [ὅσ]αι

16 ἐὰν ὦσι, ἐ[κ]φ[ο]ρίου
[τ]οῦ παντὸς κατ' ἔτος
ἀσπερ[μ]εὶ κριϑῆς ἀρταβ(ῶν)
[ἐ]ννέα μέτρῳ δρό[μ]ωι

20 τετραχ(οινίκῳ) καὶ ἐπιτε[λέ]σω
τὰ κατ' ἔτος γεωργικὰ
ἔργα π[ά]ντα ὅσα καϑή-
κι ἐκ [τ]οῦ ἰδίου, βλάβ[ο]ς

24   μηδ[ὲν] ποιῶν, σπε[ί]ρων
      ἐπὶ μ[ὲν] τὰ πρῶτ[α ἔτ]η
      δύ[ο] ο[ἶς] ἐὰν αἱρῶ[μα]ι
      γένεσ[ι π]λὴν κνήκου,
28   τῶι δὲ ἐσχάτωι ἔ[τ]ει
      τῆς μ[ισθ]ώσεως κριθῆ,
      καὶ τὰ [κα]τ' ἔτος ἐκφ[όρ]ια
      ἀποδώ[σω ἐν] μηνὶ Παῦνι
32   ἐφ' ἅλῳ [τῶν] ἀρουρ(ῶν) νέα καθα-
      ρὰ ἄδο[λ]α, καὶ μετὰ [τὸ]ν
      χρόνο[ν π]αραδώσω ἀπ[ὸ]
      συνκ[ομι]δῆς, ὡς πρόκ[(ειται),]
36   ἐὰν φαίν[η]τ(αι) μισθ(ῶσαι), βεβαιουμέ-
      νης μ[ο]ι [τ]ῆς μισθώσεω(ς)
      ὑπὸ σο[ῦ καὶ] ἀπὸ δημ[ο]σίων
      πάντων ἔξω δημοσί[ω]ν φολέ(τρων)
40   τῶν κα[ὶ ὄν]των πρὸ[ς ἐμ]ὲ
      τὸν μεμισ[θ(ωμένον)].

- - - - - - - - - - - - - - - - - - - -

1   Διδα^τ   2   κυρι^ο   3   Αρποχρατ   6   αναγρ^ς
9   read τρία   11 read εἰσιόντος   h^L   13 read σοι
14 κληρ^ο   18 αρτα^υ   20 τετραχ   22f. read καθή|κει
32 αρουρ‿   35 seemingly προκ   36 seemingly φαινη^τ   μισ⸑
37 μισθωσε‿   49 seemingly φολ⸍

       To Thermoutharion daughter of Didas, with her guar-
dian, her husband Harpochras son of Harpocration, from
Heron son of Sarapion, grandchild of Heron, registered
in the quarter of Tharapia, Persian of the epigone. I
wish to lease from you the two arourae or thereabouts
cleros-land belonging to you near the village Persyai
for three years, three crops, from the next eighth year
of Antoninus Caesar the lord, at a total yearly rent,
not including seed, of nine artabae barley by the four-
choinix dromos-measure. I will perform all the annual
agricultural operations that are fitting at my own expense, doing nothing injurious, sowing in the first two
years with any crop I choose except safflower, and in
the last year of the lease barley. I will pay the yearly
rent in the month of Pauni on the threshing-floor of the
arourae new, pure and unadulterated; at the end of the
period I will deliver it after the harvest, as aforesaid,

if you consent to the lease, the lease being guaranteed
by you for me and free from all public dues except the
public freightage which shall be borne by me, the lessee.

6. For the quarter of Tharapia in Arsinoe, cf. C. Wessely, *Die
   Stadt Arsinoe (Krokodilopolis) in griechischer Zeit* (Wien
   1903, repr. Milan 1975) 27.

7. Πέρσης τῆς ἐπιγονῆς shows the inferior status of the lessee.
   By analogy even the lessor in leases with payment in advance
   is so designated; cf. J. F. Oates, *YCS* 18 (1963) 5-129; idem
   in the introduction of *P. Yale* 67; O. Montevecchi, *La papirologia* (Torino 1973) 227; P. W. Pestman, *Aegyptus* 43 (1963) 15-
   53; Calderini, *JEA* 40 (1954) 19ff.; W. van Rengen, *Cd'E* 40
   (1965) 355; G. M. Browne, *P. Mich.* XI 585.4 n.; E. Bresciani,
   La Parola del Passato 27 (1972) 123ff.

14f. Cf. *BGU* III 919.15 (II AD) περὶ κ[ώμη]ν Περσύας τῆς ʿΗρακ-
   (λείδου) μερίδος. Grenfell and Hunt (*P. Tebt.* II, p. 395)
   suppose that this village was probably located in the southern
   part of the Heraclides division. One might now infer that its
   location was relatively close to Arsinoe where the lessee was
   a resident (line 6). The same editors point out that this
   village was called Περσέα in the Ptolemaic, Περσέαι or Περσύαι
   in the Roman period.

20ff. All the agricultural work on grainland fell usually upon the
   lessee, except under leases with payment in advance, where it
   was borne by the lessor; cf. D. Hennig, *ZPE* 9 (1972) 111ff.;
   J. Herrmann, *Bodenpacht* (MB 41, München 1958) 125ff.

27 κνῆκος: The cultivation of safflower was forbidden probably
   according to monopoly regulations and the lessor wanted to
   avoid the additional load of charges; see D. Hagedorn, *ZPE* 17
   (1975) 85ff.; *P. Soterichos* 3.24f. n.

31 Pauni is the usual month for payment in nearly all documents
   of the Roman and Byzantine period from the Arsinoite and Oxyrhynchite nomes; cf. D. Hennig, *Bodenpacht* (Diss. München
   1967) 22f.; J. Herrmann, *Bodenpacht*, 107ff.

34f. ἀπ[ὸ] συνκ[ομι]δῆς: see D. Hennig, *ZPE* 9 (1972) 125f.

36f. For the βεβαίωσις-clause in general, see J. Herrmann, *Bodenpacht*, 107ff.; L. Mitteis, *Grundzüge* (Leipzig-Berlin 1912)

188ff., 269; F. Pringsheim, *Sale* (Weimar 1950) 358; R. Taubenschlag, *Law* (Warsaw[2] 1955) 326, 335f., 361, 386 etc.
38ff. The public charges were ordinarily to be borne by the lessor
(J. Herrmann, *Bodenpacht*, 122f.; S. Waszynski, *Bodenpacht*
[Leipzig-Berlin 1905] 115ff.). The stipulation that the public freightage fall upon the lessee occurs only in the Arsinoite
nome (J. Herrmann, *Bodenpacht*, 123). T. Kalén states, in *P.
Berl. Leihg.* 19.32ff. n., that this stipulation was important
in that nome more than in the others, because of the relatively
long distances from towns and villages in the Fayum to ports
on the Nile.

Cairo/Treves   Sayed Omar

A PETITION TO THE STRATEGUS OF THE LYCOPOLITE NOME
CONCERNING AN UNAUTHORIZED SALE OF PROPERTY IN JOINT OWNERSHIP*

P. Eg. Soc. Pap. 236   9.5 x 14.5 cm.   Oct. 23, 221 A.D.
Lycopolis

Upper, lower, and part of the right margin of this papyrus is extant. The ink is partly abraded so that many readings remain obscure, making restorations difficult and details of interpretation tentative. The writing is parallel to the fibres; there is no writing on the back.

The document consists of two unrelated parts: lines 1-3 are the beginning of the preamble of a letter by Caracalla, and lines 4-18 contain the petition of a certain Aurelius Ptolemaeus who is requesting the intervention of the strategus of the Lycopolite nome in order to recover property, or payment for property, which he and his wife owned jointly and the latter had sold without his consent.

I. TEXT, TRANSLATION, AND NOTES

1 m_1 → [Αὐτοκρά]τωρ Καῖσαρ Μᾶρκος Αὐρήλιος
      [Σεουῆρος] 'Αντωνῖνος Σεβαστὸς
      [ἀρχιερεὺ]ς δημαρχικῆς ἐξουσίας

4 m_2 [..... ....]..... στρα(τηγῷ) Λυκοπολ(ίτου) *vac.*
      [παρὰ Αὐρηλίου] Πτολεμαί(ου) Θεοδώρου τῶν ἐν Λύκων Πόλ(ει)
              κατο[ίκ(ων)]
      [..... ....]..... 'Ελένη Παλοῦτος ἀπὸ κώ(μης) 'Ιβιῶ(νος)
              Σε[σ]ε[μ]βύθεω[ς]
      [..... ....]ας[.].. κοινῇ παραβαλοῦσα τροφεῖα παρελάμ-
              [βανεν]

8 [παρ' ἐμοῦ πολλὰ] ὑπὲρ λόγου τροφείων ἀναλώσαντος τοις...α()
              [....]
      [..... ἡ προγεγρ]αμμέ(νη) γυνή μου κοινωνὸς τῆς ἡμισείας
              κληρ[ονο-]

---

* In my absence, this paper was read by Professor L. Koenen, who, on the basis of photographs also made many suggestions for readings, restorations, and interpretations.

[μίας (?) μου ..... δι' ἀ]σχολίαν ἀπελθοῦσα πέπρακεν
                              χω[ρ]ὶς ἐμ[οῦ]
[..... .... παν]τοδαπήν. τοσαύτης οὖν μοι βίας καὶ
                              πλεονεξία[ς]
12   [καὶ ἁρπαγῆς (?) γενομ]ένης ἐπιστέλλω ... τὸ βιβλίδιον
                              ἀξιῶν ...
     [συντάξαι ....]ασασαν .[..]αι Αὐ[ρη]λίαν 'Ελέν<η>ν
                              Παλοῦτος
[..... .... δ]ημοσι.. ....η τὴν τιμήν μοι ἀποκατα-
[στῆσαι ἵνα μὴ ἀδικηθῶ.] διευτύχει. (ἔτους)ε' Αὐτοκράτορος
                              Καίσαρος
16   [Μάρκου Αὐρηλίου 'Αντ]ωνίνου Εὐσεβοῦς Εὐτυχοῦς Σεβαστοῦ
                              καὶ Μάρκου
     [Αὐρηλίου 'Αλεξάνδρου] Καίσαρος Σεβαστοῦ, Φαῶφι κς̄.
                              Αὐρήλ(ιος) Πτολ(εμαῖος)
     [ἐπιδέδωκα.   ] vac.

4 στὴ λυκοπο⌃   5 πτολεμαι⌐ (though the hook, or part of it,
could be residual ink from a previous use of the papyrus)   πο⌃
6 κω̄ Ιβι⌣   9 προγεγρ]αμμε (the abbreviation is apparently not
marked)   17 αυρη⌃ πτο⌐

Translation of lines 4-18:
     [To NN,] strategus of the Lycopolite nome [from Aurelius]
Ptolemaeus son of Theodorus of the settlers in Lycopolis. After
my wife Aurelia Helena, daughter of Palous from the village of
Ibion Sesembytheōs, had entrusted in mutual agreement (?)---she
received alimentation [from me and,] on account of her alimentation, I incurred [many expenses ---]. When my aforesaid wife, the
joint owner of [my] half share of an inheritance (?), left [on]
business, she sold, without my consent, [(property of various
categories).] Since I [suffer] an act of such great violence,
greediness, [and theft (?),] I submit this (?) petition and ask
[you to order that ---] my wife (?) Aurelia Helena daughter of
Palous restore to me [either the land (?), with] all taxes paid (?),
or its price [so that I may not suffer injustice]. Fare well!
Year 5 of Imperator Caesar [Marcus Aurelius] Antoninus Pius Felix
Augustus and Marcus [Aurelius Alexander] Caesar Augustus, Phaophi
26. I, Aurelius Ptolemaeus, [have submitted this petition].

3: [ἀρχιερεὺ]ς: The title *pontifex maximus* is regularly given in
    imperial letters. For this short Greek version see, e.g., the
    epistula Augusti ad Sardianos (R. K. Sherk, *Roman Documents
    from the East* [Baltimore, Maryland, 1969] 68; *SB* X 10615 (Nero);
    cf. *P. Oxy.* XLII 3020 (earlier first cent.); *P. Oxy.* XLVII
    3361 (Antoninus Pius; damaged) = J. D. Thomas, *BICS* 19 (1972)
    103ff. (see 105 n. on line 10). For ἀρχιερεὺς μέγιστος, the
    longer version, see, for example, Claudius' letter to the Alex-
    andrians (*P. Lond.* VI 1912 = *CPJud* II 153) and *P. Oxy.* XXVII
    2476.18 (letter of Claudius, copied in 289 A.D.; damaged).
    According to H. J. Mason (*Greek Terms for Roman Institutions*
    [Am. Stud. Pap. 13 (Toronto 1974)] 115), the long version "is
    the regular form in official documents" after Vespasian; this
    statement now needs correction.

4: [..... ....]....: The traces are extremely ambiguous. A
    certain Aurelius Sarapion also called Sarapammon was strategus
    of the Lycopolite nome in 229 A.D. (G. Mussies, "Supplément à
    la liste des stratèges" in *Studia pap. varia* [Pap. Lugd.-Bat.
    14 [1965] 24 no 212b). Though according to the edict of Ti-
    berius Julius Alexander the tenure of the office of strategus
    was restricted to three years (lines 34f.), longer occupancies
    of 6 or 7 years are attested: for example, Aelius Aphrodisius
    (148/9-154), Aurelius Harpocration (218-225), and Aurelius
    Leonides (229-236/7), all in the Oxyrhynchite nome (J.E.G.
    Whitehorne, *ZPE* 29 [1978] no. 50, 77, and 81, pp. 174 and 178f.;
    also the same author's contribution in the present *Proceed-
    ings*; N. Hohlwein, *Le stratège du nome* [Pap. Brux. 9 (Brussels
    1969)] 21ff.). Hence Aurelius Sarapion alias Sarapammon could
    have been in office as early as Oct., 221 A.D. and as late as
    July, 229 A.D., either continuously for eight years or in two
    separate terms, and [Αὐρηλίῳ Σαρα]πίωνι might be considered as
    a possible restoration. The extant traces, however, neither
    confirm nor preclude this suggestion.

6: Possibly [ἡ ... γυνή μου] Ἀὺρηλί(α). In this case the abbre-
    viation would apparently be unmarked (cf. pal. app. on line 9
    and 13 n.).

       Σε[σ]ε[μ]βύδεω[ς] or Σε[σ]υ[μ]βύθεω[ς]; for this village
    in the Hermopolite nome, see M. Drew-Bear, *Le nome Hermopolite*,
    toponymes et sites (Am. Stud. Pap. 21, Missoula, Montana 1979)
    127f.; *Diz. dei nomi geogr. et topogr.* III 13.

7: παραβαλοῦσα: The scribe originally wrote παραβαλετ, as it
    seems, perhaps intending παρ<έ>βαλε τροφεῖα. When he reached
    the τ, he apparently recognized his mistake and corrected it,
    changing λε into λου, deleting the τ, and adding σα.

       παρελάμ[βανεν] or παρέλαβ[εν].

8: τοις...α() [....]: palaeographically rather τοις χουςα()[
    (which yields no sense) than τὸ ἴσον ουςα()[or τοῖς δὲ ουςα()
    The α is raised, but it is not certain whether the scribe
    meant to indicate an abbreviation. τ could be read instead of
    ς, and the traces could perhaps be interpreted as τοῖς χορτά-
    [σμα|σιν. To my knowledge, however, this word is not used for
    human food in the papyri (but see Bauer, *Wörterb. NT*, s.v.).

9:     προγεγρ]αμμέ(νη) γυνή: on the photograph (see p. 248), the let-
       ters μμε are covered by two bits of papyrus folded over from
       the back. See the pal. app.

9-10: κληρ[ονο|μίας μου: λ or α, followed by a vertical stroke
       and a rounded bottom of a letter or cursive connection between
       two letters. καιϲ [, καιρ [(ρ as in Αὐρηλ() of line 17, see
       17 n.), καπ [, κλερ [, or κλη [(the bottom of the second ver-
       tical of η, in this hand, is normally less rounded) are among
       the possibilities. κοινωνός raises the expectation that Au-
       relia Helena participated in her husband's trade, but this
       apparently is not borne out by τῆς ἡμισείας (not followed by
       the genitive of the article). Hence κληρ[ονο|μίας has a
       chance of being correct.

11:    Possibly [γῆν (?) πολλὴν καὶ παν]τοδαπήν, implying that this
       land belonged to the inherited share owned jointly by Aurelius
       Ptolemaeus and Aurelia Helena. Or [ταύτην οὖσαν παν]τοδαπήν.

12:    The supplement, which is meant to be *exempli gratia*, could be
       slightly longer.

             The traces after ἐπιστελλῶ suit rather τουτο (sc. τοῦτο
       τὸ) than τόδε τὸ or σοι τό. At the end of the line, μὲν (not
       σε) seems to be quite clear, but its syntactical function is
       obscure.

13:    Possibly [σε συντάξαι (or *similia*) τὴν διαρπ]άσασαν (or τὴν
       ἐμὲ βι]άσασαν or *similia*) γ[υν]αῖ(κα). No trace of an abbre-
       viation mark is visible (cf. line 6 n.).

14:    If η is to be interpreted as ἤ, Aurelius Ptolemaeus asked for
       two alternative solutions (cf., e.g., *P. Col.* VII 169.15f. and
       170.21f.). One might expect him to demand his wife's return
       and/or the restitution of the property which had already been
       sold or, alternatively, payment for this property; e.g. [ἤ τὴν
       γῆν καθαρὰν ἀπὸ δ]ημοσίων ἐ[δῶν ἤ τὴν τιμήν μοι ἀποκατα|[στῆ-
       σαι. The reading ἐ[δῶν is difficult, though δω may be written
       very cursively (cf. lines 5 and 11) and the second part of ν
       could have disappeared in an abraded spot which looks like a
       blank (on face value it looks like γῆν). πλη[ρ]ῆ (i.e.
       [ἐπαναγκασθῆναι ὑπὸ δ]ημοσίων πλη[ρ]ῆ τὴν τιμήν μοι ἀποκατα|-
       [στῆσαι, "that (she) be forced by officials to pay the price
       in full") is a less satisfying reading.

17:    The signature seems to have been written by the same hand as
       the body of the petition, though the letter forms, in part,
       look slightly different (see ρ and τ; the latter looks almost
       like λ).

II. THE PREAMBLE OF AN IMPERIAL LETTER BY CARACALLA

The first three lines contain the titles of Caracalla in the nominative case, written in a large chancery hand.[1] Line 3 ends with δημαρχικῆς ἐξουσίας; the next line would have had to begin with τὸ plus the year of the *tribunicia potestas*, followed by a consular year, possibly by honorary titles, the dative of the people to whom the imperial letter was directed, and finally χαίρειν. Instead line 4 begins a petition written in the 5th year of Elagabalus and Severus Alexander. The second scribe, writing in a much smaller, cursive, professional though irregular hand, used a piece of old paper which perhaps contained only the three first lines of Caracalla's preamble and, hence, was merely an incomplete copy imitating a chancery hand. Alternatively, the papyrus originally carried the text of the imperial letter which was washed off for the purpose of recycling the papyrus--at the latest by the scribe who wrote out the petition for Aurelius Ptolemaeus in 221 A.D. (see below, III). Between lines 3 and 4, remnants of ink belonging to the previous text may still remain (see pal. app. on line 5). If this assumption is correct, the letter of Caracalla had a remarkably short life; it survived the emperor by not more than four years, and probably by a much shorter span of time. At this point it may be worthwhile to recall that the name of Caracalla was erased from an inscription from Middle Egypt.[2]

The titles of Caracalla in the present preamble follow a short version which is rare and, because of lacunose papyri, has aroused critical suspicion. In particular, it should be stated that the new papyrus rehabilitates the restoration of this version of

---

1 For the form of the titles also, cf. *P. Gen.* 40.1 (?; P. Bureth, *Les titulatures impériales* [Brussels 1964] 103), *P. Alex.* 20.25. Occasionally Εὐσεβής precedes (*SB* 9626.8f.; Bureth, 104) or follows Ἀντωνῖνος (*SB* 993.2f.; Bureth, 103 and below, n. 2). *BGU* XI 2056.13 ends on Σεβαστοῦ μεγίστου, but this looks like a scribal omission of Παρθικοῦ before μεγίστου. For other types of Caracalla's title see Bureth. The restoration of the title in *P. Giss.* I 40 was disputed by H. Wolff, *Die Constitutio Antoniniana und P. Giss. 40 I* (Diss. Köln 1976) I, 120ff.; the question is important since the restoration determines the width of the lost left part of the column and, consequently, influences restorations and interpretations.

2 *SB* 993.3ff. (= *IG Rom* 1136) ὑπὲρ σωτηρίας ⟦[Μ]ά[ρ]|[κ]ου Αὐρ[ηλ]ίου [Σεουήρου]⟧ | Ἀντωνίνου Σεβαστοῦ | Εὐσεβοῦς.

Caracalla's titles in *P. Giss.* I 40: [Αὐτοκράτωρ Καῖσαρ Μά]ρκος
Αὐρήλι[ος Σεουῆρος] ᾿Αντωνῖνο[ς] Σ[εβαστό]ς. This is not the
place to draw conclusions for the interpretation of the Giessen
papyrus and its possible connection with the *Constitutio Antoniniana.*

In the new papyrus the last title is *pontifex maximus,* as is
customary in imperial letters (see line 3 n.).

III. THE PETITION OF AURELIUS PTOLEMAEUS TO THE
STRATEGUS OF THE LYCOPOLITE NOME

This petition is dated on Phaophi 26 of the 5th year of
Elagabalus and Severus Alexander (Oct. 23, 221 A.D.), several
months before Elagabalus died violently to be succeeded by Severus
Alexander on March 12, 222 A.D. The petition, therefore, is entirely unconnected with the preamble of Caracalla's letter.

It is, of course, unlikely that the petition submitted to the
strategus was written on recycled papyrus which still carried complete lines from its previous use in the reign of Caracalla. The
present document is either a draft or, since it shows no signs of
drafting, a copy for the private use of the petitioner. This conclusion is confirmed by line 17f. where the petitioner signed the
document: Αὐρήλ(ιος) Πτολ(εμαῖος) | [ἐπιδέδωκα]; this signature was
apparently written by the same hand as the main body of the document (see line 17 n.).

The titles of the emperors offer a minor variant. Normally
Σεβαστοί follows at the end of the combined series of titles attributed to each of the emperors,[3] whereas in the present document
each emperor is individually called Σεβαστός at the end of his own
series of titles.

The poor state of preservation makes it difficult to reconstruct the case of Aurelius Ptolemaeus son of Theodorus, an owner
of catoecic land near Lycopolis. He complains about actions taken
by his wife Aurelia Helena daughter of Palaus from, it seems, Ibiōn
Sesembytheōs, a village in the Hermopolite nome (see line 6 n.).
The reading of the name of this village is admittedly doubtful and,
in the Hermopolite, Oxyrhynchite, Arsinoite, and Heracleopolite

---

3 Αὐτοκράτωρ Καῖσαρ Μάρκος Αὐρήλιος ᾿Αντωνῖνος Εὐσεβὴς Εὐτυχὴς
καὶ Μάρκος Αὐρήλιος ᾿Αλέξανδρος Καῖσαρ Σεβαστοί (*SB* 9212 and Bureth,
loc. cit. [see n. 1], 107).

nomes, as well as elsewhere, there are a great number of villages
with compound names beginning with Ibiōn. Sesembytheōs, however,
suits the traces best.

The prehistory of the case is complicated by the fact that in
documentary papyri παραβάλλειν (line 7) is used in different meanings: "going to a place," "deliver," "entrust," "add," "give up,"
"collate," and perhaps even "sue." In connection with the form
παραβαλοῦσα (see line 7 n.) and depending on what precedes at the
beginning of the line, the dative κοινῇ could either denote an addition to the property being held in joint ownership or under joint
power of disposal, or it is being used adverbially, "a mutual
agreement." Whatever the precise meaning, Aurelia Helena, it seems,
"gave up" some property and "added" it to the family property or
"entrusted" it to her husband. Since, in the same context, Aurelius Ptolemaeus twice mentioned his own expenses for the alimentation of his wife (lines 7 and 8), this contribution might refer to
the wife's dowry, whether it was paid before or at the wedding, or
some time later during the marriage. The terminology itself is
reminiscent of συγγραφαί τροφίτιδες of the Egyptian law.[4] In the
Egyptian contracts, neither the sum of money which the wife paid
to the husband "in order to become a wife," i.e. for her maintenance, nor other matrimonial properties were regarded as joint po-
sessions.[5] Hence, under Egyptian law, at least an understanding
of].. κοινῇ παραβαλοῦσα in the strict sense of an addition to the
joint property is precluded. It is, however, very unlikely that,
at the time of our document, συγγραφαί τροφίτιδες and the pertinent
conceptions of the Egyptian law were still known. Even for Ptolemaic times there are indications that the payments by the wife or
her family were either fictitious or symbolic.

---

4 P. W. Pestman, *Marriage and Matrimonial Property in Ancient
Egypt* (Pap. Lugd. Bat. 9 [Leiden 1961] 32-50. E. Seidl, *Ptolemäische
Rechtsgeschichte* (Ägyptologische Forsch. 22, Glückstadt-Hamburg-New
York 1962) 52; idem, *Rechtsgeschichte Ägyptens als römischer Provinz*
(Sankt Augustin 1973) 214.

5 Pestman, loc. cit. (see n. 4) 90ff., particularly 100, 104,
107f., 143ff., and 151. In Greek terms, the wife's payment for her
maintenance could be regarded as δάνειον (Pestman, 36 and 45; G.
Häge, *Ehegüterrechtliche Verhältnisse in den griechischen Papyri
Ägyptens* [Köln-Graz 1968] 111ff., 117f., 122f. and 199f.). For gifts
by the bride's father to his son-in-law, see Pestman, 142; such
gifts as well as gifts by the wife are apparently not meant in the
present papyrus as is evidenced by the references to τροφεῖα.

It is, therefore, more appropriate to seek an explanation for
the present case in the customary marriage law as it developed in
Greco-Roman Egypt. In the Ptolemaic period, joint ownership of the
family possessions was occasionally stipulated, and it may very well
have been that, in Roman times, this simply was taken for granted.[6]
For example, in *P. Tebt.* I 104.15 (92 B.C.), the wife is κυριεύουσα
μετ' αὐτοῦ κοινῇ τῶν ὑπαρχόντων αὐτοῖς.[7] Such stipulations should
have resulted in a restriction of the husband's power to use, and
to dispose of, the φερνή as he pleased. In the case of divorce,
the φερνή was to be given back to the woman. Strictly speaking, it
was her property, though her husband had the right of disposal
alone or jointly with his wife, as long as the marriage lasted and
the wife's interests were safeguarded. In practical terms, the
dowry could therefore be regarded as owned jointly. Given the ambiguity of κοινῇ in the present petition, it is more important that
the φερνή, like the wife's payment for maintenance in Egyptian contracts, was considered as creating the husband's obligation to provide sustenance for his wife: τὸν Διονύσιον ἀπεσχηκότα τὴν προκει-
μένην φερνὴν τρέφειν καὶ ἱματίζειν τὴν 'Ισιδώραν ὡς γυναῖκα γα[με-
τὴν] κατὰ δύναμιν (*BGU* IV 1050.11ff. = *M. Chr.* 286; time of
Augustus).[8]

The crucial beginning of line 7 is lost. There the papyrus
did not necessarily use any such technical term as φερνή, but the
idea of an interrelationship between the dowry and the wife's alimentation seems to underlie the argument made by Aurelius Ptolemaeus. Next he refers to what was possibly an inheritance divided
between two parties. Aurelius Ptolemaeus shared his part with his
wife (lines 9-11; see lines 9-10 n.). We are not told what made

---

6 H. J. Wolff, *Written and Unwritten Marriages* (Philol.
Monogr. IX, Haverford 1939) 52; for a different opinion, see G.
Häge, loc. cit. (see n. 4) 144ff.

7 = *M. Chr.* 285 = *Sel. Pap.* I 2 = J. Hengstl, *Griech. Pap.
aus Ägypten* (München 1978) no. 72; cf. *P. Giss.* 2.16f. (173 B.C.);
UPZ I 123.12 = *M. Chr.* 280 (157/6 B.C.). Häge, loc. cit. (see n.
5) 66ff. According to Egyptian Law, the woman seems to have been
entitled to part (usually one third) of her husband's property, including acquisitions during the marriage, if she herself did not
dissolve the marriage (Pestman, loc. cit. [see n. 4] 128 and 139).

8 There is, so far as I know, no indication that the προσφορά,
consisting of slaves, real estate, etc. and remaining property of
the wife, constituted a similar claim for her maintenance. Hence
it need not be discussed in the present context.

her his κοινωνός, but we may safely assume that, if she was not
named in a will together with her husband, she nevertheless participated in his share of the inheritance (?) as in his other po-
sessions (see above). The inheritance consisted perhaps of various
types of land (see line 14 n. and 11 n.).

Apparently it was this joint share of the inheritance (?) that
caused a domestic quarrel. Aurelia Helena left her husband on
business (line 1: δι᾽ ἀ]σχολίαν ἀπελθοῦσα) and, without her husband's consent, sold their joint share. The latter is indicated by
χωρὶς ἐμ[οῦ in line 10, which is used similarly in a sentence of P.
Mich. 477.10f. (early 2nd cent.): χωρὶς γὰρ αὐτ[ο]ῦ οὐ δύναμ[αι
αὐτὸ κατα]χωρίσα[ι]: "For without him, I am unable to register it."
In the present petition, we do not learn how Aurelia Helena was
able to sell the joint property without her husband's approval.
The relationship between husband and wife had probably deteriorated
to the point where, under the excuse of business, she seems to have
left him (line 10, ἀπελθοῦσα). In marriage contracts it was frequently stipulated that a woman should not leave her husband's
house for a day or night without his consent,[9] and it is safe to
assume that this expectation corresponded to the general expectations in marriages with or without contracts. Aurelia Helena could
be described as ἑκουσίως ἀπαλλασσομένη.[10] Many contracts specify
the time within which the husband was to return the dowry, after
his wife had voluntarily left him and laid claim to it.[11] Did,
then, Aurelius Ptolemaeus not repay the dowry, and had Aurelia Helena tried to recover what was rightfully hers by selling their
joint share of the inheritance? According to many contracts, the
wife had the right of execution upon all her husband's property as
if by legal decision.[12] Aurelia Helena seems to have taken the law
into her own hands. We may not speculate any further, but our

---

9 For example, BGU IV 1052.24ff. (= Sel. Pap. I 3; 13 B.C.)
and 1050.19f. (see above); P. Tebt. I 104.27 (see n. 7).

10 P. Ryl. II 154.25f. = Sel. Pap. I 4 (66 A.D.).

11 Häge, loc. cit. (see n. 5) 165ff., particularly 166 n. 28.

12 See, for example, BGU IV 1052.19ff. (see n. 9), 1050.17
(see above), and 1045.26f. = M. Chr. 282 (154 A.D.).

assumptions could explain both the action of Aurelia Helena who
might have thought that she was acting in accordance with accepted
procedure, and the outrage of her husband (lines 11f.).

Whatever the validity of Aurelius Ptolemaeus' claim, in lines
12-15 he demanded the help of the strategus in recovering at least
payment for the property his wife had sold. The alternative action he calls for is not clear. In face of the restricted space
on the papyrus it is simplest to assume that, alternatively, he
demanded the return of the property free from public dues (see line
14 n.). So far as we can see, Aurelius Ptolemaeus did not make any
allowance for the fact that his wife participated in the ownership.
He might have thought that she lost her title when she left him.

I may finish with a note of sociological interest. Aurelia
Helena seems to have moved out under the pretext, or for the reason,
of business travel: δι᾿ ἀ]σχολίαν ἀπελθοῦσα. Such a family situation seems to be more characteristic of the modern world than we
are inclined to assume for the ancients.

Alexandria and Cairo   Zaki Aly

PART 5

PTOLEMAIC EGYPT

Proceedings of the XVI Int. Congr. of Papyrology (Chico 1981) 251-258

UN NUOVO ARCHIVIO PAPIRACEO DEL II SECOLO AV. CR.
(P. MED. BAR.)

Nella Collezione dell'Istituto di Papirologia dell'Università
Cattolica del S. Cuore è pervenuto recentemente un archivio papiraceo[1] di notevole interesse, risalente al II secolo av. Cr. Si
tratta di 16 pezzi, di cui 10 di una certa ampiezza, più un gran
numero di frammenti, il tutto ricavato da cartoni di mummia.[2] E'
una serie di documenti, forse in origine incollati l'uno appresso
all'altro a formare un rotolo; alcuni di essi erano stati utilizzati anche nel *verso* per stendere minute di altri documenti. Per
la maggior parte sono petizioni, più qualche lettera d'ufficio,
conti, e due ordinanze reali finora sconosciute.

I documenti provengono dall'ufficio di un funzionario greco
dell'amministrazione militare, di nome Pankrates, a cui sono indirizzate la maggior parte delle petizioni scritte nel *recto*. La
grafia rimanda al II sec. av. Cr.; uno dei documenti ha conservato
la data: anno 28°, 20 Pauni; i personaggi che vi ricorrono permettono di attribuire con sicurezza l'anno di regno a Tolemeo VIII
Evergete II: siamo dunque nel 143/2[a], precisamente il 14 giugno 142,
tre anni dopo il ritorno sul trono dell'Evergete stesso. La menzione dell'anno 28° si legge anche nel corso di un altro documento,
e in un terzo quella dell'anno [.]7: tutto fa supporre che l'intero
archivio appartenga a un giro di tempo abbastanza ristretto intorno
all'anno 143/2.

Particolare curioso e nuovo: un frammento porta scritto, sul
verso e secondo le fibre (dunque nella parte esterna, visibile
quando il rotolo era chiuso), a grandi lettere (altezza cm 2) alquanto spaziate, così da estendersi per cm 8, la parola ἀχρεῖα:

---

1 L'archivio porterà il nome di *Papyri Mediolanenses Barelli*
(*P. Med. Bar.*) in memoria di Armida Barelli, confondatrice dell'
Università Cattolica del S. Cuore, e in segno di gratitudine verso
la famiglia Barelli che validamente si adoperò per assicurare all'
Università questi documenti.

2 Il lavoro di distacco e di restauro è stato compiuto dal
dott. Michael Fackelmann, che qui pubblicamente ringrazio.

"inutili." Probabilmente fu scritta all'estremità del rotolo
quando questo venne messo da parte perchè ormai vecchio. Come
dire: "buttar via," "al macero."

La località donde proviene l'archivio è l'Arsinoite, distretto
di Polemone. Sono nominati Kerkesoucha e Areos kome (che risultano
avere un'amministrazione unica), Oxyrhyncha, dello stesso distretto,
e Boubastos, del confinante distretto di Eraclide, che ricorre a
proposito di una permuta di terreni.

Il nostro archivio ha qualche importante aggancio con altri
papiri sparsi in diverse collezioni, di cui alcuni pubblicati molti
decenni or sono: lo rivelano sei personaggi che in essi ricorrono.
Si tratta dei documenti seguenti; tutti provenienti dal distretto di
Polemone: *P. Tebt.* I 32 (= *W. Chrest.* 448), del 145; *P. Tebt.* I 61
b; 62; 64 a; 72; 79; *P. Tebt.* III 736, del 143; 788, del 144 ex. o
143 ex.; 801, del 142/1; 972. Inoltre: *P. Meyer* 1, del 144; *P.
Würzb.* 4; *P. Rein.* I 7; *BGU* VI 1250; P. Lille inv. 65 A-G; 74 A-B;
102 A-B, editi da B. Boyaval in *ZPE* 28 (1978) 187-93: questi ultimi
sono frammenti che potrebbero provenire dallo stesso ufficio dei
nostri documenti, dato che vi compare più volte il nome di Pankrates.

I personaggi in questione, già registrati nella *Prosopographia
Ptolemaica* di W. Peremans e E. Van 't Dack, e in quella di L.
Mooren,[3] sono:

1. Ἀπολλόδωρος, ἐπιστάτης, destinatario di una petizione in
cui porta il titolo aulico τῶν πρώτων φίλων (*P. Med. Bar.* 2 verso),
e nominato nel corso di un'altra petizione inviata allo stratego
Ptolemaios (*P. Med. Bar.* 4 verso). Già noto come ἐπιστάτης καὶ
γραμματεὺς τῶν κατοίκων ἱππέων da *P. Meyer* 1 (aprile 144); *P. Tebt.*
I 32 = *W. Chrest.* 448 (145); *P. Tebt.* I 61 b (senza data); 72
(senza data); *P. Rein.* I 7 = *M. Chrest.* 16 (dopo il giugno 142);
e dall'iscrizione da lui posta in onore di Tolemeo VIII Evergete II:

---

3 *Prosopographia Ptolemaica* par W. Peremans et E. Van 't Dack
(Lovanii 1950-1975); L. Mooren, *The Aulic Titulature in Ptolemaic
Egypt: Introduction and Prosopography* (Bruxelles 1975). Cf. anche:
L. Mooren, *La Hiérarchie de cour ptolémaïque. Contribution à l'étude
des institutions et des classes dirigeantes à l'époque hellénistique*
(Lovanii 1977).

CIG III 4698 = *OGIS* I 128 = *SB* V 8302 (senza data: terminus post quem 146).

Cf. *Pros. Ptol.* II 2454 = 2465; *Pros. Mooren* 0233; Mooren, *La Hiérarchie de cour ptolémaïque*, 167-69; H. Bengtson, *Die Strategie in der hellenistischen Zeit* (München 1967[2]) III, 51.

2. Δημήτριος καὶ Στέφανος, ἐπιστάται del villaggio di Oxyrhyncha. Destinatari di una petizione (*P. Med. Bar.* 8 recto). Già attestati, associati, in *P. Tebt.* III 786.23-24 (c. 138[a]); Demetrio da solo compare in *P. Tebt.* III 802.2-3, come τῶν διαδόχων καὶ ἱππάρχης ἐπ' ἀνδρῶν καὶ ἐπιστάτης.

Cf. *Pros. Ptol.* 659 e 715; *Pros. Mooren* 0156.

3. Διονύσιος, ἀρχισωματοφύλαξ καὶ γραμματεὺς τῶν κατοίκων ἱππέων, nominato nella petizione *P. Med. Bar.* 1.31-33 (142). Già noto da *P. Meyer* 1.18 (cf. Introduzione, p. 4), del 144, e da *P. Tebt.* I 62.67; 63.60; 64 a.31; 79.51-53; *P. Tebt.* III 972.23 (?).

Cf. *Pros. Ptol.* 2516, 2455 (?); *Pros. Mooren* 0239; Mooren, *La Hiérarchie*, 25-26, 101, 168-69; J. Lesquier, *Les Institutions militaires de l'Egypte sous les Lagides*, 196.

4. Παγκράτης, ἀρχισωματοφύλαξ καὶ πρὸς τῇ συντάξει τῶν κατοίκων ἱππέων, destinatario delle petizioni *P. Med. Bar.* 1 (142); 2 recto; 3 recto; 5 recto; 10 recto; nominato nelle petizioni 3 verso e 15 recto; mittente della lettera 14 recto. Il nome Pankrates (senza titolo) compare anche in una lista di persone (*P. Med. Bar.* 13 recto). In questi documenti, come nei *P. Lille* ed. Boyaval, porta il titolo aulico di ἀρχισωματοφύλαξ, mentre in *P. Würzb.* 4 (senza data) è insignito del titolo più elevato di τῶν ἰσοτίμων τοῖς πρώτοις φίλοις, il che ci permette di fissare il 142 come *terminus post quem* per la datazione dello stesso *P. Würzb.* 4. Pankrates è già noto (oltre che da *P. Würzb.* 4 e dai *P. Lille* ed. Boyaval) da *P. Tebt.* I 32 = *W. Chrest.* 448 (145).

Cf. *Pros. Ptol.* 2499; *Pros. Mooren* 0235 = 00116; Mooren, *La Hiérarchie*, 22 n. 3; 97 e n. 1; 168 e nn. 1, 2.

5. Πτολεμαῖος Πύρρου, τῶν πρώτων φίλων καὶ στρατηγὸς dell' Arsinoite, destinatario della petizione *P. Med. Bar.* 4 verso. Il mittente della lettera d'ufficio *P. Med. Bar.* 16 verso (minuta), Ptolemaios, potrebbe essere la stessa persona. Già noto, con lo

stesso titolo aulico, da *P. Tebt.* III 736 (143); 788 (144 ex. o 143
ex.); 801 (142/1); *BGU* VI 1250 (data sconosciuta), e dai frammenti
P. Lille ed. Boyaval.

Cf. *Pros. Ptol.* I 317 = 316 (v. Addenda p. 47); *Pros. Mooren*
070; Mooren, *La Hiérarchie*, 168 n. 2.

6. Στέφανος: v. sopra Δημήτριος καὶ Στέφανος.

Compaiono per la prima volta in questo archivio i personaggi
seguenti:

1. Ἀγασίας, mittente di una lettera a Ptolemaios (lo stratego?)
   insieme con Νίμμος (?), Αιγ... e forse altri. *P. Med. Bar.* 7
   recto.

2. Αιγ...: v. sopra Ἀγασίας.

3. Ἀντίμαχος Ἀριστομήδου, macedone, della 5° ipparchia, hekatontarouros, mittente di una petizione a Pankrates insieme con
   Herakleides figlio di Ariston. *P. Med. Bar.* 1 recto (142).

4. Ἀντίοχος, forse destinatario di una lettera (in forma di
   hypomnema) di Ptolemaios (lo stratego?). *P. Med. Bar.* 16 verso.

5. Ἀντίπατρος, ὁ πρὸς τῇ συντάξει, nominato nella petizione *P. Med.
   Bar.* 1 recto 29 (142).

6. Ἀρχῦψις, ἱερεὺς Ἡρακλέους θεοῦ μεγάλου, mittente, insieme con
   un altro sacerdote di cui è caduto il nome, di una petizione
   allo stratego Ptolemaios. *P. Med. Bar.* 4 verso.

7. Ἀταρρίας, nominato, insieme con Νικάνωρ, come avversario in
   una petizione inviata forse al logeutes Κοινός da almeno due
   persone. *P. Med. Bar.* 15 recto 36.

8. Ἐριεμοῦνις ὁ.....γραμματεὺς, nominato nella petizione *P. Med.
   Bar.* 1 recto 27-28 (142).

9. Ἡρακλείδης Ἀρίστωνος, trace, della 5° ipparchia, orphanos,
   che ha come prostatis la madre Thais; mittente di una petizione
   a Pankrates insieme con Antimachos figlio di Aristomedes. *P.
   Med. Bar.* 1 recto (142).

10. Θαΐς Ἀπολλωνίου, madre di Herakleides figlio di Ariston, προσ-
    τάτις del figlio nella petizione *P. Med. Bar.* 1 recto (142).

11. Κοινός, λογευτῆς, nominato nella petizione *P. Med. Bar.* 5 recto,
    e forse destinatario della petizione *P. Med. Bar.* 10 recto.

12. Μαρρῆς, συναλλαγματογράφος, nominato nella petizione *P. Med.
    Bar.* 3 verso 6.

13. Μεγχῆς, nominato nella petizione *P. Med. Bar.* 3 verso 7: Μεγχῆν τὸν νῦν ἁ[ν]τειληφότα τὴν κωμογραμματείαν.

14. Μενοίτιος Ὀλυμπιοδώρου, orphanos, titolare di un kleros di cui è amministratore Ptolemaios macedone ogdoekontarouros. *P. Med. Bar.* 5.

15. Νικάνωρ: vedi sopra Ἀταρρίας.

16. Νικόλαος, ἐπιστάτης della 5° ipparchia, nominato nella petizione *P. Med. Bar.* 1.13-14 (142).

17. Νίμμος (?), vedi sopra Ἀγασίας.

18. Παλλώσιος, mittente della lettera *P. Med. Bar.* 6 recto.

19. Πα..φ..ς, γραμματεὺς Ἄρεως κώμης καὶ Κερκεσούχων. *P. Med. Bar.* 1.22-23 (142).

20. Πετεάρχης, destinatario della lettera *P. Med. Bar.* 6 recto.

21. Πετεσοῦχος, destinatario della lettera *P. Med. Bar.* 14 recto, scritta da Pankrates.

22. Πε.εμούθης, τοπογραμματεύς. *P. Med. Bar.* 1 recto 25-26 (142).

23. Πτολεμαῖος Πτολεμαίου, macedone, τῶν κατοίκων ἱππέων, mittente di due petizioni a Pankrates (*P. Med. Bar.* 2 recto; 3 recto), di una ad Apollodoros (*P. Med. Bar.* 2 verso), e di una a Demetrio e Stefano, epistatai di Oxyrhyncha (*P. Med. Bar.* 8 recto).

24. Πτολεμαῖος, macedone, ogdoekontarouros, mittente di una petizione a Pankrates. *P. Med. Bar.* 5 recto.

25. Σώστρατος Ἀ.γρικῶντος, tessalo. *P. Med. Bar.* 1 recto 34-35 (142).

Ed ecco un breve cenno sui singoli documenti:

--*P. Med. Bar.* 1 recto. Petizione a Pankrates da parte di Antimachos f. di Aristomedes, macedone, della 5° ipparchia, hekatontarouros, e di Herakleides f. di Ariston, trace, della stessa ipparchia, orfano, avente come prostatis la madre Thais. Riguarda una permuta di kleroi. cm 38,5 x 31. Una colonna (43 rr.) e parte di una seconda (12 rr.). Nel verso 3 righe che si riferiscono probabilmente al documento del recto.

--*P. Med. Bar.* 2 recto. Petizione a Pankrates da parte ˙di Ptolemaios f. di Ptolemaios. Assai rovinato, con molte lacune. 1ᵃ col. 29 rr.; 2ᵃ col. 15 rr. Nel verso petizione su due colonne ad Apollodoros τῶν ᾱ φίλων, da parte di un Ptolemaios

per terreni situati ad Oxyrhyncha. Sono menzionati documenti
mandati a Pankrates. Minuta, con correzioni. cm 35,5 x 29.
1^a col. 22 rr.; 2^a col. 20 rr.

--*P. Med. Bar.* 3 recto. Petizione a Pankrates da parte di Ptolemaios f. di Ptolemaios, macedone, τῶν κατοίκων ἱππέων. 1^a col.
28 rr.; 2^a col.: l'inizio di 27 rr. Nel verso: seconda colonna
di una petizione, nel corso della quale è nominato Pankrates.
Con correzioni: minuta. 16 rr. cm 33 x 31.

--*P. Med. Bar.* 4 verso (il recto non porta alcuno scritto).
Petizione a Ptolemaios f. di Pyrrhos da parte di Harchypsis e
di un altro, sacerdoti di Eracle. I petenti chiedono a Tolemeo
che ordini di scrivere all'epistates Apollodoros affinchè
questi disponga che essi non vengano più molestati (per motivi
fiscali?). Minuta. 21 rr. cm 18 x 30.

--*P. Med. Bar.* 5 recto. Petizione a Pankrates da parte di Ptolemaios macedone ogdoekontarouros, amministratore del kleros di
100 arure di Menoitios f. di Olympiodoros, orphanos, a Oxyrhyncha. Pare si lamenti per imposizioni fiscali ingiuste ad opera
dei grammateis. Sono nominate imposte come la ἀνιππία, lo
στέφανος, il χειριστικόν. 26 rr. cm 21 x 30.

--*P. Med. Bar.* 6 recto. Lettera di Pallosios. 21 rr., alquanto
svanite. Nel verso: Πετεάρχει, e un altro nome. cm 10,3 x 28,5.

--*P. Med. Bar.* 7 recto. Lettera di Agasias, Nimmos (?) ed altri
Πτολεμαίῳ ἀδελφῷ. 18 righe alquanto svanite con qualche can-
cellatura e aggiunta interlineare. Nel verso: περὶ τοῦ ἐκ ρ꞊
ἐπιστολή. cm 10,8 x 15,5.

--*P. Med. Bar.* 8 recto. Petizione agli epistatai di Oxyrhyncha
Demetrio e Stefano da parte di Ptolemaios f. di Ptolemaios,
macedone, τῶν κατοίκων ἱππέων. 14 rr. Nel verso una lunga
petizione quasi illeggibile perchè molto svanita. 25 rr.
cm 24 x 31.

--*P. Med. Bar.* 9. Conti, sia nel verso come nel recto. cm 13 x
13.

--*P. Med. Bar.* 10 recto. Inizio di una petizione a Pankrates, da
parte di Ptolemaios, macedone, ogdoekontarouros, per terreni
situati ad Oxyrhyncha; è nominato un tale, f. di Apollodoros,
orphanos: cf. n° 5. 5 rr. mutile a destra. cm 13,3 x 5.

--*P. Med. Bar*. 11 recto.   Inizio di 4 rr., probabilmente di conti.

--*P. Med. Bar*. 12 recto.   Forse lettera, completa ai lati, scritta
con tratto grosso; la scrittura è molto svanita.   23 rr.   cm
5,5 x 18.

--*P. Med. Bar*. 13.   Lista di nomi, tra cui Pankrates ed Hera-
sippos.   8 rr.   cm 10 x 15,5.

--*P. Med. Bar*. 14.   Inizio di una lettera di Pankrates a Pete-
souchos.   8 rr. scolorite, con qualche lacuna.   cm 13 x 11.

--*P. Med. Bar*. 15 recto.   Petizione, rivolta da più persone al
logeutes Κοινός.   E' nominato Pankrates, a cui sarebbe stato
mandato un hypomnema.   La petizione pare avere lo scopo di
difendere gli interessi di un orphanos contro la πλεονεξία dei
tutori, che sembrano essere Atarrias e Nikanor.   Alquanto svanita la prima parte, al centro una grande lacuna, meglio conservate le ultime 10 righe.   39 rr.   Nel verso alcune lettere
(forse conti).   cm 21 x 30.

--*P. Med. Bar*. 16 recto.   Due prostagmata, il primo dell'anno 20,
il secondo dell'anno 13.   Riguardano ambedue il divieto di
alienazione di ἱερὰ γῆ.   29 rr.   cm 15 x 29.   Nel verso una
lettera d'ufficio, in forma di hypomnema, da parte di Ptolemaios.   E' nominato un Antiochos.   Minuta.   20 rr.

--*P. Med. Bar*. 17.   Nel verso, ma scritto lungo le fibre, si
legge ἀχρεῖα.   cm 16,3 x 5.

--*P. Med. Bar*. 18 verso.   Vi si legge: τὸ ἐπιδοθὲν.[| ὑπόμνημα[
cm 5 x 14.

--*P. Med. Bar*. 19 recto.   Poche tracce di conti.   cm 5,5 x 13.

--*P. Med. Bar*. 20 recto.   Scarsissime tracce di scrittura.   cm
11,5 x 10.

--*P. Med. Bar*. 21 recto.   Tracce di conti.   cm 8 x 12.

--*P. Med. Bar*. 22 recto.   Tracce di conti.   cm 5,3 x 7.

--*P. Med. Bar*. 23-36.   Piccoli frammenti con qualche parola.

--*P. Med. Bar*. 37-52.   Frammenti minimi.

I *P. Med. Bar*. ci forniscono nuovi elementi per una migliore
conoscenza di alcuni problemi amministrativi e giuridici dell'
Egitto in questo periodo.   E precisamente:

1. Evoluzione del kleros da concessione a possesso ereditario. In
questi documenti siamo in fase di transizione già avanzata.
2. Titolatura aulica e sua evoluzione. In *P. Med. Bar.* 1, datato
20 giugno 142[a], Pankrates porta il titolo di ἀρχισωματοφύλαξ, mentre
sappiamo che in seguito, pur mantenendo la stessa funzione, ebbe
quello più più elevato di τῶν ἰσοτίμων τοῖς πρώτοις φίλοις (*P.
Würzb.* 4, non datato). Il nostro papiro porta a supporre che le
innovazioni dell'Evergete II, e in particolare l'inserzione del
titolo τῶν ἰσοτίμων τοῖς πρώτοις φίλοις tra τῶν πρώτων φίλων e
ἀρχισωματοφύλαξ, siano state attuate dopo il 142.
3. Significato e compiti del funzionario πρὸς τῇ συντάξει: problema
trattato in questo Congresso da Giovanni Geraci (pp. 267-76).
4. Significato del termine ὀρφανός, di cui si è occupata in questo
stesso Congresso Lucia Criscuolo (pp. 259-65).
5. Significato del termine προστάτις, qui attestato per la prima
volta nei papiri. Di questo intendo occuparmi io stessa in un articolo che uscirà prossimamente in *Aegyptus.*

Frattanto mi è sembrato opportuno dare questa prima informazione sul contenuto e le caratteristiche dei *P. Med. Bar.*,[4] sia per
offrire senza indugio agli studiosi la possibilità di tener conto
di quanto già emerge da una rapida descrizione dell'archivio, sia
per fornire dei dati che permettano di riconoscere eventuali relazioni e collegamenti con documenti di altre collezioni, editi o
inediti, e giovino ad una migliore comprensione degli uni e degli
altri.

Orsolina Montevecchi

---

4 I papiri Med. Bar. sono ora allo studio per opera di un'
équipe che fa capo alla sottoscritta, coadiuvata da Sergio Daris e
Giovanni Geraci; ne fanno parte Carla Balconi, Gerardo Casanova,
Lucia Criscuolo, Anna Di Bitonto Kasser, Silvia Strassi.

ORPHANOI E ORPHANOI KLĒROI: NUOVI ASPETTI
DELL'EVOLUZIONE DEL DIRITTO CLERUCHICO*

Uno dei contributi più rilevanti che il materiale papiraceo
arreca alla scienza dell'antichità è quello lessicale, e non solo
per la quantità di nuove parole che dai papiri sono testimoniate,
ma talvolta per il completamento delle rispettive sfumature seman-
tiche o per la loro precisazione. Questa indagine trae origine
proprio dall'esigenza di chiarire ulteriormente una espressione le
cui implicazioni giuridiche condizionano grandemente l'attuale interpretazione dell'organizzazione cleruchica sviluppatasi nel regno
tolemaico durante il III e il II secolo a.C.

In un documento, *P. Med. Bar.* 5, recentemente acquisito dal-
l'Università Cattolica di Milano e di cui mi è stata affidata la
pubblicazione, è contenuta una petizione rivolta a Pankrates, ὁ
πρὸς τῆι συντάξει, da Tolemeo, Macedone, *ogdoekatontarouros* e
"προεστηκὼς τοῦ Μενοίτου τοῦ 'Ολυμπιοδώρου ὀρφανοῦ (ἑκατονταρούρου)
κλήρου περὶ 'Οξυρύγχα." Il papiro, ancora inedito, risale probabilmente al 29° anno di regno di Tolemeo VIII Evergete II, 142/41
a.C., e fa parte dell'archivio dell'ὁ πρὸς τῆι συντάξει τῶν κατοίκων ἱππέων Pankrates.[1] La petizione, come spesso in questo genere
di documenti, contiene il resoconto dei soprusi subiti dal cleruco
a causa degli errori commessi, non certo involontariamente, dai
grammatei. Ma è l'intestazione che, a mio avviso, suscita il maggiore interesse: Tolemeo infatti vi figura, oltre che come cleruco
titolare di un fondo di 80 arure, anche come "amministratore del

---

* Desidero ringraziare il Governo degli Stati Uniti d'America,
il National Endowment for the Humanities e il Comitato Organizzatore
del XVI International Congress of Papyrologists per il generoso
contributo concessomi, grazie al quale mi è stato possibile partecipare attivamente ai lavori del Congresso.

1 Per questo personaggio e per la sua funzione rimando alle
comunicazioni presentate dai proff. Montevecchi (*infra*, pp. 251-58)
e Geraci (*infra*, pp. 267-76), oltre che, naturalmente, all'articolo
di B. Boyaval, "Παγκράτης ἀρχισωματοφύλαξ καὶ πρὸς τῆι συντάξει,"
ZPE 28 (1978) 187-93.

kleros di Menoitas, figlio di Olympiodoros, orfano, *ekatontarou-ros.*"[2]

Molti interrogativi sorgono dall'uso del termine ὀρφανός in questo come in tanti altri documenti: riveste esso un peculiare significato quando venga usato in ambito cleruchico oppure, più semplicemente, sta solo a designare il figlio privo di padre? Implica una procedura successoria del possedimento cleruchico automatica, puramente accertata e accettata dallo stato? O, al contrario prescinde ormai da ogni accezione giuridica, quale invece gli era propria nella Grecia classica, ove ὀρφανός stava a indicare il minore senza padre e quindi bisognoso di un tutore?[3] Inoltre, esaminando la documentazione relativa agli ὀρφανοί, mi sono imbattuta nell'espressione "κλῆρος ὀρφανός," usata due volte in *P. Tebt.* III 815, del 222 circa a.C. Quale senso poteva avere in questi casi l'aggettivo ὀρφανός?

Per rispondere a questi interrogativi, o per tentare di farlo, ho confrontato i testi più significativi e verificato su di essi quanto la dottrina ha fino ad ora asserito. Come è noto la analisi del sistema cleruchico, della sua evoluzione ed articolazione ha portato, principalmente da parte del Lesquier e della Préaux, a una sistemazione unanimemente accettata; l'opera dell'Uebel ha però

---

2 La traduzione proposta è basata sulla seguente costruzione che, a mio parere, meglio si adatta, considerati anche gli esempi simili, al significato qui inteso: προεστηκὼς τοῦ κλήρου Μενοίτου, τοῦ Ὀλυμπιοδώρου, ὀρφανοῦ, (ἑκατονταρούρου). La soluzione (ἑκατονταρούρου) è qui adottata in quanto si tratta per il momento di quella più documentata: Menoitas avrebbe però già il titolo connesso con l'estensione dell'appezzamento paterno, usato qui solo indicativamente. Un'altra possibile soluzione, suggeritami dal prof. E. Van 't Dack, che qui desidero ringraziare, sarebbe invece (ἑκατονταρουρικοῦ) riferito perciò a κλῆρος, per cui cf. P. J. Sijpesteijn, "Neue Eponyme Priester," *Cd'E* 54 (1979), particolarm. P. Moen inv. nr. 17, 9 e p. 105, in cui la parola è scritta per esteso, e idem, "Ἑκατονταρουρικοί and εἰκοσιπενταρουρικοί κλῆροι," *ZPE* 37 (1980) 284, in cui l'autore suggerisce la forma aggettivale in soluzione di abbreviazione anche per *P. IFAO* III 35, dove però è giustificata da una sequenza difficoltosa. Una scelta tra le due soluzioni è ancora aperta.

3 Cf. per una sommaria trattazione A. Dorjahn, "Ὀρφανός," *RE* 18,1 (1939) 1197-1200.

successivamente preparato il campo a ulteriori approfondimenti, grazie al quasi totale riordino del materiale relativo ai cleruchi.[4]

Da un esame anche sommario della documentazione ho tratto due essenziali conclusioni: 1) il termine ὀρφανός non designa alcuna speciale qualifica militare; 2) il termine ὀρφανός non presuppone alcuna particolare condizione giuridica.

Per quanto riguarda la prima considerazione essa si fonda sulla constatazione che se anche è vero che, per l'epoca tolemaica, gli ὀρφανοί sono ricordati prevalentemente in ambito militare,[5] tuttavia non mancano esempi di cui si può escludere la personale appartenenza all'esercito,[6] né va poi trascurato il fatto che sia nelle regioni di lingua greca da cui i soldati tolemaici provenivano sia, successivamente, nei testi di epoca romana ὀρφανός sta a indicare sempre e soltanto la persona priva di padre (o comunque priva di qualcosa): troppo lungo sarebbe illustrare gli esempi epigrafici di ὀρφανοί di cui è impossibile stabilire un qualsivoglia legame con l'esercito,[7] per non parlare delle fanciulle definite ὀρφαναί.[8]

Che dunque alcuni di questi personaggi fossero destinati a succedere ai padri nella carriera militare, ovvero nella classe

---

4   J. Lesquier, *Les Institutions militaires de l'Égypte sous les Lagides* (Paris 1911) particolarm. capp. II, VI, VII; C. Préaux, *L'Économie royale des Lagides* (Bruxelles 1939) 468-80; F. Uebel, *Die Kleruchen Aegyptens unter den ersten sechs Ptolemäern* (Abh. Deut. Akad. Wiss. 1968, n. 3, Berlin 1968). Un ultimo sintetico lavoro, benché assai più succinto, è dovuto a E. Van 't Dack, "Sur l'evolution des institutions militaires Lagides," *Armées et fiscalité dans le monde antique* (Paris 1977) 77-105.

5   Cf. *BGU* VI 1261 = VIII 1734 = *SB* IV 7421; *BGU* VI 1266; *P. Petr.* II 39(e), II 6; *P. Petr.* III 110(a), I; *P. Enteux.* 68.

6   *P. Enteux.* 9 (218[a]); *PSI* XIII 1310 (135/34[a]); *BGU* VIII 1813 (post 62/61[a]); *BGU* VIII 1849 (48-46[a]).

7   Si veda ad esempio per l'Egitto *SB* III 6986 (epigrafe sepolcrale per un orfano treenne); E. Bernand, *Inscriptions métriques de l'Égypte gréco-romaine* (Paris 1969) nn. 55 e 58, entrambe di epoca imperiale avanzata. Un esempio interessante, sempre per l'Egitto, è costituito poi dal n. 42 della medesima raccolta: un'epigrafe del 5[a] invita a compiangere una giovane donna che ha molto sofferto in vita essendo, tra l'altro, rimasta "ὀρφανικὴ μητρός" da bambina.

8   *P. Enteux.* 32.14 (219/18[a]); *SB* VIII 9790 (I[a] med.).

cleruchica, pur rappresentando un dato sociologicamente rilevante,
non costituisce comunque un presupposto per considerare tutti gli
ὀρφανοί già inseriti in un preciso meccanismo di reclutamento, come
fa ad esempio il Gueraud[9] mal intendendo le osservazioni del Lesquier.[10] Accettando infatti un tale postulato dovremmo concludere
che una divisione testamentaria di lotti cleruchici del I secolo
a.c. doveva inevitabilmente portare, almeno in teoria, a un incre-
mento dell'organico militare, cosa che deve ancora essere verificata.[11]

Anche la seconda conclusione, che cioè ὀρφανός non designi un
figlio minore sotto tutela e in attesa di prendere il posto del
padre a tutti gli effetti, è fondata su alcuni documenti che esplicitamente lo dimostrano: ricordo il *P. Enteux.* 9 in cui un abitante
di Crocodilopolis rivolge una petizione al sovrano, siamo sotto il
regno del Filopatore, rivendicando la proprietà di una casa usur-
pata dalla zia paterna. Egli non è cleruco e sollecita la simpatia
nei confronti del suo caso in quanto la zia lo ha disprezzato, come
egli afferma, "ἐπὶ τῶι ὀρφανόμ με εἶναι,"[12] "perché sono orfano"
(un uso molto simile di ὀρφανός compare in un'altra *enteuxis*, *P.
Enteux.* 32: due cleruchi, tutori di una loro sorella concludono
motivando la loro richiesta "affinché l'orfana non subisca ingiu-
stizie").[13] Ugualmente a titolo personale in *P. Enteux.* 68 un cleruco

---

9 Cf. commento a l. 1 di *P. Enteux.* 68: "l'orphelin est fils
d'un clerouque militaire."

10 In realtà Lesquier si limita sempre ad asserire che gli
orfani di cleruchi *potevano* godere di qualche privilegio assicurato
dai meriti del padre (cf. Lesquier, *Les Institutions,* 36 n. 3 e
233), ma non arriva mai a definire gli ὀρφανοί come una categoria
particolare legata all'esercito tolemaico.

11 Cf. Van 't Dack, "Sur l'évolution des institutions," 88 e
n. 7: la divisione attestata dal papiro demotico avviene tra figli
che sono già militari e figli che non lo sono: per questi ultimi
non sappiamo in realtà se sia l'eredità a farne dei soldati. E similmente per i due cateci di *P. Tebt.* I 62.59, 63.55 non possiamo
sapere se ereditano, dividendoselo, il *kleros* paterno perché sono
cateci o se lo diventano in quanto hanno ereditato l'appezzamento:
la distinzione è forse pedantesca ma, a mio avviso, necessaria.

12 L. 6.

13 L. 14, sopra citata.

Trace, ma che si definisce anche ὀρφανός, scrive una protesta contro un suo vicino di *kleros* il quale non rispetterebbe i confini.
Abbiamo quindi due casi di persone che, se pure si proclamano ὀρφανοί, non sono rappresentate da κύριοι o tutori di alcun genere, ma
agiscono in materia legale autonomamente. ʿΟρφανός dunque in sé
non riveste alcun significato limitativo della capacità giuridica,
così come non indica sempre un militare.

Quanto poi all'esistenza di una categoria di κλῆροι ὀρφανοί
essa si fonda sulla menzione del *P. Tebt.* III 815, fr. 2, *verso*,
col. I.19, in cui è registrato un debito contratto da un tal Dorion
"nei confronti degli *ekphoria* del *kleros orphanos* di Antiphanes."
Credo però che sia opportuno osservare che *kleros* è in soluzione di
abbreviazione delle lettere κλ, e che in altri estratti di contratti, di cui come è noto *P. Tebt.* 815 è composto, tali lettere possono essere sciolte anche in κλ(ηροῦχος):[14] e se sostituiamo questa
soluzione alla precedente avremo: "πρὸς τὰ ἐκφόρια τοῦ ʿΑντιφάνους
κλ(ηρούχου) ὀρφανοῦ."

Qualora venisse accettata questa diversa interpretazione resterebbe un solo caso di κλῆρος ὀρφανός, quello del fr. 14 di *P.
Tebt.* 815. Il frammento però è solo descritto e anche qui *kleros*
compare come soluzione delle lettere κλ. Non credo quindi che ci
siano testimonianze sufficientemente sicure perché si possa anno-
verare il *kleros orphanos* tra le altre categorie di possessi cleruchici. Tra l'altro anche dal punto di vista del linguaggio buro-
cratico, sempre così esatto in quest'epoca, un simile uso dell'aggettivo *orphanos* avrebbe reso poco "amministrativa" una tale categoria, dal momento che quel termine veniva usato contemporaneamente,
come si è visto, anche per esprimere e descrivere realtà soggettive
e perfino poetico-sentimentali.

La mia conclusione, per quanto riguarda i *kleroi orphanoi*, è
pertanto che fino ad un'ulteriore e inequivocabile verifica sul fr.
14 di *P. Tebt.* 815, essi non possano testimoniare uno slittamento
del significato di *orphanos*, che come si è già detto veniva contemporaneamente usato in ben altri contesti, da *kleros* senza padre a
kleros senza assegnatario, né tanto meno che essi vadano comunque

---

14 Cf. fr. 2, *recto* 51, 57; fr. 6, 5; fr. 7, 28; fr. 10, col.
II, 17.

considerati come una classificazione amministrativa finché non ne
venga comprovata l'esistenza. Del resto sappiamo che nel momento in
cui moriva il cleruco titolare, la prassi prevedeva che, in caso di
eredi in grado di prenderne il posto nell'esercito e nella condu-
zione del fondo, il *kleros* ritornasse allo stato fino al momento in
cui l'erede o gli eredi stessi non avessero regolato la loro posizione presso gli organi amministrativi.[15]

L'ipotesi che vorrei qui avanzare è che proprio in questa cir-
costanza venisse nominato un προεστηκώς, vale a dire un amministratore, un intendente, responsabile, per il periodo di vacanza del
titolare (periodo anche di molti mesi) dello sfruttamento del
kleros, del puntuale pagamento delle imposte che su di esso grava-
vano e, in somma, garante della continuità di resa che ogni anche
minima area di terreno demaniale doveva allo stato. Non a caso,
forse, tutti i προεστηκότες, accertati o presunti, di beni cleruchici, sono a loro volta cleruchi titolari di appezzamenti;[16] essi
cioè non vanno considerati come privati al servizio di altri privati, ma come temporanei sostituti di colleghi. E' importante
perciò sottolineare che il Tolemeo, προεστηκώς nel *P. Med. Bar.* 5,
non è tutore dell'όρφανός, bensì, se così si può dire, tutore del
kleros: la costruzione della frase non lascia dubbi al riguardo.[17]

Una tale ricostruzione confermerebbe quanto il Lesquier aveva
sostenuto nella sua opera sulle istituzioni militari tolemaiche
(contraddicendo peraltro sè stesso),[18] e che in seguito si è venuto
confondendo con una malintesa interpretazione "realistica" del

---

15 Cf. il famoso *P. Lille* 4.30-33.

16 Cf. *P. Enteux.* 8 e 75. Anche in considerazione del contesto, lamentevole e stranamente impreciso, non saprei se accettare
il suggerimento del Gueraud di nota a l. 1 di *P. Enteux.* 59: il
possibile προεστηκώς è infatti chiamato semplicemente "Δημήτριος
τις," il che sarebbe un po' poco anche per un amministratore civile.
Più probabile è invece il Polyanthes di *BGU* VI 1266, per cui cf.
Uebel, *Die Kleruchen*, nn. 1396, 1397.

17 La possibilità che si tratti di un semplice rapporto di
dipendenza per cui Tolemeo sarebbe il fattore del *kleros* di 100
arure appartenuto a Olympiodoros mi lascia un po' perplessa, soprattutto in considerazione della quasi parità di grado: Tolemeo infatti possiede 80 arure.

18 Cf. *Les Institutions*, 232; per contro sostiene l'eredi-
tarietà dei *kleroi* dalla fine del IIIª a pp. 60 e 232.

diritto cleruchico, tesa a semplificare ad ogni costo la procedura di successione dei *kleroi*: solo dalla fine del II secolo a.C., e non prima, si può considerare il possedimento cleruchico come un bene legalmente trasmissibile sia ai figli sia ad altri consanguinei senza una sanzione statale a verifica di certi requisiti.

Quanto poi ai προεστηκότες dei *kleroi* la documentazione è per il momento troppo scarsa per esaminarne la figura. Sono convinta però che la loro esistenza contribuisca a una più attenta e puntuale analisi del diritto cleruchico, tanto apparentemente scontato quanto in realtà nuovamente da considerare.

Università di Bologna   Lucia Criscuolo

L'ὁ πρὸς τῆι συντάξει: NOTE SULL' AMMINISTRAZIONE
MILITARE NELL' EGITTO TOLEMAICO*

E' di recente entrato a far parte della collezione dell' Istituto di Papirologia dell' Università Cattolica di Milano un piccolo
archivio papiraceo risalente alla metà del II secolo a.c. e probabilmente proveniente dall' ufficio di un funzionario greco del-
l'amministrazione militare, di nome Pankrates, ὁ πρὸς τῆι συντάξει
τῶν κατοίκων ἱππέων, del resto già noto da altre testimonianze.[1]

La presente comunicazione prende lo spunto dallo studio tuttora in atto di tale omogeneo lotto di testi, purtroppo spesso
mutili e sbiaditi come talora accade in seguito a distacco da un
cartonnage, e dalla conseguente esigenza di meglio identificare il
loro contenuto tramite una più precisa analisi del ruolo e delle
competenze dell' ὁ πρὸς τῆι συντάξει nella storia amministrativa
militare dell' Egitto tolemaico, quali traspaiono dai documenti
finora pubblicati relativi al funzionario.

---

* Mi è gradito rivolgere un sincero ringraziamento al Governo
degli Stati Uniti d'America, al National Endowment for the Humanities e al Comitato Organizzatore del Congresso per avere cortese-
mente consentito, con il loro aiuto finanziario, la mia diretta
partecipazione ai lavori congressuali a New York.

1 L' archivio porta il nome di *Papyri Mediolanenses Barelli*
(*P. Med. Bar.*); su di esso vd. le notizie fornite in O. Montevecchi, "Un nuovo archivio papiraceo di età tolemaica in una collezione milanese," *Rend. Ist. Lombardo*, Sc. Lett., 113 (1979) di
imminente pubblicazione, e nella comunicazione dal titolo "Un nuovo
archivio papiraceo greco del II secolo a.C.," che compare in questi
stessi *Atti* (pp. 251-58); cf. anche G. Geraci, "Due nuovi prostagmata tolemaici nell' archivio di Pankrates, ὁ πρὸς τῆι συντάξει,"
Scritti in onore di Orsolina Montevecchi (Bologna 1981) di prossima
edizione; L. Criscuolo, "'Ορφανοί e ὀρφανοὶ κλῆροι: nuovi aspetti
dell' evoluzione del diritto cleruchico," in questi *Atti* (pp. 259-
65). Su Pankrates si vedano *Pros. Ptol.* II 2499; L. Mooren, *The
Aulic Titulature in Ptolemaic Egypt. Introduction and Prosopography*
(Brussel 1975) nn. 0235, 0067a, 00116; idem, *La Hiérarchie de cour
ptolémaïque. Contribution à l'étude des institutions et des classes
dirigeantes à l'époque hellénistique* (Lovanii 1977) 22 n. 3, 168;
e, da ultimo, B. Boyaval, "Παγκράτης ἀρχισωματοφύλαξ καὶ πρὸς τῆι
συντάξει," *ZPE* 28 (1978) 187-93; idem, "P. Lille 65/D et 65/E,"
ZPE 37 (1980) 271-72.

Scarsa e in parte invecchiata la bibliografia: le uniche trattazioni d' insieme si limitano ad alcune pagine ad esso dedicate dal Lesquier nel 1911,[2] a due brevi articoli apparsi nel 1932 nella Pauly-Wissowa ad opera del Seidl[3] e dello Schwahn,[4] a cui vanno aggiunte le sporadiche osservazioni degli editori dei testi in cui il funzionario è menzionato e, più recentemente, un breve accenno dello Handrock[5] e le notazioni sulla sua titolatura aulica formulate dal Mooren.[6]

Una prima delimitazione del campo d' azione dell' ὁ πρὸς τῆι συντάξει[7] può derivare da una più accurata separazione delle competenze di questo funzionario da quelle degli οἱ ταγέντες πρὸς τῆι προσλήψει,[8] distinzione che nê il Lesquier[9] nê il Meyer[10] avevano

---

2 J. Lesquier, *Les Institutions militaires de l'Égypte sous les Lagides* (Paris 1911) 196 ss.

3 E. Seidl, "Συντακτικός," *RE* 4A,2 (1932) 1452; idem, "Ὁ πρὸς τῇ συντάξει τῶν κατοίκων," *RE* 4A,2 (1932) 1452-53.

4 R. Schwahn, "Σύνταξις," *RE* 4A,2 (1932) 1453-56, particolarm. 1455-56.

5 P. Handrock, *Dienstliche Weisungen in den Papyri der Ptolemäerzeit* (diss. Köln 1967) 86-89.

6 Mooren, *The Aulic Titulature*, nn. 0235-0238; idem, *Hiérarchie*, 22 n. 3, 168-69.

7 Nella maggior parte dei documenti il funzionario è denominato, spesso indifferentemente, ὁ πρὸς τῆι συντάξει o ὁ πρὸς τῆι συντάξει τῶν κατοίκων ἱππέων. In un solo caso, *P. Lille* I 4 (per cui vd. *infra*), l' ὁ ἐπὶ συντάξεως si occupa del *kleros* di un *hyperetes* dei Macedoni triacontaruri che parrebbe non essere cavaliere. Lo stato attuale e la consistenza numerica delle attestazioni relative agli οἱ πρὸς τῆι συντάξει non consentono per il momento conclusioni più generali; sembra comunque da escludere che la mancanza della specificazione τῶν κατοίκων ἱππέων implichi automaticamente l' allusione ad un altro ufficiale con competenza specifica soltanto su categorie diverse dai cavalieri cateci.

8 Lesquier, *Institutions*, 188 ss.; *Pros. Ptol.* II 2514-31; VIII 2514a-2526a; Mooren, *The Aulic Titulature*, 0239; idem, *Hiérarchie*, 168-69; e vd. anche *P. Tebt.* IV 1108.119-20; 1110.18-19, 101-102, 197-98; 1114.76-77; 1115.56-57, 146-48.

9 Lesquier, *Institutions*, 196.

10 *P. Meyer* 1, introd., p. 4. Contro l' ipotesi del Meyer cf. Mooren, *The Aulic Titulature*, 0239, e soprattutto idem, *Hiérarchie*, 26 e n. 1, 168-69. L' identità della titolatura aulica con l' ὁ πρὸς τῆι συντάξει non fa difficoltà se il distretto

ben chiara, tanto da confondere i due funzionari in una sola
rubrica.

Al contrario l' esame dei documenti restringe senza ombra di
dubbio i compiti dell' ὸ πρὸς τῆι προσλήψει alle sole operazioni di
primo stanziamento di nuovi contingenti cleruchici, laddove all'ὸ
πρὸς τῆι συντάξει spetta la responsabilità amministrativa sui
cleruchi già stanziati e già possessori di κλῆρος e sui terreni già
inseriti nella cleruchia, anche quando questi siano soggetti a cambiamento di titolare. Un' altra verifica di tale affermazione può
essere ricercata nel confronto tra l' ὸ τῆς προσλήψεως στέφανος che
compare in alcuni testi del I volume dei *P. Tebt.* e che indica lo
στέφανος dovuto dal cleruco al momento del suo ingresso su terre
attribuite novellamente alla cleruchia, e l' ὸ τῆς συντάξεως στέφανος, attestato da *BGU* VIII 1851 che concerne un mutamento di
possesso di terreno cleruchico e che quindi è dovuto per un fondo
comunque già appartenente alla cleruchia.

Una ulteriore precisazione potrebbe venire dalla individuazione dell' esatto significato del termine σύνταξις nel titolo del
funzionario.[11] Il Wilcken[12] sulla base di *WO* II 320 che è una
ricevuta di versamento (in forma chirografa) dello στέφανος agli
οἱ παρὰ Πάτρω(νος) τοῦ πρὸς τῆι συντά(ξει) inferiva che il vocabolo
andasse inteso come "contributo" e riteneva che l' ὸ πρὸς τῆι
συντάξει fosse appunto l' addetto alla riscossione di tali imposizioni fiscali. La sua ipotesi era però ben presto contestata da
Grenfell e da Hunt[13] che preferivano tradurre l' intera espressione
in "superintendent of the *arrangement* of catoeci" o "*of the assignment of land to the catoeci.*"[14]

---

di competenza di entrambi i funzionari era, come pare, il nomo;
cf. l' evoluzione della titolatura dello stratego dell' Arsinoite
alla medesima epoca.

11 I vari significati generali del vocabolo sono stati più
volte passati in rassegna: cf. Preisigke, *Fachwörter*; idem, *Wörterbuch*, s.vv. συντακτικός e σύνταξις; Schwahn, "Σύνταξις," 1453-56;
Cl. Préaux, *L'Économie royale des Lagides* (Bruxelles 1939) 594, 602,
s.v. σύνταξις e particolarm. 384.

12 *WO* I, pp. 296-97.

13 *P. Tebt.* I, p. 122, commento a l. 6.

14 *P. Rein.* I, p. 62, commento a l. 12.

Le varianti con cui la parola compare nel titolo sono, nei
testi finora editi, sostanzialmente tre: ὁ πρὸς τῆι συντάξει, nella
stragrande maggioranza dei casi, ὁ πρὸς ταῖς συντάξεσιν, al plurale,
in *P. Rein.* I 7 e ὁ πρὸς τῶι [σ]υγτάγματι τεταγμένος... in *P. Tebt.*
III 815, fr. 10, col. I.6-7. L' interpretazione più ovvia sarebbe,
alla luce di quanto sopra osservato, "colui che sovrintende alla
terra cleruchica, intesa come σύνταξις concessa ai militari": a
sostegno di essa potrebbero citarsi espressioni come τῶν ἀρουρῶν
φερομένων ἐν τῆι τῶν μαχίμων συντάξει[15] e le menzioni di soldati
προσληµφθέντες εἰς τὴν τῶν μαχίμων σύνταξιν.[16] Tuttavia l' esistenza della variante πρὸς τῶι [σ]υγτάγματι τεταγμένος può far sor-
gere il dubbio che il concetto esatto che il titolo vuol esprimere
sia quello di "preposto al complesso (dove σύνταξις = σύνταγμα) dei
cateci,"[17] anche se la forma al plurale ὁ πρὸς ταῖς συντάξεσιν
farebbe piuttosto propendere per la prima soluzione.

Nessuna sostanziale differenza sembra riscontrarsi nelle competenze del funzionario quando esso è designato come ὁ ἐπὶ (τῆς)
συντάξεως.[18] L' epiteto è documentato da tre soli testi, uno dei
quali *P. Cair. Zen.* I 59073, è da eliminare dal computo perché si
riferisce ad ᾿Αρτεμίδωρος, amministratore della σύνταξις di Apollonios nella δωρεά del nomo menfita.[19] *P. Lille* I 4 (243-42 o
218-17 a.C.)[20] è un *liber litterarum missarum et adlatarum*[21] in cui

15 Cf. Preisigke, *Wörterbuch*, s.v. σύνταξις; Lesquier, *Institutions*, 196 n. 1.

16 Cf. *Pros. Ptol.* II 2525, 2531; *P. Tebt.* IV 1108.119-20;
1110.197-98; 1115.147-48.

17 Cf. Lesquier, *Institutions*, 92, 100.

18 Cf. ibid., 196; Seidl, "᾿Ο πρὸς τῇ συντάξει," 1452.

19 *Pros. Ptol.* II 2492; cf. E. Wipszycka, "The Δωρεά of Apol-
lonios the Dioeketes in the Memphite Nome," *Klio* 39 (1961) 156 ss.;
F. Uebel, *Die Kleruchen Ägyptens unter den ersten sechs Ptolemäern*
(Berlin 1968) 33 n. 2; *Pros. Ptol.* VIII 2492.

20 = *W. Chrest.* 336 = Meyer, *Jur. Pap.* 56b; cf. *Pros. Ptol.*
II 2498; VIII 2498.

21 Meyer, *Jur. Pap.*, p. 187.

Lamiskos l' ὁ ἐπὶ συντάξεως[22] notifica (ll. 24 ss.) l' avvenuto decesso di un *hyperetes* dei Macedoni triacontaruri e la conseguente rivendicazione del *kleros* allo stato da parte dell' economo e del basilicogrammateo, fino al momento dell' iscrizione degli eventuali figli aventi diritto alla successione a termini di legge.[23] Infine *WO* II 1229 (II o I secolo a.c.), se le integrazioni proposte sono giuste, conserva la ricevuta, proveniente dalla Tebaide, di una somma di danaro εἰς τὸν λόγον... di 'Ηρᾶς, ὁ ἐπὶ τῆ[ς probabilmente συντάξεως τῶν κατοίκων] ἱππέων.[24]

La forma con ὁ πρὸς seguito dal dativo è indubbiamente assai più attestata. Una rassegna dei papiri in cui essa ricorre, condotta per quanto possibile in ordine cronologico, può essere utile per comprendere in dettaglio i compiti e gli incarichi attribuiti al funzionario e per verificare se sia mai esistita in essi una qualche evoluzione.

P. Tebt. III 815 (circa 223-22 a.C.) viene dalla meris di Themistos, nell' Arsinoite,[25] e contiene una raccolta di *excerpta* di contratti depositati negli uffici locali. In uno di essi (fr. 10, col. I) alle ll. 4-7 in un passo alquanto mutilo si parla di ...ἐντεύξεως [ἢ]ν ἀνένεγκεν εἰς τὸ τοῦ βασιλέως ὄνομα 'Αφθο[ν]ήτωι τῶι στρατηγῶι καὶ Ζήνωνι τῶι πρὸς τῷι [σ]υγτάγματι τεταγμένωι τῶν.... Ammesso che le letture siano esatte[26] e che si abbia veramente a che fare col nostro funzionario, sfugge il movente preciso per cui egli viene chiamato in causa, anche se dal contesto sembrerebbe

---

22 Per gli altri personaggi del *dossier* cf. U. Wilcken, "Referate. Papyrus-Urkunden," *Arch. f. Pap.* 5 (1913) 222-23, 241; *W. Chrest.*, p. 395 n. 4; Meyer, *Jur. Pap.*, p. 186 n. 2, 187, 188 n. 20. Più corrette mi sembrano però le interpretazioni di Uebel, *Kleruchen*, 250, 351 n. 3; cf. *Pros. Ptol.* II 2482. Che lo Stratios che compare in *P. Lille* I 14 sia un ὁ ἐπὶ συντάξεως (cf. *P. Lille* I, p. 82; Meyer, *Jur. Pap.*, p. 186 n. 2) mi sembra tutt' altro che certo.

23 Cf. Lesquier, *Institutions*, 196; Préaux, *Économie*, 468-69; Uebel, *Kleruchen*, 250.

24 Cf. *Pros. Ptol.* II 2496; J. K. Winnicki, *Ptolemäerarmee in Thebais* (Warszawa 1978) 61 e n. 54.

25 Cf. *Pros. Ptol.* II 2495, e soprattutto VIII 2495.

26 Cf. *P. Tebt.* III 815, fr. 10, col. I, commento a ll. 6-7.

potersi ipotizzare l' avvenuto risanamento di una situazione debi-
toria (tra cleruchi?), che aveva forse dato origine all' ἔντευξις.
In *P. Tebt.* III 793 (183 a.c.), che è un registro di corrispondenza
ufficiale, alle coll. III.19-IV.11 è conservata una serie di lettere relative all' ἀναμέτρησις dei κλῆροι degli ogdoecontaruri del
villaggio di Ibion Argaiou, ordinata a quanto pare da 'Αλέξανδρος ὁ
πρὸς τῆι συ(ντάξει) (il titolo è qui abbreviato συ)[27] e dallo
stratego Πτολεμαῖος. Posteriore al 173 a.c. è *WO* II 320, di cui si
è già fatto cenno e che attesta un versamento εἰς τὸν τοῦ βασιλέ(ως)
χρυ(σοῦν) στέφα(νον) agli οἱ παρὰ Πάτρω(νος) τοῦ πρὸς τῆι
συντά(ξει).[28]

Un rapporto debitorio nei confronti del pagamento degli ἐκφόρια si riscontra anche in *P. Tebt.* III 952 (circa 155 a.c.).
Apollonios, un cateco, scrive a [...]τρος ὁ πρὸς τῆι συ(ντάξει) (di
nuovo il titolo è abbreviato συ)[29] informandolo di avergli già inviato un ὑπόμνημα in cui denunciava il mancato versamento degli
ἐκφόρια (dovutigli?) da parte di un ecatontaruro della terza ipparchia e chiedeva provvedimenti a riguardo; non avendo ancora
ricevuto alcuna soddisfazione dalla controparte, egli domanda ora
più drastiche misure.

P. Tebt. I 79.86-92 (151-50 a.c.)[30] in un contesto assai frammentario riferisce il caso di un soldato dell' Arsinoite μεταβε[β]η-
κὼς εἰ[ς τοὺς ἐν τ]ῶι 'Οξυρυγχίτηι κ[α]τοίκ[ους ἱππεῖς], il cui avvenuto trasferimento sembra essere notificato da [...]καιος ὁ πρὸς
τῆι [συντάξει] forse al basilicogrammateo del nomo in cui si trova
il *kleros* che il cleruco ha abbandonato. La situazione è dunque
sostanzialmente diversa da quella descritta dal Lesquier:[31] l' ὁ
πρὸς τῆι συντάξει non "fait passer un soldat de l' Arsinoïte parmi
les catoeques de l' Oxyrhynchite," ma pare limitarsi a comunicarne
lo spostamento al funzionario civile competente della registrazione

---

27 Cf. *Pros. Ptol.* II 2489.

28 Cf. *Pros. Ptol.* II 2500; Winnicki, *Ptolemäerarmee*, 61 e
n. 54.

29 Cf. *Pros. Ptol.* II 2504.

30 Cf. *Pros. Ptol.* II 2503.

31 Lesquier, *Institutions*, 196.

fondiaria nel nomo, affinché questi provveda per quanto di sua pertinenza.

Del tutto simile è l' intervento dell' ὁ πρὸς τῆι συντάξει nelle operazioni di iscrizione dei cambiamenti di proprietà risultanti da παραχωρήσεις tra cleruchi, attestato in *P. Tebt.* I 30 (116 a.C.), 31 (112 a.C.), 239 (prima del 115-14 a.C.); IV 1100 (114 a.C.),[32] documenti sui quali si è a tal punto soffermata l' attenzione degli studiosi da dispensarmi dal trattarne diffusamente in questa sede. In essi l' azione del funzionario è sollecitata dagli interessati, che non si vedono riconosciuto il possesso dagli ufficiali del servizio civile. E' da notare soltanto che in un caso, *P. Tebt.* I 30, la carica sembra esercitata collegialmente da due titolari Πτολεμαῖος[33] ed 'Εστιεῖος,[34] fatto che non ha parallelo in alcuno degli altri testi finora editi. Seguendo la medesima procedura in *P. Tebt.* I 32 (145 a.C.?) l' ὁ πρὸς τῆι συντάξει Pankrates[35] registra e fa registrare agli scribi civili la promozione di un efodo divenuto cateco e la sua incorporazione nella quinta ipparchia degli ecatontaruri.[36] Meno chiaro, per le lacune del papiro, mi sembra il caso descritto in *P. Tebt.* I 61b.261 ss.

Lo stesso Pankrates è chiamato in causa in *P. Würzb.* 4: un ecatontaruro della prima ipparchia, da Philadelphia, denuncia un ogdoecontaruro della ottava ipparchia che si è introdotto nella sua casa e gli ha sottratto un candelabro del valore di 3000 dramme, per inserirlo tra le offerte dovute per il suo insediamento a capo di una associazione cleruchica, di cui entrambi sono membri. La confisca dell' oggetto è tuttavia motivata da un preteso debito del petente nei confronti dell' avversario, che se ne è dunque

---

32 Cf. rispettivamente *Pros. Ptol.* II 2494 e 2502; VIII 2494 e 2502, e *Pros. Ptol.* II 2491; VIII 2491. Sulla struttura dei documenti vd. le rispettive introduzioni e cf. Lesquier, *Institutions*, 196-98; Handrock, *Dienstliche Weisungen*, 87-88; Uebel, *Kleruchen*, 173 n. 1; L. Criscuolo, "Ricerche sul komogrammateus nell' Egitto tolemaico," *Aegyptus* 58 (1978) 58-59.

33 *Pros. Ptol.* II 2502; VIII 2502.

34 *Pros. Ptol.* II 2494; VIII 2494.

35 *Pros. Ptol.* II 2499; VIII 2499.

36 Cf. Lesquier, *Institutions*, 196-98; Handrock, *Dienstliche Weisungen*, 87-89; Uebel, *Kleruchen*, 178.

impadronito [πρὸς] χα(λκοῦ) δραχμὰς ρν, ἃς οὐδὲ ὤφιλον...διορθωσά-
μην [ὃ γέ]γονεν ἐμοὶ ὀφίλημα.[37] La singolarità della situazione
sembra perciò da ridimensionare (il papiro è mutilo in basso e
manca la circostanziata richiesta al funzionario), mentre è mani-
festamente infondata l' affermazione del Wilcken, nell' introduzione al papiro, che l' ὁ πρὸς τῆι συντάξει si occupi in questa
occasione di soldati in servizio attivo e non piuttosto insediati
in κλῆροι.

In tre casi, *BGU* VI 1218, 1221, 1222 (145-44 a.c.) subalterni
dell' ὁ πρὸς τῆι συντάξει Πτολεμαῖος[38] presenziano, assieme ad altri funzionari del nomo o a loro rappresentanti, alle vendite al-
l'asta di terreni demaniali, probabilmente in quanto competenti del-
l'amministrazione e della registrazione degli appezzamenti cleruchici.

P. Rein. I 7 (dopo il 142 a.c.)[39] è un' ἔντευξις al re in cui
uno dei μισθοφόροι dell' Ermopolite denuncia un ipparco dei cavalieri cateci dello stesso nomo che continua ad esigere da lui un
debito che egli protesta di aver saldato; egli chiede che l' avversario sia fatto comparire dinanzi all' ἐπιστάτης e γραμματεύς dei
cavalieri cateci, affinché questi, convocatolo per mezzo di ˙Ηρά-
στρατος l' ὁ πρὸς ταῖς συντάξεσιν, gli renda giustizia. La forma,
al plurale, del titolo non è sufficiente a mio avviso per sostenere
l' opinione del Reinach[40] che si abbia a che fare qui con un funzionario dell' amministrazione centrale, quasi un preposto alle
συντάξεις. La trafila suggerita nella petizione è normale e chiama
in causa in ordine gerarchico i più diretti responsabili dell' ambito amministrativo a cui l' ipparco, come cleruco stanziale, appartiene.

In *BGU* VIII 1734 (I secolo a.C.) un ὑπόμνημα è inviato ad
᾿Αρχίβιος ὁ π[ρὸς τῆι συντάξει τῶν κατοίκων ἱππέων][41] da parte di

---

37 Cf. Uebel, *Kleruchen*, 115 e nn. 6-7.

38 *Pros. Ptol.* II 2501; cf. *Pros. Ptol.* II 2505-2506.

39 Cf. *Pros. Ptol.* II 2497; VIII 2497; e vd. Seidl, "˙Ο πρὸς
τῇ συντάξει," 1453.

40 *P. Rein.* I, p. 62, commento a l. 12; cf. *Pros. Ptol.* II
2497.

41 *Pros. Ptol.* II 2493.

una donna a nome, pare, di un ὀρφανός minorenne, e concerne la
παραχώρησις di un κλῆρος, le cui condizioni sembra non abbiano potuto essere soddisfatte a causa della morte del padre dell' ὀρφανός.
Infine nel 48-47 a.C.(?),[42] ormai alla vigilia dell' ingresso
dell' Egitto sotto il dominio di Roma, *BGU* VIII 1769 ci attesta,
se le integrazioni proposte assai dubitativamente dagli editori
sono esatte, un 'Απίων che è stato nominato πρὸς τῆι συγ[τάξει τῶν
ἐν τῶι] Μεμφ[ί]τηι καὶ τῶν ἐγ τῶι 'Ηρακλεοπολίτηι κατοίκων ἱππέων
ὁμοίως δὲ [καὶ πρὸς τοῖς] καταλοχισμοῖς τούτων...ἀπὸ Μεχεὶρ τοῦ ε
ἕως Τῦβι τοῦ [ς (ἔτους)]. Si tratta molto probabilmente di un funzionario (a mandato speciale?) che cumula le due cariche su nomi
diversi e per un anno[43] (in nessun altro caso si trova una determinazione temporale dell' ufficio) e che prefigura già la situazione
dell' età romana,[44] in cui la mancanza di nuovi stanziamenti e la
cristallizzazione ammistrativa delle varie categorie privilegiate
del suolo implica l' adozione di uno schema sostanzialmente diverso
da quello della prima epoca tolemaica.

Al quadro fin qui delineato non contaddicono né i frammenta-
rissimi *P. Lille* editi recentemente dal Boyaval[45] né i dieci nuovi
P. Med. Bar.[46] in cui compare Pankrates ἀρχισωματοφύλαξ καὶ πρὸς
τῆι συντάξει τῶν κατοίκων ἱππέων. Questi ultimi, se mai, una volta
definitivamente pubblicati, per la varietà e complessità dei casi
in essi contenuti dovrebbero contribuire ad aumentare o a meglio
articolare le nostre conoscenze sul funzionario.

Il territorio su cui pare esercitarsi l' azione dell' ὁ πρὸς
τῆι συντάξει sembra essere il nomo. Tale affermazione è suffragata
dal confronto di *P. Tebt.* I 32 con *P. Würzb.* 4: in entrambi agisce
Pankrates, nel primo caso a Kerkeosiris, nel secondo a Philadelphia,

---

42 Cf. *Pros. Ptol.* II 2490.

43 Cf. *BGU* VIII, p. 49, commento al papiro.

44 Per cui vd. Lesquier, *Institutions*, 275 ss.; Seidl, "Συντακτικός," 1452; idem, "'Ο πρὸς τῆ συντάξει," 1452-53.

45 Boyaval, "Παγκράτης ἀρχισωματοφύλαξ," (supra, n. 1).

46 *P. Med. Bar.* 1 recto, 2 recto, 2 verso, 3 recto, 3 verso,
5 recto, 10 recto, 13 recto, 14 recto, 15 recto.

dunque con competenza su tutta l' Arsinoite. L' evoluzione della titolatura aulica del funzionario, studiata pochi anni orsono dal Mooren,[47] e che subisce uno sviluppo analogo a quella dello stratego, rafforza indiscutibilmente questa ipotesi. Nessuna indicazione emerge al contrario dalla documentazione, se si eccettua la dubbiosissima integrazione del *BGU* VIII 1769 testé citato, che la sfera d' influenza dell' ὁ πρὸς τῆι συντάξει abbia mai superato l' ambito del nomo.[48]

Misteriosi, nonostante la continua pubblicazione di nuovi testi, permangono infine i συντακτικοί[49] di *P. Tebt.* I 120.50; 191; 253 (tutti I secolo a.c.) sia per quanto concerne i loro compiti specifici, sia nei loro rapporti con l' ὁ πρὸς τῆι συντάξει.

Università di Bologna Giovanni Geraci

---

47 Vd. supra n. 6.

48 Al contrario di quanto ipotizzato, sia pur dubitativamente, da Mooren, *The Aulic Titulature*, 164-65.

49 Su cui vd. *P. Tebt.* I, p. 122, commento a l. 6; Lesquier, *Institutions*, 196 n. 1; Preisigke, *Fachwörter*; idem, *Wörterbuch*, s.v. συντακτικός; Seidl, "Συντακτικός," 1452; idem, "Ὁ πρὸς τῆ συντάξει," 1452.

Proceedings of the XVI Int. Congr. of Papyrology (Chico 1981) 277-280

DOCUMENTS FROM THE PTOLEMAIC PERIOD
IN THE HELSINKI UNIVERSITY COLLECTIONS

In 1978 Helsinki University acquired a collection of unpublished Ptolemaic papyri. The collection is not a large one. It consists of thirty-seven numbers, many of which contain documents on both sides. But the pieces of papyrus are largely complete and they include documents which are unique or hitherto only rarely encountered. The papyri were obtained from the cartonnage of two mummies. The collection thus consists of two units, the older one, which possibly can be dated to the third century B.C., comprising three documents from the Arsinoite nome (Nrs. 1-3).

Nr. 1 is a unique text. In this ὑπόμνημα the writer requests an investigation before the bench of *chrematistae* (lines 27-28 ἐπὶ τῶν τὰ προσοδικὰ κρινόντων χρηματιστῶν) into the conduct of a certain Petamus who on the plea of a δανείου συγγραφή has demanded before the bench of the *laocritae* the complainant's wife to act as an ἔγγυος (lines 19-24 ἐπισευδμενος καὶ συκοφαντῶν πεποίηται καταβόησιν ἐπὶ τῶν λαοκριτῶν κατ' Ἀύγχιος τῆς γυναικός μου φάμενος ταύτην ἔγγυον γεγενῆσθαι διὰ τῆς τοῦ δανείου συγγραφῆς ἧς ἐγραψάμην αὐτῷ μετὰ τῶν μετόχων τοῦ ἐπιβάλλοντός μοι μέρους τρίτου). The writer refers to the ἡ πρόσοδος ἡ Φιλαδέλφου.

Nr. 2 is reminiscent of the oft-cited *P. Enteux.* 82 (= *P. Magd.* 33 = *Sel. Pap.* 269) in which Philista complains to the king about a bathman who had emptied a jug of hot water over her and scalded her stomach and left thigh down to the knee, thus endangering her life. In this text, Dionysius, son of Zoilus, ὁ ἀντιγραφόμενος παρ' οἰκονόμου τὴν ἀπόμοιραν τῶν περὶ Θεογονίδα τόπων, complains to Philon, the *archiphylacites* about an assault in the so-called New Baths of Aristodemus (lines 7-8). He was taking a bath, perfectly quietly (the lamps had already been lighted), and he was in the process of using a jug of hot water, when one of the soldiers, a man named Philon, ordered him to serve as his bathman. Dionysius refused to obey and therefore (lines 13-19) προσπηδήσας μοι μετ' ἄλλων ὧν τὰ ὀνόματα ἀγνοῶ ἔτυπτόν με πυγμαῖς τε καὶ λακτίσμασιν εἰς ὃ ἂν τύχοι

277

μέρος τοῦ σώματος καὶ ἐκπάσαντές με ἐκ τοῦ βαλανείου εἷλκον ὡς ἐπὶ τὴν κατὰ τὸ Σαμοθράικων πύλην. But they then came up against the police. The soldiers found a way out of the critical situation. They had poor Dionysius arrested as a troublemaker.

Nr. 3 is less dramatic than the other two papyri from the older cartonnage. It consists of accounts.

The documents from the other cartonnage (Nrs. 4-37) all belong to the second century B.C. One of these texts (Nr. 15) is a bilingual Greek-demotic document, a demotic contract with a Greek docket of twelve witnesses. All the other documents are written in Greek. The texts come from the Heracleopolite nome, and the group contains material that must have belonged at one time to the archive of the *oeconomus*. The documents range in date from B.C. 163-159.

The archive is of great interest. It contains, for instance, eleven property returns (ἀπογράφαι), of which seven are practically complete. "Returns of property have been conspicuous by their absence in the later Ptolemaic period," write the editors in the introduction to *P. Tebt.* III 806.

In 1935 S. Avogadro could only list thirteen property returns of the Ptolemaic period (*Aegyptus* 15 [1935] 131-206). A new text has been published by P. J. Sijpesteijn in *Cd'E* 53 ([1978] 307-12). The archive thus enlarges our material to a considerable degree. The form of these property returns corresponds to that of *P. Tebt.* III 806. They are all addressed to the *oeconomus* Dionysius in Θωύθ of the 19th year; this should be the 19th regnal year of Ptolemaeus VI Philometor (B.C. 163), since another text from the same cartonnage (Nr. 17, dated to the 6th year) mentions the βασιλικὸς γραμματεύς Erasykhis, who is already known in *P. Tebt.* III 857.5 (31 January B.C. 162, 18th year of Philometor) as γενόμενος βασιλικὸς γραμματεύς in the 7th year, the last and incomplete year of the joint reign of Philometor and his brother.

The declarant is identified by his name, by the name of his father and by a status designation (ἀρχιφυλακίτης, ἡγεμών or simply τῶν ἐξ Ἡρακλέους πόλεως). The properties declared consist of fruit trees (τὰ πεφυτευμένα ἐν τῷ ἀμπελῶνι), deserted (ἔρημος) gardens or gardens with date palms, baths (βαλανεῖον, λουτρωνίδιον) and a deserted dovecote (περιστερεῶν ἔρημος). They are taxed with the usual ἕκτη on the fruit trees and τρίτη on the baths (εἰς τὸ βασιλικόν). In one text (Nr. 8) there is mention of a prior tax assessment (cf. *P. Ryl*. IV 575, introduction): ἀνθυφαιρουμένων μοι τῶν πεφιλανθρωπημένων ὑπὸ τοῦ βασιλέως ἐπιπέμπτων (lines 12-14). The properties are situated in the villages Βουσῖρις and Θμοιναυσῖρις, Καλαγή (hitherto known only from the third century A.D. in *CPR* I 247) and Τεχῦμις (a new name).

There is one text which is representative of the declarations in our archive and which, because of its somewhat curious formulation, I will discuss in greater detail. It is Nr. 6. In this property return, Harmiysis, son of Plabous, ἡγεμών, declares to Dionysius, *oeconomus*, for the 19th year a bath (λουτρωνίδιον is a new word), situated in his homestead (περίστασις) in the village of Busiris, and estimated at a value of one talent χαλκοῦ πρὸς ἀργύριον, for which he will pay to the royal funds the 1/3 tax amounting to 2000 copper drachmae. He himself will provide the fuel (lines 11-12 χωρηγουμένου μου τὰ ἐνκαύματα). If the tax collectors do not agree with him on these conditions, he will take from them 4000 copper drachmae for the two parts belonging to him and will let them keep the λουτρωνίδιον, working with their own fuel and at their own expense (lines 12-22 ἐὰν δὲ οἱ ἐξειληφότες τελῶναι μὴ ὑπομένωσιν συνχωρῆσαι μοι ἐπὶ τούτοις, ὑπομένωι λαβεῖν παρ' αὐτῶν τῶν καθηκόντων μοι δύο μέρων χαλκοῦ (δραχμὰς) ΄δ, παρέχειν αὐτοὺς τὸ λουτρωνίδιον ἐνεργὸν τοῖς ἑαυτῶν ἐνκαύμασιν καὶ ἀναλώμασιν). Therefore, he requests that the *oeconomus* enter the return (τὸ ὑπόμνημα) in the records so that the tax collectors will not be able to accuse him of not making his declaration (lines 22-26). There follow three lines, the last two lines preserved only in part, before the papyrus breaks off.

Nr. 17 (B.C. 162), in which the known βασιλικὸς γραμματεύς Erasychis appears, concerns the delivery of corn to soldiers (lines 3-4 τὰ μετρήματα τῶν στρατιωτῶν ἐκ τοῦ ἐν ᾽Αλιλάει θησαυροῦ--cf. *P. Ryl*. II 87, introduction) stationed in τὸ ἐν ῾Ιερᾶι Νήσωι φρούριον. The papyrus provides us with the name of ῾Ηρώιδης ἀρχισωματοφύλαξ καὶ διοικητής, known from *UPZ* 110.1 (B.C. 164), and with names of officials hitherto unknown: ῾Ηρώιδης καὶ ᾽Αλέξανδρος σιτολογοῦντές τινας τόπους τῆς ἄνω ᾽Αγήματος (see *P. Hib*. I 101.2-3) and ῟Ωρος ὁ παρὰ ᾽Ερασύχιος τοῦ βασιλικοῦ γραμματέως ἀντιγραφόμενος. The name of the addressee Philippus, in the dative case, is written with

large letters on the back of hte papyrus. In the upper part of
the papyrus is a notation of a secretary, written in a different
hand and attesting the date of the receipt (see G. Parássoglou in
BASP 7 [1970] 97 n. 45) ἐλ(ήφθη) (ἔτους) ς 'Επείφ κ, as well as
the dispatch of Philippus, the addressee of the document (called
ἀναφορά or simply ἐπιστολή) to Erasychis: 'Ερασύχει β(ασιλικῶι)
γρα(μματεῖ). ἧς γεγράφασιν ἡμῖν ἐπιστολῆς 'Ηρώιδης καὶ 'Αλέξαν(δρος)
σιτολογοῦντές τινας τόπους τῆς ἄνω 'Αγή(ματος) τὸ ἀντίγραφον ὑποτε-
τάχαμεν. ἐὰν φαίν(ηται) καλῶς ποιήσεις συντάξαι 'ἐπιστεῖλαι τοῖς
παρὰ σοῦ ' συντάξαι συνχρηματίζειν αὐτοῖς τὰ καθήκοντα φόρε(τρα)
καθότι γράφουσι καὶ πρὸ τῆς τῶν ὑδάτων εἰς τὰ πέδια ἐμβολῆς.

Nr. 18 is a list of tax payments from the 19th of Θωύθ in the
19th year (B.C. 163), arranged according to village and including
such taxes as ζυτηρά, ἰχθυηρά, τίμη κριθῆς, νιτρική, ποταμοφυλακία.
The villages are situated in the 'Αγκυρῶν πόλις district which is
named in col. II.18, and they are arranged in three τόποι: Κωίτης,
Τεχθῶ Νῆσος and Πέρα. Several of these villages are already known
from published papyri, especially the Hibeh Papyri, but some of the
names are new. There are also some officials, for instance, Δύδυ-
μος ὁ πρότερος τραπεζίτης named in the Κωίτης (col. I.6-8) and
Κύδιος ὁ σιτόλ(ογος) (col. II.17).

Most of the Helsinki Papyri deal with the taxing and transport
of tax corn. The lists are arranged κατ' ἄνδρα or according to
village. It goes without saying that the other texts not discussed
in this paper also contain names of persons, villages and officials,
and that the archive as a whole furnishes much information which is
helpful in providing insights into the social and economic history
of the later Ptolemaic period.

Our archive contains three interesting texts (Nrs. 21, 22 and
37) from the 23rd year of Philometor (B.C. 159), addressed to the
oeconomus Alexandros.[1]

Helsinki   Jaakko Frösén

---

1 A problem upon which these texts shed new light is discussed by Prof. M. Kaimio in her paper, see below, pp. 281-87.

ON THE SURETIES OF TAX CONTRACTORS IN PTOLEMAIC EGYPT

The regulations concerning the system of tax farming in Ptolemaic Egypt are known to us mainly from the Revenue Laws of Ptolemy II Philadelphus (year 259)[1] and from the set of regulations of Ptolemy V Epiphanes (year 204).[2] The former apply to Egypt as a whole, whereas the latter concerns the tax farming of the Oxyrhynchite nome only, although similar regulations were probably enforced in other nomes too.[3] In addition, many documents of different kinds illustrate the practical applications of these regulations.[4]

It was obligatory for the tax contractor to produce sureties for the sum he had offered to pay to the state for the tax.[5] The newly acquired Helsinki papyri contain three documents which clarify the system used in the enlisting and registering of these sureties, by giving examples of steps hitherto known only from the

---

1 Ed. B. P. Grenfell, Oxford 1896; re-ed. J. Bingen, *P. Rev. Laws*, *SB*/Bh. 1 (1952).

2 *P. Paris* 62, re-ed. U. Wilcken, *UPZ* I 112 (1927). For the dating, see also E. Bikerman, "L'avénement de Ptolemée V Epiphanes," *Cd'E* 29 (1940) 128; A. E. Samuel, *Ptolemaic Chronology* (Münch. Beitr. 43 [1962] 111f.).

3 Cf. G. M. Harper Jr., *Aegyptus* 14 (1934) 50 with n. 3.

4 For a general survey of the system of tax farming, see U. Wilcken, *Griechische Ostraka* (1899) I, 513-70; M. Rostovtzeff, *Geschichte der Staatspacht in der römischen Kaiserzeit bis Diokletian* (Philologus Erg. band 9 [1902]); G. M. Harper Jr., "Tax Contractors and their Relation to Tax Collection in Ptolemaic Egypt," *Aegyptus* 14 (1934) 49-64; idem, "The Relations of Ἀρχώνης, Μέτοχοι, and Ἔγγυοι to each other, to the Government and to the Tax Contract in Ptolemaic Egypt," *Aegyptus* 14 (1934) 269-85; W. Lotz, "Studien über Steuerverpachtung," *Sitz. Bayer. Akad. Wiss.*, Ph.-hist. Abt. 1935, 4; C. Préaux, *L'économie royale des Lagides* (Brussels 1939) 450-59.

5 *P. Rev. Laws* 34.2-6, 56.14-15; *UPZ* I 112 I.13ff. In some cases, the sureties probably covered the whole amount of the tax, together with the 5% or 10% mentioned in the sources. In other cases, a security covering only a part of the tax was considered adequate; cf. U. Wilcken, *UPZ* I, p. 511; B.-J. Müller, *Ptolemaeus II. Philadelphus als Gesetzgeber* (Dissertation 1968) 33.

regulations. The documents come from the office of the *oikonomos* of the Heracleopolitan nome, who was responsible for the supervision of the tax contracts of his nome, and date from the 23rd year of Ptolemy VI Philometor (159/8).[6] This *oikonomos*, named Alexandros, is not previously known from the papyri.

P. Hels. Inv. No. 21 and 37 are reports in the *hypomnema* form supplied by the tax contractor to the *oikonomos*. They are clearly written in identical formulas, although in no. 37 one line is missing from the beginning, three or four lines from the end, and lines 6-16 are almost unreadable. No. 21 is virtually complete; only the final greeting is lost. I give the preliminary text of no. 21.

P. Hels. Inv. No. 21   Heracleopolis
21 x 11.5 cm.   October 15, 159 B.C.

→ (m. 1)   ἐλ(ήφθη) (ἔτους) κγ Θωὺθ ιδ⁻

  (m. 2)   ᾿Αλεξάνδρωι οἰκονόμωι

            παρ᾿ ῾Ηρακλείδου τοῦ ῾Ηρα-

        4   κλείδου τοῦ ἐξειληφότος

            μετὰ μετόχων τὸ εἰσαγώγιον

            τοῦ οἴνου καὶ τὴν (ἕκτην) τῶν

            παραδείσων καὶ τὴν (τρίτην) τῶν

        8   βα[λ]ανείων· ἐπεὶ ὑποτί-

            θεται ἐν διενγυήματι

            ὑπὲρ ἐμοῦ εἰς τὰς δηλου-

            μένας ὠνὰς Τνεφερῶς

        12 Μαρρέους ἐπὶ ὑποθή(κη) οἰκίαι

            καὶ αὐλῆι ἐν ἧι σιτοβολὼν

            ἐν ῾Ηρακλέους πόλει πρὸς (τάλαντα) λ,

            ἀξιῶ γράψαι ὧι καθήκει

        16 ἐνενεγκεῖν σοι τὴν

            ἐγγύην.

            -

---

6 Philometor is confirmed as the regent in other Helsinki papyri coming from the same office and from the same or neighbouring years, especially P. Hels. Inv. No. 17, bearing the date 20th Epeiph, 6th year, which must be the year 164 B.C., since the text mentions the *basilikos grammateus* Erasykhis (ll.1,6,9), known from *P. Tebt.* III 857.5 from the year 163 (W. Peremans-E. Van 't Dack, *Prosopographia Ptolemaica* I, 442).

1 ε (6   7   9 1. διεγγυήματι   12 υποθ

14 Z

After mentioning his name and the sphere of his obligations, the tax contractor (in no. 21, with his μέτοχοι) informs the *oiko-nomos* of the person who is acting as his surety, the mortgages offered by the surety as security, and the amount thus guaranteed, using the formula (21, 8) ἐπεὶ ὑποτίθεται ἐν διενγυήματι ὑπὲρ ἐμοῦ εἰς τὰς δηλουμένας ὠνὰς ὁ δεῖνα...ἀξιῶ γράψαι κτλ. This form of report has not hitherto been found in the papyri; a similar formula is found in the oath of surety for a military person in *UPZ* II 217. 2f. (cf. 19f.) ὀμνύω...ἤ μὴν ὑποτεθεῖσθαι ἐν δ[ιεγγυήματι...] ὑπὲρ τοῦ δεῖνα (year 131).[7] Thus, our documents fulfill the require-ments made in *UPZ* I 112 I.13 - II.2 as regards the presentation of sureties to the *oikonomos* and *basilikos grammateus*. P. Hels. Inv. No. 21 contains in the upper margin the date when this report was received at the office of the *oikonomos*. The date was important in view of the time limit of thirty days, divided into six periods of five days each, during which the sureties had to be found in order that the tax contract should remain valid. Our document was re-ceived on the 14th Thoth, that is, rather early if the auction of taxes took place at the beginning of the Egyptian year.[8]

At the end of the document, after reporting on the security which he has acquired, the tax contractor makes a request to the *oikonomos* (21, 15) ἀξιῶ γράψαι ὧι καθήκει ἐνενεγκεῖν σοι τὴν ἐγγύην. Of the letters of the last word, only the upper parts are visible, but I feel sure that this is the word intended. Thus, the declaration concerning the security must be "brought to" the *oiko-nomos* or "entered in the records" of the *oikonomos*. ἐγγύη refers

---

7 Cf. the Zois papyri (*UPZ* I 114 I col. I.16): διὰ τὸ δεδό-σθαι ἐν διεγγυήματι ὑπὸ Θανούβιος τῆς Ἰθορῶυτος ὑπὲρ Δωρίωνος κτλ., and II col. I.15f.

8 In *P. Rev. Laws* 57.4 the ἐλαική is sold for a period begin-ning with Mesore; in *UPZ* I 112, the tax contracts were sold for the 1st and 2nd financial year, the period beginning with Mesore, i.e. apparently for the second half of the first financial year, begin-ning with Mesore, and the first half of the second year, beginning with Mecheir; see U. Wilcken, *UPZ* I, p. 502f. and E. Bikerman, *Cd'E* 29 (1940) 128. In the 2nd century, there was no such thing as a financial year.

to the written declaration presented by the surety to the magistrates, that is, the *symbolon* required in *UPZ* I 112 II.2. We have
examples of such declarations, containing various formulas, probably in *P. Hib.* I 94, 95, *P. Petr.* III 58a-d; in *P. Petr.* III 57a
the part containing the actual declaration is missing, but we have
the oath sworn by the surety guaranteeing the freedom of his security from other obligations, and the ὑπογραφή of the surety, containing the summary of the given declaration.[9] In P. Hels. Inv.
No. 21, 15 the phrase ὧι καθήκει probably refers to the relevant
magistrate, usually in the plural form οἷς καθήκει, not to the person acting as surety. Anyway, the contents of the request imply
that the surety had to present to a magistrate, possibly the *basilikos grammateus*, his written declaration, occasionally at least
endorsed with the royal oath, and the magistrate had to mark it as
received on a certain day, to be subsequently examined and approved
and, after a certain number of days, deposited at the bank (*UPZ* I
112 II.2-11).

Thus, the proper procedure in the enlisting of sureties seems
to have been that the tax contractor himself first informed the
magistrates of the sureties as soon as he had found them, as in our
documents, and that the surety himself then submitted his written
declaration to the officials. *UPZ* I 112 III.3-5 states the consequences of disobeying the rules concerning the reporting of the
sureties to the magistrates. P. Hels. Inv. No. 21 and 37 are examples of the strict observance of these rules, which are thus seen
to be valid not only in the Oxyrhynchite nome, but in the Heracleopolitan nome as well.

The third document, P. Hels. Inv. No. 22, is mutilated at the
top and the bottom, but there are probably not many lines lost.
There is a *kollesis* in the middle of the papyrus. There were apparently at least three columns in this document. Of the first
column, only minimal traces can be seen; the lines of the middle

---

9 ἔγγυος εἰς ἔκτεισιν τοῦ δεῖνος ὁ δεῖνα *P. Hib.* I 94 (258/7),
95 (257/6), *P. Petr.* III 58c + III p. 8 (236), *SB* III 6094 (231 or
230); ἐγγυᾶται τὸν δεῖνα ὁ δεῖνα *P. Petr.* III 58a (236?), 58d
(236/5); ὁμολογεῖ ὁ δεῖνα ἐγγυᾶσθαι *P. Petr.* III 57b; ὑπογραφή to a
σύμβολον of the surety *P. Petr.* III 57a = II 46a-b = *W. Chrest.* 110
(204) ὁμολογῶ ἐγγυᾶσθαι εἰς ἔκτεισιν τὸν δεῖνα. Cf. F. Uebel, *Act.
X Congrès de Pap.*, 76 n. 34.

column are complete, while at the beginning of the lines of the
third column enough of the letters can be seen to render it probable that they were written by the same hand as the lines of the
middle column. The text of the middle column runs as follows.

P. Hels. Inv. No. 22, Col. II   Heracleopolis
20.5 x 14.5 cm.   159 B.C.

- - - - - - - - - - - - - -
μετὰ μετόχ[ων τὴν
ἐπιζήτησιν εἰς τὸ κγ (ἔτος)·
ἔστιν τὸ καθὲν ὧν τίθημι
4   ἐν διενγυήματι εἰς τὴν
αὐτὴν ὠνήν· Φῦς Ταῆσις
Ὥρου ἐπὶ ὑποθήκῃ
ἀμπελῶνος συμφύτου
8   ἀρουρῶν ς πρὸς (τάλαντα) κ
καὶ παρὰ Ἀῦγχιος τῆς
Θ..μου... οἰκίας καὶ
τόπων ψιλῶν, ἐν οἷς οἴκη-
12   [μα] καὶ αἰγοβοσκεῶν καὶ
περιστερεῶν ἔρημος καὶ
φοινικῶν, τὸ γ μέρος
καὶ τὰ τῆς οἰκί[α]ς καὶ τὰ
16   [συ]νκ[ύ]ροντα .....[
- - - - - - - - - - - - - -

2 └   4 l. διενγυήματι   8 𐤊

The first two lines of the text reveal a construction similar
to that of the two reports of the tax contractors, with the exception that here the year is added. The contents of the following
lines are also of a similar nature, and are concerned with the
sureties and the amount secured by them with mortgages. Despite
these similarities, however, this document probably represents
another type. It does not have the formula ἐπεὶ ὑποτίθεται ὑπὲρ
ἐμοῦ εἰς τὴν δηλουμένην ὠνὴν ὁ δεῖνα, which was obviously typical
of the reports of the tax contractors. Instead, the securities are
listed after the heading (22, 3ff.) ἔστιν τὸ καθὲν ὧν τίθημι ἐν
διενγυήματι εἰς τὴν αὐτὴν ὠνήν. This sounds more like an official

register;[10] τιθέναι ἐν is often used of listing in a certain category,[11] and the first person is often used by the compiler of such
a list.[12] I do not think that the contractor would report the
sureties he found with the words τίθημι ἐν διεγγυήματι, "I present
as my security," although e.g. ἐνέχυρον τίθημι is a common phrase.
Nor is it likely that Taesis mentioned in line 5 would be the subject of τίθημι. On the other hand, as the words of a magistrate
compiling a list, the phrase could be translated as "there follows
a detailed list of the persons (or properties) which I register
under the securities given for the abovementioned tax."

The rest of the column contains the securities. In the preserved part two persons are mentioned: Taesis offering to mortgage
a vineyard, and Aynchis offering the third part of a house and a
plot. These entries are made in different formulas: the first
surety is mentioned in the nominative, the second one in the genitive with παρά. Before the name of Taesis in line 5, the village
Phys is mentioned, which suggests that the sureties were listed by
village, both these women belonging to Phys, and that other villages
followed in the next column, the district of this tax contractor
consisting of several villages.

Apparently, this list is based on the written *symbola* given by
the sureties. This being the case, it may be part of the register
which the *oikonomos* was required to deposit at the bank together
with the declarations of the sureties (cf. *UPZ* I 112 II.2-4 τούτων
δὲ τὰ σύμβ[ολα] τεθήσετα[ι...]...μετ' ἀναγραφῆς). Wilcken in his
note (p. 513) surmises that this register contained the main details of these declarations. Another possibility is that this is
the list which the banker was required to enter into his monthly
records (cf. *UPZ* I 112 II.5ff. οὗτος δ[ὲ] προσθή[σε]ται ἐ[ν τοῖς
μη]νιείοις τὸ καθ' ἓν τῶν συμβ[όλων] εὐσήμως (it is a rather

---

10 Cf. e.g. the land survey list *P. Tebt.* I 61a.163: τούτων
ἐστὶν τῶν τιθεμ[έ]νων ἐν ἐπιστάσει καὶ ἐν ἀπολογισμῶν ὧν τὸ καθ'
[ἓν κ]αὶ ὡς συνέστηκεν ἐπ' [ἐσ]χάτωι τέτακται κτλ.

11 Cf. e.g. *P. Tebt.* I 66.76: τεθε<ι>μ<έν>ων ἐν [το]ῖς
ἐκφο(ρίοις); 66.91: ἐν τοῖς [ἐν]θαῦτα τίθεται; 74.62, 75.80:
τίθεται ἐν τῶι ὑπολόγωι.

12 E.g. *P. Tebt.* I 61b.44: τίθεμεν δὲ [ἐν]ταῦθα χά[ριν] τοῦ
συνκριθῆναί τι.

beautiful, clear hand) ὅσα [ἐπὶ τῶν ὑ]ποθηκῶν ἐστιν καὶ τίνες ο[ἱ]
βεβαιωταὶ [καὶ] τ̣[ίνας ἕκα]σ̣τοι εἰς τὴν βεβαίωσιν ὑποθήκας.[......
...] δ̣εδώκασιν κτλ.

Such a list or a copy of it could well be found among the papers in the *oikonomos'* office. In this case, the list would re-
introduce the problem whether the *bebaiotai* mentioned in *UPZ* I 112
II.8 are to be considered as the guarantors of the mortgages offered as security, who in their turn offer other mortgages as their
security, or as the sureties (ἔγγυοι) of the tax contractor. Our
list mentions the amounts, the persons and the mortgaged properties
as required in *UPZ* I 112, but it clearly refers to the securities
of the contractors, not those of their sureties (cf. P. Hels. Inv.
No. 22, 4). Wilcken argues against the possibility of an indis-
criminate use of βεβαιωτής, βεβαίωσις and ἔγγυος, διεγγύημα, empha-
sizing the fact that in Greek law, the functions of *bebaiotes* and
eggyos were quite distinct, as Partsch points out in his *Griechisches Bürgschaftsrecht* (p. 340ff.); the function of *bebaiotes* was
to guarantee the mortgages as being free from other obligations.[13]
Understood in this way, the rules laid out in *UPZ* I 112 II.5ff.
clearly presuppose that the guarantors of the sureties, too, were
mentioned in the sureties' declarations. No such *symbolon* has
hitherto come down to us; what we do have is the oath preserved in
P. Petr. III 57a, where the surety swears to the freedom of the
mortgage he is offering, thus acting as his own guarantor. Thus,
the problem of whether P. Hels. Inv. No. 22 could be an example of
the banker's register required by *UPZ* I 112 II.5ff. is connected
with the larger problem of the concept of suretyship in Ptolemaic
Egypt.

Helsinki   Maarit Kaimio

---

13 In his commentary, *UPZ* I, p. 512f., *Griechische Ostraka* I,
553f.; cf. J. Partsch, *Griechisches Bürgschaftsrecht* (1909) I, 343.

PTOLEMAIC FAMILIES

When Ptolemy IV Philopator died in 204 B.C. and was succeeded by his five or six-year-old son Ptolemy V, real power rested with the courtiers Sosibios and Agathokles. The former had already reached a high position under Ptolemy III and, as is well-known, became Philopator's prime minister.[1] In that capacity he soon had to share power with Agathokles,[2] who belonged to a Samian family which in all probability migrated to Egypt before Philopator's accession. The events around the king's death and the queen's murder, as described by Polybius,[3] make it clear that the affairs of state were now controlled, or at any rate mainly controlled, by members of these two families. That of Agathokles had the lead role, presumably because of Sosibios' decease. Agathokles' mother Oinanthe[4] and sister Agathokleia[5] dominated court life, as they undoubtedly already did during Philopator's lifetime. Agathokleia had been the king's mistress and now, together with her mother, she looked after the young Ptolemy, whom she had nursed in his infancy. But their days were numbered. The hate that provoked the murder of queen Arsinoe and the repugnance caused by the conduct of Agathokles and his relatives led the Alexandrian people to revolt. Agathokles, Oinanthe, Agathokleia, and their kin were butchered.[6]

---

1 For Sosibios, see W. Huss, *Untersuchungen zur Aussenpolitik Ptolemaios' IV.* (Munich 1976) 242-51; L. Mooren, *The Aulic Titulature in Ptolemaic Egypt. Introduction and Prosopography* (Brussels 1975) 63-66 no. 018.

2 Huss, op. cit., 251-53; Mooren, op. cit., 67-69 no. 020.

3 Polybius XV 25-36.

4 *Prosopographia Ptolemaica* VI 14731.

5 *Pros. Ptol.* VI 14714.

6 Polybius XV 33.13; cf. 33.7, where ἀδελφαί of Agathokleia are also mentioned. Among the executed relatives was Nikon, ὁ συγγενὴς τῶν περὶ τὸν Ἀγαθοκλέα, who was appointed ἐπὶ τοῦ ναυτικοῦ (XV 25.37; see *Pros. Ptol.* V 13778 and VI 16284). Another relative was Philon (XV 30.6; cf. 33.2).

Other families, however, stood ready to fill the gap. During
Agathokles' rule it had become clear that the court was divided into factions. Anticipating trouble, Agathokles had removed the most
prominent members of the circle of the Royal Friends, replacing
them with his own adherents.[7] Thus Ptolemaios, the son of Agesarchos, was sent to Rome in the hope that he would travel no further
than Greece after greeting his relatives and friends there.[8] Another Ptolemaios, a son of Sosibios, was dispatched to king Philip V
of Macedon,[9] while Pelops, the son of Pelops, was sent on a mission
to king Antiochos III of Syria.[10] Some of Agathokles' accomplices
in the murder of Arsinoe were also gotten out of the way. Philammon, who had done the deed, was appointed Λιβυάρχης in Cyrene.[11]
But other members of the clan were allowed to share in Agathokles'
glory in Alexandria itself. First of all Aristomenes, the son of
Menneas, an Acarnanian who had come to Egypt after 216 B.C. and won
Agathokles' friendship. He was the first, so Polybius tells us, to
present his protector with a crown of gold at a dinner party and to
wear a ring with his portrait; when a daughter was born to him he
named her Agathokleia. He was appointed a σωματοφύλαξ, a Gentleman
of the Bodyguard, of the young king. When Agathokles' position became precarious Aristomenes remained loyal and was willing to intervene with the Macedonian troops on his behalf.[12] In those days
another prominent family also stood by Agathokles, namely that of
Polykrates, the son of Mnasiadas. This family had migrated from
Argos to Egypt about 220 B.C., and soon after his arrival Polykrates

---

7 Polybius XV 25.15 and 20-21.

8 Polybius XV 25.14; cf. *Pros. Ptol.* VI 15068 and 16944; E.
Olshausen, *Prosopographie der hellenistischen Königsgesandten* (Leuven 1974) I, 59-60 no. 37.

9 Polybius XV 25.13; cf. *Pros. Ptol.* VI 14779; Olshausen,
op. cit., 63-64 no. 42.

10 Polybius XV 25.13; cf. *Pros. Ptol.* VI 15064; Olshausen,
op. cit., 57-58 no. 35; idem, *RE* Suppl. 12 (1970) 1019-21.

11 Polybius XV 25.12; 26a.1; cf. *Pros. Ptol.* VI 15082.

12 Polybius XV 31.6-12; cf. Chr. Habicht, "Der Akarnane Aristomenes," *Hermes* 85 (1957) 501-4; Mooren, op. cit., 76-77 no. 036.

was entrusted by Sosibios and Agathokles with a high military command.[13] We hear that his female relatives, not yet aware of the
imminent danger, tried to console Oinanthe, who had retreated to
the Thesmophoreion; but Oinanthe rebuffed them, which of course
hardly served to stimulate their kind feelings.[14]

Less clear seems to have been the attitude of Sosibios' family.
As said above, his son Ptolemaios was appointed ambassador to king
Philip. The other son, Sosibios, stayed at court where he was a
member of the Gentlemen of the Bodyguard. We believe that he remained loyal, or at least neutral, until there was no hope left for
Agathokles. It was he who asked the king, in the presence of the
mob assembled in the stadium, whether those guilty of offences to
him or his mother should be handed over to the people.[15]

The subsequent bloodbath did not affect every family that had
been on good terms with Agathokles. Philammon, who had returned
from Cyrene, was murdered together with his wife and son.[16] But
others managed to maintain their position or even improve on it.
The younger Sosibios was thus entrusted by the new regent, Tlepolemos, with the royal seal.[17] Polykrates started a new career as
strategos of Cyprus, succeeding Pelops, who held the post before
being sent to Antiochos III by Agathokles--and it is not impossible
that it was Agathokles who appointed Polykrates strategos of the
island.[18] Nevertheless, it gradually became clear that the last

---

13   Polybius V 64.4-7; 65.5; 82.3; 84.8; cf. *Pros. Ptol.* II
2172.

14   Polybius XV 29.8-14.

15   Polybius XV 32.6-8; for the younger Sosibios, cf. Mooren,
op. cit., 75-76 no. 035.

16   Polybius XV 33.11-12.

17   Polybius XVI 22.1-2; for Tlepolemos, cf. *Pros. Ptol.* I 50
and 337, II 2180, VI 14634, VIII 50.

18   Pelops as strategos of Cyprus: see *Pros. Ptol.* VI 15064;
Ino Michaelidou-Nicolaou, *Prosopography of Ptolemaic Cyprus* (Gote-
borg 1976) 96-97 no. 18; R. S. Bagnall, *The Administration of the
Ptolemaic Possessions outside Egypt* (Leiden 1976) 252-53 no. 1.
Polykrates: see *Pros. Ptol.* II 2172 and VI 15065; Michaelidou-
Nicolaou, op. cit., 99-100 no. 34; Bagnall, op. cit., 253-55 no. 2.

word had not yet been spoken and that the families which once belonged to Agathokles' clan were out to regain control of the court
and of state affairs. The sons of the great Sosibios took on Tlepolemos after Ptolemaios had returned from his mission to king
Philip. Although they managed to get the court circles on their
side, Tlepolemos prevailed for the time being and took away the
royal seal from Sosibios.[19] But about 201 B.C. the situation had
changed completely and Aristomenes, once Agathokles' most notorious
flatterer, took charge. He revealed himself to be an excellent
statesman.[20] In 197 B.C. the king was proclaimed of age, and at
his *anakleteria* the most prominent role was played by Polykrates,
who had recently returned from Cyprus.[21] His place there was taken
by Ptolemaios, the son of Agesarchos, whom we met earlier as Agathokles' ambassador to Rome (and who, despite the latter's hopes, had
returned).[22] Shortly before Ptolemy's *anakleteria*, the famous trial
of Skopas took place in Alexandria; that event too revealed that
Polykrates could well be the coming man.[23] In fact, between 196
and 192, Aristomenes fell into disgrace[24] and was replaced as "prime
minister" to king Ptolemy V by Polykrates. And Polykrates continued
to hold that post until the end, or nearly the end, of Epiphanes'
reign.[25]

The story we have just told is based mainly on Polybius' *His-
tories*. It reveals two things: Firstly, to quote Sir Ronald Syme,
that a monarchy rules through an oligarchy;[26] and consequently, that

---

19   Polybius XVI 22.

20   See the references in Mooren, op. cit., 76-77 no. 036.

21   Polybius XVIII 54.1; 55.4.

22   Ptolemaios as strategos of Cyprus: see *Pros. Ptol.* VI 15068;
Michaelidou-Nicolaou, op. cit., 103 no. 59; Bagnall, op. cit., 255-
56 no. 3.

23   Skopas was accused before the royal συνέδριον by the king,
by Polykrates and by Aristomenes (Polybius XVIII 54.1); for Polykrates' "rising star," see also XVIII 55.5-7.

24   Diodorus XXVIII 14; Plutarch, *Moralia* 71c-d; for the date
see Chr. Habicht, *Hermes* 85 (1957) 504 n. 2.

25   See Polybius XXII 17.

26   *The Roman Revolution* (Oxford 1939) 8.

for the reconstruction of history it is equally important to know
the oligarchs or aristocrats as the monarch himself, whatever his
title may be. To be sure, we are but rarely so well informed as to
what went on on the Ptolemaic political scene--and even behind it!--
as in the present case. Incomplete though the reconstruction may
be, it can still stand as a model for what we want to know. Not
just some isolated names with titles or offices, but people: persons, families, and the connections between them. In this respect,
as in others, the literary sources and the papyrological and epi-
graphical evidence serve to flesh out each other.

Staying with the persons and families already mentioned, it
can be further demonstrated how they took charge of public life and
to what extent the state relied on them for the working of its institutions. Polykrates' family was warmly welcomed in Egypt because
of its antiquity and reputation, his father Mnasiadas being a famous athlete.[27] This Mnasiadas, son of Polykrates, was appointed
eponymous priest in Alexandria as early as 218/17 B.C.[28] When Polykrates was sent to Cyprus about 203 B.C., at least a large part of
his family accompanied him. In that period and in the following
years the family really began to stand out. His sons Ptolemaios[29]
and Polykrates[30] both served on the island, the former bearing the
court rank of ἀρχισωματοφύλαξ, the latter that of τῶν πρώτων φίλων.
His wife Zeuxo, a native of Cyrene, and his daughters Zeuxo, Eukra-
teia and Hermione all won Panathenaic contests in Athens,[31] as did
his sister[32] and perhaps another sister or daughter.[33] A Hermione,

---

27 Polybius V 64.4-6.

28 See W. Clarysse, *Enchoria* 6 (1976) 1-2; cf. *Pros. Ptol.* IX
5200b.

29 *Pros. Ptol.* VI 15770; Mooren, op. cit., 209 no. 0389;
Michaelidou-Nicolaou, op. cit., 104-5 no. 64.

30 *Pros. Ptol.* VI 15233; Mooren, op. cit., 209 no. 0390;
Michaelidou-Nicolaou, op. cit., 100 no. 35.

31 See *Pros. Ptol.* VI 17211, 17212, 17210, 17209. The wife
Zeuxo and the daughters Zeuxo and Hermione are also attested on
Cyprus; see, in addition to the above references, Michaelidou-
Nicolaou, op. cit., 62 no. 3 and no. 2, 59 no. 20. The same is
true of his father Mnasiadas; cf. 84 no. 40.

32 *Pros. Ptol.* VI 17247a.

33 *Pros. Ptol.* VI 17248a.

daughter of Polykrates, was athlophore in Alexandria in 170/69;[34]
she may be identical with Polykrates' daughter just mentioned,
though it is perhaps more likely that she was the daughter of Polykrates' homonymous son, the πρῶτος φίλος.[35] The latter also had a
son named Polykrates, and his epitaph has survived. He had reached
the rank of ἀρχισωματοφύλαξ and may be identical with an eponymous
military commander of the mid-second century B.C.[36] On the whole,
then, the activities of this family can be followed from about 220
to about 150 B.C.

The Pelops we encountered as strategos of Cyprus and as ambassador to king Antiochos III served under Ptolemy III in Cyrenaica.[37]
He was of Macedonian origin. His father Pelops, perhaps the son of
the early third-century eponymous commander Alexandros,[38] was one
of the Φίλοι of Ptolemy II and commanded Ptolemaic troops on Samos
between 281 and 259; in 264/63 he was eponymous priest in Alexandria.[39]   Pelops the son married Myrsine,[40] daughter of Hyperbassas,
who also served on Samos under Ptolemy II.[41] Pelops' sister-in-law,
Iamneia, was appointed canephore in Alexandria in 243/42.[42] His son
Ptolemaios was honored in Paphos.[43]

---

34   *Pros. Ptol.* III 5119.

35   See J. IJsewijn, *De sacerdotibus sacerdotiisque Alexandri
Magni et Lagidarum eponymis* (Brussels 1961) 103-5 no. 117.

36   Mooren, op. cit., 179 no. 0307.

37   See *Pros. Ptol.* VI 15064.

38   *Pros. Ptol.* II and VIII 1829.

39   *Pros. Ptol.* III and IX 5227, VI 14618; Mooren, op. cit.,
60-61 no. 011.   Taurinos, son of Alexandros and eponymous priest
in 260/59, might be Pelops' brother (see *Pros. Ptol.* III 5278 and
IX 5227).

40   Michaelidou-Nicolaou, op. cit., 85 no. 50.

41   *Pros. Ptol.* VI 15772; Michaelidou-Nicolaou, op. cit., 121-
22 no. 2.

42   *Pros. Ptol.* III and IX 5151 (= 5153?).

43   *Pros. Ptol.* VI 15769. For the family, see IJsewijn, op.
cit., 67-68 no. 22; P. M. Fraser, *Ptolemaic Alexandria* I, 104 (with
II, 191 n. 85); Bagnall, op. cit., 252-53.

Then we have the family of the Ptolemaios, son of Agesarchos, whom Agathokles sent to Rome and who succeeded Polykrates as strategos of Cyprus. He was a Megalopolitan. His father Agesarchos has been identified with an eponymous commander of the reign of Ptolemy III.[44] His daughter Eirene is attested as eponymous priestess of Arsinoe Philopator in Alexandria from 199/98 to 171/70.[45] During Ptolemaios' governorship, we find his grandson Andromachos[46] on Cyprus with the court rank τῶν διαδόχων and serving as an administrative officer in the armed forces. Later, perhaps the same Andromachos was sent by Ptolemy VI to Rome on a diplomatic mission. He was appointed tutor to Ptolemy Eupator and possibly finished his career about 145 B.C. as strategos of Cyprus.

The great Sosibios, who is called an Alexandrian, had a daughter Arsinoe who became canephore in 215/14;[47] he himself had been eponymous priest in 235/34.[48] Agathokles held that post in 216/15,[49] Aristomenes in 204/203.[50]

The picture we have sketched of some leading families, working outwards from the reign of Ptolemy V Epiphanes, can easily be enlarged. To add just one more example: When in 197 B.C. the trial of the Aitolian Skopas was due to take place, Aristomenes, so Polybius tells us, dispatched Ptolemaios, the son of Eumenes, with a corps of νεανίσκοι to bring the accused to court.[51] An inscription from Elephantine, published in 1970 by H. Maehler[52] and dating from the reign of Ptolemy VIII Euergetes II (145-116 B.C.), mentions the

---

44 *Pros. Ptol.* II and VIII 1825; cf. IJsewijn, op. cit., 89-90 sub no. 88.

45 *Pros. Ptol.* III and IX 5104.

46 *Pros. Ptol.* VI 14637; Mooren, op. cit., 204-5 no. 0376; Bagnall, op. cit., 255, 258.

47 *Pros. Ptol.* III and IX 5027.

48 *Pros. Ptol.* III and IX 5272.

49 *Pros. Ptol.* III and IX 4986.

50 *Pros. Ptol.* III and IX 5020.

51 Polybius XVIII 53.8-11.

52 *MDAIK* 26 (1970) 170-71 no. 2.

son and grandsons of this Ptolemaios.   It is a dedication, set up
by the phrourarch of Elephantine on behalf of Ptolemaios, the son
of Ptolemaios and grandson of Eumenes, τῶν πρώτων φίλων καὶ στρατηγός, and of his sons Ptolemaios, Timarchos and Kallikrates, all
three of the class of the ἰσότιμοι τοῖς πρώτοις φίλοις.[53] An inscription from Philae, published by A. Roccati,[54] has now thrown
more light on this family. This dedication honors king Ptolemy V
Epiphanes and his wife Kleopatra I and was set up by the phrourarch
of Philae on behalf of Ptolemaios, the son of Eumenes, Καστόρειος
(i.e. an Alexandrian deme), τῶν πρώτων φίλων καὶ ἀρχικυνηγός, his
wife Agathokleia, and their son Ptolemaios, ἀρχισωματοφύλαξ καὶ
ἀρχικυνηγός. These "chief huntsmen" are known from two other inscriptions, one, which is rather doubtful, from Philae,[55] the other
from Alexandria;[56] both date, like the new Philae document, from
the latter part of Epiphanes' reign.[57] We do not know if the elder
Ptolemaios, the son of Eumenes, was already chief huntsman in 197
B.C., but it may be safely assumed that he belonged to the court
circles[58] and, perhaps, that he was a protégé of Aristomenes, who

───────────────

53 The inscription can be dated between ca. 135/4 and 131; see
L. Mooren, *La hiérarchie de cour ptolémaïque. Contribution à l'étude
des institutions et des classes dirigeantes à l'époque hellénistique*
(Leuven 1977) 116-17. Ptolemaios and his three sons are listed in
my prosopography under no. 0121 (cf. *Pros. Ptol.* VIII 317a) and
nos. 0320-0322.

54 *Hommages à Maarten J. Vermaseren* (Leiden 1978) III, 990-91
no. 1.

55 A. Bernand, *Inscriptions de Philae* I 9; see now J. Bingen,
Cd'E 54 (1979) 305-6, who prefers to remove this inscription from
the dossier on the two ἀρχικυνηγοί.

56 *OGIS* I 99 (*SB* V 8274), reedited by H. De Meulenaere, *Cd'E*
52 (1977) 122-24, thanks to whom there is no doubt left concerning
the (long disputed) provenance of the inscription.

57 Leaving aside *Inscr. Philae* 9 (which would antedate the two
other inscriptions), the document published by Roccati can be situated about 187 (see Bingen, loc. cit.), while the Alexandrian inscription, because of the reference to τέκνα of the Kings, must be
dated between 186 and 180 (cf. my *Hiérarchie de cour ptolémaïque*,
174-75). See my prosopography, nos. 0290 and 0291.

58 F. W. Walbank, *Hist. Commentary on Polybius* II, 625 ad
53.8, is inclined to consider Ptolemaios a member of the royal
council.

was then the ἐπίτροπος of the king and who ordered Ptolemaios to
bring Skopas to trial. Here the name of Ptolemaios' wife, Agathokleia, becomes important. We know from Polybius that Aristomenes
had given this very name to his daughter, who must have been born
after 216. About 187 Ptolemaios' son was old enough to join his
father as ἀρχικυνηγός. But as he was still active as a στρατηγός
in the thirties of the second century, he must have been a very
young man indeed in the eighties. (Perhaps he was "appended" to
his father to be instructed in the ἀρχικυνηγία.) Thus the hypothesis becomes possible that Aristomenes' daughter and the Agathokleia
of the Philae inscription were one and the same person. At any
rate, there can in my view be little doubt that Ptolemaios' wife
was a relative of a member of Agathokles' clan.

Ptolemaios and his son perhaps prepared the visit of the Royal
Couple to the Thebaid after the great revolt, or were in some way
involved in the final offensive against the rebels. Both, but especially the father, played a role in Ptolemaic policy towards the
Lycian League which, as the Alexandrian inscription shows, thanked
them for services rendered.[59] The aulic titles and the activities
of father and son prove beyond doubt that they were very prominent
men at the Alexandrian court.

Some fifty years later, the son is strategos in the Thebaid
and has also attained the rank of τῶν πρώτων φίλων. His three sons
are one step below him as ἰσότιμοι. Now some papyri mention a Ptolemaios, eponymous commander in the Thebaid between 139 and 133 B.C.,
together with his sons.[60] E. Van 't Dack presumes that this is our
family and, if so, that the father should be regarded not as a nome
strategos, but as a military strategos. Unfortunately, we know
nothing of the court ranks of the purely military strategoi, but
comparison with the aulic titles borne by military commanders in

---

59 One will note that the League erected a statue of the son,
but on account of the merits and goodwill of the father. As the
provenance of the inscription is Alexandria, and not Cyprus (cf. my
Hiérarchie de cour ptolémaïque, 175 with n. 3), the κοινὸν τῶν
Λυκίων can hardly be anything else than the Lycian League (cf. Bagnall, op. cit., 110 n. 111).

60 See *Pros. Ptol.* II 1994 (ὁ δεῖνα τῶν Πτολεμαίου καὶ τῶν
υἱῶν).

the same period makes the hypothesis quite plausible.[61] On the
other hand, we encounter a Ptolemaios, son of Ptolemaios, as eponymous priest in Ptolemais in 153/52 B.C.[62] Since our family has
shifted its activities to the Thebaid, it is perhaps justifiable to
identify this priest with the strategos Ptolemaios or his homonymous
son.

Let us now return to the grandfather, Eumenes. The mere fact
that he is mentioned in the inscription of his grandson and great-
grandsons suggests that he was once a man of some importance. We
find an eponymous commander named Eumenes in the Arsinoite nome in
the forties and thirties of the third century B.C.; he is probably
identical with the Eumenes who was sent to Ethiopia on an elephant-
hunting expedition about 246 B.C.[63] If he is to be identified with
the Eumenes Polybius mentions as father of Ptolemaios,[64] then the
activity of our family can be followed for more than a century. It
served at least five kings and survived such court quarrels as the
replacement of Aristomenes by Polykrates and the conflicts between
Ptolemy VI Philometor and his younger brother. These troubles may
have left some traces. Why had the younger ἀρχικυνηγός, already
ἀρχισωματοφύλαξ around 187, not advanced beyond the πρῶτοι φίλοι
fifty years later? And why did the family have to leave Alexandria
for the distant Thebaid? Was this a kind of demotion or exile, or
was it simply because they were needed there? These and other
questions, such as the further elaboration of the family tree, remain open and will be discussed elsewhere by E. Van 't Dack and
myself. But this case has made it clear once again that the point
of view set out here must be given due attention when writing the
history of the Ptolemaic state.[65]

---

61 See, e.g., the military officer Inarôs, in 129 one of the
πρῶτοι φίλοι in the Panopolite nome (no. 0226 in my prosopography).

62 *Pros. Ptol.* III and IX 5247.

63 *Pros. Ptol.* II and VIII 1899, 1904 and 4419a.

64 Cf. IJsewijn, op. cit., 87-88 sub no. 84.

65 Compare, e.g., the examples adduced by P. M. Fraser, *Ptolemaic Alexandria* I, 104-5 (with II, 191-93 nn. 85-95) and the
stemma elaborated by L. Koenen, *Eine agonistische Inschrift aus
Ägypten und frühptolemäische Königsfeste* (Meisenheim am Glan 1977)
20.

I am now assembling such families and studying their composition, their interrelationships and their role in the public life
of Hellenistic Egypt. To enter into consideration at least two
active members must be known, of the same or of different generations. Also, these members must be state officials, more specifically high-ranking officials. Criteria of selection are therefore
the upper echelons of the administration, the aulic titles and the
eponymous priesthoods. Other indications are certain kinds of
possessions, such as δωρεαί[66] or ships,[67] or special honors bestowed within the Ptolemaic empire or abroad. My main working instrument is of course W. Peremans and E. Van 't Dack's *Prosopographia Ptolemaica* and some studies based thereon such as J. IJsewijn's work on the eponymous priests[68] and my own prosopography of
the bearers of aulic titles. And for Ptolemaic Cyprus we now have
the prosopography published by Ino Michaelidou-Nicolaou in 1976.

The planned study will, I hope, through the systematic assem-
bly of leading families, shed new light on the characteristics and
the evolution of the Ptolemaic state. As far as politics and the
higher administration in the broad sense are concerned, the Ptolemies never sought real cooperation with the native Egyptian aristocracy. Only from the time of Ptolemy VIII Euergetes II is some
modification of this attitude noticeable.[69] Even if this situation
should be partially explained by the Egyptian aristocracy's

---

66 Cf. M. Wörrle, *Chiron* 8 (1978) 207ff.; Claire Préaux, *Le
monde hellénistique. La Grèce et l'Orient de la mort d'Alexandre à
la conquête romaine de la Grèce, 323-146 av. J.-C.* (Paris 1978)
I, 379-81.

67 Cf. H. Hauben, *ZPE* 16 (1975) 289-91; idem, *AncSoc* 10 (1979)
167-70. In 187 a ship owned by Ptolemaios τῶν (πρώτων) φίλων trans-
ported a load of grain from the Koptite nome to Syene (my prosopography, 178 no. 0306; *Pros. Ptol.* V 14138; for the date, cf. my
Hiérarchie de cour ptolémaïque, 78-79); I think there is reason to
identify this Ptolemaios with our homonymous ἀρχικυνηγός (the
father).

68 New lists of eponymous priests, brought up to date, are
forthcoming. In addition to *Prosopographia Ptolemaica* IX (by W.
Clarysse), which provides addenda and corrigenda to vol. III, mention may be made here of G. Van der Veken-S. Vleeming-W. Clarysse,
The Eponymous Priests of Ptolemaic Egypt (compiled at the Papyrological Institute of the University of Leiden).

69 Cf. *AncSoc* 5 (1974) 149-52.

unwillingness to collaborate, the fact remains that it was replaced
by Hellenic immigrants who entered the service of the Ptolemies.
Thus a new aristocracy emerged in Egypt, bound not so much to the
soil as to the king and the machinery of state and forming, in essence, a nobility of office, comparable in a way--although the circumstances in which it developed were wholly different--to the
Roman *nobilitas*.

In the beginning, the golden age that was the third century
B.C., the relationship between the king and this new nobility was
rather unilateral. Of course the king needed these people; he
needed the most capable men of the Greek world to help build the
new state. But the attraction of Egypt was so great that he could
afford to be choosy. From the end of the third century, however,
immigration fell off considerably,[70] and it may be surmised, even
though the Alexandrian court and the higher offices of state will
have maintained their appeal, that the influence of the established
families grew. They at least had experience in running the appara-
tus of state, and the king, we may assume, became increasingly dependent upon them. Two other factors must also be taken into account: both externally and internally the state faced a crisis. To
counter it, the state needed its traditional supporters. On the
other hand, the monarchy, as an institution, developed its absolute
character, and to maintain the momentum of this evolution also required the cooperation of the establishment. All this may have led
to a more balanced relationship between the crown and the high society.[71] We know that the king made some concessions in order to
tie the nobility more closely to his person. The creation of the
court hierarchy in the early second century B.C. can be seen as a
measure advantageous to both parties. The higher officials were
now clearly distinguished from the lesser mortals; elevated to the
rank of courtiers, their importance and unique position were con-
secrated. The king, on his side, could hope that their industry

---

70 See, e.g., M. Rostovtzeff, *The Social and Economic History
of the Hellenistic World* II, 624-25.

71 Disregarding such "accidents" as those which accompanied
the takeover by Ptolemy VIII Euergetes II in 145/44 (cf. P. M.
Fraser, op. cit., I, 61-62, 121, and the references given in *AncSoc*
5 [1974] 149 n. 66).

and loyalty would get a fresh boost.[72]

The evolution of the Ptolemaic nobility, and therefore of the Ptolemaic state, can further be demonstrated by the appearance, from the end of the second century, of some Egyptian families in the upper strata of officialdom.[73] Their road had been long and arduous.

These few main lines that conclude this paper may serve to illustrate the overall framework within which my study of the Ptolemaic nobility will be elaborated.

Leuven   Leon Mooren

---

72 Cf. my *Hiérarchie de cour ptolémaïque*, 50ff.

73 See, e.g., my prosopography, nos. 0123, 0124, 0127, 0128, 0129, 0137, 0138.

Proceedings of the XVI Int. Congr. of Papyrology (Chico 1981) 303-312

LE CONFLIT JUDEO-SYRO-EGYPTIEN DE 103/102 AV. J.-C.

L'histoire des années 116 à 80 av. J.-C., qui couvre les
règnes de Cléopâtre III, de Ptolémée IX Sotèr II et de Ptolémée X
Alexandre I et dont la première partie jusqu'à la mort de Cléopâtre III a été traitée dans l'ouvrage fondamental de W. Otto et
H. Bengtson,[1] a fait l'objet de plusieurs mises au point durant ce
dernier quart de siècle.

Faute de temps, nous nous limiterons à un conflit international qui a dû se produire en 103/102 av. J.-C. Vers cette date Antiochos VIII Grypos et Antiochos IX Cyzicène se disputaient le
trône en Syrie. Alexandre Jannée qui venait de prendre le pouvoir
royal en Judée, profita des difficultés des Séleucides pour envahir
le territoire du littoral et pour attaquer e.a. le port de
Ptolémaïs-Akè. Cette ville fit appel à Ptolémée IX Sotèr II qui,
chassé d'Alexandrie par sa mère Cléopâtre III, s'était retiré à
Chypre. L'arrivée de ce dernier en Syrie provoqua l'intervention
de Cléopâtre III qui se rendit sur place et ordonna à son fils cadet et co-régent Ptolémée X Alexandre I de naviguer vers la Phénicie avec une flotte considérable. Comme l'Egypte se trouvait dé-
garnie de ses forces armées, Sotèr II jugea le moment opportun pour
rentrer au pays, mais son expédition--un premier essai de recon-
quérir le trône--n'obtint pas le succès espéré.

Dans ce rapport préliminaire, nous ne voulons que donner un
aperçu des catégories de sources disponibles et établir autant que
possible la chronologie des événements.

Concernant ce conflit nous possédons deux sources littéraires.
Il y a d'abord Flavius Josèphe qui donne un aperçu assez détaillé
dans ses *Antiquitates Iudaicae* XIII 320-364 et auquel nous avons
emprunté le résumé ci-dessus des événements.

A noter spécialement le rôle de Ptolémaïs-Akè, convoitée, as-
siégée ou occupée tour à tour par Alexandre Jannée, Ptolémée IX
Sotèr II et Cléopâtre III.

---

1 *Zur Geschichte des Niederganges des Ptolemäerreiches*
(München 1938) 145-93.

Le lecteur attentif du récit est frappé par deux lacunes. Il
y a d'abord le silence presque total sur les rois séleucides. Seuls
les chapitres 325-327 relatent qu' Antiochos VIII Grypos et Antiochos IX Cyzicène, qui se combattent l'un l'autre, ne peuvent venir
en aide à Ptolémaïs. Josèphe les compare à des athlètes qui sont à
bout de forces mais qui, honteux d'abandonner, prolongent la lutte
en multipliant les phases d'inactivité et de repos.

Manquent aussi les données chronologiques, du moins en ce qui
concerne les exploits lagides. Ce n'est qu'au chapitre 352 que
nous apprenons que Ptolémée IX Sotèr II, après l'échec de son expédition en Egypte, hiverne à Gaza. Il est vrai que les chapitres
suivants sont peut-être plus précis sur ce point, mais ils ne sont
plus d'aucune utilité directe pour fixer les étapes des campagnes
des Ptolémées. Ainsi l'auteur mentionne au chapitre 356 la prise
de Gadara par Alexandre Jannée après un siège de dix mois et au
chapitre 364 celle de Gaza après une année de siège. Mais avant
d'attaquer Gaza, Alexandre Jannée s'était déjà rendu compte que
Ptolémée IX Sotèr II avait quitté Gaza pour Chypre et que sa mère
était retournée en Egypte.

Signalons ensuite le résumé assez intéressant que Justin a
fait du livre XXXIX de Trogue-Pompée. Au chapitre 4 nous apprenons
au moins quelques faits nouveaux. Nous sommes enfin fixés sur les
alliances politiques: d'une part Antiochos IX Cyzicène est soutenu
par Ptolémée IX Sotèr II, tandis que Cléopâtre III et Ptolémée X Alexandre I viennent en aide à Antiochos VIII Grypos; Cléopâtre ne lui
envoie pas seulement des *ingentia auxilia* mais aussi sa fille, jadis la femme de Ptolémée IX Sotèr II, *Selenen uxorem, nupturam
hosti prioris mariti*. En même temps le résumé fait état de la
fuite de Ptolémée X Alexandre I *territus hac matris crudelitate* et
de son rappel par la reine mère: *Alexandrumque filium per legatos
in regnum revocat*. Suit enfin le meurtre que le fils cadet aurait
commis sur sa mère après son retour.

On pourrait invoquer d'autres textes, mais ils se rapportent
sans doute à d'autres événements.

Ainsi nous passons sous silence le Prologue de ce même livre
XXXIX de Trogue-Pompée qui dans un bout de phrase--*in Syria bello
petitus* (*scil.* Ptolémée IX Sotèr II) *ab eadem*--n'apporte rien de
neuf. Le passage se rapporte sans doute à la poursuite du fils

aîné lorsqu'en 107, expulsé d'Alexandrie et obligé même de s'enfuir de Chypre, il partit en direction de la Syrie.

C'est sans doute à ce même épisode que fait allusion un passage de Diodore XXXIV/XXXV 39a qui raconte le complot dont faillit être victime Πτολεμαῖος ὁ πρεσβύτερος en Séleucie.[2]

Depuis que la séparation éphémère de Cléopâtre III et de Ptolémée IX Sotèr II en 110 av. J.-C. et le remplacement très temporaire de ce dernier par son frère cadet ont été mis en cause,[3] il devient plus difficile qu'auparavant de situer précisément un passage de Strabon XVII 794 (= I 8): ἐσύλησε δ' αὐτὴν (scil. πύελον) ὁ Κόκκης καὶ Παρείσακτος ἐπικληθεὶς Πτολεμαῖος, ἐκ τῆς Συρίας ἐπελθὼν καὶ ἐκπεσὼν εὐθύς, ὥστ' ἀνόνητα αὐτῷ τὰ σῦλα γενέσθαι. Nous n'osons toutefois pas suivre M. L. Strack qui jadis avait rapporté ce texte à l'invasion ratée de Ptolémée IX Sotèr II.[4] Ces sobriquets conviennent-ils vraiment à celui-ci? Pourrait-on supposer que ses troupes eussent pénétré dans le pays jusqu'à atteindre Alexandrie?[5]

Nous éliminons aussi du débat le texte de Diodore XXXIV/XXXV 20, passage qui signale une victoire totale sur les forces alexandrines et une série successive de mesures de clémence de la part du vainqueur.

---

2 Cf. W. Otto et H. Bengtson, o.c., 169-70, 184 avec n. 5.

3 La datation nouvelle du P. Rein. 22 et du PSI IX 1018 en 107 av. J.-C., date proposée par P. W. Pestman, P.L.Bat. XIX (1978), pp. 21-22, nous oblige à revoir la thèse de W. Otto-H. Bengtson, o.c., 160-71, selon lesquels Ptolémée IX Sotèr II aurait été expulsé et remplacé temporairement par son frère cadet en 110 av. J.-C.

4 Dyn. (reprod. 1976) 91 n. 32, 93-95 n. 36; thèse refutée e.a. par W. Otto-H. Bengtson, o.c., 167-68.

5 D'autres solutions restent plus ou moins possibles: une première dissension entre Cléopâtre III et son fils aîné en 112 av. J.-C., qui ne semble toutefois pas avoir entraîné l'effacement total de ce dernier (cf. L. Koenen, "Kleopatra III als Priesterin des Alexanderkultes," ZPE 5 [1970] 61-84, surtout 75 n. 20 et 76-77); l'expulsion de Sotèr II en 108 lorsqu'il s'imposa à Cyrène, sans qu'on puisse conclure directement à son remplacement éphémère par Alexandre I sur le trône d'Alexandrie (cf. W. Otto-H. Bengtson, o.c., 173-75, 178 n. 3; P. M. Fraser, Berytus 12 [1958] 114 et n. 5; R. S. Bagnall, The Administration of the Ptolemaic Possessions outside Egypt [Leiden 1976] 30 n. 16); peut-être les événements de 88 av. J.-C.

Laissons donc ces informations des auteurs anciens et tournons-
nous vers la documentation non-littéraire qui nous apporte incontestablement quelques précisions grâce aux archives sur papyrus
d'un groupe de militaires en provenance de Gebelen.

Référence	Auteur(s) des lettres	Date		Lieu d'origine
n°1 P.Amh. 39 + P.Grenf. I 30 (cf. Archiv 2 [1903] 517)	Πόρτεις ἡγεμὼν τῶν ἐν προχειρισμῶι καὶ οἱ [ἐκ] τοῦ σημείου νεανίσκοι	an 14 = 11, Pauni 15	29 juin 103	Hermônthis
n°2 DP BM 040 + DP Berl. 13381 (cf. Festschr. 150j. Bestehen Berl. äg. Mus., 289-291)	Panobchounis f. de Pmois, prostatês de Souchos	an 15 = 12, Thôth 10	27 sept. 103	Ptolémaïs-Akè
n°3 P.Grenf. I 32	[Πετε]σοῦχος ἡγεμὼν et ...οἱ στρατιῶται...	an 15 = 12, Pharmouthi 2	17 avril 102	Pélousion
n°4 DP Heid. 746 (cf. ZÄS 42 [1905] 47-49)	Nechthyris f. de Psenmônthês	an 15, Epeiph 30 (?)	13 août 102	le Nord (Mendès ?)
n°5 DP Heid. 742b + 781a + fr. sans numéro d'inventaire (cf. Festschr. 150j. Bestehen Berl. äg. Mus., 291-292)	Panobchounis f. de Pmois (cf. n°2)	an [16] = 13, Thôth 6	23 sept. 102	Mendès ("départ vers le sud le 10 Thôth")
n°6 P.Grenf. I 35	?	an 16, Thôth 8	25 sept. 102	Ptolémaïs
n°7 P.Louvre 10593 (cf. Archiv 2 [1903] 515-516)	Philammôn (prob. chef militaire)	an 16, Choiak 28	13 janv. 101	?

Il s'agit incontestablement d'archives au sens strict du mot:
car les adressés sont apparemment les mêmes. Patês et Pachratês,
manifestement les principaux interlocuteurs, figurent dans 4 des 7
documents au moins (nos 1,2,5 et 7). Les nos 3 et 6 semblent à
première vue faire exception. Mais au no 3 les premiers noms des
destinataires ont disparu dans une lacune de quelque 73 lettres;
le texte ne reprend qu'avec l'adressé Poêris, le fils de Ne[choutês]
qui figure aussi soit en troisième, soit en quatrième, soit en si-
xième et dernière position parmi les destinataires des nos 2,4 et 5.
Au no 6 toute la partie supérieure de la lettre, y compris les noms
des expéditeurs et des destinataires, est perdue de sorte qu'on
hésite un peu à joindre ce document au dossier.

Avant et après la campagne, les destinataires résident dans
le Pathyrite. Parmi eux se trouve, selon le papyrus démotique no 2,
Hôros, le fils de Nechoutês, un personnage assez bien connu par
ailleurs.[6] Il apparaît comme contractant jusqu'au 29 Choiak de

---

6 Cf. *Pros. Ptol.* II 4145 et VIII add.; IV 11152; P. W. Pestman, "A proposito dei documenti di Pathyris, II. Πέρσαι τῆς ἐπιγονῆς," *Aegyptus* 43 (1963) 15-53, surtout 51-53 no 130; arbre géné-
alogique dans P. W. Pestman, "Les archives privées de Pathyris à
l'époque ptolémaïque. La famille de Pétéharsemtheus, fils de Panebkhounis," dans *P.L.Bat.* XIV (1965) 47-48 n. 5.

l'an 14 = l'an 11 (14 janv. 103) dans *P. Adler dem.* 7 et à nouveau
à partir du 28 Thôth de l'an 17 de la reine et de Ptolémée X Alexandre I (14 oct. 101) dans *P. Adler gr.* 11.[7] La lettre démotique
no 2 (27 sept. 103) des archives prouve qu'entretemps la compagnie
doit avoir quitté l'Egypte sans qu'on puisse déterminer précisément
le nouveau lieu de résidence.

Quant aux auteurs des lettres, nous avons deux fois affaire à
un hégémon et à ses soldats (nos 1 et 3). Deux autres lettres ont
été rédigées par le même personnage, gérant du dieu Souchos, le
grand dieu, *N3-nḫt-f-r-w* (nos 2 et 5), qui se trouve manifestement
en contact direct avec un milieu militaire; W. Clarysse a restitué
ce même titre sous la forme προστάτης [τοῦ με]γίς[του θεοῦ] Νεχθη-
ραῦτος au no 1. Ni l'auteur du no 4, Nechthyris, le fils de Psen-
mônthês,[8] ni celui du no 7, Philammôn, ne nous est connu par ailleurs; à en juger d'après le contenu du dernier texte, Philammôn
doit avoir été un officier. Enfin, même si le début de la lettre
no 6 manque, les quelques lignes qui nous en restent suggèrent
encore une fois un milieu de militaires.

La localisation de ces auteurs nous paraît intéressante. Celui du texte no 2 se trouve apparemment à Ptolémaïs (ligne 17). A
première vue, puisqu'il s'agit de documents de Gebelen, on pense à
Ptolémaïs Hermiou en Haute-Egypte. Dans son édition, Madame U.
Kaplony-Heckel rejette manifestement cette solution trop facile,
parce que à la ligne suivante (ligne 18), elle lit le nom du district de Thémistos du Fayoum; elle songe donc à une localité dans
l'Arsinoïte. Or, cette hypothèse n'est plus valable depuis que
J. K. Winnicki[9] et W. Clarysse, indépendamment l'un de l'autre,

---

7 Le *P. Adler gr.* 19 date même de l'an 16 Phamenôth; mais se
basant sur le rapport avec d'autres actes, on a attribué à juste
titre cette année à Ptolémée X Alexandre I seul. Le *P. Cairo dem.*
30652, datant du 13 Phaôphi de l'an 16 d'un Pharaon masculin, doit
être situé dans ce même règne.
D'autres cas, comparables à celui de Hôros fils de Nechoutês,
sont cités par U. Kaplony-Heckel, *Festschrift zum 150jährigen
Bestehen des Berliner Ägyptischen Museums*, 295-96.

8 Voir E. Van 't Dack, *Le retour de Ptolémée IX Sotèr II et
la fin de Ptolémée X Alexandre I* (à paraître).

9 Cf. infra, 547-52.

ont déchiffré à l'endroit précité le nom de Damaskos au lieu de
celui de Thémistos. Il faut par conséquent situer Ptolémaïs plus
près de cette ville syrienne et l'identifier de préférence avec le
port de Ptolémaïs-Akè. Le no 3 vient de la ville frontière Pélousion. Le no 4, qui de toute façon est écrit "dans le Nord," vient
peut-être de Mendès comme le no 5. Le no 6, qui, répétons-le, ne
fait pas nécessairement partie du dossier, est originaire d'une
ville Ptolémaïs, tandis que dans le no 7 il n'y a, hélas, aucune
indication précise.

Notons--en passant--le bout de phrase du no 2 ligne 18: "le
roi alla vers Damas." Il ne peut s'agir que de Ptolémée X Alexandre I, convoqué d'après Josèphe en Phénicie par sa mère. Quelle
est la signification exacte de ce communiqué? Quelle en est la
valeur? Le roi a-t-il apporté à Antiochos VIII Grypos les renforts
dont parle Justin? A-t-il accompagné sa soeur Sélènè, *nupturam
hosti prioris mariti*? Ou s'agit-il de la fuite du fils cadet pour
sa mère? Le caractère analytique et fragmentaire de la documentation papyrologique ne nous a, en l'occurrence, certainement pas
comblés.

Les données concernant la localisation deviennent importantes
surtout lorsqu'elles sont combinées avec les dates des différentes
lettres. Ainsi le 27 septembre 103 nous assistons au siège ou à
l'occupation de Ptolémaïs-Akè (no 2). Le 17 avril 102, après l'invasion avortée de Ptolémée IX Sotèr II en Egypte, au moment où, de
son quartier d'hiver à Gaza, il menace toujours la frontière est
de l'Egypte, des troupes lagides veillent à Pélousion à la sécurité
du pays (no 3). Le 23 septembre 102 des unités militaires sont
encore présentes à Mendès du Delta, mais d'après l'auteur de cette
lettre (no 5) elles seront sans doute démobilisées quatre jours
plus tard; de toute façon elles navigueront vers le Sud "ramant et
faisant voile." Si le papyrus no 6 appartient au dossier, il semble
y avoir encore des forces armées lagides à Ptolémaïs-Akè le 25 septembre 102. Il est dommage que le no 7 ne contienne aucune information permettant de localiser les faits relatés. S'agit-il--ce 13
janvier 101--d'un autre ordre de démobilisation? Ce texte suggère-
t-il la raison pour laquelle la démobilisation s'est si longtemps
différée et révèle-t-il une pénurie de moyens de transport?

La technique de datation soulève un léger problème. Car les
dates doubles alternent avec les dates simples ou plutôt, depuis
les derniers mois de l'an 15, nous ne relevons plus qu'une seule
date double (no 5), émanant du prostate de Souchos qui avait auparavant eu recours à la même technique (no 2). Les trois autres
textes (nos 4,6 et 7) utilisent une date simple. On a toujours
situé ces trois documents sous le règne de Ptolémée X Alexandre I
seul (resp. le 12 août 99, le 24 sept. 99, le 12 janv. 98); mais
est-on vraiment en droit d'admettre, dans ce cas, une lacune d'environ trois années complètes (no 5, dernier texte avec une date
double: 23 sept. 102) dans la correspondance de ce groupe de militaires qui ne paraît pas avoir subi de changement notoire depuis le
début du dossier (no 1: 29 juin 103)?

Si nous optons provisoirement pour une datation sous Cléopâtre
III, nous ne voudrions pas immédiatement accorder une signification
politique à ce détail d'ordre technique. D'autre part, nous ne
voudrions pas l'exclure non plus. Il faudra attendre d'autres
informations plus amples et plus convaincantes.[10]

Quant aux inscriptions, nous serons plus bref puisque leur
importance se situe plutôt sur le plan de la composition de l'armée
lagide que sur celui de la chronologie de la campagne.

Pour l'aspect qui nous occupe présentement, la stèle démotique
3709 du Sérapeum de Memphis reste toutefois de première importance.
La date proposée par W. Spiegelberg[11] est le 6 Mecheir (?) de l'an
15 correspondant à l'an 12, soit le 20 février 102. L'inscription
précède donc le papyrus no 3 de presque deux mois. A ce moment le
roi Ptolémée X Alexandre I surveille, à la tête de ses troupes à

---

10 Si la datation d'après la seule année de règne de la reine
n'est pas due au désir de simplification, on pourrait penser éven-
tuellement à la fuite d'Alexandre I ou à l'influence grandissante
de Cléopâtre III. (Voir à ce dernier sujet, L. Koenen, *o.c.* dans
le présent article n. 5.)
    Les trois documents précités ne seraient d'ailleurs pas les
seuls à être datés uniquement d'après les années de règne de Cléopâtre III. Aussi le *P. Adler gr.* 11 renvoie sans plus à la 17e
année de la reine, apparemment déjà morte à ce moment, et d'Alexandre I. De même dans *P. Cairo dem.* II 30627 plus endommagé: 16e
année de Cléopâtre III et d'Alexandre I. Cf. W. Otto-H. Bengtson,
o.c., 189 n. 1, 191 n. 2.

11 "Ein historisches Datum aus der Zeit des Ptolemaios XI
Alexandros," *ZÄS* 57 (1922) 69.

Pélousion, son frère ennemi, hivernant à Gaza.[12]

La seconde inscription--grecque--provient de Hassaia, la
nécropole d'Apollônopolis Magna, et fait partie d'un groupe de
quatre épigrammes écrites par le poète Hêrôdês.[13] Le texte de la
stèle en question a été édité en dernier lieu par E. Bernand, *Inscriptions métriques de l'Egypte gréco-romaine*, no 5 et commenté
d'une manière détaillée par J. Yoyotte, "Bakhthis: Religion égyptienne et culture grecque à Edfou," dans *Religions en Egypte hellénistique et romaine* (Paris 1969) 127-41.

Ptolemaios, père du défunt Apollônios, paraît avoir reçu des
Evergètes le συγγενικῆς δόξης ἱερὸν γέρας (11.4-5). Or, Boêthos
est le premier stratège de la Thébaïde entière à être promu au rang
de συγγενής. En 135/134 av. J.-C. il doit avoir été le seul à porter ce titre en Haute-Egypte.[14] Nous supposons que l'octroi de ce
même titre à Ptolemaios, qui n'était certes pas placé aussi haut
dans la hiérarchie militaire, est plus récent.

Le fils Apollônios a participé, non avec son père qui était
sans doute déjà trop âgé, mais avec des amis de son père, à une
expédition militaire en Syrie qui eut le trône comme enjeu et pendant laquelle périt sans doute Apollônios: 11.11-12 πατρὸς ἐμοῦ
γνωτοῖσι συνεκπλεύσαντα, ..., ὅτε σκάπτρων ἦλυθ᾽ ῎Αρης Συρίην.

A la suite de U. von Wilamowitz,[15] cette campagne a été con-
sidérée souvent--si elle n'a pas été située à une date antérieure[16]
--comme un épisode des querelles dynastiques qui opposaient

----

12 Cf. W. Otto-H. Bengtson, *o.c.*, 186.

13 Trois d'entre eux mentionnent explicitement son nom;
l'autre peut lui être assignée grâce à des arguments d'ordre
stylistique.

14 Cf. L. Mooren, *The Aulic Titulature in Ptolemaic Egypt.
Introduction and Prosopography* (Verhand. Kon. Acad. Belg., Kl. Lett.
XXXVII, no 78, Brussel 1975) 90-91 no 053.

15 "Zwei Gedichte aus der Zeit Euergetes' II.," *Archiv* 1
(1901) 219-25, surtout 222 comm. no 2.11-12.

16 L. H. Vincent, *MIFAO* 67 (1934-1937) 48-49 n. 7 (= *Mélanges
Maspéro* II): dernier quart du 3e siècle. Une datation plus vague:
P. Mouterde, *Mél. Univ. Beyrouth* 16 (1932) 100: second siècle avant
l'ère chrétienne. *Pros. Ptol.* II 1847 = VI 15181 = VIII 2110a et
II 1997 = VIII 2134b; L. Mooren, *o.c.*, 159 no 0227: 2e moitié du 2e
siècle (145/116?).

Cléopâtre II et Evergète II entre 129 et 123 av. J.-C.[17] Même
cette date-ci nous paraît assez haute. Compte tenu de la titulature aulique de Ptolemaios, une date plus basse conviendrait mieux.
D'autre part, puisque la carrière du père connaît son apogée sous
le règne d'Evergète II, on ne peut s'écarter trop loin de 116 av.
J.-C. Le conflit de 103/102 av. J.-C. semble répondre de manière
suffisante aux conditions susmentionnées.

Il y a enfin une inscription hiéroglyphique, inédite encore,
sur une statue de Karnak en l'honneur d'un personnage originaire du
Delta, prêtre et militaire à la fois.[18] Avec la permission de MM.
H. De Meulenaere et J. Quaegebeur, nous citons la traduction d'une
partie de la col. II: "il alla au pays de Khar (la Syrie) en compagnie de la femme pharaon (ou bien: pour être auprès de la femme
pharaon); il entra dans la région étrangère comme un faucon divin;
il régna sur (ou: soumit?) la ville 'la forteresse de P-sj de Ptolémaïs;' il abattit des (ennemis) innombrables et piétina des cen-
taines de milliers." Et plus loin: "la grande épouse du roi lui
donna de multiples cadeaux ainsi qu'à son père et à son armée...."
La mise en évidence de la reine, le bulletin de victoire, la prise
de Ptolémaïs s'insèrent encore une fois aisément dans la campagne
de 103/102 av. J.-C. Il n'y a que la mention de "la grande épouse
du roi" qui pourrait soulever des doutes. Mais d'après les éditeurs, il ne s'agit ici que d'une expression banale pour indiquer
toute reine.

L'ensemble sera commenté plus amplement dans un petit volume
qui comportera aussi la réédition revue de tous les documents grecs
sur papyrus et l'édition première de l'inscription hiéroglyphique.
Pour le moment nous hésitons à rééditer en plus tous les documents
démotiques; mais dans un commentaire approfondi de chaque texte
nous signalerons les corrections que nous proposons. Nous nous

---

17 Cf. W. Otto-H. Bengtson, *o.c.*, 98-99 et n. 4. J. Ijsewijn,
De sacerdotibus sacerdotiisque Alexandri Magni et Lagidarum eponymis
(Verhand. Kon. Vl. Acad., Kl. Lett. 42, Brussel 1961) 114 no 149,
attribue à tort le titre de *syngenês* au fils (de même J. K. Winnicki, *Ptolemäerarmee in Thebais* [1978] 82) qu'il identifie ainsi avec
le prêtre éponyme d'Epiphane à Ptolémaïs en 138/37 av. J.-C. (*Pros.
Ptol.* III 5009); voir aussi P. M. Fraser, *JEA* 48 (1962) 151; J. Yoyotte, *o.c.*, 130-31.

18 Muzeo egizio di Torino 3062.

conformerons aux voeux exprimés au précédent congrès.[19]

A cette étude collaboreront: W. Clarysse (Leiden-Leuven),
G. M. Cohen (Cincinnati), H. De Meulenaere (Gent), J. Quaegebeur
et moi-même (Leuven). Au cours de ce congrès Monsieur J. K. Winnicki a présenté un rapport assez semblable.[20] Il est évident que
dans le cadre de l'*amicitia papyrologorum*, nous voulons bien chercher une solution qui puisse contenter toutes les parties en cause
et inviter Monsieur J. K. Winnicki à rejoindre notre groupe.
L'union fait la force.

Leuven   E. Van 't Dack

---

19 W. Peremans-E. Van 't Dack, "La papyrologie et l'histoire
ancienne. L'heuristique et la critique des textes sur papyrus,"
dans *Actes du XVe Congrès international de Papyrologie* IV
(Bruxelles 1979) 7-25.

20 Cf. infra, 549-54.

Proceedings of the XVI Int. Congr. of Papyrology (Chico 1981) 313-318

THE POLITICAL BACKGROUND OF THE PLURALITY
OF LAWS IN PTOLEMAIC EGYPT

My starting point is a fact well-known to all papyrologists, namely the national dualism which was the outstanding characteristic of the legal life of the Ptolemaic monarchy during the whole period of its existence. It cannot, of course, be my intention to enter upon a discussion of all the problems and as yet unsettled controversies involved in this historical phenomenon. What I propose to do in the short time allowed to me for this paper, is to suggest an answer to the question of what political conditions made both possible and inevitable such a coexistence of disparate legal traditions.

Let us cast a quick glance at the factual situation. As I have pointed out elsewhere, in agreement with J. Modrzejewski,[1] the two strands never merged into one unified legal system. But no more were they, at least as a matter of legal principle, mutually exclusive. They may have been so, in fact, during the first few decades of the monarchy. However, this merely reflected the initial separation of the immigrants--Greeks and others who were hellenized-- from the Egyptians. The closer the contacts grew, and the more the populations mixed, the more the barriers between "Greek" law and Egyptian law fell. As I have also tried to show in earlier publications,[2] the principle of the "personality of laws," as postulated by L. Mitteis[3] and most papyrologists down to Taubenschlag and Seidl (with the sole exception of E. Bickermann,[4] who denied it more than fifty years ago) did not in fact govern the legal life of Ptolemaic Egypt.

---

1 Modrzejewski, *IVRA* 15 (1964) 46ff.; *Essays in Honor of C. Bradford Welles* (New Haven 1969) 157ff.; Wolff, ibid., 75ff. = *Opuscula Dispersa* (Amsterdam 1974) 111ff.

2 *RIDA*[3] 7 (1960) 217f.; *Essays Welles*, 70 = *Opusc.*, 106.

3 *Reichsrecht und Volksrecht in den östlichen Provinze des römischen Kaiserreichs* (Leipzig 1891 [1935, 1963]) 51.

4 *APF* 8 (1927) 227ff.

What did exist was only the division of jurisdiction between
the *laokritai* and the Greek *dikasteria*. Each of these courts dis-
pensed justice according to its own *lex fori*, but--as evidenced at
least for the *laokritai* by the famous *prostagma* on jurisdiction,
P. Teb. I 5.207-220--they were open to litigants of the other nationality as well as of their own. The *chrematists* were the royal
judges who meted out justice to all; they probably applied the
royal laws which apparently included the τῆς χώρας νόμοι, as the
native laws were called. The same goes for the judicial activities
of administrative officials; witness the lawsuit of Hermias. Last
but not least, private individuals could avail themselves of forms
and types of transaction taken from either sphere, as they pleased.

More than anything else, it is this last-mentioned fact that
renders understanding of the situation difficult to the mind of
today's jurist. For it means that there were two separate sets of
institutions, forms of contract, and methods of documentation,
representing divergent traditions, expressed in different languages,
and yet all of them equally at the disposal of all the people, regardless of their nationality. Moreover, they always remained
parallel and independent of each other, so that there never came
into existence anything like a coherent system of rules and forms
which could be called "the law of the land," as we understand this
term.

So much for the background. As regards the causes of this
peculiar legal dualism, I must emphasize that it was by no means
the effect of any deliberate policy on the part of the Ptolemaic
government. It was the result of, so to speak, a natural growth on
both sides. No more than other Hellenistic rulers did the Ptolemies ever try to impose on their subjects a codification which
would have provided them with a common and unified system of private law. What was the reason behind this omission?

In an article, published in 1958 under the title "Pourquoi n'y
eut-il pas de grandes codifications hellénistiques?," Cl. Préaux
offered an answer to the question.[5] According to her, there was,
on the one hand, a narrow traditionalism characterizing the attitude of the various peoples living in the territories ruled by the
Seleucids and the Ptolemies which would of necessity have condemned

---

5 *RIDA*[3] 5 (1958) 365ff.

to failure any attempt to overcome hereditary habits by a new and
uniform legislation. She found another, and perhaps even stronger,
reason in the official ideology of the period which, in line with
a general weakening of the rationalistic spirit, insisted on vague
ideas of φιλανθρωπία and ἐπιείκεια and was not interested in enact-
ing a rational legal order. Now in view of Philadelphus' comprehensive regulation of the modes of procedure and enforcement, referred to in the sources as τὸ διάγραμμα, I cannot help doubting
Miss Préaux's second thesis, at least as far as the Ptolemies were
concerned. Her first thesis is, in my opinion, more suggestive.
The decisive reason, however, should rather be looked for in the
very concept the Ptolemies had of the constitutional nature of
their government, if I may use this anachronistic and inexact expression. It seems to me this concept was not only apt to hinder
any notion of establishing a uniform code of private law for the
country, it must also have led to the belief that precisely the
coexistence of different traditions was a natural condition in a
country inhabited by peoples so different in language, culture, and
religion.

To understand the concept in question, we have to realize that
there was, in the historical experience of the Greeks, no precedent
for the new kingdoms that had risen from the ruins of Alexander's
empire. The emergence of those huge monarchies, extending over immense territories and inhabited by numerous and diverse populations,
had within only a few years, and most turbulent years at that,
brought to the Greeks a type of political order which so far was
known to them only from the distant and foreign Persian kingdom.
Such must have been the impression the vast territorial domains
governed despotically by a centralized bureaucracy made on the
Greeks. Thus a chasm had opened between their traditional concepts
shaped by the polis and the political realities which surrounded
them. They were unable to bridge this chasm by adapting their traditional concepts to the new situation: in other words, they did
not devise a new type of political organization which would have
been appropriate to the new political needs while firmly rooted in
the Greek tradition.

Such a state in the true sense of the word might conceivably
have evolved, had it been possible to set up an administration which,
though headed by a monarch, could have received its legitimation

from serving the common interest. This, however, was unthinkable
under the circumstances. For one thing, it was incompatible with
the character of the diadochs themselves who were pursuing purely
personal goals. Even more important: the political ideology of the
period was in strict opposition to any such concept.[6] According to
this ideology the lands occupied by the Hellenistic kings were co-
sidered to be their personal, even private, property, "gained by
the spear" (δορίκτητος), as the Greeks said. Egypt, as is well-
known, was primarily an object of economic exploitation by the dynasty. Current philosophy of course expected the king to display
fatherly goodwill (φιλανθρωπία), fairness (ἐπιείκεια), and love
(εὐστοργία) for his subjects. We may leave aside the question of
the extent to which these ideals were realized. What is decisive
is the fact that Hellenistic thought, even among its most outstanding representatives, was not geared to developing an abstract and
objective idea of the "state," such as the philosophy of the En-
lightenment later conceived in demanding that the 18th century king
be, in the words of Frederick the Great, "the first servant of the
state." The Ptolemaic king was a god and above the rest of mankind.
The effect of all this was that the concept of a "state," in our
sense of this term, could not emerge.[7]

We arrive at the same result when we look at the political
status and corresponding role of the population of Ptolemaic Egypt.

It is true that, for practical purposes, the administrative
and fiscal system of the Ptolemies, relying on a tightly-knit bureaucracy and operating according to fixed rules, was not dissimilar
to that of a normal territorial state, as we know it. Nonetheless,
this organizational achievement of the Lagid kings (which, as is
well-known, was in many respects simply continuing along the lines
laid down by their pharaonic predecessors) could not change the
basic fact that there was no such thing as a "Staatsvolk," in other

----

6 Suffice it to remind the reader of Cl. Préaux's comprehensive discussion of the subject in the chapter entitled "Le Roi" in
her last work, *Le Monde hellénistique* (Paris 1978) I, 181ff., 192ff.

7 Cf. Préaux's brief statement,(op. cit., II, 681): "Les
royaumes ne sont ni des 'Etats,' ni des 'nations' et encore moins
des 'patries.' Il y a des rois, leurs 'affaires' (*ta pragmata*) et
ceux qui leur sont soumis ou alliés."

words, that the people living under their rule did not form a com-
pact body belonging to the country of Egypt as a political unit and
subject, in this capacity, to the latter's government. We may pass
over the special status of the citizens of the three more or less
self-governing Greek poleis, Naukratis, Alexandria, and Ptolemais.
What matters is the fact that even the people of the *chora* were
divided into several unconnected groups which differed not only as
to their ethnic origin but also with respect to their political
status and consequently, in their relationship to the king and the
country.[8] There was, on the one hand, the mass of the Egyptians
who, in the eyes of the royal administration, were no more than objects of exploitation; for their part, they were loyal to their
priests; and, while possibly recognizing the king as their divine
pharaoh, they did not consider themselves as belonging to the country as a political entity governed and represented by the Ptolemaic
king. On the other hand, there were the majority of the Greeks and
other immigrants. It is important to note that not only were they
not defined ethnically, as a group of their own, but in the course
of time they were even joined by an increasing number of ethnic
Egyptians who had succeeded in more or less hellenizing themselves.
The common denominator of all these elements was the fact that they
formed the military and civil following of the king to whom they
were personally loyal, an attachment, however, which again did not
by any means involve any loyalty to Egypt as a "state."[9] Finally,
in addition to these two categories of people, there were other
non-Egyptians who lived in Egypt as peasants and tradesmen; some
of them, such as the so-called Hellenomemphitai,[10] had in fact been
in Egypt for centuries, antedating the conquest of the country by
Alexander. They were, like the natives, subject to the direct authority of the king's functionaries, but had to some extent

---

8 As to the following remarks, cf. Bickermann, op. cit.,
216ff.; M. Rostovtzeff, *The Social and Economic History of the
Hellenistic World* (Oxford 1941) I, 266, 316ff., II, 1309; W. Peremans
in H. Maehler-V. M. Strocka, eds., *Das ptolemäische Ägypten* (Mainz
1978) 45.

9 Cf. Wolff, *Das Justizwesen der Ptolemäer* (München 1962,
1970) 57.

10 Cf. U. Wilcken, *Grundzüge* (Leipzig 1912) 18; W. Peremans,
Vreemdelingen en Egyptenaren in Vroeg-Ptolemaeisch Egypte (Louvain
1937) 224ff.

succeeded in preserving their own identity and traditions, especially those of a religious nature.

There was no bond unifying all these elements other than that of being subject to the king who was the divine and absolute ruler over them all. In this respect I should like to emphasize a circumstance which seems to me to be of paramount importance. It is the fact that to all appearances it made no difference whether a person was present in Egypt as a permanent resident or merely as a transient. The modern distinction between nationals (Inländer or Staatsangehörige) and foreigners (Ausländer) seems to have played no part in ancient legal thought. There was of course in the poleis a distinction between citizens and non-citizens. Beyond that, however, and especially in the Hellenistic monarchies, the fact of being an alien apparently did not affect a person's legal position.[11]

I think that the facts which I have been discussing allow me to draw the following conclusion. At least under the conditions which prevailed in Egypt during the first century of Ptolemaic rule there was simply no room either politically or sociologically or psychologically for an all-encompassing code of private law. This situation did not last, to be sure. There was, on the one hand, the political resurgence of the Egyptians which gained momentum at about the start of the second century B.C. On the other hand, there must have been a growing consciousness among the immigrants, or rather among their descendants, that they really belonged to the country. An increasing tendency to intermarriage with the natives was its concomitant. All this could not but lower the barriers separating the various elements of the population. Accordingly, in the middle and later Ptolemaic era a unifying legislation may no longer have been as inconceivable as it had been in the opening decades. At that time, however, the dynasty was torn by internal strife and no longer produced any outstanding figures. Both intellectually and politically the strength needed for such legislation was lacking. There is indeed no indication that anything of the sort was ever even taken into consideration.

Freiburg-i.Br.   Hans Julius Wolff

---

11 It seems significant that Préaux, in dealing with the "régime des étrangers en pays royal" in *Recueil Bodin* IX: *L'étranger* (Brussels 1958) I, 189ff., did not even mention this type of alien.

PART 6

ROMAN EGYPT

LA HAUTE ADMINISTRATION DES EAUX EN EGYPTE
(D'APRES LA DOCUMENTATION PAPYROLOGIQUE AUX
EPOQUES GRECQUE, ROMAINE ET BYZANTINE)

Pour essayer de voir clair dans la structure et le fonctionnement de l'administration des eaux en Égypte, nous tenterons d'utiliser des notions courantes aujourd'hui. Puisque, selon la remarque
d'un haut fonctionnaire égyptien du IIIe siècle de notre ère,
"l'irrigation efficace apporte la plus grande partie, sinon tout,
dans l'abondance des récoltes,"[1] on peut considérer l'exploitation
des eaux du Nil comme une vaste entreprise. Toutefois, ce qui
concerne le financement sera ici laissé de côté. Je chercherai
seulement à exposer de manière très générale comment étaient struc-
turées la conception et la réalisation de cette entreprise, ainsi
que le contrôle qui s'exerçait sur elle. La hiérarchie administrative étudiée pour cette recherche se situe au niveau le plus élevé,
des autorités du nome au Souverain.

1. La conception.

Elle est le propre des instances au pouvoir. Dans le millénaire où se situe la documentation papyrologique, la conception du
système d'irrigation est un héritage pharaonique, depuis longtemps
en place. C'est aux étyptologues qu'il appartient de l'étudier,
et les travaux récents de W. Schenkel[2] et de E. Endesfelder[3] pour
les idées générales, de M. Bietak pour les réalisations décelées
par l'archéologie,[4] ont commencé cette étude que la philologie

---

1 P. Yale inv. 447: G. Parássoglou, *Cd'E* 98 (1974) 338-41.

2 "Die Einführung der Künstlichen Felderbewässerung im Alten
Ägypten," *Göttinger Miszellen* 11 (1974) 41-46; *Die Bewässerungs-
revolution in Alten Ägypten* (1978).

3 "Zur Frage der Bewässerung in pharaonischen Ägypten," *Actes
du Ier Congrès International d'Égyptologie* (Berlin 1979) 203-08.

4 *Tell el Dab'a* II (1979).

égyptienne a à peine abordée.[5] Lorsque les Grecs, puis les Romains, devinrent maîtres de la vallée, le Nil est toujours "l'eau du Souverain."[6] Le système d'irrigation en conséquence apparaît comme le moyen de distribution de la richesse potentielle du Souverain; il est l'instrument essentiel de la production fiscale et le demeurera. La conception, en matière d'organisation du réseau d'irrigation, ne cessera pas d'être le propre du Souverain; l'essentiel est fait avant la domination grecque et particulièrement le réseau du Fayoum entre 1850 et 1800.[7] Les papyrus ne font connaître que des aménagements nouveaux de l'adduction des eaux vers les terres, voulus par les Souverains : Ptolémée II vers 260 avant notre ère dans le nord du nome Arsinoïte,[8] Trajan,[9] Philippe l'Arabe.[10] Il y a peu d'intérêt pour l'emploi de moyens techniques nouveaux, telle la sakieh qui, après avoir laissé le Souverain indifférent,[11] a été ensuite diffusée prioritairement dans les domaines impériaux,[12] semble-t-il.

Un autre élément conceptuel dans l'administration des eaux est la prévision du moyen de production, l'eau. Elle était fournie par l'ensemble des mesures des progrès de la crue observées aux nilomètres,[13] dont l'établissement officiel était conçu et exécuté par

---

5 Quelques mots sont repérés par D. Meeks, *Le grand texte des donations au temple d'Edfou* (1972).

6 *Mw (n) Pr ꜥꜣ* (*P. Deir el Medineh* 28.8; 8 mai 106 av.n.è.).

7 Di. et Do. Arnold, *Der Temple Qasr el Sagha* (1979) 20-21.

8 Voir Cl. Préaux, *Le Monde Hellénistique* (1978) 379.

9 Voir P. J. Sijpesteijn, "Trajan and Egypt," *P. Lugd. Bat.* XIV (1965) 106-13.

10 Voir P. Parsons, "The Wells of Hibis," *JEA* 57 (1971) 180.

11 *P. Edfou* 8, qui me paraît concerner l'utilisation de la sakieh, est resté sans effet.

12 Le premier reçu de pièce de sakieh parvenu jusqu'à nous émane des terres de la *domus divina* (*P. Med.* 64 = *SB* VI 9503; 6 décembre 440).

13 Voir D. Bonneau, *Le Fisc et le Nil* (1971) 21-65; "Le nilomètre : aspect architectural," *Archeologia* (Varsovie) 27 (1976) 1-11.

la volonté des rois.[14] Ces mesures, tout au long du millénaire qui
nous occupe, étaient notées en trois points : à la première cata-
racte où un second nilomètre a été récemment trouvé,[15] à Memphis et
dans le Delta;[16] le faisceau des renseignements obtenus réunis
était transmis au roi ou, selon les époques, à l'empereur par
les soins du préfet d'Égypte.[17] La conséquence de la prévision
des eaux est la possibilité de la prévision fiscale; celle-ci
dépend souverainement du pouvoir au sommet, puisque la hauteur
qui détermine la normalité globale des prélèvements fiscaux est
décidée par le Souverain lui-même, de même que la défaillance du
Nil est reconnue, du point de vue fiscal, comme une insuffisance
notoire par le Souverain et par lui seul. La règle des 12 coudées
(= 6 m) domine constamment, malgré des variations passagères, la
perception fiscale.[18] Elle apparaît déjà au IIIe siècle avant
notre ère où l'économe est alors le centralisateur des renseignements et le décideur de cette hauteur satisfaisante de 12 coudées.[19]

Ce lien administratif établi entre une certaine hauteur du Nil
en crue et la prévision fiscale ira en se resserrant au cours des
siècles; c'est en ce sens qu'en Égypte, l'eau se transforme en blé
de manière globalement mathématique et que l'évolution générale de
l'administration de l'eau tendra à dégager un schéma économique
simplifié : "Tant d'eau, tant de blé". Ce schéma sera le seul que
retiendra l'administration impériale à Byzance, tout le reste demeurera alors l'affaire des Égyptiens entre eux. La conception de
l'entreprise d'exploitation des eaux en Égypte demeure le fait du

---

14 Diod. Sic. I 36, 11: "A cause de l'inquiétude causée par
la crue du fleuve, les rois ont fait construire un nilomètre à
Memphis."

15 Jaritz et Bietak, "Zweierlei Pegeleichungen zum Messen der
Nilfluthöhen im Alten Ägypten," *MDAIK* 33 (1977) 47-62.

16 Voir o.c. ci-dessus n. 13, 39 et 60.

17 Pour avoir omis de transmettre ces renseignements, le préfet d'Egypte Ekdikios reçut une lettre ironique de l'empereur Julien en 362 (*Lettre* 108, Bidez).

18 *C.Th.* 9, 32, 1.

19 *PSI* V 488.18.

prince, ainsi que les décisions essentielles. Mais au fur et à
mesure que l'Égypte est insérée dans un ensemble politique plus
vaste, la décision est déléguée aux hauts fonctionnaires, puis par
ceux-ci à leurs collègues ou à leurs subordonnés. Les papyrus nous
offrent très rarement des témoignages de la concertation nécessaire
à la réalisation au niveau des plus hauts fonctionnaires. Toutefois un exemple de ce qu'on pourrait appeler un "conseil régional"
sur ce sujet est donné pour la Thébaïde du nord, en 300.[20]

2. La réalisation.

   La réalisation de l'exploitation de l'eau comporte diverses
étapes : amenée de l'eau vers les terres, mise en réserve pour une
utilisation à moyen terme et distribution. Les papyrus montrent
surtout l'exécution sur le terrain des tâches tendant à ce triple
but, à l'intérieur du nome.[21] Mais le découpage administratif ne
suit pas seulement la division en nomes; cela tient à la nature
même du réseau d'irrigation et à la prédominance, selon les époques,
de tel ou tel mode de distribution, par exemple la division en bassins ou l'irrigation par sakieh. Ce découpage proprement égyptien
est vraisemblablement à l'origine des toparchies et de la *méris*; il
demeure en vigueur pour des raisons techniques, aux époques grecque
et romaine, et a une administration spécifique difficile à percevoir dans nos documents. C'est dans le nome Arsinoïte qu'elle apparaît le plus clairement, puisque, au-dessus des trois *méris* con-
trôlées en matière d'irrigation par les stratèges, se trouve
l'"administrateur général des eaux", l'*aigialophylax*.

   Du point de vue des réalisations techniques, elles sont, à
l'époque ptolémaïque entre les mains de l'ingénieur, *architektôn*,[22]
à l'époque romaine, aux IIIe et IVe siècles, dans celles du *chomatépiktès*; ce dernier a même rang hiérarchique que le stratège.
C'est que l'administration des eaux est en quelque sorte une

---

20 *P. Panop. Beatty* 2.222.

21 Par exemple pour l'entretien et la surveillance: l'*hydro-
phylax*.

22 Voir par exemple Kléon (*Pros. Ptol.* I 534), Komoapis (*Pros.
Ptol.* I 535; VIII p. 60).

administration parallèle, dont l'analyse peut s'appuyer sur la
terminologie administrative: l'*épistolè* par exemple émane des
bureaux de l'*épitropos Kaisaros*, haut fonctionnaire de l'*idios
logos*). Un fonctionnaire de rang égal ou supérieur à un autre lui
écrit "pour information" (ἵν᾽ εἰδῇς), parcequ'il le tient au courant de ce qui se fait en matière d'irrigation dans le ressort de
la compétence du destinataire, mais cela ne signifie pas que la
voie hiérarchique de l'administration des eaux passe obligatoire-
ment par lui. En effet, lorsqu'il s'agit de l'eau, l'administration est très souple; le cheminement des papiers ne progresse pas
forcément par tous les échelons.[23] D'autre part, la documentation
parvenue jusqu'à nous appelle une remarque : les papiers officiels
que nous avons ne sont pas toujours des papiers de routine, mais
le témoignage de démarches occasionnelles causées par des circonstances particulières souvent urgentes. Les requêtes et les
plaintes passent alors par-dessus la tête des échelons intermé-
diaires et, adressés à des fonctionnaires très importants comme
l'*épitropos* (*Kaisaros*)[24] ou le *dioikètès*,[25] ces papiers sont en
même temps communiqués à l'administration locale, stratèges et
épistratèges pour transmission.[26] Ces papyrus concernent: les
travaux exceptionnels, les travaux neufs, les demandes d'eau urgentes, et tout ce qui est frauduleux ou simplement irrégulier.[27]

---

23 Sur la souplesse administrative, D. Bonneau, "Liturges et
fonctionnaires de l'eau à l'époque romaine," *Akten des XIII.
Papyrologenkongress* (1974) 35-42.

24 Exemple: que le fonctionnaire responsable de la distribution des eaux dans le nome Arsinoïte (*aigialophylax*) soit accusé
de négligence, il faut adresser la réclamation au procurateur des
biens impériaux (*P. Wisc.* I 34 et 35).

25 Exemples: que le Nil se retire plus vite que prévu, il
faut atteindre un haut fonctionnaire pour obtenir une circulation
plus rapide des eaux de bassins en bassins (*P. Oxy.* XLIV 3167.10).
Sur les circonstances de ce genre, Barois, *Irrigations*, 68-69 et
373. Le fonctionnaire du bureau local de la dioikèsis est probablement l'auteur de cette lettre, de rang supérieur au stratège à
qui il écrit pour information. Cf. encore *P. Oxy.* XII 1409.

26 Par exemple: *P. Ryl.* II 81.8-10.

27 Par exemple: *P. Oxy.* XLIV 3167.9-12.

Plus on monte dans la hiérarchie, plus les responsabilités
concernant l'efficacité de l'utilisation de l'eau paraissent être
attachées à d'autres responsabilités qui, elles, sont fiscales. En
effet, lorsque nous trouvons dans les papyrus le nom grec de "l'administration des eaux", διοίκησις τῶν ὑδάτων, dont je connais deux
exemples,[28] ce n'est pas un ministère indépendant contrairement à
ce qu'on pourrait attendre, ni sous les rois Ptolémées, ni sous le
préfet d'Égypte. Elle semble n'être qu'un des bureaux de l'organe
essentiel du fisc, l'*idios logos*[29] et plus particulièrement du
kyriakos logos, aussi longtemps qu'il a existé,[30] ce qui s'explique
par le fait que l'eau du Nil ne cessa jamais d'être au Souverain
d'Égypte. L'*idios logos* était intéressé dans le "management" des
digues, comme à une branche importante des finances publiques.[31]
L'*idios logos* paraît donc le point le plus élevé de la hiérarchie
administrative des eaux.

Au IVe siècle, au-dessous du *praeses* qui occupe le sommet administratif, est le *katholikos*, "autorité financière suprême",
unique pour toute l'Égypte;[32] on peut soupçonner que c'est alors
lui le point le plus élevé de l'administration de l'eau. Au Ve
siècle, la succession de cette responsabilité est assurée par le
magistôr (ancien *épitropos* (*Kaisaros*)) et l'*officialis*, fonctionnaire de la *dioikèsis*, concernés par le programme d'entretien des
digues.[33]

Du point de vue des réalisations techniques, le *chomatépimé-
lètès*, qui dépend de la *dioikèsis* et de l'*idios logos*,[34] tient le
rôle qu'avait l'ingénieur au IIIe siècle avant notre ère; il est
ensuite remplacé, avec des modifications, par le *chomatépiktès*,

---

28 *P. Mich.* III 174.5 (145-147); *P. Oxy.* XLIV 3167.18 (c.
195-198).

29 P. Oxy. inv. 50.4B.24B(3-4).24-25 (*ZPE* 24 [1977] 49).

30 Voir D. Bonneau, "Recherches sur le kyriakos logos (P.
Oxy. 2847)," *JJurPap* 19, sous presse depuis 1974.

31 Hübner, *ZPE* 24 (1977) 44.

32 Cela ressort de *P. Panop. Beatty* 2.222-225; voir Jouguet
(*P. Théad.* pp. 95-96) sur l'importance décroissante du *dioikètès*.

33 *SB* V 8262.

34 Voir Hübner (o.c. ci-dessus n. 31) 43-53.

souvent romain. Aux niveaux inférieurs, l'exécution relève des
Égyptiens; mais, comme nous venons de le voir, la spécifité nécessaire aux réalisations dans le système d'irrigation, paraît s'éva-
porer aux hauts échelons de l'administration.

3. Le contrôle.

C'est grâce au système de contrôle que l'organisation de
l'utilisation des eaux a toute son efficacité, sous réserve des
incidences climatiques ou politiques. Là encore, pas de hiérarchie spécifique; tout haut fonctionnaire à partir du stratège ac-
complit une tâche de contrôle en rapport avec l'inondation, comme
c'est le cas aussi aux échelons modestes des villages. Tout liturge
ou tout fonctionnaire qui a place dans la réalisation des décisions
de cette énorme entreprise des eaux a en même temps devoir et pouvoir d'en contrôler l'exécution. La part la plus lourde revient au
stratège dont le rôle sur ce point a autrefois été analysé;[35] les
papyrus édités depuis n'ont rien changé à cette analyse à condition
d'interpréter les nouveaux documents comme des éléments du système
de contrôle, et non pas comme le résultat d'ordres donnés par ce
fonctionnaire. Il est le transmetteur des ordres venus de la *dioikèsis,* le lieu de rencontre du cheminement des papiers administra-
tifs : circulaires venues d'en haut qu'il faut diffuser, plaintes
ou états descriptifs ou résultats d'enquête venus d'en bas qu'il
faut acheminer. Il n'est donc pas seulement un organe de contrôle
technique ou financier, mais, plus qu'un rouage bien huilé, il est
la courroie de transmission de la machinerie.[36]

Le contrôle entraîne la connaissance des irrégularités; là
encore le stratège est au courant, témoin attentif des arrangements
de heurts au niveau du nome; mais si les conflits ne peuvent être
réglés à l'intérieur de sa juridiction, il transmet le cas à une
juridiction plus haute. C'est alors qu'intervient l'épistratège,[37]
que l'on voit confondu peu à peu sur ce point avec l'*épitropos*
(*Kaisaros*),[38] car en matière d'eau, l'urgence dispense de remonter

35 Voir Hohlwein, *Le stratège du nome* (1926 [1969]) 122-23.

36 Le basilicogrammate, ayant un rôle limité au financement
du système d'irrigation, est ici laissé de côté.

37 P. Yale inv. 1529 (*AJP* 92 [1971] 665).

38 Voir ci-dessus, n. 24.

lentement la voie hiérarchique; au-delà encore, il faut s'adresser
au préfet[39] pour les litiges risquant de léser sérieusement le
fisc; car c'est le préfet et lui seul qui, en lieu et place de
l'empereur, tranchera.[40]

4. Conclusion.

Cette trop rapide synthèse permet cependant quelques constats:

a) Il n'y a pas d'administration des eaux indépendantes des
autres sections de l'administration; pas de ministère des eaux.

b) L'administration des eaux reste accrochée presque directement à l'administration centrale royale, puis impériale; elle est
une partie de l'administration fiscale aux époques étudiées ici.
Et à l'époque byzantine, ceux qui continuent les tâches de distribution des eaux ou de responsabilité de surveillance et d'entretien, et qui continuent à utiliser le vocabulaire impérial pour
les remplir, ceux-là ont remplacé la hiérarchie administrative précédente, mais au lieu de donner à l'empereur les résultats de la
gestion de l'eau, ils lui donnent les résultats en sous d'or; ce
qui était "tant d'eau, tant de blé" sous Dioclétien est devenu
"tant d'eau, tant de sous" aux VIe et VIIe siècles.

c) La grande loi de ce système administratif est la recherche
du profit pour le maître de l'Égypte. On a dit que le Souverain
de ce pays, au IIIe siècle avant notre ère, le gérait comme un
"domaine"; on peut dire que, jusqu'au IIIe siècle de notre ère, il
le gère comme une "entreprise" impériale.

d) Il en ressort que la nécessité de l'exploitation de l'irrigation qui est "la plus grande partie, sinon le tout, dans
l'abondance des récoltes", n'est pas le point de départ d'un type
de gouvernement donné, mais seulement le point d'appui constant de
tout système politique de l'Égypte antique.

Saint-Cloud   Danielle Bonneau

---

39   *P. Mich.* III 174.1.

40   Voir D. Bonneau, "Le préfet d'Egypte et le Nil," *Études
offertes à J. Macqueron* (1970) 141-51.

A VETERAN'S EXEMPTION FROM EPIKEPHALAIA

P. Oslo inv. 1518   14 x 17.3 cm.   A. D. 10 January 149

['Αν]τίγραφον. Αὐρήλιος Πετρώνιος [....]
    Διοφάντωι βασιλικῶι γραμματεῖ ['Αρσ(ινοίτου) 'Ηρ(ακλείδου)]
μερίδος χαίρ(ειν). 'Αχιλλᾶς 'Αρποκράτο[υς]
4 [ἱ]ππεὺς εἴλης Οὐοκουντίων πρὸ τῆ[ς στρα-]
[τ]είας κληθεὶς 'Οροννοῦς 'Ραπαλιω[..]ς
μητρὸς Ταμεστρεμφι ἀπὸ κώμης Συγνα
[ἐ]δηλώθη ἐστρατεῦσθαι ἔτεσι πλείος[ι εἴκο-]
8 [σ]ι πέντε· ἀκόλουθον οὖν ἐστί γρ(άψαι) κατὰ
τὴν χάριν τοῦ μεγίστου Αὐτοκράτορος
περιαιρεθῆναι αὐτὸν ἐκ τῆς δόσε-
ως ἐπικεφαλίων.

12   (2nd h.) 'Ερρῶσ(θαί) σε εὔχομαι
(3rd h.) ("Ετους) ιγ Αὐτοκράτορος Καίσαρος Τίτου Αἰλίου
'Αδριανοῦ 'Αντωνείνου Σεβαστοῦ Εὐσεβοῦς Φαῶφι δ

Aurelius Petronius (...) to Diophantos, royal scribe
of the division of Herakleides in the Arsinoite nome, greeting. Achillas, son of Harpokrates, cavalryman of the *Ala
Vocontiorum*, before his military service called Oronnous,
Rhapalion's son, his mother being Tamestremphis, from the
village of Syngnas (?), has proved to have served for more
than twenty-five years.
    Therefore it is suitable that you should give a
written order that in accordance with the grant of the
greatest Emperor he is exempted from paying *epikephalia*.
    (2nd hand) Farewell. (3rd hand) The 13th year of
Imperator Caesar Titus Aelius Hadrianus Antoninus Augustus
Pius, the 4th of Phaophi.

Apart from the fact that this letter contains remarkable
names,[1] as well as an example of a soldier adopting a Greek name
instead of a Roman one, it is interesting and puzzling because of
its subject: exemption from some tax-payment "in accordance with an
imperial favour," granted to a veteran, or to veterans generally.

I have not been able to trace the writer of the letter, Aurelius Petronius, in any prosopography, but he probably belonged to
the staff of the prefect in Alexandria, since veterans, tax-
exemptions and financial matters were the direct concern of the
prefect. Aurelius Petronius was most likely either some high official to whom the prefect had delegated his authority, or an experienced imperial freedman who had an important function in the
financial administration (cf. P. A. Brunt, *JRS* 65 [1975] 139f.).
The main question, however, is: what kind of a χάρις is meant?

Unfortunately we do not know much about *epikephalaion* other
than the fact that it was a tax, paid per head. In the first two
centuries A.D. it often appears to be identical with the poll-tax,
laographia, but sometimes the plural *epikephalaia* (or *-lia*) seems
to indicate capitation taxes in general, or various *merismoi*.
Capitation taxes, however, were not paid by Roman citizens, and
since Achillas was a veteran and presumably a Roman citizen, he
should be exempt from paying capitation taxes. What, then, was the
purpose of this imperial grant? If the exemption from *epikephalaia*
was a privilege that did not form part of the general privileges of
Roman citizenship or the traditional privileges of veterans, it
nevertheless must be a grant of a sort appropriate for ordinary
auxiliary veterans to acquire.

The period of Pius is far from well known in respect to its
military policy. Lesquier suggested the possibility of strong limitations of the veterans' privileges, but regretted as well the
paucity of our information; on the other hand, Mason Hammond (*The
Antonine Monarchy*, 171) felt that Pius did not "concern himself
with military reforms." However, I do not think we must take this
alleged lack of interest in military reforms too seriously. We

---

1 The names Oronnous and Tamestremphis seem to be hitherto
unattested.

know, after all, of one important military reform: some time between A.D. 140 and 144 a change was introduced in the wording of
military diplomata. Before that time all veterans who had served
in the *auxilia* obtained citizenship for themselves, their wives,
parents and children. The traditional grant of Roman citizenship
was reduced so as to concern only the veteran himself; the clause
ipsis liberis posterisque was removed from the diplomata.

I cannot here give a full evaluation of this reform, but generally it seems to have been a rather sensible measure. For sons
of veterans it meant that they now had to win citizenship by their
own merits instead of inheriting it. Many of them would no doubt
have chosen a military career anyway, because of the economic advantages and the lack of other possibilities (for their daughters,
however, no such alternative existed). Another effect of the reform may have been that service in the legions became more attractive again, because it put an end to the favouring of children of
the auxiliaries as compared to legionaries' children, who were *not*
granted citizenship even after the discharge of their fathers.

It seems to me that the reform also agreed with the general
attitude and character of this emperor, his sense of justice, and
his irritation at demands for undeserved rewards. We have evidence
of this in replies to petitions and other letters, but I think it
is formulated quite adequately in the *Historia Augusta* (Cap. 7.7):
Salaria multis subtraxit quos otiosos videbat accipere, dicens
nihil esse sordidius, immo crudelius, quam si rem publicam is
adroderet qui nihil in eam suo labore conferret. Also other regulations give evidence of Pius' dislike of unnecessary expenditures
and unjustified privileges, yet these are balanced by acts of generosity and humanity when justified. As for military matters, he
put a stop to the practice of keeping soldiers in service beyond
their legal term.

A policy adopted by an emperor is, nonetheless, not only the
result of his personal taste or preference. Military policy is
also dependent on a number of interacting factors, as well as a reflection of the economic and political situation. Pius had become
emperor through adoption and had not required the troops for his
elevation; neither was he dependent on their favour because of

important campaigns. He is unlikely to have had strong appeal to
or popularity with his soldiers. On the other hand, the economic
crisis was probably not yet very perceptible so that Pius could afford to grant public favours to his troops. He apparently felt no
urge to coax them, nor was there any necessity for him to do so. He
was, however, reasonable enough to give ear to justified demands.

To return to the nature of the *charis* bestowed on Achillas and
his fellows: there is no reason to suppose that the emperor granted
these auxiliary troops an important privilege in addition to their
usual rewards. Perhaps Achillas was not yet a "complete" veteran,
and the long procedure of discharge was still in progress: first,
the discharge itself, *missio*, usually in December-January; then the
waiting in camp, often for several months, for the diploma, the
evidence of his military service and of his new status as a Roman
citizen; and finally the *epikrisis*, control and registration of the
new citizen conducted by the prefect or some high officer, usually
in the spring. The period from the day of discharge until the
final formalities could occupy as much as a year. We might suppose
that Pius had granted discharged soldiers exemption from capitation
taxes, and perhaps other privileges, for the current year, while
they were waiting for the time when they could settle down and en-
joy their new life as civilians and Roman citizens. Such a grant
is not unreasonable after 25 years of service, and not unlikely
either, for Pius also stopped the undue prolongation of active service practised by his predecessors.

To conclude I will mention another possibility: Achillas may
have belonged to the mysterious category of veterans who were said
to be χωρὶς χαλκῶν. Different explanations for this term have been
surveyed by S. Daris (*Aegyptus* 40 [1960] 67ff.), but the only fact
we know is that these veterans had no diploma to present at their
epikrisis; yet they were granted citizenship all the same. It seems
noteworthy that the only two documents which refer to such veterans
are dated A.D. 140 and 148 (Wilcken, *Chrest.*, 458 and 459). Again
the *charis* of the emperor which exempted Achillas from *epikephalaia*
would presumably have assisted him in the period of transition from
auxiliary cavalryman to civilian and to full Roman citizenship--if,
in fact, Achillas belonged in the category of veterans χωρὶς χαλκῶν.

Any explanation of the imperial grant which benefitted Achillas through an exemption from *epikephalaia* must be provisional until further evidence is found, but after studying the attitude of Pius, I think that a *charis* which bestowed neither undue favours nor lavish gifts, but rather removed an inequity based on formal criteria, would have been in the spirit of this emperor.

†Martha H. Eliassen

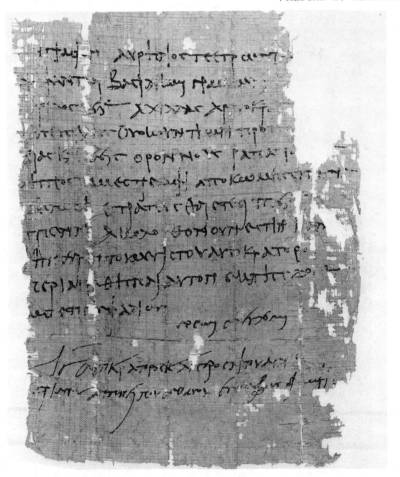

SULLA DIFFERENZA TRA TASSI DI INTERESSE IN NATURA
E IN MONETA NELL' EGITTO GRECO-ROMANO[*]

Solo l'Egitto, praticamente, ci conserva un'ampia documentazione sul credito in natura, almeno per il periodo greco-romano-bizantino. E' questo un tipo di credito che ha un'estesa applicazione nelle fasi premonetali dello scambio: crediti su pegno e senza interesse nell'Assiria dell XIV-XIII sec.;[1] crediti al 33-1/3% in Mesopotamia;[2] crediti al 50% di interesse già nell'Egitto faraonico;[3] forme forse simili anche nella prima Repubblica romana.[4]

Ma anche con il dilatarsi del volume della circolazione monetaria, il credito in natura mantiene una sua considerevole presenza: senz'altro durante il feudalesimo, nella forma tipica del prestito di sementi,[5] ma anche dopo il Rinascimento, quando, come osserva il Braudel "...le dialogue de la monnaie parfaite (si elle existe) et de l'imparfaite éclaire nos problèmes jusqu'en leurs racines."[6]

Nell'Egitto greco-romano troviamo diversi tipi di credito in natura: quello semplice, con possibile multa pagabile in denaro, quello misto natura-denaro e il pagamento anticipato di futuri prodotti (τιμή). Queste ultime forme si sviluppano più tardi, nel periodo romano-bizantino.

---

[*] Queste pagine sono dedicate ad H. C. Youtie, del cui magistero chi scrive serberà un ricordo indelebile.

1 C. Saporetti, "Il prestito nei documenti privati dell'Assiria del XIV-XIII sec.," *Mesopotamia* 13-14 (1978-79) 1-90.

2 R. Bogaert, *Les origines antiques de la banque de depôt* (Leyde 1966) 52.

3 B. Menu, "Le prêt en droit égyptien," *CRIPEL* 1 (1973) 87-89, 124-25.

4 F. De Martino, *Storia economica di Roma Antica* (Firenze 1980) 146.

5 G. Duby, *L'economia rurale nell'Europa medievale* (trad. it. Bari 1970) 391.

6 F. Braudel, *Civilisation materielle, économie et capitalisme XVe-XVIIIe siècle* (Paris 1979) III, 388.

Netta è la prevalenza di crediti di cereali per la semina, con
contratti normalmente stipulati in autunno-inverno e restituiti in
primavera-estate, dopo il raccolto. Ma non mancano crediti di vino,
aglio, verdure, legumi, foraggi, fieno, canne, lino, sale....

Nel 150 d.C. troviamo anche un credito, senza indicazione di
interesse (P. *Tebt*. II 395), stipulato attraverso διαγραφή bancaria,
di una certa quantità di olio, malgrado l'interdizione del paragrafo
103 del Gnomon dell'Idios logos,[7] dove, tra l'altro, si definiscono
i tassi di interesse monetari (§105), senza far cenno a quelli in
natura.

Diacronicamente osserviamo che in epoca tolemaica i crediti in
natura costituiscono circa il 60% di tutti i crediti conservati,
mentre nel periodo romano-bizantino i rapporti tra numero dei crediti in natura e numero dei crediti in denaro si ribaltano e, nello
stesso tempo, si amplia la quantità di crediti misti natura-denaro.
Per tutte le epoche prevalgono, in modo consistente, i contratti
ἄτοκοι, o senza alcuna indicazione di tasso di interesse, rispetto
a quelli in cui viene chiaramente espresso il tasso di interesse.
Sul mercato del credito si presenta un notevole sventagliamento dei
tassi di interesse.

Per i crediti in natura abbiamo tra i due poli dominanti dello
zero e del 50% (qualunque sia la durata--in genere qualche mese--
del credito) una varia articolazione di valori: del 40% (P. *Gen*. 9,
251 d.C.); del 33,3% (P. *Stras*. I 71; IV 588, II d.C.; P. *NYU* 22,
329 d.C.); del 25% (P. *Oxy*. XXXI 2566, 225 d.C.; XLV 3251, II/III
sec.); del 16,6% (*BGU* XII 2197, VI sec.). In un caso (P. *Oxy*. XXXVI
2775, del tardo III sec. d.C.) il tasso non viene fissato quantita-
tivamente, ma si fa riferimento al tasso che risulterà tra i conta-
dini locali, come a sottintendere l'esistenza di un mercato flut-
tuante.

Per i crediti in denaro, accanto agli interessi piu usuali
dello zero, del 24% (in epoca tolemaica) e del 12% (in epoca romana)
troviamo, più raramente, un ampio spettro di tassi di interesse

---

7 Il papiro potrebbe confermare il 150 d.C. come *terminus*
post quem per la datazione del Gnomon.

annuali:[8] del 6% (*P. Vindob.* L 135, in *ZPE* 36 [1979] 109 ss., 27
d.C.); dell'8% (*CPR* I 12, 93 d.C.); del 9,5% (*SB* XII 11228, 204
d.C.); del 10% (*PSI* XIII 1328, 201 d.C.); del 18% (*P. Mich.* V 336,
27 d.C.; *P. Lond.* III 1273 [p. 174] 29 d.C.; *P. Lond.* II 202 [p.
247] 98-117 d.C.); del 22% (*P. Lond.* II 202 [p. 247] 98-117 d.C.)
e anche tassi di interesse usurai del 48% (*P. Fouad* 26, 157-159
d.C.) e del 50% (*P. Lips.* 13, 366 d.C.).

Questo sventagliamento di tassi di interesse è il fenomeno che
deve essere spiegato attraverso l'analisi economico-sociale. Ma in
prima istanza occorre fare almeno tre precisazioni filologiche.

1) Come ha mostrato il Pestman[9] il termine ἄτοκος è un termine
ambiguo che può significare sia "che non porta interessi" (potendo
questi essere già computati nel capitale prestato) sia "che non
paga interessi" (v. Pseudo-Arist., *Economico*, 1350 a 11). Frequentemente si può pensare che gli interessi fossero capitalizzati.
Esemplare è il caso di P. Mich. inv. 1410[10] dove si contratta un
credito di 46 talenti e 4000 dracme (nel 326 d.C.) precisando che
il credito è ἄνευ τόκου, mentre sul *verso* dello stesso documento
si specifica che si tratta di un credito di 35 talenti cui si aggiungono interessi, per 8 mesi, di 11 talenti e 4000 dracme (50%
annuo).

Ma già il Pestman individuava alcuni casi di probabili crediti
gratuiti. A questi pensiamo vadano aggiunti quei documenti in cui
esplicitamente si precisa che il credito è senza alcuna aggiunta,
con espressioni del tipo "κεφαλαίου αἷς οὐδὲν τῷ καθόλου προσῆκται"
(*P. Princ.* II 32.9-10) o con locuzioni simili.[11]

---

8   V. anche Johnson, *ESAR* II, 450 n. 58.

9   P. W. Pestman, "Loans bearing no Interest," *JJP* 16-17
(1971) 7-29.

10   Edito da J. C. Shelton, *JJP* 18 (1974) 157-62.

11   Κεφαλαίου αἷς οὐδὲν προσῆκται (*SB* XII 11228.6-7); 'τὰς
ἴσας χ'' (*P. Oxy.* XXXI 2566 I.10). Nel caso che sia aggiunto l'interesse, questo viene espressamente indicato: κεφαλαίου αἷς οὐδὲν
προσῆκται τόκου τριωβολείου κτλ. (*P. Oxy.* III 506.12); τὰ προκείμενα
κεφάλαια σὺν τοῖς συναχθησομένοις διαφόροις (*P. Oxy.* VI 988 II).

Probabilmente si deve aggiungere anche *P. Oxy*. XXXI 2566 da
cui appare che le stesse persone stipulano nello stesso anno e
nello stesso mese due contratti di credito in natura, uno senza
interessi e uno con interessi ridotti al 25%.
Del resto il concetto di credito senza interesse risale alla
migliore tradizione della Grecia, dove, come nota il Finley, i crediti *eranos* furono per loro natura liberi da interessi[12] e dove
anche un banchiere come Pasion poteva concedere un credito a Timoteo senza interessi (Demostene, *Contro Timoteo*).

Certamente ogni documento deve essere analizzato con sospetto.
Bisogna però evitare di ingabbiare una realtà pre-industriale
dentro le categorie di quella che il Polanyi ha chiamato "la nostra
obsoleta mentalità di mercato."

2) L'espressione greca ἐκ τρίτου (e simili, v. *P. Stras*. I 71;
IV 588; *P. NYU* 22) per indicare il tasso di interesse è diversa
dalla latina *tertia pars*. Mentre infatti il greco si riferisce al
solo capitale prestato, il latino si riferisce invece alla somma
che già capitalizza gli interessi. Ἐκ τρίτου dà quindi un tasso
del 33,3%; *tertia pars* un tasso del 50% (*C. Th*. II 33,1).

Del resto in greco la più normale ἡμιολία è riferita al capitale, di cui appunto costituisce il 50%.[13]

3) L'ultima notazione filologica riguarda l'espressione tolemaica ἡμιόλιον ἢ τὴν ἐσομένην πλείστην τιμήν impiegata per indicare
la multa che dovrà pagare il debitore inadempiente. Sempre questa
espressione è stata intesa come "il 50% in più oppure il massimo
prezzo che ci sarà." Sarebbe quindi una clausola diversa dalla più

---

12 M. I. Finley, *Studies in Land and Credit in Ancient Athens*
(New Brunswick 1951) 85.

13 Inspiegabilmente tuttavia in un papiro tolemaico (*P. Rein*.
I 16.19-21) l'interesse τρίτον risulta uguale al 50%. Abbiamo infatti: capitale = artabe 166-2/3; interesse τρίτον = 83-1/3; somma
= 250. Ma qui forse è un semplice errore che tuttavia a noi può
servire come spia di un interesse τρίτον piu diffuso di quanto
risulti dai documenti.
Finckh, *Zinsrecht*, 97, lo ritiene un caso di *Diskontberechnung*,
e con lui concorda Rupprecht, *Darlehen*, 75-76 n. 12; sarebbe però
il primo e forse unico esempio di questo sistema di computo nei
papiri, e resterebbe una .testimonianza isolata nell'archivio di
Dionysos di *P. Rein*. I.

usuale "ἡμιόλιον τὴν ἐσομένην πλείστην τιμήν" = "il 50% in più del
massimo prezzo che ci sarà."[14]

Proponiamo di rendere equivalenti le due formule intendendo la
particella ἤ come comparativa invece che come disgiuntiva e tradu-
cendo: "il 50% in più del massimo prezzo futuro."

Una costruzione parallela può essere trovata in Senofonte
(*Hell.* V,3,21): "τὸν ἥμισυν...σίτου τελεῖν ἤ πρόσθεν" (v. Schwitzer,
Grammatik, II, 566). Del resto, al momento del raccolto, quando
venivano restituiti i debiti, si verificava un tale crollo dei
prezzi da non lasciare al creditore alternativa reale tra il 50%
in più del credito e il maggior prezzo di mercato.

Precisato così il campo problematico restano da spiegare almeno due contraddizioni economiche: in primo luogo come potessero coesistere tassi monetari al 24 o 12% annuale accanto a tassi in natura del 50% per pochi mesi di durata; in secondo luogo come possano essere credibili dei crediti senza interesse.

Già gli antichi avevano individuato la causa di una così sen-
sibile maggiorazione dei tassi di interesse in natura. Il Codice
di Giustiniano cita una risposta di Diocleziano e Massimiano del
294: "Oleo quidem vel quibuscumque fructibus mutuo datis incerti
pretii ratio additamenta usurarum eiusdem materiae suasit admitti"
(Codex IV,33,23).

Al momento del raccolto, quando in genere si restituivano i
crediti in natura, più che un'incertezza dei prezzi si verificava
un vero crollo.

Il fenomeno era generale nel mondo antico: "post messem, summa
in vilitate, cum aratores frumentum dare gratis mallent" (Cicerone,
Act. in Verrem, II,3,215).

In Sicilia si avevano crolli dei prezzi anche del 60%.[15]
Simili le fluttuazioni calcolabili per l'Egitto.[16] Per questo il

---

14 *BGU* VI 1281; *P. Grenf.* II 29; *P. Adler* 15; *P. Amh.* II 46,
47; *P. Grenf.* I 18.

15 R. P. Duncan-Jones, "The Price of Wheat in Roman Egypt
under the Principate," *Chiron* 6 (1976) 243.

16 Fr. Heichelheim, *Wirtschaftliche Schwankungen der Zeit von
Alexander bis Augustus* (Jena 1930) 64.

debitore che non restituiva puntualmente un credito in natura doveva ripagarlo in denaro con un'addizionale del 50% sul prezzo del
mercato.

Su questo dato possiamo costruire una semplice equazione teorica per calcolare i passaggi di valore nel caso di credito in
natura (A) e nel caso di credito in moneta (B):

IPOTESI: - credito di 10 artabe di grano;

        - 1 art. = 7,5 dr. in autunno = 5 dr. in primavera;

        - tasso di interesse in natura 50%, in moneta 12%.

CONSEGUENZA: caso (A): 10 art. = 75 dr. in autunno = 15 art. = 75
                      dr. in primavera.

           caso (B): 50 dr. = 10 art. in primavera = 50 + 12% =
                  56 dr. = 11 art. in primavera successiva.

Cioè, *in termini di valore naturale (reale)*:

    il debitore: caso (A): prende 10 rende 15;

                 caso (B): prende 10 rende 11;

    il creditore: caso (A): dà 10 prende 15;

                caso (B): dà 10 prende 11.

In termini di valore monetario (in dracme):

    il debitore: caso (A): prende 75 rende 75;

                 caso (B): prende 50 rende 56;

    il creditore: caso (A): dà 75 prende 75;

                caso (B): dà 50 prende 56.

Se asseconda il proprio interesse individuale il creditore
predilige quindi il credito-natura qualora possa tesaurizzare o
attendere la più favorevole congiuntura del mercato monetario. Se
non può tesaurizzare predilige il credito-moneta a scadenza inferiore all'anno.

Per il debitore sembra più vantaggioso il credito-moneta.
Infatti impegnerebbe un valore di 56 dr. contro uno di 75 dr., con
un risparmio di 19 dr. (circa il 25%). Sempre al debitore conviene
però il credito-natura se in autunno, a prezzi alti, si trova
sprovvisto di semi; infatti 10 artabe gli costerebbero fino a 84
dr. (75 + 12%) con il credito-moneta, mentre con il credito-natura
solo 75 dr. (e al tasso tolemaico del 24% il vantaggio sarebbe
ancora superiore).

Frequentemente il debitore si ritrova in questo secondo caso.
Per diverse motivazioni:

1) scarsa liquidità monetaria e/o scarsi *surplus* agricoli;

2) difficoltà ad acquistare sul mercato (v. *P. Amh.* II 130,
   del 70 d.C.);

3) speculazioni e turbative sul mercato;[17]

4) razionalità economica tradizionale, misurata sulla scala
   stagionale e non su una scala temporale media in funzione
   del massimo profitto.

Sembra esistano due percezioni diverse del tempo: da una parte
il tempo del contadino debitore, vissuto sulle scadenze agricole.
Rispetto a questo tempo soggettivo, scandito da semina e raccolto,
un interesse del 50% non è lesivo del debitore: né in termini monetari, per via del deprezzamento stagionale, né in termini reali,
perché (dato un rapporto 1:10 tra seme e prodotto) l'interesse in-
ciderebbe sul prodotto solo per il 5%.

Vi è poi il tempo soggettivo del creditore che, dando a credito i suoi *surplus* in natura li aumenta del 50% se li può conser-
vare come scorte rinnovate e di una quota praticamente uguale
(quando il tasso di inflazione sulla lunga durata è insignificante[18])
se può attendere il più favorevole andamento del mercato per scambiare la merce in moneta.

Vi è insomma un risucchio del 5% del prodotto agricolo da parte
del capitale di credito. Ma nello stesso tempo vi è da parte del
coltivatore un risparmio delle 10 artabe che avrebbe dovuto accan-
tonare per la semina, cioè di circa il 10% del prodotto.

In questi termini la situazione sembra favorevole ad entrambi
ed in particolare al debitore.

Se però computassimo anche il valore della terra (10 arure
nell'esempio), degli strumenti e degli equipaggiamenti (certo
qualche migliaio di dracme), osserveremmo che questo capitale in-
vestito in agricoltura ha una resa che in pratica remunera solo il

---

17 Per casi di quasi raddoppio dei prezzi in settembre v.
Duncan-Jones, op. cit., 244.

18 Tra il I° e II° secolo d.C. il tasso di inflazione sembra
inferiore all'1%; v. Duncan-Jones, op. cit., 246.

lavoro a livelli di susistenza, non produce *surplus* ed è molto meno
redditizio del capitale di credito.

La situazione del coltivatore-debitore peggiora ulteriormente
quando il rapporto seme-prodotto si abbassa rispetto ad una *ratio*,
da ritenersi buona, di 1:10.

Ma, in genere, una realtà produttiva in cui il tasso del profitto è inferiore sensibilmente al tasso di interesse è una realtà
di stagnazione o di declino: il profitto dell'investimento non ri-
paga il tasso di interesse. Sulla lunga durata il capitale commer-
ciale e creditizio agisce come un tarlo lento sulla produzione.

Trova qui giustificazione economica anche il credito senza
interessi: il creditore può rinnovare le scorte disponibili senza
costi, il coltivatore-debitore può sopravvivere senza bruciare len-
tamente il valore delle sue terre. E' questa una situazione economica stagnante, ma che può essere--come fu--estremamente duratura.

Per quanto riguarda questi crediti senza interesse, essendo
destinati allo scacco filologico i tentativi di negarne la presenza,
si tratta di comprenderli uscendo dall'ottica del nostro tipo di
calcolo economico e ricordando ancora che significativamente la
cultura antica non si pose mai il problema del massimo profitto.

In quel mondo le forme dello scambio non si ridussero mai al
solo mercato monetario. Già nel 253/2 a.C. una lettera di Nikarios
a Zenone (*PSI* IV 356) ci informa che nessuno vuole scambiare fieno
con grano, ma invece con denaro. Eppure lo scambio merce contro
merce ebbe vitalità per secoli e proprio nell'Egitto tolemaico i
crediti in natura ebbero una grossa consistenza. Evidentemente,
come in tutte le civiltà pre-industriali, sono sempre esistiti
diversi livelli di scambio che mai si ridussero ad un unico scambio
monetario di mercato.

Sommariamente possiamo ritenere con Max Weber che la civiltà
ellenistico-romana, eminentemente urbana e con un buon livello di
monetizzazione nelle aree costiere, presenta invece un retroterra
rurale vastissimo, dove perdurano nei secoli rapporti e culture
antiche, antropologicamente "primitive."

Il credito senza interessi, quello in natura in genere, è un
indizio di questa realtà, mai completamente estinta, nemmeno all'
acme dell'Impero romano. In questo quadro si può cercare di comprendere "l'irrazionalità" del credito senza interessi.

Nei villaggi della campagna egiziana non si è mai estinta una mutevole e variegata forma di vita comunitaria[19] che costituirà ancora la base della responsabilità fiscale collettiva.

In questo contesto il credito assumeva verosimilmente valenze non immediatamente economiche, ma si inseriva in una rete di relazioni sociali collettive, esprimendo *status*, gerarchie, relazioni interpersonali e familiari.[20]

La nostra documentazione offre poche piste per una simile ricerca che, finora, è però stata scarsamente sondata.

E' significativo comunque che in un documento raro (una denuncia di tassi di interesse usurai) la vittima spieghi il fatto senza ricorrere a motivazioni economiche (scarsa liquidità, alta domanda, estremo bisogno...) ma ricordando la prepotenza, fondata sul prestigio e l'influenza locale, del creditore usuraio.[21]

Simili contesti sociali possono spiegare sia il credito illegale che quello senza interesse.

In tali assetti sociali l'aspetto materiale della transazione non viene affatto rimosso, ma si deve armonizzare con un codice etico-sociale che contempla disinteresse e benevolenza: come in *P. Grenf.* I 26 (111 a.C., v. *BL* VI 45), dove il creditore esenta dal pagamento della multa un debitore che restituisce in ritardo.[22]

Pisa   Daniele Foraboschi
Milano   Alessandra Gara

---

19 V. A. I. Pavlovskaya, "Elements of Communal Organization in the Fourth Century Egyptian Kome," *VDI* 4 (1978) 43-60 (in russo con riassunto inglese).

20 Cicerone, *ad Fam.*, V,6,2. Per un'analisi antropologica del debito v. E. E. Evans-Pritchard, *Introduzione all'antropologia sociale* (trad. it. Bari 1975[3]) 129-32.

21 *P. Fouad* 26 del 157-59 d.C. Vedi anche Cicerone, *ad Atticum*, I,12,1.

22 Solo un cenno, per motivi di spazio, alla bibliografia papirologica essenziale: N. Lewis, Σὺν ἡμιολίᾳ, *TAPA* 76 (1945) 126-39; C. Michurski, "Les avances aux semailles," *Eos* 48,3 (1956) 105-38; R. S. Bagnall, "Sales on Delivery," *GRBS* 18 (1977) 85-96. Il tema sarà inoltre ripreso ed ampliato in un articolo sull'economia dei crediti in natura di prossima pubblicazione su *Athenaeum*, a cui rinviamo anche per l'elenco dei documenti utilizzati.

EVIDENCE FOR A REDUCTION IN LAOGRAPHIA AT PHILADELPHIA
IN GAIUS' SECOND YEAR

Two hundred fifteen villagers of Philadelphia in the Fayum
were asked to pay eight drachmas less for laographia and related
charges which they owed to Rome for the second year of Gaius'
reign. The evidence is derived from two large, partially preserved, tax registers: document I is made up of P. Mich. inv. 875
and inv. 862; document II, of P. Mich. inv. 904 and BM inv. 2248.
Male villagers at Philadelphia between the ages of fourteen and
sixty-two annually paid 44 drachmas, 6 chalkoi, for laographia and
related charges; the payments consisted of 4 drachmas or multiples
of 4 drachmas, and during this period the chalkoi and pig tax of 1
drachma, 1 obol, were usually paid at the end of the year.[1] The
villagers also paid 6 drachmas, 4 obols, for dike tax.[2] These
capitation taxes were based on the Roman census instituted under
Augustus and regularized under Tiberius.[3] In the texts from Philadelphia which span a period from the middle of Tiberius' reign to
the middle of Nero's, laographia paid at the highest rate and pig
tax which were not collected during the year in which they fell due
were computed as arrears of 45 drs., 2 obs.[4]

---

1 S. L. Wallace, *Taxation* (Princeton 1938) 121-26, and
intro. to *P. Corn.* 21, p. 154. Laographia when paid at its highest
rate and the related charges were also called syntaximon; C. W.
Keyes, *AJP* 52 (1931) 263-69; see also intro. to *P. Mich.* XII 640,
pp. 48-50.

2 Wallace, *Taxation*, 140-45.

3 For the census, see M. Hombert and C. Préaux, *Recherches
sur le recensement dans l'Égypte romaine* (= *Pap. Lugd. Bat.* V,
Leiden 1952), and now also O. Montevecchi, *Aevum* 50 (1976) 72-84.

4 For example, *ZPE* 15 (1974) 229-48, or *P. Ryl.* IV 595. For
the archive from Philadelphia, see *Actes du XVe Congrès*
(Brussels 1979) II, 97-102. A rate of 45 drs., 3 obs., appears in
P. Osl. inv. 1100, A.D. 57/58, from an unnamed Fayum village
(*Symbol. Osl.* 52 [1977] 97-102).

345

Document I contains eight columns of a list of arrears for
year 1 and year 2 of an unnamed emperor; entries are readable for
185 men, and the rubrics under which they were listed reveal that
over half of the 185 were currently residing in localities away
from Philadelphia and from the Arsinoite nome.[5] For year 1 the 185
men whose names appear were posted as each owing 45 drs., 2 obs.,
for arrears of laographia and pig tax, plus 6 drs., 4 obs., for
dike tax. For year 2, however, the arrears posted for these same
185 men is 37 drs., 2 obs.; this amount is 8 drs. less than the
arrears posted in other years.[6] Although document II (see below)
shows that the remission of 8 drs. affected only the laographia in
Gaius' second year, but not the pig tax, that document contains no
information on dike tax.[7] Dike tax may have been remitted at
Philadelphia for year 2; receipts for dike tax for year 2 of Gaius
at Thebes show that dike tax was paid there in that year.[8] Alternatively, the omission of dike tax among the arrears for year 2 in
document I may be due to the fact that this tax at Philadelphia was
often paid in the year following, as opposed to laographia and pig
tax which were collected in the year in which they fell due; document I may have been compiled in year 3, when poll tax for year 2
was in arrears, but dike tax for year 2 was still expected.

---

5 H. Braunert (*Binnenwanderung* [Bonn 1964] 150-52) analyzed
the movement of villagers away from Philadelphia in the first
century A.D. from the evidence in *P. Princ.* 8, 9, and 13.

6 For example, from col. ii:
καὶ τῶν ἐν ἄλλοις νομοῖς καταγεινομένων
Ἡρακλεοπολείτου νομοῦ Τιλώθεως
Πετσῖρις Ὀρσενούφεος α (ἔτ.) (δρ.) με = χω(ματ.) (δρ.) ϛϝ, β(ἔτ.)
  (δρ.) λζ =
Πετεσοῦχος Κερᾶτος α (ἔτ.) (δρ.) με = χω(ματ.) (δρ.) ϛϝ, β(ἔτ.)
  (δρ.) λζ =
Μύσθας Πασίωνος α (ἔτ.) (δρ.) με = χω(ματ.) (δρ.) ϛϝ, β(ἔτ.) (δρ.) λζ =

7 Collections for dike tax were recorded separately; see *P.
Mich.* XII 640, or P. Mich. inv. 816 plus P. Gen. inv. 217, with
the heading χωματικοῦ ιβ(ἔτ.)/μη(νὸς) Νέου Σεβαστοῦ/ ιγ (ἔτ.).

8 *WO* 1553, dike tax of year 2, paid in year 2, 6 drs., 4 obs.;
O. Theb. dem. 52, dike tax of year 2, paid in year 2, 6 drs., 4
obs.; *O. Bodl.* 592, dike tax of year 2, paid in year 2, 5 drs.,
4 obs.; *Pap. Lugd. Bat.* XIX 27 (dem.) dike tax of year 2, paid in
year 3, 6 drs., 4 obs.; *WO* 1373 (plus *BL* II 106), dike tax of year
2, paid in year 3, 5 drs., 2 obs.

Document II contains seven full columns and one partial column of a year-ledger, recording payments which 95 men contributed for laographia and for pig tax in year 2 of an unnamed emperor.[9] That the emperor is Gaius is assured by the presence of the month name Gaïos for Phamenoth,[10] in combination with the date of the text on the verso, Claudius' letter to the Alexandrians (P. Lond. VI 1912). The covering letter for that text from the prefect L. Aemilius Rectus was dated 10 November (= 14 Neos Sebastos) 41, early in Claudius' second regnal year in Egypt, while the register on the recto included payments dated as late in year 2 as 9 August (= 16 Mesore). Hence the text on the recto must date from year 2 of the preceding emperor Gaius. Eight of the 95 entries are damaged and will not figure below; the entries for 87 tax payers can be summarized as follows:

(1) Twelve individuals were labelled ἀπολύσιμοι, and no payments were credited to them;[11] the entries are marked with a single stroke.

(2) Eleven individuals have no payments credited to them.

(3) Forty-five individuals have double strokes drawn by their names, a conventional method for showing payment in full.[12] These men had paid 44 drs., 6 chalk., for laographia and 1 dr., 1 ob., for pig tax prior to 16 Mesore; no payments were made after that date. Fifteen of the forty-five were said to reside elsewhere than Philadelphia.

(4) Nineteen individuals paid part of their assessment; twelve had paid 32 drs. or more by 16 Mesore; none paid after that date.

---

9   The format of document II is similar to that in P. Prince 8.

10   The month name Gaïos did not survive long into the reign of Claudius: O. Bodl. 474, O. Stras. 68, SB X 10430, all year 1 of Claudius. The occurrences of Gaïos in document II are now the earliest examples: O. Bodl. 469, 470, year 3 of Gaius, and 472, year 4 of Gaius, have Γάϊος Σεβαστός, as does the demotic receipt O. Mattha 65, year 3. These four last-mentioned ostraka are all from Thebes. (P. Tebt. II 492 is undated.)

11   For the current state of the discussion, see G. Parás-soglou, Imperial Estates (Amsterdam 1978) 61-64. Two phrases involving the ἀπολύσιμοι were used in document II; no attempt will be made to clarify the matter here.

12   See the plate in P. Col. II, opposite p. 60.

The notation $\Gamma^{\mathsf{L}}{}_{//}$ was written by a different hand in the margin near twenty-seven entries from category (3). The notation $\Gamma^{\mathsf{L}}{}_{//}$
was also placed next to the entries for two men from category (4):
one is said to be a priest and he had paid 32 drs.;[13] the other,
Nekpheros, s. of Mysthas, had paid 44 drs. for laographia, but
neither chalkoi nor pig tax. His entry never received the double
strokes because he was still owing. Further, the notation $\Gamma^{\mathsf{L}}{}_{/}$
is found next to the entry for Pnepheros, s. of Akousilaos, also
of category (4): he had paid 40 drs., but neither the final 4 drs.,
6 chalk., nor pig tax. I suggest that the notation $\Gamma^{\mathsf{L}}{}_{//}$ signifies
"for year 3: (credit of) 2 (payments of laographia)," i.e., 2 pay-
ments of 4 drs. each, or 8 drs., and $\Gamma^{\mathsf{L}}{}_{/}$ "for year 3: (credit of)
1 (payment of laographia)," i.e., 1 payment of 4 drs.[14] The pig
tax of 1 drs., 1 ob., was to be collected as usual, as the entries
for Nekpheros and Pnepheros show, but to twenty-nine men who had
paid more than 36 drs. for laographia in year 2 and to the priest,
a credit was given for that tax in year 3.

In document I every tax payer listed was asked to pay 8 drs.
less for year 2, regardless of his current place of residence. In
document II not all the entries for men who paid more than 36 drs.
for laographia during year 2 bear the notation which signifies a
credit for year 3. There is, however, a marked correlation between
the appearance of the notation and residence in or near Philadelphia: of the thirty instances where the note appears, twenty-eight
of the entries have no geographical designation; presumably the men
lived near the village and paid to local tax authorities. Con-
versely, of the fifteen who paid in full and who were said to dwell
elsewhere than Philadelphia, the entries for only two, resident in
Sebennytos and Bakchias, villages also in the Herakleides division
of the Arsinoite nome, bear the mark. This distinction, between
men who reside in or near the village and those who live away from
the village which was their idia, reflects bookkeeping practices

---

13 Presumably the priest paid at a reduced rate (Wallace,
Taxation, 119).

14 For the tetradrachm as the unit of payment for the laographia, see H. C. Youtie, *ZPE* 15 (1974) 117.

in the tax office, as well as arrangements for collection.[15] If
document II fails to provide information about the credit for year
3 for those living away from Philadelphia, document I demonstrates
that place of residence was not a factor in the receiving of the
reduction of 8 drs.

This coincidence, involving 8 drs. of laographia, seems to
bind together these two documents from year 2: document I, in which
185 men, over half of whom were resident outside of Philadelphia
and all of whom were in arrears for laographia and related charges
for year 2 in the amount of 37 drs., 2 obs., instead of the usual
45 drs., 2 obs.; and document II, in which thirty men received a
credit toward their payments of laographia in year 3 if they had
paid their assessment at Philadelphia in year 2. When taken together, the two registers show that 215 tax payers were asked to
pay 8 drs. less for laographia in A.D. 37/38. If the reduction
came selectively to some peasants of Philadelphia, the basis on
which the selection was made is not evident: rather, the two documents show that the reduction extended to villagers who had already
paid their taxes for year 2 and to those who had not, to those
resident in the village and to those living away from Philadelphia.
As in the case of dike tax (above, p. 346), receipts on ostraka show
that in Upper Egypt, where laographia was paid at a rate much lower
than in the Fayum, the tax was collected at the normal low rate
during the course of years 2 and 3.[16]

---

15 See the distinction in P. Princ. 14 i.13 καὶ πρὸς [κ]ώμην
and iii.20 καὶ τῶν ἐν Ἀλεξα[νδρείᾳ], and also in P. Mich. inv.
887.28, Proceedings of the 14th Congress (London 1975) 152. Analogous are the arrangements for collections made by four practors
at Tebtynis some years later (P. Tebt. II 391, with F. Preisigke,
Girowesen [Strassburg 1910] 265-66); cf. as well, J. C. Shelton,
A Tax List from Karanis II (Bonn 1977) 4.

16 Year 2: Elephantine, where the rate was 16 drs. per year
(Wallace, Taxation, 128): O. Bodl. 451, 16 drs.; SB VI 9604, no.
13, 8 drs.; subdivision of Memnonia (= Jême) at Thebes, where the
rate was perhaps 24 drs. per year, although receipts for 16 drs.
are common (Wallace, Taxation, 130): O. Theb. dem. 5, 16 drs.; O.
Theb. dem. 52, 16 drs.; subdivision of Charax at Thebes, where the
rate was 10 drs. per year (Wallace, Taxation, 129): O. Stras. 66,
10 drs.; O. Mattha 64 = SB I 5291, 10 drs.; O. Deissmann 85, amount
lost. Year 3: Elephantine, WO 10 (plus BL II 46), 8 drs.; Memnonia,
Thebes: O. Theb. dem. 37, 16 drs.; Charax, Thebes, O. Mattha 65
(dem.) and O. Bodl. 469, 470, 471, all 10 drs.

Although our evidence of a reduction in taxes for the second
year of Gaius is confined to the laographia as it was paid in that
year at Philadelphia, nonetheless, several considerations lead to
the possibility that the reduction may have been a benefice granted
by the emperor. First, document II, the year-ledger of payments,
shows that the villagers were unaware of the reduction until very
late in the Egyptian year. The pattern of payment in year 2 was
similar to that in other years and the villagers paid the full
amount of 44 drs., 6 chalk., and pig tax, until the 16th day of the
final month of Gaius' second regnal year in Egypt, 9 August 38. No
payments were recorded after that date. Document I, the list of
arrears, however, shows that the reduction was intended for year 2,
and the notations in document II reveal that local authorities
could extend the reduction to year 3 through a credit, for the
profit of those who had been prompt with their payments. This in-
sistence that the reduction belong to year 2 disregarded the administrative problems produced at Philadelphia by the fact that the
reduction was announced when regnal year 2 in Egypt was nearly completed. If the reduction were a celebratory and an inaugural gesture, it would be important to celebrate it either in Gaius' first
regnal year in Egypt which was only five and one-half months long,[17]
or in his second regnal year in Egypt which was also his first full
year as emperor and the first year which he did not share with his
predecessor.[18] That second year in Egypt began on 29 August 37,
two days before his 26th birthday on 31 August. The second anni-
versary of his rule at Rome, however, fell on 18 March 38, after
his serious illness in his eighth month on the throne, and his

17 His *dies imperii* was 18 March 37. The writer of *P. Ryl.*
II 141, a petition from Euhemeria and dated 2 Pachon, year 1 of
Gaius (27 April 37), was aware of Gaius' accession forty-two days
after Tiberius' death. A delegation from Alexandria was apparently
in Italy during spring, 37: see H. Musurillo, *Acts of the Pagan
Martyrs* (Oxford 1954) no. III, pp. 8-17 and 105-16, and the new
fragment from Yale, *ZPE* 15 (1974) 1-7.

18 The customary eastern method was to count the period from
a monarch's accession to the next New Year's Day, whenever that
was celebrated, as his first regnal year; the subsequent regnal
years, except the last, were calendar years.

subsequent recovery in the early months of 38.[19]   The date of the
last payments made at Philadelphia and recorded in document II,
16 Mesore (= 9 August 38), coincided with the visit of Agrippa I
to Alexandria on his way to Judaea, an event which Philo joined to
the downfall of the prefect, Avillius Flaccus, later in the same
fall.[20]   The reduction in laographia belonged to year 2 and in its
conception was part of the early days of Gaius' reign.

In addition to the fact that the reduction had to be placed
in year 2, regardless of the inconvenience to the tax collectors,
a second consideration may also lead to Gaius as the likely author.
The edict of Hadrian, A.D. 136, was a response to an unfavorable
economic situation due to low flooding of the Nile for two successive years: in it the emperor announced that money taxes for the
year were to be deferred.   The arrangements for the postponed payments differed in the Thebaid, the Heptanomia, and the Delta, varying in accordance with the degree of hardship endured.[21]   Although
the decision to change tax contributions from Egypt was the emperor's prerogative, the prefect, as the emperor's deputy, and his
assistants, did function in cases where individuals attempted to
vindicate privileged status in taxation; the prefect could also
arrange for adjustments and postponements in collections in time
of economic difficulties.[22]   The main thrust of the prefect's

---

19   Philo *Leg.* 14; cf. Dio 59.7.9-8.1.   See also E. M. Smallwood, *Legatio ad Gaium* (Leiden 1970) 164-66 (news of his recovery
spread before the opening of the sailing season in March); A. M.
Dabrowski, *Problems in the Tradition about the Principate of Gaius*
(Diss. Toronto 1972) 162-64 (Gaius' failure to assume the consul-
ship only in 38 was due to protraction of his illness).

20   For the visit of Agrippa I, see Josephus *AJ* 18.238 and
Philo *In Flacc.* 26, and cf. Smallwood, *Legatio ad Gaium*, 17 and
252 (commentary to sect. 179).   For the relation between the visit
and the recall of Flaccus, see *In Flacc.* 27-43.

21   The edict is known in several copies; see *P. Osl.* III 78
(= *SB* III 6944).

22   Edict of Ti. Julius Alexander, lines 26-29 (see G. Chalon,
L'édit [Olten and Lausanne 1964] 144-52), and *Pap. Lugd. Bat.* VI 42
(A.D. 180).   For adjustments and postponements, *SB* IV 7462 (= *Sel.
Pap.* 281, A.D. 56-59), *BGU* III 903 (ca. 168/69, plus *BL* I 80), P.
Berol. inv. 16036 (A.D. 168) in *Festschrift 150 jähr. Bestehen
Berl. Aeg. Museums* (Berlin 1975) 425-29 (and now N. Lewis, *ZPE* 38
[1980] 244-54), *PSI* I 103 and 104 (170/71, plus *BL* I 391), *BGU* II
486 (2nd cent.).

activities, however, was to discover ways by which taxes could be collected.[23] The reduction at Philadelphia has the appearance of a gift rather than a response to a troubled economy: first, because men who had paid in excess of 36 drs. for year 2 received a credit for year 3; second, because rates of collection seem as high in Gaius' second year as at the end of Tiberius' reign.[24] References to ἀνακεχωρηκότες are not frequent, and both documents I and II imply that laographia which had fallen into arrears was for the most part collectable, even from those not currently residing in the village.[25]

If the reduction at Philadelphia was due to imperial beneficence, one would expect Gaius to extend his generosity further than one small village.[26] Villagers in Philadelphia, who were normally assessed at a rate of 44 drs., 6 chalk., for laographia received a reduction of 8 drs. By contrast, payments for laographia in Upper Egypt, where peasants were assessed, for the most part at rates of 10 drs. and 16 drs. per year, remain unaffected in Gaius' second and third years (above, note 16). If Gaius were the author of the gift, the application of the benefit was apparently left to the prefect and to the eklogistai to apportion. At present, the evidence for an imperial benefice admittedly derives only from the tax accounts of Philadelphia.

---

23 Philo *In Flacc.* 133.

24 Compare, for example, two alphabetical registers, *P. Princ.* 9, collections for year 16 of Tiberius (29/30), and P. Mich. inv. 876r, for year 4 of Gaius (39/40); cf. also the summary of document II, above p. 347. Philo (*Leg.* 9) claimed that at Gaius' accession revenues from the empire were pouring in "as if from inexhaustible springs" (cf. Smallwood, *Legatio ad Gaium*, 158, note ad loc.).

25 As also in *P. Princ.* 11 and *P. Corn.* 21v, after 30 August 35, as republished in *ZPE* 37 (1980) 243-45.

26 For example, Augustus is said to have reduced the tribute of the entire island of Kos by 100 talents in return for Apelles' painting of Aphrodite Anadyomene which he removed from the Asklepieion (Strabo 14.2.19). Claudius later cancelled all tribute for the inhabitants of the island as a favor to his physician, Xenophon (Tacitus *Ann.* 12.61; cf. E. Koestermann, *Annalen* III [Heidelberg 1967] 215).

At the same time, the sources for the life of Gaius mention his interest in Alexandria and Egypt.[27] Gaius accompanied his father Germanicus to Syria in A.D. 18 (Suet. *Cal.* 10.1). As a child of six he heard about his father's visit to Alexandria and Egypt, even if he did not personally witness the emotionally stirring scenes.[28] The interest endured throughout Gaius' short life and he was preparing to depart for the east and Egypt at the time of his assassination.[29] These same sources are replete with examples of Gaius' acts of demagogic generosity.[30] Gaius advertised his cancellation of a .5% tax, the duocentesima, on bronze quadrants, issued after 18 March 39, and from there on until his death; on the obverse was a pileus, signifying that the abolition would be a popular one.[31] Dio set his account of this remission in the events of 38 (58.16.2), and in both timing and mood, the abolition of the tax joins the reduction seen at Philadelphia. Suetonius listed the cancellation of the duocentesima among those of Gaius'

---

27 Philo *Leg.* 338 and Suet. *Cal.* 49.2; for a detailed discussion of that theme, see E. Köberlein, *Caligula und die ägypt. Kulte* (= Beitr. klass. Phil. III [Meisenheim 1962]).

28 H. Willrich, *Klio* 3 (1903) 88; for Germanicus, see D. G. Weingärtner, *Die Ägyptenreise des Germanicus* (= *PTA* XI, Bonn 1969).

29 Josephus *AJ* 19.81.

30 For Gaius' *donativa*, *congiaria*, and other benefits at Rome, see Dio 59.2.1-4, Suet. *Cal.* 17.2, and cf. A. Garzetti, *From Tiberius to the Antonines* (London 1974) 82. Whenever Gaius restored kings to their thrones, he gave them arrears of taxes and revenues from the area (Suet. *Cal.* 16.3).

31 E. M. Smallwood, *Documents* (Cambridge 1967) no. 35; and, for the history of the tax, including its apparent variation between .5% and 1%, see M. Gelzer, *RE* X (Stuttgart 1917) 391. Galba advertised the cancellation of the *quadragesima Galliarum* on bronze issues; the image of Libertas and the legend Libertas Augusta extended Gaius' symbol of the pileus; see R. Mowat, *Rev. numis.* 13 (1909) 75, and A. U. Stylow, *Chiron* 1 (1971) 285-90. Nero proposed the cancellation of the *vectigalia* throughout the empire; Tacitus *Ann.* 13.50-51.1 (see especially the commentary by Koestermann, *Annalen* III, 334-35, notes ad loc.). Instructive for continuity in the history of the inaugural acts of emperors is Herodian's account of the initial projects of Pertinax, which included the remission of all customs tariffs (2.4.6-9).

354   A. E. Hanson

actions which were designed to arouse men's devotion because of
their deliberately popular nature; his notice of the remission
limited it to sales at auction in Italy (*Cal.* 15.1 and 16.3).
Gaius responded to an embassy despatched by the koinon of Central
Greece at the time of his accession that he considered the number
of statues offered him to be excessive; he gave as the reason for
refusing, "That you burden yourselves less with expenses" (καὶ
ἑαυτοὺς ἧττον ἀναλώμασι βαρυνεῖτε).[32] In his fiscal generosity to
his subjects and in his expressions of concern for their welfare
in the early days of his reign, Gaius' acts recall Ptolemaic decrees of φιλάνθρωπα, issued at beginnings of reigns, or at a significant turning point within a reign.[33] His declarations of amnesty can also be paralleled in the decrees of φιλάνθρωπα.[34] Roman

---

32 Smallwood, *Documents*, no. 361, and J. H. Oliver, *GRBS* 12
(1971) 222. For a similar expression from Nero, as he rejected a
gold crown from the metropolis of the Arsinoite nome, see *SB* XII
11012.8-10 (plus commentary ad loc. in the ed. prin., *Aegyptus* 50
[1970] 19-20; for corrections to the text, E. G. Turner, *HSCP* 79
[1975] 11 n. 32). The refusal of gold crowns or remission of sums
offered in place of a crown was a common inaugural gesture of generosity, for which we have evidence for Roman emperors from Octavian (*RG* 21.3) to Alexander Severus (*P. Fay.* 20 and J. H. Oliver,
AJP 99 [1978] 474-85); see also A. K. Bowman, *BASP* 4 (1967) 59-74,
and F. Millar, *The Emperor in the Roman World* (Ithaca 1977) 140-42.
Four demotic receipts for "crown" from Upper Egypt and dated to
year 2 of Gaius suggest that he accepted a proffered crown (*Archiv*
6 [1920] 131).

33 For Roman parallels to the philanthropa, especially the
edict of Ti. Julius Alexander, see L. Koenen (commentary to *P.
Kroll* 9 and note 8, 14-15, 27-28, 36) and followed by Chalon,
L'édit, 85-88. For reductions and remissions in taxes as celebra-
tory gestures, see the commentary to *P. Kroll* 29-30; compare also
H. Kloft, *Liberalitas Principis* (= Kölner histor. Abhand. XVIII,
Köln 1970) 89-132.

34 The recall of those condemned for maiestas under Tiberius,
the dismissal of untried cases and the destruction of evidence, the
restoration of the ashes of his mother and brother, banished by
Tiberius, to the family mausoleum on the Tiber (Suet. *Cal.* 15.1 and
4); cf. Köberlein, *Caligula und die ägypt. Kulte*, 39-43. For Octavian's amnesty to Alexandria, see Julian 433D-434A ("ἀφίημι τὴν
πόλιν αἰτίας πάσης"), and quoted indirectly by Plutarch, *Ant.* 80.1;
for other references to the speech, cf. G. W. Bowersock, *Augustus
and the Greek World*, 33 and n. 1. The beginning of Octavian's
reign in Egypt was made to coincide with the Egyptian New Year's
Day, 1 Thoth 30 B.C. (T.C. Skeat, *JEA* 43 [1953] 98-100). For Vespasian's amnesties in Alexandria, see Dio 66.9.1; cf. A. Henrichs,
ZPE 3 (1968) 74-75.

traditions for the inauguration of a reign were being shaped by
the Julio-Claudian emperors,[35] and the celebrations attending both
Gaius' accession and his recovery from illness were remembered
with a joy which spread over the empire.[36] It seems possible that
Gaius responded by reducing the tribute owed to Rome, as signalled
in the registers from Philadelphia.[37]

Fordham University/Lincoln Center   Ann Ellis Hanson
Princeton University Library

---

35 ·Note, for example, the similarities in inaugural ceremon-
ies for Gaius (V. Ehrenberg-A.H.M. Jones, *Documents* [Oxford 1976]
43, the notice from the *fasti Ostienses*; Dio 59.3.8, Suet. *Cal.*
15.1, and Josephus *AJ* 18.236) and for Nero (Tacitus *Ann.* 13.3-4.2).
Gaius addressed the people, but Nero spoke in the Senate.

36 See in particular the account in Philo *Leg.* 11-20; the
notes in Smallwood (*Legatio ad Gaium*) are very useful--ad 11, for
a list of inscriptions which corroborate Philo (but one inscription is cited twice, p. 161: *ILS* 8792 = *IG* VII 2711) and ad 13,
where Philo's statement that "the 'age of Cronos' described by the
poets ceased to be regarded as a poetic fiction" is provided with
post-Hesiodic parallels which include Vergil *Georg.* 1.121-59, *Aen.*
8.319-27, Tibullus 1.3.35-50, Ovid *Metam.* 15.96-110, etc. Dio reported that in the year before Tiberius' death the phoenix was
sighted in Egypt (58.27.1): εἰ δέ τι καὶ τὰ Αἰγύπτια πρὸς ῾Ρωμαίους
προσήκει, ὁ φοῖνιξ ἐκείνῳ τῷ ἔτει ὤφθη καὶ ἔδοξε πάντα ταῦτα τὸν
θάνατον τῷ Τιβερίῳ προσημῆναι (for the significance of the phoenix
as the precursor of the beginning of a new age, after a time of
trouble, see Köberlein, *Caligula und die ägypt. Kulte*, 18 and 43).

37 The sources for Gaius which represented senatorial traditions (Dio, Tacitus, Suetonius, and Seneca) were justifiably hostile, as were Philo and Josephus who recorded the reaction to his
reign from the Jews of the Diaspora. When discussing the bridge
of boats which Gaius made from Baiae to the mole at Puteoli, Seneca
claimed that Gaius' action threatened Rome with famine, and his
verdict was that Gaius...viribus imperii ludit (*de brev. vit.* 18.5).
If the senatorial tradition had noticed the reduction of laographia
at Philadelphia, the reaction might have been similar to the response which Nero's proposed cancellation of *vectigalia* received;
Tacitus *Ann.* 13.50-51.1 (above n. 31). Nonetheless these same
sources tend to see the beginning of Gaius' reign in a positive
light, if only to contrast it with the dismal ending and the return
of tyrannicide to Roman politics. See also Plutarch's comment on
Gaius, *Ant.* 87.8, "Of Germanicus' children, Gaius reigned with distinction, but for a short time only, and was then put to death with
his wife and child" (τῶν δὲ Γερμανικοῦ παίδων Γάϊος μὲν ἄρξας ἐπιφανῶς οὐ πολὺν χρόνον ἀνηρέθη μετὰ τέκνου καὶ γυναικός, pace C. P.
Jones, *Plutarch and Rome* [Oxford 1971] 80 and n. 50). The tax reduction at Philadelphia may itself represent one more detail,
hitherto unrepresented in the discussion of the beginning of Gaius'
reign.

A PETITION FROM PRIESTS TO HADRIAN WITH HIS SUBSCRIPTION

The text to be discussed is one of the Berlin Papyri, property of the Staatliche Museen in Berlin. The papyrus bears inventory number P. 16546. It has been entrusted for publication, along with other items, to the Institute of Papyrology, Warsaw University.[1] This paper is intended as a preliminary presentation of the text, which will be published in a future volume of the *BGU*.

The item in question is an almost rectangular scrap of papyrus measuring 14 x 11.5 cm. The text is written in regular hand. There are almost no problems in transcription, for the text was clearly written. Except for two mistakes in lines 3 and 5, the preoccupation of the scribe to produce a final copy is apparent. On the left only a few letters (ca. 2-3) are lost from each line. The large space above the first line shows that this is the beginning of the column. The contents reveal, however, that the extant fragment is but the conclusion of the whole and must be a continuation from a previous column which has been lost. It is also broken at the bottom, and these lacunae unfortunately leave us lacking much which would have been of interest. The back is blank.

→ Σω]τῆρα καὶ Εὐεργέτην ἐλεῆσαι ἡμᾶς καὶ τὸν ἡμέ-
τερ]ον θεὸν Σόξειν καὶ ἐπιτρέψαι κ̣[α]ὶ̣ ἡμεῖν ἃς ποιού-
με]θα ὑπὲρ τοῦ ἱεροῦ δαπάνας παρὰ [τ]ῶν αὐτῶν κω,-

4   μη]τῶν λαμβάνειν ἵνα δυνηθῶ[μ]εν τὰς ὑπηρεσίας ‵τω[ς]′,
ποι]εῖσθαι καὶ τὰ ὀφειλόμενα τῶι φίσκωι ἀμέμπ〚τῶς〛
ἀπο]διδόναι ἐκ τῆς σῆς εὐεργεσίας. (vac.) διευτύχει.
ἀ]ντίγρ(αφον) ὑπογρ(αφῆς). ὑπέγραψ(α). προτεθήτωι.
                (vac.)

8   Αὐτ]οκράτωρ Καῖσαρ [Τρ]αιανὸς Ἀδριανὸς Σεβαστὸς
ἱ]ερεῦσι (vac.) [   ]τ̣ο̣ς̣ [
                · · · · · · ·

4 ἵνα   7 προτεθητωι 1. προτεθήτω   8 Τραϊανος

1 For permission to publish the text, my thanks are due to Dr. hab. Wolfgang Müller, head of the Papyrus-Sammlung, Staatliche Museen.

1   The formula which served as a link between the missing first
    column and the extant part of the text must have been some-
    thing like: καὶ ἀξιοῦμέν (or δεόμεθά) σε | [Σω]τῆρα καὶ
    Εὐεργέτην κτλ.

3   At the end of the line an irregular sign which follows κω
    should probably be considered as a simple trace of ink,
    perhaps a remainder of an intended and miswritten μ. The
    rest of the word κω[μη]τῶν should certainly be read in
    line 4.

5   At the end of the line three letters of ἀμέμπτως have been
    crossed out by the scribe and then rewritten above.

7   The abbreviation ὑπεγραψ( ) should probably be resolved as
    ὑπέγραψ(α).

Thus the text may possibly be translated as follows:

> (We beg you, the) Saviour and Benefactor to show pity
> on us and on our god Soxis, and order that we also may
> collect from the aforesaid villagers the amount which we
> spend for the temple in order that we may be capable of
> performing the services and paying appropriately the taxes
> due the Treasury, by your leave. Farewell.
>
> Copy of subscription. Signed. To be posted.
>
> Imperator Caesar Traianus Hadrianus Augustus to
> priests....

The petitioners request the right to collect certain sums
which they used for the temple from some κωμῆται who have been mentioned in the lost portion of the text and who certainly were the
inhabitants of the locality in which the temple was situated.

The petition seems to be a request for the right to collect a
new temple tax, substantiated with a reference to a similar privilege granted to somebody else. Such taxes are known and have been
thoroughly discussed by Otto and Wallace.[2] These temple-taxes could
be collected from the people directly by the priests, though in the
Roman period, according to Otto, this must have been infrequent.[3]

---

2   W. Otto, *Priester und Tempel* (Leipzig 1905) I, 340-66; S. L.
Wallace, *Taxation in Egypt from Augustus to Diocletian* (Princeton
1938) 239.

3   Cf. Otto, op. cit., 341 n. 3, 360 n. 1, 361; Wallace, ibid.

Anyway, the expression ἐπιτρέψαι...ἡμεῖν...δαπάνας παρὰ τῶν... κωμητῶν λαμβάνειν (lines 2-4) may be understood literally as indicating the direct collection of taxes from κωμῆται without involvement of the State tax-collecting system.

The legal character of the payment (whether a proper tax or another kind of contribution) is difficult to qualify. The amount in question is not stated in the preserved text. It was common practice to substantiate requests on the grounds that the petitioners would not in the long run be able to perform their duties and to pay taxes to the State unless their request was granted. These statements in our text may have been a reflection of this practice, or they may represent true economic difficulties at the temple. It is common knowledge that expenses involved in running a temple were considerable.[4]

Also the duties of the temple to the Treasury, stressed in the text, may be considered as a *signum temporis*.[5] In this respect, however, the text does not add much to our knowledge. As we know, petitions directed to the emperor were usually answered by subscript attached to the request itself.[6] This document, in which the emperor's ὑπογραφή follows the request, provides us with an example of this practice. From line 7 we learn that the copy was to be posted. Usually the imperial answers were fashioned into a roll and posted for a certain time after which they were filed in the archives where they were accessible to interested parties.[7] This papyrus, however, can hardly be considered a fragment of such a roll of ἀποκρίματα (or ὑπογραφαί).

The regularity of the hand seems to point to its being an official copy rather than a private copy made from the posted text. The document, however, must not be considered an internal bureau paper or official circular. The official version--according to Wilcken and supported by Schiller--was never transmitted to the

---

4   Otto, op. cit., (1908) II, 6-14.

5   Ibid., 43-70.

6   A. Arthur Schiller in W. L. Westermann and A. A. Schiller, *Apokrimata* (New York 1954) 39.

7   Schiller, op. cit., 46; cf. Wilcken, *Archiv* 9 (1930) 19f.; v. Premerstein, "Libellus," *RE* 25 (1926) 42.

petitioner.[8] Schiller states: "He could, however, have a transcript
made and certified while the rescript was posted or after it had
been lodged in the archives." It seems possible that the Berlin
papyrus under discussion is such a transcript.

The content of the emperor's reply has been lost. In the last
line, after ἱ]ερεῦσι, there is a blank space. What remains after
the blank is only the tops of three letters, probably τος. It could
be a remnant of [Σόξι]τος which makes sense with ἱ]ερεῦσι. In such
a case the blank would seem unnecessary, unless it was intended to
separate the first word of the line from the name of the god which
had been placed at the center of the line. Another space would
separate Σόξιτος from the next word (χαίρειν?) which may have closed
the line.

The petitioners themselves are of some interest to us since the
temple in question is that of a little-known divinity named Soxis.
He was one of the crocodile gods of the Fayûm, an aspect of Sobk or
Σοῦχος.[9] The god is known from three edited documents: (1) an inscription from Euhemeria (69 B.C.), now in the Graeco-Roman Museum
in Alexandria, mentioning the local temple of Psosnaus, Pneferôs
and Soxis, θεοὶ Κροκοδείλοι (SB I 5827.8-9, reedited with corrections, cf. SB III 6154); (2) a papyrus from the 2nd century, without a known origin, containing a question to the oracle, was addressed Σούξει θεῷ μεγάλῳ μεγάλῳ (lines 1-2: P. Lond. III 1267 d =
Wilcken, Archiv 4 [1908] 559); (3) a dedicatory inscription of 72
B.C. found in the North-West temple at Karanis. This text recently
made possible the identification of that temple as a place of wor-
ship of Σόξεις θεὸς μέγας μέγας (G. Wagner, S.A.A. El-Nassery, "Une
nouvelle dédicace au grand dieu Soxis," ZPE 19 [1975] 139-42).

Unfortunately, the provenance of the Berlin papyrus is unknown.
It is more likely that this papyrus came from Karanis, as many other
of the Berlin papyri do, than from Euhemeria which is less frequently represented. It is also probable that the temple in question is
that in Karanis, dedicated to Soxis alone and not to three gods as
in Euhemeria.

---

8 Schiller, op. cit., 40; U. Wilcken, "Zu den Kaiserreskripten," Hermes 55 (1920) 1-42.

9 E. Kiessling, "Suxis," RE 5 A,996-97; Kees, "Suchos," RE
7 A,540-60.

The Karanis temple was of considerable size, as the ruins show, and thus fits the circumstances of the document. If this is the case, the κωμῆται would be the inhabitants of Karanis.

The fact that a petition concerning some obscure financial problems was directed by priests of a minor temple in the χώρα to the emperor is certainly a point of interest in this text. As we know from literary sources, e.g., the correspondence of Pliny with Trajan, the emperors used to take a great deal of interest in provincial finance. While one cannot compare Nicomedia or Prusa with Karanis, the emperor's involvement does throw some light on the date of the text in question. It points to 130 A.D., Hadrian's visit to Egypt, as a possible time for this petition and subscription.

Hadrian's reign was a period marked by the increased interest of the central authorities in the temple affairs in Egypt and by the reorganization of the offices to which the temples were subject even earlier than the emperor's visit to the province.[10] The Berlin papyrus not only supports that picture, but also gives new testimony for the cult of the great god Soxis.

Warsaw   Adam Łukaszewicz

---

10 J. Scherer, "Idiologue et archiereus," *BIFAO* 41 (1942) 60–66; G. M. Parássoglou, "A prefectural edict regulating temple activities," *ZPE* 13 (1974) 21–37 (A.D. 120).

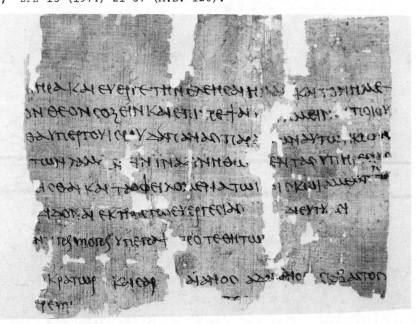

REFLECTIONS OF CITIZEN ATTITUDES IN
PETITIONS FROM ROMAN OXYRHYNCHUS[1]

Scholars have assumed that Roman rule in Egypt brought with it, right from the start, an extreme degree of fiscal oppression.[2] Although there is scant evidence for such an assumption with regard to Roman Oxyrhynchus,[3] nevertheless, such an assumption has precluded investigations to determine how the contemporary citizen perceived the matter.

It is the intent of this paper to attempt to determine to what extent the citizens of Oxyrhynchus felt themselves to be the victims of an oppressive imperial government. Petitions[4] have been selected as the basis for this investigation because such documents represent occasions on which individuals formally requested the government to intervene in their lives, and in such a request there is the obvious expectation that some benefit will result. Furthermore, such documents reflect individual perceptions of rights and the role of government in their protection.

---

1 I wish to express appreciation to the National Endowment for the Humanities for providing financial support for the research of this paper through a 1979 Summer Seminar at Columbia University. Also, my deepest appreciation goes to Professors William V. Harris, the Director of the Seminar, and John F. Oates, Duke University, for reading early drafts of this paper and for making invaluable suggestions for its improvement.

2 For modern prejudices regarding the term "imperialism," see P.D.A. Garnesey and C. R. Whittaker, *Imperialism in the Ancient World* (Cambridge 1978) 1.

3 Royce L.B. Morris, "The Economy of Oxyrhynchus," *BASP* 15 (1978) 263-73.

4 The value of petitions for our understanding of the social history of Egypt was pointed out almost a half century ago by H. I. Bell, "Proposals for a Social History of Graeco-Roman Egypt," *IV International Congress of Papyrology* (Florence 1935) 39.

First Century[5]

The nineteen separate petitions from this period cover many
aspects of personal rights which individuals felt were guaranteed
by the government.[6] Five of these petitions were submitted by one
man, Tryphon, a weaver from Oxyrhynchus, over the course of twenty
years. It would be unusual indeed for one man to continue to appeal to a government he perceived to be unresponsive so many times
over such an extensive period. For our purpose, therefore, it may
be useful to look in some detail at the petitions of this man.

At some point between A.D. 30-35 (II 282), Tryphon's wife deserted him, a fact that would have been of little consequence to
the government;[7] however, when she left, she apparently took several articles belonging to Tryphon, and the protection of private
property would have been, at least in Tryphon's view, a matter of
concern to the government. This letter concludes with the request
that Demetrous be brought before the strategus in order that "she
may receive her deserts and return my property to me."[8]

The continuing conflict between Tryphon and Demetrous is the
subject of two subsequent petitions by Tryphon to the strategus
(II 315, A.D. 37; II 324, A.D. 50). In the first, he complained
that his present wife, Saraeus, had suffered an assault from his
former wife and her mother. It concludes with the request that
they "may receive their deserts (?)." In the second, Tryphon complained that he and his present wife had both been assaulted by a

---

5 My treatment of petitions of the first century separate
from those of the second century is not entirely arbitrary. John
White (*The Form and Structure of the Official Petition* [SBL Dissertation Series 5, 1972]) makes a stylistic distinction between the
petitions of these two periods.

6 All unspecified references in the notes and text consisting
of Roman numerals followed by Arabic numbers will refer to volume
and document number of *The Oxyrhynchus Papyri*. In chronological
order, the petitions from the first century are: *P. Mert.* 104, *P.
Oxy. inv.* 34.4b 73 lb (12)a, II 281, 282, XIX 2234, II 315, *P.
Fouad.* I 27, II 283, XLII 3033, II 394, II 393, I 38, II 324, II
284, 285, II 316, *P. Fouad.* I 28, XLII 3064, II 286.

7 I.e., there was no marriage contract to enforce as in II
281 (A.D. 20-50), which is addressed to the archidicastes, not the
strategus.

8 All translations in the text are those of the editors of
the various documents noted.

woman (Demetrous?) and other persons (Demetrous' mother?). This petition concludes with a request for the strategus "to proceed against them however seems best."

Whether the Roman government of the first century was approachable and responsive to its citizens or not is not demonstrable from these petitions; however, it is indisputable that this citizen believed that it was. It is clear that he believed that the government was interested in him and his petty domestic problems. Moreover, he demonstrates a conviction that the government was concerned with the protection of his private property and individual rights.

The final petition from Tryphon (I 38, A.D. 49-50) is addressed to the prefect. In the year preceding, Tryphon had been involved in a trial before the strategus concerning the disputed identity of a child whom Tryphon claimed as his own. Although the strategus rendered a judgment in favor of Tryphon and his wife, the opponent in the litigation evidently failed to abide by the decision and continued to harass Tryphon. Tryphon, therefore, appealed directly to the prefect. In his petition, Tryphon simply stated, "Syrus, however, refused to comply with the judgment and hinders me in my trade. I therefore come to you, my preserver, in order to obtain my rights."[9]

Tryphon, although illiterate,[10] crude, and common in many respects, was a man who felt that he had certain rights, the protection of which was a matter of concern to the government. When he felt these rights had been violated, he did not hesitate to take his case to the prefect if necessary, "in order to obtain my rights." His knowledge of his rights and his unrelenting and unhesitating demands for their protection say more for the Roman government than for Tryphon. It says quite clearly and emphatically that the government had created an atmosphere in which a Tryphon, a first-century citizen, believed that it was concerned with him and his rights as an individual.

---

9 The significance of this document is to be seen in its unformulaic construction. It relates not at all to White's paradigm for a petition from this period (*Form and Structure*, 16-17).

10 II 324 (A.D. 50).

There must have been many persons like Tryphon, and the Roman
Government must have expended tremendous amounts of administrative
energy dealing with a myriad citizen conflicts, from important dis-
putes over property rights to the most trivial interpersonal conflicts and domestic bickering. More important than these, however,
are those that illustrate that persons did not hestiate to approach
the government with complaints against violent and rapacious
government officials.

There are five such petitions from the first century. The
first (XIX 2234, A.D. 31) is addressed to the Centurian Quintus
Gaius Passer[11] from a certain Haemon. Haemon complained that a
fisherman and a soldier have poached fish from his pond and physically assaulted him. He requests that the accused be brought before the centurion, that he be reimbursed for the lost fish, and
that the two in the future "keep their hands off my property."
Whatever may have been the eventual results of this petition, Haemon
obviously felt that his rights were such that their violation, even
by a soldier of Rome, would not be tolerated.[12]

The other four petitions of this type were complaints of ex-
tortion against tax-collectors during the years A.D. 49-50. The
collector Apollophanes is charged in A.D. 50 (II 284) by the weaver
Alexandros of extorting sixteen drachmae. A second charge is levied
against him in the same year (II 285) by the weaver Sarapion. The
final two petitions (II 393, 394, A.D. 49) are severly damaged;
however, that they deal with the same problem is clear. Although
these documents have traditionally been viewed as illustrative of
Roman fiscal oppression in the first century,[13] they simply will not
bear the weight of such an interpretation.[14] It is important to
note that these petitions are not against government, but are against

---

11 For the competency of the centurion, see Meyer, *JurPap*,
281-82.

12 In support of this attitude, see II 240 (A.D. 37), an
investigation into illegal activity by a soldier.

13 H. I. Bell, "The Economic Crisis in Egypt Under Nero,"
JRS 28 (1938) 5.

14 Morris, "Economy of Oxyrhynchus," 265-66.

officials of government[15]--a distinction that seems to have been clear to the people involved, but a distinction that has not been clearly perceived by modern scholars.

The fact that many persons, like Tryphon, did not hesitate to approach the government for the protection of their person and property, and for protection from oppressive officials demonstrates that an atmosphere of stability existed in the first century. This atmosphere may have been created to facilitate economic exploitation, but the citizens themselves do not seem to have been aware of such a motive.

Second Century

The petitions from the second century[16] reveal that the government continued to deal with the many problems common to human beings living in community: neighborhood brawling, charges of fraud, and the ever present problem of theft.

There are, however, a number of petitions from the second century that reflect attitudes and conditions distinct from those observed in the first century. These changes in attitude seem closely linked to a growing problem of economic and administrative instability.[17] Whatever the reasons for the change, clearly a number of petitions from this period reveals persons who lack the confidence of a first-century Tryphon, both personal confidence and confidence in the government's role as the guardian of individual rights.

The first petition (I 76, A.D. 179) reflecting some external pressure on the individual citizen is unique in what one expects in petitions; i.e., it does not deal with a complaint of physical suffering or material loss. Rather it deals with an attempt to avoid material gain. In this unusual letter to the strategus, Apia, the daughter of Horion, informs the strategus, Theon, that her father who owned a room in her own house was near death. She states that she does not wish to inherit and requests information regarding

---

15   Supra n. 11; also II 298 (I cent.), and II 239 (A.D. 66).

16   XXII 2342, XXXVI 2758, XXIV 2410, III 592, VI 898, I 68, III 486, III 484, X 1272, III 487, III 594, VII 1032, *PSI* 1033, XXXVI 2708, XXXI 2563, XXIV 2411, XXXVI 2760, I 76, IV 718, II 237, I 69, VI 899, IV 705, III 488.

17   J. D. Thomas, "A Petition to the Prefect of Egypt and Related Imperial Edicts," *JEA* 61 (1975) 221.

what steps to take "in order to free me from responsibility after
his death."

Personal loss resulting from administrative incompetence is
the subject of a number of petitions from this period. Dionysius
Amynthianus, recently discharged from the cavalry, was in charge of
the delivery of blankets for the army from Oxyrhynchus. In A.D. 179
(XXVI 2760), he appealed to the prefect because he had been in Alexandria with the blankets for forty days but had been unable to have
them received. He precedes his request to the prefect with the
statement that "I and those with me are short of means of subsistence."

The largest number of petitions against official incompetence
deals with land. In A.D. 162 (VII 1032), Ammonius and Morthius
complain to the epistrategus that fifteen years previous to this
petition they had converted 7/16 aroura of grainland to vineland
upon proper registration and the payment of the appropriate fee;
nine years later, however, the land was listed by the komogrammateus as improperly converted land.

Sometime between A.D. 180-192 (IV 718), Antistius Primus, also
called Lollianus, complained to the epistrategus Ti. Claudius Xenophon that four arourae of *basilike ge* had been improperly assigned
to his private land. Forty years previous to the petition, Antistius had purchased 52-1/2 arourae of grainland and 1/2 aroura of
building land, all of which had been declared "free from any obligation to cultivate royal, usiac and sacred land";[18] forty years
later, however, the komogrammateus had assigned to the land the
very obligation for which it had been declared free.

In the final petition of this type (III 488, III), also addressed to the epistrategus, Senphibis, the daughter of Thartaeus,
states that she has purchased some land; in the process of registration, however, she was listed as possessing one aroura more than
she in fact possessed.

In addition to the frustration reflected in these petitions,
several aspects of petitions from the second century reveal persons

---

18   That the assignment of such land to private land had become
a significant economic liability by the middle of the second century
is clearly indicated. See III 506 (A.D. 143), X 1270 (A.D. 159),
III 633 (II cent.), *P. Wisc.* 9 (A.D. 183). Also see A. K. Bowman,
"The Crown Tax in Roman Egypt," *BASP* 4 (1967) 59-74.

who felt themselves to be oppressed by government, and such attitudes are explicitly reflected in a number of petitions of complaint
against government itself.

Although there were complaints in the first century against
government officials, there were no complaints against government
itself. The weavers of the mid-first century did not complain of
excessive demands of the government. They complained of the excessive and illegal demands of individual tax-collectors. In the second century, even when the formal complaint deals with another issue, there is the frequent reference to the fact that the persons
involved feel that the government has been excessive in its demands
and that this excessiveness has resulted in personal suffering and
loss.

In A.D. 156 (III 487), a certain Nicias petitioned the epistrategus for release from a public appointment. Unlike any first-
century petition, his case is in no way based on a point of law,
but on the plea that burdensome debts have resulted from this service. On the other hand, Apollonarion (VI 899, A.D. 200), although
her petition to be relieved of the obligation to cultivate *basilike*
ge seems based on an appropriate point of law,[19] nevertheless felt
the need to strengthen her case by a similar complaint against the
government. She states that her performance of this duty to date
has reduced her to a state of poverty because of the extra levies.

In A.D. 200-202 (IV 705), a well-to-do citizen of Oxyrhynchus
petitioned Septimius Severus and Caracalla to allow him to establish
an endowment to aid the people of the land who were being exhausted
by the "burdensome demands of the annual liturgies."

A further distinctive characteristic of petitions from the
second century may be viewed in two ways: an appeal to pity--an aspect that is totally uncharacteristic of first-century petitions,
or a veiled threat--also uncharacteristic.[20] This aspect of second-
century petitions can be seen in several documents where the final
appeal is predicated upon the statement that unless the petition is
acted upon favorably, the persons involved will be forced to abandon their home and land. This fear or threat of joining the

---

19 *BGU* 648 (A.D. 164 or 196).

20 XLIV 3164 (A.D. 73) introd.

growing ranks of the homeless is expressed in the following way:

1. in order that we may be able to remain in our own
    home (XXIV 2410);
2. that you may not make me an outcast from my home and
    property (III 487);
3. in order that I may not become a wanderer (VI 899);
4. there is the danger of their being ruined as far as
    the treasury is concerned and leaving the land un-
    cultivated (IV 705);
5. I am in danger of abandoning the land (III 488).

The appeal to pity not to make them homeless is clear in each;
the threat, however, is most explicit in IV 705, where it is stated
that the abandonment of the land will result in a loss to the treasury. Obviously these petitions reflect the problem of the growing
ranks of the homeless and the economically nonproductive persons of
the late second century.[21] They also obviously reflect persons who
have lost confidence in themselves and in the government.

The most striking difference between the petitions of the
first and second century is the fact that the level of confidence
with which a first century citizen petitioned to "obtain his rights"
has disappeared. In its place is a rather pathetic plea that the
government take pity and grant some kind of relief. The primary interest of the citizen of Oxyrhynchus from roughly mid-second century
becomes, not the protection of their rights, but the avoidance at
all costs of extreme poverty and loss of home; and as MacLennan has
pointed out, the people "clung with pathetic tenacity to what they
had...."[22] If, in fact, the Roman government was oppressive during
the first two centuries of its rule, its affect does not manifest
itself in the attitudes of the people until the mid-second century.

Emory and Henry College, Virginia   R.L.B. Morris

---

21 Thomas, "Petition to the Prefect," 216 and n. 27; also see
Naphtali Lewis, "Μερισμὸς ἀνακεχωρηκότων" ("An Aspect of Roman Oppression in Egypt"), *JEA* 23 (1937) 63-75.

22 Hugh MacLennan, *Oxyrhynchus: An Economic and Social Study*
(Princeton 1935, repr. ed. Chicago 1968) 23.

SALES OF LAND IN THEIR SOCIAL CONTEXT

Despite the importance of the sale of agricultural land to the understanding of the agrarian economy of Roman Egypt, the subject has received relatively little attention from historians and papyrologists for several decades.[1] The survival of a few hundred documents of sale and cession may seem adequate testimony to the mobility of land, and it has been assumed that land was available for increased investment to occur in the financially unstable years of the third century A.D.[2] Yet Finley has expressed doubts about the use of the term "investment," and the existence of a land market even in late Republican and Imperial Italy; and, although other scholars have not been so sceptical, it is surely legitimate to enquire how far there can have existed a land market in Egypt, a province where the high proportion of public land restricted the amount of land available for private purchase.[3] We must consider

---

1 The most recent major works are already more than thirty years old; F. Pringsheim, *The Greek Law of Sale* (Weimar 1950); O. Montevecchi, "Ricerche di sociologia nei documenti dell'Egitto greco-romano III: I contratti di compra-vendita. c) Compra-vendite di Terreni," *Aegyptus* 23 (1943) 11-89. This contrasts with the leases of land, which since 1958 have formed the subject of a book, a thesis, and numerous articles. Sale from the legal point of view is treated in the standard legal works; e.g. R. Taubenschlag, *The Law of Greco-Roman Egypt in the Light of the Papyri 332 B.C. - 640 A.D.* (Warsaw[2] 1955) 317ff.; E. Seidl, *Rechtsgeschichte Ägyptens als römischer Provinz* (Sankt Augustin 1973) 181ff.

2 M. Hombert and C. Préaux, "Un petit propriétaire égyptien du milieu du IIIe siècle de notre ère, Aurelius Serenus Sarapion," *Antiquité Classique* 17 (1948) 333; I. Fikhman, "Quelques données sur la genèse de la grande propriété foncière à Oxyrhynchus," *Le monde grec. Hommages à Claire Préaux* (Bruxelles 1975) 787; H. MacLennan, *Oxyrhynchus; an economic and social study* (Diss. Princeton 1935) 18; A. C. Johnson, *Roman Egypt*, Tenney Frank ed., *An Economic Survey of Ancient Rome* (Baltimore 1936) II, 146; but Johnson excludes privately-owned land as a source of investment in "Roman Egypt in the third century," *JJurPap* 4 (1950) 157; see also K. Hopkins, "Brother-sister marriage in Roman Egypt," *Comparative Studies in Society and History* 22/3 (July 1980) 342f.

3 M. I. Finley, *The Ancient Economy* (London 1973) 118ff.; dissent is expressed by M. Frederiksen in his review, "Theory, evidence and the ancient economy," *JRS* 65 (1975) 157.

not only how many sales survive, but also the context in which the
recorded transactions took place. Was there, for example, a perceptible reluctance to sell land, a characteristic observed in many
peasant societies?[4] How important a part did land sales play in
the economic activity of the provincials of Egypt? An answer to
the latter question, especially, would contribute much to our understanding of the mechanism by which accumulation of land in a few
hands apparently increased in the third century.

A reexamination of the documents with this in view must take
account of one particularly relevant feature. It has been noted
that many sales of all kinds of real property involved more than
one member of the same family.[5] Family involvement took various
forms; for instance, close relatives together sold land which was
in joint ownership, and wives consented to the alienation of their
husbands' property. The participation of family members in these
sales is clearly the result of practices associated with the dis-
position of property by inheritance or at marriage; heirs might
retain joint ownership for a lengthy period, and a wife obtained
a claim on her husband's property as security for her dowry.[6]

But here I am concerned with some other cases of family involvement; the sale of land by close relatives to each other, and
the purchase by parents on behalf of their children. These, too,
may be interpreted in the light of marriage and inheritance practices, with implications that are fundamental for our understanding
of the nature of the Egyptian land market.

---

4 H. T. Fei and C-I. Chang, *Earthbound China; a study of
rural economy in Yunnan* (London 1948) 125.

5 Montevecchi, op. cit. (n. 1) 54 and 64ff. The work by
Montevecchi on sale, both of land and buildings (for which see
Aegyptus 21 [1941] 93-151; also "Contributi per una storia sociale
ed economica della famiglia nell'Egitto greco-romano," *Aegyptus* 17
[1937] 338-48), discussing the involvement of the family, is directed towards an understanding of the nature of the Egyptian family rather than towards an elucidation of the significance of sale
within the total economy.

6 E. Weiss, "Communio pro diviso und pro indiviso in den
Papyri," *Archiv* 4 (1907-8) 356f.; Taubenschlag, *Law*, 220ff., 127.

The most plentiful documentation of family involvement is
provided by late Ptolemaic Pathyris,[7] but it must be emphasized
that the same phenomena can be found in the Roman period, not only
in the Fayum, but even in the relatively hellenized metropoleis of
Middle Egypt. This may be illustrated by examples from Oxyrhynchus, concerning catoicic land, which could be expected to be most
subject to hellenization. These are derived from the notices of
cession addressed to the agoranomoi and other officials in the late
first century A.D.[8]

   P. Oxy. I 46 records the cession of just over 1-1/4 arouras
of productive catoicic land near the village of Palosis by a priest,
Harthothes the younger, to his full brother, Harthothes the elder,
also a priest. The land was part of 6 arouras held in common between the two brothers and other persons. In another notice of
cession, *P. Oxy.* I 47, the ceded land was also in joint ownership,
between the vendor and the father of the buyer. It is not stated
that these persons were related, and none of the patronymics coincide, implying that any relationship was not through the male line.
But joint heirs need not have been full brothers; in a society
where mortality was high, and divorce was easy, second marriages
were common; and cousins could become joint heirs if their parents
were already dead.[9] Another transaction between members of a family seems to be recorded in a notice to Taroutillios, the superintendent of the καταλοχισμός, although textual difficulties raise
some doubt about this (*P. Oxy.* XII 1462). If the reading ἀ[δ]ελ-[φοῦ
(lines 19f.) is correct, an agreement was made between the purchaser and his brother to buy land on behalf of his young daughter.

---

7 Montevecchi, *Aegyptus* 23 (1943) 64ff. Also P. W. Pestman,
"Les archives privées de Pathyris à l'époque ptolémaique. La fa-
mille de Pétéharsemtheus, fils de Panebkhounis," *Pap. Lugd. Bat.* 14
(Leiden 1965) 47-105; Pestman, "A Greek testament from Pathyris,"
JEA 55 (1969) 129-60; U. Kaplony-Heckel, "Demotische Texte aus
Pathyris," *MDAIK* 21 (1966) 133-70.

8 *P. Oxy.* I 45-47, 165, 174-76; II 341-42, 344, 346-47; III
641; XII 1462. But only the first three and the last provide information in the published versions about the names of the people
involved.

9 M. Hombert and C. Préaux, *Recherches sur le recensement
dans l'Egypte romaine*, *Pap. Lugd. Bat.* 5 (Leiden 1952) 168; *P. Oxy.*
III 503.

All these transactions seem to have had the effect of reunit-
ing in the hands of one person property divided or placed in joint
ownership among heirs; the reunification would come about either
immediately or after one more stage in the process of inheritance.
But was this effect intentional, and if so, why was it thought
desirable?

One possible explanation is that the transactions reveal an
attempt to prevent property becoming fragmented through inheritance.
This could take two forms. Land could be divided physically into
units which were uneconomically small; or the ownership of a parcel
which retained physical unity might have been fragmented among a
number of persons. The evidence suggests that it was the latter
which produced more concern. Sale certainly could have been used
to eliminate minute plots; but many landholders continued to cultivate their scattered, diminutive holdings.[10] Had the physical consolidation of land been thought important, we should expect a much
higher proportion of sales and cessions to neighbours; and even
some of the few surviving sales to neighbours suggest the consolidation of relatively large areas rather than the unification of
small plots.[11]

Relevant to this is an edict of the prefect Avidius Heliodorus,
probably dating from 137 A.D., which confirmed prior rights of purchase to joint owners of common property and, failing them, to the
neighbours.[12] Joint ownership was commonly created by inheritance,

---

10 *P. Oxy*. VII 1044, with L. C. Youtie, "P. Oxy. VII 1044,"
ZPE 21 (1976) 1ff. I have some reservations about assuming this to
be typical; this and one other contemporary document, dealing mostly
with the same village, *P. Oxy*. 1459, together account for 33% of the
attested agricultural plots in the nome of less than 1 aroura area,
but only 10% of the plots for which an area is recorded at all.

11 To those listed by Montevecchi (*Aegyptus* 23 [1943] 54) add
P. Mich. 263, 267-68, *P. Oxy*. 2723. In the last (if the transaction
was ever completed; the surviving papyrus contains a copy, with some
details omitted), the purchaser was L. Calpurnius Gaius on behalf of
his son, L. Calpurnius Firmus. The family was prominent in both
local and provincial offices, and participated in an endowment for
the city of Oxyrhynchus, along with Aurelius Horion and his sons;
P. Oxy. 2848. The family was clearly wealthy. The area of the
vineyard conveyed was relatively large; 11-3/4 arouras, although it
was neglected; and land already belonging to Calpurnius Gaius ad-
joined it on three sides.

12 *P. Oxy*. 2954; see J. Herrmann, "Zum Edikt des Präfekten
Gaius Avidius Heliodorus," *ZSS* 92 (1975) 260ff.

and seems to have been regarded as more appropriate among close
relatives than among individuals not otherwise associated.[13] The
highest priority implied by the edict was that a sale should both
reduce the total number of shares and keep ownership confined to
the original partners, who were likely to be relatives; secondly
that the share should be taken by someone with whom the joint
owners would already be familiar, and whose other land was as close
as possible to the shared parcel; only as a last resort could a
total outsider obtain a share.

An alternative explanation of the cessions between close relatives must be considered; one which assumes that there was no intended preference for relations. If the number of landowning families in a village was very small, and these had intermarried, the
probability that the purchaser of land was related to the seller
would be greatly increased; especially if, as is likely, information about land for sale passed by personal contact. There is some
substance in these considerations, particularly with regard to a
village, such as Tebtunis.[14] But the Oxyrhynchite examples are
more likely to have concerned inhabitants of Oxyrhynchus itself,
where the circle of landowning families was much greater; and even
villagers did not confine their sales to fellow-villagers, but had
dealings also with inhabitants of the metropolis.[15] Conscious
preference seems to have played a greater part than chance in pro-
ducing sales between brothers and other close relatives.

---

13 H. C. Youtie, "P. Mich. inv. 148, verso; the rule of precedent," *ZPE* 27 (1977) 124ff.; the remarks of the advocates Apollonius
(col. ii 1.19-col. iii 1.1), and Nilus (col. v 1.11ff.) imply that
family members were thought to have some special right in shares of
joint property. Advocates' remarks are likely to be tendentious,
but not implausible.

14 Many of the documents from the Tebtunis γραφεῖον archive
concern members of four families; those of Lysimachus son of Didymus,
Heracleides the younger, son of Maron, Psyphis also called Harpo-
chration, Eutychus and Thermouthis; the first two were connected by
more than one marriage; *P. Mich.* V, Introduction, pp. 16ff. A small
number of families are similarly prominent in the Pathyris documents; O. Montevecchi, *La Papirologia* (Torino 1973) 250f.

15 *P. Harr.* 138, *P. Oxy.* 1208, 1636, *SB* III 6612; also sale
by a villager to an Alexandrian, *PSI* 897 ii. No certain examples
from the Oxyrhynchite nome attest the sale of agricultural land from
one villager to another; no doubt because records of such transactions would be preserved in the village rather than in the metropolis.

Nevertheless, it need not be supposed that all sales between
relatives represent a desire to reunify property shared out through
partible inheritance. This is only one aspect of a much more general use of sale to modify the operation of relatively inflexible
inheritance and marriage customs.

This can be seen if we turn to another sort of family involvement in sale, the purchase of land by a parent on behalf of a child,
or by a child with the assistance of a parent. Clearly, representation by a parent was a legal requirement if minors were to purchase land; but why should they wish, or their parents wish them,
to do so at all? It is striking how many more minors at Oxyrhynchus are recorded as buying land than selling it, and that in all
but one case, the recipient was a girl.[16]

In the long term, the effect of the purchases would be the
same as if the parent, usually the father, had bought the land in
his own name, to be inherited on his death by the child. In the
short term, however, it enabled parents to provide their offspring
with property in their own lifetime without detracting from their
own land, as did, for instance, the gift from mother to daughter
in P. Oxy. 273.

The fact that so many of the recipients were female suggests
a more precise reason for the purchase. Land does not seem to have
formed part of a dowry proper, although it might be given in addition, ἐν προσφορᾷ.[17] A gift to the daughter before her marriage
had certain advantages over this. A girl who already owned land
might prove more attractive to potential husbands than one with

---

16 Only one sale from Oxyrhynchus by a minor is yet published;
P. Oxy. 1208. Land bought for or by female minors; P. Harr. 138.
11ff., P. Oslo 114, P. Oxy. 633, 1208, 1462, 1470. P. Oxy. 2723 is
the only case of land bought for a minor son (see n. 11). The purchases by or for girls must be distinguished from the case of P.
Amh. 95 (from Hermopolis), a sale by a father to his married daughter, in which the dowry he owed her formed at least part of the
purchase price; see Montevecchi, Aegyptus 23 (1943) 84. The girls
in the examples from Oxyrhynchus were unmarried, although marriage
may have been in view, and their fathers parted with money rather
than with land. P. Amh. 95 may represent an effort to avoid the
situation, discussed below, where provision of a daughter's dowry
denuded the family landholding of necessary financial support.

17 G. Häge, Ehegüterrechtliche Verhältnisse in den griechischen Papyri Ägyptens bis Diokletian (Köln 1968) 47ff., 250ff.

whom land was merely promised; and, if the marriage was unsuccessful, there would perhaps be less possibility of dispute over the ownership of the land if it had been hers alone before marriage.

Both sets of sales and cessions discussed above can be seen to have provided a means of intervening in the normal course of property devolution; modifying it to produce specific advantages (in the case of purchases for young girls), or to eliminate unwanted effects, as with the consolidation of fragmented property ownership. Where the wealth of a family was largely derived from landowning, the existence of several children among whom the land and other property would be divided seriously threatened the continued wealth and social status of the younger generation.[18] Sale permitted greater flexibility in strategies to conserve and increase family wealth against such an eventuality, and allowed for the disposal of plots which were unduly small or otherwise inconvenient.

But no strategy could wholly overcome the impoverishing effects of a large family; among several sons and daughters, parental resources, both in land and money, were bound to be spread more thinly under a system of partible inheritance. Moreover, the practice of granting a dowry to daughters in precious metals rather than land meant that, unless some land was sold to pay for the dowry, the inheritance of the sons would consist of little wealth other than land.

The results of such a situation can perhaps be seen in an involved series of transactions recorded through the γραφεῖον of Tebtunis in the mid-first century A.D.[19] The family of Lysimachus son of Didymus consisted of five brothers and a sister, Hero, who was married to one of the brothers, Didymus the younger. A contract of 35/36 A.D. shows that about two years previously, Didymus had ceded to his wife 10 arouras of catoicic land near Theognis. Part of the price was said already to have been paid; further payment took the form of a valuation of jewellery which Didymus and Hero had received from their father as dowry at their marriage eleven years

---

18 Cycles of family prosperity from wealth to poverty through the generations as a result of partition among offspring is a phenomenon familiar to anthropologists; Fei and Chang, *Earthbound China*, 117; J. Goody, *Production and Reproduction* (Cambridge 1976) 133.

19 *P. Mich.* 262 (35/36 A.D.), 232 (36), 266 (38).

previously. This can perhaps be connected with a transaction
of the following year in which Didymus the younger, along with his
two brothers, Didymus and Lysimachus, and his three nephews, the
heirs of a dead brother, gave up to creditors a total of 82 arouras
inherited from their father after defaulting on a loan at interest
of the large sum of 2 tal. 1,200 dr. Two years later, Hero was
ceded more land, by her brother Lysimachus, who had earlier been
ceded the same plot by Didymus the husband of Hero. Whether Didymus had received a price from Lysimachus is not recorded, but Hero
certainly did not pay a price to Lysimachus.

Hero had not been involved in the loan on which the brothers
defaulted, and indeed seems to have received no land from her father, taking the dowry instead. The brothers, however, inheriting
a large amount of land, but presumably little cash, soon seem to
have felt the need of a loan, which they borrowed from men apparently unrelated to them. But their financial difficulties continued,
and they were not even able to keep up the tax payments on their
mortgaged land.[20] Hero would also have been in a position to offer
them financial assistance; perhaps in fact these "sales" of land
were recompense for help given to her brothers at the time of their
financial embarrassment.

I have argued that the sales and cessions discussed above were
undertaken as adjustments to the "normal" transmission of property
at marriage or through inheritance. Few of these sales were actually fictitious, and to the extent that the adjustments led to
the disposal of land by one family to one unrelated to it, the land
market may even be said to have been stimulated. But if it is essential to a market that the land should be available for purchase
by anyone who wishes to buy, and that the price be determined by
comparison with other transactions of the same kind, rather than by
other social relationships between the contracting parties, then
sales between relatives were clearly not market transactions. The
actual mobility of land was more circumscribed than at first appears
from the number of sale documents which has survived, and I doubt
that there was ever an opportunity for widespread investment purchase of private land.

The Queen's College, Oxford   Jane Rowlandson

---

20 *P. Mich.* 232.20.

DIE ANANEOSIS IN DEN GRÄKO-ÄGYPTISCHEN PAPYRI

Mit der wörtlich übereinstimmenden Feststellung, die *Ananeosis* müsse nun neu betrachtet werden, schlossen 1911 Hunt und genau 60 Jahre später Shelton ihre Kommentare zu *P. Oxy.* VIII 1105 bzw. *P. Mich.* XI 625. Wenn ich der darin enthaltenen Aufforderung folge, so weil es mir möglich erscheint, gerade aufgrund der neuen Urkunden wenigstens für Ägypten eine der bisher hauptsächlich vertretenen Meinungen als unwahrscheinlich auszuschließen; die Duratexte muß ich hier aus Zeitgründen beiseite lassen.

I

Um an die beiden genannten Autoren anzuknüpfen, sie bezeichnen auch die Pole der Meinungen in der *Literatur* für die Texte aus römischer Zeit. Hunt sieht die *Ananeosis* als Erneuerung der Hypothek, Shelton als einen Schritt in der Zwangsvollstreckung aus der Hypothek.

Shelton ist damit zu der älteren und überwiegenden Meinung in der Literatur zurückgekehrt. Der Ausgangspunkt dieser Lehre läßt sich eindeutig festlegen: 1901 deutete Wessely[1] anhand der Klausel in *P. Flor.* I 1.6f. aus dem Jahre 153 p.C. (ἐὰν δὲ μὴ ἀποδοῖ τῆς προθεσμίας ἐνστάσης, εὐθέως ἐξέστω der Gläubigerin ...μὴ προσδεομένοις ἀνανεώσεως ἢ διαστολικοῦ ἢ ἑτέρου τινὸς ἁπλῶς...ἐπικαταβολὴν ποιήσασθαι) die *Ananeosis* als "Mahnung," wobei er von ἀνανεοῦν in einer Polybiosstelle (5,36) ausging, das er als "ins Gedächtnis rufen" faßte. In der Folgezeit verdichtete sich diese Auffassung-- bei aller Betonung der Unsicherheiten--zu der Annahme eines öffentlichen Anerkenntnisses und der Erneuerung der Eintragung im Grundstücksregister,[2] bzw. Erneuerung/Anerkennung der Hypothek zum

---

1 *Anz. der phil.-hist. Classe der Wiener Acad. d. Wiss.,* Jahrg. 1901, 1ff. S. auch Koschaker, *SZ* 29 (1908) 29--allerdings mit erheblichen Reserven (s. auch Anm. 4)--, dem Preisigke (vgl. Anm. 6), *Girowesen im griech. Ägypten* (1910, Neudr. 1971) 321 anscheinend folgt; Rabel, *Verfügungsbeschränkungen des Verpfänders* (1909) 102 = *P. Bas.* 7 Anm. zu Z. 18-19, S. 40.

2 Costa, *BIDR* 17 (1903) 7 und *Mem. Classe Scienze morali della R. Acc. delle Scienze dell' Istituto di Bologna* 1909, 217ff.; auch Mitteis, *SZ* 23 (1902) 302, s. aber auch Anm. 4.

Nachweis ihrer Gültigkeit als Voraussetzung der Zwangsvollstrek-
kung,[3] oder auch nur eines nicht näher bestimmten Schrittes in der
Zwangsvollstreckung.[4] Sie wurde auch als dinglicher Akt--jedoch
ohne nähere Qualifikation gefaßt.[5]

Für die Gegenmeinung, die in der *Ananeosis* vornehmlich eine
zeitliche Verlängerung des Vertragsverhältnisses sieht, ist als
erster Vertreter Preisigke[6] anzuführen, dem P. M. Meyer,[7] Mitteis[8]
und später auch Welles[9] folgten. *P. Enteux.* 15 (= *P. Magd.* 31) ließ
diese Auffassung dann für die ptolemäischen Texte allgemein werden.[10]
Zu einem komplizierten System baute Schönbauer[11] sie aus, der die

---

3 Vitelli, *Atene e Roma* 6 (1903) 333f. Nur von Anerkennung
als Gegenstück zur ἀντίρρησις spricht Welles, *YCS* 2 (1931) 22ff.,
entsprechend in *SZ* 56 (1936) 99ff.; aufgegeben in *P. Dura* S. 114.
Anerkennung und Bekräftigung des alten Vertrags als Schritt in der
Zwangsvollstreckung: Harmon, *YCS* 2 (1931) 28ff.

4 Mitteis, *Grundzüge und Chrestomathie der Papyruskunde* II 1
(1912) zunächst 162f., dann aufgegeben dort XI; Koschaker, *Über einige griechische Rechtsurkunden aus den östlichen Randgebieten des
Hellenismus* (Sächs. Akad. der Wiss., Abh. der phil.-hist. Klasse
42. Bd. Nr. 1, 1931) 65ff.

5 Schwarz, *Hypothek und Hypallagma* (1911) 118; er schließt
die *Ananeosis* in *Symb Osl.* 14 (1935) 77 nicht mehr ohne weiteres in
diesen Zusammenhang ein; *Aegyptus* 17 (1937) 244: Immer noch unklar,
inwieweit die *Ananeosis* eine Voraussetzung für die Geltendmachung
der Hypothek war.

6 *P. Stras.* I 52.7, wobei er allerdings eine Novation unter
Einschluß rückständiger Zinsen anzunehmen scheint. In *FWB* s.v.
ἀνανέωσις noch weitere Varianten: Erneuerung unter Umschreibung auf
neuen Namen (zu *P. Magd.* 31) und jährlich fällige Erneuerung (zu *P.
Oxy.* VIII 1105). S. auch oben Anm. 1.

7 *JurPap* S. 205, unter Hinweis auf *P. Lips.* 33.6ff.

8 *SZ* 32 (1911) 344 und *Grundzüge* XI (s. auch oben Anm. 4).

9 *P. Dura* (1959) S. 114.

10 Koschaker, *Über einige griechische Rechtsurkunden*, 65ff.;
Welles, *YCS* 2 (1931) 22ff.; *SZ* 56 (1936) 124; Harmon, *YCS* 2 (1931)
28 unter Betonung der "Anerkennung"; San Nicolò, *SZ* 52 (1932) 463;
Guéraud, Anm. zu *P. Enteux.* 15 und Shelton zu *P. Mich.* XI 625.
Außerdem siehe auch Flore, *Festschr. Pugliatti* (1978) V, 266. Auf
die ältere Literatur zu *P. Magd.* 31 ist nach der Publikation der
vollständigen Urkunde als *P. Enteux.* 15 nicht mehr einzugehen.

11 S. nur *Beiträge zur Geschichte des Liegenschaftsrecht im
Altertum* (1924) 90ff.; *SZ* 52 (1932) 341; *SZ* 53 (1933) 433ff. Ihm
scheint Taubenschlag, *Law*[2] (1955) 282 für die ptolemäische Zeit zu
folgen.

unter öffentlicher Kontrolle vorzunehmende Erneuerung als Voraussetzung des Fortbestandes der Hypothekenhaftung ansah, wobei die
Hypothek seiner Meinung nach nur für jeweils ein Jahr wirksam bestellt werden konnte.

Wenger[12] konstatierte ein *non liquet*, neigte aber zu der Möglichkeit eines formellen Schuldanerkenntnisses mit Novationswirkung.
Seidl[13] schließlich faßt die *Ananeosis* vom Namen her als Novation--
auch bei Texten, die diesen Ausdruck nicht gebrauchen.

II

Das nicht sehr umfangreiche und sogleich vorzuführende Urkun-
denmaterial ist der Zahl nach seit den Dreißigerjahren nicht
wesentlich vermehrt worden, bietet aber durch die neuen Michigan-
Texte nun die Chance einer Lösung.

(1) Wir haben an Quellen aus *ptolemäischer Zeit*: *P. Enteux.*
14,15 und *P. Ryl.* IV 584, sowie einen Vermerk über die Zahlung
eines τέλος ἀνανεώσεως in *P. Tebt.* III 1 814, alles Urkunden aus
dem 3. Jh. a. C. In allen vier Belegen handelt es sich um Hypotheken.

In *P. Enteux.* 15 (= *P. Magd.* 31),[14] dem wohl bekanntesten Fall,
hatte der verstorbene Bruder des Petenten dem Gläubiger einen Weingarten für ein Darlehn von 3.000 Dr. hypotheziert. Der Schuldner
war verstorben und von seinem Bruder, dem minderjährigen Petenten
beerbt worden. Die Fälligkeit der Schuld nahte[15] und der Gläubiger
ἐπιχωρεῖ συνανανεώσασθαι (Z. 5). Die *Ananeosis* konnte aber vom
Erben wegen seiner Minderjährigkeit nicht abgeschlossen werden,
deshalb drohte die ἐπικαταβολή des Pfandes. Der Antrag, dem anscheinend entsprochen wurde, richtete sich auf die Genehmigung zur
Vornahme der *Ananeosis* durch den Gläubiger auf den Namen des Erb-
lassers Hermias.

---

12 Wenger, *APF* 10 (1932) 134f.

13 *Ptol. RG*[2] (1962) 135f., 122.

14 S. hierzu Schönbauer, *Liegenschaftsrecht*, 91ff. u. auch
oben Anm. 10. Vgl. auch H. J. Wolff, *Das Recht der griechischen
Papyri Ägyptens* II (1978) 81 Anm. 2 mit weiterer Literatur; hier
nur Verbuchung in öffentlichen Registern anzunehmen, erscheint zu
eng.

15 Henne, *Eos* 48,2 (1956) 95ff.

P. Enteux. 14 ist die Eingabe eines Soldaten, der seinen
Stathmos in einem hypothezierten Hause hatte. Dieses Haus war dem
Gläubiger anheim gefallen, der nach Fälligkeit der Schuld die *Ana-*
neosis abgelehnt und später den Soldaten hinausgeworfen hatte.
Soweit der sehr fragmentarische *P. Ryl.* IV 584 erkennen läßt,
ist ein Weingarten als Hypothek gegeben. Falls die Schuldnerin das
Grundstück ordnungsgemäß bearbeitet, soll vom Gläubiger die *Ananeo-*
sis--evtl. auf ein weiteres Jahr--durchgeführt werden; diese Ver-
pflichtung des Gläubigers ist mit einer Strafklausel zugunsten der
Schuldnerin bewehrt.

P. Tebt. III 1 814.59ff.: Die Schuldnerin zahlt das τέλος ἀνανεώσεως von 2% für ein mit Hypothek belastetes Haus. Das zugrunde
liegende Darlehn lief--ausweislich der erwähnten Zinsen--bereits
zwei Jahre; ob schon eine *Ananeosis* vorausgegangen war, ist nicht
ersichtlich, ebenso wenig ob und warum nun eine *Ananeosis* vorge-
nommen wurde.

Allen diesen Texten ist gemeinsam, daß die *Ananeosis* hier
jedenfalls keinen Schritt in der Zwangsvollstreckung darstellt. In
P. Enteux. 15 und *P. Ryl.* IV 584 wird gerade deutlich, daß der
Pfandverfall ausgeschlossen werden soll. Nach inzwischen allge-
meiner Meinung bedeutet *Ananeosis* hier eine Vertragsverlängerung,[16]
allerdings nicht in der technischen Form einer Novation,[17] sondern
eher durch Hinausschieben der Fälligkeitsfrist.

(2) Aus *römischer Zeit* sind zu nennen: Die drei durch Hypothek
gesicherten Darlehn in *P. Flor.* I 81 (103), *P. Stras.* I 52 (151)
und *P. Flor.* I 1 = *MChr.* 243 = *JurPap* 68 (153), alle aus Hermopolis
Magna, und die Steuerquittungen: *P. Oxy.* VIII 1105 (81-96), II 274
= *MChr.* 193 = *JurPap* 60 = *FIRA* III 104 (89/97), *P. Oslo* III 118
(111/112), *P. Mich.* XI 625 (121) und der noch unveröffentlichte P.
Mich. Inv. 138 (wohl etwa der gleichen Zeit). Sonstige Belege sind
aus Ägypten[18] nicht bekannt geworden. Die bereits oben genannte

---

16 S. oben Anm. 10.

17 So z.B. Preisigke *FWB* s.v.: Novation durch "Umschreibung
auf andere Namen." Zur Novation s. Rupprecht, *Untersuchungen zum*
Darlehn (1967) 146f.

18 Aus Palästina s. *P. Mur.* 115 = *SB* XII 10305 (124): Wieder-
heirat nach vorangegangener Scheidung zwischen denselben Partnern:
ἐξ ἀνανεώσεως καταλλάξαι.

einschlägige Klausel der drei Verträge lautet: ἐὰν δὲ μὴ ἀποδοῖ τῆς προθεσμίας ἐνστάσης, εὐθέως ἐξέστω der Gläubigerin ...μὴ προσδεομένοις ἀνανεώσεως ἢ διαστολικοῦ ἢ ἑτέρου τινὸς ἁπλῶς...ἐπικαταβολὴν ποιήσασθαι (*P. Flor.* I 1 u. 81) bzw. μετεπιγραφῆναι (*P. Stras.* I 52).

Von den Steuerquittungen bezieht sich eine auf eine Hypothek allein (*P. Oxy.* II 274), zwei auf Hypotheken mit ἐνοίκησις (*P. Oslo* III 118, *P. Oxy.* VIII 1105) und zwei auf bloße ἐνοίκησις (*P. Mich.* XI 625 und Inv. 138), wobei uns für Nummer 625 auch in *P. Mich.* III 188 der entsprechende Vertrag erhalten ist. Die Urkunden stammen aus dem Arsinoites und aus Oxyrhynchos.

Für diese Texte ist nun, wie bereits gesagt, streitig, ob *Ananeosis* als Vertragsverlängerung oder als Schritt in der Zwangsvollstreckung, jeweils mit Entstehung einer Steuerschuld, zu fassen ist.

Wenn man als Ausgangspunkt die ptolemäische Deutung wählt, dann liegt auch hier der Gedanke einer Vertragsverlängerung im Sinne des Hinausschiebens der Fälligkeit nahe. Also wie Preisigke formulierte, der Gläubiger kann die ἐπικαταβολή, den Anfall des Pfandes an sich[19] herbeiführen, ohne sich auf eine Vertragsverlängerung einlassen zu müssen.[19a]

Wenn man eine neue Bedeutung annehmen will--und dies ist nach drei Jahrhunderten ja nicht ausgeschlossen--dann jedenfalls ist ein Beweis hierfür zu erbringen.

Die Bedeutung von ἀνανέωσις und ἀνανεοῦσθαι in den Inschriften und bei den Schriftstellern hat Daux untersucht[20] mit dem Ergebnis, daß bei völkerrechtlichen Verträgen, Proxenieverleihungen u.ä. ein fast technischer Befund festzustellen war i.S. von: einem Recht,

---

19 Meyer, *JurPap*, S. 205f.

19a Als Ausschluß einer Vertragsverlängerung könnte auch die in demot. Pachtverträgen der Ptolemäerzeit mitunter begegnende Wendung: "nicht soll ich sagen können: ein Pachtvertrag, der umzuwenden ist um 1 Jahr, ist das..." (*P. Rein.* dem. 1.18 und 5.24) aufzufassen sein (Hinweis von Herrn Zauzich). Vgl. hierzu Sethe-Partsch, *Urkunden zum Bürgschaftsrecht vornehmlich der Ptolemäerzeit* (Sächs. Akad. der Wiss., Abh. der phil.-hist. Klasse, 32. Band, 1920) 197; Mattha, *The Demotic Legal Code of Hermopolis West* (1975) Col. II 32.

20 *Mélanges Desrousseaux* (1937) 117f. S. auch die Solon zugeschriebene eheberaterische Anordnung bei Plutarch, *Amat.* 769A.

das nicht mehr ausgeübt aber auch niemals abgeschafft wurde, seine
Wirksamkeit zurückgeben, bzw. einen Vertrag mit neuem Leben er-
füllen. Wo ἀνανεοῦσθαι--wenn auch zahlenmäßig von sehr viel geringerer Bedeutung--i.s. von von "erinnern" benutzt wird, heißt es
aber konkret, "sich erinnern" und nicht "anderen ins Gedächtnis
zurückrufen."

In den Papyri begegnet *Ananeosis* vornehmlich bei der Wieder-
herstellung von Bauwerken.[21] Das scheint mir auf unsere Frage ge-
wendet, zumindest nicht für "Mahnung" und "Anerkenntnis" als einen
notwendigen Schritt im Rahmen der Zwangsvollstreckung zu sprechen,
sondern eher für ein "am Leben erhalten" durch Verlängerung der
Laufzeit eines Vertrages.

Nun noch näher zu den juristischen Papyri im einzelnen: Die
Klausel der drei Vertragsurkunden ist zeitlich auf die Jahre 103-
153 und örtlich auf Hermopolis Magna beschränkt; sie ist in dieser
Gestalt sonst nicht belegt. Schon dies spricht gegen eine besondere
Bedeutung im Rahmen der Zwangsvollstreckung. Die sonst auftretenden
Erleichterungen für den Gläubiger in der Zwangsvollstreckung[22] sind
technisch scharf gefasst und stellen auf die Befreiung von διαστολή,
πρόσκλησις, παραγγελία ab. Eine Identifizierung mit diesen Begrif-
fen erscheint willkürlich, wie schon Koschaker[23] bemerkte, wenn-
gleich der Zusammenhang dazu verleiten mag. Ein als *Ananeosis*
eines Vertrages deklarierter Akt liegt bislang nicht vor.[24]

---

21   S. nur *SB* V 8318 (164), 7791 (159); *Stud. Pal.* V 95 (II/
III); *APF* 2 445 Nr. 67 (II); *P. Panop. Beatty* 2.224 (III). Weitere
Belege s. Preisigke *WB* s.v. Unklar bleiben *BGU* VI 1222.23 (II a.C.),
P. Tebt. I 5.186 (118 a.C.).

22   *BGU* IV 1131 II.54 (13 a.C., Alexandria), 1158 = *MChr.* 234
= *JurPap* 67.15 (9 a.C., Alexandria); *P. Fouad* I 44.27 (44, Oxy.);
P. Bas. 7.18f. (II, Fayum). Vgl. auch Schwarz, *Symb Osl.* 14 (1935)
77f.; Koschaker, *Über einige griechische Rechtsurkunden*, 65ff.;
Rabel, *P. Bas.* S. 40f.

23   S. Anm. 22; s. auch Meyer, *JurPap* S. 205.

24   Vom Herausgeber wird eine *Ananeosis* für möglich erachtet
bei *P. Oslo* II 40 A/B (150, Oxy.) (Anm. zu Z. 63ff.). 40 A (13.
Jahr): Darlehn bis zum 30. Mesore des 13. Jahres gesichert durch
eine Sklavin. Am 3. epagomenen Tag des 13. Jahres, d.h. drei Tage
nach Fälligkeit wird ein Darlehn bis zum 30. Mecheir des 14. Jahres
gegeben unter Sicherung durch Hypothek auf Land (40 B.). 40 B Z.
63ff. wird die Praxis vorbehalten für die Schuld aus 40 A. Damit
wird diese Urkunde über den Fälligkeitstermin hinaus aufrecht

Nun zu den Steuerquittungen: Für die Hypothek war eine Steuer
(ἐγκύκλιον) von 2% der Schuld zu entrichten, die Zahlung erfolgt in
der Regel durch den Gläubiger.[25] So auch in den Steuerquittungen
über *Ananeosis* der Hypothek bzw. der ἐνοίκησις. Aus der Tatsache
der Zahlung durch den Gläubiger läßt sich allerdings kein zwingendes
Argument ziehen,[26] denn damit ist noch nichts über die endgültige
Lastenverteilung gesagt. So haben wir drei Fälle, in denen der
Schuldner letztlich die Hypothekensteuer zu tragen und sie dem
Gläubiger zu erstatten hat.[27]

Der erste bekannt gewordene Beleg für das τέλος ἀνανεώσεως (*P.
Oxy.* II 274), ein Diastroma, wurde fast allgemein für die Erklärung
i.S. der Vollstreckungslösung in Anspruch genommen. Auf dem Per-
sonalfolium des Gläubigers ist eine Hypothek für drei Forderungen
aus den Jahren 88 und 89 vermerkt. Am 28.8.93 zahlt der Gläubiger

---

erhalten. Eine ausdrückliche Fristverlängerung findet nicht statt,
auch nicht die Festsetzung eines Tages, bis zu welchem der Gläubiger nicht vollstrecken wird. Ob hier in der Tat eine *Ananeosis*
stattgefunden hat, muß offen bleiben; der Gläubiger hatte gegen
weitere Sicherheit ein neues Darlehn gegeben und klargestellt, daß
damit keine Novation des ersten Darlehns beabsichtigt war, da auch
diese Urkunde noch in Kraft war. Eine *Ananeosis* im Sinne einer
Verlängerung der Laufzeit des Darlehns kommt hier nicht zum Ausdruck, ebensowenig ein Schritt in der Zwangsvollstreckung. Zur Urk.
s. auch Schwarz, *Aegyptus* 17 (1937) 248f.

25 Vgl. Wallace, *Taxation in Egypt* (1938) 229f. und Schwarz,
Hypothek u. Hypallagma, 58ff. S. auch *P. Oxy.* II 243, *P. Lond.* III
1201 (S. 3), 1202 (S. 5). Sehr unsicher ist *P. Mert.* III 109.23ff.;
anders der ptolemäische Text *P. Tebt.* III 1.814, s. oben II 1.

26 In dieser Richtung aber Wessely a.a.O. (s. oben Anm. 1);
Koschaker, *Über einige griechische Rechtsurkunden*, 65ff.; Welles,
SZ 56 (1936) 124ff. Siehe auch Shelton, Komm. zu *P. Mich.* XI 625.

27 *P. Oxy.* III 510 (101): Darlehn mit Hypothek auf 1 Jahr;
der Gläubiger hatte die Steuer entrichtet und quittiert nun bei Darlehnsrückzahlung auch die Erstattung der Steuern. *P. Flor.* I 86.
21 (I): Drei Hypotheken wurden bestellt und die Steuern gezahlt (Z.
12); der Erbe des Gläubigers mahnt nun den Schuldner zur Zahlung
der Schuld und verlangt auch Erstattung der Steuern, die nur für
die Hypothek gezahlt worden sein können; ob auch für *Ananeosis* der
Hypothek ist nicht gesagt. *P. Flor.* I 56.15 (234): Die Zwangsvollstreckung soll auch wegen der Steuern stattfinden. *P. Oxy.* III
511 (103) ist in diesem Zusammenhang nicht aussagekräftig, da bei
der Darlehnsaufnahme für τέλος ὑποθήκης nicht deutlich wird, ob der
Darlehnsnehmer Gläubiger oder Schuldner der hypothekengesicherten
Forderung ist.

die Steuer für *Ananeosis*,[28] am 28.8.94 das τέλος ἐπικαταβολῆς, und
am 10.1.97 erfolgt die ἐμβάδεια in das Grundstück. Der Zusammenhang legt einen Akt der Zwangsvollstreckung nahe, beweist ihn aber
nicht. Über die Laufzeit der Darlehn und der Hypothek ist nichts
gesagt; eine schon vorhergehende Verlängerung, die--wenn wir *P.*
Oxy. VIII 1105 glauben dürfen--jährlich zu erfolgen hat, ist nicht
ausgeschlossen, ihre Nichterwähnung aus der Tatsache der Übertra-
gung aus dem alten Diastroma auf das neue Folium vielleicht erklärlich, eine Verlängerung der Hypothekenfrist auch möglich angesichts
der sonst recht kurzen Laufzeit der Hypotheken; dazu aber gleich.

P. *Oxy.* VIII 1105 enthält die Anweisung zur Anagraphe eines
hypothekarisch gesicherten Darlehns auf drei Jahre mit Zinsantichrese durch Wohnrecht unter der Bedingung jährlicher Zahlung der
Steuer für die *Ananeosis*.[29] Diese jährliche Steuer für die Erneuerung ist sonst nicht belegt, die nicht recht sichere Lesung wurde
deshalb auch angezweifelt.[30] Das Fehlen sonstiger Belege ist jedoch erklärlich aus der Übung, Hypotheken sonst nur recht kurz-
fristig zu bestellen. So sind von 16 Hypotheken mit angegebener
Laufzeit 10 für bis zu einem Jahr bestellt, und nur 6 für eine längere Zeit.[31] Vom Gläubiger gewährte Verlängerungen durch Hinausschieben der Fälligkeitsfrist werden nur in Ausnahmefällen vorge-
kommen sein, so wenn der Gläubiger auf den lukrativen Pfandverfall
zu verzichten bereit war. Im konkreten Fall hier war also aus fiskalischen Gesichtspunkten zumindest eine Steuer für die *Ananeosis*
jährlich zu entrichten--um so eine Angleichung an die übrigen Fälle
wenigstens steuerlich zu erreichen, wenn auch eine *Ananeosis* angesichts der dreijährigen Laufzeit tatsächlich nicht erfolgt sein mag.

Von Interesse ist ferner, daß das τέλος ἀνανεώσεως sich auch
in *P. Oslo* III 118, *P. Mich.* 625 und P. Mich. Inv. 138 auf Fälle

---

28 Vgl. v. Woess, *Untersuchungen über das Urkundenwesen und*
den Publizitätsschutz im röm. Ägypt. (1924) 246.

29 Z. 20f.: [ἐ]φ᾽ ᾧ κατ᾽ ἔτος τὴν ἀναγε[ώσ]εως τάξεται...;
vgl. auch zur Berechnung des Betrags den Kommentar zu Z. 21.

30 S. Shelton zu *P. Mich.* XI 625; für jährliche Steuerzahlung
schon Naber, *APF* 1 (1901) 314.

31 Eine andere Frage ist es, ob die Darlehnsrückzahlung in
diesen Fällen auch fristgerecht erfolgte.

mit ἐνοίκησις bezieht. *P. Oslo* III 118 ist die Quittung für die
Steuer für das vergangene Jahr; leider ist das Datum der Vertragsur-
kunde und die Laufzeit des Darlehns nicht bekannt. Antichresen nun
laufen vorwiegend über längere Zeit als die gerade genannten Hypotheken, so von 14 Verträgen mit erkennbarer Laufzeit 11 mehr als
ein Jahr, bzw. auf unbestimmte Zeit, nur 3 bis zu einem Jahr. Ob
aus der auch aus *P. Mich.* XI 625/Inv. 138 folgenden steuerlichen
Gleichbehandlung von Hypothek und ἐνοίκησις auch materiell-recht-
liche Schlüsse gezogen werden können, kann hier dahinstehen. Die
Steuer für ἐνοίκησις entspricht jedenfalls der für Hypotheken: 2%
des Darlehnsbetrags.[32] Ich darf einstweilen festhalten, sowohl *P.
Oxy.* VIII 1105 als auch *P. Oslo* III 118 sind unter steuerrechtlichen
Gesichtspunkten einleuchtend zu erklären als Steuer für die *Ananeosis* des Vertrags i.S. einer Vertragsverlängerung, die im Einzelfall
nicht nötig gewesen sein mag; ein Schritt in der Zwangsvollstreckung
erscheint hier ausgeschlossen.

Nun zu der die neue Diskussion auslösenden Urkunde: *P. Mich.* XI
625. Am 19.9.121 wurde die Steuer für ϑέσις ἐνοικήσεως καὶ ἀνανεώσεως gezahlt; der zugrunde liegende Vertrag stammt vom 18.8.120,
nämlich *P. Mich.* III 188, ein Darlehn mit Zinsantichrese durch Wohnrecht an einem ganzen Haus, wohl bekannt aus einer Reihe von
Michigan-Texten. Shelton[33] glaubt hier die *Ananeosis* als Schritt
der Zwangsvollstreckung erklären zu müssen, da der Vertrag selbst
auf unbestimmte Zeit abgeschlossen worden war. Dies erscheint unwahrscheinlich. Einmal verwundert, daß die Steuer für eine Maßnahme
der Zwangsvollstreckung schon mit der Steuer für den Abschluß des
Vertrags fällig werden soll. Zum anderen:[34] Die Gläubigerin aus Nr.
188 gibt im Jahre 123 (Nr. 189) der Tauris ein Darlehn von 60 Dr.
auf unbestimmte Zeit, gekoppelt mit einer Zinsantichrese für ein
Wohnrecht an 4/27 eben dieses Hauses. Die Steuerquittung Inv. 138
letztlich wird ausgestellt für τέλος ἀνανεώσεως für ein Darlehn der
gleichen Gläubigerin an die gleiche Schuldnerin über 200 Dr.--also

---

32 Siehe auch Wallace, *Taxation in Egypt*, 230.

33 *P. Mich.* XI S. 100.

34 So schon in meiner Besprechung von *P. Mich.* XI in *SZ* 89
(1972) 401f.

nicht identisch mit Nr. 189[35]--gleichfalls mit Zinsantichrese durch
Wohnrecht an 4/27 wohl des gleichen Hauses. Wenn die *Ananeosis* in
Nr. 625 ein Teil der Zwangsvollstreckung gewesen wäre, warum hat
die Gläubigerin nicht das ganze Haus erworben, wo doch das Wohnrecht das ganze Haus erfasste? Wieso auch gibt sie noch zweimal
Darlehn, offensichtlich um ein Wohnrecht an 4/27 zu erwerben?
Wahrscheinlich jedenfalls ist, daß sie Inhaberin der anderen 23/27
dieses Hauses ist, denn sie zahlt wirtschaftlich in Nr. 189 einen
um ein Drittel höheren Mietzins als in Nr. 188 und in Inv. 138 ein-
en viermal höheren.

Die Erklärung scheint mir wieder im fiskalischen Bereich zu
liegen. Das τέλος ἀνανεώσεως wurde fällig--gegebenenfalls jährlich
--ohne Rücksicht auf die von den Parteien gewählte Vertragsdauer,
dies schon um Umgehungsgeschäfte zu vermeiden. Daß die sogen.
wirtschaftliche Betrachtungsweise des Steuerrechts auf diese Art
und Weise schon in das 2. Jahrhundert nach Chr. zurückverlegt wird,
mag nicht für jedermann tröstlich sein. Die *Ananeosis* ist, wie hier
deutlich wird, kein Schritt in der Zwangsvollstreckung, sondern
eine Verlängerung der Vertragsdauer durch Hinausschieben der Fälligkeit, entsprechend also der ptolemäischen Bedeutung. Damit erklärt
sich auch zwanglos, daß es bisher noch nicht gelungen ist, einen
Platz der *Ananeosis* im Verfahren der Zwangsvollstreckung deutlich
zu machen,[36] und die Anknüpfung an die *reparatio temporum* in *P.
Lips.* I 33.6 (ἀνανέωσις τῶν χρόνων)[37] liegt nahe.

                                        Hans-Albert Rupprecht

---

35 Die in *SZ* 89 (1972) 401 noch vertretene Verbindung wird
aufgegeben.

36 Vgl. Schwartz, *Aegyptus* 17 (1937) 244 Anm. 2; der Ansatz
von Harmon, *YCS* 2 (1931) 28 ff. bezieht sich auf die ptolemäische
Zeit, wo aber der gegenteilige Sinn feststeht.

37 So schon Meyer, *JurPap* S. 205; vgl. auch Kaser, *Römische
Zivilprozeßrecht* (1966) 459.

Proceedings of the XVI Int. Congr. of Papyrology (Chico 1981) 389-403

GREEKS AND ROMANS AT SOCNOPAIOU NESOS

The point of departure for this paper is a passage in Wessely's monograph on Karanis and Socnopaiou Nesos in which he remarks on the number of Roman names found among the papyri from these two villages.[1] His observation seems entirely consistent with the prevailing notion that the Roman presence in Egypt, and particularly in the fertile oasis of the Fayum, was extensive. Indeed, recent studies on the land-holding populations of Karanis and Philadelphia in the late second and early third centuries have pointed to the fact that Roman citizens owned a large amount of land in those villages. Boak, writing in 1955,[2] had counted seventy-two Roman citizens paying property taxes on the Karanis tax rolls for the years 171-174, as against about 600 Greco-Egyptian poll-tax payers. Thus based on his calculations we could suppose that Romans constituted perhaps eight percent of the total population of Karanis at this time. A more recent study by Geremek,[3] based on a more extensive analysis of the same tax rolls, has revealed that among the Karanis land-holders the Roman names increase proportionately with the size of the properties, which indicates that the Romans figured prominently among the large landowners around that village.

---

1 Karl Wessely, *Karanis und Soknopaiu Nesos* (Vienna 1900) 45, "Römische Namen treffen wir allenthalben."

2 A.E.R. Boak, *Historia* 4 (1955) 159. His analysis is based on the information provided by the Karanis tax rolls published in *P. Mich.* IV. Boak does not indicate what proportion of the property owners of Karanis the Roman citizens represent, but merely what is the proportion of Roman property holders in comparison with Greco-Egyptian taxpayers.

3 H. Geremek, *Karanis, Communauté Rurale de l'Egypte Romaine au IIe-IIIe Siècle de Notre Ere* (Warsaw 1969) Annexe, 105ff. and esp. tables IX, X, XII. Note that Geremek's statistics are presented in terms of percentages whereas Boak discusses only numbers of individuals, so it is somewhat difficult to correlate the two analyses. Nevertheless, they concur that there were significant numbers of Roman property owners in Karanis at the time.

A similar situation is suggested for Philadelphia in the early
third century. Oates has made a study[4] of property ownership in
Philadelphia based on an unpublished Yale papyrus (P. Yale Inv. 296)
which contains a list of 167 Philadelphia residents who own private
land in the years 216/217 A.D. Among these, thirty-three are identifiable as Roman citizens, because they are designated as veterans
or soldiers. Thus at least twenty percent of the property owners
of Philadelphia at this time were Romans.

As for the Greeks in these villages, the hellenization of the
Fayum is so thoroughly taken for granted that Boak, Geremek and
Oates all follow the usual practice of describing the indigenous
(i.e. non-Roman) population as Greco-Egyptian, since the distinction between Greeks and hellenized Egyptians had become blurred by
the Roman period.[5]

In the absence of evidence to the contrary, we are inclined
to assume that what has been shown to be the situation for one village is equally true for all of the other villages in the vicinity.
Thus we would automatically assume that Socnopaiou Nesos would be,
like Karanis and Philadelphia, a village with a significant Roman
population and a hellenized indigenous population. This is not the
case at all. Socnopaiou Nesos was, in fact, astonishingly unaffected by the Roman occupation of Egypt, and only peripherally affected
by its previous hellenization. In this respect, and in others as
well, I believe that it is distinctly different from the villages
to the east, such as Karanis and Philadelphia. Wessely's observation about the numbers of Romans is based partly on the deceptive

---

4   J. F. Oates, *Atti dell'XI Congresso Internazionale di Papirologia* (Milan 1966) 451-74, and *Proceedings of the XII International Congress of Papyrology* (Toronto 1971) 385-87.

5   On the question of interrelationships between Greeks and
Egyptians, the literature is extensive, though mostly for the Pto-
lemaic period; see esp. W. Peremans, *Cd'E* 11 (1936) 151-62; idem,
"Egyptiens et Etrangers dans l'Egypte Ptolemaïque," *Fondation Hardt,
Entretiens* 8 (Geneva 1961) 121-55; idem in *Recherches sur les Struc-
tures Sociales dans l'Antiquité Classique* (Caen 1969) 213-23; idem,
Ancient Society 1 (1970) 25-38; Dorothy Crawford, *Kerkeosiris, An
Egyptian Village in the Ptolemaic Period* (Cambridge 1971) ch. IX
"Nomenclature," 132-38 (with the references cited therein); A. E.
Samuel, *Proceedings of the XII International Congress of Papyrology*,
443-53; V. Martin, *Akten des VIII Internationalen Kongresses für
Papyrologie* (*MPER* N.S. 5, Vienna 1956) 85-90.

impression created by amalgamating the papyri from the two villages
and treating them as reflections of a single phenomenon. It is
also the result of failing to distinguish between those whose names
merely appear in some context in connection with the village and
those who are demonstrably residents of it.[6] If we are to obtain
an accurate picture of the life of the village, it is critical that
we make such distinctions.

This paper is based on a study of all of the Greek papyri
which can be identified as having a connection with Socnopaiou
Nesos, a total of about 1000 documents at this point. Since all
but twenty-five of these texts are from the Roman period, the analysis which follows will not take into consideration any of the
evidence from the Ptolemaic period. Among these numerous texts
from the Roman period (the latest of which is dated 239 A.D.),
there occur about 6500 names, of which perhaps 600 could be said
to be Greek or possibly Greek, and a handful are Roman. All of the
rest are authentically Egyptian. If one tabulates only those individuals who are specifically identified as residents of the village
of Socnopaiou Nesos, then the proportion of Egyptian to non-Egyptian
names is even greater.

The most decisive way of demonstrating the thoroughly Egyptian
character of this village is to examine the ethnic composition of
the property-owning class of the population. It would be gratui-
tous to present an analysis of the number of state farmers who were
Egyptians, since one would expect to find little evidence of hellenization or romanization at the lowest level of the society.[7] Furthermore, the statistics derived for Romans in Karanis and Philadelphia were, as we have seen, based on an analysis of landholders

---

6 Of the nineteen documents cited by Wessely (supra n. 1),
only seven involve Socnopaiou Nesos, and of these seven, five are
lists of names (P. Lond. II 369 [p. 265], BGU II 426, BGU II 630,
SPP XXII 67, 181) in which the "Roman" name which he cites is actually conspicuous for its rarity on a roster of otherwise completely Egyptian names. Thus the significance of the names which
he cites, when examined in the contexts in which they appear, is
that they indicate the paucity, rather than the abundance, of Romans
in the village.

7 Peremans in Recherches (op. cit., n. 5) 213, points out that
for the Ptolemaic period the population is increasingly Egyptian as
you descend the social scale; but see infra, n. 27.

in these villages; thus for the purposes of comparison we must look at the analogous segment of the Socnopaiou Nesos population.

The first point of difference between our village and the other two can be detected when one looks at the kind of evidence which is available about owners of property. We do not have for Socnopaiou Nesos any of those large lists of landholders which we have for Karanis and Philadelphia, and for other villages of the Fayum such as Theadelphia, Tebtunis, or Kerkeosiris. There is some significance to the absence of such documentation, and I will come to this point further on. In the absence of such lists, we can only compile an index of property owners from more diverse sources: not only are there pieces of farming land, but also houses within the village, camels and donkeys, slaves, and capital. If we look at all the various documents which give evidence for these forms of property ownership, we can compile a list of those who owned property of one sort or another, and from this list we can determine with some accuracy the ethnic composition of what must have been the highest stratum of the society.[8]

There are thirty-two documents[9] involving real estate transactions, from which we can obtain the names of people who owned

---

8 All the works cited supra, n. 5 discuss the difficulties involved in determining ethnic from names. In the case of Socnopaiou Nesos, however, the proportion of completely unhellenized Egyptian names is so overwhelming that the question of the ethnic identity of those with apparently hellenized names is perhaps not so critical for an understanding of the general character of the village population.

9 Throughout these tabulations I include only those documents where the text is complete enough to allow us to identify the parties involved; the figures given represent total individuals, so a person who, for example, appears in two documents as a buyer of property (as, e.g. the buyer in *SB* 5247 and *P. Vindob. Tandem* 25) will only be counted once. The documents involving sales of property within the village (listed in chronological order) are: *SB* I 5246, *SB* I 5231, *SB* I 5108, *P. Ryl.* II 160a, *P. Ryl.* II 160c, *P. Ryl.* II 310 descr., *P. Ryl.* V 160b, *P. Stras.* IV 265, *P. Stras.* VII 602, *P. Ryl.* II 160d (= *SB* I 5109 + *SB* I 5110), *BGU* III 854, *P. Vindob. Tandem* 24 (incl. *CPR* I 217), *SB* I 5247, *P. Vindob. Tandem* 25, *CPR* I 4 = *M. Chr.* 159, *SB* I 5117, *BGU* I 184/*P. Stras.* IV 208 (different stages of the same transaction), *PSI* XIII 1319 = *SB* V 8952, *P. Ryl.* II 161, *BGU* XI 2095, *P. Ryl.* II 313 descr., *PSI* XIII 1320 = *SB* V 8950, *P. Ryl.* II 312 descr., *CPR* I 220, *BGU* I 350, *P. Vindob. Tandem* 26, *P. Ryl.* II 162, *P. Lond.* II 334 (p. 211; a receipt for deposit on a property), *P. Amh.* II 97 (application to buy confiscated

houses in Socnopaiou Nesos. In addition there are twelve property
registrations[10] and seventeen census declarations,[11] all of which
record home ownership in the village. There are surprisingly few
documents which either record or imply ownership of agricultural
land by Socnopaiou Nesos residents, and none of the land in these
documents is in Socnopaiou Nesos itself. There are only ten texts[12]
which contain this kind of information, and these include mortgages,
rental agreements, and a receipt for naubion. There are also seven

---

property), *SPP* XXII 42 (deposit on sale of property), *SB* X 10571,
P. Vindob. Tandem 25a (incl. *CPR* I 221). In order not to inflate
the statistics, I have not included among the property buyers the
fifty-one S.N. priests who sell an empty lot to a S.N. person in
P. Vindob. Tandem 25a.

10 Property registrations are: *SPP* XXII 175, *BGU* XI 2098,
BGU XI 2100, *BGU* XI 2097, *P. Ryl.* II 107, *BGU* II 536 (including
shares of five houses and 1 5/6 arouras of *catoecic land near Heraklia*), *SPP* XXII 25, *SPP* XXII 23 (report of income from rental), *P.
Gen.* 27, *BGU* XI 2094, *BGU* III 870 (extract from public records),
SPP XXII 34. The parties involved in *BGU* XI 2098, 2100, 2097 are
all members of the same family; each is counted only once. From
this list I have excluded *BGU* II 420, a fragmentary registration
of land near Kerkesoucha in which the registrant is identified as
being from S.N. on the basis of the tenuous reading at line 4, ἀπὸ
Σ[οκνοπ(αίου) Νήσου(?)].

11 Census declarations are: *BGU* III 706, *P. Amh.* II 74, *BGU*
XIII 2227, *P. Grenf.* II 55 (= *BGU* I 90, 224, 225, IV 410, 537),
BGU XIII 2221, *BGU* XIII 2228, *P. Flor.* III 301, *P. Flor.* I 102, *P.
Rein.* I 46, *SB* III 6696, *BGU* XI 2090, *SPP* II, pp. 28-31 (includes
census declarations of five priests of the 3rd phyle).

12 Documents in this group are: *BGU* II 644 (rental of 20 arouras of catoecic land around Philopator Apias, owned by S.N. men),
CPR I 240 (rental of 6-1/2 arouras of catoecic land around Heraklia),
P. Ryl. II 192 (receipt for payment of naubion on catoecic land in
Heraklia), *BGU* III 959 (extract from public records; receipt for
rent on 3 arouras of catoecic land near Apias), *P. Grenf.* I 47 (petition to dekadarch regarding a kleros of 4 arouras near Heraklia),
P. Lond. II 311 (p. 219, a loan secured against 5 arouras of catoecic land near Heraklia and two slaves), *P. IFAO* I 33 (sale of property near Heraklia), *SB* VI 9582 (registration of dry land; 5-1/4
arouras of catoecic land near Heraklia), P. Mich. Inv. 6167 = *ZPE*
33 (1979) 198f. #3 (declaration of uninundated land; 5 arouras catoecic land near Apias), *P. Bour.* 17 (offer to rent 5 catoecic
arouras near Heraklia). In all cases here the owner of the property in question is a resident of S.N. (five of these are priests).

documents[13] in the category of wills, marriage contracts, or divisions of property, in which property owned in Socnopaiou Nesis is
involved. In addition to the documents which involve real estate
holdings, we have fifteen Socnopaiou Nesos residents attested as
slave owners.[14] We also have several different types of document
which reflect ownership of camels or donkeys. There is a total of
seventy-three documents[15] providing this sort of information, among
which there are sales of camels or donkeys, payments of the camel
tax, and registrations of camels. A further type of property ownership is reflected in loans and loan repayments, of which we have a
total of fifty-one papyri from the Roman period.[16] Thus we have all

---

13 This group includes *BGU* I 251 = *BGU* III 719, *BGU* I 183
(these three papyri involve the same family; marriage contract and
division of property), *P. Vindob. Tandem* 27 (will), *CPR* I 11 (division of property), *P. Ryl.* II 155 (gift of house property), *BGU* I
86 (will and division of property).

14 S.N. slave owners are attested in *BGU* III 773, *P. Stras.*
IV 249a, *BGU* III 706, *SPP* XXII 8, *BGU* III 805, *SPP* XXII 36, *BGU* III
855, *P. Lond.* II 311 (p. 219; see also supra n. 12 and infra n. 16),
SPP XXII 40, *P. Lond.* II 325a (p. 106), *BGU* XIII 2228, *BGU* II 467,
P. Grenf. II 59, *BGU* II 630, *SPP* XX 39.

15 Sales of camels: *SPP* XXII 30, *P. Gen.* 29, *P. Gen.* 30, *P.
Lond.* III 1132B (p. 141), *BGU* I 87, *BGU* I 88, *BGU* II 416, *SPP* XXII
48 = *BGU* I 153, *SB* VI 9640, *BGU* II 453, *P. Lond.* II 320 (p. 198),
P. Vindob. Worp 9, *BGU* II 427, *P. Stras.* IV 201, *P. Amh.* II 102,
SPP XXII 17, *P. Lond.* II 333 (p. 199); sales of donkeys are *SPP*
XXII 22, *P. Lond.* II 303 (p. 195), *SPP* XXII 20, *BGU* III 982, *P.
Flor.* I 22; also *BGU* III 912 (rental of donkey where owner is S.N.
man).
    Registrations of camels: *P. Grenf.* II 45, *BGU* I 352, *P. Grenf.*
II 45a, *BGU* I 355, *BGU* I 354, *BGU* I 357, *BGU* I 353, *BGU* I 51, *SB* VI
8977, *BGU* III 852, *P. Lond.* II 304 (p. 72), *SPP* XXII 90, *BGU* I 52,
P. Lond. II 309 (p. 73), *BGU* I 358, *BGU* III 869, *BGU* XIII 2235,
2236, *SPP* XXII 15, *BGU* II 629, *SPP* XXII 28, *BGU* XXII 2237, *P. Lond.*
II 327 (p. 74), *BGU* III 762, *P. Lond.* II 328 (p. 74), *BGU* I 89, *SPP*
XXII 91, *P. Aberd.* 48, *BGU* XIII 2238, *SPP* XXII 98, *SPP* XXII 97,
P. Lond. II 368 (ined. p. 76), *BGU* I 266.
    Payments of camel tax: P. Monac. gr. inv. 14, *P. Grenf.* II 48,
P. Lond. II 318 (p. 87), *P. Lond.* II 319 (p. 80), *P. Youtie* 40, *P.
Lond.* II 323 (p. 81), *BGU* II 654, *BGU* I 219 (2 receipts), *SPP* XXII
155, *P. Basel* 12, *BGU* II 521, *BGU* III 770, *BGU* II 461, P. Monac.
gr. inv. 26 (ined.), *SPP* XXII 122, *SPP* XXII 108, *P. Lond.* II 468
(p. 81). N.B. when a single individual appears in several documents
he is only tabulated once in the total of camel/donkey owners.

16 Loans are: *SB* I 5244, *BGU* I 189, *SB* I 5243, *SB* I 5245, *BGU*
III 911, *P. Lond.* II 277 (p. 217), *P. Ryl.* II 326 descr., *PSI* IX
1051, *P. Ryl.* II 160 c col. ii, *BGU* III 713, *SB* I 5110, *BGU* XI 1044,

together a total of 217 Greek documents which can give us information about the people who owned property in Socnopaiou Nesos in the
Roman period. From these I think we obtain a fairly accurate picture of the kind of village it was.

The statistics derived from tabulating the names in these 217
documents are presented below (see Table I). The figures given include only those people who can with some certainty be regarded as
inhabitants of Socnopaiou Nesos. Thus, for example, in a document
like *SB* 7, a loan executed at Arsinoe where the lender is Gaius
Julius Satorneilos, a veteran, and the borrower is Sotas son of
Apunchis of Socnopaiou Nesos, my assumption is that the lending
party is a resident of Arsinoe (since his place of residence is not
specified as is that of the borrower, and therefore he must live in
the place where the transaction takes place); I would therefore not
include Gaius Julius Satorneilos in my tally of Romans found in
Socnopaiou Nesos. Furthermore, where it was possible to determine
that several occurrences of the same name involved a single individual, then that person was only counted once.

In order to give the broadest possible scope for the manifestation of non-Egyptians among the residents, I have broken down the
figures into as many categories as possible. By "Roman" I mean
identifiable as Roman, either by the *tria nomina* or by a designation of status such as that of a soldier or veteran, or a single
Roman name with a Roman parent's name. I did not find a single
person with a name of this sort. Under the category of "possibly
Roman" I class those names which have some Roman element; there is
only one such name among the documents involving property ownership:
Sempronius, son of Panas, grandson of Sempronius, is a priest of

---

SB XII 10804, *P. Amh.* II 110 (repayment), *SB* V 8952 (= *PSI* XIII
1319 col. ii), *BGU* XIII 2330 (loan and sale with advance payment),
BGU XIII 2331 (loan and sale with advance payment), *P. Ryl.* II 327
descr., *SPP* XXII 46 (repayment), *P. Amh.* II 112 (repayment), *P.
Amh.* II 111 (repayment), P. Monac. gr. inv. 32 (ined.), *P. Stras.*
IV 293, *SPP* XXII 83, *P. Ryl.* II 174a (repayment), *SPP* XXII 78, *P.
Vindob. Worp* 10, *SPP* XXII 36, *P. Lond.* II 308 (p. 218), *BGU* II 445
(repayment), *P. Lond.* II 311 (p. 219) = *M. Chr.* 237 (see also above
at nn. 12 and 14), *CPR* I 15, *P. Stras.* V 383, *BGU* I 290, *BGU* XI 2043
(loan)/*SPP* XXII 45 (partial repayment), *P. Amh.* II 113 (repayment),
CPR VI 3, *CPR* I 16, *CPR* I 14 (repayment), *P. Lond.* II 332 (p. 209;
repayment), *P. Lond.* II 336 (p. 221), *SB* VI 9369 = *PSI* XIII 1324 (repayment), *P. Flor.* I 42, *SPP* XXII 69, *SPP* XXII 76, *BGU* III 853, *P.
Ryl.* II 334 descr., *SPP* XXII 41, *SB* I 7, *P. Ryl.* II 337 descr.

the local cult with a brother whose name is Stotoetis (*SPP* XXII 41,
A.D. 216). In view of the otherwise completely Egyptian character
of the local priesthood, it is hard to imagine that this man is
anything other than Egyptian.[17] Similarly, in the category of
"possibly Greek," I have included all those names which have any
Greek element, although in virtually every instance the person in
question has a father and/or mother with a totally Egyptian name.
Here I include Hellenistic Greek names like Sotas, Soterichos,
Ptolemaios, and adjectival Greek names like Melas, Demas, and Harpalos.[18] Even in this category we find only twelve names.

There is only one name which one could call authentically
Greek among property owners of Socnopaiou Nesos: Artemidoros, son
of Artemidoros, buys a fifth-share of an empty lot in Socnopaiou
Nesos from Taapis, daughter of Horos in A.D. 52 (*CPR* I 14 = *M. Chr.*
159). It is not entirely clear that he is a resident of the village, since the transaction was carried out at the grapheion of
Heraklia, but the property in question is definitely in Socnopaiou
Nesos, so one must certainly include him on a list of people who
owned property in the village. If indeed he was really a Greek,
one cannot help but think of how out of place he must have felt
in the neighbourhood!

---

17 This is one of the pieces of evidence cited by Wessely as
an indication of the ubiquitousness of Roman names (supra n. 6),
but in fact it is quite anomalous among S.N. documents.

18 Here I follow the general distinction employed by Peremans
(see esp. *Recherches*, 219ff.) in differentiating between Greek and
"peut-être grécisés" names; cf. on the other hand, A. E. Samuel
(op. cit., 444 n. 2), who in analyzing the population of Hibeh in
the Ptolemaic period defines as Greek names only those of which all
components are Greek and which were attested in the Greek area before the Hellenistic period. Thus for him Ammonius is not a Greek
name, whereas for Peremans it is classified as "possibly Greek."
It is only in these categories of "possibly Greek" or "possibly Roman" that there exists any ambiguity as to the ethnic identity of
the individual in question. On this point, see Crawford (op. cit.,
133f.), who remarks (inter alia) that, e.g., "Demas is a good Greek
name but in all cases one would expect the holder to be native."
This certainly concurs with my own interpretation of the Egyptian
identity of the bearers of such names. Corroboration for such a
view can be found merely by looking up these names in the indices
of the Karanis tax rolls (*P. Mich.* IV) where they occur frequently
and always in the context of Egyptian fathers or sons.

Against the grand total of fourteen possible non-Egyptians,
our list includes a total of 309[19] Egyptians who can be identified
as living in Socnopaiou Nesos and owning property in the first 225
years of the Roman era. That is the extent to which we can talk
about Greeks and Romans at Socnopaiou Nesos.

Two further pieces of statistical information are included in
the table, with the idea that they may supplement the picture of
the landholders by shedding some light on other elements of the
population. First of all, I have made an analysis of the ethnic
origin of all of the *hypographeis* who countersign Greek documents
drawn up at Socnopaiou Nesos; here if anywhere we would expect a
preponderance of Greeks, but in fact even here we find only six[20]
authentically Greek names, and three of these[21] must surely represent successive generations of the same family. Even in this capacity, then, the indigenous Egyptians are strongly in the majority.
Similar evidence of the ethnic integrity of the native population
can be found among lists of local officials, such as tax collectors,
chief of police, and other village functionaries, among whom Egyptian names predominate.[22] Only in the case of officials connected
with the central administration, who pass through the village to
carry out a particular responsibility, do we find non-Egyptian
names. For instance, among the nineteen individuals whose names

---

19 Actually the total is probably closer to 300, allowing for
the fact that a few documents listed above appear in more than one
category (see esp. *P. Lond.* II 311 [p. 219], a loan secured against
land near Heraklia and slaves, and therefore causing the party in
question to be listed separately under property owners, borrowers,
and slave owners).

20 Zosimas son of Philadelphos (*SB* XII 10882), Charimedon
(*BGU* III 912), Leontas son of Eirenaios (*BGU* III 854), Leonidos
(*SB* I 5246), Zoilos son of Leonidos (*BGU* III 713, *SB* I 5247, *CPR*
I 4), Leonidos son of Zoilos (*BGU* II 526, *BGU* XIII 2330).

21 Leonidos who is μονογράφος καὶ συναλλαγματογράφος of S.N.
in 3/2 B.C. must surely be the father of Zoilos who is ὑπογραφεύς
in 41-52 A.D. (in *BGU* III 713, Ζωΐλος [   ] must certainly be
[Λεωνίδου]), and grandfather of Leonidos who is ὑπογραφεύς in the
years 86-89.

22 Here we have twenty-five purely Egyptian names, ten possibly Greek (e.g. Sotas, Harpalos, etc.), one Greek (Dioskoros),
two possibly Roman (Tourbon son of Herieus, Tryphon son of Sempronius). There are five chiefs of police attested, all with Egyptian
names.

appear on the bottom of penthemerous certificates as having verified the dike work of a resident of Socnopaiou Nesos, we find nine
Greek names and two Roman ones.[23] But if we distinguish, as we
must, between those people who are temporarily active in the village and those who are permanently resident there, then we see how
minimal was the impact of the Greek or Roman presence in Egypt upon
the everyday lives of the people in this little community at the
edge of the desert.

A final item which appears on the statistical analysis concerns the data derived from an archive of tax documents from the
years 207-209, which provides the names of 101 residents of the
village who paid taxes.[24] This list does not include priests,[25]
but I suspect that it is probably a more or less complete list of
all the taxpayers of the village in this two-year period. Here we
find one person with an authentically Greek name, Dionysios son of
Dionysios. There are a few men with "possibly Roman" names, such
as Ioustos, Turbon, and Antonius, and a greater number with "possibly Greek" names, but in every one of these cases the names of

---

23   Greek names are Diomedes, Dioskoros (two of this name),
Dionysios, Didymos (two), Phanias, Korax, Stratos; Roman names are
Longinus, Ailius.

24   I exclude from these tabulations those people on the lists
whose payments are recorded under the headings for one of the other
villages, such as Nilopolis or Heraklia, on the assumption that
such persons were not permanently registered in S.N. but were working there temporarily. For a list of all the taxpayers in this archive, and a discussion of the possible significance of their payments, see my article in *BASP* 14 (1977) 161-207.

25   *BGU* II 392 and II 639, which are κατ' ἄνδρα reports from
the tax collectors of the village to the strategus of the nome,
list large sums paid on behalf of the priests. These sums are at
the end of each document and are not itemized like the payments of
the individuals. In each case the sum paid for the priests is almost equal to the sum of all the individual payments listed above
it; since we are not entirely clear as to the basis on which these
payments were assessed (see my article cited in n. 24), it is hard
to know whether the priests paid at the same rate as other residents of the village; but, assuming that they would at least not be
paying at a *higher* rate, we can infer that the number of priests may
may have been roughly equal to the total of other adult male residents of the village at the time.

the fathers and other men in the same family are totally Egyptian.[26]
Even so, it is interesting to note that hellenized names appear so
much more frequently at the bottom than at the top of the social
structure; I suspect that the explanation for this may lie in the
fact that people at the lower end of the social scale are forced by
economic circumstances to be more mobile than those above them.[27]
People who own property tend to stay in one place, whereas those
who work another person's land may have to move from one place to
another depending on agricultural conditions; similarly people who
own camels stay home, but those who drive camels have to move
around. The end result of this difference in resources might be
that those who own property are more endogamous than those who do
not; thus we see more of the influence of the neighbouring villages
on the names of the lowest levels of taxpayers than on those of the
families who own property in the village. However, speculation of
this sort has no direct bearing on the question of Greeks living in
Socnopaiou Nesos, since at best these "possibly Greek" names probably show nothing more than the influence of the Greek language on
Egyptian fashions in the naming of children.

It remains to consider why there is such a conspicuous absence
of Greeks and Romans among the residents of our village. I think
there are two explanations for this. First of all, there is the
fact that the village from its inception centered around the cult
of the crocodile god Souchos, and the consequent existence of a
local priesthood presumably placed a certain native stamp upon the

---

26 E.g. Sotas, son of Apunchis, Tourbon, son of Herieus,
Ioustos, son of Pabous, Melas, son of Pakusis. On the other hand,
there is Sotas whose mother is Dioskoros (no father named), but
this is the only instance of a parent who is not certainly Egyptian.

27 There is much evidence for the mobility of the δημόσιοι
γεωργοί; in the tax archive cited above (n. 24), we see that there
are people from Heraklia, Nilopolis and Karanis residing temporarily in S.N. *CPR* I 33 (A.D. 215) and *SPP* XXII 174 (A.D. 219) are
lists of grain payments for S.N. (ἀπαιτήσιμα) which include people
from the village of Philopator. H. Braunert (*Die Binnenwanderung*
[Bonn 1964]) collects and discusses all the evidence for this phenomenon, but does not distinguish between the Egyptian property
owners and their social inferiors, nor does he discuss the effects
of such relative degrees of mobility on the marriage patterns of
the different classes of the society.

character of the community. An analysis of the names connected
with property ownership indicates that much of the property in the
village belonged to members of priestly families.[28]

Why, one might ask, did the central government (whether Greek
or Roman) allow the indigenous priesthood to assume such a position
of prominence? The answer to this lies, I believe, in the quality
of agricultural land in the area around Socnopaiou Nesos. I mentioned earlier the absence of any large lists of landholders among
the numerous papyri from Socnopaiou Nesos, and I suggested that
such an absence was more than an accident. In fact, I think it is
significant that among the 1000 documents we have from this village
there is not one bit of evidence for the existence of privately-
owned agricultural land in Socnopaiou Nesos. People owned houses
and courts in the village, but whenever a Socnopaiou Nesos resident
is involved in the ownership or rental of a piece of agricultural
land, it is always in one of the neighbouring villages such as
Heraklia or Apias or Boubastos.[29] The only agricultural land which
is ever mentioned within the village is *aigialos*-marginal shoreland

---

28   The evidence on this point is too extensive to be discussed here, and will form the subject of a separate study. For
example, though, among the extant census declarations from S.N. all
but 3 involve families of priests; among 134 people from S.N. involved in loans, 25 are identified as priests, but many more have
names which are those of priestly families, etc. (see above at the
end of no. 12).

29   In addition to the evidence presented above in n. 12,
other evidence of the absence of agricultural land around S.N. (all
second-century documents): *BGU* III 834 (a complex sitologos receipt
involving a number of farmers from S.N., where the payments of
wheat are made to the thesauroi of Boubastos or Heraklia), *P. Stras.*
IV 267 (an offer by some state farmers of S.N. to rent palm trees
around the village of Psenuris), *P. Oxf.* 13 (lease of a palm-grove
near Boubastos by some S.N. residents), *P. Lond.* II 314 (p. 70) =
W. Chr. 356 = *M. Chr.* 149 (a sublease of S.N. public land which is
situated around Bacchias), *P. Aberd.* 57 (an application by a man
from S.N. for sublease of palm and olive trees growing on public
land near Boubastos).
   Furthermore, in the well-known document of A.D. 207, *P. Gen.*
16, a petition of Socnopaiou Nesos state farmers concerning the
shoreland which they had been cultivating for some years, and which
has been taken over by someone else during their absence from their
idia, the importance of this land to them is stated in terms of the
fact that the village has no other kind of land, ἕνεκ[α τοῦ] μὴ
ἔχιν τὴν κώμην μήτε ἰδι[ω]τικὴν μήτε βασ[ιλ]ικὴν μηδὲ ἄλλην εἰδέαν
(lines 16f.).

at the edge of the lake which was public land and was cultivated
by state farmers.[30]   Even what little evidence there is about temple
lands points to the fact that the holdings were in other villages.[31]
Similarly, the large estates whose names occur in Socnopaiou Nesos
give no evidence of having been agriculturally productive, but are
mentioned only in connection with pasturage or boats.[32]

I have found only one possible piece of evidence to contradict
this image of a village without any private agricultural land, and
that is contained in *P. Vindob. Tandem* 27.6, a division of property
of the first century. The document is broken at the left margin
and is lacking some 40-55 letters at the beginning of some of the
first lines. In line 6 after the break we find the reading

]ὲγ μίᾳ σφ[ραγίδι κλήρο]υ κατοικικοῦ ἀρούρας [δέκα δ]ύω

The entries preceding and following this one specify properties in
S.N. However, it must be noted that the portion of the text which
is missing is precisely that part (i.e. right before the statement
of the extent of the holding) where one ordinarily finds the statement of its location. Furthermore, the individual owns at least
some property outside of S.N. (a share of something in Nilopolis,
line 3). Thus in the face of all the evidence to the contrary, I
see no reason to assume that the catoecic land here must have been
in S.N.

30   Documents involving *aigialos* are *SB* VI 8976, *BGU* II 640,
BGU III 831, *SPP* XXII 49, *P. Gen.* 16, *SB* I 4284, *P. Lond.* III 924
(p. 134), *BGU* I 35, *CPR* I 32, *CPR* I 239, *P. Lond.* II 350 (p. 192) =
W. Chr. 353, *BGU* II 659, *CPR* I 33, *SPP* XXII 174, *SPP* XXII 26 + 88,
BGU I 175.

31   There are, in fact, only two S.N. papyri which contain
references to temple lands, and both are second century B.C. and
from the same find. In one (*P. Amh.* II 35), there is a reference
to ἱερὰ γῆ in the village of Dionysias, owned by the temple of Socnopaiou Nesos. In *P. Amh.* II 40 there is a complaint addressed to
the priests of Socnopaious that the Greeks have been allotted the
best portion of land and left the worst for the god, εἰς τοῦ θεοῦ
κλῆρον, but in this case it is not specified where the land is. A
similar absence of evidence regarding temple lands is noted for
the nearby village of Euhemeria by N. Hohlwein (*JJP* 3 [1949] 80f.)
despite the fact that this village had three temples.

32   Here are the documents which connect ousiac land to S.N.:
SB VI 8978 and *SPP* XXII 176 (both receipts for φόρος βωμῶν), *SPP*
XXII 120 (receipt for φόρος οὐσιακός), *BGU* I 212 and *P. Aberd.* 24
(both receipts for φόρος πλοίων), *P. Bour.* 29, *BGU* III 810, *BGU*
XIII 2298, *BGU* I 63, *BGU* XI 2102, *P. Lond.* II 312 (p. 80), *BGU* I
102 (all receipts for φόρος προβάτων and/or φόρος νόμων). In *SB* I
4284 the state farmers of S.N. speak of an *ousia* on which they pay
2400 drachmas a year and which is used for pasturing a great many
cattle (line 12f.). Estates do not occur in any other contexts
among Socnopaiou Nesos documents.

The truth is, then, in my opinion, that Socnopaiou Nesos
(which was, after all, at the far side of Lake Moeris on the extreme end of the irrigation system and at the edge of the desert)
had very little desirable land, and thus it was of no interest to
the Greeks and Romans. It is interesting that a very similar suggestion has been made by Biezunska-Malowist[33] for Oxyrhynchus: she
has pointed to the relative paucity of farm land in the area around
Oxyrhynchus (in comparison with the more fertile land of the Fayum)
as a possible explanation for the small number of Romans attested
in the papyri from Oxyrhynchus.

It is not within the scope of this paper to discuss how a
village of the sort I have described could survive economically
without the revenue derived from land holdings. For the present I
merely point to the commercial activities generated by the temple
itself (e.g. the weaving industry), as well as the possibilities
for transportation services created by the existence of the customs
house at the gate of the village. At any rate, it seems clear from
the evidence I have brought together here that Socnopaiou Nesos was
a thoroughly Egyptian village in the Roman period, and that there
were virtually no Greeks or Romans resident there. The picture I
have drawn of the village should indicate that it was very different from Karanis and Philadelphia. Perhaps this will serve as a
caution to us against assuming that all of the little villages in
the Fayum must have been alike.

York University, Toronto   Deborah H. Samuel

---

33 I. Biezunska-Malowist in *Le Monde Grec, Hommages à Claire
Préaux* (Brussels 1976) 747. See also E. G. Turner, *JEA* 38 (1952)
86; he counts only eleven veterans and seventeen other Roman citizens, including women, at Oxyrhynchus in the first three centuries
A.D.

TABLE I

GREEKS AND ROMANS AT SOCNOPAIOU NESOS

	E	PG	G	PR	R
S.N. houseowners buyers	28	1	1	-	-
(32 documents) sellers	40	1	-	-	-
S.N. property registrations current owners	11	-	-	-	-
(12 documents) previous owners	7	-	-	-	-
agricultural land owned by S.N. residents (none in S.N.) (10 documents)	11	-	-	-	-
census declarations (17 declarations)	17	-	-	-	-
S.N. camel/donkey owners (73 documents)	61	5	-	-	-
S.N. slave owners (15 documents)	15	-	-	-	-
loans and repayments lenders	37	4	-	-	-
(51 documents) borrowers	81	1	-	1	-
wills, marriage contracts, divisions of property (7 documents, 5 families)	5	-	-	-	-
TOTAL S.N. PROPERTY OWNERS	313	12	1	1	-
ὑπογραφεῖς at S.N.	21	7	6	-	-
S.N. taxpayers of 207-209 A.D. (7 documents, 122 names, of which 101 are S.N. inhabitants)	70	27	1	3	-

E = Egyptian   PR = Possibly Roman
PG = Possibly Greek   R = Roman
G = Greek

THE PREFECT'S HORSE-GUARDS AND THE SUPPLY
OF WEAPONS TO THE ROMAN ARMY

Recently the correct reading of the papyrus *Stud. Pal.* XXII 92
was established by R. W. Daniel in the following form.[1]

Φλάυϊος Σιλβανὸς σημηαφόρος ἱππέ[ων σιν-]
γλαρείων ἡγεμόνος πρεσβυτέροις κώμης
Σεκνοπέου χαίρειν. ἀπέσχον παρ' ὑμῶν τὰ ἐπι-
μερισθέντα ἡμῖν ἀκόντεια ἐκ φύνεικος
ὧν κατέβαλλον ἡμῖν τὴν ὡρισμένην τει-
μὴν δημοσείας.

Ἔτους β̄ Μεχὶρ κε.

1-2 ἱππέ[ων σιν]γλαρείων: ὑπὸ 'Ιλαρείων(ος) *ed. pr.*

Flavius Silvanus, standard bearer of the Prefect's
horse-guards, to the elders of the village of Soknopaios,
greetings. I received from you the palm-wood shafts
assigned to you and have paid you the agreed sum from
the public treasury.

The Prefect's horse-guards (*equites singulares praefecti*) had
not been recognized in this text previously, for in their place the
name Hilarion had been read. However, the reading ἱππέων σινγλαρείων is confirmed beyond doubt by another, very similar, Fayum papyrus of the Freiburg collection (soon to be published by R. W.
Daniel) in which the same standard bearer sends a parallel letter
to the elders of Theadelphia. The interest of the new reading for
our knowledge of the Roman army is discussed in the following.

A *signifer equitum singularium* has not been known reliably
among the eighty-odd inscriptions and papyri that mention the

1 R. W. Daniel, "Notes on the Guilds and Army in Roman Egypt,"
BASP 16 (1979) 37-46, esp. 44f. I am grateful to Dr. Daniel for
having sent me a manuscript copy of his forthcoming publication of
the *P. Freiburg* from the commentary of which I have learned a great
deal. This paper was researched with the help of a grant by the
National Endowment for the Humanities (Research Materials Program).

provincial *singulares*-guards. The horse-guards in major military
provinces could be some 500 men strong, and we know that they
served under a *praepositus*. But how were they organized into tactical units? The soldiers were selected from the *alae* and cohorts
of their province and continued to belong to their regular centuries and *turmae* to which they would return eventually after service
in the guards.[2] Yet while in the capital they may have formed new
tactical squadrons. The presence of decurions, or squadron leaders, among them was no solid proof for this, since such decurions
might have been detached to the guards because of their rank. Now,
however, that we learn the *singulares* had *signiferi*--standard bearers of the squadrons--, we may infer that they were indeed organized
into tactical squadrons, i.e. *turmae*. To be sure, a cavalry man
thus belonged to two *turmae*, one in his original unit and one in the
guards, but inconvenient as this may have been, it was apparently
necessitated by the duties of the provincial horse-guards which included intensive training and actual fighting--one papyrus even reports war casualties of the *singulares* at some time during the later
third century A.D.[3] For fighting technique the Roman cavalry relied
on the individual squadrons to train and manoeuvre,[4] but now we may
assume that this was so in the Prefect's horse-guards as well.

The *equites singulares* of a province formed a *numerus*. But
since *numerus* means no more than "unit" and is not a technical term
like *ala* or *cohors*, the word is frequently omitted in the naming of
such units.[5] This fact is confirmed by our two texts that call the
standard bearer simply σημηαφόρος ἱππέων σινγλαρείων ἡγεμόνος. Unfortunately, both texts are datable only roughly to the second or

---

2 M. P. Speidel, *Guards of the Roman Armies* (Bonn 1978) 33.

3 *P. Ross. Georg.* III 1 (= Speidel, *Guards*, no. 71).

4 Vegetius 2.14: *Eligendus est decurio qui turmae equitum
praeponatur, inprimis habili corpore, ut...possit...turmales suos,
id est sub cura sua equites positos erudire ad omnia quae equestris
pugna deposcit.*

5 Speidel, *Guards*, 22f.

third century A.D.[6] so that we do not gain new dates for the practice of omitting the term *numerus*. The problem may seem inconse-
quential were it not for the many accounts of the Roman army that
treat the *numeri* as if they were a class of units all by themselves.[7]

The shafts bought are called ἀκόντια. The word is the diminutive form of ἄκων and may mean javelin.[8] Yet is it likely that
villagers in the Fayum produced weapons for the Roman army? Dio
Cassius (69.12) tells us that the Jews just before the Bar-Kochba
revolt in A.D. 131 made weapons for the Roman army but purposely
made them of inferior quality so that the Romans would reject them
and the Jews could have them for their own use in the coming revolt.
The story, if it is not an empty *topos*, would show that provincials
manufactured weapons for the army and that there existed a quality
control.[9] Yet the Fayum villagers very likely produced only the
wooden shafts of spears and this is not only a possible meaning of
the word ἀκόντια,[10] but the one that goes best with the fact that
the shafts are of palm-wood which is not suited for real spears.
In Latin ἀκόντιον is *hastile*, and an ostrakon from Wadi Fawakhir
seems to show that *hastilia* were indeed sent from one military out-
post to another as an item of military supplies.[11] What is more,
Arrian in his *Tactica* (34.8ff.) shows that ἀκόντια were used in
cavalry shows and exercises as lighter-than-usual shafts without

6 Wessely, *Stud. Pal.* XXII 92 dated the papyrus to the third
century, but Daniel opts for 2nd/3rd century. *Singulares* guards of
the governors existed throughout the first three centuries of the
empire and thus provide no framework for the dating of the papyrus.

7 M. Speidel, *TAPA* 106 (1976) 339-48.

8 LSJ, 53; see also below, n. 15.

9 R. MacMullen, *AJA* 64 (1960) 23-40. J. Oldenstein, *BerRGK*
57 (1976) 49-284, esp. 68-85.

10 *ThLL* VI, 2557, 31f. where ἀκόντιον is equated with *hastile*; cf. ibid., 2556, 80f. See also S. Lauffer, *Der Maximaltarif
des Diokletian* (Berlin 1971) Text 15,14 and commentary 253f.; H.
Blümner, *Der Maximaltarif des Diokletian* (Berlin² 1958) 135f.

11 *O. Faw.* 9. The editor mistook these *hastilia* for plants,
but cf. Blümner and Lauffer, locc. citt., on Diocletian's edict 14,4
and 4: ἀστίλιον κράνειον; ἀστίλιον ἰς κόντον: both shafts for
spears.

metal tips: since intensive training, in part just for such shows, was one of the distinguishing features of the horse-guards,[12] our two documents may refer perhaps to such parade-weapons as mentioned by Arrian.

In his justly famous book on the Roman army in Egypt, J. Lesquier remarked in the chapter on military supplies that by 1913, when he wrote, papyri had produced some information on clothing and food, but nothing yet on the weapons supply.[13] Thus when our papyrus became available in 1922, its importance was recognized and it has been quoted as a first-rate source in studies on the supply of weapons to the Roman army.[14] It proves that the army organized and controlled the weapons supply, even though the individual soldier had to pay for his weapons.[15] We now learn that a *signifer* of the Prefect's *equites singulares* did the buying in the Fayum while his unit was stationed at Alexandria, at the seat of the governor. A good parallel to this is a receipt for barley by a horseman of ala Gallica, stationed at Alexandria--a receipt made out to the elders of the same village of Soknopaios.[16] Apparently, units of the Alexandria garrison made routinely requisitions in the Fayum.

Very possibly, the shafts were for the use of the Prefect's horse-guards, but if conditions at Alexandria resembled those in Rome then there was a central armory in the city from which all units of the garrison received their arms and into which, of course, all such deliveries as this one would go.[17] In either case we learn

---

12 Speidel (*Guards*, 43) on *hastiliarii* among *singulares* (see ibid., 30).

13 J. Lesquier, *L'armée romaine d'Egypte* (Cairo 1918) 349.

14 MacMullen, *AJA* 64 (1960) 26; Oldenstein, *BerRGK* 57 (1976) 81.

15 See MacMullen, *AJA* 64 (1960); D. J. Breeze, *Britannia* 7 (1976) 93-95.

16 *P. Grenf.* I 48 = Wilcken, *Chrest.* 416.

17 For the *armamentaria* in Rome, common to all units, see Tacitus, *Hist.* 1.38: *aperiri deinde armamentarium iussit. rapta statim arma, sine more et ordine militiae, ut praetorianus aut legionarius insignibus suis distingueretur: miscentur auxiliaribus galeis scutisque....* The interpretation of this passage by A. v. Domaszewski, *Westdeutsche Zeitschrift für Geschichte und Kunst* 14

from the two papyri a new function of the members of the Prefect's
horse-guards: to run the weapons supply from the Fayum to Alexandria.[18] As in other cases, epigraphy may give us a more balanced
picture of the Roman institutions, but papyrology provides the
sharper and livelier details.

University of Hawaii   Michael P. Speidel

(1895) 1-124 (= *Aufsätze zur römischen Heeresgeschichte* [Darmstadt
1972] 81-209) 87 n. 351, followed by M. Durry, *Les cohortes pré-
toriennes* (Paris 1938) 115, must be wrong, for MacMullen and Oldenstein, locc. citt., have shown how the provincial units procured
their own arms. For *armamentaria*, see also M. Speidel and A.
Dimitrova-Milčeva in *ANRW* II/16 (1978) 1542-55, esp. 1552.

18 A *signifer* was particularly suited for such financial
tasks, see e.g. J. F. Gilliam in *Bonner Historia Augusta Colloquium*
1964/65 (Bonn 1966) 91-97. R. W. Daniel in his manuscript of the
P. Freiburg edition gives a good account of the literacy of the
signiferi.

Proceedings of the XVI Int. Congr. of Papyrology (Chico 1981) 411-418

THE HIGH PRIEST OF ALEXANDRIA AND ALL EGYPT

The policy of the Roman government towards the Egyptian clergy was of increased control of their activities and secularisation of their resources. Under Augustus most of the sacred land was confiscated and the priests were made to rely on the government subvention, *syntaxis*, as their chief form of livelihood.[1] The amount of exemption from taxation and liturgies was restricted and special taxes were levied on the priests.[2] Besides these constraints the degree of bureaucratic intervention in temple affairs increased, culminating in the creation of a special official to head the administration of religion: the High Priest of Alexandria and all Egypt.

The office probably developed from a need to administer various prefectural decrees of the first and early second centuries AD which were concerned with religious matters. These decrees served two purposes. Some regulated the behaviour, dress and powers of the clergy,[3] while others required the registration of all temple personnel, their families and property. These registers were mainly for taxation purposes, but they also served as a check on the abuse of priestly privileges by those who falsely claimed attachment to temples.

The first known edict of this kind is that of the Prefect C. Turranius in 4 BC (*BGU* IV 1199), which required the registration of temple personnel only. This list was updated and extended in the Neronian period by a decree of C. Caecina Tuscus.[4] At this time a register of priests' property was included and probably also an

---

1 W. Otto, *Priester und Tempel in Hellenistischen Ägypten* (Berlin 1905-8) I, 366ff.

2 S. L. Wallace, *Taxation in Egypt from Augustus to Diocletian* (Princeton 1936) chap. 14.

3 *PSI* X 1149 (1st cent. AD); *P. Oxy.* VIII 1155 (AD 104); Yale Inv. 1394V + *P. Fouad* 10 (AD 120).

4 J.E.G. Whitehorne, *Cd'E* 53 (1978) 321ff.

account of the dues owed to the State by the temples. From these registers probably developed the annual γραφαὶ ἱερέων[5] which had to be submitted to several government officials, by order of the High Priest.

The first known High Priest of Alexandria and all Egypt is Julius Vestinus, a relative of the Prefect of the same name, who served under Nero.[6] Vestinus was in office during the late 120s AD, which could imply that the post of High Priest was created under Hadrian. This view is confirmed by P. Yale Inv. 1394V.[7] This document is an edict of the Prefect T. Haterius Nepos, dated to AD 120, which regulates temple affairs. Lines 2-6 of the edict imply that the post of High Priest was instituted at that time. If so, then the decree may well have set forth and explained the new official's terms of reference. As the date of this edict is AD 120 and Julius Vestinus' last year in office was probably AD 130, it is unlikely that he was the first High Priest of Alexandria and all Egypt, unless he was in office for ten years.

It has been argued that the office of High Priest of Alexandria and all Egypt was created as a part of the department of the *Idios Logos* and that it never existed as an independent post.[8] A less extreme view is that although the High Priest was originally a separate official, his department was merged with that of the *Idios Logos* at the beginning of the third century.[9] A strong body of evidence, which I do not have time to discuss here, points to the view that the two posts were always intended to be separate.[10]

---

5   O. Montevecchi, *Aegyptus* 12 (1932) 31ff.

6   *PIR* IV, nos. 623 + 622.

7   G. Parássoglou, *ZPE* 13 (1974) 21ff.

8   G. Plaumann, *Der "Ἴδιος Λόγος*, Abh. Preuss. Akad. Wiss. Phil-Hist. Kl. 17 (1918) 36ff.; H. Henne in *Mélanges offerts à Nicholas Iorga* (Paris 1933) 435ff.

9   U. Wilcken, *Hermes* 23 (1888) 600; idem, *Grundzüge*, 127; idem, *Chrest.*, 87 introd.; W. Otto, *Priester und Tempel* I, 61ff., 172ff.; O. Reinmuth, *The Prefect of Egypt from Augustus to Diocletian*, Klio Beiheft 34 (1935) 27ff.

10   The evidence is cited and discussed by P. Swarney, *The Ptolemaic and Roman Idios Logos* (Toronto 1970) 130f. See also P. Parsons, *Cd'E* 49 (1974) 146-47; Parássoglou, *ZPE* 13 (1974) 33f.

Unification can be demonstrated in one instance only: Modestos, the
Idios Logos in October 183 (*PSI* VIII 928), is described in *SB* VIII
9658 as ὁ γενόμενος πρὸς τῷ ἰδίῳ λόγῳ διαδεξάμενος καὶ τὰ κατὰ τὴν
ἀρχιερωσύνην (lines 24-25). Nevertheless, as the term διαδεξάμενος
implies, he was only acting as temporary head of the High Priest's
department, no doubt during an emergency.

It also seems likely that the office of High Priest of Alexandria and all Egypt outlasted that of the *Idios Logos*. The latest
surviving reference to the *Idios Logos* is in *P. Oxy.* XLIII 3133,
dated to AD 239, and it has been suggested that the post was abolished during the reforms of Philip the Arab, ten years later.[11]
There are, however, three more High Priests attested in the later
part of the third century AD,[12] and a recently published document,
P. XV Congr. 22, indicates that the post of High Priest still existed in the early part of the fourth century. If this document,
dated to the 330s AD, does indeed refer to the High Priest of Alexandria and all Egypt, then it seems reasonable to suppose that the
post continued until Christianity became the official religion of
the empire and the pagan temples were dismantled.

The High Priest of Alexandria and all Egypt appears to have
taken over most of the religious, administrative functions of the
Prefect, but there is no evidence that he assumed the Prefect's
cult functions.[13] These the latter probably retained as he was the
formal representative of the emperor-Pharaoh in Egypt. Nor does it
seem as if the ἀρχιερεύς normally acted as High Priest of the Imperial cult in Egypt, although one or two of them did hold that
office.[14]

The most widely attested duty of the High Priest of Alexandria
and all Egypt was consideration of requests to circumcise candidates
for the priesthood. The procedure for entry into the Egyptian

---

11 P. Parsons, *JRS* 57 (1976) 134ff.

12 Iulius Ruf-, AD 251/2 (*P. Tebt.* II 608 descr.); Gessius
Serenus, AD 259 (*P. Ryl.* II 110); Flavius, late 3rd cent. AD (*P.
Tebt.* II 418 introd.).

13 O. Reinmuth, *The Prefect of Egypt*, 3.

14 Unknown in P. Yale Inv. 1394V; Flavius Melas: *SPP* XXII 66.

clergy was highly formalised and intended not only to preserve the
purity of the clergy but also to implement two aspects of Roman
policy: the abolition of all forms of bodily mutilation and control
of the numbers of Egyptian priests allowed to serve the gods. The
origin of the elaborate examination of candidates for the priesthood in the Roman period was an edict of Antoninus Pius which for-
bade circumcision to members of the Roman empire, except Jews and
Egyptian priests.[15] It was only permitted to the latter as it was
an essential part of their initiation rite. Nevertheless, from the
time of the edict, written permission was required from the High
Priest in order to perform the ceremony.

Acquisition of this permission required a great deal of time
and expense. Further, not all members of a priestly family were
granted permission, only those with a definite chance of entering
the clergy and not those who intended to enter some other branch of
temple service. The process whereby the permission of the High
Priest was obtained is well known and I need not describe it here.[16]
Suffice it to say that in this capacity the High Priest of Alexandria and all Egypt was the main instrument of the policy of con-
trolling the numbers and thereby the power of the clergy. The High
Priest also kept a check on priests' qualifications once they were
in office. *P. Tebt.* II 291 preserves part of a letter written by
the High Priest, concerning the fitness of certain priests to continue serving the gods. The reason why they were challenged does
not survive, but they appear to have satisfied their judges. One
by giving proof of a knowledge of Egyptian by reading from a hieratic book, the other by giving proof of his parentage.

Although the High Priest acted as a control on the Egyptian
clergy, the Roman government did not aim to crush it completely, as
this could provide a cause for rebellion. The High Priest was,
therefore, concerned with the welfare of the priests, especially in
connection with their right to exemption from liturgies. The
sources of this immunity were the ἱεροὶ νόμοι and prefectural
edicts.[17] This right was also reaffirmed several times by the High

---

15   J. Foucart, *JSav* (1911) 5ff.

16   *P. Tebt.* II 292 introd.

17   *P. Aberd.* 16 (ca. AD 134); *OGIS* 664 (1st cent. AD).

Priest. The privilege was, however, abused and the High Priest
had to call on the *strategos* to ensure that local officials did not
use violence against the priests, or in any other way force them to
undertake manual labour (*P. Bacch.* 20 + 21).

The High Priest not only stood between temples and the government, but also between temples and the lay population. In *SB* VIII
9659 the High Priest, Ulpius Serenianus, issues instructions that
certain defaulters, who owed something to a temple, be prosecuted.
Another case is that of a certain Tastous (*P. Mich.* IX 531).[18] She
had requested the jurisdiction of the High Priest on a question of
land, probably as a result of a dispute between herself and a temple. She failed, however, to appear for an audience at the appointed time and the High Priest wrote to her nome enquiring as to
her whereabouts. Five months later she was discovered in Alexandria. Unfortunately the penalty for not appearing before the High
Priest could be high, as one Cathytes found out in *P. Achmim.* 8.
He was fined 1000 drachmae.

Finally in the fourth century document, *P. XV Congr.* 22, already mentioned, the High Priest appears to have taken over some of
the duties that used to belong to the *Idios Logos*. Column IV relates how the priestly family of Aurelius Ammon was trying to purchase the Propheteia of the main temple in Panopolis from the High
Priest for Ammon's nephew Horion. Sale of priesthoods has been
identified by Swarney as one of the religious duties of the *Idios
Logos*.[19] If the office of *Idios Logos* did indeed become defunct in
the middle of the third century, then it seems possible that some,
if not all of that department's religious duties should have passed
to the High Priest.

In the performance of his duties the High Priest of Alexandria
and all Egypt worked closely with a number of officials. The most
notable of these was the *Idios Logos*. The interest of this department in religion was purely financial, in keeping with its general
character. The *Idios Logos* acted as the agent for the sale of
priestly posts. His office collected the fees from the auction of

---

18 *P. Mich.* IX 531, revised by P. Parsons, *Cd'E* 49 (1974)
136-37.

19 Swarney, *The Ptolemaic and Roman Idios Logos*, 59.

non-hereditary posts and the *eiskritikon* payment on the passage of
hereditary ones. The *Idios Logos* was also concerned with the discipline of priests, especially cases in which the penalty was a
fine.

The officials most widely attested as working with the High
Priest (and *Idios Logos* in his religious duties) are the *strategos*
and *basilicogrammateus*. These worked on behalf of the central religious administration in the nomes and as liason officers between
local temples and Alexandria. The *strategos* was the main interme-
diary between candidates for the priesthood and the central bureaucracy. The candidate's family wrote to the *strategos* with a
request that a letter be sent to the High Priest in order to obtain
his permission to circumcise the boy. The *strategos* then had to
organise the preliminary investigation of the child's eligibility.
Once this was satisfactorily completed the case could then be
passed to the attention of the High Priest.[20]

Both the *strategos* and the *basilicogrammateus* were called upon
to investigate priests' misdemeanours, or questions about their
eligibility to continue serving the gods. The information was then
passed back to the High Priest or *Idios Logos* for judgement.[21]
Finally the *strategos* was required to protect the rights and privileges of the priests, once these had been determined by the Prefect
or High Priest. The most notable example of this known to us is
from the Bacchias archive. This concerns the abuse of the priests'
right to freedom from liturgies. The *strategos* was required to see
that force was not used against the priests and that they were not
made to undertake manual labour.

Finally, I would like to discuss an official whose importance
in the religious hierarchy of Egypt has only recently been recog-
nised and who must have had very close relations with the High
Priest of Alexandria and all Egypt. This is the *Archiprophetes*.[22]
Archiprophetai have been identified at Memphis, Oxyrhynchus,

_____

20   *P. Tebt.* II 292; *P. Tebt.* II 293; *BGU* I 82; *SB* I 15,16,17;
BGU XIII 2216; *W. Chr.* 77.

21   *P. Tebt.* II 291; *SB* VIII 9658; *BGU* I 16; *BGU* I 250.

22   A. Bülow-Jacobsen in *Actes du XVe Congrès International de
Papyrologie, IVe Partie* (Brussels 1979) 124ff.

Heliopolis, Panopolis, Alexandria and Philae. Their titles indicate that they held an important position in the Egyptian hierarchy. Indeed, one of them, the *Archiprophetes* and *Orapis* of Memphis, may have been the head of the Egyptian clergy in the Roman
period and author of the sacred law (Semenuthi). He would therefore have been the religious counterpart of the administrative High
Priest of Alexandria and all Egypt.

Nevertheless, the *Archiprophetai* had certain administrative
functions which affected the temples in their area. They organised
the levy of *byssos* for the mummification of the dead Apis and
Mnevis bulls.[23] They also issued a certificate to priests which
stated that they were eligible to serve the gods.[24] The exact nature of this document is unknown, but it paralleled the certificate
of circumcision which had to be obtained from the High Priest.
Lack of either one of these documents caused an official enquiry.[25]
The document issued by the *Archiprophetes* was required at the same
time as the candidate was approved by the High Priest. Its introduction may have been an innovation of the *Idios Logos*, Modestos,
when he was acting as High Priest in AD 184/5.

Finally, the *Archiprophetai* are known to have received copies
of γραφαί ιερέων from the temples in their district. It is stated
in both cases that these reports had been demanded by the High
Priest (*PSI* IX 1039; *P. Ryl.* II 110). The *Archiprophetai*, then,
may have been bishop-like figures, responsible for the religious
direction of the priests in their areas, but were nevertheless tied
to the government's strict control of temple affairs from Alexandria.

In conclusion, the creation of the post of High Priest of
Alexandria and all Egypt marks an important phase in the subjec-
tion of Temple to State. In many ways the power and prestige of
the clergy had already been sapped by loss of land and tax exemptions, but from the mid-second century AD their activities were

---

23 *SB* VI 9346 (AD 156-70); *W. Chr.* 85 (AD 170); *P. Tebt.* II
313 (AD 210/1).

24 *SB* VIII 9658 (AD 193); P. Oxy. ined. 50 4B 30/71 (1-26)
(AD 131).

25 *SB* VIII 9658 (AD 193); P. Oxy. ined. 19 79 J19/4/04.

subject to the jurisdiction of this one man who, despite his title, was a bureaucrat.

British Museum, London   Miriam Stead

THE ROLE OF THE STRATEGIA IN ADMINISTRATIVE
CONTINUITY IN ROMAN EGYPT[*]

In his survey of recent British papyrology,[1] Peter Parsons
ended by noting the current tendency among scholars to see the
Roman empire in less clearcut and positive terms than was the case
earlier this century.

Nowhere is this trend more evident in our own field than in
Brunt's 1975 paper on the prefects of Egypt.[2] His conclusion,
based on a review of their known careers, that the majority of prefects, and their immediate subordinates, had never before set foot
in Egypt and can have known little of the country's complex fiscal
system, stands in marked contrast to Reinmuth's 1935 picture of
Roman Egypt as "a modern well organised business corporation" controlled by prefects who were "by and large men of outstanding
ability."[3]

It is perhaps mistaken to look for specialisation in the modern sense in the government of Roman Egypt. Yet the notion of a
country as important to Rome as Egypt, left in the hands of gifted
amateurs seems both unlikely and anachronistic. The need for a
minimal level of competence and continuity is present in any administrative structure, Roman Egypt's included. So granted Brunt's
conclusion, that for one year in three the prefects of Egypt can
hardly have been in real control of the province, I wish to ask
whether we can see any attempt being made to provide for continuity
in the country's administration at the middle level of government,
in the nomes. It was here that the strategi and royal scribes

---

    * I am most grateful to the National Endowment for the Hu-
manities, and to the University of Queensland, for their generous
financial assistance.

1 *StPap* 15 (1976) 95-102.

2 *JRS* 65 (1975) 92-106.

3 *The Prefect of Egypt from Augustus to Diocletian* (Klio
Beiheft 34; Leipzig 1935) 128.

carried out the essential business of collating returns of land,
crops, animals, and men, and summarising their results for the
central administration in Alexandria. It was these officials, too,
more than any other, who were responsible for implementing the instructions of the prefect, the idiologus and the other financial
procurators.

     If an attempt had been made to ensure continuity at this mid-
dle level of government, then we might expect to find traces of
this surviving in what is known of the careers of individual strategi. For instance, we might find men appointed to the strategia
because of appropriate local knowledge or special administrative
skills. Or we might find those royal scribes, who had deputised
for absent strategi or acted as interim strategi (as so many did),[4]
being given preference for that office themselves in due course.
Competent strategi might have their terms extended. Incoming prefects might be expected to confirm their predecessors' appointments
to the strategia, or at least to abide by their choice for a decent
interval in the interests of continuity. Finally strategi who had
proved their worth might be asked to serve again at a later date.

     These are all elementary procedures to maximise administrative
efficiency. They are also the sort of procedures of which we may
reasonably expect to find identifiable traces in our evidence. The
fasti of the strategi are of course still very far from complete,
but we now have the names and dates of about 400 strategi of Roman
Egypt. About many of these we know enough to make it worth asking
whether that professionalism which we can see slowly developing in
and around the imperial household in Rome was ever extended into
the local internal administration of the country that was effectively that household's greatest and most valuable possession.

     Taking the above points one by one, we may immediately dis-
count local knowledge as a criterion of any great importance in the
choice of strategi. As Tait demonstrated,[5] a strategus was normally
posted for service outside his *idia*, presumably to minimise the
danger of corruption. There is also a prohibition in the Gnomon

---

4   See now M. H. Eliassen - De Kat in *Actes XVe Congrès*
(Brussels 1979) IV, 116-23.

5   *JEA* 8 (1922) 166-73.

(§10) against officials acquiring property or lending money in
their area of appointment.

On the other hand the social background of those who became
strategi must have meant that most appointees, if not all, were
landowners with a general knowledge of estate management on which
they could draw in their new post. During much of the first century their names suggest that strategi came mainly from Alexandria
rather than the metropoleis but, as we know, wealthy Alexandrian
citizens often owned lands in the *chora*. Even if such people did
not reside permanently on their country estates they may have had
more local knowledge of a general kind than we may perhaps now ap-
preciate. However it was probably no more than that, a general
knowledge. It was not a familiarity with the conditions and problems of the particular area to which they had been sent.

On the matter of special skills, we have evidence from all
periods to show that some strategi at least had previous administrative experience of a type which would have been useful. They
are found serving in many of the main posts in Alexandria and the
metropoleis (see Appendix), but what seems to me more remarkable is
the paucity of evidence throughout the whole period for a progression from royal scribe to strategus. I have found only two examples where it is expressly stated that the same man held both posts,
one where a progression seems certain, and another five where there
may be a progression.[6] This despite the broad overlap between the
areas of responsibility of the two offices, and the fact that it
was almost invariably the royal scribe who acted as deputy for the
strategus in his absence.

---

6 Lucretius and Apollonius minor (Appendix Nos. 7, 19) are
sure. Heracleides (No. 18) seems certain, although the name is a
common one. Possible examples of progression are:
    1. Pasion: ex-b.g., str. or acting str., Ars(H), 37 (*P. XV.
Congr*. 13, 4: see Eliassen - De Kat (supra n. 4) 117 n. 2).
    2. Hermaeus alias Dryton: b.g., Ars(H), 119 (Henne 67, Mussies
no. 366) = str., Memphite, 131/2 (Mussies no. 215), unless latter =
str., Busirite, 151 (Mussies no. 158).
    3. Archibius: b.g., Ars(Th), 128-133 (Henne 70) = str. Ars(H),
146 (Bastianini 38).
    4. Herminus: b.g., Ars(H), 133-138 (Henne 67, Mussies no. 367)
= str., Memphite, c. 154/5 (Mussies no. 216).
    5. Aur. Achilleus: b.g., Ars(H), 244/5 (Henne 70) = str.,
Heracleopolite, 258/9 (Henne 17), unless former = str., Heracleopolite, 232/3 (Henne 17).

Strategi then were sometimes men who had already proved their
capacity for administration but, as far as we can tell, there was
no regular cursus through which they had to pass before appointment.
Nor is there any strong link discernible in one area where we might
expect to have found evidence of a progression in Roman times, that
is from royal scribe to strategus.

The next point is the extension of tenure of strategi who had
proved their competence. On this we must first ask what was a
normal term for the strategia. The water has been unnecessarily
muddied here by the well known Edict of Ti. Julius Alexander, in
lines 34-35 of which Alexander established the term of office for
a strategus as three years. Despite much discussion of this passage, Alexander's three year rule is still accorded a status which
it does not deserve. In fact, all that his ruling proves is that
before 68 the prefect had the power to retain a strategus for as
long as he chose, which is something we knew already from the fasti.

These same fasti show, too, that for the period after Alexander, his three year rule was treated with as little respect as some
of his other pronouncements. It is true that after 68 many strategi are found serving three years but they do not appear to constitute a clear majority. Many others lasted less than this so-called
normal term and some few lasted more. Indeed so great and so numerous are the variations that if we did not have the Edict it is very
unlikely that scholars would ever have seriously entertained the
notion of a regular term for this office.

Whatever the intention behind Alexander's three year rule, it
seems to have been something of a dead letter. Alexander's successors continued actively to exercise their powers of discretion in
regard to the term for the strategia. Nor does there seem to be any
support for Chalon's view,[7] that the ruling reaffirmed a pre-
existing principle that strategi should serve for a three year
period.

One may certainly calculate an average term for the strategia,
and come up with a figure of slightly less than three years, but in
view of the amount of variation in individual cases it would be

    7 *L'Edit de Tiberius Julius Alexander* (Olten and Lausanne
1964) 181-82.

most unwise to equate "average" with "normal" and to speak of ex-
tensions or curtailments of a normal term, of three years or otherwise. The best one can do is to follow Oertel[8] and Hohlwein[9] in
noting the great discrepancy found in lengths of tenure. The longest term attested remains that of Dionysodorus who served continuously in the Heracleides *meris* between May/June 12 and 25/6. His
case seems to have been exceptional but the evidence of twenty
other cases of service of between three and eight years helps to
put it into context.[10]

At the other end of the scale there are now several more examples to add to the two strategi known to Hohlwein who lasted
little more than a year.[11] Generally speaking as we get more
prefects serving for shorter periods so we seem to get more

---

8 *Die Liturgie* (Leipzig 1917) 293-95.

9 *Le Stratège du Nome* (Brussels 1926; repr., *Pap. Brux.* IX,
1969) 22-23.

10 See *AULLA 20 Proc. Papers, Newcastle, Australia, 1980*
(Newcastle 1980) I, 76-82.

11 Hohlwein (supra n. 9) 23. Strategi known to have served
less than two years include:
1. Iunius Hestiaeus: Oxy., 88/9, after 87/8 and before Oct
89; Whitehorne no. 30.
2. Antamon: Oxy., 98/9, after late 97 and before Nov 99;
Whitehorne no. 33 bis.
3. Asclepiades: Ars(H), Feb 108, after Jan 107 and before
Oct 108; Bastianini 22.
4. Heracleides: Ars(ThP), July/Aug 137, after 136/7 and before Oct 138; Bastianini 50.
5. Dion: Ars(H), 139-140, after Feb 139 and before Jan 141;
Bastianini 37.
6. Aelius Sarapion: Ars(H), Jan/Feb 145, after May 144 and
before Jan 146; Bastianini 38.
7. Archibius: Ars(H), Jan 146, after Jan/Feb 145 and before
May 146; Bastianini 38.
8. Sarapion: Ars(H), 170-171, after Nov 169 and before June
171; Bastianini 42.
9. Hieracapollon: Ars(ThP), Oct 181, after July 181 and before July 182; Bastianini 55.
10. Claudius Ischyrion alias Artemidorus: Oxy., July 190,
after 188/9 and before Aug/Sep 190; Whitehorne no. 63 bis.
11. Discorus: Ars(H), 190, after June-Aug 189 and before Feb
191; Bastianini 45.
12. Apollophanes alias Sarapammon: Ars(H), 209, after Mar 208
and before Dec 209; Bastianini 47.
I have not attempted to make this list exhaustive.

strategi doing likewise, and although there are of course many
cases where the tenure of a strategus overlaps two or even more
prefectures, particularly in the last quarter of the second century
when prefects were changed with great rapidity, there are also
plenty of examples where the turnover in strategi can be tentatively linked to a change of prefects.

To what extent, though, would a new prefect have been willing
to serve the interests of administrative continuity by delaying the
immediate replacement of his predecessor's appointees? A correlation of the fullest lists of known strategi, those of the Oxyrhynchite and Arsinoite, with the prefectural fasti,[12] can give a partial answer at least.

I present only a couple of examples here.[13]

(1)

Septimius Vegetus
8 Feb 85 - [before Apr/May] 88
        /([Feb/Mar] 89?)

Claudius Macedonius, Oxy.
(July 83)/25 June 86/(87/88)

Titus Flavius Heracleides, Oxy.
(25 June 86)/87/88 - [9 Mar 89?]
                   /(88/89)

Mettius Rufus
([Apr/May] 88)/[Feb/Mar] 89?
        - 91/92

Iunius Hestiaeus, Oxy.
([9 Mar 89?])/88/89/(31 Oct 89)

Claudius Areius, Oxy.
(88/89)/31 Oct 89 - 93/94

(2)

Iunius Rufus
26 Feb 94? - 21 June 98
        /([Oct-Dec] 98)

Ti. Claudius Hermias, Ars(H).
([89-91])/Nov [90-96]/(15 May 98)

Arrius Heracleides, Ars(H).
([90-96])/15 May 98 - 21 June 98
                    /(14 Sept 98)

---

12 For the Arsinoite, see G. Bastianini, *Gli strateghi dell'
Arsinoites in epoca romana* (*Pap. Brux.* XI, Brussels 1972); for the
Oxyrhynchite, my listing in *ZPE* 29 (1978) 167-89; and for the pre-
fects of Egypt, Bastianini, *ZPE* 17 (1975) 263-328, and Brunt (supra
n. 2) 142-47. Addenda and corrigenda are regularly noted by J.
Modrzejewski in part 2 of his "Chronique" in *RHD*.

13 Date = date attested in office; (Date) = *terminus post* or
ante; [Date] = date based on circumstantial evidence, e.g. document
type.

Pompeius Planta   Claudius Areius, Ars(H).
(21 June 98)/[Oct-Dec] 98   (21 June 98)/14 Sept 98 - July 101
    - 14 Feb 100

In the first, it is clear that whether his arrival in Egypt is
dated to summer 88 or early 89 Mettius Rufus must have made at
least one appointment to the strategia within his first year in the
country, that is during the period in which, on Brunt's thesis, he
would still have been inexpert in the administration of his province.

In the second case, it looks as though it may have been Pompeius
Planta who was responsible for replacing the strategus of the Heracleides *meris*, and that he did so within a very short time of taking
office. It is obvious from these examples, and others, that prefects did not always feel constrained to abide by their predecessors'
appointments, even though by doing so they might have been able to
minimise the possible disruptive effects of their own inexperience.

Finally it may be asked what attempt was made to capitalise
upon experience in the strategia by reappointment to a second term.
Homonymity means that there is often no way of knowing in some
cases whether there is iteration or not. Nevertheless there are
now eighteen cases where iteration is certain or probable, and
another thirteen which I would accept as possible.[14] Doubling this
figure to allow for examples concealed by homonymity would give us
a maximum of fifteen-sixteen percent of the total of known strategi,
which is perhaps enough to indicate a trend but hardly a regular
policy of iteration. Indeed the paucity of titles of the form γενόμενος στρατηγὸς τοῦ δεῖνος νομοῦ, ἔναρχος στρατηγὸς τοῦ δεῖνος
νομοῦ seems to support the conclusion that iteration was the exception rather than the rule.

Summing up, most strategi might be expected to have some general knowledge of the *chora*, and some, perhaps even many of them,
might have had previous administrative experience. Yet these were
incidental qualities, not prerequisites for appointment. They are
unlikely to have been familiar with their particular areas of

---

14 I am grateful to the editor for drawing my attention to
the latest example of iteration to be confirmed. Vegetus alias
Sarapion was already known as str., Ars(H), 28 Jan - 21 Oct 137
(Bastianini 37). P. Cairo S.R. 3049 inv. 43,2, edited here by A.H.
el-Mosallamy (pp. 215-29) now shows him as str., Ars (Th), 26 Aug
135. I hope to discuss iteration in the strategia more fully
in a forthcoming paper in *ZPE*.

appointment, and there was no regular cursus for the strategia, such as there was for the Alexandrian offices. Indeed there is surprisingly little flow on to the strategia from the post most closely associated with it, that of royal scribe. Furthermore there was no normal term for the office, despite the apparent attempt by Ti. Julius Alexander to establish one. Turnover in strategi shows little evidence of any desire to promote administrative efficiency, and finally the relatively small number of extended or double terms also underlines the apparent lack of concern for, or perhaps lack of perception of, a need to maintain administrative continuity at this level.

In short the typical strategus was just as much an amateur to modern eyes as Brunt's typical prefect, who at least made up in varied experience for what he lacked in local knowledge. Given such a combination, we must surely wonder not that the administration of Roman Egypt was so inefficient, but that it ever managed to function as effectively as it did.

University of Queensland   J. E. G. Whitehorne

APPENDIX

NOME STRATEGI HOLDING OTHER OFFICES BEFORE OR CONCURRENTLY
WITH THE STRATEGIA, LISTED BY DATE.

1. Heracleides: Heracl., after 15/14 B.C.; ἐπὶ τῶν προσόδων;
   Henne 16.

2. Ptolemaeus: Tentyrite, 13-10 B.C.; syngenes, prophetes, agent
   of Caesar in Denderah, ἐπὶ τῶν προσόδων; Henne 38.

3. Corax: Tentyrite, n.d. (but son of preceding); syngenes,
   prophetes; Henne 38.

4. Theon: Heracl., 1 B.C./1; ἐπὶ τῶν προσόδων; Henne 16.

5. Apollonius s. of Ptolemaeus: Ombite, Eleph., and Philae,
   before 2; paralemptes of Erythraean Sea; Henne 25.

6. Sarapion: unknown nome, 6; gymnasiarch; Mussies no. 344.

7. Lucretius: unknown nome, 15; centurion, b.g.; *SB* I 5954,11.

8. Didymus s. of Hierax: Ars(Th), 38; member of Museum;
   Bastianini 11.

9. C. Iulius Asclas: Ars(H.Th), 39/40; exegetes, archiereus
   of Gaius; Bastianini 10-11.

10. Ti. Claudius Philoxenus: Ars(Th), 42; epistates phylakiton;
    Bastianini 11.

11. C. Iulius Asinianus: Ars(H), 57-59; ex-exegetes ? Bastianini
    14.

12. Ti. Claudius Ammonius: Oxy., 59; ἐπὶ τῶν προσόδων; Whitehorne
    no. 20.

13. Philoxenus: Ars(Th), 63/64; ex-cosmetes; Bastianini 15.

14. Papiscus: Oxy., 66; ex-cosmetes (Alex.); Whitehorne no. 23.

15. Ti. Claudius Sara[pion: Oxy., i-ii; ex-agoranomus of Alex. ?;
    Whitehorne no. 36.

16. Claudius Chrysermus: Coptite, 103; paralemptes; Henne 13.

17. Lucretius Cerealis: Ars(H), 104-107; τῶν κεχιλιαρχηκότων;
    Bastianini 20.

18. Heracleides: Ars(H), 149-151; ex-b.g. and acting str. (Ars(H):
    (147-148)); Bastianini 39. See Eliassen - De Kat (supra n. 4)
    121 n. 4.

19. Apollonius minor: Sethroite, before 170; ex-gymnasiarch, b.g.
    (Bubastite); Mussies no. 321, 394.

20. Isidorus: Apoll., before 170; ex-archiereus; Henne 3.

21. Alexander: Apoll. and Sethroite, before 170; ex-gymnasiarch, agoranomus; Henne 3.

22. Aur. Asclepiades: Heracl., before 170; ex-gymnasiarch; Henne 16.

23. Apion: Antaeopolite, 193/4; ex-gymn. (Oxy.; before 199); Whitehorne no. 3A. It is possible that Apion's strategia antedates his gymnasiarchy.

24. Lucretius Nilus: Oxy., 197-198; ex-agoranomus, gymnasiarch, and royal banker (Arsinoe; 194) ? Whitehorne no. 67.

25. Dioscorus s. of Apollonius: Heliopolite, before 210/11; ex-gymnasiarch; Henne 15.

26. Sarapion alias Phanias: unknown nome, 211; ex-gymnasiarch (Oxy.; 203) ? ; Whitehorne no. 4A.

27. Aur. Spartiates alias Chaeremon: Herm., 258-259; ex-gymnasiarch, bouleutes (Oxy.; ca. 258-260); Mussies no. 198, *P. Oxy.* XLVI 3290.1n.

28. Aur. Olympius; Oxy., 280; ex-hypomnematographus; Whitehorne no. 102.

29. Aur. Heracleides: Oxy., 288/9; exegetes (Alex.); Whitehorne no. 106.

30. Aur. Apollonius: Oxy., 290; ex-hypomnematographus; Whitehorne no. 107.

31. Aur. Diogenes: Mendesian (διοικῶν), iii; ex-hypomnematographus; Henne 23.

32. Theon alias Plutarch: Tanite, iii; ex-hypomnematographus; Henne 37.

33. Aur. Hermias: Oxy., 323-325; ex-gymnasiarch; Whitehorne no. 120.

PART 7

BYZANTINE EGYPT

L'EGYPTE AU IVe SIECLE: FISCALITE, ECONOMIE, SOCIETE

Invité à participer au colloque sur le IVe siècle, j'avais d'abord projeté un rapport général sur l'économie et la société égyptiennes durant la période. Il m'est apparu bientôt que la fiscalité se situait à un point de convergence de ces deux thématiques et que son approche se trouvait renouvelée par la documentation papyrologique la plus récente. A mon projet initial de rapport-bilan s'est donc progressivement substituée une remise en question générale des idées admises sur la fiscalité romaine tardive. Les limites d'espace, dans les *Actes* comme dans l'exposé oral, ne permettent plus d'accueillir l'ensemble de ces propositions. En attendant de pouvoir publier l'exposé intégral, j'en donnerai ici les grandes lignes.

On sait que trois théories ont été développées concernant la fiscalité égyptienne dans son rapport avec la "capitation": (a) la fiscalité de Dioclétien aurait été appliquée à l'Egypte dès le début, et l'édit d'Aristius Optatus en fournirait la preuve;[1] (b) la fiscalité de Dioclétien n'aurait jamais été introduite en Egypte;[2] (c) l'Egypte aurait été tenue à l'écart du système en 287, mais lui aurait été plus tard soumise; ce serait chose faite au milieu du IVe siècle, puisque des *képhalai* sont mentionnées en 359, des *terrena iuga* en 377.[3]

Avant de préciser le mode d'assiette de la fiscalité égyptienne du IVe siècle, il n'est pas inutile d'opérer une classification des diverses contributions exigées des provinciaux, et de mieux définir la nature de certaines d'entre elles.

---

1 J. Karayannopulos, *Das Finanzwesen des Frühbyzantinischen Staates* (München 1958). R. Rémondon dans *Proceedings of the XII [1968] Intern. Congress of Papyrology* (Toronto 1970) 431-36. Mais son raisonnement plaide tout autant en faveur de la non-application à l'Egypte de la "Capitation."

2 A.H.M. Jones, "*Capitatio* and *Iugatio*," *JRS* 47 (1957) 88-94 (= *Roman Economy*, 280-92).

3 J. Lallemand, *L'administration civile de l'Egypte byzantine*, 184-85; A. Deléage, *La Capitation de Dioclétien*, 112-14.

I. Les différentes formes de fiscalité et parafiscalité en Egypte
au IVe siècle

A. *L'impôt proprement dit (en nature ou en espèces)*

L'Etat lève en nature les denrées qui lui sont utiles, sur les
terres qui les produisent, là où elles lui sont utiles, ou faciles
à transporter. Il commue en espèces (*adaeratio*) ces mêmes denrées
dans tous les autres cas, c'est-à-dire: quand l'impôt pèse sur une
terre non-productrice de la denrée en question (τιμὴ πύρου, τιμὴ
κρέως, ἀναβολικόν en espèces); quand le produit imposable n'est pas
susceptible d'utilisation par l'Etat (φόρος προβάτων sur les ovins
et les chèvres); quand le coût du transport rend plus avantageux de
lever en espèces l'équivalent des *species* qu'on achètera, par réquisition remboursée, à proximité de leur lieu d'utilisation. C'est
pourquoi je juge tout à fait aléatoires les tentatives d'évaluation
statistique des pratiques d'*adaeratio*. Pour assurer leur perti-
nence, il faudrait retenir uniquement les cas dans lesquels l'*adaeratio* représente un choix politique véritable, et non pas la pratique normale, imposée, techniquement inévitable.[4]

D'autre part, l'Etat entretient sa trésorerie par des impôts
en espèces. Certains de ces impôts ont une destination spécifique
et ne se mêlent jamais aux autres: ainsi, le groupe des "impôts
militaires": *aurum tironicum*, *primipilon*, χρυσὸς βουρδόνων. D'autres, au contraire, sont très génériques, comme l'indiquent leurs
titres: ὑπὲρ ἀργυρικῶν τίτλων.[5]

B. *La réquisition remboursée* (coemptio, συνωνή)

Elle ne constitue pas une nouveauté, au IVe siècle. Dans le
domaine du ravitaillement militaire, on peut même dire, qu'elle a
reculé par rapport aux siècles précédents, remplacée par la fiscalité en nature.[6] On y a encore recours dans des circonstances

---

4 C'est la raison essentielle des réserves que j'ai déjà ex-
primées ("Le rôle économique de l'armée dans l'Egypte romaine,"
dans *Armées et Fiscalité* [Paris 1977]), à l'encontre des conclusions de R. MacMullen, "Some Tax Statistics from Roman Egypt,"
Aegyptus 42 (1962) 98-102.

5 Formule présente dans *SPP* XX 93; à restituer dans *P. Cair.
Preis.* 33, par similitude avec P. Vindob. Inv. G. 13094.

6 *Armées et Fiscalité*, 375.

particulières (opérations militaires, transit de troupes) ou, plus
régulièrement, pour l'approvisionnement d'Alexandrie.

Cependant la forme la plus originale de *coemptio*, au IVe
siècle, c'est incontestablement l'achat obligatoire d'or et de
billon d'argent, réparti au prorata de l'impôt en blé dû par chaque
contribuable.[7] Actuellement, les attestations papyrologiques de
cette pratique vont de 300 à 329 (si l'on accepte l'interprétation
donnée par R. S. Bagnall et K. A. Worp du P. Vindob. Inv. G 27879).
Or une allusion à ces mêmes réquisitions doit être tirée, me
semble-t-il, d'une loi beaucoup plus tardive (377), *Cod. Theod.* VII
6, 3. De ce texte fort riche, je retiendrai pour le moment la mention d'un *aurum comparaticium* qui, pris littéralement, ne peut désigner autre chose qu'*auri coemptio*, χρυσοῦ συνωνή. Cette institution n'aurait donc pas été limitée à l'Egypte, puisque la plupart
des provinces orientales y sont soumises. Comment concilier cette
donnée juridique avec l'absence de toute mention de ces réquisitions dans les papyrus après 329? Je suggérerai l'explication suivante: en 377, on peut appeler encore *aurum comparaticium* une levée
devenue purement fiscale, par disparition graduelle du remboursement, mais qu'une pieuse fiction rattache au souvenir de la χρυσοῦ
συνωνή. Je montrerai plus loin qu'effectivement dès les deux premières décennies du siècle, le tarif de remboursement ne cesse de
s'éloigner du prix réel des métaux précieux.

P. *Oxy.* XLVI 3307, a été dissocié à juste titre des réquisitions de métaux précieux par J. R. Rea, qui le date du "début du
IVe siècle." Or, on imagine difficilement que la *coemptio* véritable
et les levées fiscales d'or aient pu coexister. On notera, d'autre
part, que la même proportion observée dans ce document entre l'or
et l'argent (1:12) se trouve également dans P. *Vindob.* G 13174 V°,
datable de ca. 335, et typique de la fiscalité constantinienne en
espèces.[8]

---

7 J. R. Rea, "*PSI* IV 310 and Imperial Bullion Purchases,"
Cd'E 49 (1974) 163-74; R. S. Bagnall, "Bullion Purchases and Land-
holding in the Fourth Century," *Cd'E* 52 (1977) 322-36.

8 P. J. Sijpesteijn et K. A. Worp, "Ein neues Archiv: Hermias
und Maximos, Söhne des Sarapions," *ZPE* 32 (1978) 250, n° 6.

C'est pourquoi je proposerai déjà de reconnaître dans *P.*
Vindob. G 27879, pour l'expression χρυσὸς συνωνῆς, la même signification qu'*aurum comparaticium* dans le *Code Théodosien*, et d'y voir
un témoignage de l'évolution vers l'impôt pur et simple. De fait,
le versement est intitulé χρυσὸς συνωνῆς ιϛ ἤτοι γ ἰνδικτίονος,[9]
donc intégré à l'indiction fiscale annuelle.

C. *Impôt et réquisition combinés*

Nous trouvons enfin des systèmes complexes combinant impôt
monétaire et réquisition de travail--c'est le cas de la *vestis
militaris*--, ou impôt en espèces, fourniture en nature et indemnité
compensatoire--dans la *praebitio tironum* et la *comparatio equitum
sive mularum.*

1. *La* vestis militaris

L'opinion la plus courante voudrait que la *vestis militaris*,
dans l'Egypte du IVe siècle, ait été perçue en nature, les imposi-
tions fractionnaires étant seules converties en espèces.[10] Un ré-
examen de la documentation papyrologique suggère un tout autre
fonctionnement de l'institution.

Dans un premier temps, un impôt en argent était levé, selon un
tarif précis d'équivalence entre les divers types de vêtements et
leur prix (c'est pourquoi les reçus de paiement sont exprimés non
en valeur monétaire, mais en unités et fractions de vêtements).
Seuls des versements en argent peuvent expliquer la multitude de
fractions de *vestes* acquittées dans *P. Oxy.* XII 1448, en 314--c'est
l'exemple le plus frappant. Dans les registres mêmes où les versements ne sont pas fractionnaires (par exemple, *P. Stras.* V 618 et
695) la formule ἐξοδιάσθη nous assure qu'il s'agit bien de paiements en espèces.

P. Oxy. XVI 1905, document bien connu, nous a conservé un
barême de perception de la *vestis militaris* qui paraît appliqué
dans le *P. Stras.* V 695, ainsi que dans P. Mich. Inv. 418 verso,
daté de 353/4, mais que nous ne retrouvons ni au début du IVe

---

9 R. S. Bagnall et K. A. Worp dans *Cd'E* 52 (1977) 319-21.

10 A. C. Johnson et L. C. West, *Byzantine Egypt*, 221; R. Mac
Mullen, "The Anabolicae Species," *Aegyptus* 38 (1958) 184-98.

siècle, ni en 377.[11] Le taux de levée a donc varié au cours du IVe
siècle, de même que sa justification: ainsi, en 359, *SB* V 7756 di-
vise l'impôt dû pour la *vestis* entre prix du matériau (ἀναβολικόν),
et prix pour la confection (τριμιτάριοι).

La deuxième phase de l'opération voit l'administration s'a-
dresser à des tisserands professionnels, citadins ou villageois,
pour tisser les vêtements, contre paiement de leur travail. Le
document le plus éclairant, à cet égard, est *P. Ross. Georg.* V 61,
que je daterais personnellement du dernier quart du IVe siècle.[12]
Parmi plusieurs autres συνῶναι ou *coemptiones*, figurent des paiements effectués à des tisserands, selon un prix voisin d'un sou
d'or, ce qui constitue un prix courant, et prouve qu'il s'agit d'un
paiement complet (matériau et travail). D'autres documents attestent des prix fort inférieurs à ceux du marché: dans *P. Oxy.* XLIV
3194, en 323, 4000 et 5000 drachmes par *sticharion* et *pallion* res-
pectivement (soit les mêmes prix qu'en 301); encore moins en 324,
dans *P. Ant.* I 39. Dans les cas de ce genre, je suggérerai que ces
remboursements couvraient seulement le prix de la confection (comme
pour les orfèvres fabriquant une couronne d'or dans *P. Oxy.* XLIII
3121). La déduction des ἑκατοσταί, appliquée au montant versé,
irait dans le sens de cette interprétation.

Les deux opérations sont totalement indépendantes l'une de
l'autre, si bien que nous ne pouvons pas estimer la surface imposable d'un village d'après le nombre des *vestes* qu'il produit
(par exemple, *P. Cair. Isid.* 54); ce nombre peut être tout à fait
hors de proportion avec le montant de l'impôt dû par le même village au titre de la *vestis militaris*.

---

11 H. C. Youtie, "P. Mich. Inv. 418 Verso: Tax Memoranda,"
ZPE 38 (1980) 285-86. R. S. Bagnall, qui a récemment cherché à
resserrer la datation du *P. Oxy.* 1905 ("P. Oxy. XVI 1905, SB V 7756
and Fourth Century Taxation," *ZPE* 37 [1980] 185-98), propose les
années 356/357 et 371/372. Je serais personnellement enclin à retenir 356/357, sans exclure 341/342.

12 En raison du prix de l'or dans ce document (je compte re-
venir ailleurs sur ce point). Le document a été arbitrairement
rattaché à la période 300-340 par R. Mac Mullen, "The Anabolicae
Species," 196 n. 4) et interprété comme une *adaeratio* de la *vestis*.

2. Χρυσὸς τιρόνων (aurum tironicum) *et* χρυσὸς βουρδόνων (comparatio mularum sive equitum)

Hommes et chevaux représentent les deux fournitures les plus difficiles à obtenir de la population. Dans les deux cas, la réquisition représente un amoindrissement des facultés productives de la cellule contributive. Chacun cherche à s'y soustraire, et toute injustice est ici plus durement ressentie qu'ailleurs. Ainsi s'expliquerait la profonde similitude que je propose de voir entre les mécanismes de la *praebitio tironum* et ceux de la *comparatio equitum*, similitude qui permet de les éclairer l'une par l'autre. Le langage de l'*Anonymus de rebus bellicis* prouve qu'une telle assimilation existait dans l'esprit des contemporains.[13]

Le gouvernement impérial fait peser sur tous l'*adaeratio* des recrues militaires: c'est l'*aurum tironicum*, dont le produit sert, pour une part, à financer les dépenses d'enrôlement, pour une autre part, bien plus considérable, à verser une indemnité compensatoire au groupe qui fournit la recrue effective (30 *solidi* sur 36, dans *P. Lond.* III 985 [p. 228], comme dans *Cod. Theod.* VIII 13,7). Un système identique expliquerait les prix considérables, bien supérieurs aux prix du marché, que les lois impériales fixent pour les chevaux militaires. L'hypothèse d'un *interpraetium* scandaleusement pratiqué par l'Etat deviendrait alors inutile.[14]

Aucun document égyptien ne fait état de la *comparatio equitum*. Une loi de 290, *Cod. Iust.* XI 55,1, indique cependant que des mules pouvaient être également requises: *mularum fiscalium vel equorum ministerium*. L'impôt intitulé χρυσὸς βουρδόνων a généralement été considéré par les papyrologues et les historiens comme un impôt de transport de denrées militaires. Il me paraît beaucoup plus naturel de voir en lui, par comparaison avec le χρυσὸς τιρόνων, l'or destiné à rembourser les mulets réquisitionnés.[15]

---

13 *Anonymus de rebus bellicis*, édition R. Schneider, p. 8: *tironum comparatio, equorum vel frumenti coemptio*.

14 C'est l'explication de S. Mazzarino, *Aspetti sociali del quarto secolo*, 145-49.

15 Il faudrait donc rectifier, dans ma communication au colloque *Armées et Fiscalité*, le tableau de la p. 383, dans lequel je plaçais encore le χρυσὸς βουρδόνων parmi les impôts non militaires; on comprendrait mieux, en outre, l'association du χρυσὸς βουρδόνων avec le χρυσὸς πριμιπίλου, indiquée dans ma communication au *XVe* [1977] *Congrès Int. de Papyrologie de Bruxelles* (*Actes* IV, 169).

Il convient, au total, d'insister sur la souplesse de l'appareil fiscal, qui permet, par exemple, d'assurer l'entretien des armées par l'impôt en nature ou par des fournitures en espèces; par l'impôt ou par la réquisition. Cette complexité rend plus inutile encore la théorie de l'*annona militaris* comme impôt séparé.

II. Situation de la fiscalité égyptienne au regard de la *iugatio-capitatio*

A. *Position du problème*

Je tiendrai pour acquis les deux principes suivants: La *iugatio sive capitatio* constitue un tout dont on ne peut isoler les éléments.[16] C'est l'équivalent du mot composé grec ζυγοκεφαλή. Les registres fonciers épigraphiques nous montrent que si l'assiette est d'abord estimée en *iuga* pour ce qui se mesure, en *capita* pour ce qui se compte, le but final est d'exprimer l'ensemble de la matière imposable en ζυγοκεφαλαί. Seules des attestations de ζυγοκεφαλαί en Egypte pourraient prouver dans cette province l'application d'un système d'assiette "bivalente," d'une *capitatio sive iugatio*.[17]

J'ajouterai un troisième principe dont je suis personnellement convaincu, mais qu'il me faudra prouver: *capitatio* et *iugatio* peuvent coexister dans une même province, comme deux modes d'assiette distincts, servant chacun à lever des impôts différents.[18]

Il faut par ailleurs tenir compte d'une grande rapidité d'évolution sémantique du langage fiscal, au IVe siècle, dans les lois impériales comme dans les papyrus égyptiens.

B. *L'arouratio*

Les historiens de la "capitation" ont généralement cru que toutes les provinces de l'Empire avaient été soumises au système de la *capitatio sive iugatio* pour le calcul de l'assiette. C'est

---

16 Jones, "*Capitatio* and *Iugatio*," passim.

17 Ibid., 89 (= *Roman Economy*, 283-84) et 93 (= 290-91).

18 C'était même là, à mon avis, le système en vigueur dans la majorité des provinces, la *iugatio sive capitatio* se limitant essentiellement aux provinces d'Asie Mineure.

manifestement faux pour l'*Italia suburbicaria*, et Jones pensait de
même pour l'*Africa*.[19]

Roger Rémondon, au Congrès d'Ann Arbor, avait établi la persistance jusqu'au VIe siècle de l'*arouratio* comme assiette de la
fiscalité égyptienne. Les documents publiés depuis 1968 n'ont pas
démenti cette appréciation, qui n'est cependant nullement incompatible avec l'existence d'un multiple de l'aroure, le *iugum*, et qui
demande à être complétée par une définition plus précise des
mérismoi.

De fait, lors de la réforme fiscale de 287, l'Egypte est dé-
meurée plus que jamais une province redevable de *species*. Les
céréales, sans jamais constituer une monoculture, demeurent la production largement dominante. Les différences mêmes de fertilité,
soigneusement classifiées dans les îles grecques (cadastre de Théra)
ou en Syrie (*Livre de droit Syro-Romain*, FIRA II^2 [1968] pp. 795-
796), sont tenues pour négligeables par la réglementation fiscale
égyptienne.

Le seul coefficient de la surface cultivée règle donc, pour
toute l'imposition livrable en nature ou adérée--je laisse de côté
l'imposition en espèces--le problème de l'assiette fiscale,
épargnant ainsi à l'Egypte le lourd système de cadastration et
d'assiette de la *iugatio sive capitatio*. Le principe comme l'application de ce système étant simples et connus, un seul point me
retiendra ici: que représentent les *terrena iuga* sur lesquels repose en 377 (*Cod. Theod.* VII 6,3) l'imposition de la *vestis militaris*, en Egypte comme dans les autres provinces orientales? Deléage a comparé ce texte à *P. Oxy.* XVI 1905, en supposant à tort
que 3 *vestes* (1 chlamyde, 1 tunique, 1 *pallion*) étaient exigées
pour 2183 aroures, ce qui donne une parité d'un *iugum* pour 72
aroures 23/30.[20] Le papyrus ne peut se comprendre que d'une seule
manière: 1925 aroures sont soumises au paiement d'1 *pallion*, 11
tuniques et 8 chlamydes, soit 1 *vestis* pour 96 aroures 1/4. Rappe-
lons ici que Jones rend "approximativement" cohérent le registre de

---

19   Jones, "*Capitatio* and *Iugatio*," 91 (= *Roman Economy*, 287).

20   Deléage, *Capitation*, 115. De plus, le calcul repose sur
une erreur textuelle (1 chlamyde pour 83 aroures, au lieu de 243).

Théra en supposant pour le *iugum* une valeur de 100 jugères de terre arable:[21] 100 jugères sont très proches de 96 aroures. Si 1925 aroures représentent 20 *iuga*, le tarif de *P. Oxy.* 1905, comparé à celui de 377, serait plus lourd d'un tiers. Mais la loi de 377 est explicitement présentée comme un allègement fiscal pour certaines provinces, cependant que d'autres, la Thrace, par exemple, s'y voient maintenir l'imposition de 20 *iuga*. En Egypte même, dans le *P. Oxy.* XVI 1905 toujours, les 36 *solidi* correspondant au tarif d'un *tiro*, à raison d'1 gramme d'or pour 20 3/4 aroures, représentent la contribution de 2988 aroures, où l'on retrouve 30 *iuga* de 100 jugères.

Cette loi a été écrite dans les bureaux de Constantinople. Ses termes doivent pouvoir s'appliquer aux divers systèmes fiscaux en vigueur dans les provinces. Nous pouvons être certains que, une fois passée la frontière égyptienne, les *iuga* étaient convertis en aroures. On peut citer un autre exemple de dispositions impériales appliquées à l'Egypte, et qui cette fois conservent les termes de l'original: c'est *P. Oxy.* XVII 2117: pour le financement de transports militaires à destination de Byzance et Héraklée du Pont, en 316, le barème fiscal conserve des unités d'imposition (1 olivier, 1 aroure de pâturage, etc.) rencontrées en Syrie, mais inconnues ou inusitées en Egypte.

C. Mérismoi *et* épiképhalaion

Indépendemment de l'*arouratio*, nous rencontrons un autre mode d'assiette: le *mérismos*, fondé sur une répartition entre κεφαλαί (*capita*). Ces *mérismoi* ont-ils un rapport avec la *iugatio sive capitatio* dioclétianienne?

1. Ἄνδρες *et* κεφαλαί

On a souvent invoqué ce terme de *képhalé* pour affirmer l'existence, au IVe siècle, d'un impôt individuel de taux uniforme.[22] Un document tout récemment publié, *P. Oxy.* XLVI 3307, me paraît

---

21 A.H.M. Jones, "Census Records of the Later Roman Empire," *JRS* 43 (1953) 50 (= *Roman Economy*, 230).

22 J. Lallemand et R. Rémondon ont cependant rejeté un tel raisonnement.

contredire définitivement cette théorie. Nous y voyons un impôt en
or et en argent (et non une *coemptio*) levé dans le 8e *pagus* oxyrhynchite, et réparti entre les villages et *epoikia*. L'intitulé
est nouveau dans les papyrus: κατ' ἄνδρα κήνσου παγαρχίας Τήεως,
mais le latin *census* prend couramment le sens d'"impôt en espèces"
(cf. par exemple *Cod. Iust.* XI 52,1, *Cod. Théod.* XIII 10,2, de 313,
et le *Panégyrique* VIII). La répartition est faite sur 346 ἄνδρες
ὑποτελεῖς: 129 à Teeis, chef-lieu du *pagus*; 186 dans d'autres villages, et 31 dans les *epoikia*. Chaque ἄνηρ est imposé de 2 grammes
d'or et 24 grammes d'argent. Ces ἄνδρες ne sauraient être des contribuables individuels payant l'impôt à un taux uniforme, comme
dans l'ancienne λαογραφία. Nous ne pouvons pas penser un seul instant qu'un *pagus* entier comptait seulement 346 contribuables, un
village 4, etc. L'ἄνηρ ὑποτελῆς est une unité abstraite d'imposition, qui permet d'exprimer une répartition de quotités entre les
divers groupements humains. De même, en latin, *tributarius* est
synonime de *caput* dans *Cod. Theod.* VII 4,32.

        Aussi nous faut-il reconsidérer *P. Théad.* 17 (= *P. Sakaon* 44),
daté de 332: εἰσφέρομεν ὑπὲρ ὅλης τῆς κώμης ἀρούρων πεντακοσίων καὶ
μηδὲ συνπροσχοριζομένων καὶ τοῦ κατ' ἄνδρα σὺν ταμιακοῖς ἀνδράσι
εἴκοσι πέντε. Ces 25 ἄνδρες ne constituent pas un témoignage dé-
mographique; ils expriment la part d'imposition de Théadelphie par
rapport à l'imposition de la pagarchie dont elle dépend; de même,
dans *P. Oxy.* 3307, des villages comptaient pour 65, 64, 23, 19, 11
et 4 ἄνδρες. Inversement, quand Sakaon déclare 9 contribuables
vivant sous son toit, il ne dit pas ἄνδρες ὑποτελεῖς, mais ὑποτελεῖς tout court. Notons encore que trois familles de cette ampleur
constitueraient à elles seules la population entière de Théadelphie,
si les ἄνδρες ὑποτελεῖς étaient des individus.

        Une explication du même type me paraît inévitable dans le cas
du célèbre *BGU* I 21, dont la 1ère colonne peut se résumer ainsi:

        Mois de *Pâchôn*: 125 1/2 ἄνδρες, à 25 talents.

        Pour les trois mois de *Pauni, Epeiph, Mésoré*: 100 ἄνδρες re-
spectivement à 15, 12 et 15 talents.[23]

---

23 Deléage, *Capitation*, interprétait ces ἄνδρες comme des
soldats, ce qui ne donne aucun sens.

Une variation subite de la population entre *Pachôn* et *Epeiph*
est une hypothèse absurde. Le détail du calcul s'explique par le
montant total à prélever, 7337 1/2 talents, et par la recherche de
diviseurs permettant de le répartir sur un quadrimestre. Le document n'est pas de même nature que *P. Oxy.* XLVI 3307 (c'est une
simple répartition interne), mais le terme d'ἀνήρ y a le même sens,
purement arithmétique, de fraction, d'unité par rapport à un tout.[24]

Dans tous ces textes, la fraction représente un certain montant
d'impôt, dont la valeur n'est pas fixe ni universelle. En effet, au
lieu de calculer l'impôt à lever en fonction de la richesse imposable, un *mérismos* part d'un montant déterminé d'imposition, qu'il
répartit sur le total de *capita*. En d'autres termes:

$$\frac{\textit{montant total à prélever}}{\text{nombre d'ἀνδρες ou de κεφαλαί}} = \text{unité de levée fiscale}$$

Notons encore que la répartition constitue une chaîne ininter-
rompue, depuis le diocèse (cf. la *communis formula* du *Panégyrique*
VIII) jusqu'à la collectivité locale, l'échelon de base. Au niveau
de la perception concrète, les liturges ont à répartir entre leurs
administrés la contribution globale de la communauté, qui résulte
d'un calcul simple: x unités x valeur de l'unité. Tout le problème
est alors de savoir sur quels critères se fait cette répartition en
l'absence des coefficients précis que définit dans d'autres provinces la *iugatio sive capitatio*. Il est exclu que la contribution
aux *mérismoi* ait été indexée sur l'*arouratio*. Et la surface possé-
dée n'est qu'un facteur parmi d'autres de la fortune imposable. Je
souscris donc, sur ce point, aux constatations formulées par Rémondon, malgré les critiques que lui a adressées R. S. Bagnall.[25] Une
chose est en tout cas certaine: la moyenne des versements individuels est bien inférieure à 1 κεφαλή ou 1 ἀνήρ. C'est pourquoi ces
termes disparaissent au niveau de la perception, et font place à
des expressions du type: τὸ μέρος, τὸ αἱροῦν μέρος, τὰ αἱροῦντα.

---

24 Ce sens arithmétique de *caput* a été clairement dégagé par
E. Faure, *Etude de la capitation de Dioclétien d'après le Panégyrique VIII* (Paris 1961), en particulier p. 96. Même conclusion
pour ἀνήρ dans l'article de R. S. Bagnall cité n. 11 (pp. 192-93).

25 Rémondon, art. cité n. 1; Bagnall, art. cité n. 11, pp.
190-95.

2. *Epiképhalaion kômês*

J'essaierai d'établir qu'aucune preuve n'existe, au IVe siècle, de la survie d'une capitation générale de taux individuel uniforme, pourtant admise par la plupart des historiens.[26] L'expression *épiképhalaion kômês*, pour commencer par elle se rencontre dans *P. Théad.* 48 (= *P. Sakaon* 9) et *P. Cair. Isidor.* 72. Elle signifie, à mon avis, la récapitulation de divers impôts, tarifés séparément, mais prélevés ensemble (comme dans *SB* V 7756) sur les contribuables en tant qu'individus et non en tant qu'unités de levée. Ce sens de κεφαλή existait déjà sous le Haut-Empire, comme dans P. Berol. Inv. 16036 verso.[27]

Ces deux sens de *képhalé* se combinent dans l'Edit d'Aristius Optatus, *P. Cair. Isidor.* 1. Dans la section perdue du texte étaient publiés, tout d'abord le tarif de l'impôt foncier (ποσὰ οὖν ἑκάστῃ ἀρούρᾳ πρὸς τὴν ποιότητα τῆς γῆς ἐπεβλήθη), ensuite le tarif de l'imposition personnelle (πόσα οὖν ἑκάστῃ κεφαλῇ τῶν ἀγροίκων). Nous pouvons raisonnablement imaginer ce tarif sur le modèle de *SB* V 7756, fixant des taux κατὰ κεφαλήν ou πρὸς κεφαλήν. Une allusion directe à ce tarif de 297[28] est faite trois ans plus tard dans *P. Panop. Beatty* 2.229: l'unité de levée (ποσότης) de l'ἀργυρολογία-- c'est-à-dire de l'*epiképhalaion*--a été précisée par un édit impérial toujours en vigueur.

Ainsi, les impôts non assis sur l'*arouratio* étaient indifféremment dénommés tantôt par la forme monétaire de leur versement: ἀργυρολογία, ἀργυρικοὶ τίτλοι, κῆνσος, plus informellement encore ἔχθεσις (ἀργυρίου ou χρυσοῦ)

---

26 Par exemple, Jones, "*Capitatio* and *Iugatio*," 93 (= *Roman Economy*, 291) bien qu'il l'exclue dans certains cas: ibid., 90 (284). Quoiqu'il en soit, il interprète toujours κεφαλή dans le sens d'"individu."

27 = A. Swiderek dans *Festschrift 150 jähr. Bestehen Berl. Aeg. Museums* (Berlin 1975) 425-29. Nous trouvons dans ce texte, pour κεφαλή, le sens d'"individu," "particulier," et non celui de "part." De la même façon, *Cod. Theod.* utilise couramment *capitatio* au sens d'"impôt individuel" par opposition à l'impôt foncier.

28 297, soit dix ans après la réforme fiscale de Dioclétien, au terme de la deuxième *épigraphé* de cinq ans.

tantôt par la modalité de leur assiette, qui était de répartition:

ἐπικεφάλαιον, μερισμὸς κατ' ἄνδρα, négligeamment abrégé en τὸ κατ' ἄνδρα.

Dans *P. Stras.* III 337 (330/331), un reçu récapitulatif, ἀποχὴ παντοίων μερισμῶν, est délivré contre paiement des ἀργυρικοὶ τίτλοι, de l'ἐξαργυρισμὸς πατρεμουνίου (*sic*), de divers ναῦλα et diverses adérations.

Sans avoir ici le temps de développer mon argumentation, je voudrais également indiquer qu'à mon avis les impôts recouvrés dans l'important registre fiscal du village de Skar, *CPR* V 26[29] sont ceux-là mêmes que d'autres documents appellent *mérismos*, ou *épiképhalaion*.

3. *Epiképhalaion poléôs*

Les données du problème semblent ici plus contradictoires. Premier élément du dossier: dans un groupe de documents jusqu'à maintenant exclusivement oxyrhynchites, datant de 296/7 à 315/6, les citadins résidents paient un impôt qui porte le nom d'*épiképhalaion poléôs* sans rien avoir d'une taxe municipale. J. R. Rea, à qui nous devons l'essentiel de nos connaissances sur ce sujet, avait d'abord admis une gamme diversifiée des paiements; il est finalement revenu à l'idée de Deléage d'un impôt de taux uniforme rappelant la *laographia*.[30] Dans son introduction aux *P. Oxy.* XLII 3036-3045, il rassemble la documentation selon la chronologie. Son tableau suggère une augmentation graduelle du montant exigé:

de 298 à 304: 1200 drachmes/tête (on ajoutera maintenant
        P. Oxy. Hels 28, et *P. Oxy.* XLIV 3184 V°);
de 304 à 312: 1600 drachmes/tête (on ajoutera de même
        P. Genova I 19, de 305);
de 313 à 316: 2400 drachmes/tête.

Deuxième élément: une loi impériale de 313, *Cod. Théod.* XIII 10,2, confirme, au bénéfice de la *plebs urbana*, l'exemption de *census pro capitatione* accordée par Dioclétien.

---

29 = P. J. Sijpesteijn, *Der Papyruskodex P. Vindob. G.* 39847 dans *CPR* V Teil 2. Le sigle *CPR* V 26 a été proposé par l'éditeur lui-même et R. S. Bagnall dans un article commun, "Currency in the Fourth Century and the Date of CPR V 26," *ZPE* 24 (1977) 111-24.

30 J. R. Rea, commentaires aux *P. Oxy.* XLIII 3142 et XLIV 3184 V°. R. S. Bagnall, *Cd'E* 52 (1977) art. cité n. 7.

Plebs urbana   sicut in Orientalibus quoque provinciis observatur minime in censibus pro capitatione sua conveniatur sed iuxta hanc iussionem nostram immunis habeatur sicuti etiam sub domino et parente nostro Diocletiano seniore Augusto eadem plebs urbana immunis fuerat.

Comment concilier ces deux données? On ne peut croire au caractère abusif de l'*épiképhalaion poléôs* d'Oxyrhynchos. La période d'oubli des dispositions dioclétianiennes correspond-elle aux années 296-313? Mais pourquoi paierait-on encore en 316? D'autre part, cet impôt n'est spécifique d'aucune catégorie particulière (artisans, commerçants, etc.). Je suggérerais donc la solution suivante: Dioclétien aurait accordé aux résidents citadins l'exemption des *mérismoi* pesant sur les villages où ils étaient propriétaires et où ils payaient l'impôt foncier. (C'est l'une des oppositions de sens possibles entre *iugatio* et *capitatio*.) Ils ne pouvaient pas être considérés comme contribuables, pour l'impôt personnel, là où ils n'étaient pas résidents.[31]

P. Oxy. XLIV 3184 V°, du début du IVe siècle--je préciserais: avant 304--atteste simultanément la perception de l'*épiképhalaion* à un taux uniforme en ville (quatre versements de 1200 drachmes), à un taux variable, proportionnel à la richesse, dans les campagnes. Les trois versements enregistrés ὑπὲρ ἐποικίου Σαραπίου (2400 drachmes pour deux parts, 2000 et 2600 drachmes pour une seule part) inciteraient à conclure que les paiements villageois étaient en moyenne plus élevés que le tarif citadin.

L'uniformité d'imposition citadine apparaît dès lors comme une exception, et non plus comme l'application d'un principe fondamental de la fiscalité dioclétianienne. Je proposerai de voir en elle une manifestation de l'idéologie poliade revivifiée au cours du IIIe siècle, qui affirmait emphatiquement l'égalité civique absolue entre les membres de ce corps privilégié que constituait la *plebs urbana*.[32]

---

31 Séparation entre impôts de la métropole et impôts du nome à rapprocher des registres fonciers d'Hermoupolis: P. J. Sijpesteijn et K. A. Worp, *Zwei Landlisten aus dem Hermopolites* (*P. Giss. 117 und P. Flor. 71*) (Stud. Amst. 7, Zutphen 1977).

32 Cf. mon article, "Les distributions alimentaires dans les cités de l'Empire romain tardif," *MEFRA* 87 (1975) 995-1101.

La tradition d'égalitarisme poliade confère à l'*épiképhalaion poléôs* les formes extérieures d'un impôt de taux uniforme, ce qu'il n'est pas en principe.

En fonction de ces analyses, comment répondre à la vieille question, rappelée en introduction, des rapports de la fiscalité égyptienne du IVe siècle avec la réforme de Dioclétien?

C'est bien sous Dioclétien que l'Egypte a connu, comme l'ensemble de l'Empire, des changements majeurs dans son organisation fiscale. Il devient donc nécessaire de dissiper les équivoques qui entourent le terme de "capitation." La *iugatio sive capitatio* est seulement un mode de calcul de l'assiette parmi d'autres, et elle ne s'applique que dans certaines provinces. C'est assez dire qu'elle ne constitue pas l'essentiel de la réforme fiscale de Dioclétien, encore moins son principe fondamental.

L'exemple égyptien, qui n'est nullement isolé, nous permet de saisir ce que fut cette réforme dans les autres provinces, celles où le système de *iugatio sive capitatio* ne se justifiait pas. La réforme a tendu, ici, à rationaliser la levée des *species annonariae et canonicae* selon la *iugatio*, et à rendre plus équitable la distribution *per capitationem* de l'impôt complémentaire en espèces sur les diverses catégories de la population. Dans les deux cas, la préoccupation militaire est centrale: *annona militaris*, levée d'or et d'argent pour les *donativa*, fiscalisation des fournitures de recrues et de montures, etc.

Cette organisation fiscale, plus complexe et se voulant plus rigoureuse que la précédente, nécessitait un appareil administratif plus développé. La généralisation des *mérismoi* demandait un personnel d'exécution jusqu'à l'échelon local, qui explique la création des liturges villageois, contemporaine de la réforme fiscale. C'est là une transformation administrative considérable, l'érection des principaux villages des *pagi* au rang de *metrocomiae* (terme apparaissant dans *Cod. Theod.* XI 24,6), qui entraîne a son tour d'importantes conséquences économiques et sociales.

L'unité d'inspiration apparaît donc de mieux en mieux dans la politique de Dioclétien, à travers les réformes administratives, militaires, fiscales et monétaires. Le lien entre ces deux derniers

aspects ne peut être développé ici. Je me contenterai, à son sujet,
d'indiquer que l'*aurum comparaticium* comme les tarifs officiels
d'*adaeratio* et de *coemptio* cherchent à imposer au public les valeurs
et rapports monétaires souhaités par le pouvoir impérial. Dans le
même sens joue l'adération forcée de certaines rétributions militaires (τιμὴ ἀννώνης de *P. Panop. Beatty* 2) ou civiles (τιμὴ νομισ-
ματίου de P. Vindob. gr. Inv. 13187), comme si les tarifs d'Etat
pouvaient ralentir l'inflation. Cette prétention--naïve ou
sensée?--a pour effet d'instituer un double cours de l'or: le cours
officiel et en quelque sorte fiscal, et le cours sur le marché
libre. Voici quelques étapes de leur évolution respective:

En 300 (*P. Panop. Beatty* 2.215-222), les stratèges avaient
payé 42 talents (= 63.000 deniers) par livre d'*aurum comparaticium*.
Ils sont réprimandés par le Catholicus, qui limite le remboursement
à 40 talents (= 60.000 deniers), alors qu'en 301 l'*Edit du Maximum*
tolère un prix de 72.000 deniers.

En 304-306, l'*aurum comparaticium* est remboursé 66 talents la
livre, prix assez proche du prix de marché. Mais vers 313 (*P. Ryl.*
IV 616), il n'est que de 73 talents, tandis que cette même année un
cheval se vend 70 talents: un cheval n'a jamais coûté une livre
d'or!

En 324 (*P. Oxy.* XII 1430), l'*aurum comparaticium* est remboursé
209 talents la livre, tandis qu'en 316/318 l'or coûtait déjà 288
talents au marché libre.

De ces quelques chiffres, une première conclusion se dégage:
en 324, l'*aurum comparaticium* était devenu, de fait, un impôt dé-
guisé. Le principe du remboursement dut lui-même disparaître
ultérieurement.

La deuxième conclusion est de méthode: on ne peut plus con-
tinuer à construire une courbe unique du prix de l'or à partir de
ces deux séries de valeurs, comme ont fait jusqu'ici les historiens
de l'économie égyptienne.

Firenze   Jean-Michel Carrié

Proceedings of the XVI Int. Congr. of Papyrology (Chico 1981) 447-456

ON THE MELITIANS IN P. LONDON VI (P. JEWS) 1914:
THE PROBLEM OF PAPAS HERAISCUS

Until 1924 our knowledge of the Melitian[1] schism was based
exclusively on orthodox sources which include several official ecclesiastical documents and the writings of Athanasius which are
often biased.[2] Only Epiphanius seems to have used some Melitian
material.[3] In 1924, however, H. I. Bell, in collaboration with
W. E. Crum, published a series of seven Greek and three Coptic papyri,[4] to which Crum later added another Coptic text (*JEA* 13 [1927]
19-21); all the texts dated from the years 330-40, and they belonged
to the archive[5] of Aurelius Pageus (Apa Paiêous),[6] head of the

---

1 For the spelling "Melitius" and "Melitians" (rather than
"Meletius" and "Meletians," often retained for convenience; see H.
I. Bell, *P. London* VI 39 n. 1 [below n. 4]), cf. S. L. Greenslade,
Schism in the Early Church (London 1953) 51 n. 41.

2 A survey and an evaluation of the sources for the genesis
of the schism will be found in e.g. Bell, *P. London* VI 38 (below
n. 4), and L. W. Barnard, *JEA* 59 (1973) 181. For the later stages
of the schism and for the Coptic sources, see Bell, *P. London* VI
40-45, and W. E. Crum, *JEA* 13 (1927) 21-25.

3 F. H. Kettler, *ZNTW* 35 (1936) 157 and 167, cf. 184; Greenslade, *Schism*, 53.

4 H. I. Bell, *Jews and Christians in Egypt...with Three Coptic Texts edited by W. E. Crum* (= *P. London* VI = *P. Jews*) (London
1924) 38-39: "The Meletian Schism," nos. 1913-19 and 1920-22.

5 J. Van Haelst, "Les sources papyrologiques concernant
l'Eglise en Egypte à l'époque de Constantin," *Proceedings of the
Twelfth International Congress of Papyrology* (Toronto 1970) 499,
nos. 29-35; Orsolina Montevecchi, *La Papirologia* (Torino 1973) 258,
no. 70; E. A. Judge-S. R. Pickering, *JbAC* 20 (1977) 48, no. 12.

6 Aurelius Pageus (no. 1913) and Apa Paiêous (spelled variously in the other documents) are one and the same person: U. Wilck-
en, *Archiv* 7 (1924) 310, and endorsed by H. I. Bell, *JEA* 11 (1925)
95-96 n. 2, thus revising his original view (above n. 4 [51, line 2,
comm.]); likewise G. Ghedini, *La Scuola Cattolica* 53 (Ser. VI, Vol.
VI [1925]) 261-80, passim; K. Holl, *Gesammelte Aufsätze zur Kirchen-
geschichte* II. *Der Osten* (Tübingen 1928) 283-97 (= Sitzb. Berl.
Akad., Phil.-hist. Kl. [1925] 18-31) esp. 293; W. E. Crum, *JEA* 13
(1927) 20 n. 14. Even so, this identification has not become sufficiently familiar: e.g. Judge-Pickering, *JbAC* 20 (1977) 57 and Judge,
ibid., 84 (identification only with reservations).

monastery called Hathor in the Upper Cynopolite nome. He is now
commonly thought to have been the general superior of all Melitian
monks as well.[7] For the first time information was available from
the Melitian camp.

By far the most interesting document in the archive is no.
1914.[8] It is a letter from Callistus, a Melitian monk or priest,
to Paiêous and the priest Patabeit; it describes in highly emotional terms the abuses suffered by the Melitians in Alexandria in the
period May-June 335, shortly before the synod of Tyre. The document offers an abundance of information which is often open to divergent interpretations, largely because of the emotionalism and
confused nature of the letter.

In this paper I limit myself to the problem of *papas* Heraiscus.
The existence of a *papas* Heraiscus (as he is called in line 25) in
Alexandria on the eve of the synod of Tyre is intriguing. Until
the publication of this papyrus the man was completely unknown:
Athanasius makes no mention of him, and he appears only here in the
archive, a fact which is not so surprising in itself since this is
the only document to originate from Alexandria. Heraiscus, who
occupies a central position in the letter, clearly played a leading
role in the Melitian community in the metropolis. The crucial
question, however, is whether or not he had episcopal status, for
if he did, he should be considered an antipope to Athanasius.

Bell did not come to a final conclusion on this matter.[9] Later writers reexamined the problem and a few, principally Holl and
Ghedini, decisively opted for the view that Heraiscus was the Melitian bishop of Alexandria; their arguments, nonetheless, do not
seem wholly conclusive.[10] The continuing doubt about his status is

---

7 Holl, *Gesammelte Aufsätze*, 295; Ghedini (supra, n. 6) 270-71;
idem, *Aegyptus* 6 (1925) 276; Paola Barison, *Aegyptus* 18 (1938) 84.

8 For a recent evaluation of this document, see Barnard,
JEA 59 (1973) 186-87; cf. also N. H. Baynes, *JHS* 44 (1924) 312-13.

9 Bell, *P. London* VI, 63-64 (line 7, comm.), 65 (line 25,
comm.), 69-70 (lines 48-50, comm.).

10 Holl, *Gesammelte Aufsätze*, 287-90, esp. 288-89; Ghedini
(supra, n. 6) 263-66 and cf. *Aegyptus* 6 (1925) 276.

the reason why most publications mention Heraiscus fleetingly,[11] and often with a measure of reserve;[12] some even ignore him completely.[13] The consequences of Heraiscus' episcopacy have seldom, if ever, been exploited as fully as they might be if it were certain that he was a bishop.

According to the list Melitius delivered to Alexander shortly before his death in 327 or 328, there was no Melitian bishop in Alexandria at that time.[14] Further, we cannot adduce the notice about Theonas, because the historicity of this Melitian antibishop has not received total acceptance.[15] The title of *papas* does not prove that Heraiscus was a bishop, because the term was still used

---

[11] Thus F. H. Kettler, *ZNTW* 35 (1936) 171; G. Bardy in A. Fliche-V. Martin, *Histoire de l'Eglise depuis les origines jusqu'à nos jours* (Paris 1950) III, 109 n. 2: only the name, without allusion to possible office; E. Stein, *Histoire du Bas-Empire* I. *De l'Etat romain à l'Etat byzantin 284-476* (Paris 1959) 102: the author wrongly suggests that Alexandria would have had its own Melitian bishop as early as 313; Annik Martin, "Athanase et les Mélitiens 325-335," *Politique et théologie chez Athanase d'Alexandrie. Actes du Colloque de Chantilly 23-25 septembre 1973*, Théologie historique 27, édités par Ch. Kannengiesser (Paris 1974) 59.

[12] So K. M. Girardet, *Kaisergericht und Bisschofsgericht. Studien zu den Anfängen des Donatistenstreites 313-315 und zum Prozess des Athanasius von Alexandrien 328-346*, Antiquitas I,21 (Bonn 1975) 55 and 57: follows Holl, but with some reservations; and Martin, "Athanase" (see above n. 11), 59: "un certain Héraïskos, dont il semble bien qu'il fût également évêque résidant à Nikopolis, sinon à Alexandrie"; Heraiscus is not mentioned on p. 51.

[13] Thus H. Lietzmann, *Geschichte der alten Kirche* (Berlin[4-5] 1975) [=1932-44], 770-79 [= III, 116-25]; E. R. Hardy, *Christian Egypt: Church and People* (New York 1952); W. Telfer, *HThR* 48 (1955) 227-37; W.H.C. Frend, *Martyrdom and Persecution in the Early Church* (Oxford 1965) esp. 540-41; and "Athanasius as an Egyptian Christian Leader in the Fourth Century," *Religion Popular and Unpopular in the Early Christian Centuries* (London 1976) 20-37 [= *New College Bulletin* VIII/1 (Edinburgh 1974)] esp. 30; and L. W. Barnard, *JEA* 59 (1973) 181-89. There is no entry for Heraiscus in the *RE*.

[14] In that list the Melitian church of Alexandria had a cadre of no more than three deacons and five presbyters, one of whom was active in the *parembole* of Nicopolis, where the incidents described in no. 1914 took place; see Martin, "Athanase," 32; cf. 37.

[15] The existence of Theonas, who is merely mentioned in passing by Epiphanius, could surely be made acceptable by proving that Heraiscus was a bishop (see below), but the reverse does not hold (thus Ghedini [supra, n. 6] 266).

for both bishop and priest in the fourth century.[16] Neither does
his leading position automatically imply episcopal office. He
could be a priest, for the Alexandrian presbyters enjoyed an exceptionally powerful and privileged status.[17] In emergencies some of
them acted on behalf of the bishop when he was prevented from gov-
erning his diocese in person,[18] and specifically, John of Memphis,
the leader of the parallel church, whom Melitius had designated as
his successor shortly before his death,[19] was abroad in 335.[20]
Hence, we could be dealing here with an instance of delegation by
a presbyter.[21]

The solution of the problem, therefore, exclusively depends on
an interpretation of the relevant passages in our document.

                                1
5   μετὰ
γὰρ τὴν ἡμέραν ἐκίνη<ν> ἐν τῇ τ{ρ}ετράδι καὶ εἰκάζι τοῦ
Παχ[ὼ]ν μηνὸς ᾿Ισὰκ

---

16 A. Deissmann, *Licht vom Osten* (Tübingen[4] 1923) 186-87;
Bell, *P. London* VI, 65, line 25, comm.; Holl, *Gesammelte Aufsätze*,
288; Ghedini (supra, n. 6) 265-66; Judge-Pickering, *JbAC* 20 (1977) 70.

17 The "parish churches" gave their priests a high level of
prestige and independence, and for a long time the priests apparently held the right to consecrate the new patriarch. Although
opinions on the procedure for consecration of the bishop of Alexandria in the earliest period differ, the privileged position of the
clergy there remains beyond dispute: e.g. F. Cabrol, *Dict. d'Arch.
chrét.* (Paris 1907) I, 1204-10 [s.v. Alexandrie-Election du patri-
arche]; J. Faivre, *Dict. d'Hist. et de Géographie ecclés.* (Paris
1914) II, esp. 336-37 [s.v. Alexandrie]; Bell, *P. London* VI, 64; K.
Müller, *ZNTW* 28 (1929) 274-96, passim; Kettler, *ZNTW* 35 (1936) 171-
74; Lietzmann, *Geschichte* (above n. 13), 376-78 [= II, 54-56]; E.W.
Kemp, *JEH* 6 (1955) 138-39; Telfer, *HTR* 48 (1955) 230; Martin,
"Athanase," 46; H. Brakmann, *JbAC* 22 (1979) 143-49. The latter
rightly points out how the existence of such highly independent
"parish churches" could foster schisms (144-45).

18 E.g., Kettler, *ZNTW* 35 (1936) 168.

19 See Bell, *P. London* VI, 40; Barnard, *JEA* 59 (1973) 184
and 185-86; Martin, "Athanase," 37 with n. 15; cf. 38-39 and 44.

20 As is apparent from no. 1914, line 34; cf. Martin,
"Athanase," 51.

21 This would imply that John felt himself in one way or
another linked to the See of Alexandria, a problem which will be
dealt with below.

ὁ ἐπίσκοπος ἀπὸ Λητοῦς ἦλθεν πρὸς Ἡραείσκον ἐν
  Ἀλεξα[νδρ]ίᾳ, καὶ ἠθέλησεν
8 γεύσασθαι μετὰ τοῦ ἐπισκόπου ἐν τῇ παρεμβολῇ.

6. 1. ἐκείνην   εἰκάδι   7. 1. Ἡραίσκον   Ἀλεξανδρείᾳ.

2

24 θλιβόμεθα οὖν πάνυ διειρ[γμέ]νοι ὑπὸ αὐτῶν κατὰ τόπον. ἐπιλοιπούμεθα οὖν {ουν} ὅτι οὐκ ἐπιτρέπουσιν ἡμῖν
     πρὸς τ[ὸν] πάπαν Ἡραείσκον ἀπελθῖν
καὶ ἐπισκέψασθαι αὐτόν. ἐν τῇ νυκτὶ γὰρ ἐν ᾗ ὑβρίσθησαν
  οἱ ἀδελφοὶ ὁ πραι[π]όσιτος τῶν στρατιοτῶν ἔπεμ-
σεν φάσιν τῷ ἐπισκόπῳ λέγων ὅτι "ἡμάρτησα καὶ ἐπαρυνήθην
  ἐν τῇ νυκτὶ ὅτι τοὺς ἀδελφοὺς
28 ὕβρισα." ἐποίησεν δὲ καὶ ἀγάπην ἐν ἐκίνη τῇ ἡμέρᾳ
  Ἕλλην ὢν δ[ιὰ] τὸ ἀμάρτημα ὃ ἐποίησεν.

25. 1. ἐπιλυπούμεθα   Ἡραίσκον   ἀπελθεῖν
26f. 1. στρατιωτῶν ἔπεμψεν   27. 1. ἐπαροινήθην

3

44   καὶ μέχρις
τῆς ὀγδόης καὶ εἰκάδος τοῦ Παχὼν μηνὸς καὶ Ἡραείσκος
     συνκεκλισμέ-
νος ἐστὶν ἐν τῇ παρεμβολῇ--εὐχαριστῶ μὲν τῷ δεσπότῃ θεῷ
  ὅτι ἐπαύθησαν ἐ πλη-
γαὶ ἃς εἶχεν--καὶ ἐπὶ τῇ ἑυδόμῃ καὶ εἰκάδι ἐποίησεν
  ἐπισκόπους ἑπτὰ ἀποδη-
48 μῆσαι· Ἕμις καὶ Πέτρος εἰς αὐτούς ἐστιν, υἱὸς Τουβέστις.
  μὴ ἀμελήσηται οὖν
περὶ ἡμῶν, ἀδελφοί, ἐπιδὴ τὰ ψωμία ἀφῆκαν ὀπίσω, ἵνα
  διὰ τὸν ἐπίσκοπον μή-
πως ἔξω ἀρθῇ ἵνα τυρῇ αὐτὰ μετ' αὐτοῦ.

45. 1. Ἡραίσκος   45f. 1. συγκεκλεισμένος
46. 1. αἱ   47. 1. ἑβδόμῃ   48. 1. Τουβεστίου(-ίας?)
ἀμελήσητε.   50. 1. τηρῇ

Who is the bishop mentioned by Callistus in lines 8, 27, and 49? Bell rightly pointed out that Athanasius cannot enter into consideration, as he is nowhere in the letter explicitly called bishop.[22] This is by no means surprising, since the validity of his election and consecration was contested by the Melitians.[23] The only two persons who are cited before line 8 and who can be taken into consideration are Isaac, explicitly referred to as "bishop of Letopolis," and Heraiscus.

In line 8 one could possibly take τοῦ ἐπισκόπου to refer to Isaac; but this would imply a change of subject which, though not impossible, is rather unlikely. The connection with Heraiscus seems more obvious.[24] Although it would be possible to think of Isaac in lines 27 and 49 as well, he, unlike Heraiscus, is never mentioned again by name after line 6.[25] In line 49 τὸν ἐπίσκοπον connects logically with Heraiscus (line 45): the thanksgiving-phrase (lines 46-47) forms a parenthesis and the term cannot refer to the seven banished bishops.[26]

Lines 24-28 deserve particular attention. The sentences beginning with ἐπιλοιπούμεθα (= ἐπιλυπούμεθα) and ἐν τῇ νυκτί would appear wholly unrelated, were it not that the use of γάρ (line 26)

---

22 Bell, *P. London* VI, 69 (lines 48-50, comm.); cf. Ghedini (supra, n. 6) 264.

23 E.g. Martin, "Athanase," 40-44, and Girardet, *Kaisergericht* (above n. 12), 52-57. We might add that it would have been senseless for the *praepositus* to send his apologies to Athanasius in lines 26-28 for brutalities suffered by Melitians.

24 Thus also Holl, *Gesammelte Aufsätze*, 288-89, and Ghedini (supra, n. 6) 265-66.

25 The fact that the reference in each case is to "the" bishop does not necessarily point to Heraiscus, as Holl assumed (*Gesammelte Aufsätze*, 289).

26 J. G. Winter (*Life and Letters in the Papyri* [Ann Arbor 1933] 175) suggested that Ἔμις καὶ Πέτρος (line 48) is a double name, and this view could resolve many difficulties (cf. Bell, *P. London* VI, 69, line 48, comm.). Emis (= Emês) would most likely be the original name, Petrus the baptismal. Even so, the τὸν ἐπίσκοπον in line 49 can hardly refer to Emis-Petrus, who is only mentioned in passing in connection with the banishment of the seven bishops. He is unlikely to have been involved in the seemingly important distribution of the ψωμία. In addition, Emis-Petrus is first mentioned in line 48, while "the bishop" has already been referred to twice before.

explicitly links them together.[27] Γάρ gives the reason for a
thought which Callistus felt, but failed to express: e.g. "(We
hadn't expected that and all seemed to be going well), *for* on that
night the *praepositus* offered his apologies to the bishop."[28]
Their annoyance and grief stem particularly from the fact that the
praepositus had expressed his regrets to the bishop; this action
had raised their hopes for the future. Their subsequent fall from
these previous high expectations led to despair at their present
situation and heightened their sorrow at their obvious isolation.
In fact, the contrast between the officer's repentant attitude toward "the bishop" and the barring of the Melitians from visiting
Heraiscus takes on its full meaning only when "the bishop" is
Heraiscus.

Callistus' letter was written under considerable emotional
stress. While such conditions often result in writing which is
unstructured and lacking in coherence, emotional writing is much
more susceptible to spontaneous mental associations. It can hardly
be mere chance that the mention of "the bishop" is on all three
occasions preceded by the name of Heraiscus (lines 7/8, 25/27,
45/49), while the name Heraiscus appears only once without being
followed by a reference to "the bishop" (line 36). There obviously
existed in Callistus' mind a close association between the name
"Heraiscus" and the title "bishop." We may, therefore, conclude
that *papas* Heraiscus was indeed the Melitian bishop of Alexandria.
This fact, in turn, enables us to eliminate several other uncertainties regarding the Melitian schism.

1. The Question of Theonas

Epiphanius (Pan. 68.7) mentions a certain Theonas, who was
appointed bishop of Alexandria by the Melitians immediately after
the death of Alexander--and in the absence of the Catholic candidate
Athanasius. He is said to have died only three months later.

---

27   J. D. Denniston, *The Greek Particles* (Oxford 1966 [=
1954][2]) 58-62 (cf. explanatory γάρ including elliptic use). An
anticipatory γάρ (ibid., 68-73) is ruled out by the use of δὲ καί
(line 28), indicating that the sentence beginning with ἐποίησεν is
only an extension of the one beginning with ἐν τῇ νυκτί.

28   My thinking about lines 24-28 has been influenced by a
letter from Prof. L. Koenen (8 October 1980), endorsing the view
presented here.

Epiphanius tells a similar story in his discussion of Arianism
(Pan. 69.11): a certain Achillas was put on the throne by the Ari-
ans, and he also passed away after three months. One of the two
stories is probably a doublet of the other. The historicity of
the Arian Achillas has often been denied because, among other reasons, there would be some confusion with the homonymous predecessor
of Alexander;[29] Kettler has argued in the same way against Theonas.[30]

On the basis of Heraiscus, we can now accept the existence of
Theonas. His appointment must be dated shortly after 17 April 328
(death of Alexander),[31] and his successor, or one of his successors,
was Heraiscus.[32] But unlike Theonas, the latter may be regarded as
an "antibishop" or "antipope" in the full sense of the word.

2. The See of St. Mark in the Eyes of the Melitians

When Theonas and Heraiscus were elevated to the episcopate of
Alexandria, the leader of the Melitian church was Melitius' successor, John Archaph, the bishop of Memphis. This means that John
himself apparently never nursed the ambition of occupying the See
of St. Mark.[33] The Melitians had evidently disconnected the

---

29 H. M. Gwatkin, *Studies of Arianism* (Cambridge[2] 1900) 70 n.
2; Faivre, *Dict. d'Hist.* (above n. 17), 307; B. J. Kidd, *A History
of the Church to A.D. 461* (Oxford 1922) II, 51; Kettler, *ZNTW* 35
(1936) 183; W. Telfer, *JEH* 3 (1952) 11; Kemp, *JEH* 6 (1955) 132;
Martin, "Athanase," 40-41 n. 24.

30 Kettler, *ZNTW* 35 (1936) 171 n. 45. Most scholars, however, accept the historicity of Theonas or give Epiphanius' item
without further comment: thus Gwatkin, *Studies of Arianism*, 70 n. 2;
Faivre, *Dict. d'Hist.*, 307; O. Seeck, *Geschichte des Untergangs der
antiken Welt* (Stuttgart[2] 1921) III, 436 (who reverses the chronology
and considers the consecration of Theonas as a reply to that of
Athanasius); Kidd, *History of the Church*, 51; Ghedini (supra, n. 6)
266; W. Ensslin, *RE* 5A (1934) 2085 (s.v. Theonas 5); Bardy in
Fliche-Martin, *Histoire de l'Eglise*, 99 n. 2; Martin, "Athanase," 40.

31 See V. Grumel, *La chronologie*, Traité d'études byzantines
1 (Paris 1958) 442.

32 Epiphanius' observation in this context (Pan. 68.7) that
Alexandria, unlike other cities (cf. Martin, "Athanase," 33 and 39)
never had two bishops at the same time, may not be construed as an
argument against Heraiscus' episcopate. Rather, the statement ap-
plies only to the period prior to Theonas and during his episcopacy.

33 Thus also Barnard (*JEA* 59 [1973] 185-86, 187-88), who reacts against the view of Telfer (*HThR* 48 [1955] 235-36), according
to whom John would have had prospective rights to the See of
Alexandria.

episcopacy of Alexandria from the leadership of the Egyptian church,[34] and this notion is confirmed by the fact that Heraiscus probably took no part in the synod of Tyre,[35] although he was considered a very dangerous opponent by the Catholics (lines 35-36) and though his title of *papas* proves his great prestige among his own flock.

In this affair the Melitians remained true to their convictions: since one of the causes of the schism lay in their rejection of the claims of the Alexandrian pope which had been ratified at Nicaea, they could not possibly attach the same importance to "their" metropolitan See as the Catholics did to theirs. The fact that the epicenter of their following was in the Egyptian chora[36] will also have influenced their attitude toward the See of St. Mark.

3. The Appointment of a Melitian Pope of Alexandria as the Final
   Stage in the Development of the Schism

The secession of the Melitians was a gradual process and three main breaking points can now be distinguished. (1) The consecration of bishops by Melitius, possibly as early as 308 in Palestine, and certainly in 311, after Melitius' return and before the death of Peter. These consecrations brought about a parallel hierarchy.[37] (2) The nomination of John Archaph as Melitius' successor in 327 or 328, despite the stipulations at Nicaea. By this action Melitius perpetuated the schism.[38]   (3) The designation of Melitian antipopes in Alexandria from 328. Although the Melitian bishop of Alexandria had only a subordinate position within the Melitian church, his appointment must have seemed a straight provocation to the Catholics. To them the authority of the See of St. Mark was

_____

34 So, properly, Kettler (*ZNTW* 35 [1936] 170-71) even though he fails to carry this development back to Melitius.

35 For the participants in the synod of Tyre, see Martin, "Athanase," 51 n. 48.

36 See esp. Barnard, *JEA* 59 (1973) 185.

37 Kettler, *ZNTW* 35 (1936) 168 and 190-92; Greenslade, (above n. 1), 54; Frend, *Religion Popular and Unpopular* (above n. 13) 29.

38 Bell, *P. London* VI, 40; Martin, "Athanase," 37.

inviolable. The psychological repercussions of this challenge,
fortified by the fact that Athanasius was apparently incapable of
chasing his opponent from the capital, must have made many Catholics realize that a point of no return had been reached. The unity
of the Egyptian church seemed irrevocably lost. Although most Melitians would eventually return to the fold, the schismatic church
as such would never be reincorporated into the Catholic community.

Katholieke Universiteit Leuven   Hans Hauben
Belgium

DER PAPYRUS-KODEX BGU 1024-1027 AUS HERMUPOLIS MAGNA

Im 4. Band der *BGU* (1912) hat Wilhelm Schubart Fragmente eines
Papyruskodex aus Hermupolis Magna in Transkription veröffentlicht
und, dem damaligen Charakter dieser Reihe entsprechend, nur gering-
fügige Bemerkungen beigegeben. Diese Fragmente waren von Otto
Rubensohn aus dem Papyrusfonds für die Berliner Museen im Jahre
1902 erworben und nach konservatorischer Behandlung zwischen Glasplatten montiert worden. W. Schubart hatte den Text der besser erhaltenen Seiten mitgeteilt, unter denen sich Prozeßprotokolle,
Quittungen, Zaubertexte und ein amtliches Schreiben befinden. In
der vom Editor zu *BGU* 1024-1027 gegebenen Textübersicht heißt es:
"... Die übrigen Seiten werden von Rechnungen ausgefüllt, z.T. von
1., z.T. von 5. Hand." Eine Überprüfung dieser Aussage ergibt, daß
auf 9 Seiten Rechnungen, Quittungen oder Aufstellungen zu finden
und daß 6 Seiten frei sind, schließlich daß eine ganze Seite mit
einem, zwar stark fragmentierten, Text versehen ist, über den sich
aber doch einige Aussagen gewinnen lassen.

Einzelne Teile des Kodex sind nach Revision des Textes wieder
abgedruckt worden, so Quittungen in *W. Chr.* 422, ebendort 424 das
amtliche Schreiben, schließlich der Zaubertext im 2. Band der *PGM*
(XXIIa). Die Prozeßprotokolle fanden Eingang in die Behandlung
einschlägiger juristischer Fragen,[1] jedoch fehlen bis heute ein
Komentar sowie eine zusammenfassende Würdigung des Kodex.

In letzter Zeit hat sich durch Reedition und Neupublikation
von Urkundenkodizes aus Hermupolis Magna, z.B. der in den *P. Herm.
Landl.* herausgegebenen Kodizes aus Gießen und Florenz und des Wiener Kodex aus Skar, das Interesse verstärkt auch dieser Gattung
zugewandt.[2] So werden einige zusammenfassende Bemerkungen zu ver-
waltungsgeschichtlichen und kulturhistorischen Aspekten des Berliner

---

1 Dazu hauptsächlich: R. Taubenschlag, *The Law of Greco-Roman
Egypt in the Light of the Papyri*, 2nd ed. (Warszawa 1955) mit weiterer Literatur.

2 P. Giss. Inv. Nr. 4 und *P. Flor.* I 71 in: P. J. Sijpesteijn
u. K. A. Worp, *Zwei Landlisten aus dem Hermupolites* (*P. Landlisten*)
(Zutphen 1978); P. Vindob. G 39847 = *CPR* V 26.

Kodex unter Berücksichtigung der noch nicht edierten Texte nicht
unwillkommen sein, zumal dieser Kodex im Vergleich zu den eben genannten anderen schon wegen seines verschiedenartigen Inhaltes besondere Aufmerksamkeit verdient.
      Zunächst: Was ist uns von dem Kodex heute erhalten? Vorhanden
sind 4 Doppelblätter in mehr oder weniger fragmentiertem Zustand
und 6 einfache Blätter. Die Größe des einzelnen Blattes beträgt
durchschnittlich 24 cm in der Höhe, 13 cm in der Breite; wenn man
die von E. G. Turner in seinem Werk *The Typology of the Early Codex*
(Philadelphia 1977) zugrunde gelegte Gruppierung verwendet, so gehört dieser Kodex zur Gruppe 8, deren Breite die Hälfte der Höhe
beträgt (S. 13ff.). Klebungen sind auf den Blättern bzw. Doppelblättern nachzuweisen, so daß ihre Herstellung aus einer Papyrus-
rolle gesichert ist. Ferner sind paarig angeordnete Heftlöcher zu
erkennen. Die konservierten Blätter sind mit den Seitenzahlen von
1-28 versehen; dieser Zählung folgt auch Schubarts Edition. Das
Original enthält keine Seitenzählung, so daß für die Rekonstruktion
der Seitenfolge heute nur das Äußere des Kodex wie die aus dem Verlauf des Textes gewonnenen Indizien zur Verfügung stehen; denn Aufzeichnungen des Editors sowie des Konservators über den Erhaltungs-
zustand und die Beschaffenheit des Kodex existieren nicht. Dies
ist bedauerlich, da seine Rekonstruktion auf Schwierigkeiten stößt.
Die über mehrere Seiten fortlaufenden Texte bieten dabei die besten
Anhaltspunkte und die sichere Gewähr dafür, daß es sich überhaupt
um einen Kodex handelt. Im einzelnen können die Beobachtungen hier
nicht dargestellt, vielmehr soll nur das Ergebnis skizziert werden.
      Die 4 Doppelblätter gehören zu einer Lage, in die 3 Einzel-
blätter an 2 verschiedenen Stellen eingefügt wurden, ein Blatt in
der ersten Hälfte und 2 Blätter in der zweiten Hälfte der Lage, so
daß nach S. 4 ein Einzelblatt mit den Seiten 5/6, nach S. 12 zwei
Einzelblätter mit den Seiten 13/14 und 15/16 folgen. Insgesamt ergeben sich 22 Seiten. Da die Heftränder der Einzelblätter sehr
breit sind und über die Heftmitte der Lage reichen, ist es durchaus
möglich, daß die Lage ursprünglich aus vollständigen Doppelblättern
bestand und erst später Seiten aus der gehefteten Lage entfernt
wurden. Die 3 noch nicht berücksichtigten Einzelblätter mit den
Seiten 23-28 gehören wahrscheinlich auf Grund der anders angeordne-
ten Heftlöcher einer zweiten Lage an.

Aufschlußreich ist nun die Beobachtung, daß der Freirand zwischen Heftung und Schriftspiegel bei den einzelnen Texten variiert. Möglicherweise läßt das den Schluß zu, daß die Seiten mit schmalerem Rand vor der Heftung, die Seiten mit breiterem Rand nach der Heftung beschrieben wurden.

Die Herkunft des Kodex aus Hermupolis Magna ist durch zahlreiche Angaben gesichert: durch die Nennung von Ratsherren dieses Ortes in den Quittungen sowie durch ein amtliches Schreiben an die Kurie von Hermupolis Magna, ferner durch eine bisher nicht publizierte Übersicht über Fleischlieferungen von verschiedenen Orten des Hermupolites,[3] schließlich durch den für den Hermupolites charakteristischen Personennamen Hyperechios in einem ebenfalls unpublizierten Abschnitt.[4]

Die Datierung des Kodex durch die *Editio princeps* in das IV./V. Jh. u.Z. konnte bereits Ulrich Wilcken, *APF* 3 (1906) 302, präzisieren: der in der Quittung (S. 16) genannte Ratsherr Aurelios Philammon, Sohn des Hermes, als ἐπιμελητής tätig, ist in *P. Lips.* 62 ebenfalls genannt, der in die Jahre 384/5 u.Z. zu datieren ist. Dieser Mann ist jedoch meines Wissens noch in 2 anderen Urkunden belegt: *P. Lond.* III S. 228 (357 p.) als διαδότης Φιλῶν und *P. Flor.* 75 (380 p.) als ἐπιμελητής σίτου Ἀλεξανδρείας, also über einen Zeitraum von 27 Jahren, in denen er mehrmals liturgische Ämter bekleidete.

Da diese Quittungen nur aktuelles Interesse beanspruchen konnten, wird man die Abschriften der Prozeßprotokolle und damit auch den gesamten Kodex in das Ende des 4. Jh. datieren, worauf auch der Schriftcharakter weist.

Alle Texte, einschließlich der Zaubertexte, sind kursiv geschrieben. Fünf Hände lassen sich unterscheiden, wobei sich die Handschriften der Prozeßprotokolle, Quittungen und Zaubertexte sehr gleichen. Den von W. Schubart unerwähnt gelassenen Text möchte ich der 3. Hand zuweisen, welche die Zaubertexte verfaßt hat.

Zum Inhalt selbst: Der umfangreichste Text, 6 Seiten (3-8), umfaßt eine Sammlung von Sentenzen eines ἡγεμών in Kapitalprozessen,

---

3 Es werden genannt: Πακή, Πεεντᾶλις, Σιναπή, Τωοῦ (χωρίον).

4 Vgl. die Bemerkungen *CPR* V 21 Einl. und *CPR* VI (Archiv des Apollonios aus Pesla).

denen jeweils eine Charakteristik des Einzelfalles vorangeht. W.
Schubart und U. Wilcken (*APF* 3 [1906] 302) nahmen für die Sentenzen
eine wörtliche Wiedergabe aus den ὑπομνηματισμοί an, dagegen folgen
die Charakteristiken in freier Form meist dem Schema πρός τινα ...
ἡγεμών. Mit einer einzigen Ausnahme (S. 4) sind die abgeurteilten
Verbrechen an weiblichen Personen begangen; doch spricht nichts dagegen, daß auch der hier erwähnte Leichnam ein weiblicher gewesen
ist.

Die Ähnlichkeit der geschilderten Fälle läßt vermuten, daß die
Auszüge aus Anlaß eines ähnlichen Prozesses hergestellt worden sind,
also auf die Praxis zurückgehen und daher als Quelle rechtsgeschicht-
licher Erkenntnis gelten können.

Welcher Beamte unter dem ἡγεμών in diesen speziellen Fällen zu
verstehen ist, läßt sich nicht eindeutig beantworten. Verschiedene
Beamte kommen in Frage, wie denn auch die Fälle zeitlich auseinander
liegen mögen. Eine zeitliche Klammer für diese Vorgänge bildet
allerdings die Person des Zephyrios, der im 1. und letzten Fall auftritt (S. 3-6ff.). Nach der Vorgeschichte des letzten Falles, der
in Alexandria spielt, möchte Wilcken im ἡγεμών gern den Augustalis,
nicht den Praeses der Thebais sehen. Da aber Präfekt wie Praesides
in Zivil- und Strafsachen urteilen, ist es durchaus möglich, wie
Jaqueline Lallemand vorschlägt, daß ἡγεμών in dieser Sammlung von
Rechtsfällen nicht präzis gebraucht ist und den Präfekten wie den
Praeses bezeichnen kann.[5] Leider bleibt die Organisation des Straf-
prozesses undeutlich, ebenso wird über die Durchführung der Prozesse nichts gesagt.

Die nächste Textgruppe, 2 Seiten umfassend (15+16), bilden 4
Quittungen von διαδόται, die Ratsherren von Hermupolis sind, an
ἐπιμεληταί mit der Bestätigung, die *annona* empfangen zu haben, und
mit der Verpflichtung, die Lieferung an die Militärlager, darunter
Syene, weiterzuleiten.

Mit der Einführung der Kommunalordnung war für die Beschaffung
der *annona* die Kurie verantwortlich, die ἐπιμεληταί als Liturgen
mit der Verteilung an die Soldaten betraute. Sie hafteten für die
Durchführung der Lieferung, wurden jedoch durch die Gesamthaftung

---

5 J. Lallemand, *L'administration civile de l'Egypte de
l'avènement de Dioclétien à la création du diocèse (284-382)*
(Bruxelles 1964) 141 Anm. 2.

der βουλή gestützt, wie die Seiten 26 und 27 des Kodex zeigen (=
BGU 1027). Seit Ende des 3. Jh. nachweisbar, übernimmt ein neu-
geschaffenes Kollegium, das der διαδόται, die Lieferungen von den
ἐπιμεληταί, bevor sie an die Soldaten verteilt werden. Die Mit-
glieder dieses Kollegiums, ebenfalls Liturgen, werden wie die ἐπιμεληταί für die Dauer einer Indiktion von der Kurie nominiert, zu
der sie gehören, und für bestimmte Orte eingesetzt, in unserem Falle
für Syene. Die διαδόται stellten für die empfangenen Lieferungen
die vorliegenden Quittungen aus und empfingen von den ἐπιμεληταί
Gegenquittungen. διαδόται lassen sich bis ins VI./VII. Jh. nach-
weisen. Welche Last diese Liturgie für die Kurie bedeutete, wird
ebenfalls aus dem genannten Abschnitt des Kodex (S. 26-27) deutlich,
in dem der sonst nicht weiter belegte Praeses der Thebais Flavius
Domittius Asclepiades[6] die Exaktoren und den Rat von Hermupolis ta-
delt, daß sie 3 Jahre den Soldaten die fällige *annona* nicht ausge-
liefert hätten. Er hebt die dadurch entstandene Gefahr hervor und
verlangt, daß die Lieferungen in kürzester Frist zu erfolgen hätten,
sonst würden Beamte die Schuld eintreiben und sie selbst der höch-
sten Strafe zuführen (S. 27). Eine Spezifizierung der Lieferungen
folgte in einem nicht erhaltenen *breve*.

Zu den 2 Seiten umfassenden Zaubertexten (22+23) möchte ich
nur erwähnen, daß der eine ein Mittel gegen Blutfluß unter Verwendung von Homerzitaten behandelt, der andere eine hymnische Helios-
Anrufung enthält.

Von den bisher nicht in Transkription mitgeteilten Texten sind
einige so zerstört, daß sich kein Sinnzusammenhang ergibt. Jedoch
können von 3 Seiten, die listenartige Aufstellungen und Notizen
enthalten, genauere Aussagen getroffen werden. Zunächst (S. 20)
finden wir eine Aufstellung über die Verladung von Fleisch aus Orten verschiedener Toparchien des Hermupolites,[3] dann (S. 25) eine
Aufstellung über Einzelposten von Naturalien; genannt werden Wein,
Fleisch und Spreu, spezifiziert nach Einzelpersonen, schließlich
noch eine Aufstellung über Spreu (S. 28) aus dem Θαλλοῦ κώμη genannten Ort des Hermupolites. Ferner wird nach 2 Kurznotizen (S.
25; 28) der Arzt Theodosios mit einer Lieferung Fleisch, wahrscheinlich als Honorar, bedacht.

---

6 Lallemand, op. cit., 62 und 255 Nr. 24.

Können diese in den Kodex eingestreuten Aufstellungen in einen
Zusammenhang mit den die *annona* betreffenden Urkunden gebracht werden? Die zitierten Texte, die Quittungen der διαδόται an die ἐπιμεληταί, sind Quittungen für Fleisch, Spreu und Wein; das Schreiben
des Praeses, zum Schluß hin fragmentiert, erwähnt Spreulieferungen.
Wie wir wissen, war die *annona* im 4. Jh. allgemein eine Natural-
leistung, die erst später durch die Geldleistung ersetzt wurde. So
ist es durchaus möglich, daß die noch nicht edierten notizenartigen
Aufstellungen mit der Eintreibung der *annona*-Lieferungen in Verbindung stehen, zu denen sowohl Einzelpersonen wie Ortschaften herangezogen wurden.

Hingewiesen hatte ich bereits auf einen von W. Schubart unerwähnt gelassenen Text (S. 11). Leider gewährt uns sein fragmentarischer Zustand keine einzige vollständige Zeile. Wie schon bei
der Behandlung der Handschrift gesagt, weist dieser Text Ähnlichkeiten mit der Hand der beiden Zaubertexte auf. Ferner scheinen
Wortwahl und Kürzungen auf die Gattung der Zaubertexte hinzudeuten.
Vielleicht ermöglicht besonders hier die weitere Beschäftigung eine
genauere Aussage.

Zum Gesamtbefund des Kodex ist folgendes zu sagen: U. Wilcken
bemerkte in seinem Urkundenreferat *APF* 3 (1906) 302, daß in diesem
Kodex "die verschiedensten Akten in privaten Abschriften, dazu
Zaubertexte, Rechnungen usw. in buntem Durcheinander stehen." Daß
sich die Aufstellungen und Listen zwischen den anderen Texten befinden, ist wahrscheinlich so zu erklären, daß der Schreiber hinter
den Haupttexten Platz für noch weitere Eintragungen dieser Art gelassen hat, dieser Freiraum jedoch später für die listenartigen
Aufzeichnungen verwendet wurde. Außer dem Besprochenen bieten die
Texte auch noch zahlreiche Einzelheiten, die hier unerwähnt bleiben
müssen. So ergab die erneute Beschäftigung mit dem Kodex bisher
neben der Gewinnung neuer Texte eine Präzisierung seiner Datierung
sowie zahlreiche Hinweise für die Rekonstruktion.

Berlin-DDR   Günter Poethke

Proceedings of the XVI Int. Congr. of Papyrology (Chico 1981) 463-468

LES OSTRACA GRECS DE DOUSH[*]

Cette communication est le fruit de l'étude des O. Doush menée
conjointement par Jean Gascou et Guy Wagner qui ont déjà rendu
compte des apports de cette documentation dans le "Rapport Préliminaire de la Campagne de Fouilles 1976" (*BIFAO* 78 [1978] 28-32 et
pl. VIII) ainsi que dans le "Rapport Préliminaire des Campagnes de
Fouilles 1978/9 et 1979," à paraître dans le *BIFAO* 80 (1980).

Les ostraca grecs trouvés lors des trois campagnes de fouilles
menées sur le tell de Doush proviennent du temple, de sa tribune et
de ses abords ainsi que de la forteresse et de son angle extérieur
sud-ouest. Ces documents, au nombre d'environ 600 pièces, doivent
être datés du milieu et surtout de la deuxième moitié du IVème s.
de notre ère. Cette documentation frappe par sa très grande cohérence: administrative, à la fois fiscale et comptable, elle re-
garde presque exclusivement le ravitaillement de l'armée, que ce
soit la garnison stationnée à Kysis ou les détachements de la Vallée
venus effectuer des missions ponctuelles en ce point du *limes*.

Parmi ces textes, nous avons reconnu différentes catégories de
documents:

LES ORDRES DE PAIEMENT

Adressés par un épimélète à un redevable au bénéfice de militaires

- dossier de l'épimélète Isokratès et de Sippas (le meilleur
  exemple est l'ordre adressé au bénéfice du *signifer* Iakobios
  O. Doush 68)

- dossier de l'épimélète Chrestos et de Paniskos (8 pièces en
  bon état trouvées dans le même local, le meilleur exemple est
  l'ordre adressé au bénéfice d'un *signifer* O. Doush 672)

Adressés par un diadotès à un redevable au bénéfice d'un militaire

  (O. Doush 664)

---

[*] Presentation des O. Doush - Campagnes de Fouilles à Doush 1976 -
1978/1979 - 1979.

Adressés par un diadochos à un épimélète au bénéfice de militaires

- dossier du *diadochos* Horos à l'épimélète Peteuris (une trentaine de pièces, les attributions sont des annones de pain,
  un des bénéficiaires est l'*optio* Petros, O. Doush 365, 1 à 30
  et en particulier n° 30)

Adressés par un optio à un épimélète au bénéfice de militaires

- dossier d'Aios, *optio* de Thèbes, à l'épimélète Patechôn (les
  attributions sont des annones de pain, O. Doush 501)
- dossier de l'*optio* Pachmounis à l'épimélète Peteuris (annones
  de pain)
- dossier de l'*optio* Demetris à l'épimélète Chrestos (O. Doush
  1978, 63; 64; 69)

*Adressés par d'autres petits gradés, optio, signifer, simples
stratiôtai, à l'autorité civile au bénéfice de civils*

- le meilleur exemple: le *signifer* Petros ordonne à l'épimélète
  Chrestos de délivrer 1 *marion* de vin au *hiereus* Apellôs
  (O. Doush 559; cf. aussi O. Doush 320 et 753)

LES REÇUS

Délivrés par un épimélète

- par l'épimélète Chrestos au titre de l'annone de Kysis (des
  artabes de blé, Chrestos étant épimélète de la boulangerie
  militaire, *pistrina*, O. Doush 70) et au titre de l'annone
  d'Hibis (O. Doush 69)

Délivrés par un diadotès

- par le diadotès (pour du vin annonaire, O. Doush 79; pour
  du blé au titre de la ferme d'un bain, O. Doush 650)

Reçus d'un type particulier: la formule ἔσχον καὶ ἐρόγευσα
                                  (O. Doush 1978, 29; 128; 137, dans
                                  dans un contexte toujours mutilé)

LES LISTES DE MILITAIRES

- listes simples avec mention de grades (O. Doush 72)
- listes avec mention de grades et d'attributions (O. Doush 86;
  721 etc...)

LES COMPTES

- tenus par les épimélètes où ils consignent soit les quantités
  de denrées perçues auprès des redevables (en particulier
  lorsqu'y figurent des noms de femmes, O. Doush 1978, 62 et
  surtout les comptes de coton, O. Doush 83) et les quantités
  de denrées redistribuées (O. Doush 87; 193, boulangerie

publique et boulangerie militaire; 588 + 639, les comptes
de blé de l'épimélète Peteuris; O. Doush 689, compte complexe où se mêlent les noms de plusieurs épimélètes ou
diadotai connus par ailleurs, à ceux de simples redevables).
- tenus par une autorité indéterminée, soit civile, soit
  militaire: comptes d'annones, de livres de viande de porc,
  de chèvre, de vin en *xestai*, de blé, d'orge etc...

LES BILLETS DE LOGEMENT

Deux billets de logements pour, dans un cas, 3 groupes de
quatre soldats, dans l'autre, un groupe unique de cinq
soldats (O. Doush 250), illustrent la pratique du *metatum*,
en l'occurence le droit à l'*hospitalitas* pour les militaires
dans les maisons des habitants de Kysis.

LES LETTRES PRIVEES ET LES LETTRES = ORDRES DE PAIEMENT
Les lettres privées

Les lettres privées au sens strict du terme sont fort rares.
Le seul document qui mérite cette appellation est sans doute la
lettre de Sophia à Isokratès où elle se plaint des barbares et
supplie qu'on lui envoie des dattes, car elle est dans le besoin
(O. Doush 185). Même son de cloche pour obtenir de l'huile et un
peu de blé, "car tu sais dans quelle indigence....."

Une lettre d'affaires faisant allusion au commerce entre Kysis
et la Vallée du Nil, accuse reception de "ceintures de papyrus",
en réclame 20 autres ainsi que 2300 talents d'argent (O. Doush 520).
Une autre lettre d'affaires, sur écorce, commence par des saluta-
tions (O. Doush 747).

Les lettres privées = des ordres de paiement déguisés

Une lettre chrétienne où un père demande "à son fils bien-aimé"
de livrer du vin et 20 *ti/ophagia* (sens inconnu, O. Doush 23). Une
lettre où un soldat ordonne à un redevable de livrer des annones de
pain à l'épimélète se termine par la clause: "je souhaite que tu
te portes bien beaucoup d'années" (O. Doush 753); il en va de même
pour une autre lettre très voisine (O. Doush 1978, 145).

LES MARQUES DE JARRES

Les marques de jarres sont soit incisées soit inscrites à
l'encre noire. Pour les incisions, il s'agit d'un simple anthro-
ponyme, Premn[..]eiôs (O. Doush 814), ou d'un nom avec une

indication du métier, Apollon le charpentier (O. Doush 151). Pour
les inscriptions à l'encre, il y a des anthroponymes, mais aussi des
indications de denrées et de quantités (O. Doush 653; 750 etc...).
La tranche chronologique à l'intérieur de laquelle se situent
les O. Doush est mince : si le texte le plus ancien est de 304
(O. Doush 755, années 21 et 20 de Dioclétien et Maximien) et si les
ostraca assignables à la 1ère moitié du IVème s. sont très peu nombreux, l'immense majorité des documents date de la 2ème moitié du
IVème s. ou du début du Vème s.

Les militaires étaient souvent montés: il y avait des *drome-
darii* (O. Doush 520), des *kamêlitai* légèrement équipés, *armaturae*
(O. Doush 366). Les grades sont ceux de centurion, de *princeps*,
de *primicerius*, d'*optio*, de *tesserarius*, de *signifer*, de *portaren-
sis*, d'*armatura*, de simple soldat ou de *tiro*.

Les soldats de Kysis étaient souvent originaires de la Vallée.
Ces corps auxiliaires mobiles habitués à patrouiller dans le désert
venaient de Tentyris (O. Doush 51; 129; 90 + 364; 709), de Thèbes
(O. Doush 501), d'Hermonthis (O. Doush 580) et d'Asphynis. D'autres
documents, épigraphiques ceux-là, de la région de Kysis nous apprennent qu'il en venait aussi de Latopolis et surtout d'Apollônos Anô.
Nous avons la trace d'un recrutement local en la personne d'un
Oasite bénéficiaire d'annones (O. Doush 498). Parmi les allogènes,
nous n'avons guère que le Saracène Abram (O. Doush 90 + 364) et,
peut-être, un Mazique (O. Doush 639 + 588). Les liens entre Kysis
et Hibis nous sont connus par un ordre de paiement délivré par
Peteuris, ἐπιμελητὴς κάστρων ῎Ιβεως (O. Doush 596).

Outre l'*hospitalitas* dont ils bénéficiaient chez l'habitant
(cf. *supra* les billets de logement), ces militaires touchaient
leurs rations annonaires à Kysis, pain, vin, huile et souvent de
la viande, de porc (O. Doush 239 etc...) ou de chèvre (O. Doush
662). Ils encaissaient également leur solde en talents d'argent
(O. Doush 690) et en myriades de deniers (O. Doush 216).

L'anthroponymie de ce milieu atteste la coexistence de la religion traditionnelle et du christianisme. Les noms chrétiens ne
sont pas rares chez les soldats : Abraam, Isak, Ioseph, Iakôb,
Petros, Paulos etc... Leurs noms sont aussi souvent très égyptiens, caractéristiques parfois de la Thébaïde: Epônychos,

Patelôlis, Peteuris, Pachmounis, Petechôn, Papnouthis, Pachoumis, Psennêsis etc...

Les notables civils de Kysis, épimélètes et autres agents liturgiques, portent volontiers des noms grecs, parfois recherchés: Isokratès, Chrestos, Paniskos, Sippas, Agathemeros etc... A ce titre le curieux ordre de paiement adressé par le *signifer* Petros à l'épimélète Chrestos au bénéfice du prêtre païen Apellôs est significatif (O. Doush 559).

A l'arrière plan de l'organisation annonaire qui absorbe ses productions apparait la paysannerie de Kysis, ses *geôrgoi* et ses propriétaires fonciers, ses *geouchoi* (O. Doush 320, 369, 787). Notons cependant que les textes mentionnant la paysannerie Kysite sont très rares.

Des textes isolés nous apprennent l'existence à Kysis d'un bain affermé (O. Doush 650) d'une part, de l'autre, d'un commerce de ceintures de papyrus acheminées à dos de chameaux depuis la Vallée (O. Doush 520). Enfin, une lettre privée fait allusion aux excès commis par les troupes cantonnées chez l'habitant (*barbaroi*), à moins qu'il ne s'agisse d'un raid des tribus nomades du désert (O. Doush 185).

Un mot, pour finir, des relations entre nos ostraca et les points de fouille où ils ont été mis au jour. Ils ne nous aident guère, sauf en ce qui concerne la datation, à mieux comprendre leur environnement archéologique, car ce sont des pièces de rebut jetées après usage. Pourtant le dossier du *diadochos* Horos a été découvert en 1978 dans la Cour I du temple, dans quelques pièces à l'est du local II; la trouvaille semblait homogène, mais en 1979 d'autres ostraca du même dossier ont été mis au jour à l'ouest de la tribune.

Disons cependant, sans entrer dans les détails, que, si nous n'avions pas les ostraca, nous ne saurions certainement pas que toutes les constructions en briques crues qui ont envahi les Cours I et II du temple de Kysis datent du IVème s. et constituent les bureaux de l'intendance militaire de la place forte. Il y a mieux: le dossier de l'épimélète du vin Chrestos et de Paniskos, 8 pièces datées d'une année indictionnelle 7, a été découvert groupé, au sol, dans la salle V du carré K22, à l'intérieur de la forteresse; de

même, de nombreux ossements d'animaux ont été trouvés dans les
cuisines des locaux I à III de la désserte du fort, locaux où ont
précisement été mis au jour des ostraca qui font mention de livrai-
sons de viande aux soldats.

Strasbourg   Guy Wagner

LES CAUTIONNEMENTS POUR LES <u>COLONI ADSCRIPTICII</u>[1]

Les colons adscrits sont mentionnés dans la documentation
papyrologique dès 469 (probablement dès 441)[2] jusqu'à 616 dans des
textes divers: reçus d'outillage d'irrigation, cautionnements,
prêts, contrats de livraison de vin, pétitions etc. Ce sont les
cautionnements dans lesquels les colons figurent en qualité de garantis, de garants ou--parfois--garantis et garants à la fois qui
ont la plus grande importance pour l'étude de la condition des
énapographes égyptiens. Nous disposons au moins d'une quinzaine de
cautionnements dont quelques uns inédits. La plupart des textes
appartiennent aux archives des Apions mais il y a des cautionnements provenant d'autres archives aussi, surtout des archives de
Fl. Anastasia.[3] Chronologiquement les cautionnements édités
s'échelonnent de 568 à 613. Les cautionnements pour les colons
adscrits constituent une variété des ἐγγύαι εἰς παράστασιν.[4]

---

1 Cette communication constitue un extrait abrégé de notre
étude "Pripisnye kolony (adskripticii-enapografy) po dannym papiru-
sov [Les *coloni adscripticii* d'après les données des papyrus]" (sous
presse) où sont largement citées la bibliographie et les sources
respectives. V. aussi notre commentaire à l'édition de *P. Oxy.* VI
996, "Une caution byzantine pour des *coloni adscripticii*: *P. Oxy.*
VI 996" dans *Miscellanea Papyrologica* (Firenze 1980) 67-77 et en
russe dans *Vizantijskij Vremennik* 42 (1981). [For the ἐκαπόγραφος
γεωργός, see also J. G. Keenan, "On Village and Polis in Byzantine
Egypt," infra, 479-85. Ed.]

2 *P. Oxy.* XXIV 2724 (469); dans *P. Mil.* I 64.4-5 = *SB* VI 9503
(441, v. R. S. Bagnall, K. A. Worp, "Ten Consular Dates," *ZPE* 28
[1978] 226-27) le mot est dans la lacune.

3 Les textes restent inédits, v. J. van Haelst, "De nouvelles
archives: Anastasia propriétaire à Oxyrhynchus," *Atti dell'XI Congresso Internazionale di Papirologia*... (Milano 1966) 587 qui mentionne quatre cautionnements (ou cinq si on y compte P. Giss. Univ.
inv. 44 [588] aussi). O. Eger, "Papyri der Giessener Universitäts-
bibliothek," *Archiv* 5 (1913) 572 parlait de six cautionnements.

4 Sur les cautionnements v. O. Montevecchi, *La Papirologia*
(Torino 1973) 192-93 et la bibliographie citée là; sur les cautionnements pour les *coloni adscripticii*, v. E. Seidl, *Der Eid im
römisch-ägyptischen Provinzialrecht* (München 1935) II, 86-87
(MBPAR 24). Une liste des cautionnements des V-VI siècles est

Nous disposons des cautionnements suivants mentionnant des colons adscrits: *P. Lond.* III 778 (568), *P. Oxy.* I 135 = *W. Chrest.* 384 = *Sel. Pap.* I 26 = *FIRA* III 13 (579), VI 996 (584), XLIV 3204 (588), XXVII 2478 (595, v. *BL* V 82), *PSI* I 59 (596, v. *BL* I 390), P. Giss. Univ. inv. 45, 49),[5] *P. Merton* II 98 (tous: la fin du VIe s.), *P. Oxy.* I 200 = *SB* XII 10944 (VIe s.), *P. Heid.* 248, *PSI* III 180 (VIe-VIIe s.), I 61 (609), *P. Oxy.* XVI 1979 (613), *PSI* I 62 (613, v. *BL* I 390). A cette liste on devrait ajouter probablement P. Giss. Univ. inv. 41 (590),[6] peut-être *P. Oxy.* XVIII 2203 (VIe s.)[7] et quelques autres textes. Tous les cautionnements furent rédigés selon un formulaire unique mais dans le cadre de ce formulaire on peut constater deux variantes de rédaction--une plus détaillée, l'autre plus courte. Comme exemple de la rédaction plus détaillée on peut citer le *P. Oxy.* I 135; de la rédaction plus courte, *PSI* I 61. Le *P. Oxy.* VI 996 dont l'édition intégrale fut préparée indépendamment par G. Bastianini et nous[8])constitue dans ce sens (à ce temps) un document unique--une compilation artificielle dans un seul et même texte de deux cautionnements donnés par des garants différents pour deux colons adscrits originaires de localités différents.[9] Vu que le formulaire des cautionnements pour colons fût bien mis en évidence par les études précédentes nous passons directement à l'étude des données socio-économiques qu'on pourrait tirer de ce type de documents.

---

publiée par G. Bastianini, "Una malleveria dall'archivio degli Apioni (P. Oxy. VI 996)," dans *Miscellanea Papyrologica* (Firenze 1980) 25-27. V. aussi *P. Turner* 54 (Ant., VIe s.).

5 V. J. van Haelst, "De nouvelles archives," 587.

6 Ibid.

7 Le début du texte est perdu. Le fait que le garant est un *archisymmachos* admet encore une autre interprétation: cautionnement pour un *symmachos*.

8 V. G. Bastianini, "Una malleveria" et I. F. Fikhman, "Une caution byzantine," citées plus haut.

9 J. van Haelst, "De nouvelles archives," 587, écrit que P. Giss. Univ. inv. 43 représente "un type spécial" et P. Giss. Univ. inv. 45 "un type rare" mais il ne précise pas en quoi consiste la particularité de ces textes.

Tout d'abord il faut souligner que les cautionnements pour
colons ne doivent nullement être interprétés comme conséquence de
la méfiance des maîtres contre les paysans[10] ou comme indice d'une
capacité juridique limitée des colons qui n'ayant pas le droit
d'assumer d'obligations à l'égard de leur maître sont forcés de
recourir à des cautionnements. Dans beaucoup de cas les maîtres
étaient pleinement satisfaits par les obligations écrites des colons et ne demandaient pas de cautionnements comme en témoignent
les reçus d'outillage d'irrigation, les prêts, les contrats de
livraison de vin etc.

On a avancé l'hypothèse que les cautionnements constituaient
une procédure destinée à fixer la situation de dépendance du colon
adscrit.[11] M. Pallasse appelle même les cautions "contrats d'as-
cripticiat," les considère une "imitation de la pratique impériale"
et pense qu'à la suite du cautionnement "le nouvel adscrit se
transportera sur le domaine du maître avec son épouse, ses enfants,
ses animaux et tout son mobilier, qu'il y demeura etc." Sans doute
y avait-il des contrats établissant des relations d'adscripticiat
mais il est peu probable qu'ils aient pris la forme de cautionnements, plus vraisemblablement ces relations étaient instituées par
des contrats de bail ou de louage, v. *CJ* XI 48 (47), 22 (531).
Dans tous les cautionnements pour colons adscrits il y est question
non de personnes qui s'obligent de devenir des *enapographoi geôrgoi*

---

10 C'est l'expression (à propos d'un autre type de contrat)
de G. Rouillard, *La vie rurale dans l'Empire byzantin* (Paris 1953)
38. G. Geraci, "Economia e società nei papiri greci d'epoca bizantina: linee di una problematica," *Corsi di cultura sull'arte ra-
vennate e bizantina Ravenna 1977* (Faenza 1977) 213, voit dans les
cautionnements un indice de la méfiance des grands propriétaires
contre l'efficacité de la législation impériale et de la capacité
de l'administration d'en assurer l'application.

11 M. Pallasse, *Orient et Occident à propos du colonat romain
au Bas Empire* (Lyon 1950) 67 (Bibliotheque de la Fac. de droit de
l'Univ. d'Alger, 10). V. aussi pp. 63 et 87 où il y est question
de "l'installation d'un cultivateur sur la terre." Cf. et M. Kaser
Das römische Privatrecht II, *Die nachklassischen Entwicklungen*[2]
(München 1975) 145 n. 24 sur "l'eidliche Unterwerfung" des colons.
A. R. Korsunskij, "O kolonate v Vostočnoj Rimskoj imperii V-VI
vekov" [Sur le colonat dans l'Empire romain oriental aux Ve-VIe
siècles], *Vizantijskij Vremennik* 9 (1956) 48 croit que "les magnats
emprisonnaient souvent dans leur prison des paysans et les forçai-
ent à se reconnaître leurs colons."

mais d'énapographes réels détenus dans la prison privée du maître
et qui ont besoin d'un garant pour sortir de cette prison. Vu que
c'est la contravention à ses obligations qui soit la cause de la
mise en prison du colon[12] sa libération pouvait avoir lieu seulement dans le cas où quelqu'un le prenait sous caution, c'est à dire
garantissait l'accomplissement par le colon de ses obligations ou
l'indemnisation du dommage. En d'autres termes les cautionnements
ne constituaient pas une procédure normale et obligatoire[13] mais
au contraire une procédure extraordinaire qui avait pour condition
des circonstances spéciales, fait noté par les chercheurs.[14]

Qui jouait le rôle des garants? Les colons étant de règle
organisés en κοινά τῶν γεωργῶν ou κοινά τῶν γεωργῶν καί ἀμπελουργῶν,
on s'attendrait que ce rôle fût assumé par les corporations respectives obligées de venir en certains cas à l'aide à ses membres.[15]
Mais dans tous les cautionnements dont nous disposons il ne s'agit
pas de *koina* mais de garants isolés, le plus souvent d'une seule
personne,[16] parfois de deux ou quelques personnes.[17] La fonction

---

12 Selon M. Pallasse, *Orient et Occident*, 68, la mise dans la
prison privée est une sanction des obligations énumérées dans les
cautionnements et non la cause primaire de la rédaction des cautionnements.

13 Selon toute apparence c'est l'opinion de A. C. Johnson,
L. C. West, *Byzantine Egypt: Economic Studies* (Princeton 1949) 31
(Princeton Univ. Studies in Papyrology, 6) lorsqu'ils affirment que
"his tenancy was guaranteed by sureties (on the side of the lessor)."

14 Par ex. E. Seidl, *Der Eid*, 86-87, G. Rouillard, *La vie
rurale*, 39-40.

15 V. I. F. Fikhman, "K voprosu o korporativnoj vzaimopomošči
v vizantijskom Egipte" [Sur l'aide mutuelle dans les corporations
de l'Egypte byzantine] *JJP* 15 (1965) 91-97; idem, *Egipet na rubeže
dvukh spokh. Remeslenniki i remeslennyj trud v IV - seredine VII v.*
[L'Egypte aux confins de deux époques. Les artisans et le travail
artisanal du IVe - au milieu du VIIe siècle] (Moskva 1965) 178-82.

16 *P. Lond.* III 778.7-9 (568), *P. Oxy.* I 135.8-10 (579), VI
996.10 (584), XXVII 2478.7-9 (595), *PSI* I 59.6-7 (596), *P. Merton* II
98.19-20, 23 (fin du VIe s.), *P. Oxy.* XVIII 2203 (VIe s.) si c'est
un cautionnement pour un colon, *P. Heid.* 248 (VIe-VIIe s.), *PSI* III
180.8 (VIe-VIIe s.), I 61.10-12 (609), I 62.13-14 (613), probablement aussi P. Giss. Univ. inv. 41 (590).

17 *P. Oxy.* VI 996.10 (584), P. Giss. Univ. inv. 45, 49 (fin
du VIe s.), *P. Oxy.* I 200.1-2 (VIe s.), peut-être P. Giss. Univ.
inv. 44 (588) aussi.

de garant était assumée par un colon adscrit[18] de la même localité,[19] d'une autre localité,[20] par une personne dont l'appartenance aux colons adscrits n'est pas mentionée[21] ou par un habitant de la ville.[22] Quoique on ne puisse pas exclure complètement l'hypothèse d'une pression de la part du grand propriétaire qui forçait "uns des habitants du domaine accepter le rôle de garants d'autres habitants du domaine"[23] le fait que le rôle de garant était assumé aussi par des personnes n'ayant aucune relation au domaine y compris des citadins, nous incite à supposer que le plus souvent les garants étaient choisis par les garantis eux-mêmes. Quant aux garantis dans la plupart des cas il s'agit d'un seul colon,[24] parfois de deux ou de quelques colons.[25]

A. C. Johnson et L. C. West ont émis l'hypothèse que les cautionnements seraient rédigés seulement dans le cas où il y avait dans la localité respective un si petit nombre de colons qu'ils ne pouvaient pas constituer une corporation.[26] Dans maints cas

---

18 L'affirmation de A. Segrè, "The Byzantine Colonate," *Traditio* 5 (1947) 111 et de M. Pallasse, *Orient et Occident*, 68, que le rôle de garant était souvent assumé par des "hommes libres" n'est pas tout à fait correcte car dans la majorité des cas il s'agit de colons adscrits.

19 *P. Oxy.* VI 996 (584), I 200 (VIe s.), *PSI* I 61 (609); dans *P. Merton* II 98 (fin du VIe s.) le garant est de la même localité mais nous ignorons s'il est colon.

20 *P. Lond.* III 778 (568), *P. Heid.* 248 (VIe-VIIe s.) (?).

21 *PSI* I 59.6-7 (596), III 180 (VIe-VIIe s.); sur *P. Merton* II 98 v. plus haut.

22 *P. Oxy.* I 135.8-10 (579), XLIV 3204.6-8 (588) mais il est au service du grand propriétaire, XXVII 2478.7-9 (595), *PSI* III 180.13 (VIe-VIIe s.) (?).

23 A. R. Korsunskij, "O kolonate," 67.

24 *P. Lond.* III 778.13-14 (568), *P. Oxy.* I 135.8-10 (579), XLIV 3204.11 (588), XXVII 2478.7-9 (595), *PSI* I 59.10-11 (596), *P. Oxy.* I 200.10-11 (VIe s.), XVIII 2203 (VIe s.) si c'est un cautionnement pour un colon, *P. Heid.* 248.2-3 (VIe-VIIe s.), *PSI* III 180.2-3 (VIe-VIIe s.), I 61.18-20 (609), 62.13-15 (613), probablement P. Giss. Univ. inv. 41 (590).

25 *P. Oxy.* VI 996.10 (584), P. Giss. Univ. inv. 45, 49 (fin du VIe s.), *P. Merton* II 98.1-2 (fin du VIe s.).

26 A. C. Johnson, L. C. West, *Byzantine Egypt*, 31, 153.

l'explication est plausible; tout de même on ne peut pas la considérer comme la seule possible. Malheureusement nous ne connais-
sons pas le nombre des colons dans tel ou autre hameau au moment de
la rédaction des cautionnements mais dans certains hameaux il y
avait sans doute un nombre suffisant pour constituer une corporation. A Mouchis et à Paggouleiou il y avait sans doute des corporations de paysans[27] néanmoins dans les cautionnements se référant
aux colons originaires de ces localités (P. Oxy. VI 996 et PSI I 61)
la fonction de garants est assumée non par les corporations respectives mais par des garants privés. L'absence de la mention des
corporations dans ce cas doit être probablement expliquée d'une
autre façon: par exemple par l'expiration du terme prévu par le
statut de la corporation pour la durée de l'aide ou par le fait que
la corporation n' a pas accompli ses obligations de garant ce qui
amenait à la nécessité de chercher un garant privé.

Les cautionnements nous apportent d'importantes informations
sur les obligations des colons adscrits. Ces obligations étaient
bien connues par toutes les parties intéressées (grand domaine,
colons adscrits et garants), elles dérivaient de la condition de
enapographos geôrgos. C'est pourquoi dans une série de cautionnements on indique que le garanti est responsable εἰς ἅπαντα τὰ
ὁρῶντα τὸ αὐτοῦ πρόσωπον ἤτοι τὴν τοῦ ἐναπογράφου τύχην.[28] Cette
formule n'est pas une invention des notaires égyptiens mais s'inspire de la terminologie officielle. Dans les Novelles de Justinien
(les documents chronologiquement les plus proches de nos cautionnements) le mot τύχη est souvent employé pour désigner le statut (la
condition) des hommes libres, des esclaves, des adscripticii, des
curiales et d'autres groupes de la population. Le mot τύχη de même
que son équivalent latin fortuna est mentionné aussi dans le Codex
Justinianus où cependant le terme condicio prédomine.

Les cautionnements contiennent aussi des données plus dé-
taillées sur la condition et les obligations des colons adscrits.

---

27 Par ex.: Mouchis: PSI VIII 954.42 (568), Paggouleiou:
P. Oxy. VI 999 (616-17).

28 P. Lond. III 778.17 (568), P. Oxy. I 135.19 (579), XLIV
3204.15-16 (588), P. Merton II 98.7-9 (fin du VIe s.), P. Heid.
248.8-9 (VIe-VIIe s.).

Tout d'abord ils confirment l'attache héréditaire des colons à la
terre. Si la clause ἀδιαλείπτως παραμεῖναι καὶ διάγειν...καὶ μηδα-
μῶς...καταλεῖψαι...μήτε μὴν μεθίστασθαι εἰς ἕτερον τόπον figure
aussi dans des cautionnements pour non-colons,[29] l'addition μετὰ
τῶν αὐτοῦ φιλτάτων καὶ γαμετῆς καὶ κτηνῶν καὶ πάσης τῆς αὐτοῦ ἀπο-
σκευῆς est ajoutée seulement dans les cautionnements pour colons.
Il est vrai que l'obligation de demeurer sur le domaine avec sa
famille et son avoir n'est pas incluse dans tous les cautionnements
pour colons sans exception.[30] Mais les *enapographoi geôrgoi* constituaient du point de vue de leur statut et situation un groupe
homogène, surtout les colons d'un seul et même grand domaine. Il
est inconcevable que le maître ayant la possibilité de s'appuyer
sur la législation impériale attachant héréditairement le colon à
la terre impose au colon dans certains cas la résidence sur le domaine avec sa famille et son avoir et que ce même maître dans
d'autres cas ne demande que la résidence du colon seul, en libérant
de cette obligation sa famille et son avoir. La clause de la résidence témoigne à notre avis l'attache héréditaire du colon au domaine et contredit l'affirmation de A. C. Johnson et L. C. West que
"the ἐναπόγραφοι γεωργοί were free tenants."[31]

Ensuite les cautionnements imposent au colon l'accomplissement
d'une série d'obligations envers le grand domaine. Parfois ces obligations ne sont pas précisées, on les mentionne d'une façon générale dans la clause pénale qui prévoie qu'en cas de fuite et de
non-présentation du colon par le garant celui-ci s'oblige ὑπεύθυνος
εἶναι πᾶσιν τοῖς πρὸς αὐτὸν ἐπιζητουμένοις ἀποκρίνασθαι.[32]

---

29 Par ex. *P. Oxy.* XXIV 2420.13-15 (611) cautionnement pour
deux orfèvres.

30 Elle est mentionnée dans *P. Oxy.* I 135.17 (579), XLIV
3204.14 (588), *PSI* I 59.13 (595), *P. Merton* II 98.4 (fin du VIe s.),
P. Heid. 248.7 (VIe-VIIe s.).

31 A. C. Johnson, L. C. West, *Byzantine Egypt*, 31.

32 *P. Merton* II 98.16-18 (fin du VIe s.), *PSI* I 61.31-32
(609), I 62.23-24 (613). La clause est mentionnée aussi dans *P.
Oxy.* XVIII 2203.5-6 (VIe s.) mais nous ne pouvons pas affirmer ca-
tegoriquement qu'il s'agit d'un cautionnement pour un colon. Dans
certains cautionnements (*PSI* I 59, *P. Oxy.* I 200, *P. Heid.* 248,
PSI III 180) la clause pénale ne nous est parvenue.

Dans certains cautionnements les obligations sont énumérées d'une façon plus ou moins détaillée, par ex. dans *P. Oxy.* XXVII 2478.17-21 (595). Le colon doit labourer avec soin la terre, payer régulièrement les fermages etc. Irrésolu reste le problème des corvées des colons: devraient-ils au surplus travailler gratuitement sur les terres que le grand domaine exploitait lui même? Les *operae* des colons sont citées dans les inscriptions africaines du Haut Empire se référant aux saltus impériaux. Dans la législation impériale les *operae* des colons sont mentionnées dans *CJ* XI 53 (52), I (371) se rapportant à l'Illyricum. Quant à l'Egypte les opinions divergent. Certains auteurs (par ex. A. C. Johnson et L. C. West, M. V. Levčenko) admettent l'existence du devoir d'accomplir des corvées,[33] d'autres la denient.[34]

N'ayant pas la possibilité--par manque de place--d'analyser ici toutes les données respectives[35] nous nous limitons à exprimer l'opinion que *P. Oxy.* XXVII 2478.19-21 (595) donne une réponse affirmative à la question. Le garant indique que le colon est obligé de εὐγνωμονεῖν...κ[αὶ τ]ὰς διδομένας παρ᾽ αὑτοῦ ἐξ ἔθους γεουχικὰς ὑπηρεσίας πάσας. L'auteur traduit "shall...perform all the estate tasks usually presented by it," c'est à dire selon lui παρ᾽ αὑτοῦ = παρὰ τοῦ πωμαρίου. Selon nous παρ᾽ αὑτοῦ = παρὰ τοῦ πωμαρίτου, c'est à dire il s'agit de travaux effectués par le πωμαρίτης. Vu que le texte mentionne plus haut l'obligation du colon d'accomplir πᾶσαν φιλοκάλειαν καὶ καλλιέργειαν nous supposons que dans les lignes 19-21 il y est question non pas de travaux dans le πωμάριον mais des *operae* que le colon doit faire pour son maître.

---

33   A. C. Johnson, L. C. West, *Byzantine Egypt*, 65; M. V. Levčenko, "Materialy dlja vnutrennej istorii Vostočnoj Rimskoj imperii V-VI vv." [Matériaux pour l'étude de l'histoire intérieure de l'Empire romain oriental aux Ve-VIe siècles], *Vizantijskij sbornik* (Moscou-Léningrad 1945) 26.

34   Par ex. A. Segrè, *Byzantion* 21 (1951) 211; A. I. Tjumenev, "Perednij Vostok i antičnost'" (strany rečnykh kul'tur [Dvureč'e i Egipet] v ellinističeskuju i rimskuju epokhu)" [Le Proche-Orient et l'antiquité (les pays des cultures rivéraines: Mésopotamie et Egypte) aux époques hellénistique et romaine] *Voprosy istorii* 1957 N9, p. 52.

35   V. plus détaillement I. F. Fikhman, "Byli li objazany barščinoj egipetskie kolony adskripticii?" [Etaient-ils obligés les colons adscrits égyptiens de faire des corvées?] (à paraître dans *Klio* 63 [1981]).

Les considerations ci-dessus nécessairement succintes ne sont pas certes, exhaustives quant aux informations contenues dans les cautionnements pour colons adscrits.

Leningrad Institut des Sciences orientales   I. F. Fikhman
de l'Academie des sciences de l'URSS

ON VILLAGE AND POLIS IN BYZANTINE EGYPT

On page 316 in the final chapter of his book *Die Binnenwande-rung*, Professor H. Braunert remarked upon the continued importance of economic exchanges between city-dwellers (πολῖται) and villagers (κωμῆται) in Egypt during the Byzantine period, exchanges that, for reasons of geographical proximity, most frequently linked *politai* and villagers of the same polis-territory--Hermopolite villagers to Hermopolis, Oxyrhynchite villagers to Oxyrhynchus, and so forth. Ten pages later, Braunert makes the same point in much the same way, this time stressing further the importance of the Egyptian poleis as "market-centers" for those who dwelt in surrounding villages. Villagers would travel for brief sojourns in cities to take out loans or to sell livestock and other merchandise. They would re-turn home, cash in hand, on completion of those transactions.

It is true that evidence for more permanent links between vil-lagers and nearby poleis, through the establishment of long-term residences, is not lacking. This evidence sometimes consists of leases of house property to villagers in cities. From these we learn, for example, of the man from the Panopolite village Psonis who leased for three years a house in Panopolis; of the man from the Hermopolite village Nagogis who took out a lease of indefinite term on a house located (evidently) in Hermopolis; of the lady from the Heracleopolite village Ibichis who took out a lease on part of a house in the Pammenes Garden district of Oxyrhynchus; of the vinedressers from Ibion Sesembythis of the Hermopolite territory who took out a five-year lease on vineland with appurtenances (in-cluding a house) in Antinoopolis.[1] At other times, the evidence is supplied by the filling in of notarial formulas in contracts, in those instances where it is indicated by such terms as καταμένων, οἰκῶν or διάγων that a contracting party or witness originates from a village, but is now present as long-term visitor or resident in a

---

1 *P. Köln Panop.* 13 (*ZPE* 7 [1971] 32-34); *P. Lond.* V 1872 descr.; *P. Oxy.* XVI 1961; *P. Hamb.* 23.

polis.[2] But, despite the existence of these and other types of
evidence for long-term presence of villagers in poleis, it is clearly the evidence for visits of short duration that is more abundant,
and there is no reason to doubt that the relative proportion of the
evidence is a reasonable reflection, if not a precise measurement,
of actual conditions.

It is possible, after a fashion, to begin illustrating this
pattern of village-to-polis movement (and back again) by citing a
type of document that first makes its appearance in the Byzantine
period, that which is commonly referred to as a "receipt for agricultural machinery." These receipts appear as early as A.D. 440/41
in a Milan papyrus already in the form that is standard in later
documents.[3] An individual, usually identified as a registered tenant (ἐναπόγραφος γεωργός) of a great landowner, indicates that he
has found need of some piece of agricultural equipment--a handmill,
an axle, a windlass.[4] He acknowledges that he has received the
needed piece of machinery from his landlord (or indirectly, through
his landlord's agent). For present purposes, the question whether
these documents are to be construed as recording contracts between
ἐναπόγραφοι and their landlords, or were simply receipts to assist
in the management of the landlords' estates is not important.[5]
What is important is that the formulary for these documents included
reference to the tenant as "having gone up" (usually ἀνελθών) from
his rural habitat (his assigned κτῆμα or ἐποίκιον) "to the city"
(ἐπὶ τῆς πόλεως) to ask for and to receive the specified equipment.[6]

---

2 E.g. *P. Cair. Masp.* II 67155; *BGU* XII 2200; *P. Stras.* III
317; *P. Stras.* I 40; *P. Wisc.* I 10. Fuller discussion in my forthcoming chapter in *ANRW*.

3 Cf. analysis of the form by S. Daris, *Aegyptus* 37 (1957) 89ff.

4 Cf. *P. Oxy.* XVI 1983, 1985, 1988-89, 1991; *P. Lond.* III 774
(pp. 280-81), 776 (p. 278), among other texts. See the detailed
list in I. F. Fikhman, *Egipet na rubezhe dvukh epokh* (Moscow 1965)
227-48.

5 Contracts: A. C. Johnson and L. C. West, *Byzantine Egypt:
Economic Studies* (Princeton 1949) 29ff.; A. C. Johnson, *Egypt and
the Roman Empire* (Ann Arbor 1951) 99-100. Receipts: H. I. Bell,
JRS 43 (1953) 205.

6 For the term ἐποίκιον and its various meanings, see now M.
Lewuillon-Blume, *Actes du XVe Congrès international de papyrologie*,
Pt. 4 (Papyrologie documentaire), Pap. Brux. 19 (1979) 177-85. It
is sometimes interchangeable with κώμη (see p. 177 n. 2), at other
times it stands for a kind of *villa rustica* (p. 182).

It is true, however, that the bond between an *enapographos georgos* and his landlord was one of more than usual dependency; moreover, that the extant examples of agricultural machinery receipts are all of Oxyrhynchite provenance and that most of these concern the properties and tenants of the imposing Apion family. It is necessary therefore to proceed to determine whether this pattern of country or village-to-city movement had any broader geographical application and whether it concerned parties not so closely bound, socially, economically, juridically, administratively, one to the other as the *enapographos* was to his landlord.

Immediately, the pattern with its implications, is clear in the type of transaction, sometimes referred to as "sale on delivery," whose prices were the subject of a recent discussion by Roger S. Bagnall (*GRBS* 18 [1977] 85-96). Papyri recording "sales on delivery" are to be found in the Greek papyri of the Ptolemaic, Roman, and Byzantine periods, but it is in the last-named that they are the most common. By the standard form, one party acknowledges receipt of an acceptable sum of money from a second party, to be repaid at an established future date, not in currency but in kind-- in wine, barley, fodder, vegetable seed, jars, soap, or in some other commodity. The formulas of the documents recording these transactions are patterned on those of the simple loan-contract; and, according to Bagnall, this is essentially what the contract is--a loan, but one designed to dodge the legally established 12% annual rate of interest on money loans. The price (or the amount lent) typically remains unstated (except for its agreeableness) in Byzantine documents, so there was no possibility for an outsider to determine the amount "paid" and its relationship to the value of the commodity to be delivered (the reverse calculation, of course, would probably have been relatively easy to make). "For the lender," Bagnall writes

> there was the security of the crop, a good rate of interest, and repayment in a non-depreciating commodity. For the borrower there was at least relatively easy access to cash which would be inaccessible at 12 per cent and illegal at a higher rate. It was easy to obey the letter of the law in this way: no interest was being charged in money.

"The contract of loan in money with repayment in kind," Bagnall continues,

is most correctly to be seen as one of the manifestations
of the ingenuity of the population of Roman Egypt in avoiding laws which were wholly contrary to actual conditions.
But while one may admire this ingenuity, the conditions
which made it necessary are anything but laudable. The
perennial shortage of capital and the continuing inflation
which helped make this contract profitable are not earmarks
of economic health and stability. Worse still, one may
suspect that these loans form part of a worsening cycle of
economic dependence of the farming class on the wealthy.

If Bagnall is right (or even right in a majority of cases),[7]
then we may further extend his statement about the "economic dependence of the farming class on the wealthy" to cover an attendant
and overlapping economic dependence of Byzantine Egyptian villagers
(artisans as well as village farmers) on their respective territorial *politai*. This is because in virtually all instances in
which a villager and a *polites* are found to engage in "sales on
delivery," it is the *polites* who stands as the creditor-buyer, the
villager as the debtor-seller. A cluster of probative examples (at
least seven in number)[8] from sixth-century Hermopolis may be found
by repairing to *BGU* XII and the pattern there evident supported by
other Hermopolis documents, and still more generally by Byzantine
documents of other proveniences, from the fifth through the seventh
centuries.[9] Additionally, though at the risk of obscuring or com-
plicating the simple point that is being pressed here, it may be
noted that several of the texts[10] illustrate that the pattern of
politai as creditor-buyers to villagers as debtor-sellers partly
overlaps another pattern for some time familiar in Byzantine Egyptian contracts--the one whereby in contracts between parties with

---

7   I suspect some texts, e.g. the Michigan papyrus edited in
ZPE 34 (1979) 142-46, evidence genuinely commercial transactions.

8   *BGU* XII 2198-99, 2205, 2207-10.

9   E.g.: <u>Arsinoite</u>: *P. Lond.* II 390 (p. 332) (6th or 7th c.),
BGU II 370 (630); <u>Heracleopolite</u>: *SB* VIII 9773 (405), *P. L. Bat.*
XIII 15 (435); <u>Hermopolite</u>: *P. Lond.* III 999 (p. 270) (538), 1001
(pp. 270-71) (539); V 1774 (570); <u>Oxyrhynchite</u>: *P. Lond.* V 1777
(434), P. Oxy. inv. 14. 113. 209/c (f), in *ZPE* 30 (1978) 205-6 (492);
P. Oxy. X 1320 descr. (497), XVI 1974 (499); P. Mich. inv. 3769, in
ZPE 34 (1979) 143-44 (557).

10   *BGU* XII 2205, 2208-10; *P. Lond.* III 1001; the papyrus edited by R. Hübner in *ZPE* 30 (1978) 205-7. Cf. also *CPR* IV 34, a bilingual (Greek-Coptic) document, a formulary according to its editor, W. Till (reference owed to Gladys Frantz-Murphy).

the *nomen* Flavius and those with the *nomen* Aurelius, the former
consistently appear economically (and socially) more dominant.

Even more so than in "sales on delivery" (cf. *ZPE* 13 [1974]
288 and n. 163), however, the Flavius-Aurelius pattern is noticeable (it was first in fact succinctly noted by E. Bickermann in his
inaugural dissertation, *Das Edikt des Kaisers Caracalla in P. Giss.
40* [Berlin 1926] 35) in contracts of lease and loan.[11] In turn,
again, the Flavius-Aurelius pattern in leases partly overlaps the
pattern that is being illustrated here, for in contracts of lease
between *politai* and villagers the former are regularly the lessors,
the latter are regularly the lessees. Examples are very common in
leases of land. Again one may repair to *BGU* XII, wherein at least
eleven contracts have Hermopolite *politai* leasing land to villagers,[12]
and richly support the illustration of that pattern by numerous
other Byzantine contracts from Hermopolis and other proveniences.[13]

The pattern of *politai* as lessors to villagers as lessees, were
it studied more intensively and the results of such study presented
at greater length than is possible here, might contribute somewhat
to our knowledge about "absentee landlordism" in Byzantine Egypt.
But even without that intensive study, the pattern alone would seem
to indicate that quite a few villagers were probably themselves
landless (or landowners on a very small scale) and earned (or supplemented) their income by tenant sharecropping. Even others, those
who were medium-class landowners, may have made a practice and a
profit from sharecropping leases arranged with absentee landlords
or with ecclesiastical and monastic institutions.[14] Moreover, in
view of the rarity of landleases *between* villagers, one may conclude
that villager-landowners, when physically able, almost without

---

11   The pattern is now more fully discussed in *ZPE* 13 (1974)
283ff.

12   *BGU* XII 2147-48, 2152, 2155-56, 2159-60, 2174, 2181, 2186-87.

13   E.g. *P. Ant.* I 89 (= *CPJud.* III 517); *BGU* I 306, 311; *P.
Cair. Masp.* I 67113; *P. Coll. Youtie* 89-90; *P. Berl. Frisk* 5; *P.
Grenf.* I 57-58; *P. Hamb.* 23; *P. Lips.* 20; *P. Lond.* III 979 (pp. 234-
35), 1003 (pp. 259-60); V 1689, 1766-67, 1770; *P. Oxy.* VI 913; *P.
Ross. Georg.* III 32, 40, 51; *PSI* I 77, IV 316, IX 1078; *SB* I 5139,
III 7167, VI 9269, 9596; *P. Stras.* 557, 579; *P. Thead.* 6; *P. Vindob.
Bosw.* 5.

14   Like Aurelius Phoibammon, son of Triadelphus, of sixth-
century Aphrodite. Cf. my discussion in *BASP* 17 (1980).

exception farmed their plots themselves. In addition, because the
Flavius-to-Aurelius pattern often also comes into play in these
leases from *politai* to villagers (as sometimes in the "sales on
delivery"), these contracts would appear to have something to say
about the relative proportion of Flavii to Aurelii in poleis and in
villages. It would appear that Flavii were relatively scarce in
village communities; when they do occur in village "contexts" they
tend to be outsiders--absentee landlords, provincial governors and
officials, soldiers.[15] On the other hand, Flavii, often on government salary, were no doubt proportionately more common in poleis,
especially in those like Antinoopolis and Oxyrhynchus, which were
administrative centers, or in cities where military units were
stationed (e.g. Hermopolis, Syene).

Finally, and all too briefly, the *polites*-to-villager pattern
sketched already for land-leases, sales with deferred delivery, and
receipts for agricultural machinery, is also common in money loans
and in loans in kind.[16] In these the *politai* are regularly the
creditors, the villagers the debtors. Thus the many instances of
the pattern in these varieties of document-types clearly point to,
but without precisely defining, the importance of *politai* in village economic life. Whether they constituted the dominant factor
in any given village or villages is at present hard to establish.
What is clear enough, however, is that on those many documented
occasions when villagers and *politai* were in economic contact, the
politai were the superior parties, the ones who stood in the long
run to profit from the transactions. What the villagers "gained"
of course, from some of the transactions, was an immediate receipt
of cash. Thus, in what may be an overstatement of the case,[17] these

---

15 Not absolutely conclusive on this point, but well worth
perusing for partial confirmation is V. A. Girgis, *Prosopografia e
Aphroditopolis*, R. Università di Pisa, Facoltà di Lettere (Berlin
1938).

16 Money loans: *BGU* I 314, II 365, III 736; *P. Erl.* 9 = 67; *P.
Grenf.* II 74; *P. Lond.* I 113. 6 (c); *P. L. Bat.* XIII 7; *P. Oxy.* XVI
1982; *SB* I 4498, X 10524; *SPP* XX 90; *P. Warren* 10. Loans in kind:
P. Grenf. II 86; *P. Lond.* III 975 (p. 230); *P. NYU* 24; *PSI* I 42, VI
703; *SB* VI 9593.

17 As one of Eric Ambler's characters maintains, "...it is
sometimes agreeable to talk in primary colours even if you have to
think in greys" (*The Mask of Dimitrios*, Fontana edition, p. 71).
Cf. *P. Soterichos*, pp. 22-23, for an analysis of the economic and
social character of comparable transactions in first-century Theadelphia.

transactions, taken as a whole, probably served to keep the cycle
of village economies going, to render possible the payment of taxes
due in money or the commutation of those due in kind, and to facilitate the acquisition of goods not accessible through barter. They
may have retarded the slide of village economic life to natural subsistence levels and the reduction of many sale transactions to
barter--at how great an individual or communal price we cannot guess.
This was not a local trend, it was widespread; it was not restricted
in time, it was chronic. It was a fact of Byzantine Egyptian village life. Nevertheless, it is not this paper's intent in its short
compass to explore the wider consequences of the pattern that has
been sketched. Its main purpose has simply been to point out the
consistency with which Byzantine Egyptian *politai* dominated their
contemporary villagers in a variety of economic relationships. The
implications of that consistency must be reserved for future study.

Loyola University of Chicago   James G. Keenan

Proceedings of the XVI Int. Congr. of Papyrology (Chico 1981) 487-490

RECU POUR LIVRAISON DE BLE AU TITRE DE L'ANNONE

P. Gen. inv. 204   551 ap. J.-C.

En 1929, Victor Martin publiait le P. Gen. inv. 210 qui appartient aux archives de Dioscore.[1] L'éditeur signalait que le texte avait été acquis en Egypte par Jules Nicole en 1907 précisément, dans les années où à Kôm Ischgau on découvrait les pièces qui constituent ce lot et qui ont été dispersées entre plusieurs collections. Il ajoutait que d'autres textes genevois, alors non déchiffrés, semblaient appartenir au même ensemble.[2] C'est en reprenant les papyrus byzantins de Genève - au nombre de cinquante environ et pour la plupart inédits - que mon attention a été attirée par le P. Gen. inv. 204.[3]

Avant de présenter le document, il me reste à remercier M. P. J. Sijpesteijn pour les remarques précieuses que lui a inspirées la lecture de ma transcription.

Le P. Gen. inv. 204 est un reçu établi au nom du pagarque Julianus par son subalterne X attestant qu'Apollôs a versé 20 artabes 15/48 de blé pour l'annone de la 15e indiction.

Le papyrus, haut de 8 cm, large de 30,5 cm, offre quatre lignes complètes sur six. Le reçu est écrit en cursive, aux lettres grandes, serrées et verticales, disposées dans le sens de la longueur des fibres. Le dos est blanc.

Depuis que la photo a été prise, l'extrémité inférieure gauche, déjà fort réduite, s'est détachée du document et n'a plus été retrouvée.

---

1 V. Martin, "A Letter from Constantinople," *JEA* 15 (1929) 96-102. Cf. G. Malz, "The Papyri of Dioscorus: Publications and Emendations," *Studi in onore di Aristide Calderini e Roberto Paribeni* II (Milan 1957) 348, n° 21.

2 Martin, "Letter," 98 n. 2.

3 Cf. Cl. Wehrli, "L'état de la collection papyrologique de Genève," *Actes du XVe congrès international de papyrologie, Papyrologica Bruxellensia* 18 (Bruxelles 1979) 24.

Texte

1 ✝ δέδωκεν ᾿Απολλῶς Διοσκώρου δι(ὰ) τῶν κληρ(ονόμων) αὐτοῦ
   εἰς λόγον ἐμβολῆς

2 πεντεκαιδεκάτης ἰνδ(ικτίονος) (ὑπὲρ) κωμ(η)τ(ικῶν) κώμ(ης)
   Φθλᾶ δι(ὰ) προσγράφ(ου) Τιμοθέου γραμ(ματέως)

3 κώμ(ης) ᾿Αφροτίτ(ης) σίτου κανόνος ἀρτάβας εἴκοσι τέταρτον
   τετραεικοστὸν

4 τεσσαρακοστόγδ[οο]ν γί(νονται) σίτου κανό(νος) [(ἀρτάβαι)]
   κ δ' κδ' μη'. ὁ ἐνδοξ(ότατος) πάγαρχος ᾿Ιουλιανὸς

5 ᾿Ιλλουστρ(ίου) δι' ἐμοῦ ...νίννου βοηθ[οῦ ....] ...
   οἰκί[....]✝ο-

6 [ἐγρά(φη) μ]ην[ὶ ...]ι κα' [ιε' ἰνδ(ικτίονος)]

        1 Διοσκόρου   3 ᾿Αφροδίτης

Traduction

Apollôs, fils de Dioscore, a donné par l'intermédiaire de ses
héritiers au compte de l'annone de la 15e indiction pour les taxes
villageoises du village de Phthla, sur déclaration écrite du scribe
Timothée, du village d'Aphroditô, vingt artabes un quart, un vingt-
quatrième et un quarante-huitième de blé au titre de la contribution annuelle soit artabes 20 1/4 1/24 1/48. Le très glorieux
pagarque Julien, fils d'Illoustrios, par l'intermédiaire de moi...
(ninnos), son assistant.

Ecrit le 21 du mois de..., indiction 15.

Commentaire

1. L'intitulé de notre texte ressemble aux reçus 67045 et
67046 des *P. Cair. Masp.* et aux quittances 1665 et 1666 des *P.
Lond.* V. A propos de l'"*embolè*," cf. G. Rouillard, *L'administration civile de l'Egypte byzantine,*[2] ch. 3, passim, et plus spécialement, pour la perception du blé, p. 131 à 136.

Sur la permutation ω>o, cf. Fr. Th. Gignac, *A Grammar of the
Greek Papyri of the Roman and Byzantine Periods* I (Milan 1978)
276 sq.

2. Les gens d'Aphroditô acquittaient deux sortes d'impôts:
les κωμητικά, pour les dépenses de leur village (cf. *P. Lond.* V

1665 et 1666) et les ἀστικά, pour l'entretien d'Antéopolis, la
métropole (cf. *P. Cair. Masp.* 67045). La famille de Dioscore pos-
sédait des terres dans le village de Phthla qui appartient à la
commune d'Aphroditô.

Le scribe Timothée se rencontre à ma connaissance pour la
première fois dans les papyrus qui appartiennent aux archives de
Dioscore.

3. Sur la permutation τ>δ, cf. Fr. Th. Gignac, op. cit., 80-
83. Sur κανῶν, cf. L. Wenger, *Canon in den römischen Rechtsquellen
und in den Papyri,* Sb. Akad. Wiss. Wien, Phil.-hist. Kl., Bd. 220,2
(1942) 24-33. Sur Aphroditô, cf. A. Calderini, *Dizionario dei nomi
geografici e topografici dell'Egitto Greco-romano* (Madrid 1966)
302-414.

4. Sur la forme τεσσακοστόγδοον, cf. H. C. Youtie, *ZPE* 38
(1980) 284. Julianus Flavius, pagarque d'Antéopolis, est bien
connu par les *P. Lond.* V 1660.6 et 1661.5 (553 ap. J.-C.) et aussi
par les *P. Cair. Masp.* 67024 r.31 (vers 551) et 67046 (14e indiction).

5. Ἰλλούστριος est ici un nom propre, non un titre. Cf. *P.
Würzb.* 19.15.

6. Pour les restitutions de cette ligne, cf. R. Rémondon,
"Reçu de versement pour l' 'embolè,'" *BIFAO* 50 (1952) 67.

Genève   Claude Wehrli

P. Gen. inv. 204

Proceedings of the XVI Int. Congr. of Papyrology (Chico 1981) 491-498

PAPYRUS FRAGMENTS FROM THE MONASTERY OF PHOEBAMMON[1]

In the 1947-1948 season, the Society for Coptic Archaeology, under the direction of our President, Mirrit Boutros Ghali, and the field supervision of the then General Secretary, Charles Bachatly, undertook excavations at the site of the monastery of St. Phoebammon near Jeme, Western Thebes. Abundant evidence for the activities of this monastic foundation, especially in the sixth, seventh, and eighth centuries, is furnished by the Jeme papyri in Crum and Steindorff's *Koptische Rechtsurkunden des achten Jahrhunderts aus Djême (Theben)* [*KRU*] of 1912, the correspondence of Pesynthius of Coptos first published by Revillout, many letters in Crum's *Coptic Ostraca*, and the famous *P. Lond.* I 77, the testament of Bishop Abraham of Hermonthis, who was also abbot of St. Phoebammon's monastery. (For a list of monastic superiors of the foundation, see W. C. Till, *Datierung und Prosopographie der koptischen Urkunden aus Theben* [Vienna 1962] [*SB. Österr. Akad. d. Wiss., phil.-hist. Kl.*, 240.1] 236.)

It was thought desirable even then to find out something about the physical surroundings in which the monastic life, with all its concomitant economic activities, was carried on in Late Antiquity in a flourishing center of population in Upper Egypt. Excavation results are usually unhappily slow in reaching published form, and ours are, alas, no exception: the final volume should be out this academic year, thirty-three years after the fact. The volumes have appeared in reverse order: first III, scientific analyses of the organic remains and soils; then II, the graffiti and ostraca, hitherto our only forms of text from the Phoebammon site. Volume I will comprise the plans of the monastic buildings, the layout of the complex, the chronology (the surviving fabric of the buildings is sixth- and seventh-century), and what is known of the find-spots of artifacts. Among the objects for which no find-spot was recorded are forty-four fragments and scraps of papyrus, many uninscribed,

---

1 My sincere thanks to Professor L. Koenen, whose many suggestions are incorporated in this paper.

many more bearing a trace of only a single letter or two. Photographs of these fragments are to appear as Plates CVI-CXII of
Volume I of the Phoebammon publication. Here I present only those
fragments yielding enough text to add something to our knowledge of
the Phoebammon community's use of the written word and its interactions with the world outside.

The three fragments belong to the historical epos known as the
Blemyomachia (edd. Livrea, Meisenhein 1978; E. Heitsch, *Die griechi-*
schen Dichterfragmente, XXXIII, p. 99), and they are written by the
same hand of the 4th/5th century as the fragments published in 1881
(P. Berol. 5003; L. Stern, *ZÄS* 19 [1881] 70ff. [with a plate facing
p. 75]).[2] On the new fragments, punctuation appears in fr. 1 ↑ 5
(ψυχη· [high stop], → 3 (εερσην· [middle stop]), 5 (εσται· [high
stop]), 7 (ικεσθαι. [low stop]), 8 (ϊανθη· [middle stop]), fr. 2 →
4 (not transcribed, see photograph), and fr. 3 → 2 (εργων· [high
stop]). *Tremata* are preserved above ι (ϊ) and υ (ϋ): fr. 1 ↑ 4 and
→ 8; an apostrophe is extant in fr. 1 ↑ 8 (δ'). For a comparison
with the same features in the old fragments, see footnote 3.

On the side written across the fibres (↑), the three fragments
preserve the beginning of lines and, on the other side written
along the fibres (→), the end of lines. Parts of the margins are
extant. I found neither an indication for the relative order of
the three fragments nor for the priority of side → or side ↑,
though all three fragments might come from the same page of the
codex. Some readings and the body of notes which follow the trans-
scription of the fragments were provided by Prof. L. Koenen (K.)
and Mr. M. Petrini (P.), a participant in K.'s papyrological seminar, on the basis of the photographs.

---

2   E. G. Turner dated the hand to ± 400 (see Livrea p. 9 and
footnote 16). A photograph of P. Berol. 5003,1 ↑ is to be found in
R. Seider, *Paläographie der griechischen Papyri* II, *Literarische*
Papyri (Stuttgart 1970) 160 no. 62 (pl. XXXIII).

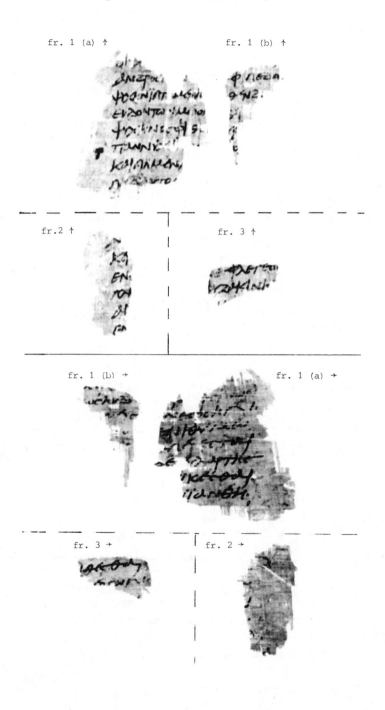

fr. 1 (a) ↑

fr. 1 (b) ↑

fr. 2 ↑

fr. 3 ↑

fr. 1 (b) →

fr. 1 (a) →

fr. 3 →

fr. 2 →

fr. 1 (a+b) ↑   fr. 1 (a+b) →
- - - - - - - - - - - - - - -   - - - - - - - - - - - - - - -
1 ...[..... ....].[1]....[..... .....].....
   ἀνδρὸς .[..].[....].σφι πεδο.[π]ροσηύδα [....]..[..]ρσι....
   ψυχὴν ἱπταμένη[ν ἐ]γθένδ[(ε)   ].εις[...]ν ἐέρσην·
4 εὐδόντων μεροπ[..]ϋϊ[4   ]..[...] ἐνὶ θυμῷ
   ψυχή· νόσφι θ.[...]υξ[   ]..[....]ε περ ἔσται·
   παννυχι..... [.....]ο[ἡ]δὲ [Π]υλάρτης
   καὶ πῇ μὲν .[.....].[   ].ικέσθαι.
8 πῇ δ᾽ αὐτο.[8   ]ν ἴάνθη·
- - - - - - - - - - - - - - -   - - - - - - - - - - - - - - -

fr. 2 ↑   fr. 3 ↑   fr. 3 →
- - - - - - -   - - - - - - - - -   - - - - - - - -
1 α[1].ἐφλέγεο.[1].θεσθαι
  κει.[   ]φυζακινη[   ] ἔργων·
  εν.[   ]...[   ].[
4 πλι[- - - - - - - - -   - - - - - - - -
  αν[
  εν
- - - - - - -

fr. 1 ↑

The fragments a and b were separated by K. on the photograph.

3 ἱπταμένη[ν ἐ]γθένδ[(ε): supplemented by K. and (ἐ]γθένδ[ε) P.
   The final ε was either elided or lengthened by following conso-
   nants; for the observance of Hermann's bridge in the *Blemyomachia*,
   see Livrea, p. 19.

   ἱπταμένην is, of course, late. Here, as in Homer, the ψυχή
   flies away, seemingly in the moment of death; cf. Π 856 = Χ 362
   ψυχὴ δ᾽ ἐκ ῥεθέων πταμένη Ἄιδόσδε βεβήκει and see also Quint.
   Smyrn. 7,41f. ἄιστος | ψυχὴ οἱ πεπότηται ἐς ἠέρα and 8,202f.
   ψυχὴ δὲ δι᾽ ἕλκεος ἐξεποτήθη | ἐκ μελέων. In *Blemyom.* (P. Berol.)
   12f., however, the author accepts the unhomeric idea of the
   θυμός flying away (τῆλε δὲ οἱ προλιπὼν χρόα θ[υμὸς ἀπέπτη | ἠύτ]ε
   κοῦφος ὄνειρος; cf. λ 221ff. ἐπεί κε πρῶτα λίπῃ λεύκ᾽ ὀστέα
   θυμός, | ψυχὴ δ᾽ ἠύτ ὄνειρος ἀποπταμένη πεπότηται. In Homer,
   ἔπτατο θυμός [Π 469; κ 163; τ 454; cf. ψ 880] always refers to
   dying animals; see B. Snell, *Die Entdeckung des Geistes*

[Göttingen[4] 1975] 19ff.); similarly Quint. Smyrn. 6,636 καὶ
θυμὸς ἀπέπτατο and Nonnos, *Dion.* 11,90. The author of the
Blemyom. seems to treat ψυχή and θυμὸς as exchangeable variants,
as did Quint. Smyrn., partly in adaptation of Homeric phrases
(see Snell); cf. 8,202f. (quoted above) with 8,312f. σὺν δ'
αἵματι θυμὸς | ἔκθορεν ἐκ μελέων, 1,746 αἶψα δ' ἄναλκις ἀπὸ
μελέων φύγε θυμός, and 3,318f. ἔσπετο δ' αἰχμῇ | θυμὸς ἀπὸ
μελέων; 11,206 ψυχὴ δὲ καὶ ἄλγεα κάλλιπον ἄνδρα with 6,429 λίπε
θυμός· ἔβη δ' ἄφαρ "Αιδος εἴσω (see H 131; *Meropis* fr. 4, 5 [*P.
Köln* III 126 = L. K.-R. Merkelbach in *Coll. Pap.* ... *in Honor of
H. C. Youtie*, Bonn 1976, 1] "Αϊδόσ[δε δ' ἀπή]λυθε θυμὸς ἀναιδής.
In Homer it is normally the soul that goes to Hades; see Snell),
8,408, and 10,362; and further 1,253f. ψυχὴ δ' ἐμίγη πολυαέσιν
αὔραις with 11,465f. στονόεις δὲ οἱ ἤέρι θυμὸς | αἶψα μίγη (for
ψυχή cf. also 10,280f. and for θυμὸς 11,33 and 13,364ff.).
Nevertheless, the hope for the eternal life of the blessed is
only ascribed to the soul: 7,87ff. καὶ γὰρ ῥα πέλει φάτις ἀνθρώ-
ποισιν, | ἐσθλῶν μὲν νίσσεσθαι ἐς οὐρανὸν ἄφθιτον αἰεὶ | ψυχάς,
ἀργαλέων δὲ ποτὶ ζόφον. On the whole topic, see also Livrea on
Blemyom. 12-13.

4 εὐδόντων: thus K. and P. - μεροπ[. .] (μερόπ[ων]) P. Cf. Quint.
Smyrn. 7,83 μερόπων δὲ πανόλβιος οὔ τις (μ. in the same metrical
position); in Homer the word is part of formula μερόπων ἀνθρώπων
which occurs seven times in the *Iliad* (Α 250 etc.), twice in the
Odyssey (υ 49 and 132), and once in the hymns (*h. Cer.* 310; cf.
h. Apoll. 42 Μερόπων ἀ. and *Meropis* fr. 1 [see above on line 3]
- - - Μερόπων κατὰ νή[ριτ]α φῦλα; for Μέροπος in the same metrical position as in the new pap., see Β 831 and Λ 329.

]ϋϊ[: the inclination of the ϋ seems to indicate that it was
connected with the preceding letter, which, in this case, could
not be ν. Possibly there was an additional letter in the lacuna.
At this point the writing seems to be spaced less closely than
in the same area of the following line.

5 νόσφι θε[ῶν? Cf. M 466. - The slightly enlarged shape of what
remains of υ leads us to expect that this letter is the beginning of a word.

6 For παννυχι- in this position, see H 476 and 478; Σ 315 and 354;
  Ψ 105 and 217; β 434; μ 429; *h. Merc.* 141; Quint. Smyrn. 2,634.
  There seems to be a dot above the υ (apparently without meaning);
  another dot and a T-shaped thick mark appear on the left margin.

7-8 The words were divided by K. For πῇ δέ at the beginning of
  the line, see Quint. Smyrn. 10,319. E. Livrea refers for πῇ μὲν
  --- πῇ δὲ to Nonnos, *Dion.* 14,155 and 159; 16, 15 and 17; 29,11
  and 13; 30,4f.; 34,311f. etc.; see W. Peek, *Lex.* s.v. (letter
  of February 11, 1981).

8 αὐτο. [: only the upper part of the final letter is extant; it
  gives the impression of σ, though, among others, ι cannot be
  ruled out (υ is excluded).

fr. 1 →

2 π]ροσηύδα: thus P.

3 ειϲ[: ι or ρ. - ἑέρσην· K. In Homer, various cases of the word
  occur at the end of lines.

4 ἐνὶ θυμῷ: a Homeric formula in this position; B 223; Θ 430; N
  337; O 561 and 661; P 254 and 451; Ω 672; α 119, 200, 311, 320
  etc.

5 περ ἔσται: K.'s division of the words.

6 ἠ]δὲ [Π]υλάρτης: supplemented by K. and P. on the basis of Λ 491
  and Π 696 ἠδὲ Πυλάρτην, where this Trojan is killed twice in
  battle. A person of this name is also killed in *Blemyom.* (P.
  Berol.) 6 Περσίνοος δ' ὄλεκεν Δολίον κρατερόν τε Πυλάρτην. If it
  were not for the remote possibility that in the *Blemyomachia*
  "Pylartes" could also have met his death twice it could be in-
  ferred that the new fragment 1 ↑ precedes the Berlin fragment
  5003,1 →.

7-8 Both ἱκέσθαι and ἰάνθη appear frequently in this position in
  Homer. For ἱκέσθαι (A 19; I 652; M 221; O 58, etc.; Quint.
  Smyrn. 1,830; 2,19; 3,69 and 141; 10,273; 12,123; 13,97; 14,335)
  followed by ἰάνθη (θυμὸς ἰάνθη Ψ 600; Ω 321; ο 165. ἦτορ ἰάνθη
  δ 840; cf. δ 549) cf. Quint. Smyrn. 4,494f. ποτὶ νῆας ἱκέσθαι |
  - - - πάμπαν ἰάνθη | - - -. The letter preceding ἰάνθη looks
  like ν, though ι cannot be ruled out.

fr. 2

Side ↑ is not transcribed here as it offers only insignificant traces of the last letters of 7 or 8 lines. The last letter of line 3 (or 4) is a final ν̥ (see footnote 3).

fr. 3

The final ν of → 2 (cf. fr. 1 → 3) and the little blank at the end of line 1 indicate the end of lines. Hence the other side (↑) must contain the beginning of verses (cf. footnote 3).

fr. 3 ↑

1].ε: as, in all likelihood, ἐφλέγεο is preceded by only one letter (see above) and the trace seems to belong to the lower end of a diagonal stroke descending from the left to the right corner (κ̥, λ̥, χ, perhaps α̥, hardly δ̥), we hesitantly consider κ᾽ ἐφλέγεο (for κἀφλέγεο).

2 φυζακινῇ[ς ἐλάφοισιν as in N 101f. Τρῶας - - -, οἳ τὸ πάρος περ | φυζακινῆς ἐλάφοισιν ἐοίκεσαν?

fr. 3 →

1]ι: γ or ι̥

(for the preceding notes: L. Koenen and M. Petrini)

   The new fragments are from an epos which is hellenistic or later (see note on fr. 1 ↑ 3), closely imitates Homer and is seemingly influenced by Quintus Smyrnaeus (see passim in the preceding notes). Fr. 1 ↑ 3 seems to narrate a death, possibly in a battle scene (see the note), and fr. 3 ↑ 2 indicates flight in battle (see note). A warrior named Pylartes (fr. 1 → 5) is killed in the Berlin papyrus of the *Blemyomachia* (see note). These observations, which were pointed out to me by K., confirm the tentative conclusions which I had reached on palaeographical grounds:[3] the new fragments belong

---

   3 The new and the old fragments show the same system of punctuation with clear distinctions between high, middle and low stops, use apostrophes for elisions, and employ tremata on top of υ and ι; but they have no accents and breathings (see above and cf. Livrea, p. 8). For the characteristic final ν (fr. 1 → 3, fr. 3 → 2, also 3 → 3 or 4 [see photograph]), cf. P. Berol. 5003,1 → 6 and ↑ 9.

to the *Blemyomachia*; moreover they are from the same codex as the
Berlin papyrus of the same poem, probably from a part preceding the
Berlin fragment(s) [see note on fr. 1 → 6). Of course, the question is
immediately raised of how it could have been possible for Ludwig
Stern to buy the Berlin papyrus fragments, supposedly found at
Thebes, on the Luxor antiquities market a hundred years ago (1880),
and then for fragments to be left on the site of the original find-
spot, apparently the monastery of Phoebammon, to be found sixty-seven
years later. If the papyrus codex in which the epic poem was contained formed a part of the monastery library, was copied in it or
acquired by it, this would lead to interesting conclusions about
the role and value of classical learning in the monastic community.

Of the Coptic documentary material, only a single scrap, apparently from a letter, affords enough text to provide a phrase or
two, longer than the one or two letters visible on the other inscribed fragments (none of which appear to belong to the same document or be in the same hand). The text of the letter is written
along the fibres (→), and reads:

    ]ү ероκ ν꜅ꜗϩⲁⲣⲉϩ [
    ]ⲙⲙⲟⲧⲛ̄ ⲛ꜅[
    ]ⲕⲉ ⲉⲧⲏϫ ⲉϩⲟⲩⲛ ⲡ.[
    ]ⲙⲙⲟⲛ ⲉⲓⲙⲏⲧ[ⲓ
    ]ⲧⲉⲓ ⲛ̄ⲙⲙ[

The docket on the other side (also along the fibres, turned 90°) reads:
    ⳨ ⲧⲁⲁⲥ ⲛ̄ⲛⲉⲛ̄ⲙ[ⲉⲣⲓⲧ...

Unfortunately, no personal names remain to help date or place the
letter prosopographically.

I have not yet been able to examine the Phoebammon papyri
autoptically, and have worked only from photographs.[4] The originals
are believed still to be in a safe at the Society for Coptic Archaeology, which up to the present moment has proved unopenable. It is
hoped that the originals will be retrievable shortly and that a
full and proper study of the papyri can be made: this is only a
preliminary report on work in progress.

Society for Coptic Archaeology   Leslie S.B. MacCoull
Cairo

---

4 For this reason no measurements can be given here.

Proceedings of the XVI Int. Congr. of Papyrology (Chico 1981) 499-508

DUE ROTOLI COPTI PAPIRACEI DA DUBLINO
(LETTERE DI HORSIESI)

La presentazione di questi due manoscritti nell'ambito del
presente Congresso, mentre è in preparazione da parte nostra l'edizione,[1] è sembrata conveniente perché da un lato il lavoro di edizione sembra ritardato da alcuni problemi strettamente connessi
alla conservazione dei manoscritti; dall'altro l'interesse che essi
rivestono sotto molteplici aspetti consiglia di diffonderne una
conoscenza, sia pure preliminare.

I manoscritti furono acquistati in Egitto da Chester Beatty,
il noto collezionista, e posti nella sua biblioteca, in un primo
tempo a Londra, poi a Dublino, dove tuttora si trova ed è divenuta
pubblica istituzione.[2] A quanto ci risulta, i due manoscritti
furono restaurati presso il British Museum;[3] essi furono srotolati
e posti sotto vetro, ed i frammenti furono inseriti dove sembrava
essere il loro posto originario. Fra il *verso* dei papiri ed il
vetro fu posto un foglio di cartone. I due manoscritti furono così
rimandati alla biblioteca, chiusi in apposite scatole di legno, che
rimasero sigillate fino ad una mia visita alla biblioteca nel 1975,
insieme con Hans Quecke, fatta allo scopo di rendermi conto di
tutto il materiale copto ivi esistente.

Dopo che vidi i due rotoli, decisi di pubblicarli, in un libro
che contenesse anche il materiale Pacomiano scoperto recentemente.
Hans Quecke si incaricò del commento grammaticale e Adalbert De
Vogüé di quello contenutistico. A Roma iniziai il lavoro sulla

---

1 In un volume intitolato *Pachomiana coptica* di T. Orlandi
(edizione di due lettere di Horsiesi e una lettera di Teodoro;
introduzione e traduzione; studio letterario), H. Quecke (commento
grammaticale; edizione della lettera 11B di Pacomio), A. De Vogüé
(studio della spiritualità), J. Goehring (commento storico).

2 Cf. R. J. Hayes, *The Chester Beatty Library* (Dublin 1971)
5-6.

3 I manoscritti restaurati furono accompagnati da note dattiloscritte (talora con una traduzione preliminare) di A. F. Shore.

base di buone fotografie, che resero possibile la trascrizione ed
anche la sistemazione di un certo numero di frammenti che erano
stati collocati fuori posto nel restauro. Ma allo scopo di ottenere una trascrizione sicura ed una traduzione definitiva mi resi
conto che era necessaria una seconda visita alla biblioteca, con
la possibilità di aprire i vetri e ricollocare fisicamente i frammenti, con un nuovo studio delle fibre. Per questo riuscii ad
ottenere la collaborazione di Stephen Emmel, che mi accompagnò a
Dublino nel giugno 1980. Tuttavia a causa della ristrettezza del
tempo il lavoro non è stato concluso, ed è prevista una nuova (e
si spera finale) visita alla biblioteca.

Per questi motivi l'edizione dei due manoscritti ha subito un
ritardo rispetto alla scadenza che ci eravamo proposti. Tuttavia
sono state nel frattempo pubblicate due traduzioni preliminari dei
testi (sulla base della mia trascrizione e traduzione italiana preliminare), una da parte di A. De Vogüé ed una da parte di A. Veilleux.[4] Del resto, le informazioni di carattere generale che vengono fornite qui non dovrebbero essere contraddette dal nuovo restauro che è stato intrapreso.

Il primo rotolo (segnatura: Ac. 1494) contiene tre colonne di
scrittura; la colonna centrale è molto più larga di quelle late-
rali, e la terza finisce (con la fine del testo) alcuni centimetri
prima del margine inferiore ed è la più stretta delle tre. Il
secondo rotolo è più lungo (segnatura: Ac. 1495) e contiene cinque
colonne di differente larghezza. Anche in questo caso l'ultima
colonna è la più stretta e finisce (con la fine del testo) prima
del margine inferiore. Ambedue i rotoli sono scritti sulla super-
ficie che presenta le fibre orizzontali. Il primo rotolo ha
un'iscrizione nel verso, scritta "trasversalmente" all'inizio del
rotolo in modo da essere visibile a rotolo chiuso e da formare il
titolo, che diceva: "Lettera scritta da Horsiesi...". Il verso del
secondo rotolo è attualmente tutto coperto dal cartone (cf. sopra),
ma per tale motivo crediamo non porti alcuna iscrizione. Ad ogni

---

4 La traduzione di A. De Vogüé in *Studia Anselmiana* 70 (1977)
244-57. Di quella di A. Veilleux non possiamo al momento dare gli
estremi precisi.

modo è questo uno dei fatti che devono essere accertati col nuovo
restauro, anche perché l'inizio del rotolo è la parte più danneg-
giata.

Paul Kahle jr. osservò nel 1948 che "rolls are extremely rare
in Coptic",[5] tanto che egli ne conosceva solo otto esempi, molti
dei quali non potevano però essere considerati rotoli letterari
veri e propri. Due infatti erano composizioni magiche;[6] due erano
scritti sul retro di testi greci precedenti;[7] altri due erano degli
estratti che non appaiono prodotti per il normale "mercato" dei
manoscritti.[8] Dunque solo due manoscritti erano conosciuti, para-
gonabili ai nostri. E dopo di allora solo altri quattro rotoli
sono stati scoperti, per quanto ne sappiamo. Uno è un altro rotolo
magico della collezione di Colonia;[9] un altro è un frammento della
collezione Doresse alla Vaticana, del quale ignoriamo le caratteristiche.[10] Gli altri due sono assai interessanti e simili fra
loro. Essi sono scritti "transversa charta"[11] e contengono delle
lettere circolari (forse delle *Epistulae festales*) scritte da vescovi egiziani. Questi due rotoli possono essere paragonati a uno

---

5   Paul E. Kahle, *Bala'izah* I (London 1954) 175.

6   *P. Mich.* 1190, ed. W. H. Worrell, *Orientalia* 4 (1935) 1-37
e 184-94 (v. p. 4 sgg.). - London, British Library, Or 6796 (Crum
Cat. n° 523), ed. A. Kropp, *Ausgewählte koptische Zaubertexte* I
(Bruxelles 1931) 35-49.

7   Cf. H. I. Bell - H. Thompson, *JEA* 11 (1925) 241-46.
- Collezione privata (von Scherling) di Leiden, n° 128, ed. Lefort
(cit. alla nota 13).

8   Paris, Bibl. Nat. Copte 135, ed. P. Lacau, *BIFAO* 8 (1911)
43-109. - London, British Library, Or 9271, ed. da ultimo L. Th.
Lefort, *Les Pères apostoliques en copte* (CSCO 135, Louvain 1952)
32 sgg.

9   Papyrussammlung Rheinisch-Westfälische Akad., Inv.-Nr.
2242.

10   Cf. il contributo di P. Canart in *Miscellanea Papyrologica*,
ed. R. Pintaudi (Firenze 1980).

11   Cf. E. G. Turner, *The Terms Recto and Verso; the Anatomy
of the Papyrus Roll* (Papyrologica Bruxellensia 16, Bruxelles 1978)
26-53. - Berlin, Staatliche Museen, P 11346, inedito. - Manchester,
John Rylands Library, Suppl. 47-48, inedito.

di quelli conosciuti dal Kahle, cioè il rotolo di Vienna,[12] che
tuttavia era utilizzato su entrambi i lati, cioè nel cosiddetto
recto, in colonne (*epistula festalis*, forse) e "transversa charta"
(testo omiletico indirizzato a monaci). L'ultimo esempio, già
conosciuto dal Kahle, è invece un vero rotolo, in dialetto achmi-
mico: contiene una composizione poetica, che il Peterson tendeva
ad attribuire a Ieraca, il monaco eretico del III secolo.[13]

Sembra di poter osservare che il rotolo fosse usato dai Copti
per ragioni speciali. Da un lato esso poteva essere usato per le
Lettere festali (o comunque lettere circolari di vescovi), ed in
questo caso la tendenza era a scriverli "transversa charta". Dall'
altro per la trasmissione di estratti, forse per uso liturgico.
Per ciò che riguarda i nostri testi Pacomiani, pensiamo alla volontà di mantenere una tradizione antica, che era ancora usuale ai
tempi di Pacomio e dei suoi primi successori. Aggiungeremo che per
Pacomio stesso e per Teodoro, abbiamo esempi di *pergamene* in rotolo,
scritte "transversa charta",[14] cosa che diverrà abituale in ambiente bizantino.

La scrittura dei nostri due rotoli è la ben nota *maiuscola
alessandrina* del tipo unimodulare;[15] in questo caso essa può essere
assegnata al VII secolo, sebbene vi siano ragioni per spostare la
datazione sia più in alto (il tipo di testo e il materiale stesso)
sia più in basso (lo sforzo conservativo, osservabile anche nell'
ortografia della I lettera).

Il contenuto delle lettere, negli obiettivi e nel carattere
generale, è sufficiente a provare che esse provengono da un ambiente
monastico molto antico. Gli elementi che permettono di fare delle
congetture più precise sono: - l'*inscriptio* della I lettera; - le

---

12 Wien, Österr. Nationalbibliothek, K 10157, ed. W. Till,
Osterbrief und Predigt in achmimischem Dialekt (Leipzig 1931).

13 Collezione privata (von Scherling) di Leiden, n° 127; ed.
L. Th. Lefort, *Le Muséon* 52 (1939) 1-10. Cf. E. Peterson, *Le
Muséon* 60 (1947) 257-60.

14 Cf. sotto (nota 18).

15 Cf. G. Cavallo, *Jahrb. der Österr. Byzantinistik* 24 (1975)
23-54.

persone nominate in ambedue le lettere. Come abbiamo visto, l'*in-scriptio*, sebbene incompleta, indica chiaramente un Horsiesi come autore. Non vi è alcun elemento nel contenuto che contrasti la naturale identificazione con il successore di Pacomio alla testa del monastero di Pbau. Anche il paragone con quanto sappiamo della letteratura pacomiana sorregge questa identificazione. Quanto alla seconda lettera, le analogie esterne ed interne con la prima consigliano fortemente l'ipotesi che essa sia frutto dello stesso autore.

Il significato generale dei testi non è facile da determinare. Per quanto vediamo, nella prima lettera è possibile enucleare gruppi successivi di citazioni bibliche relative a determinati soggetti, cucite da brevi frasi originali. I soggetti toccati sono: la concordia fra i monaci; la preparazione al giudizio finale; i monaci come nuova comunità d'Israele, erede della speciale protezione di Dio; la posizione centrale di Gesù Cristo nella vita dei cristiani.

Il manoscritto della seconda lettera è assai più frammentario, e non è possibile ricostruire la parte superiore delle prime tre colonne. Si può solo dare qualche esempio dei temi trattati nelle parti rimaste: la purificazione generale, probabilmente in vista di una delle due assemblee annuali; la vera saggezza, che non è individuale ma di tutta la comunità; la punizione per coloro che non si comportano secondo la santità della comunità; la necessità per ciascuno di stare nel luogo che gli è stato destinato.

Allusioni a personaggi e fatti storici ne abbiamo soprattutto nella seconda lettera. Per esempio: III,35 "...sapendo che il nostro Padre (*scil.* Pacomio) che ci riunì ... è giusto e piacque a Dio; egli che ci insegnò il Dio che non conoscevamo". - III,42 "Ricordiamoci del nostro padre Petronio che passò il suo breve tempo fra noi ... e del nostro padre Teodoro che ci scrisse..." All'inizio della prima lettera abbiamo invece una probabile allusione alla malattia finale di Teodoro (che è nominato).

La letteratura delle comunità pacomiane era poco nota fino a pochi anni addietro. Gli studi su questo soggetto erano basati esclusivamente sulle *Vite di Pacomio*, che ricordano le raccomandazioni di Pacomio sulla meditazione delle Scritture, e riportano

alcune delle sue allocuzioni alle assemblee di monaci. Dunque la
cultura dei monaci, oltre che sulle Scritture, sembrava basata
anche sulle catechesi di Pacomio e dei suoi successori, ma nessun
tale testo sicuramente genuino era conosciuto. Unica eccezione
sembrava il *Liber Horsiesi*, giunto nella traduzione latina di Gero-
lamo;[16] le lettere di Pacomio giunte nella stessa traduzione erano
troppo strane ed incomprensibili per trarne testimonianza della
spiritualità pacomiana.

Un progresso in questo senso fu rappresentato dalla pubblicazione in cui Lefort riunì tutti i testi conosciuti in copto.[17]
Ma essi erano tramandati quasi esclusivamente in codici tardi (IX
secolo), oltre che frammentari; ed era noto che quel genere di
codici era pieno di opere pseudepigrafe, e la loro testimonianza
andava dunque presa con la massima cautela.

La situazione diviene più chiara con la scoperta dei nuovi
codici, che non solo sono assai antichi, ma provengono da un ambiente diverso da quello del Monastero Bianco, che ci ha tramandato
gli altri, menzionati sopra. Essi ci testimoniano la continua
esistenza delle lettere di Pacomio nella tradizione copta, oltre
all'esistenza di opere di Teodoro ed Horsiesi la cui autenticità è
difficilmente contestabile.

Se noi confrontiamo il contenuto dei manoscritti di Dublino
(i nostri due papiri ed un altro rotolo pergamenaceo) con le opere
pubblicate da Lefort, si può concludere la non autenticità della
grande *catechesi* attribuita a Pacomio, ed in generale di quei testi
che riproducono nella forma le "normali" composizioni omiletiche
del IV e V secolo.[18] Essi furono probabilmente prodotti più tardi,
quando si volle colmare quella che appariva una lacuna nella letteratura pacomiana. Noi pensiamo in effetti che Pacomio ed i suoi
primi successori non amassero la retorica grecizzante, il cui uso

---

16   Ed. A. Boon, *Pachomiana Latina* (Louvain 1932).

17   L. Th. Lefort, *Oeuvres de S. Pachôme et de ses disciples*
(CSCO 159, Louvain 1956).

18   Il Prof. Ludwig Koenen ha attirato la nostra attenzione
sul fatto che alcune opere di Didimo (in *Patrol. Graeca* vol. 39)
sono caratterizzate da uno stile simile a quello delle nostre due
lettere.

si diffondeva allora presso gli strati colti cristiani anche dell'
Egitto; mentre lo stesso movimento monastico negli stadi successivi
si adeguò alla nuova moda letteraria.

E' possibile così seguire quello che appare lo sviluppo della
letteratura pacomiana, dai modi di comunicazione essenziali usati
dal fondatore, nei quali i testi si caricavano anche di significati
mistici, attraverso l'attività di Teodoro ed Horsiesi, che pure
scrissero lettere molto scarne ma più esplicite nel loro scopo e
significato, fino all'ultima opera di Horsiesi (il *liber*) di stile
normalmente omiletico.

Non è possibile in questa sede soffermarsi sui problemi storici
che queste lettere sollevano o aiutano a risolvere: quello delle
due grandi riunioni annuali dei pacomiani, e quello di una grave
crisi organizzativa seguita alla morte di Pacomio.

Gioverà invece riassumere la documentazione in greco ed in
copto, che è divenuta accessibile successivamente alla pubblicazione delle edizioni di Boon-Lefort e di Lefort. In primo luogo
il rotolo pergamenaceo verticale contenente una raccolta di lettere
di Pacomio in greco, pubblicato da Hans Quecke.[19] Lo stesso studioso riconobbe l'originale copto di tre lettere di Pacomio in due
rotoli pergamenacei verticali di Colonia, pubblicati da Kropp e
Hermann. Nella raccolta della Chester Beatty Library a Dublino si
trovano anche due lettere di Pacomio in copto ed i frammenti di una
terza;[20] oltre ai nostri due rotoli papiracei e ad un altro rotolo
pergamenaceo verticale contenente una lettera di Teodoro in copto.
Quest'ultimo testo è contenuto anche in un altro rotolo pergamenaceo verticale pubblicato dal Krause da una collezione non identi-
ficata.[21] Finalmente, l'originale copto di un'altra lettera di Pacomio e stato trovato presso la Bibliotheca Bodmeriana di Ginevra.[22]

---

19 Hans Quecke, *Die Briefe Pachoms (Anhang: Die koptischen
Fragmente und Zitate der Pachombriefe)* (Regensburg 1975).

20 Ed. Quecke (cf. nota 19).

21 In corso di stampa nel volume di studi in onore di H. J.
Polotsky (ed. D. W. Young).

22 Epist. 11A (cf. sopra, nota 1).

Come si vede, la nostra conoscenza dell'antica letteratura pacomiana è molto cresciuta in questi ultimi anni. Ed il fatto che molti manoscritti siano conservati a Dublino fa pensare che provengano da una stessa biblioteca di qualche monastero. Ma la valutazione storica e letteraria di questo materiale richiederà ancora parecchi sforzi e tempo agli studiosi.

Roma   Tito Orlandi

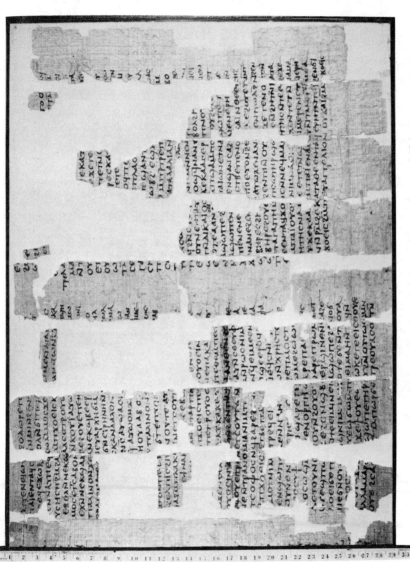

Dublin, Chester Beatty Library, Ac. 1495

Proceedings of the XVI Int. Congr. of Papyrology (Chico 1981) 509-516

HISTORIANS AND THE PAPYRI ON THE
FINANCES OF EGYPT AT THE ARAB CONQUEST

It has repeatedly been lamented by previous scholars, such as Johnson and Jones, that no total or global estimates of the revenue or of the imperial tribute of sixth century Egypt are available.[1] For the early Arab period Nabia Abbott has also added, "What proportion of the total was spent on local, provincial and imperial purposes there is no way of telling."[2]

In view of such assertions, it was tempting to consider anew some of the few estimates of Egypt's revenue in money at the time of the Arab conquest, i.e., of 'Amr's governorship, as preserved by the earliest Arab historians: Ibn 'Abd al-Ḥakam, Ṭabarī and Balādhurī.

In a well-known statement by Ibn 'Abd al-Ḥakam, who wrote some two hundred years after the Arab conquest, we are assured that "'Amr confirmed the perpetuation of the Byzantine taxation system in Egypt."[3] Fortunately, papyrological evidence from Aphrodito of the first century of the Arab rule establishes the veracity of this statement.[4] In view of this, other data provided by early Arab historians on the finances of Egypt may also be of value to fill in gaps in our knowledge about Byzantine Egypt. Unfortunately, because of glaring discrepancies among the estimates preserved, their evidence has generally been disregarded.[5] For example, for 'Amr's

---

1 A. C. Johnson, *Egypt and the Roman Empire* (Ann Arbor 1951) 125; A.H.M. Jones, *The Later Roman Empire* (Oxford 1964) I, 463.

2 Nabia Abbot, *The Ḳurrah Papyri from Aphrodito in the Oriental Institute* (Chicago 1938) 97.

3 Ibn 'Abd el-Ḥakam, *Futūḥ Miṣr...*, ed. C. C. Torrey (New Haven 1922) 152-53.

4 *P. Lond.* IV, Bell's introd., pp. XVIIff.; Abbott, *The Ḳurrah Papyri*, 92ff.

5 A. J. Butler, *The Treaty of Miṣr in Tabari* (1913), published with separate pagination in his *Arab Conquest of Egypt* (Oxford² 1978) 52; S. I. Kashef, *Egypt at the Dawn of Islam*, 15f.

governorship alone we have the following different estimates:
first, according to Ibn ʿAbd al-Ḥakam, ʿAmr levied 12,000,000 (p.
161; see n. 3); second, according to Ṭabarī, the text of the treaty
of surrender stipulated that the people of Egypt should pay taxes
amounting to 50,000,000;[6] whereas, third, according to Balādhurī,
ʿAmr levied in Egypt 2,000,000 as total of both land and capitation
taxes (*kharāj* and *jizyah*).[7] To add to the confusion, these figures
are not followed by the monetary unit of account, and so according
to the usual practice, they have been assumed to be in gold dinars
(solidi; Butler, *Conquest* [see n. 5] 321). In order to illustrate
the grave suspicion expressed by modern scholars of the estimates
of the Arab historians, I may quote Johnson who stated: "If these
figures were divided by ten they might be more credible" (*Egypt*,
126).

Yet are all the figures really fictitious or wildly exaggerated? One might, of course, argue that when dealing with these Arab
historians, one should take into consideration the fact that they
all wrote some two centuries after the Arab conquest, and may not
have been too familiar with either the language or the conditions
before or at the time of the conquest. An initial difficulty they
met with would be the Greek language in which most of the surviving
archives of that time were written, and which was practically unknown at the time of the historians. Severus, the Coptic church
historian, complains in the tenth century of the scarcity among his
fellow Christians of those who could help him translate into Arabic
the earlier Greek and Coptic sources.[8] This is not the place to
discuss the limitations of Arab knowledge of, and interest in,
Greek learning which flourished in the ninth and tenth centuries.
For our present purpose, however, the Arabic papyri of the ninth
and tenth centuries provide ample evidence on the continued employment of Greek numerals for writing dates and numbers in a

---

6   al-Ṭabarī, Abu Djafar Mohammed ibn Djarir, *Taʾrīkh al-rusul
wa-al-mulūk*, ed. M. J. de Goeje et al. (Leiden 1879-1901) I, 2588.

7   al-Balādhurī, Aḥmad ibn Yaḥyā, *Futūḥ al-buldān* (*Liber ex-
pugnationis regionum*), ed. M. J. de Goeje (Leiden 1866) 216.

8   Severus Ibn al Muqaffa, *History of the Patriarchs of the
Coptic Church of Alexandria* (Patrologia Orientalis I) 17 (115).

variety of accounts and payments (A. Grohmann, *Arabic Papyri* III
181-213). Yet one notices in our historians' presentation of past
conditions that they often apply contemporary terminology of dinar
and feddān to a time when solidus and aroura were the only standard
units of money and land. Given the complex monetary system and
terminology of Byzantine Egypt, the problem we are facing, I suggest, may be one of terminology and not of wrong data.

The general method of assessment was that every farm, from the
smallest peasant holding to the great estate of the nobility, was
assessed at some fraction or multiple of the fiscal unit of land.
The data were combined in various registers.[9] The chief tax was
always imposed on land and the papyri of the sixth and seventh centuries show that taxes were always rated in gold carats per aroura.
The rate differed according to the nature of the land (i.e., arable
land, vineyard, olive land, pasture land, etc.) and its quality.
In the case, for example, of the Largitionalia, which was a money
tax probably designed for the imperial treasury (cf. Johnson, *Egypt*,
125), the rate varied: at Antaeopolis it seems to have been one and
one-half carats per aroura on arable land.[10] At Aphrodito the rate
was two carats, while vineyards were taxed at eight carats per
aroura (*P. Lond.* V 1670 [ca. A.D. 570]). From the Fayyum, shortly
before the Arab conquest, a receipt indicates that the land there
was taxed at approximately three carats per aroura.[11] Practically
all other taxes in money were rated in gold carats per fiscal unit
(aroura or caput). In view of the disappearance of a silver coin
and the unstable relation of the copper to the gold coinage, the
carat may have acquired in the sixth century a practical value as
a unit of account. We may recall that it was equivalent to the
siliqua, the short-lived silver coin of the fourth century, which
was also a twenty-fourth of a solidus.[12] Later on, under the Arab

---

9 Johnson, *Egypt*, 118; Jones, *The Later Roman Empire*, 454.

10 *P. Cair. Masp.* I 67057 (reign of Justinian); cf. A. C.
Johnson and L. C. West, *Byzantine Egypt: Economic Studies* (Princeton 1949) 275.

11 *P. Lond.* I 113, 1.8ff.; cf. Johnson and West, *Byzantine
Egypt*, 258.

12 Cf. A. C. Johnson and L. C. West, *Currency in Roman and
Byzantine Egypt* (Princeton 1944) 107; Jones, *The Later Roman Empire*,
438ff.

administration, when a silver coin (the dirham) was reintroduced
in Egypt, it was equated to one carat, as a twenty-fourth of a dinar.[13] Thus it seems that the solidus was too large a coin for
fixing tax rates, and that the carat (or its value in silver) was
the tax unit in Egypt at least from the sixth to the ninth century.

Tax assessments and registers were normally made in solidi and
carats, yet there is some evidence that rentals and tax payments
were occasionally made in carats alone, even when they exceeded
twenty-four carats. A first indication of this phenomenon is found
in rentals of the early sixth century, as is seen in *P. Flor.* I 73
(Hermopolis [A.D. 505]), where half a house is rented for three
carats per annum. *P. Bad.* 95, also of Hermopolis (seventh century)
provides examples of renting κιλλία, each at five carats per annum,
on the average.[14] Similar payments of small amounts in carats come
from Aphrodito in the early eighth century, ranging between 34 and
57 carats.[15]

A second indication may be found in the form and method of
calculation employed in the tax registers of the χρυσικά δημόσια
of Aphrodito, *P. Lond.* IV 1412-1418. In these registers the main
entries are: first a sum described as ἐπιζητούμενα, i.e., tax quota
due from the ἐποίκιον in question; second, a sum or sums principally paid into the treasury (εἰς τὴν σάκελλαν) to be deducted from
the first sum; third, the remainder after the deduction of these
sums. Further the sum or sums deducted (εἰς τὴν σάκελλαν) are
stated twice, in two kinds of solidi, of which one is called
ἐχό(μενα) and the other ἀρίθμια; the latter being nearly always
larger than the former. It is curious that the ἐπιζητούμενα and
the ἐχόμενα are reckoned in solidi and carats, whereas the ἀρίθμια
are reckoned in solidi and fractions. The editor noticed that, due

---

13 A. Grohmann, *Arabic Papyri* II 96.4 et comm. pp. 102-3
(A.D. 841); and III 202.11 et comm. (ninth century).

14 A papyrus in the Wilbour collection at the Brooklyn Museum
(No. 35.1472) is a receipt of four carats of gold in payment of a
year's rent for a room, bakery, cook shop... (6th-7th century).
Also cf. G. Husson, "Traditions pharaoniques dans l'architecture
domestique de l'Egypte grecque, romaine et byzantine," below pp.
521-528.

15 *P. Lond.* IV 1419.140 (after A.D. 716): 34 carats; 197: 57
carats; 198: 40 carats; 679: 56 1/2 carats; 680: 37 1/2 carats.

to the clumsiness of the fractions, the reckoning in ἀρίθμια, where
small sums were concerned, is only approximate, as e.g. in No. 1414.
103, where 12 2/3 carats ἐχόμενα are equal to 1/2 solidus ἀρίθμια,
one-half being the nearest available fraction (P. Lond. IV 80ff.).
Since the ἐπιζητούμενα and ἐχόμενα represent the government's interests, no approximation was allowed and the exact number of carats
and their fractions is given in full. The reason may have been that
the tax quota (ἐπιζητούμενα) was originally reckoned in carats and
then changed into solidi and carats.

Third, even more important for our purpose, are a number of
lists of payments in money from Oxyrhynchus, all dated from the
sixth and seventh centuries, in which certain counts are actually
made in myriads of carats.[16] P. Oxy. XVI 1918 verso 6-13 (sixth
century) may best illustrate the case. In these lists payments
were made in four different standards of currency: the private, the
ἀρίθμια, the public, and in the Alexandrian standard. These accounts afford a good illustration of the complications entailed by
the common employment of different standards of currency. The several totals are converted successively from the private to the public and from the public to the Alexandrian standard, the result being finally expressed in terms of pounds, ounces and grammes (P.
Oxy. 1918, introd.). The different standards varied in their degree
of deficiency, the amount of which is reckoned in carats as follows:

Line 6:

(a) Total in private standard	$2,414 \frac{1}{6}$	sol. less 10,000	carats
(b) ἀρίθμια with weighing fee	$11,049$	sol. less $47,646 \frac{1}{2} \frac{1}{4}$	carats
(c) and without weighing fee	868	sol. less $3,188 \frac{1}{4}$	carats
(d) and total in public standard	$3,068 \frac{1}{2} \frac{1}{3} \frac{1}{8}$	sol. less 306	carats
(e) and in Alexandrian standard	$263 \frac{1}{3}$	sol.	

---

16 P. Oxy. XVI 1908 (sixth or seventh century); 1911 (A.D.
557); 1918 (sixth century).

Line 7: total receipts in gold:

(a) private standard with ἀρίθμια (sum of line 6, a through c)	$14{,}331 \frac{1}{6}$	sol. less 60,835	carats
(b) from which specified sums to be deducted total		$7{,}011 \frac{1}{2}$	carats

Line 8:

(a) remainder (line 7a minus b)	$14{,}331 \frac{1}{6}$	sol. less $53{,}823 \frac{1}{2}$	carats
(b) total of the carats (rebated in line 8a) in public standards		$82{,}482 \frac{1}{2} \frac{1}{4}$	carats
(c) total in public standard (from line 6d)	$3{,}068 \frac{1}{2} \frac{1}{3} \frac{1}{8}$	sol. less 306	carats

Line 9:

(a) total of gold in public standard (sum of line 8, a through c)	$17{,}400 \frac{1}{8}$	sol. less $82{,}788 \frac{1}{2} \frac{1}{4}$ carats
(b) these carats (line 9a) converted into sol. ($\div$ 24)	$3{,}449 \frac{1}{2} \frac{1}{48} \frac{1}{96}$ sol.
net amount (τὰ καθαρά) in public standard (line 9, a minus b)	$13{,}950 <\frac{1}{2}> \frac{1}{12} \frac{1}{96}$ sol.[17]

The account continues with other minor additions, and the total is converted into the Alexandrian standard, $20{,}010 \frac{1}{2} \frac{1}{8} \frac{1}{96}$ solidi (line 12), which is finally transferred into 191 pounds 5 ounces, $17 \frac{1}{2} \frac{1}{24}$ grammes of gold (line 13).

---

17 The editors printed γ͞νιβ 'ρϛ'; it should be γ͞νⳑιβ 'ρϛ' (L. Koenen).

In another account, *P. Oxy.* XVI 1908.19-21, the total is given
in the private standard as 558 solidi less 2313 $\frac{1}{2}$ carats, the re-
bate in carats is converted into the public standard 3430 $\frac{1}{4}$ carats,
i.e. 142 $\frac{1}{2}$ $\frac{1}{3}$ $\frac{1}{12}$ $\frac{1}{96}$ solidi. The net amount (τὰ καθαρά) in
public standard is 415 $\frac{1}{3}$ $\frac{1}{24}$ $\frac{1}{48}$ $\frac{1}{96}$ solidi.

These and similar accounts of the sixth and seventh centuries
perhaps justify the suggestion that the carat was employed as a
unit of account. Let us now apply this suggestion to the figures
quoted above by early Arab historians. It is perhaps of interest
to mention the circumstances surrounding the first estimate of
12,000,000 of Ibn 'Abd al-Ḥakam. It is reported that when 'Amr
collected twelve million from Egypt, the Caliph was dissatisfied
and finally deposed him. The new governor collected fourteen million, which provoked an exchange of harsh words between the Caliph
and 'Amr (Ibn 'Abd al-Ḥakam, *Futūḥ Miṣr*..., 161).

If these two figures are reckoned in carats, the first, divided by 24, makes 500,000 solidi, and the second ca. 583,000 solidi. The dissatisfaction of the Caliph in Medina, and the record of
the exchange of harsh words between the Caliph and 'Amr may indicate
that these estimates represent Egypt's annual tribute to the Caliphate's treasury in Medina. Under the Caliph Mu'āwiyah some two
decades later, the same historian is more definite. He explicitly
states twice that Egypt used to send 600,000 dinars (solidi) as annual tribute to Mu'āwiyah (Ibn 'Abd al-Ḥakam, *Futūḥ Miṣr*..., 102).
The increase may have been the result of more settled conditions
and the adaeratio principle (or commuting payment in kind for gold)
which was encouraged by the Caliphs (Balādhurī, *Futūḥ al-buldān*,
216).

Thus it would seem probable that under the early caliphate
Egypt's tribute ranged between 500,000 and 600,000 solidi (dinars).
From Byzantine Egypt we have no similar estimates, yet it was once
suggested that, if Procopius in the Secret History were to be
trusted when he alleges that in the nine years of Justin 4,000 centenaria of gold came into the imperial treasury (*h.a.* XIX), this
would imply that the annual revenue was about 400 centenaria. "If
this figure is correct," suggested Jones, "Egypt, which was certainly far the richest of the seven dioceses, would have contributed

about a fifth" (*The Later Roman Empire* I, 463). This means that Egypt's tribute to the imperial treasury under Justin was about eighty centenaria, i.e., 576,000 solidi, which is not incompatible with the estimates reached above.

The treaty of surrender as preserved by Ṭabarī stipulated that ʿAmr impose upon the people of Egypt a levy of 50,000,000 (without mention of the unit of account). On the assumption that dinars (solidi) were meant, both the figure and the text of the treaty were rejected as fictitious (Butler, *The Treaty of Miṣr*, 52f.). Once again, if the suggestion is accepted that this figure is reckoned in carats, it will amount to approximately 2,083,000 solidi. When we compare this result with Balādhurī's estimate of 2,000,000 (dinars) for Egypt's total revenue of both land and capitation taxes (*kharāj* and *jizyah*) under ʿAmr, we find them almost identical (Balādhurī, *Futūḥ al-buldān*, 216).

Finally, in an interesting passage concerning the main divisions of the Egyptian budget Ibn ʿAbd al-Ḥakam says, "...Under the rule of the kings (i.e., Byzantine emperors)...when the collection of taxes was completed, one quarter went to the king; ...another was given to the army and for other military expenses; ...a third quarter was spent upon the upkeep of the land and its cultivation: dykes, canals and dams; the last quarter was used for local and administrative expenditure."[18]

The division into four equal parts need not be taken too literally, yet the passage's broad lines bear out the estimates reached above. A tribute of 500,000-600,000 dinars is indeed about 25% of the total taxes of 2,000,000 dinars. If, accordingly, the interpretation offered in this paper is correct, we may conclude that of the total revenue of gold, ca. 25% was sent to the imperial treasury, either in Constantinople, Medina or Damascus. It will also follow that the text of the treaty of surrender as preserved by Ṭabarī is authentic.

University of Alexandria   Mostafa el Abbadi

---

18   Ibn Abd al-Ḥakam, *Futūḥ Miṣr*..., 32-33, 102, and 151-52.

PART 8

EGYPTOLOGY AND PAPYROLOGY

Proceedings of the XVI Int. Congr. of Papyrology (Chico 1981) 519-526

TRADITIONS PHARAONIQUES ATTESTEES DANS L'ARCHITECTURE
DOMESTIQUE DE L'EGYPTE GRECQUE, ROMAINE ET BYZANTINE

En Egypte, où les traditions sont particulièrement tenaces, et dans un domaine où l'évolution est lente, celui de l'architecture domestique, parler des "continuités" relève de l'évidence. Cependant, sur des points précis, les papyrus attestent des continuités qui n'ont pas encore été suffisamment dégagées. J'examinerai quatre exemples:

1. Les murets de brique crue construits comme protection autour des arbres devant les maisons;
2. La salle fraîche pour la réserve d'eau;
3. Le développement en hauteur des maisons;
4. Les maisons mitoyennes de plan uniforme.

1. *Les murets de brique crue autour des arbres*

Mon premier point ne concerne pas à proprement parler l'architecture domestique mais plutôt l'urbanisme, puisqu'il s'agit d'arbres plantés sur la voie publique. Mais ces arbres sont à côté des maisons ou d'autres édifices et forment leur décor villageois et urbain dont on ne peut les dissocier.

Sur des peintures de tombes thébaines du Nouvel Empire sont représentés, devant les façades de certaines maisons, des arbres entourés de murets de brique, et cette tradition est encore vivante aujourd'hui en Egypte et au Soudan (voir figures 1 et 2).[1] Ces murs sont évidemment destinés à protéger l'arbuste des dommages causés par les animaux, et notamment les chèvres.[2] Or cette pratique est attestée dans les papyrus grecs: selon le *P. Lond.* VII 1974, des archives de Zénon, des briques sont fournies "pour des perséas." Ces briques, livrées en petites quantités, devaient

---

1 Voir J. Cerny, "Survivance d'une ancienne pratique," *Rd'E* 22 (1970) 201-03.

2 Sur les dégâts provoqués par les animaux sur les jeunes arbres, voir *P. Tebt.* III 703.203-207 avec le commentaire de M. I. Rostovtzeff. Voir aussi M. Schnebel, *Die Landwirtschaft im hellenistischen Ägypten* (München 1925) 305.

servir à réparer ou à achever les murets entourant les arbres, murets qui étaient sans doute ajourés comme ceux de la figure 1.
D'autres exemples proviennent de papyrus d'Oxyrhynchos du début du
IVe siècle ap. J.C. qui ont conservé des engagements pris par des
habitants de la ville au sujet de perséas plantés à proximité de
leurs maisons. Dans le *P. Oxy.* XXXVI 3767 deux personnes et leurs
associés, μέτοχοι, font le serment de veiller sur un perséa qui,
disent-ils, a été planté récemment "à côté de nos maisons sur le
dromos de Psès" (lignes 15-17). Ils devront s'acquitter "du soin
et de la surveillance du pourtour de la construction (?) du dit
perséa," τὴν τήρησιν καὶ παραφυλακὴ(ν) τῆς περιβολῆς τῆς ἀν[οικοδ]-
ομῆς[3] τῆς αὐτῆς περσίας (lignes 19-21). Même si le sens exact de
περιβολή et de ἀνοικοδομή est difficile à établir, il est clair que
l'expression désigne le muret protecteur construit autour de l'arbre. Les *P. Oxy.* XLI 2969, 2993 et 2994 sont des parties de contrats parallèles.

On peut donc se référer à l'usage pharaonique des murets pro-
tecteurs pour interpréter ces textes relatifs à des perséas: comme
de tels enclos n'apparaissent ni chez les Agronomes latins ni dans
les *Geoponica*,[4] il semble bien que ce soit une survivance de la
pratique égyptienne ancienne.

2. *La salle fraîche pour la réserve d'eau*

Selon "L'Histoire de Sinouhé" traduite par Gustave Lefebvre
dans *Romans et contes égyptiens de l'époque pharaonique* (Paris
1949) 24, le héros, parvenu au faîte de la gloire, reçoit cette
marque de faveur du pharaon: "Je fus installé, dit-il, dans une
maison de fils royal qui renfermait des richesses. Il y avait là

---

3 ἀν[οικοδ]ομῆς a été restitué à la place de ἀν[αδρ]ομῆς proposé dans la lère édition à cause du contrat parallèle *P. Oxy.* XLI
2993.3: voir *P. Oxy.* 2969.16-17 n.

4 Je dois ce renseignement à M. René Martin, Professeur à
l'Université de Lille III et auteur d'une thèse de Doctorat d'Etat
sur les Agronomes latins. L'usage égyptien n'a rien à voir, à mon
avis, avec les murs ou barrières formant un enclos autour de certains arbres sacrés et les mettant ainsi à l'abri des contacts pro-
fanes (voir Daremberg et Saglio, *Dictionnaire des Antiquités
grecques et romaines* I, Arbores Sacrae, 356-62).

une salle fraîche." Selon le commentaire de Lefebvre (note 115):
"On conservait dans la 'salle fraîche' les aliments et surtout
l'eau à l'abri de la chaleur et des mouches." Erman et Grapow dans
le *Wörterbuch* (IV, 305.12) traduisent le terme *škbbwj* (la salle
fraîche de Sinouhé) par "Kühler Raum für Speisen, Getränke u.ä."
et donnent des références à des textes de l'Ancien et du Moyen Empire. Or dans quatre papyrus des époques ptolémaïque, romaine et
byzantine est attesté un terme ὑδροψύκτιον ou ὑδροψυγεῖον qui
semble désigner une pièce où l'on conserve l'eau au frais. En effet l'ὑδροψύκτιον ne peut être un bassin ou un réservoir d'eau,
selon les traductions du *Wörterbuch* de Preisigke et du Liddell-
Scott-Jones, car il est présenté comme un local pourvu de plusieurs
fenêtres (*P. Cairo Zen.* IV 59764 et 59847), couvert (*P. Ryl.* II 233
= *Sel. Pap.* I 123, ca. 118 ap. J.C.) et situé à l'intérieur de la
maison avec un vestibule situé au-dessus (*P. Lond.* II 394 [p. 330],
VIème ou VIIème siècle ap. J.C.). Dans tous les cas, la "salle
fraîche" appartient à une maison hors du commun, celle de Diotimos
à Philadelphie, la "résidence du Roi," la maison d'Apollonios le
stratège dans l'Hermopolite, une maison urbaine à quatre niveaux.
Il est d'ailleurs intéressant de noter que dans des maisons aussi
"grecques" que celle de Diotimos[5] ou la "résidence du Roi," on ait
adopté un usage proprement égyptien. En dehors des papyrus ὑδροψύ-
γιον n'est attesté que dans le *Corpus Glossariorum Latinorum*[6] où il
est glosé par *frigidarium*, c'est-à-dire "chambre froide."[7] Cette
coutume apparaît encore dans la plupart des ermitages d'Esna où une
salle spéciale semble avoir été réservée à la provision d'eau.[8]

---

5 A cause des éléments "égyptiens" de la maison de Diotimos,
notamment cette salle fraîche pour la réserve d'eau et le πυλών (*P.
Cairo Zen.* IV 59764.27), il conviendrait de nuancer l'opinion qui
en fait une maison typiquement grecque.

6 Ed. G. Loewe et G. Goetz (Leipzig 1880-1923) II, 73, 42.

7 Cf. Vitruve, 5.11.2.

8 Voir S. Sauneron et J. Jacquet, *Les Ermitages chrétiens du
désert d'Esna* I. *Archéologie et Inscriptions* (Le Caire 1972) 27.

3. *Le développement en hauteur des maisons*

Dans un article des *Metropolitan Museum Studies* 1 (1929) 233-
54, "The Town House in Ancient Egypt," Nina de Garis Davies a montré
comment dans une ville très peuplée comme Thèbes les maisons aisées
pouvaient être construites en élévation sur plusieurs étages au lieu
de s'étendre sur un vaste espace au sol: ainsi celle de Thut-mosĕ
comportait trois niveaux et une terrasse avec diverses installa-
tions. Dans les papyrus, les maisons à trois niveaux, τρίστεγοι,
sont bien attestées dans les villes comme dans les villages,[9] un
quatrième niveau, τετάρτη στέγη, apparaît à Hermoupolis,[10] à Syène[11]
et peut-être à Arsinoé[12] et une maison à sept niveaux, ἑπτάστεγος,
est mentionnée dans le *P. Oxy.* XXXIV 2719, du IIIe siècle ap. J.C.,
dans une ville qui doit être Alexandrie ou Hermoupolis. Les modèles de maisons et les lampes en forme de tours de l'époque gréco-
romaine illustrent ce type d'édifices.[13] Les maisons à étages
multiples étaient, selon les voyageurs arabes et persans, une des
caractéristiques de Fustat, l'actuel Vieux-Caire, du Xème au
XIIIème siècle: à l'οἰκία ἑπτάστεγος des papyrus correspondent précisément les maisons à sept niveaux qu'ils décrivent dans leurs relations.[14] Ainsi, plutôt qu'à l'influence des *insulae* de la Rome
Impériale ou à celle des hautes maisons yéménites familières à certains des conquérants arabes,[15] on peut rattacher les hauts immeu-
bles de Fustat à des traditions locales: entre le passé pharaonique

---

9 Par ex. *P. Ryl.* II 160b.2, Soknopaiou Nèsos, 37 ap. J.C.-
P. Oxy. I 99.15, 55 ap. J.C.

10 *P. Ryl.* II 153.8, 138-161 ap. J.C.

11 *P. Monac.* 8.13 et 9.34, VIème siècle ap. J.C.

12 *P. Lond.* II 394 (p. 330) 4, VIème-VIIème siècle ap. J.C.

13 Voir M. Nowicka, *La Maison privée dans l'Egypte ptolémaïque* (Varsovie 1969) 20-21 et *Les Maisons à tour dans le monde
grec* (Varsovie 1975) 28-29.

14 Voir les témoignages cités dans l'article d'A. Lézine,
"Persistance de traditions pré-islamiques dans l'architecture domestique de l'Egypte musulmane," *Annales Islamologiques* 11 (1972)
1-5.

15 Ibid., 6.

et l'époque arabe, les papyrus grecs sont un relais qui témoigne de la persistance d'un type de construction à travers les siècles.

4. *Les maisons mitoyennes de plan uniforme*

Les maisons de plan uniforme construites en séries constituent un type d'habitat bien attesté en Egypte depuis l'Ancien Empire, qu'il s'agisse des villages d'ouvriers de Kahoûn ou d'Amarna, de celui des ouvriers de la nécropole thébaine installés à Deir-el-Medineh, des maisons pour artisans d'Abydos ou des habitations pour le personnel des temples à Giza ou à Amarna.[16] Or plusieurs papyrus de l'Egypte romaine ou byzantine montrent, à mon avis, le prolongement de cette tradition avec les groupements de κέλλαι ou de κελλία en séries dans les centres d'exploitation des domaines. Le texte le plus explicite est le *P. Mich.* XI 620 qu'a édité John Shelton: il s'agit d'un compte de domaine situé dans la méris de Thémistès au Fayoum et datant des années 239-240 ap. J.C. Les revenus des bâtiments locatifs occupent les cinq premières colonnes du recto. La plupart de ces bâtiments sont des κέλλαι, groupés topographiquement par séries, chaque κέλλα portant un numéro dans la série. La κτῆσις de Sphex, l'une des propriétés qui composent le domaine, est divisée en deux ἐποίκια, avec dans l'un plus de 26 κέλλαι (la mention de la 26ème κέλλα est suivie d'une lacune d'environ 10 lignes) et dans l'autre 5 κέλλαι.[17] Les 30 κέλλαι de la κτῆσις d'Aristoklès sont réparties en cinq séries de nombre inégal.[18] Chaque série nouvelle est indiquée par un changement d'orientation: "à gauche au nord" (ligne 67), "à droite au nord" (75), "du sud au nord" (81), "à l'ouest" (97). Ces κέλλαι sont distinguées des bâtiments d'exploitation tels que l'atelier de tissage, ἐργαστήριον γερδιακόν (lignes 10, 94), le pressoir à vin, στεμφυλούργιον (96), la brasserie, ζυτοπώλιον (109), l'huilerie, ἐλαιούργιον (111). Elles ne sont pas non plus confondues avec les οἰκίδια, qui sont

---

16 Voir A. Badawy, "La maison mitoyenne de plan uniforme dans l'Egypte pharaonique," *Bulletin of the Faculty of Arts*, Cairo University 16.2 (December 1953) 1-58.

17 *P. Mich.* XI 620.14-54.

18 *P. Mich.* XI 620.55-119.

situés en dehors de l'ἐποίκιον, ἔξωθεν τοῦ ἐποικίου (112) et qui
sont des maisons habitées par certains προστάται, sortes de contre-
maîtres responsables d'une pièce de terre. Les κέλλαι sont alors,
sans nul doute, et c'est l'interprétation de l'éditeur, des logements où le propriétaire abrite les cultivateurs et les artisans
qu'il emploie, le plus souvent moyennant un loyer. Et l'on peut y
voir, semble-t-il, des sortes de cases toutes semblables et accolées
les unes aux autres lorsqu'elles appartiennent à la même série: le
fait qu'elles ne soient pas identifiées par une caractéristique
architecturale, mais par des numéros successifs dans le groupe considéré est un indice de cette uniformité comme le montant identique
du loyer pour nombre de ces unités d'habitation. En effet pour 29
κέλλαι le loyer de chacune s'élève à 20 drachmes, 12 jours de travail et 1/2 porc pour une durée de 6 mois. Dans quatre cas la
κέλλα est occupée par deux locataires et le nombre de jours de travail est doublé, les autres prestations restant les mêmes.[19] D'autres locataires sont dispensés de fournir les jours de travail, le
montant du loyer étant fixée à 20 drachmes et 1/2 porc comme dans
les autres cas.[20] D'autres encore ne paient pas de loyer du tout,
comme les portiers, les conducteurs de boeufs, le meunier et le
jardinier:[21] sans doute le travail dû était-il estimé à la valeur
du loyer habituel.[22]

Les papyrus offrent d'autres exemples de κέλλαι, et plus tard
de κελλία, sur des domaines. Dans le *P. Flor.* I 50.103 de 268 ap.
J.C., on trouve sur un ἐποίκιον de l'Hermopolite des bâtiments,
οἰκόπεδα, des κέλλαι, des greniers, θησαυροί, des pressoirs,
ληνῶνες etc. Les κέλλαι, distinguées des οἰκόπεδα, des θησαυροί et
d'autres bâtiments d'exploitation ne sont pas, à mon avis, des en-
trepôts, mais des logements de cultivateurs et d'artisans. Plus
significative est la mention d'un loyer de 200 artabes de blé pour

---

19 *P. Mich.* XI 620.18,19,29,31.

20 *P. Mich.* XI 620.34,42,48,53,63,68,71,79.

21 *P. Mich.* XI 620.9,50,56,86,93.

22 L'expression "une κέλλα qui est double (διπλῆ οὖσα) dans
laquelle il y a un moulin" pourrait aussi être interprétée comme un
indice de l'uniformité des κέλλαι, si l'on comprend que cette κέλλα
"double" était formée de la réunion de deux unités, l'une servant
de logis et l'autre de local pour la mouture du grain.

100 κελλία dans le *P. Oxy.* XVI 1917 des archives des Apions au début du VIème siècle: Mme Ewa Wipszycka, en citant ce texte dans un article de la *Chronique d'Egypte* de 1968,[23] estime que ce chiffre de 100 κελλία est "trop considérable pour ne pas nous inquiéter." Elle reconnaît néanmoins que "si l'on accepte la lecture et l'interprétation des éditeurs, le montant du loyer paraît tout à fait raisonnable, par rapport aux prix de l'époque." Le chiffre de 100 κελλία, je crois, s'explique, si l'on y voit de petites habitations mitoyennes de plan uniforme groupées en séries, le loyer de chacune d'elle étant le même. Dans le *P. Bad.* 95, compte d'un domaine de l'Hermopolite du VIIème siècle, le récapitulatif des loyers des κελλία à la ligne 28 indique: "loyer de 67 κελλία 1/2 à 5 carats, 14 sous 1 carat 1/2." Le 1/2 κελλίον est probablement un logement identique aux autres, mais loué à moitié prix: à la ligne 92 le loyer du κελλίον de "l'aveugle" est réduit de 2 carats 1/2, c'est-à-dire de moitié. Ces κελλία ne semblent pas être tous situés sur le même ἐποίκιον comme ceux du *P. Oxy.* 1917, mais le taux de location fixé à 5 carats par unité[24] oriente vers un type de logements identiques. C'est alors la situation du *P. Mich.* 620 et du *P. Oxy.* 1917 où le même loyer était versé pour un certain nombre d'habitations du domaine.

Ainsi, entre les maisons mitoyennes de plan uniforme de l'Egypte ancienne et les petites cases alignées régulièrement des ezbeh modernes,[25] les papyrus témoignent, peut-être, pour les époques romaine et byzantine, de la persistance d'un type d'habitat qui s'est maintenu à travers la diversité et l'évolution des structures économiques et sociales. Cependant, à l'origine de ces logements tous semblables et accolés les uns aux autres, on retrouve probablement les mêmes facteurs: un sol vierge de constructions, le souci de loger une main d'oeuvre nombreuse, de bâtir vite en économisant les matériaux, et l'initiative d'un "employeur," que ce soit

23   "Deux papyrus byzantins," *Cd'E* 43 (1968) 347-48.

24   Voir aussi tous les cas de remise du loyer d'un κελλίον soit 5 carats, lignes 91 à 96, 195 à 201. De même dans le *P. Mich.* XI 620, certains des occupants des κέλλαι étaient exemptés de loyer.

25   Voir J. Lozach et G. Hug, *L'Habitat rural en Egypte* (Le Caire 1930) 33, et J. Besançon, *L'Homme et le Nil* (Paris 1957) 197.

le pharaon, le propriétaire d'un grand domaine ou leur représentant.

Université de Rouen   Geneviève Husson

Fig. 1.   Maison peinte dans la tombe 254 à Thèbes (d'après un dessin reproduit dans N. de Garis Davies, "The Town House in Ancient Egypt," *Metropolitan Museum Studies* 1 (1929) 242 Fig. 6).

Fig. 2.   Photographie prise à Cheik-Abadeh (Antinooupolis) en Avril 1976.

Proceedings of the XVI Int. Congr. of Papyrology (Chico 1981) 527-536

DEMOTIC AND GREEK OSTRACA EXCAVATED AT ELKAB*

In 1923, on the occasion of the visit of the Queen of Belgium
to the newly discovered tomb of Tut-Ankh-Amun and on the initiative
of the well-known Egyptologist J. Capart, the "Fondation Egyptologique Reine Elisabeth" was founded in Brussels. It was only in
1937, however, that the Foundation was able to organize its first
excavations, for which Capart chose Elkab, site of the ancient town
of Nekheb (Greek name Eileithuiaspolis), some 15 km north of Edfu
on the east bank of the Nile. Under Capart's direction a few campaigns were undertaken, during which he unearthed, inside and partially outside the temple precinct, part of a Graeco-Roman
settlement.[1]

In 1964, with a view to the resumption of archaeological work
at Elkab, a "Committee for Belgian Excavations in Egypt" was set
up; two years later activities recommenced at the site under the
overall direction of Professor H. De Meulenaere. Since 1968 a spot
just east of the temple area, designated "scoriae" has been excavated; here too the remains of a village of the Graeco-Roman period
have been turned up.[2] The military situation between Egypt and

---

* Due to the omission of a large number of illustrations, it
was impossible to publish the text in its original state. Suggestions of colleagues have also led to some slight modifications.

1 On Elkab in general, see B. Porter and R. Moss, *Topographi-
cal Bibliography* V: *Upper Egypt: Sites* (Oxford 1937) 171-91, to be
supplemented by the references given in notes 2 and 10ff. On Capart's excavations, see *Fouilles de El Kab. Documents*. Fondation
Egyptologique Reine Elisabeth, Brussels, Livraison I-II (1940),
III (1954). Highly readable is his booklet *Fouilles en Egypte.
El Kab. Impressions et souvenirs* (Brussels 1946).

2 See the report "Elkab 1966-1969," *Cd'E* 45 (1970) 19-44,
esp. 36-39. See also J. Leclant, "Fouilles et travaux en Egypte
et au Soudan 1969-70," *Orientalia* 40 (1971) 242-43 and subsequent
contributions.

Israel, however, halted all archaeological activity at the site for
some time.[3]

In 1974, to the great joy of the "mudir," Professor De Meulenaere, the promising activities could be resumed. The further excavation and the study of the Graeco-Roman settlement now became
one of the main objectives. In this paper I would like to deal in
particular with the more than 400 ink inscriptions on potsherds
that have hitherto come to light at Elkab. It should be noted that
the site has not yielded a single scrap of papyrus; for that matter, no papyri are known to have come from Elkab.

Ostraca from Elkab, on the other hand, are not unknown. In
his report on the second excavation campaign, that of 1938, Capart
mentions the find of several ostraca together with the information
provided by the Egyptian demotic scholar G. Mattha.[4] In volume III
of the *Fouilles de El Kab. Documents*, a brief description is given
of four barely legible ostraca, now in the Royal Musea of Art and
History in Brussels (E 7781-7784), whereby the remark is made that
"ces quatre ostraca semblent donc se référer aux taxes dues au
temple...."[5] Compared to the recent finds, this small number is
somewhat surprising in view of the extent of the living area then
excavated.[6] Also worthy of note is that Sayce may have picked up a
small number of ostraca at the site before the turn of the century.[7]

---

3 Since the site lay in a military zone, it became inacces-
sible for foreigners. Activities were then shifted to the Theban
necropolis: see the report "Fouilles de l'Assassif 1970-1975," *Cd'E*
50 (1975) 13-64.

4 *Fouilles de El Kab* I, 28. The mention of a temple of the
phoenix could not be traced on one of the ostraca now in Brussels
(cf. n. 5).

5 *Fouilles de El Kab* III, 110.

6 *Fouilles de El Kab* II, pl. 39, 40.

7 Cf. *PSBA* 23 (1901) 211. On A. H. Sayce (1845-1933), see
W. R. Dawson and E. P. Uphill, *Who was who in Egyptology* (London
1972) 261. A letter from Mrs. J. Crowfoot Payne (8.2.1976) states
that "The Bodleian collection includes 8 ostraca from el Kab, all
of which were given by Sayce." These are now in the Ashmolean
Museum, Oxford.

Mattha published one demotic sherd in his *Demotic Ostraka* of 1945,[8] and the only published Greek piece is included in the *O. Bodl.*[9]

Before presenting the demotic and Greek ostraca found at Elkab since 1968, a brief word on the site and a few archaeological details should prove useful.

Elkab, situated on the Nile, is encircled by an almost square, rather well-preserved, enclosure wall with a side of roughly 500 m. It has now been established that the wall was built at the end of the pharaonic period.[10] Close by, to the north, lie the mountains with their rock tombs, mainly of the 2nd Intermediate Period and the New Kingdom. In one of these graves, that of Renni and not that of Paheri, is the well-known demotic graffito dedicated to a saint called *p3 rmt c3* "the great man."[11] Elsewhere too, demotic or Greek graffiti are found, for example on the walls of the desert temples; but such texts need not be discussed here.[12] Also worthy of mention is a tomb, not yet listed in the literature which, according to the decoration, presumably dates from the Ptolemaic era.[13]

---

8 Bodleian 1258 = Mattha n° 243.

9 *O. Bodl.* II 408 = *SB* I 1085; cf. J. Bingen, *Cd'E* 46 (1971) 368 n. 2.

10 In 1979, radiocarbon dating (C 14) was undertaken. The data will be published in detail elsewhere. The recent works of A. J. Spencer (*Brick Architecture in Ancient Egypt* [Warminster 1979] 104 [the date of the town enclosure is not certain, but it is presumed to belong to the Middle Kingdom]) and M. A. Hoffman (*Egypt before the Pharaohs* [London 1980] 99 [mud-brick wall...built probably in the tenth century B.C.]) are to be amended in this respect. The correct date is already found in L. Keimer, *Die Gartenpflanzen im alten Ägypten* (Hamburg 1924) 56.

11 Cf. J. Quaegebeur, "Les 'saints' égyptiens préchrétiens," *OLP* 8 (1977) 142 n. 77. This is not the only graffito in the tomb. Πρεμμαως also occurs as a person's name in Elkab.

12 See Ph. Derchain, *Elkab I: Les monuments religieux à l'entrée de l'Ouady Hellal* (Brussels 1971) 76-78 and pl. 24-26. Demotic graffiti are also found both outside (inscribed) and inside (in ink) the small desert temple of Amenhotep III. Like the many rock graffiti (including some in Greek), they have not (yet) been published.

13 The beautiful book by J. Baines and L. Málek, *Atlas of Ancient Egypt* (Oxford 1980), which I first saw after the Congress, seems to refer to this tomb (p. 81).

Later, loculi were also hewn out for crocodile mummies.[14] Other
graves of the Graeco-Roman period have not (yet) been found here.

We return to the enclosure wall of which the south corner has
been washed away by the river. Still visible, however, are the remains of a quay as well as the so-called Deir, once presumably a
small square Roman fort.[15] Within the great enclosure an ill-
preserved smaller precinct surrounds the temple area. The portion
of the village excavated since 1968 lies just beyond, to the east
of this temple wall. On this same side are the remains of a gate.
A wide road has been unearthed which ran through the village to
this gate, directly connecting the settlement with the temple area.
A few houses could be identified as potter's houses thanks to the
presence of rimmed clay pits and the discovery of loamers, used to
finish turned pottery. A large amphora oven has also been unearthed. Otherwise there is little of note to be said of the archaeological context in which the sherds with "maktub" (writing)
were found.[16] Only exceptionally were they dug up together with
pottery or has a coin come to light to aid in the dating of a house.
As will be seen below, a few groups of ostraca, mainly Greek, have
turned up; the demotic sherds are mostly isolated finds.

One of the first tasks in the processing of the material entered in the field book is the joining of fragments, which at times
is like putting together a jig-saw puzzle. It may be useful to
point out that joins are sometimes easier to achieve by working not
from the front, but from the back of the fragments, where the ridges
in the pottery may provide a good point of reference. Yet there are
other instances where the back has been completely eroded, so that
the front, and the fracture line itself, are all one has to go by.

---

14 See in this connection H. De Meulenaere, "Sébek à Elkab,"
Cd'E 44 (1969) 13-21.

15 *Fouilles de El Kab* III, 79-82. For the location, see the
map (field surveying: F. Depuydt & P. Vermeersch) of the site published in 1972. See also Spencer, *Brick Architecture*, 109-10.

16 Most of the ostraca were found at very slight depth, sometimes even before the remains of the walls were uncovered, i.e., at
a level not only higher than the ancient living level, but also
higher than the surviving house walls. Ptolemaic and Roman ostraca
are sometimes also found on the same level and are therefore not
always integrated in a stratigraphically datable layer.

The following step is photographing the ostraca. Several methods were tested, for instance photographing the sherds after wetting them with a mixture of water and alcohol, or after placing them in a flat water basin.

Often employed in the decipherment of Greek ostraca is a hand-pencilled copy; for demotic ostraca it is necessary to make real facsimiles, to be included in the final publication. Quite exceptional are cases like 5 T 004 (fig.) with two complete calligraphically written words, which pose no problems for the facsimile. For that matter, what we have here are new orthographies of apparently known words, *t3j.f 3mj.t* "his character" and *n3j.f mhw3.wt* perhaps "his families" (but how to explain the plural and the determinative pointing to a festival?). Writing and content would seem to suggest a writing exercise. The vast majority, however, are small fragments of which it is difficult not only to determine the nature of the text, but also to make facsimiles of often faded signs. A few examples show that there is sometimes writing on both convex and concave sides.

Let us now take a closer look at the ostraca themselves, both in form and in content. We will start with the demotic texts, which make up about two-thirds of the total found, that is to say some 250, and which will be published by the present writer; the information here presented on the Greek ostraca has been kindly provided by Professor J. Bingen and Dr. W. Clarysse.

First of all, it should be noted that the demotic ostraca vary considerably in form and material as well as in script and content. A comparison of two items (2 T 017 and 2 T 013) will make this clear. The first is a note written on gray-beige pottery; the variable thickness of the characters and the irregular ink distribution betray a fine reed brush. Lines 1 and 2 read as follows: *P3-šr-iḥj* son of *Ḥr-tb3* greets (*sm r*) *Ḥr-msn*. Note that the two Horus-names point to nearby Edfu. The text, like that of many other demotic ostraca, concerns *ššw* "pottery." This might point to a link with the potter's activity. The other document, on typically Roman pink pottery, was clearly written with a *kalamos* (hard reed pen). The opening formula too differs from that of the previous text: "It is *P3-iwiw-n-Ḥr* (Pinuris) who says...." At issue here is a payment for a recipient called *lkjnws*. The term occurs also as *lgjnws* in the Elkab ostraca 2 T 020 and 6 T 017[17] and is to be connected with the orthography *lgns*, which Griffith[18] identified with the Greek λάγυνος "flask, flagon."[19] On line 4 of the ostracon discussed, we read the name *Jwln* with foreign determinative. From these examples it is clear that the material itself is of importance in the dating of the ostraca: at Elkab Roman amphora pottery was much liked, as will be further confirmed by the Greek ostraca.

Important data are the regular references to cults and priests. A large sherd (6 T 016), probably part of a Roman vase-inscription containing a kind of temple inventory, clearly shows the word *m-bȝḥ* three times, followed by the names of gods, among them, as one might expect, those of Nekhbet and *ᶜȝ pḥty* "the great in might," which is the name of the local crocodile god. Another, broken, ostracon (6 T 035) contains a list of festivals. Above a list of names and numbers (3 T 069 and 5 T 007), to be dated to Ptolemaic times, we read: *nȝ sh̲.w ḥw.t-ntr* "the scribes of the temple." It is somewhat surprising to find, among known Egyptian names, that of *Pjln*, father of *Pȝ-išwr*, perhaps the Greek name Philon,[20] but without foreign determinative. There are also regular references to the division of the priests into *phylae*, for example a small fragment (3 T 129) on which virtually only the words *sȝ 4.nw* "the fourth *phyle*" have survived. An interesting piece is 7 T 034, a receipt containing a reference to the strategos. Another noteworthy title appears on 5 T 018 (fig.), of which the first line reads *d̲d Gl-šr Rȝ-in.t*: this "Calasiris of the mouth of the wadi"

17   In addition to *lgjnws* we also found on this ostracon the orthography or the word *ljnws*, which further occurs on 6 T 016.

18   F. Ll. Griffith, *Catalogue of the Demotic Graffiti of the Dodecaschoenus* I (Oxford 1937) 164 (210) = W. Erichsen, *Demotisches Glossar* (Kopenhagen 1954) 265: "Krug"; see also S. V. Wångstedt, *Ausgewählte Demotische Ostraca* (Uppsala 1954) 165 (comm. 64/3).

19   Liddell-Scott-Jones, *A Greek-English Lexicon* (Oxford 1940) 1022.

20   The name *Pjln* is borne by an eponymous priest; cf. J. Quaegebeur, "Les prêtres éponymes des années 230/229 et 171/170 av. J.-C.," *Cd'E* 55 (1980) in press. See also P. W. Pestman, "Contrat démotique relatif à un prêt d'orge," *AfP* 19 (1969) 167.

would seem, to judge from the geographical indication, to have
police or military authority.[21]

To further illustrate the diversity of the demotic texts, a
few more random examples: 5 T 001 is a well-written Ptolemaic ostracon containing the list of a woman's trousseau;[22] it mentions
clothing (the notorious *ỉn-šn*, shawl?) and jewelry, and specifies
the value of each item. Another pretty piece is 5 T 005 (fig.)
with numbers, which I take to be a school exercise. The right-hand
column has the numbers 116, 166, 169, 169 in the feminine, but then,
instead of 170, 160 - 10. I could suggest, tongue firmly in cheek,
that perhaps the Egyptians, like the French, were taught to say
"soixante-dix" instead of "septante"! Finally there are a few instances of demotic tax receipts: e.g. a receipt for salt tax from
a sixteenth year; the writing suggests the Roman period. This type
of text brings us close to the Greek ostraca.

A group apart is formed by several fragments of demotic vase-
inscriptions from the Roman period, such as 6 T 015: a number of
joining pieces containing an inventory. We also have a flattened
amphora with a Greek inscription which has had to be strengthened
with cement in situ. It is a list of payments, but the amounts are
very small. At the top there is the name of the month, followed by
a list of names with the amounts to the right. Of some interest
is the fact that this list, presumably from the second century,
contains Roman names like Primus and Rufus.

The Greek ostraca, some 180 in all, are mostly from the imperial era and almost exclusively tax receipts. A Ptolemaic example
is 3 T 044: it concerns a payment in cash and dates from the third
century B.C., as is apparent from the term πέπτωκεν.

The Greek ostraca were partly found grouped together. A large
number of sherds[23] was discovered in just two houses, now named

---

21 J. K. Winnicki, "Die Kalasierer der spätdynastischen und
der ptolemäischen Zeit," *Historia* 26 (1977) 257-68.

22 Compare M. A. A. Nur El-Din, *The Demotic Ostraca in the
National Museum of Antiquities at Leiden* (Leiden 1974) 218-20
(dowry lists).

23 Some demotic sherds were found among the Greek ostraca.

"house of Pekusis" and "house of the ostraca"; the families of the
two houses may have been interrelated. From a perfunctory study it
is already apparent that what we have here are archives, albeit
very incomplete ones. Evidence of payment of the various taxes was
clearly being kept for later reference. Noteworthy is the fact
that the Greek texts, unlike their demotic counterparts, are usually
quite precisely dated. The piece 3 T 064, for instance, comes from
the so-called "house of Pekusis" and is dated A.D. 148; it concerns
the payment by Pekusis son of Senuris of an hitherto unknown tax,
the μερισμὸς ἀφανῶν.[24] This was apparently an extra tax to compen-
sate for the unpaid poll-tax of "vanished persons," comparable or
perhaps even identical to the μερισμὸς ἀνακεχωρηκότων.

A considerable number of texts concerns a single family, from
the so-called "house of the ostraca," which can be followed over
several generations. For example: 3 T 091 is a *laographia*-receipt
for A.D. 106 of Psemonkhes son of Phthoumonthes; 3 T 087 is a similar document for 131 or 132, paid then by Siphthyris son of Psemonkhes. The latter text is incomplete due to the peeling of the
slip. Note also that the name Siphthyris is a new one and its
etymology unknown. An important text, dating from 129, is surely
3 T 105, in which several tax payments have been recorded together,
among them the dike tax (for the maintenance of dikes) and a river-
guard tax (μερισμὸς ποταμοφυλακιτῶν). The form too is interesting:
much like a letter in which the tax collectors (πράκτορες ἀργυρικῶν), after a greeting formula, acknowledge having received the
various taxes due.

What can we learn from these tax receipts? Well, in the first
place, we acquire some information on the administration and on the
tax system, which is closer to that of Elephantine than that of
Thebes, and also on the occupational activities of the populace.
In this connection reference may be made to a weaver's tax (γερδιακόν). Also striking--in the present state of the documentation--
is the minimal role of agriculture.

Before concluding, the question of the interrelationship between the Greek and the demotic ostraca must be considered. Apart

---

24 This tax is also attested outside Elkab but went hitherto
unrecognized, e.g. *O. Stras.* 137.2 (information provided by W.
Clarysse).

from a few barely legible bilingual ostraca and a few demotic texts
found amidst the Greek documents, the two groups are quite conspic-
uously distinct. This was already apparent in the circumstances of
the find itself: the demotic sherds were much more widely dispersed
and showed markedly less coherence, which is largely the result of
the nature of the texts. A second difference concerns the content:
the Greek items are almost exclusively tax receipts, from which a
few "family archives" can be isolated; the demotic ostraca vary
widely in content (lists, inventories, accounts, notes, a woman's
trousseau, etc.) and contain numerous references to the cult and
clergy of the neighboring temple area. The fact that the Greek
items are dated rather precisely, whereas for the demotic only an
approximate date can be suggested, for instance on palaeographical
grounds, is also bound up with nature of the texts. Generally
speaking, it may be stated that what is concerned with the official
administration is in Greek, anything else in demotic, which in the
second century A.D. remained the language of priestly circles as
well. Despite this rather strict distinction, some intercourse between Greek and Egyptian environments must be assumed. The Greek
tax receipts had to be understandable to a number of people, and
the presence of some Greek and Latin names also suggests a measure
of bilingualism.

The conclusion can be brief. The presently available material
should be incorporated into a social and economic study of this
village community in the Graeco-Roman period. On the social side
we have some information on the composition and living standard of
the populace; the phenomenon of "missing persons" also merits attention. Economically Elkab seems mainly to have been an indus-
trial town, in which the role of the temples appears to have been
of some significance.[25] This is apparent both from the archaeological data and from the ostraca, particularly from the tax system.
The information on clergy and cult is strikingly abundant in the
demotic texts: the cult of the crocodile god ^{c}3 pḥ.ty "the great in

---

25 Cf. J. Quaegebeur, "Documents égyptiens et rôle économique
du clergé en Egypte hellénistique," in *State and Temple Economy in
the Ancient Near East* II, ed. E. Lipiński (*Orientalia Lovaniensia
Analecta* 6, Leuven 1979) 720.

might" (in Greek transcription, απαθης)[26] is especially prominent
here. Onomastics--even apart from the new names--is also an important source of information: it reveals, among other things, the
popularity of Thot and the ties with Edfu.

K. U. Leuven   Jan Quaegebeur

---

26   This divine name is also well-represented onomastically.

Demotic Ostraca Elkab

Elkab 5 T 004

Elkab 5 T 018

Elkab 5 T 005

Proceedings of the XVI Int. Congr. of Papyrology (Chico 1981) 537-545

THE ARTABA, AND EGYPTIAN GRAIN-MEASURES

I should like to speak of the information that can be obtained from demotic texts on the grain-measure called the artaba. I shall confine my discussion to Ptolemaic Egypt, firstly because demotic texts of Roman times so far as they have been published, are not very instructive on the subject, and secondly, because we know that the grain-measures had changed drastically in the Coptic period. This would force us to examine whether the grain-measures had been left unchanged after each and every incision in the history of administration from Ptolemaic till Coptic times. It would take too long to do so here, and therefore I shall confine myself to the Ptolemaic period.

Many different artabai were in use in Ptolemaic Egypt. The artaba of 40 choinikes and the artaba of 30 choinikes (χ) were the two most conspicuous. Based on the artaba of 40 χ there were some others, for example the artaba that was measured by the μέτρον δοχικόν, which contained a fat 42 χ. I think we need not detain ourselves with these deviant artabai, whose importance would grow considerably in Roman times, witness the impressive list recently compiled by R. P. Duncan-Jones.[1] Well then, what can demotic texts contribute to our knowledge of the artaba?

Since the publication of O. Wien 14 by S. V. Wångstedt in 1965, we know of an artaba of 60 *hin*.[2] As the *hin* contained ±1/2 litre to judge from archaeological evidence,[3] this artaba contained ±30 litres.

---

1 R. P. Duncan-Jones, "Variation in Egyptian Grain-measure," *Chiron* 9 (1979) 369-72.

2 S. V. Wångstedt, *Die Demotischen Ostraka der Universität zu Zürich* (Uppsala 1965) 23f. See also *Enchoria* 9 (1979) 97f.

3 In the *Lexikon der Agyptologie* III, 1210, under n. 34, I proposed to take 1/2 litre as a rough equivalent of the *hin*, mainly for the sake of simplicity. This estimate is almost certainly too high, the *hin*-measure probably ranging from 0.45 to 0.5 litre, so all conversions into litres in these pages should be slightly reduced.

ἀρτάβη   r t b
   40 χ
29/30 χ   60 *hin* $\leqslant$ 30 l.

The place assigned to the artaba of 60 *hin* in this table is
arbitrary, because in the Greek and demotic texts there is no direct link between these measures. There do exist bilingual texts
in which the artaba occurs, but in the demotic parts of these texts
the artaba is regularly reproduced without further detail. If we
look at *O. Stras.* 304 for example, we read in the Greek text $\frac{1}{4}$ ιη∠,
to which corresponds *rtb* (*n*) *sw* 18-1/2, 18-1/2 artabai of wheat,
in the demotic subscription.[4] In bilingual texts from the Zenon-
archive an artaba of 29/30 χ is to be found, but in the demotic
halves of these texts, this artaba is referred to by means of a
special sign for choinix, and not converted into Egyptian *hin*.[5] So,
bilingual texts do not seem to offer the points of contact that
would help to calculate the capacity of the artaba on the basis of
possibly better known Egyptian measures.

The traditionally accepted capacity of the artaba of 40 χ is
±40 litres; of the artaba of 30 χ, ±30 litres. These capacities
are somewhat uncertain, because they are established by comparison
with Roman and Byzantine measures and metrologists. This is why I
draw a division line between these artabai and their assumed capacities. Similarly, I should like to point out that the Greek and
Egyptian measures are separated from each other within the demotic
text-corpus.

| | GREEK | | DEMOTIC | |
	ἀρτάβη		r t b	
40 l.	40 χ			
30 l.	29/30 χ	29/30 χ	‖	60 *hin* $\leqslant$ 30 l.

Now, why should we have to make the artaba of 60 *hin* (= ±30 l.)
equal to the artaba of 30 χ? I intend to answer this question by

4 P. Viereck, *Griechische und Griechisch-Demotische Ostraka*
etc. (Berlin 1923) no. 304.

5 *P. L. Bat.* XX 12 and 13; see P. W. Pestman's commentary,
ibid., pp. 69f. (cf. *Lex. Äg.* III, 1210 nn. 25-27).

way of the history of Egyptian grain-measures. If we speak of the history of Egyptian grain-measures, we would stress that on the basis of the facts known to us at present, it can only be a reconstruction in which dispersed facts are harmonized over a distance of some 1,000 years in time, hundreds of kilometers in space, and of various applications of the measures in their daily use. Perhaps, I need not stress the presumability and tentativeness of my exposé any further.

In the Late Period, in pre-Persian times, the Egyptians used a sack called *ẖ3r* ([hieroglyph]) to measure their wheats and barleycorns etc. This sack was divided into 4 *oipe* of 40 *hin* each. Given a *hin* of about 1/2 litre, the *oipe* contained ±20 litres, and the sack ±80 litres by consequence.

1 sack (*ẖ3r*, [hieroglyph]) = 4 *oipe* = 160 *hin* $\leqslant$ 80 litres
1 *oipe* = 40 *hin* $\leqslant$ 20 litres

In the abnormal-hieratic texts of the 25th and 26th or Kushitic and Saitic Dynasties (7th and 6th centuries B.C.), the *ẖ3r*-sign was not written regularly. We know however, that we are facing the *ẖ3r* or sack in these texts, because the masculin article was used (whereas the *oipe* would have required the feminin article), and because in all mentions of grain quantities a complementary sign is to be found. This sign is read *oipe* after a proposal by J. Černý & R. Parker.[6] The whole purport of this sign would be that the relevant quantities of grain were to be measured out in *oipe*, "with the *oipe* consisting of exactly 40 *hin*."[7] So, the sack or *ẖ3r* was tacitly assumed in this abnormal-hieratic formula; the *oipe* was only mentioned to assure the orthodoxy of the *ẖ3r* or sack.

(sack, [hieroglyph]) x [hieroglyph], *oipe*

Now, by a unique variant in an early-demotic text from Elephantine, dating from some 20 years before the Persian conquest of Egypt, this formula is connected with a formula in a number of

6 J. Černý & R. Parker, "An Abnormal Hieratic Tablet," *JEA* 57 (1971) 128-31.

7 Ibid., 129 bottom.

demotic marriage-contracts, to know: "barley x (with the *oipe* of)
40 *hin*."[8] This demotic formula was first deciphered and discussed
by M. Malinine.[9]

(sack, ⌓) x ⤳, *oipe*   (Abn. Hier.)

 - x (*oipe* of) 40 *hin*   (Demotic)

It appears that this formula lived on through Ptolemaic times
into the first half of the first century A.D. It can hardly have
concealed anything but the artaba in late Ptolemaic times,[10] and
probably the artaba was meant ever since the first Persian domination over Egypt. Here again, the formula "(measured with the *oipe*
of) 40 *hin*," was added to the presumed artaba to ascertain its exactitude, just as it was once added to the *ḥȝr* or sack. This implies that the involved artaba should have contained a multiple of
40 *hin*, and hardly anything else than 80 *hin* ≼ 40 litres. (In the
table below, I place this artaba between brackets, because its existence has been demonstrated only in an indirect manner.)[11]

    To be fair to our predecessors I have to point out that they
envisaged the meaning of our phrase, and by consequence the history

----

8 For a list of the relevant texts, see E. Lüddeckens, *Ägyptische Eheverträge* (Wiesbaden 1960) 261; add *P. Louvre* 2347 (after
P. W. Pestman, *Marriage* etc. [Leiden 1961] 148 n. 3), and *P. Louvre*
3265 (after Malinine, *Kemi* 11 [1950] Pl. 2, no. XV); *P. Köln* 1864
(ed. E. Seidl, as *P. L. Bat.* XVII, 15); and *P. Mich.* V 347 (= E.
Lüddeckens, *Ägyptische Eheverträge* [Wiesbaden 1960] doc. 12 D).
Here the words "(with the *oipe* of) 40 *hin*" are not optional
(as was the case with the sack in the abnormal-hieratic formula
discussed under nn. 6-7), but they are the interpretation of the
sign that is thought to be the descendant of the abnormal-hieratic
oipe-sign; see J. Černý & R. Parker, *JEA* 57 (1971) 131.

9 M. Malinine, "Un Prêt de Céréales à l'Epoque de Darius I,"
Kemi 11 (1950) 15-17 and Pl. 2. Malinine identified this formula
with an early-demotic phrase which was read tentatively by Griffith,
P. dem. Ryl. III, p. 242 n. 12.

10 The value of the involved quantity of grain is additional
evidence; see P. W. Pestman, *Marriage* etc. (Leiden 1961) 148 nn.
11-12 (cf. *Enchoria* 9 [1979] 98 n. 16).

11 The supposed attestation of an artaba of 8 *ḥqȝ.t* (= 80 *hin*)
in the hieroglyphic Naukratis copy of the Decree of Memphis (Roset-
tana), is based on an emendation; see *Enchoria* 9 (1979) 99 n. 19.
The measure refers to the artabieia-tax (see P. W. Pestman, *P. L.
Bat.* XIX, p. 116), whose amount (1/2 ? 3/4 artaba ?) at the time of
the stela is unknown. This prevents any conclusion, even if the
text would have seemed wholly trustworthy.

of the artaba, in other ways than I do. Going back in time we
first meet J. Černý and R. Parker who, in 1971, concentrated on the
abnormal-hieratic and early-demotic evidence.[12] They proposed a
direct development of the *oipe* into the artaba.[13] Thus, they ar-
rived at the same theory that A. H. Gardiner had put forward 23
years before: "(...) reasonably certain that, so far as capacity
goes, the artaba took over the old value of the *oipě*."[14] The old
value of the *oipe* was some 20 litres, however, and neither Gardiner
nor Černý and Parker were prepared to link this capacity to the
considerably bigger artaba, Gardiner leaving the question open,
Černý and Parker apparently ignoring it.

M. Malinine, as we have seen, devoted a lengthy note to the
formula under discussion, and its relation to the demotic sign for
artaba.[15] His theory is, I hope, faithfully paraphrased as follows.
He asks himself if the abnormal-hieratic formula could not have been
a circumlocution of "the measure whose Egyptian name escapes us,
that would be called 'artaba' later."[16] As the *ẖȝr* or sack figures
in this formula at first, it is apparently the sack, not the *oipe*,
that is the predecessor of the artaba.[17] The demotic formula from
the marriage-contracts would refer to the same measure, now safely
to be interpreted as "artaba of 40 choinikes." Presently Malinine
derives the demotic artaba-sign from this phrase.[18] The archaistic
tendency of the demotic marriage-contracts, as apparent from their
featuring old-time emmercorn, is called upon to explain the perse-
verance of the full writing of the "artaba of 40 choinikes" formula
in these texts against the use of the cursive artaba-sign elsewhere
in demotic.[19]

---

12   J. Černý & R. Parker, loc. cit. in n. 6 (*JEA* 57 [1971]).

13   Ibid., 129: "(...) direct development of *ipt* into *rtb*."

14   A. H. Gardiner, *The Wilbour Papyrus* II, *Commentary* (London
1948) 65.

15   M. Malinine, *Kemi* 11 (1950) 15-19 and 19-22.

16   Ibid., 18.

17   Ibid., 19.

18   Ibid., 19-21.

19   Ibid., 21-22.

This attractive theory contains two presuppositions I should prefer to decline. Firstly, the existence of the artaba in Egypt in pre-Persian times, and secondly the use of the word *hin* for choinix. Malinine's derivation of the demotic artaba-sign from the formula seems not sufficiently beyond doubt[20] to warrant the assimilation of the *hin* to the choinix, if only temporarily. And the existence of the artaba in pre-Persian Egypt can be easily avoided, if we take our formula as a phrase to assure nothing but the correctness of the measures involved, the Egyptian *ḫȝr* or sack of ±80 litres at first, and the artaba of ±40 litres later.[21]

The reduction of the sack or *ḫȝr* to half of its capacity and the assimilation of the name artaba to this measure, should have occurred during the Persian period. Unfortunately, we seem to know relatively little of the relevant metric subsystem of the Persians. Herodotos tells us of an artaba that contained 3 χ more than the Attic medimnos (I 192), but this particular artaba seems to be unknown from Semitic texts of the Persian Empire.[22] What is known of the Persian measures is a single *irtiba* consisting of 3 *kurrima* (BAR) or 30 *daduya* (QA), which is to be found in texts from Persepolis.[23] Its contents can be calculated to have been some 30 litres, both after the traditionally accepted values of its constituent parts,[24] and after an actual inscribed cup found in Persepolis.[25] The Aramaic documents from Egypt, which mention a *'ardab* consisting in all probability of 3 *griw* or 30 *ḥpn* (*ḥofen*), assure that this artaba

---

20   Compare for instance the obscure group in *P. dem. Ryl.* IX, 16, 18.

21   Possibly, the early Roman demotic formula *n p3 ḥy n iyp.t*, "with the *oipe*-measure" (see M. Lichtheim, *Demotic Ostraca from Medinet Habu* [Chicago 1957] p. 36, no. 65 [n. 1] etc.) was meant to express exactly the same idea as the present formula; cf. (Gr.) *O. Stras.* 331 and 332.

22   See B. Porten, *Archives from Elephantine* (Los Angeles 1968) 71 n. 54.

23   See R. T. Hallock, *Persepolis Fortification Tablets* (Chicago 1969) 72.

24   See for example R. Borger, *Babylonisch-Assyrische Lesestück* (Roma 1963) II, 103 § 44 19).

25   See E. F. Schmidt, *Persepolis* (Chicago 1957) II, 108-9.

was indeed introduced in Egypt.[26] So, I think it a reasonable conclusion to regard the artaba of 60 *hin*, which has served as our
starting-point, as the direct descendant of the Persian measure of
±30 litres. This implies a proportion between the *hofen* and the
hin of 1:2 (or, the *hin* to have been 1/2 *hofen*). This proportion
is rather important, I think, if it is assumed correctly, because
it would enable the Greeks coming to Egypt to adapt their own choinix to the Persian measure called *hofen* in Aramaic, resulting in a
proportion of 1:2 between the choinix and the Egyptian *hin* (or,
making one *hin* equal to 1/2 choinix). The choinix would accordingly
hold some 9 to 10 decilitres, or a slight litre, or roughly one U.S.
liquid quart.[27]

GREEK			DEMOTIC	ARAMAIC
	ἀρτάβη		*r t b*	
40 1.	40 χ		(80 *hin* – 40 1.)	
30 1.	29/30 χ	29/30 χ	60 *hin* – 30 1.	30 *hofen* – 30 1.

This is my reconstruction of the history of the Egyptian grain-
measures. To resume it once more for the sake of clarity, we have
seen that the Egyptians adopted the Persian *ardab* of ±30 litres. We
have come to suppose that the Egyptians halved their sack or *h3r* to
a measure of ±40 litres, probably under the influence of Persian
metrology. This measure of ±40 litres was adopted by the Greeks as
the artaba of 40 χ. Both artabai continued to be used through the
Ptolemaic period.

Factual proof of this reconstruction, be it textual or archaeological, is not known to me. Any new text could bring the
needed evidence of course, but we should rather look forward to new
bilingual texts, or bilingual text-corpora from a single town or
village of Ptolemaic Egypt. I should think of a place like

---

26 See B. Porten, op. cit., 70f. (In Pers. Fort. Tabl. 2072,
BAR is glossed *griw* in Aramaic script; *kurrima* (BAR) and *griw* are
in fact the same word; see Hallock, op. cit., 72f.) For the capacity of the *hofen*, see Porten, op. cit., 71 (nn. 52-53); cf. P.
Grelot, in *Semitica* 14 (1964) 70 n. 2 (rather than p. 63f.).

27 Compare Schmidt ("liquid quart"), op. cit., 109, with n.
3 above. The Attic choinix is known to have been 1.1-1.2 litres;
see M. Lang & M. Crosby, *Weights, Measures and Tokens* (Princeton
1964) 47-48.

Pathyris, from where also smaller texts, ostraka and such like,
seem to have been preserved in considerable numbers. Or, the
splendid demotic and Greek archives from Fayumic Hawara, as a second example, seem quite promising for our subject, even because
they are from the Fayum, and should acquaint us with new descriptions of the relevant measures.[28] It is much to be hoped that the
distinguished scholars engaged in publications of Hawara-texts will
satisfy our curiosity before very long.

A second way of attacking the uncertainties in our reconstruction would be, rather obviously I think, the measurement of actual
grain-measures. Only few of them seem to be known from Egypt. In
fact, no choinix measures have been published so far as I know, and
perhaps only one Egyptian grain-measure, from the Cairo Museum, unfortunately of Roman date.[29] Here again, it is much to be hoped,
if more grain-measures are extant, that they will be published soon,
even if their capacities are not inscribed on the objects themselves.
The measurement of a fair sample of them should reveal the capacity
of the constituent measure by their common multiple.

The capstone of metrology is of course the acquired ability to
supply all sorts of real figures to the uses attested for the measures in the documents. In dilemmas such as ours, this might be
put to the advantage of the metrologist. We may never expect very
clear results in this proceeding, however. For instance, if we
hear from texts of the Zenon-archive that 1 to 2 choinikes of grain
were the daily allowances to the employees of the estate of Apollonios the dioiketes, this would provide us with a minimum for the
choinix, admissable on our knowledge of subsistence diets, *if* we
could only be sure that the men had no other sources of income.[30]
Or, as a second example, if we are informed how many artabai it

---

28 The only instance e.g., of the demotic formula " (with the
oipe of) 40 *hin*" outside the marriage-contracts is to be found in
E.A.E. Reymond, *Embalmers' Archives from Hawara* (Oxford 1973) doc. 7.

29 See A. Lucas & A. Rowe, "Ancient Egyptian Measures of Capacity," *ASAE* 40 (1940) 77, no. 4; cf. the remarks by O. Guéraud,
JJurPap 4 (1950) 107 bottom.

30 See D. J. Crawford, "Food: Tradition and Change in Hellenistic Egypt," *World Archaeology* 11 (1979) 143.

took to sow an aroura of land,[31] we need only settle the numerous variables (such as condition of the soil, manuring, irrigation, care of the crop, climate, species of grain),[32] to be able to compare the 18th or 19th century production figures from Egypt[33] in a confident manner with classical conditions.

Along these lines, I imagine, we would overcome the uncertainties that oppress us, if to overcome them we choose.

University of Leiden   Sven Vleeming

---

31   See M. Schnebel, *Landwirtschaft* etc. (München 1925) 125 n. 5 (1-1/2 artaba per aroura), and 126 (±1.2-1.3 *dito*).

32   See the preliminary remarks by D. J. Crawford, "The Opium Poppy: A Study in Ptolemaic Agriculture," *Problèmes de la Terre en Grèce Ancienne*, ed. M. I. Finley (Paris 1973) 224-28.

33   Quantities of seed for sowing from modern Egypt are cited by P. S. Girard, "Mémoire sur l'Agriculture, *etc.*," *Description de l'Egypte* (éd. Panckoucke) T. 17 (Paris 1824) p. 49 and 51 (± A.D. 1800); and by Schnebel, op. cit., 127 under n. 3 (± 1880).

Proceedings of the XVI Int. Congr. of Papyrology (Chico 1981) 547-552

GRIECHISCH-DEMOTISCHE SOLDATENKORRESPONDENZ
AUS PATHYRIS (GEBELEN)

Im Gebiet von Pathyris und dem benachbarten Krokodilopolis befand sich bekanntlich im II. Jahrh. v. Chr. ein grosses Militär-
zentrum.[1] Die dort stationierten Truppen waren unter den Einwohnern
dieser Umgebung, meistens Ägyptern, angeworben und erscheinen in den
aus Pathyris stammenden zahlreichen Urkunden verschiedener Art. Unter ihnen sind es vor allem griechische und demotische Privatbriefe,
in denen zumindest ein Partner ein Militärangehöriger ist:[2]

1. P. Louvre 10594   vom 15. Jan. 130
   S. de Ricci, *APF* 2 (1903) 518; St. Witkowski,
   Epistulae privatae graecae (Leipzig 1911) Nr. 43;
   WChr. 10.

2. P. Heid. dem. 781b   vom 30 Dez. 110[3]
   U. Kaplony-Heckel, *Festschrift Ägyptisches Museum
   Berlin* (Berlin 1974) 289; 292, Abb. 1; Taf. 42.

3. P. New York (Pierpont Morgan Library)
   + P.BM 626   vom 29. Juni 103
   P. Amh. II 39, Taf. 7; *P. Grenf.* I 30; S. de
   Ricci, *APF* 2 (1903) 517; Witkowski, o.c., Nr. 57;
   BL I 1, 181; *BL* IV 1, 34.

4. P.BM dem. 040 + P. Berl. dem. 13381   vom 27. Sept. 103
   Kaplony-Heckel, *Festschrift Ägyptisches Museum
   Berlin*, 289-92, Abb. 2, Taf. 43.

5. P.BM 628   vom 17. April 102
   P. Grenf. I 32; *BL* I 181; *BL* V 37.

---

1 Vgl. P. W. Pestman, "Les archives privées de Pathyris à
l'époque ptolémaïque. La famille de Pétéharsemtheus, fils de
Panebkhounis," *P. L. Bat.* 14 (1965) 50; J. K. Winnicki, *Ptolemäerarmee in Thebais* (Wrocław-Warszawa 1978) 68-78.

2 Aus Pathyris stammt noch ein fragmentarischer Brief an den
Hipparchen Dryton (P. Heid. dem. 742a - *ZÄS* 42 [1905] 50-51, Facs.).

3 Zum Datum siehe jetzt P. W. Pestman, *P. L. Bat.* 19 (1978)
22.

6. P. Heid. dem. 742b + 781a   vom 23. Sept. 102
    W. Spiegelberg, ZÄS 42 (1905) 50, Facs.; Kaplony-
    Heckel, *Festschrift Ägyptisches Museum Berlin*,
    291-93, Abb. 3, Taf. 44.

7. P. Heid. dem. 746   vom 12. August 99[4]
    Spiegelberg, ZÄS 42 (1905) 48-50, Facs.

8. P. Louvre 10593   vom 12. Jan. 98[4]
    de Ricci, *APF* 2 (1903) 515-16.

9. P. BM 680   vom 21. Mai 95
    P. Grenf. II 36; Witkowski, o.c., Nr. 64;
    Sel. Pap. I 103; *BL* I 186; *BL* II 2,71; *BL* IV 35.

10. P. Leipzig 511   vom 30. Juni 95
    P. Lips. 104; Witkowski, o.c., Nr. 63; *BL* I 214;
    BL II 2,79; *BL* III 92; *BL* IV 42.

Manche dieser Briefe entstammen schon bekannten Archiven; so
Nr. 1 dem Archiv des Dryton,[5] Nr. 9 und 10 dem des Peteharsemtheus.[6]
Ein besonderes Archiv bilden die an den Hegemonen Pates adressier-
ten Nr. 3. 4. 6. 7. 8.[7]

Viel Platz beanspruchen in den Briefen die in üblichen Formeln[8]
abgefassten Grüsse an die Empfänger sowie die Mitteilung über das
Wohlbefinden der Absender. In einigen Fällen hat man sogar den Ein-
druck, dass der Briefschreiber nur den Zweck verfolgt, von sich
hören zu lassen. Doch enthalten einige Briefe einen, wenn auch

---

4 Es wird angenommen, dass sich das 15. Jahr in Nr. 7 und das
16. in Nr. 8 auf die Regierung des Alexander beziehen. Es ist aber
auch möglich, dass es sich hier um Regierungsjahre Kleopatras III.
handelt. In dieser Zeit sind die Doppelregierungsjahre üblich,
obwohl Ausnahmen vorkommen, zu denen ich aber vorliegenden Brief
nicht rechnen möchte.

5 Siehe J. K. Winnicki, *Eos* 60 (1972) 343-53.

6 Siehe P. W. Pestman, *P. L. Bat.* 14 (1965) 71, Nr. 59 und 60.

7 In den Briefen 4. 6. 7, in denen Grussempfänger mit Namen
genannt werden, kommt u.a. ein Poeris, der Sohn des Nechutes vor.
Ihn finden wir vielleicht auch in der fragmentarischen Nr. 5. Gehört dieser Brief zu dem Archiv?

8 Vgl. darüber B. Olsson, *Papyrusbriefe aus der frühesten
Römerzeit* (Uppsala 1925) 12.

fragmentierten Text von historischer Bedeutung, die ich hier behandeln will.

Zunächst ist hervorzuheben, dass Verfasser und Empfänger der
meisten Briefe keine Einzelpersonen, sondern Personengruppen sind,
wie z.B. in Nr. 3, Z. 1-4:

Πόρτεις ἡ[γ]εμὼν τῶν ἐν προχειρισ-
μῶι καὶ οἱ [ἐκ] τοῦ σημείου νεανίσκοι
Πατῆτι [καὶ] Παχράτηι καὶ τοῖς ἄλλοις
[στ]ρ[α]τιώται[ς] πᾶσι χαίρειν.

Wenn auch der Verfasser von Nr. 9 und 10 als Einzelperson erscheint,
so spricht er doch im Namen von sechs genannten Personen καὶ οἱ παρ'
ἡμῶν πάντες, die sich nach seiner Mitteilung einer guten Gesundheit
erfreuen, also mit ihm zusammen sind.

Die Anzahl von Soldaten, die in Briefen gruppenweise erscheinen
und Grüsse an Freunde und Familienmitglieder entsenden oder von
ihrem Wohlbefinden sprechen, macht deutlich, dass in den Ortschaften, in denen die Briefe geschrieben wurden, grössere Truppenkontingente stationert waren und ihr Aufenthalt sicherlich nicht mit
Privatangelegenheiten, sondern mit dem Militärberuf in Verbindung
steht.

Wie sich aus dem Inhalt der Briefe ergibt, sind sie ausserhalb
von Pathyris geschrieben. Nur gelegentlich nennen die Verfasser
ihren Aufenthaltsort. In Nr. 4 äussert der Verfasser, dass er den
Brief in *Ptlwmjs* schreibt, in Nr. 9 lädt ein anderer die Empfänger
seines Schreibens zu sich nach Diospolis zum Getreideeinkauf ein.
In beiden Fällen ist es aber ohne zusätzliche Angaben unmöglich
festzustellen, um welche Ortschaften es sich genau handelt.

Den Aufenthaltsort eines Briefschreibers können wir manchmal
aber auch der Einleitungsformel entnehmen:

Nr. 5, Z. 5-6:

] ἐρρώμεθα δὲ καὶ αὐτοὶ ὑμῶν τὴν ἀρίστην [ὑγίειαν
εὐχόμενοι] παρὰ τοῖς ἐν Πηλουσίωι θεοῖς

Nr. 6, Z. 4:

A sm r B dj m-b3ḥ B3-nb-Ḏd.t p3 ntr ᶜ3 Ḥr-p3-ḥrd
A segnet B hier vor dem Widder, Herrn von Mendes, dem
grossen Gott, und vor Harpokrates.

Nr. 7, Z. 4-5:

> *A sm r B dj m-b3ḥ Ḥr-p3-ẖrd*
> A segnet B hier vor Harpokrates.

Diese Formel nennt im allgemeinen entweder die Götter sowie den
Ort, in dem der Briefschreiber sich aufhält, oder nur den Gott, der
an dem betreffenden Ort besondere Verehrung geniesst.[9] In Nr. 5
und 6 ist der Aufenthaltsort angegeben. In 7 ist die Angabe nicht
eindeutig; denn Harpokrates war in der Ptolemäerzeit zu populär, um
ihn mit einer bestimmten Ortschaft in Verbindung setzen zu können.

Von besonderem Interesse sind die Briefe Nr. 4 und 6, von
Panebchunis, dem "Geschäftsführer (*rd*) des Suchos und des Nechtha-
raus" verfasst. In der Grussformel von 4 nennt er 24 Personen, u.a.
den Hegemon Pates, seinen Freund Pachrates,[10] einen Fähnlein-Träger
und einen "Mann, der ausgewählt ist."[11] In der Anschrift auf der
Rückseite sind sie als "Hegemon Pates und seine Genossen" bezeichnet. In 6 grüsst Panebchunis wieder Pates, Pachrates, vier weitere Personen und "ihre Genossen." In beiden Briefen zeigt sich ein
freundliches Verhältnis des Absenders zu dem Militär in Pathyris.
Es entsteht aber die Frage, welche Rolle der Absender ausserhalb
von Pathyris spielt. Hierauf erhalten wir eine ungefähre Antwort
aus seinen Briefen:

Nr. 4, Z. 17-19:

> *iw=j hb n=tn p3j bk ḥr t3 bw3 n Ptlwmjs š n=f pr-ᶜ3 r*
> *Dmsḳ3 ḥ3ᶜ=f wᶜ ḏnḥ n rmt mšᶜ (n) p3 dmj (m?) tw=w šm*
> *ḥr-r3=w*
> Ich schreibe euch dieses Schreiben auf dem Hochland von
> Ptlwmjs. Der König ging nach Dm-sḳ3. Er liess eine
> Unterabteilung von Leuten des Heeres in der Ortschaft.
> Man soll mit ihnen losgehen.[12]

---

9 Vgl. K.-Th. Zauzich, *Ägyptische Handschriften*, Teil 2
(Wiesbaden 1971) XIV-XV.

10 In allen Briefen erscheint als einer der Grussempfänger
direkt hinter Pates ein Pachrates, der in Nr. 3. 7. 8 auch in der
Anschrift genannt und dem letzten Brief als Hegemon bezeichnet wird.
Vielleicht ist Pachrates ein enger Freund des Pates.

11 Nach Frau U. Kaplony-Heckel, *Festschrift Ägyptisches Museum
Berlin*, 296h soll der Titel die ägyptische Widergabe des griechischen
ἔξω τάξεων sein. Ich teile diese Meinung nicht.

12 Die Transkription folgt der Edition mit der Ausnahme von
Dmsḳ3, das dort als *Tmst3* gelesen wurde. Die hier vorgeschlagene
Lesung, die auch W. Clarysse in Leiden unabhängig von mir angenommen
hat, scheint sicher zu sein.

Nr. 6, Z. 5-6:

tw=j šp šms (n)dr.t nȝ srtj[t]s.w dr=w m-šs
Ich empfange viele Dienstleistungen von allen Stratioten.

Aus beiden Briefen geht klar hervor, dass sich Panebchunis bei dem
Heer aufhält, wobei seine Rolle nicht untergeordnet zu sein scheint.
Möglicherweise soll er mit den Soldaten nach Dmsk̠ȝ gehen.
Aus den geographischen Angaben der Texte folgt, dass sich

der König "bei dem Heer in Pelusium"   am 20. Febr. 102,[13]
die Truppen aus Pathyris in Pelusium   am 17. April 102(5),
die Truppen aus Pathyris in Mendes   am 23. Sept. 102(6),

aufhielten. Die Anwesenheit des Königs und der Truppen kann zwei-
felsohne mit einer äusseren Bedrohung der ägyptischen Grenze in
Verbindung stehen. Tatsächlich finden wir 103/102 Ptolemaios IX.
Soter II. mit 30,000 Mann in Syrien. Er war Herrscher über Gaza
und hatte einen Vorstoss gegen Ägypten versucht.[14] 102 endete aber
das syrische Abenteuer Soters II., und wir müssen annehmen, dass
sie in den Briefen genannten Truppenkontingente schon früher, nicht
lange nach seiner Landung in Syrien, im Grenzgebiet stationiert
waren. Unter diesen Umständen können wir vermuten, dass Panebchunis am Feldzug gegen Soter teilgenommen hat. Demgemäss kann die
von ihm genannte Ortschaft Ptlwmjs, in der er am 27. Sept. 103 seinen Brief schrieb nur Ptolemais-Akka gewesen sein, das laut Josephus
(*Ant.* XIII 352) von Kleopatra erobert worden ist. Nicht weit davon
muss auch der zweite von ihm genannte Ort Dmsk̠ȝ liegen. Eine Ortschaft mit ähnlichem Konsonantenbestand kommt in den hieroglyphi-
schen Texten als Bezeichnung für Damaskus vor (Gauthier, *Dict.*
géogr. VI 42), das meines Erachtens in unserem Fall auch gemeint ist.
     Von einer späteren Militäraktion erfahren wir aus den von
Petesuchos,[15] dem Sohn des Peteharsemtheus, verfassten Briefen 9

---

     13 Die demotische Stele aus dem Serapeum in Memphis ist publ.
von W. Spiegelberg, *ZÄS* 57 (1922) 69.

     14 Vgl. W. Otto-H. Bengtson, *Zur Geschichte des Niederganges*
des Ptolemäerreiches (München 1938) 186-87; H. Volkmann, *RE* XXIII 2
(1959) 1741-42 u. 1745. Zu Einzelheiten siehe den Vortrag von E.
Van 't Dack, supra, pp. 303ff.

     15 Nur von seinem Vater weiss man, dass er Söldner gewesen
ist (siehe Pestman, *P. L. Bat.* 14 [1965] 95); es ist aber durchaus
wahrscheinlich, dass der Sohn denselben Beruf ausübt.

und 10 vom Jahr 95. Beide betreffen Privatangelegenheiten, doch
aus dem Text von 9, Z. 9-13, kann man wohl schliessen, dass der
Verfasser mit seinen Kameraden an irgendeinem Kampf teilnehmen
sollte:

μὴ λυ-
πεῖσθε ἐπὶ τοῖς χωρισθεῖσι. ὑπε|λαμβάνοσαν
φονευθήσεσθαι. οὐθὲν | ἡμῖν κακὸν ἐποίησεν ἀλλ᾿ ἐκ
τῶν | ἐναντίων ἐπιμεμέληται.

Beide Briefe sind in einem Zeitabstand von 39 Tagen geschrieben, so
kann man vermuten, dass sie von demselben Unternehmen stammen, an
dem nach 10 auch Ptolion, wohl ein Militärstratege,[16] teilgenommen
hat. Wo aber diese Aktion stattgefunden hat, ist unsicher. In 9
lädt Petesuchos die Briefempfänger, wie bereits gesagt, zu sich
nach Diospolis ein, Getreide zu kaufen, wozu in einem getreiderei-
chen Land wie Ägypten, wenn nicht in Pathyris selbst, doch sicherlich in der näheren Umgebung die Möglichkeit bestand. So wird man
in diesem Zusammenhang an Gross- oder Kleindiospolis denken.

Warschau   J. K. Winnicki

---

16   Über Ptolion siehe jetzt L. Mooren, *Ancient Society* 4
(1973) 131-32.

Proceedings of the XVI Int. Congr. of Papyrology (Chico 1981) 553-556

VORSCHLAG FÜR EINE DEMOTISCHE BERICHTIGUNGSLISTE

Wenn sich Spezialisten für die griechische und die demotische
Papyruskunde begegnen--so wie es auf diesem Kongreß geschieht--,
dann können die Demotisten leicht etwas neidisch werden, weil die
Demotistik der Papyrologie so deutlich nachhinkt. Selbst die fun-
damentalsten Nachschlagewerke, die für den Papyrologen zum selbstverständlich gewordenen und täglich gebrauchten Werkzeug gehören,
müssen für die Demotistik erst noch geschaffen werden. Immerhin,
an einem umfassenden Wörterbuch wird seit einigen Jahren wieder gearbeitet, worüber Frau Johnson hier am Samstag berichten wird. Für
ein Sammelbuch ist möglicherweise mit dem Recueil von Herrn Pestman
der Anfang gemacht.

Für die segensreiche Einrichtung der Berichtigungsliste gibt
es dagegen bisher auf demotischer Seite kein Gegenstück. Dabei
wäre ein solches Werk hier beinahe noch dringender, weil die Mög-
lichkeiten zum Irrtum bei der Entzifferung demotischer Texte un-
gleich größer als bei der Entzifferung griechischer Texte sind. Wer
Demotisch kann, weiß was ich meine--für die anderen mag der Hinweis
genügen, daß die demotische Schrift über einige Hunderte verschiedene Zeichen verfügt, die vielfach auch noch mehrdeutig sind.

Über die Notwendigkeit einer demotischen Berichtigungsliste
wird es daher keine Meinungsverschiedenheit geben, und ich brauche
darüber nicht weiter zu reden. Diskutiert werden muß dagegen die
Frage, ob die Art und Weise, wie ich ein solches Unternehmen organi-
sieren möchte, der Sache angemessen ist und den Wünschen der künftigen Benutzer entspricht. Bitte lassen Sie mich meinen Entwurf
kurz vorstellen, der im gegenwärtigen Planungsstadium noch leicht
zu verändern ist, wenn entsprechende Wünsche geäußert werden.

Daß die *Correctiones Demoticae*, wie ich das Unternehmen nennen
will, nicht einfach das Muster der griechischen Berichtigungsliste
nachahmen können, liegt in der Natur der Sache. Wollte man in
erster Linie nur die bereits irgendwo abgedruckten Korrekturen
übersichtlich zusammenstellen, so wäre die Arbeit ziemlich schnell
erledigt. Ich glaube, daß eine demotische Berichtigungsliste vor

allem danach streben muß, die ungedruckten Korrekturen allgemein
zugänglich zu machen, die die einzelnen Kollegen am Rande ihrer
Privatexemplare der Texteditionen notiert haben. Da das Verfassen
von Miszellen nicht jedermanns Sache ist, da mancher unter uns aus
Rücksicht auf irrende Kollegen sogar vor dem Schreiben von Rezensionen zurückschreckt, bleibt vieles, was längst zum Wissen einzelner Gelehrter gehört, der Allgemeinheit verborgen und muß von
anderen immer wieder neu gefunden werden. Daß dieser Umstand den
Fortschritt unserer Wissenschaft deutlich hemmt, dürfte auch dem
rücksichtsvollsten Kollegen einleuchten. Die *Correctiones Demoticae* wollen hier Abhilfe schaffen, indem sie eine Möglichkeit zur
Berichtigung von Irrtümern anbieten, die den irrenden Kollegen--das
wird jeder, der demotische Texte publiziert, gelegentlich sein--
weitgehend schont.

Aus verschiedenen Gründen habe ich vor, die einzelnen Korrek-
turvorschläge jeweils auf einzelne Blätter zu schreiben--je 200
Blatt ergeben eine Lieferung, vier bis fünf Lieferungen passen in
einen Ordner.[1] Ich hatte zuerst erwogen, Karteikarten im Format
DIN A 6 (also halb so groß wie die Ihnen vorliegenden Zettel) zu
verwenden, habe dann aber schnell davon Abstand genommen, weil das
einerseits zu teuer wird und weil andrerseits Karteikarten zu viel
Platz brauchen. Druckt man aber auf dünnes und preiswertes Papier,
so darf der einzelne Zettel aus Gründen der Handlichkeit kaum
kleiner als die Musterzettel (im Format DIN A 5) sein.[2]

Das vorgeschlagene System hat einige Vorzüge, die ich jetzt
aufzählen möchte.

(1) Jeder Kollege, der zur Mitarbeit bereit ist, braucht nur
entsprechende Formblätter mit der Hand auszufüllen und mir zu
schicken. Ich würde die Angaben dann mit der Maschine neu schreiben und in Druck geben. Der Name des jeweiligen Bearbeiters würde
in Feld 17 erscheinen. Die demotische Berichtigungsliste könnte
also eine wirkliche Gemeinschaftsarbeit vieler Kollegen werden.

---

1 Beim Vortrag in New York wurden 15 Musterzettel im Format
DIN A 5 sowie der Schlüssel für das Formblatt verteilt. Davon kann
hier nur ein Beispiel zusammen mit dem Schlüssel abgedruckt werden.

2 An dieser Stelle wurden im Vortrag die einzelnen Beispiele
kurz erörtert, um die Anwendbarkeit des Systems auf verschiedene
Quellen (ungedruckte Korrekturen, Berichtigungen aus Rezensionen,
Artikeln, Büchern) zu demonstrieren.

1 Text- art	2 Name des Museums oder der Sammlung	3 Inventarnummer		4 Zeile
5 alte Lesung (Umschrift wie in der Originalpublikation)		6 Fundstelle (ohne Verfassername)	7 Jahr	8 Seite
9 neue Lesung (Umschrift nach den Grenobler Empfehlungen)		10 Fundstelle (mit Verfassername)	11 Jahr	12 Seite

13
kurzer Kommentar zum Korrekturvorschlag, sofern erforderlich
 	
   Abkürzungen in Feld 1:
   I = Inschrift
   M = Mumientäfelchen
   O = Ostrakon
   P = Papyrus				

14 Zettel-Nr.	15 CoDe Lieferungs-Nr.	16 Monat der Lieferung	17 Bearbeiter	

I	Ann Arbor	25804		1
	m R̠-kd (?)	Demotica II	1928	37
	š˓ dt			
	"in Ewigkeit" verdeutlichende Abschrift: vgl. Glossar S. 687/8			
Muster 1	CoDe O	Juli 1980	K.-Th.Z.	

(2) Die einzelnen Zettel lassen sich nach den Inventarnummern
der Texte ordnen. Wer die Einzellieferungen regelmäßig einsortiert,
braucht später bei der Arbeit immer nur *einmal* nachzusehen.
(3) Das System ist sehr beweglich und läßt sich für verschiedene Aufgaben verwenden.
(4) Sollte sich einmal herausstellen, daß eine bestimmte Korrektur falsch, also eine "Verschlimmbesserung" war--das kann ja
schwerlich ganz ausbleiben--, so läßt sich der betreffende Zettel
später leicht austauschen.

Ich will nicht verschweigen, daß den vielen Vorzügen der *Cor-
rectiones Demoticae* ein möglicher Nachteil gegenüberzustellen ist.
Es könnte unter Umständen geschehen, daß durch das Unternehmen die
Freundschaft unter den Demotisten Schaden nimmt--und das wäre in
der Tat ein hoher, ein zu hoher Preis. Ich will versuchen, dem da-
durch vorzubeugen, daß ich als Herausgeber einige Dinge aus dem
Werk heraushalten werde, die leicht zum Ärger Anlaß geben können.
In den *Correctiones Demoticae* soll folgendes nicht vorkommen: (1)
Polemik, (2) Quisquilienkritik, (3) "bevorzugte" Behandlung einiger
Kollegen, (4) Korrekturen zu besonders fehlerreichen Publikationen,
die besser erst einmal durch eine Neupublikation ersetzt werden
sollten.

Ich hoffe, daß auf diese Weise die *Correctiones Demoticae* zu
einem nützlichen und willkommenen Hilfsmittel der Demotistik werden
und auch die Zusammenarbeit zwischen Papyrologie und Demotistik
fördern können. Wenn Ihnen mein Vorschlag im ganzen als gut und
richtig erscheint--Einzelheiten lassen sich, wie gesagt, noch
ändern--, dann bitte ich Sie schon jetzt um Ihre künftige Mitarbeit.

Am Rande des Kongresses haben die anwesenden Spezialisten für
demotische Studien den Plan der *Correctiones Demoticae* in zwei Sit-
zungen diskutiert und grundsätzlich begrüßt. Die dabei vorgetrage-
nen Wünsche der Kollegen, insbesondere die Beigabe von Indices betreffend, werden berücksichtigt werden. Gesonderte schriftliche
Einladungen zur Mitarbeit an der ersten Lieferung werden in Kürze
versandt.

Mainz   Karl-Theodor Zauzich

PART 9

THE APOKRIMATA

Proceedings of the XVI Int. Congr. of Papyrology (Chico 1981) 559-573

ON THE INTENDED USE OF P. COL. 123

I hope it may be considered an expression of *pietas* to examine once again the question to which my revered teacher, the late Professor A. Arthur Schiller, devoted one of his last publications,[1] namely the purpose of the scribe of the Columbia Apokrimata Papyrus,[2] or as it would perhaps be better to phrase it, the intended use of this papyrus. The issue was much debated by many of those who discussed the papyrus in the years immediately following its publication. That no consensus has been reached over the years is evidenced by the fact that as recently as within the last few years major scholars have taken sharply contrary views. I would like, then, to survey the various suggestions which have been given to answer this question as well as some of the arguments for and against them, and finally place the solution which Professor Schiller accepted towards the end of his life into the context of the evidence of other papyri.

What, then, could have been the intended uses of this papyrus? Several of the scholars who discussed the papyrus after its publication proposed an official initiative of one sort or another.

One suggestion is that this papyrus is the copy of a register or index of the rescripts in the archive. This is a position represented particularly by d'Ors, who presented this view as soon as the

---

1 A. Arthur Schiller, "The Copy of the Apokrimata Subscripts," *BASP* 14 (1977) 75-82.

2 *P. Col.* 123, published as *Apokrimata. Decisions of Septimius Severus on Legal Matters*. Text, translation, and historical analysis by William Linn Westermann. Legal commentary by A. Arthur Schiller (New York 1954), hereafter cited as *Apokrimata*. The text substantially revised by Herbert C. Youtie with revised legal commentary by A. Arthur Schiller, was published as "Second Thoughts on the Columbia *Apokrimata* (P.Col. 123)," *Cd'E* 30 (1955) 327-45. The revised text reprinted in Ernst Schönbauer, "Die neu gefundenen Reskripte des Septimius Severus," *AnzWien* 94 (1957) 165-97 at 167-68; *SB* VI 9526; E. Volterra, "Il problema del testo delle constituzioni imperiali," *La critica del testo: Atti II Congr. internaz. d. Soc. ital. di storia del Diritto* (Firenze 1971) 821-1097 at 922-23. Bibliography in Naphtali Lewis, "The Imperial Apokrimata," *RIDA* 3 Ser. 25 (1978) 261-78 and Schiller (supra n. 1).

papyrus appeared,[3] and as recently as in last year's *AJP*.[4] In this
view the texts in the papyrus are the sharply excerpted precis of
the original rescripts. This would explain, says d'Ors, the exces-
sively laconic and obscure character of the texts, particularly as
compared with those recorded in the codes. One would expect, however, if a register is to be more than a list of names, and our
text is clearly more than that, that the excerpts would indicate,
however briefly, the subject matter treated in the decision. This,
however, is not always the case.

Another variation of this theory that the papyrus is a register of rescripts in the archive was suggested by Levy, in fact many
years before the first publication, namely that the texts in the
papyrus are the stenographic report of the emperor's oral response
to the petitions.[5] The responses would then have been elaborated
by the bureau for placement in the archives, from which in turn the
texts of the codes were drawn. The original oral responses of the
emperor are here kept as a register of the fuller texts to be found
elsewhere. The advantage of this view is that the texts read better as a response directly referring to a petition in which the
facts of a case are presented. On the other hand, raw drafts of
responses seem odd material from which to compose a register.

Both these variations of the register theory are intended primarily to explain what their authors view as a substantial difference between the laconic style of the rescripts in our papyrus and
the fuller style of those in the codes. Not everyone felt this
difference so strongly. Professor Schiller insisted that our texts
are not any briefer than other such texts.[6] In his favor it may be
said that though the texts in the codes and the rescripts whose
texts are sufficiently intact in the papyri do generally have a
more definite meaning than do some of our rescripts, we have to keep

---

3 Alvaro d'Ors, *Emeritá* 24 (1956) 417-25 at 418-19; "Notulas
sobre los Apokrimata de P. Col. 123," *Eos* 48.3 (= *Symbolae Taubenschlag* III) (1956) 83-88 at 85.

4 Alvaro d'Ors and Fernando Martin, "*Propositio Libellorum*,"
AJP 100 (1979) 111-24 at 120.

5 Ernst Levy apud Schiller, *Apokrimata* 41 n. 7.

6 *Apokrimata* 41 n. 7, and (supra n. 1) 81.

in mind that in the selection process that went into making the
codes or the rescripts used as precedents the unintelligible or
useless rescripts were no doubt weeded out.

A second suggestion takes us to the offices of the *strategoi*
in the nome capitals of Egypt, to which, in this theory, such
copies of imperial rescripts were sent. There they would be of
obvious use to the strategos. So Arangio-Ruiz.[7]

Lewis has suggested that the copies of the rescripts were
posted in the metropoleis of the nomes where the petitions were
originally submitted, for the convenience of the addressees.[8] This
would explain why the names of the petitioners are given but not
the texts of the petitions. Each petitioner can identify his answer by his name, and he knows what his petition was. This suggestion has the great merit that it makes the procedure of the imperial
jurisdiction in Egypt similar to that of the prefect of Egypt. As
Lewis pointed out, we know for a fact that a prefect of Egypt at
about this time ordered that the decisions given on the petitions
submitted at the conventus be posted both in Alexandria and *epi
topōn*, in the localities.[9] We also know that in other respects the
emperor used the conventus procedure. Hence it is attractive to
suppose that in the matter of posting as well the imperial practice
matched that of the prefect. The problem is that otherwise it
seems that the imperial bureaucracy never took the trouble to post
rescripts anywhere except at the residence of the emperor at the
time.[10] This is what led Professor Schiller to reject this suggestion.[11] I would just say in defense of Lewis' theory that it could
well be that when the emperor was in Egypt, the prefectural bureaucracy was involved in handling the paperwork, and this bureaucracy

---

7   Vincenzo Arangio-Ruiz, *Gnomon* 28 (1956) 186-92 at 188.

8   Naphtali Lewis, "Notationes Legentis, 29," *BASP* 13 (1976)
11.

9. *P. Yale* I 61.

10   Wynne Williams, "The *Libellus* Procedure and the Severan
Papyri," *JRS* 64 (1974) 86-103 at 98-101, along the lines set by
Ulrich Wilcken, "Zu den Kaiserreskripten," *Hermes* 55 (1920) 1-42
at 18-27.

11   Supra (n. 1), 77.

does seem to have been concerned to get the rescripts to the localities.

Yet another variation of the theory that this is an official
copy was given by Seidl.[12] Our document is in his view an official
publication intended neither for the use of officials nor as notice
to the petitioners, but rather to inform the public of the disposi-
tion of these cases. The interest of the public he supposes, is
not juristic but "journalistic," that is the publication is not intended to satisfy public curiosity on the state of the law, as is
the case with modern law reports, but to satisfy the public curiosity on the outcome of cases of some notoriety. In this theory the
"In Alexandria" at the top of the page functions rather like the
date-line at the opening of a modern newspaper article. Seidl discusses the various cases individually to show the so-called journalistic interest of each. Certainly #11, the case of Comon and
Apion, could have been notorious. Seidl's case is less strong for
the others.

Most writers preferred to see in the document the product of
private initiative. For what purpose? One possibility is that
this was an effort on the part of the petitioners from a particular
locality who arranged to have all their rescripts copied at once to
save them the trouble of coming into Alexandria. This suggestion
is similar to that of Lewis in that the purpose is the information
to the petitioners, but since it assumes a private rather than official initiative, it is not susceptible to the criticism that the
imperial bureaux are not known to have been so considerate of private individuals. Schiller considered this possibility too and
rejected it on the grounds that it was unlikely that so many petitions came from one place at one time.[13] However, several points
can be made in defense of this theory, and were made by Gaudemet[14]
and by Stein.[15] First of all, the petitioners may be from one

---

12 Erwin Seidl, "Neue Klassische Konstitutionen aus den Papyri," *Studi Calderini e Paribeni* (Milan 1957) II, 307-15 at 308-9;
idem, *Rechtsgeschichte Ägyptens als römischer Provinz* (Sankt Augustin 1973) 31-40, esp. 33-34.

13 *Apokrimata*, 100.

14 J. Gaudemet, *RHDFE* 33 (1955) 475-81 at 478.

15 Peter Stein, *Am. Journ. of Comp. Law* 5 (1956) 686-90 at 690.

place but not necessarily from one time. Gaudemet wrote before the
publication of Youtie's revised readings, so that the *kai homoiōs*
Westermann read in lines 21 and 40 appeared to prove that the scribe
did not copy all the posted rescripts continuously. This consideration loses some of its force now that these are read as dates, but
on the other hand, the petitions are not all from the same day.
Secondly, even if they all are from one place at one time, why not
imagine that a group of petitioners traveled together to present
their petitions, or even that the emperor received them while he
was travelling. Finally, be it noted that the copyist paid more
attention to the names of the addressees of the rescripts than to
those of the authors of the rescripts, the joint emperors, which
he omitted entirely.

Now I have avoided presenting the arguments that the various
scholars drew from the curious fact that the official titulature
was not written by the first copyist, but squeezed in between the
lines by a second hand, because that argument can go either way.
If your theory on the purpose of the copy does not require the official titulature, you say, "See, the original scribe did not copy
it." If your theory does require the titulature you say, "Aha,
somebody took the trouble to add it in later." I only raise this
point now by way of contrast to the care given to the names of the
recipients. (Assuming them to have been carefully copied. After
all, we have no control on this except for *P. Amh.* 63.) The scribe,
so the argument can run, had uppermost in his mind the recipients,
not the emperor; therefore, he must have been a private scribe working for them, not an official clerk working for the emperor.

For those who have difficulty in accepting such a cooperative
venture by thirteen or more different litigants, there is the suggestion of Bellinger that a scribe was commissioned to report
whether a particular petition was dealt with on that day, but,
either because the instructions were not sufficiently clear, or
because the required petition was not there at all, the scribe
copied out the entire day's output of rescripts.[16]

A further step in the same direction was a suggestion of Welles
that a professional scribe, or scribal establishment, copied the

---

16 Alfred R. Bellinger, *CP* 51 (1956) 179-80.

entire output for sale to anyone interested and, Welles suggests, this may have been cheaper than copying any particular rescript to order.[17] This theory does not really stand on its own separately from all the others, for the question as I phrased it, the intended use of the papyrus, is not answered here at all. The theory refers to the way the scribe was paid--instead of being hired, he worked free-lance. Welles at this point does not say what he expects the anticipated buyer to do with it. What this theory does supply is an explanation of the variegated quality of the text. The scribe himself did not know how it would be used.

The suggestions we have dealt with so far all see the papyrus as intended in one way or another for the use of someone connected with the rescripts here recorded, whether the imperial bureaux who issued them, or the local authorities who may be called on to put them into effect, or the addressees. I move on to some suggestions that the document was intended for the use of persons unconnected to the particular rescripts.

Schiller, in his commentary to the first edition, and again in his "Second Thoughts," concluded, after weighing various alternatives, that the copy was made by a notary who wanted to have samples of the modes of expression of the imperial chancellery.[18] It had been noticed that the Greek vocabulary in the papyrus was not the usual legal usage in Egypt of this period. The suggestion is then that the notary wanted to learn this new and different usage. Though several scholars went along with it, this explanation did not arouse much enthusiasm.[19] Professor Wolff raised two objections which eventually convinced Schiller to abandon his view. First, Wolff argued, a Greek notary living before the Constitutio Antoniniana would have no reason to learn the Roman imperial usage. Secondly, the usage of our papyrus did not become the accepted usage in Egypt, as the traditional usage was too entrenched at the

---

17 C. Bradford Welles, *AJP* 77 (1956) 84-88 at 86.

18 *Apokrimata*, 101; "Second Thoughts" (supra n. 2), 345.

19 Pietro de Francisci, *IURA* 6 (1955) 184-88 at 188; Gaudemet (supra n. 14), 478; Barry Nicholas, *CR* n.s. 6 (1956) 179-80; Fritz Pringsheim, "Some Suggestions on P. Col. 123 (Apokrimata)," *Eos* 48.1 (= *Symbolae Taubenschlag* I) (1956) 237-49 at 239; Julien Guey, *REA* 61 (1959) 134-39 at 134.

end of the second century to be easily changed.[20] Neither of these
arguments is completely overwhelming. As for the first, without
getting involved in the controversy concerning the pace at which
Roman law entered Egypt, I would just note that this view is not
unanimously held,[21] and in particular there is more than one instance in our papyrus where Roman law seems to be applied to petitioners with non-Roman names. As for the second, the fact that an
attempt to adapt one's usage did not become a general practice does
not mean that the attempt was not made. But even if these specific
objections are not overwhelming, one still remains unsatisifed with
Schiller's notion that a scribe copied this whole document, complete with the precise dates and names just for a dozen or two new
turns of a phrase.[22]

In fact, Schiller himself abandoned this view toward the end
of his life, and turned instead to the view that the papyrus has to
do with the use of rescripts as precedents--to indicate the law in
cases similar to but not directly connected with those of the addressees of the rescripts.[23] This is actually the first published
view. Some years before the publication of our papyrus Professor
Westermann described it "as giving precedents for the use of up-
country judges for their use in cases which might later come before
them."[24] The attraction of this view comes not only from the modern experience of law reports, and the codes of late antiquity, but
also from the fact that several such collections of imperial rescripts have been found in the papyri, and that quite a few imperial rescripts have been found appended to petitions cited as precedents.

On the other hand, a severe objection comes immediately to the
fore--indeed Schiller raised it in the first edition[25]--very few of

---

20 Hans Julius Wolff, *ZSav* 73 (1956) 406-18 at 410.

21 E.g., Schönbauer (supra n. 2), 173-76.

22 Pringsheim (supra n. 19).

23 Supra (n. 1), 80.

24 William L. Westermann, *BSRAA* 38 (1949) 10-11; implied in
Apokrimata 5.

25 Schiller, *Apokrimata*, 100.

the rescripts here given could be of any use as precedents. #5 allowing women to borrow and lend to others, #9 conditioning the ex-
cusal of infirm from liturgical duties on their inability to attend
to their own affairs, #10 forbidding the substitution of money payments for grain payments, seem clear and useful enough. But others
are not. #3 "Obey the findings made." is no more than the denial
of an appeal and says nothing at all about any law. The same is
true of #6, "the decisions...have commonly given consideration to
Egyptians," #11 contains only the information as to who will be appointed delegated judge in some cases. Other rescripts do seem to
make substantial statements on law, but what these statements were
could not be known because the details of the cases are not given.
#4 is the most notorious of these. Though Schiller thought he
could reduce the possible interpretations to two, in fact nearly a
dozen have been offered.[26] Other decisions subject to varying interpretations are #8, 12 and 13. At any rate these and probably
others as well could be of little use as precedents. This then is
the main objection and it has been called "insuperable."[27]

Another objection that has been raised to the notion that the
papyrus is a collection of precedents is that no principle of selection seems to appear.[28] They are clearly not on one topic as
are other collections of rescripts known from the papyri. The topics here range from taxes and liturgies, to debts and mortgages,
inheritance, guardianship, and women's status. It is possible, I
suppose, to work up a case, as Welles did, for which all of the
rescripts would serve as precedents: a case of the estate of a tax
farmer, complicated by loans and mortgages contracted by his wife
in the attempt to free the estate from its obligations to the
government.[29] But even Welles himself felt it was "unduly fortuitous" that all the cases needed for the various aspects of the case
should show up among the decisions of just one day. We now know
that the decisions were given on three days, so it is not quite

---

26   d'Ors, *Eos* (supra n. 3), 84.

27   Stein (supra n. 15), 690.

28   Schiller, *Apokrimata*, 100.

29   Welles (supra n. 17), 86.

that fortuitous, but nonetheless it is rather farfetched.

Furthermore, why select only this day or these days. Indeed, Seidl argues, why does the collection not include rescripts by other emperors as well?[30]

For the record, I make mention of one further objection that has been raised, that is that the rescripts would not be valid as precedents without the petitions which they answered.[31] This is not the same objection we raised above, that without the petitions the rescripts are obscure and useless. Now the objection is that even if clear, the rescripts alone would not be valid precedents. This objection can be dismissed. The rescripts actually quoted as precedents in the papyri never have the original petitions either. Only the rescript itself stated the rule of law and so only it was quoted,[32] and, no less important, only the rescript had the imperial authority.

At any rate, the notion that the papyrus is a collection of precedents was mostly rejected, and stated this way rightly so.

However, Professor Wolff presented the precedent theory in a different form,[33] which was taken up in particular by Williams,[34] and this is the form which Schiller endorsed in 1977. Wolff's suggestion is that this is a copy of all the rescripts published on these three days, made for a lawyer in Egypt for the purpose of drawing *from* these rescripts precedents which may be useful in later cases. We have before us, then, a preparatory stage in the development of juristic literature--the preparation of the raw material. The up-country lawyer has his clerk (or as Welles suggests, a free-lance scribe does this on his own) copy all the rescripts so that he, the lawyer, can study them at his leisure. Perhaps the lawyer himself came to Alexandria and knew that like most people he does not immediately grasp all the implications of a legal text the

---

30   Seidl, *RARP* (supra n. 12), 31.

31   de Francisci (supra n. 19), 188.

32   Erich Sachers, *AnzAlt* 11 (1958) 103-6 at 105.

33   Wolff (supra n. 20), 411-12.

34   Williams (supra n. 10), 91-92. In agreement, Sachers (supra n. 32).

first time he reads it. So he copied them all even though many
would turn out to be useless. The same is true of a modern researcher of the law of 200 A.D. who lives at some distance from a
repository of the legal texts of that era, a major university library. When he has the occasion to be there to look up references,
he does not photocopy just the one page of his reference, but the
entire article in which it appears. Then he adds in the margin in
his own hand the precise data, author, title, and the like, by
which he must refer to what he copied. This, I believe, is a better model than either the court reporter of a daily journal or an
official or commercial Law Reports.

I would like to add one more consideration which must be very
tentative, but if ever proven to be correct should be decisive.
Rescripts #3, 6 and 10 are addressed to specific individuals *kai
allois*, "and others." In fact, #3 and 10 are each addressed to two
individuals "and others." Now it can of course be, and so nearly
everyone assumes, that each of these rescripts is a rescript given
to a single petition submitted by a group of people involved in one
case. If so, my argument goes no further. However, it is noteworthy that two of these, #6 and 10, are respectively the first rescripts reported for their day. #3 and 6 are remarkable for having
virtually no content other than saying "no." All deal with administrative matters, #6 and 10 certainly, #3 probably. The three are
among the four shortest rescripts on the page. Is it a coincidence
that these characteristics converge on the rescripts referred to by
kai allois? D'Ors said that it was not.[35] Rather, he suggested
that in each of these cases there were in fact several rescripts
with identical wording which were addressed to various individuals,
and the copyist made do with copying the names of one or two of the
addressees and then merely indicating that the identical rescripts
were also given to other petitions. D'Ors also observed that such
a phenomenon appears in Justinian's Code where, for instance, a rescript addressed to an individual *et aliis* is phrased in the second
person singular.[36] Now, if this is true that the *kai allois* in our

---

35 D'Ors, *Emerità* (supra n. 3), 418 and 424; idem, *Eos* (supra
n. 3), 86-88.

36 C. 2.17.1.

papyrus refers to other petitioners who received rescripts with the same wording rather than other persons in a joint petition,--this is admittedly a big if--all the explanations which relate the papyrus to the persons or agencies involved in the instant cases of the rescripts must be excluded. Because of the incompleteness, it could not be a register nor an information to strategos. It cannot be intended as a notice to petitioners, whether official notice or private, for then some of the petitioners would never find out what answers they received. On the other hand, this kind of a reference would serve the needs of precedent collectors perfectly. In Roman Egypt, as is well known, precedents were frequently cited in the course of trials and in petitions.[37] These quotations of precedents generally, though not always, include the names of the parties involved in the precedent case; and often the party who cites the precedent will make the claim that "other prefects decided the same," or "I have given you a few of many such decisions," but will then not itemize further.[38] In other words, what the collector of precedents wants is the names of one or two parties who received a rescript of a particular wording and an indication that there were others as well, and our papyrus would fit this requirement perfectly.

A few words on the citation as precedents of imperial rescripts in the papyri are in order. It is elementary Gaius that constitutions of the emperors--decrees, edicts, *epistulae*--have the force of statute, and that this has never been doubted.[39] It is also well known that this *has* been very much doubted by modern scholarship. By now there is consensus that the general enactments such as edicts and *mandata* had the force of law, and that decisions on individual cases such as *decreta* and rescripts had binding force in the instant cases for which they were given. However, whether individual decisions, *decreta* and rescripts had the force of law in other similar

---

37 Ranon Katzoff, "Precedents in the Courts of Roman Egypt," *ZSav* 89 (1972) 256-92; idem, "Sources of Law in Roman Egypt: The Role of the Prefect," *ANRW* II 13 (Berlin 1980) 807-44.

38 E.g., *P. Oxy.* II 237 vi 19 (Chaeremon); vii 14 (Dionysia); *P. Oxy.* VI 899.25; *P. Oxy.* XXIV 2411.40.

39 Gai. *Inst.* 1.5.

cases is very much disputed. Did they have the force of statute,
or only of persuasive precedent, or neither? When did they acquire
such force as they had? All these are questions on which no unani-
mity exists. As a minimum it will be admitted that the tendency
over the long term was for imperial constitutions to gain in authority.[40] I would like to sketch just a couple of lines which indicate this gain in authority reflected in the papyri.

First some numbers. A list of the instances in which rescripts
are cited as authority--petitions, reports of trial proceedings, and
collections of legal materials including imperial rescripts which
look as if they were prepared for use as precedent--compiled to see
when they are cited, reveals the following.[41]

---

40 A. Arthur Schiller, *Roman Law: Mechanisms of Development*
(The Hague/Paris/New York 1978) 506-24.

41 Petitions:
P. Harr. 67 (mid II c. A.D.)
P. Oxy. VI 899 verso (201 A.D. ?)
PSI IX 1052 (205/6-211)
SB X 10537 (214/5)
P. Flor. I 88 (215)
P. Flor. III 382 (222/3)
P. Oxy. XLIII 3105 (229-35)
P. Oxy. XII 1405 (236/7)
BGU II 473 = *M. Chr.* 375 (> 200)
PSI IV 292 (> 200)

Trial proceedings:
P. Tebt. II 286 = *M. Chr.* 83 = *FIRA* III 100 (121-38)
BGU I 19 = *M. Chr.* 85 (135)
SB V 7696 (250)

Collections:
P. Oxy. VII 1020 = *Jur.Pap.* 17 (> 200)
P. Oxy. XLII 3018 (> 200)
P. Stras. I 22 = *M. Chr.* 374 = *Jur.Pap.* 54 = *Sel.Pap.*
II 214 and 261 = *FIRA* I 85 (> 207)
P. Mich. IX 529 v 25-38 (> 232-39)
P. Tebt. II 285 = *M. Chr.* 379 = *FIRA* I 90 (> 260)

Imperial *decreta* cited as precedents are included in the list.
Rescripts appearing alone on papyri with no indication that they
were intended as precedents are excluded (e.g. *BGU* I 267; *P. Oxy.*
XLIII 3106; *SB* IV 7366). For the inclusion of *P. Tebt.* II 286:
Grenfell and Hunt in ed. pr.; Wilcken (supra n. 10), 32 n. 1; Kat-
zoff (supra n. 37), 273-75; contra Mitteis, *M. Chr.* p. 91-92; Naph-
tali Lewis, "Notationes Legentis, 55," *BASP* 14 (1977) 157. For *BGU*
I 19: below nn. 44, 45. For *P. Mich.* IX 529 v 25-38: Naphtali
Lewis, "The Michigan-Berlin Apokrimata," *Cd'E* 51 (1976) 320-30.
Perhaps it should also be listed under "Trial proceedings," as a

During the entire second century--well, since the rescript
procedure in matters of law really took hold under Hadrian, it
would be fairer to say during the last two-thirds of the second
century, there are three papyri in which imperial rescripts are
cited. (I counted the year 200 as being in the third century for
this purpose.) In the first four decades of the third century
there are eight, two in each decade. There are none from the 240s,
one each again from the 250s and 260s. None later in the principate. Another five are undated, but later than 200, and can be
statistically distributed to make three each for the first four
decades and another three from the period 250-270. The distribution curve formed by these figures--none before Hadrian, low number
for the rest of the second century, relatively high for the first
four decades of the third century, low number again for the next
three decades, and none for the rest of the principate--matches
roughly the curve formed by statistics drawn from Justinian's Code.
First, Krüger's chronological list of the contents of the Code has
116 for the second century since Hadrian, of which only twenty-three
predate Severus, nearly a thousand (969) for the first four decades
of the third century (in fact well over a thousand [1038] if you
count in the first seven years of Severus' reign), down to 416 for
the next four and a half decades. This confirms Honoré's observation that the supply of imperial rescripts and the demand for them
as precedents rise and fall together.[42]

Another tabulation--very partial surely, but interesting--
Honoré's list of constitutions in the Code in which reliance is
made on frequent rescripts, *saepe rescriptum est* and the like.[43]

---

trial in 215, in view of Lewis, "The Michigan-Berlin Apokrimata."
However, if Lewis is correct, it is not certain that the rescript
was not given for the same case Lollianus speaks in. For *SB* V 7696:
infra, n. 47. In *P. Tebt*. II 285 a rescript of Gordian indeed appears alone but several decades after its issue. I exclude *P. Mich*.
IX 529 v 39-53, in fact an edict, Naphtali Lewis, "The Severan Edict
of *P. Mich*. IX 529," *Cd'E* 50 (1975) 202-6. Perhaps *SB* XII 11069
(late II c.) should be included, J. D. Thomas, "An Imperial Constitution on Papyrus," *BICS* 19 (1972) 103-12 at 109. For the date of
P. Oxy. XII 1405: P. Mertens, *Cd'E* 31 (1956) 353.

42 Antony Maurice Honoré, "The Severan Lawyers: a Preliminary
Survey," *SDHI* 28 (1962) 162-232 at 178.

43 Ibid., 227.

None date from the beginning of Severus' reign to 210, seventeen in
the next four decades, down to three from the next three decades.
Again the same curve, but a decade later. The imperial chancellery
runs a decade behind popular feeling on the importance of imperial
rescripts as precedents.

To turn from statistics to specific papyri, I will refer to
three papyri with a spread of more than a century, which I believe
illustrate the trend. At the early end--*BGU* 19 is the record of a
trial in 135 A.D. concerning an Egyptian's right to inherit from a
grandmother. The party cites as a precedent a grant of Hadrian
given in an earlier case by way of decree or rescript, but the
delegated judge is not convinced, and refers the matter back to the
prefect, and only after the prefect rules does he act in accordance
with the Hadrianic precedent. This at least is the interpretation
I have suggested for the papyrus,[44] and though it has not gone un-
challenged,[45] I think it is defensible. If I was right, we have
here a delegated judge who not only does not consider the decision
of the emperor a binding precedent, but is not even persuaded by
it. On the other hand, the prefect does follow the precedent. Now
I by no means suggest that some up-country hick judge in Egypt represents juristic opinion in Rome, but he does illustrate something
of the popular consciousness in the matter.

At the other end--*SB* V 7696, "A Trial Before the Prefect of
Egypt Appius Sabinus, circa 250 A.D.,"[46] in a dispute between the
senate of Arsinoe and the villagers in the vicinity over the latter's liability to liturgical duties. The villagers read to the
court an oral decision given by the former Emperor Severus in the
course of a hearing, a *decretum*, in other words, in support of
their claim (lines 82, 84).[47] This is henceforth referred to by

---

44   Ranon Katzoff, "*BGU* 19 and the Law of Representation on
Succession," *Proc. XII Int. Congr. Pap.* (Am. Stud. Pap. 7, Toronto
1970) 239-42.

45   Seidl, *RARP* (supra n. 12), 225-26.

46   P. Lond. Inv. 2565, published under that title by T. C.
Skeat and E. P. Wegener, *JEA* 21 (1935) 224-47.

47   Vid. Fritz Freiherrn von Schwind, *Zur Frage der Publikation im römischen Recht* (Münch. Beitr. 31, Munich 1940) 152-53.

the prefect as a *nomos*, law. The representatives of the city try
to oppose to it contrary prefectural decisions but to no avail.
They try to say that the ruling of Severus only applied to the
economic circumstances of his day, which have meanwhile changed,
and this too is dismissed. The verdict of the prefect begins with
reference to the *nomothesia* of Severus. The precedent is law.

In between these two poles is the year 200, when Severus issues
our rescripts. During the following decades it becomes an occasional practice to preface petitions with the citation of an imperial
rescript as a precedent. People in 200 are already preparing themselves for this by collecting the rescripts--the Apokrimata, we
suggested, illustrates that. At this time, however, apparently *not*
everyone is so sure of the value of rescripts as precedents. Someone has doubts.

BGU VII 1578 dates from sometime about the turn of the second
century according to its editor. It is the petition to an acting
prefect from a man complaining about his daughter. In line 6 he
cites the authority for his claim. This was originally read τοῦ
ἱερωτάτου καθολικοῦ διὰ τοῦ μα[...--a reference to an official
titled *katholikos*. That would be the *rationalis*. But could he be
most sacred? Does he give such orders? In 1967 Parsons revised the
restoration to read τοῦ ἱερωτάτου καθολικοῦ διατάγμα[τος κελεύοντος
"Since the most sacred (that is, imperial) universal (*katholikos*)
edict orders etc."[48] This makes much more sense. But why the word
katholikos, universal? Precisely, I suggest, to point up the difference between rescripts and edicts. Our petitioner stresses that
his authority is no rescript which, who knows, may not be binding,
may be *specialis*. No, he relies on an edict, universal (*katholikos*)
in applicability and no doubt about it.

Bar-Ilan University   Ranon Katzoff

---

48 Peter Parsons, "Philippus Arabs and Egypt," *JRS* 57 (1967)
134-41 at 138-39.

Proceedings of the XVI Int. Congr. of Papyrology (Chico 1981) 575-604

APOREMATA APOKRIMATON (P. COLUMBIA 123)

I

Eine Reihe der noch offenen Fragen, die mit den *apokrimata* des P. *Columbia* 123 verbunden sind, mag aus prinzipiellen oder empirischen (Quellen-)Gründen unlösbar sein; insoweit muss sich die Forschung damit begnügen, die Probleme klar zu stellen. Andere können durch Verbreiterung der Quellengrundlage, durch genauere Interpretation der Quellen, vielleicht auch durch Verwendung eines adäquaten begrifflichen Instrumentars einer Lösung näher geführt werden. Im folgenden ist eine Auswahl zu treffen. So beschränken wir uns im wesentlichen auf vier Aspekte: Erweiterung der Quellenbasis für das Verständnis der *apokrimata* (II); Versuch einer Erklärung des Wortgebrauchs von *apokrima* (III); Einordnung der *apokrimata* unter die bekannten Konstitutionentypen (IV); die *apokrimata* als Zeugnisse für die Reskriptenpraxis (V).

Die folgenden Bemerkungen können vielfach an frühere Diskussion anknüpfen.[1] Andererseits liegt ihnen teilweise ein von den gängigen Meinungen etwas abweichendes Verständnis von der Konstitutionenpraxis zugrunde.[2] Das gilt nicht zuletzt in dem Bereich, der

---

1 Die Literatur zu den *apokrimata* hat--nach einer gewissen Stille in den sechziger Jahren--letzthin wieder sehr zugenommen. Die frühere Literatur ist in der Ausgabe der *apokrimata* von Modrzejewski in Girard (*Textes du droit romain* II [1977[7]] VIII 19 [p. 468f.]) zusammengestellt. Dazu etwa E. Seidl, *Rechtsgeschichte Ägyptens als römischer Provinz* (Sankt Augustin 1973) 31ff.; W. Williams, *JRS* 64 (1974) 86ff.; A. A. Schiller, *BASP* 14 (1977) 75ff.; N. Lewis, *BASP* 13 (1976) 11; derselbe *RIDA* 3 S. 25 (1978) 261ff.; A. d'Ors-F. Martin, *AJP* 100 (1979) 111ff. Eingebettet in die Gesamtdarstellung der Tätigkeit der römischen Kaiser treten sie auch in dem zugleich monumentalen und minutiösen Werk von F. Millar, *The Emperor in the Roman World* ([London 1977] 244f.) passim auf. Nach Verfertigung eines ersten Entwurfes überliess mir A. Honoré eine Kopie der Fahnen seines eindrucksvollen Buches *Emperors and Lawyers*, das noch im Jahre 1981 erscheinen soll; dafür möchte ich ihm auch an dieser Stelle danken. Vgl. einstweilen seinen Bericht in *JRS* 69 (1979) 51ff.

2 Ein Überblick über die Konstitutionenprobleme findet sich in jedem Lehrbuch; vgl. hier nur Schiller, *Roman Law* (The Hague 1978) 463ff.

von dem mit Recht berühmten Artikel U. Wilckens über die Reskriptenpraxis (*Hermes* 55 [1920] 1ff.) beherrscht wird. An dieser Stelle
zwingen Raum- und Zeitgründe bisweilen dazu, die eigene Meinung in
Thesenform vorzutragen. Eine nähere Begründung soll an einem anderen Ort gegeben werden. Auf den Spuren Wilckens werden wir bei
den kaiserlichen Reskripten *epistulae* und *subscriptiones* unterscheiden. Dabei wird eine gewisse historische Ungenauigkeit in
Kauf genommen. Denn nicht nur verschwindet der Terminus "*subscriptio*" für ein kaiserliches Reskript aus der Rechtssprache; auch in
der Sache kann man in der uns interessierenden Epoche nur noch mit
Bedenken von einer (echten) *subscriptio* sprechen (s.u. V.).

Eine letzte Vorbemerkung betrifft die verwendete Terminologie.
Sie folgt bei der Beschreibung des Erlasses der Konstitutionen in
lockerer Form derjenigen, die sich für die moderne Gesetzgebung
eingebürgert hat: Der Inhalt der Konstitution wird festgelegt (was
dem Gesetzesbeschluss entspricht); sie wird ausgefertigt (Beispiel:
scripsi, *recognovi*-Vermerk bei der *subscriptio*); sie wird promulgiert (veröffentlicht, an den Adressaten übermittelt). Wenn man
auf übersteigerte Präzisionsansprüche verzichtet, so wird man diese
drei Schritte regelmässig auch in der Konstitutionenpraxis wieder-
finden. Über die jeweilige (juristische) Bedeutung der einzelnen
Akte ist damit nichts gesagt.

II

Aus der Zeit des Ägyptenaufenthalts der Kaiser Septimius
Severus und Caracalla (damals etwa 14 Jahre alt) sind im Codex
Justinians eine Reihe von Konstitutionen überliefert. Sie sind
bisher m.W. zum Verständnis der *apokrimata* nicht herangezogen
worden. Die Gründe dürften mannigfaltig sein: Der Historiker hat
die Tendenz, die eigentlichen Rechtsquellen zu vermeiden; der
Rechtshistoriker neigt zur Vernachlässigung des historischen Zu-
sammenhangs (hier des Ägyptenaufenthalts der Kaiser). Beachtlicher
sind andere Motive. Der Umgang mit den Konstitutionen des *CJ* wird
dadurch erschwert, dass die Überlieferung häufig nicht erkennen
lässt, welchem Konstitutionentyp die jeweilige "*lex*" zuzuweisen
ist. Das betrifft vor allem das Verhältnis zwischen *epistula* und
subscriptio. Dazu kommen Überlieferungsmängel, die sich gerade

auch auf die Formalien der Konstitutionen (Inskription, Promulga-
tions- und Datierungsvermerk) konzentrieren.[3] Bekanntlich sind die
Formalien für die zeitliche und typologische Einordnung der Konstitutionen besonders wichtig. Nimmt man dazu die (eher radikale als
gründlich ausgeführte) These van Sickle's,[4] derzufolge die Inskriptionen in den Konstitutionen der Severerzeit in der Epoche des
Alexander Severus weithin interpoliert worden seien, so wird die
Zurückhaltung gegenüber der Verwendung des im *CJ* gesammelten Materials verständlich. Zumindest nach den Maßstäben, die man üblicherweise an die Brauchbarkeit von althistorischen Quellen legt, ist
sie aber nicht haltbar.

Vielleicht genügt es heute bereits, auf die Untersuchungen
Honoré's zur Konstitutionenpraxis des 3. Jhd. hinzuweisen. Auch
wenn man den Optimismus des Autors hinsichtlich der Trennbarkeit
von *epistulae* und *subscriptiones* nicht in vollem Umfange teilt, so
ist doch bereits die Fruchtbarkeit seiner Untersuchungen ein Indiz
für die Brauchbarkeit der Methode. Dazu kommt, dass sich tatsächlich eine Reihe von (hier nicht zu erörternden) Indizien findet,
die zumindest in einigen Fällen eine plausible Zuweisung, sei es zu
den *epistulae*, sei es zu den *subscriptiones* ermöglichen. Es ist
auch nicht bedeutungslos, dass der Unterschied von *epistula* und
subscriptio in der uns interessierenden Epoche anscheinend geringer
wird. Noch überzeugender sind die Ergebnisse Honoré's im Bereich
der Datierung (vgl. nur *JRS* 69 [1979] 51 A. 8). Zumindest wenn man
von den Tagesdaten absieht, so ist die weitaus überwiegende Mehr-
zahl der Konstitutionen relativ sicher datiert.

---

3 Über die Unzuverlässigkeit der Überlieferung des *Codex* un-
terrichtet vor allem das (häufig vernachlässigte) Vorwort zur *Editio maior* des *Codex* (1877) von P. Krüger.

4 *CP* 23 (1928) 270ff. Um nur Beispiele zu nennen: Bei einem
Zusammentreffen von Kaiser-Inskription und Konsuldatum ist stets
ein Indiz für richtige Datierung gewonnen; wenn man weiss, dass die
Konstitutionen des Septimius Severus und des Caracalla "zusammen-
geflossen" sind (dazu u. bei A. 20), so bleiben nur noch wenige
Unsicherheiten. Nicht beachtet sind die Bemerkungen von P. Krüger
in dem Vorwort zur *Editio maior* des *CJ*; das gilt vor allem auch für
die Geschichte der handschriftlichen Überlieferung (vgl. etwa die
Ausführungen zu *CJ* 7.12.1).

Grössere Vorsicht wird man hinsichtlich des Namens der Adressaten, an die die Reskripte gerichtet waren, walten lassen. Ähnliches gilt auch für die Promulgationsvermerke (*pp.*, *d.*, *a.* etc.).
Hier ist im Einzelfall stets mit Überlieferungsfehlern zu rechnen.
Doch wird damit die Existenz verschiedener Promulgationsmöglichkeiten nicht in Frage gestellt. Was schliesslich den häufig nicht
überlieferten Promulgationsort betrifft, so braucht er uns an dieser Stelle nicht zu beschäftigen; zu prüfen wäre, ob und inwieweit
aus den überlieferten Daten Extrapolationen möglich sind.

Eine letzte Unsicherheit führt in den Verantwortungsbereich
der Historiker. Es geht hierbei um die Länge des Ägyptenaufenthalts der Kaiser Septimius Severus und Caracalla. Auszugehen ist
von den papyrologischen (und inschriftlichen) Quellen;[5] die (datierten) Konstitutionen im *CJ* geben insoweit keine sicheren Anhaltspunkte.[6]

Nach den datierten Texten befanden sich die Kaiser jedenfalls
vom Dezember 199 bis zum April 200 (möglicherweise mit Unterbre-
chungen) in Alexandria; spätestens im Januar 201 waren sie wieder
in Syrien. Was den übrigen Zeitraum betrifft, so lässt sich nur

---

5 Eine Aufzählung ist hier überflüssig. Das Material lässt
sich leicht zusammenstellen aus Westermann-Schiller, *Apokrimata*,
27f.; Lewis, *RIDA* 25 (1978) 261ff.; Williams, *JRS* 64 (1974) 86ff.;
A. Birley, *Septimius Severus, the African Emperor* (1972) 201ff., s.
auch *P. Oxy.* XLVII 3364. Vgl. zum Ägyptenaufenthalt der Kaiser
auch Braunert, *Binnenwanderung* (Bonn 1964) 289ff.; D. Nörr, *Die
Entstehung der longi temporis praescriptio* (AG Forschung Nordrhein-
Westfalen [Geisteswissenschaften] H. 156, 1969) 74ff.

6 Die Digesten-Überlieferung der Konstitutionen muss wegen
des Fehlens einer präzisen Datierung hier ausscheiden; in den vor-
justinianischen Rechtsquellen habe ich nichts Einschlägiges gefunden. Bisweilen wird in der Literatur auf die aus Marcian *D.*
48.10.1.3 bekannte Verurteilung eines *praefectus Aegypti* durch
Severus wegen *falsum* hingewiesen. Angesichts anderer mehr oder
weniger gut begründeter Spekulationen über die Identität des Praefekten (vgl. nur Bastianini, *ZPE* 17 [1965] 263ff. [303]; Birley,
a.a.O., 208 Anm. 3 [mit Hinweis auf G. Grosso]) sei hier eine weitere
Spekulation angeboten. Nach Cassius Dio *epit.* 75 (76).14.2 hat
Plautian seinen möglichen Konkurrenten, den ehemaligen oder der-
zeitigen Praefekten von Ägypten, Q. Aemilius Saturninus, im Jahre
200 beseitigt. Eine Mitwirkung oder Duldung des Septimius Severus
wäre am leichtesten vorstellbar, wenn sich für die Beseitigung ein
juristischer Anhaltspunkt gegeben hätte--den Cassius Dio aus ver-
ständlichen Gründen überging.

vermuten, dass sie nicht vor dem späten Frühjahr 199 ägyptischen
Boden betraten, dann nach einem Aufenthalt in Pelusium unter vor-
läufiger Umgehung Alexandrias den Nil aufwärts fuhren und schliesslich in Alexandria einzogen.[7] Weitere Indizien (aus der Numisma-
tik, den üblichen Konventsterminen, dem Kompetenzverlust des Präfekten während der Anwesenheit der Kaiser, aus Nilfeiern und Nil-
tabus) scheinen mir sehr unsicher zu sein. Unter diesen Umständen
wird man nur Konstitutionen, die in die Zeit vom Sommer 199 bis zum
Frühsommer 200 datiert sind, mit grösserer Wahrscheinlichkeit dem
Ägyptenaufenthalt des Septimius Severus zurechnen können. Im übrigen wird man sich mit geringeren Plausibilitätsgraden zufrieden
geben müssen.

Das einschlägige Material lässt sich im wesentlichen aus der
(nicht ganz präzisen) Appendix I der *Editio minor* des *Codex* von P.
Krüger zusammenstellen. Dem durch exakt überlieferte Daten gesicherten Aufenthalt des Severus in Alexandria gehört *CJ* 8.44.1,
proponiert am 25. Februar 200, an.[8] Es geht um die Haftung beim
Erbschaftskauf. Wie bereits die Aufnahme in den *Codex* vermuten
lässt, ist hier--wie auch sonst--eine spezifische Beziehung zu
Ägypten nicht erkennbar. Das gilt auch für den Namen des Adressaten "Munatius." Weitere Konstitutionen lassen sich mit kleineren
Vorbehalten dem durch Daten bezeugten Alexandria-Aufenthalt des
Severus zuweisen. Es geht einmal um *CJ* 8.37.1 (*accepta* [!] *XVII
k. Mai.* = 15. April 200); das Reskript verweist ausdrücklich auf
einen *libellus* des Adressaten Secundus und dürfte daher eine "*subscriptio*" sein. Inhaltlich betrifft es die Wirksamkeit einer Stipulation. *CJ* 6.2.1 (*D.* [nach anderer Überlieferung: *pp*; s. *CJ Editio maior*] *XI k. Mai.* = 21. April 200) hat als Adressaten einen gewissen Theogenes; es geht um Aktionenkonkurrenzen. Folgt man einer
Überlegung Krügers (*Addenda* zur *Editio minor* p. 516), so ist *CJ*

---

7 Vgl. J. Hasebroek, *Untersuchungen zur Geschichte des
Kaisers Septimius Severus* (1921) 116ff.; K. Hannestadt, *CM* 6 (1944)
194ff.; Westermann-Schiller, a.a.O., 30; Birley, a.a.O., 205ff.;
Parássoglou, *P. Coll. Youtie*, pp. 262ff.; Lewis, *Historia* 28 (1979)
253f.

8 Das Tagesdatum ist hier wegen *CJ* 8.13.1 und *P. Flor.* 382.1ff.
von Interesse. Wegen der Überlieferungsunsicherheiten verzichte ich
im folgenden oft auf die Angabe der Tagesdaten.

8.13.1 am 26. Februar 200 proponiert (Adressat Timotheos, Pfand-
rechtsprobleme).

Weiterhin sind folgende Konstitutionen aus der Zeit zwischen
Mitte 199 und Mitte 200 bezeugt: *CJ* 9.9.2 (*pp. k. Iul.*, Adressat
Cyrus, über *lex Julia de adulteriis*); 6.47.1 (*proposita* [!] *prid.
k. Aug.*, Adressat Maximus, über den Umfang des Herausgabeanspruches
bei Vermächtnissen); 3.33.1 (*pp.* Ende September 199, Adressat Po-
sidonius, zur *cautio usufructuaria*); 6.25.1 (*pp. k. Oct.*, Adressat
Alexander, Beteiligter Anthyllos, bedingte Erbeinsetzung); 3.31.2
(*D.* [!] *k. Iul.* 200; Adressat Marcellus *miles* [Indiz für eine--
recht umfangreiche--*subscriptio*], weitere "Beteiligte" Menecrates
und Musaeus, über *hereditatis petitio*).

Die bisher genannten Konstitutionen kann man mit recht grosser
Wahrscheinlichkeit in die Zeit des Ägyptenaufenthalts des Septimius
Severus datieren. Bei den folgenden bestehen grössere Unsicherheiten. Die Konstitutionen *CJ* 2.18.3 (*pp.* 2. Hälfte Januar 199,
Adressat Hadrianus, über Rechtsverhältnis zwischen Brüdern und
Miterben) und 5.4.1 (*D.* [nach anderer Überlieferung *pp.*; s. *Editio
maior*], erste Hälfte Mai 199, Adressat Potitus, Zustimmung zur Ehe-
schliessung bei einer *puella*) dürften eher noch vor dem Ägyptenaufenthalt erlassen worden sein. Aus der zweiten Jahreshälfte von
200 datieren: *CJ* 4.55.1 (*pp.* Mitte September, Adressatin Petronia
Favilla, zu einer *lex venditionis* beim Sklavenverkauf; Hinweis auf
civitates deutet provinziales [nicht unbedingt ägyptisches] Ambiente an); 2.34.1 und 2.36.1 (*D.* [!] Mitte Oktober 200; Adressat
Longinus, weitere "Beteiligte" ein *minor* Probus und ein kaiserlicher
dispensator Rufinus; Inhalt und Stil sprechen für eine *epistula* an
den Beamten Longinus; Problem: *in integrum restitutio* zugunsten
eines Minderjährigen gegenüber dem Fiskus); am gleichen Tag proponiert ist 8.40.1 (möglicherweise wieder Fiskalprobleme; Adressat
Lysias verdächtig, da er im Text in der dritten Person erscheint;
vielleicht *epistula* an einen mit dem Fall Lysias befassten Beamten);
4.55.2 (*pp.* Ende Oktober 200; Adressat Sezus Nedymos; *lex venditionis* bei Sklavenverkauf); 2.3.1 (*pp.* Ende November 200 [?];
Adressat Philinus, beteiligt Licinius Fronto, Vergleichs-*pactum*
über Fideikommiss). Bei 4.32.3 (Adressat Serpius, Zinsprobleme, s.
Ulp. *D.* 46.3.5.2) liegt das Propositionsdatum entweder Ende September 200 oder 202 (vgl. die Anmerkung in der *Editio minor* des *CJ*).

Auch wenn man im Moment von einer eingehenden Auswertung der
einzelnen Konstitutionen absieht, lassen sich doch bereits einige
allgemeine Feststellungen treffen. Die durch die Papyri bezeugte
reiche Tätigkeit des Septimius Severus während seines Aufenthalts
in Ägypten findet im *Codex* einen gewissen Widerhall. Da wir aber
nur einen kleinen Ausschnitt dieser Tätigkeit fassen können, ist es
nicht verwunderlich, dass keines der in den Papyri überlieferten
Reskripte in den *Codex* aufgenommen wurde. Wir haben gesehen, dass
einige Konstitutionen aus der *Codex*-Überlieferung mit überaus grosser Wahrscheinlichkeit dem Aufenthalt in Alexandria zuzuweisen sind.
Die Erlasse des Septimius Severus in Ägypten stehen somit nicht
ausserhalb der sonstigen Überlieferung, konkreter, sie waren wahrscheinlich über die Archive späteren Sammlern zugänglich. Die aus
den Papyri überlieferten Konstitutionen lassen eine gewisse zeitliche Konzentration der normativen Produktivität des Severus in
Alexandria erkennen. Aus der *Codex*-Überlieferung lassen sich zeitliche Schwerpunkte schwer herauslesen. Allenfalls kann man eine
gewisse Konzentrierung in der Zeit von Mitte September bis Ende
Oktober 200 feststellen.[9]

Die *inscriptiones* der "ägyptischen" Konstitutionen des Septimius Severus aus dem *Codex* entsprechen im wesentlichen dem Usus der
apokrimata; die meisten (aber nicht alle) von ihnen wurden--ebenso
wie die *apokrimata*--"proponiert." Beides deutet darauf hin, dass
die *apokrimata* von den Konstitutionen des *CJ* nicht grundsätzlich
unterschieden sind. Aber auch wenn man die Unterschiede beider
Gruppen betonen will--die im formalen Bereich in der Sprache und in
der Datierung (bei den *apokrimata* nach ägyptischem Brauch, bei den
Konstitutionen des *Codex* nach römischem) liegen--, so kommt man
jedenfalls um die Feststellung nicht herum, dass während des Ägyptenaufenthalts auch "normale" Konstitutionen in lateinischer
Sprache (teilweise mit griechischen Adressatennamen) und mit Kon-
sulsdaten proponiert wurden.

III

Der Schreiber des *P. Col.* 123 fasste den Inhalt des Papyrus
mit den Worten: *antigrapha apokrimatōn* zusammen. Die wörtliche

---

9 Zum Problem s. Honoré, *Emperors and Lawyers*, 2. Kapitel
bei Anm. 29.

Übersetzung: *exempla* (Abschriften) *responsorum* ergibt für die uns interessierende Epoche keinen technischen Begriff.[10] Dieser ist dem *responsum* als Antwort eines Juristen (vorzugsweise mit *ius respondendi*) auf die Anfrage einer Partei vorbehalten. Der Versuch, eine eigene Konstitutionenart "*responsum-apokrima*" zu entwickeln,[11] ist bisher noch nicht geglückt. Dazu wäre es nicht nur erforderlich, dass man die Identifizierung der *apokrimata* mit anderen Konstitutionenarten ablehnt; notwendig wäre vielmehr eine (positive) Beschreibung ihrer Eigenart.

Es läge nahe, *apokrinein*, *apokrima* mit *rescribere*, *rescriptum*, *rescriptio*, also dem Wortfeld der "schriftlichen" Beantwortung zu identifizieren; dem steht entgegen, dass die technische Übersetzung hierfür *antigraphein*, *antigraphe* ist.[12] Unter diesen Umständen lässt sich eine Untersuchung des Wortgebrauches von *apokrima* nicht vermeiden. Soweit es um den griechischen Sprachgebrauch geht, kann weithin auf die sorgfältige Studie von Lewis (o.A. 1) verwiesen werden.

---

10 Anderes gilt vielleicht für das 1. oder das frühe 2. Jhd.; vgl. Titel wie ἐπὶ τῶν ἐπιστολῶν καὶ πρεσβειῶν καὶ ἀποκριμάτων (Suida D 1173). Weitere Belege bei Lewis, *RIDA* 25 (1978) 267. Wenn man hier an einen bestimmten Konstitutionentypus zu denken wagt, dann wird er sich auf die--im Gegensatz zur Epistula--mündliche Antwort auf Gesandtschaften beziehen. Zu ἀποκρίνειν als Bezeichnung brieflicher Antworten des Kaisers s. jetzt auch die kyrenische Inschrift bei J. Reynolds, *JRS* 68 (1978) 111ff. (Zeile 7 und 74). In diesen Bereich (vgl. auch u. Anm. 23) gehört auch der Hinweis bei Priscian, *Inst.* 5.66, wo neben dem *a secretis*, *a calculis*, *ab actis* auch ein *a responsis* erwähnt wird. Vgl. zur grammatikalischen Form V. Väänänen, *Ab epistulis....Ad Sanctum Petrum* (Ann. Ac. Sc. Fenn. 1977). In der Dominatszeit wird häufiger von *responsa* der Kaiser gesprochen (s. nur *CT* 2.4.4 [a. 385]; 11.30.8.1 [a. 319]; *Pan. Lat.* III 9; X 34[2]; *Not. Dig.* Pars Or. XIX). Problematisch ist die Verwendung von ἀποκρίνειν in Dittenberger *Syll.*[3] 679 II b (Sherk Nr. 7, S. 52); Arangio-Ruiz (*FIRA* III 162) übersetzt das Wort mit *vindicare*, während E. Garcia Domingo, *Latinismos en la Koiné* (Burgos 1979) 314 an ein (m.E. fragwürdiges) *abiudicare* denkt.

11 Vgl. Lewis, *RIDA* 25 (1978) 261ff. auf den Spuren von Wilcken, *Hermes* 55 (1920) 32 Anm. 1.

12 Ausführliche Belege dürften sich erübrigen. Vgl. aus den Juristenschriften nur Ulp. *D.* 48.1.1.1; Mod. *D.* 27.1.14.2, 15.2 u.ö. Für das folgende darf auf H. J. Mason, *Greek Terms for Roman Institutions* (Am. Stud. Pap. 13, Toronto 1974) verwiesen werden.

In den juristischen Texten kommt das Wort *apokrima* nicht vor.[13]
Damit ist bereits ein gewisses Indiz gegen die Technizität des Aus-
druckes gegeben. Das lateinische Äquivalent "*responsum*" wird vom
Kaiser in der uns interessierenden Epoche selten gebraucht. Immerhin ist es von Interesse, dass Diokletian einmal sein Reskript als
responsum bezeichnet (*CJ* 2.4.15; a. 290). Aus den literarischen
Quellen ist Sueton, *Vespasian* 8.3 zu erwähnen; dort wird ein Bescheid, der in der uns interessierenden Epoche in der Regel durch
ein Reskript (*subscriptio*) gegeben worden wäre, als *responsum* bezeichnet. Auch das Verbum *respondere* wird in Beziehung auf den
Kaiser nur recht selten--und dann wohl untechnisch--gebraucht.[14]
Es darf auf zwei Texte aus dem *liber decretorum* des Paulus verwiesen werden (*D.* 32.97, 49.14.50). An beiden Stellen handelt es sich
um relativ umfangreiche Protokolle kaiserlicher Gerichtsverhand-
lungen. Um das kaiserliche Urteil zu bezeichnen, bedient sich
Paulus gängiger Termini (*placuit, pronuntiavit*). In beiden Fällen
lässt das Urteil "Fragen" offen, die von den Beteiligten, bzw. von
einem Konsiliar nach der Urteilsfällung gestellt werden. Auf diese
Fragen ergeht ein weiterer--jetzt durch *respondere*--gekennzeichneter
Bescheid. An der viel erörterten Stelle *HA Macrinus* 13 (*cumque
Traianus numquam libellis respondit*) bezieht sich das Verbum
schliesslich auf Reskripte (*subscriptiones*).

Diese Belege lassen vermuten, dass *respondere, responsum*--vom
Kaiser ausgesagt--in der uns interessierenden Epoche untechnisch
ist; der blosse Wortgebrauch gibt vor allem keine Auskunft darüber,
ob wir es mit der urteilenden oder reskribierenden Tätigkeit des
Kaisers zu tun haben. Das Bild wird durch die Heranziehung der
griechischen Belege nicht eindeutiger. Für die republikanische
Epoche und die frühe Kaiserzeit hat Lewis gezeigt, dass *apokrima*--
einigermassen technisch--die Antwort an Gesandte bezeichnet. Hierfür gab es in der frühen Kaiserzeit einen Beamten, der das Wort

---

13 Vgl. G. Bortolucci, *Index verborum Graecorum...*, AG 76
(1906) 354ff.

14 Wegen der Kontamination kaiserlicher Reskripte und juri-
stischer Responsen sind die Belege aus den *libri responsorum* des
Paulus nicht verwertbar; vgl. nur *D.* 50.1.21.6 u. 7 mit *CJ* 10.41.1
u. 11.32.1 (jeweils Severus und Caracalla); s. auch *D.* 48.19.43.
Bei *CJ* 2.19.1 (a. 223) bleibt es offen, ob sich das *respondere* auf
Kaiser oder Juristen bezieht.

apokrima im Titel führen konnte;[15] er dürfte ein Vorgänger des späteren *ab epistulis* sein. Genetisch deutet der Ausdruck "*apokrima*" insoweit auf die Beantwortung von *epistulae* oder--mit einer gewissen, allerdings nicht ungefährlichen Verallgemeinerung--auf die Reskriptenpraxis schlechthin.

Mehr Fragen als Antworten produzieren die papyrologischen Belege: *P. Tebt.* II 286 (*FIRA* III 100; Mitteis, *Chrest.* 83; dazu zuletzt Oliver, *AJP* 100 [1979] 544 A. 7), *P. Mich.* IX 529.25ff.[16] und *P. Giss.* 40 II.1ff.[17]

P. Tebt. 286 beginnt mit den Worten: Ἐ]κ μέρους ἀποκρίματος θεοῦ Ἁδριανοῦ. Es folgt ein Protokollauszug über eine Verhandlung vor dem *iudex datus* Julius Theon. Der Auszug, der möglicherweise erst in nachhadrianischer Zeit (vgl. das *theou* = *divi*) verfertigt wurde, hatte den Zweck, einen im Protokoll zitierten Bescheid Hadrians festzuhalten. In ihm verweist Hadrian auf ein früher ergangenes "*epikrima*"; denkbar wäre ein Urteil (*decretum*). Weiterhin werden im Protokoll anscheinend sowohl das frühere *epikrima* Hadrians, als auch der neue Bescheid als "*apophaseis*" (*sententiae*) bezeichnet. Nur wenn man an einen präzisen Sprachgebrauch glaubt, kann man zu einer Identifizierung von *epikrima, apophasis* und *apokrima* und damit zur Gleichsetzung von *apokrima* und Urteil kommen. Das würde voraussetzen, dass man wider den ersten Anschein das Hadrian-Zitat auf einen Urteilsspruch in einem formellen Prozess bezieht, der aus einem Verhandlungsprotokoll des Kaisergerichts entnommen wäre. Trotz der recht lockeren Fassung mancher

---

15 Vgl. o. A. 10. Der letzte Beleg ist anscheinend Dessau 8860 (*OGIS* 494; Zeit Mark Aurels), wobei es allerdings um einen Beamten beim Prokonsul in Asien geht; überdies ist es unsicher, ob *apokrima* sich hier auf *epistulae* oder *libelli* bezieht. Bei Ammian (20.98) wird der *magister libellorum* als *libellis respondens* bezeichnet; vgl. auch O. Hirschfeld, *Untersuchungen auf dem Gebiet der römischen Verwaltungsgeschichte* (1877) 208 A. 1.

16 S. auch Berlin Inv. 7216 (zuerst veröffentlicht von A. Swiderek, *Proc. XIV Int. Congr. Pap.* [1974] 293ff.). Vgl. vor allem Lewis, *Cd'E* 51 (1976) 320ff. (vgl. auch 50 [1975] 202ff. und *BASP* 9 [1972] 33ff.); letztlich etwa auch Oliver, *ZPE* 31 (1978) 139f.

17 Mitteis, *Chrest.* 378; Heichelheim, *JEA* 26 (1940) 10ff.; vgl. auch *CJ* 10.61.1 und Ulp. *D.* 50.2.3.1.

kaiserlicher Urteilssprüche[18] dürfte man aber kaum geneigt sein,
Zeile 4-9 des Textes ohne weiteres als richterliche Sentenz in
einem formalen Prozess zu akzeptieren.

Der Text erinnert vielmehr an Äusserungen Hadrians in den
"*sententiae et epistulae Hadriani*" (s. *CGL* III 32, 5ff.). Zwar
kann nicht entschieden werden, ob unser Bescheid schriftlich (etwa
als *epistula* oder *subscriptio*) oder mündlich (als *interlocutio de
plano*; s. u. IV) ergangen war. Doch liegt die Antwort (*apokrima*)
auf eine schriftliche Anfrage näher. Die Bezeichnung als "*apophasis*" kann damit erklärt werden, dass der Übersetzer nach einem Begriff suchte, mit dem man sowohl ein "*epikrima*" als auch ein "*apokrima*" umfassen konnte; er wäre dabei von dem gleichsam stärkeren
Begriff des kaiserlichen Urteils ausgegangen (ähnlich Oliver o.
Anm. 16). Es darf nicht vergessen werden, dass es sich hier wohl
nicht um eine amtliche Übersetzung handelt, dass somit auch kein
Indiz für einen amtlichen Gebrauch von "*apokrima*" besteht.

Was *P. Mich.* IX 529 betrifft, darf in erster Linie auf die
eingehenden Erörterungen von Lewis (o. Anm. 16) verwiesen werden.
P. Mich. IX 529 v. enthält (39ff.) ein Edikt der Kaiser Severus und
Caracalla, das am 5. Dezember 199 in Alexandria proponiert wurde,
sowie den hier interessierenden Text (25ff.), der als ἐξ ἀπ]οκρι-
μάτων θεῶν Σεουήρου κ[αὶ 'Αντωνίνου bezeichnet wird. Dieser bringt
den Auszug aus einem Gerichtsprotokoll des Kaisergerichts mit den
Ausführungen eines Advokaten (Lollianus) und dem Urteilsspruch
(εἶπεν) des Antoninus Caracalla. Beide Konstitutionen befassen
sich mit unzulässigen Liturgien und dürften in der Zeit des Alexander Severus von einem Privatmann aufgezeichnet worden sein (s.
auch *P. Mich.* IX 529r).

Von dem uns interessierenden Text gibt es ein Duplikat in
einem Berliner Papyrus inv. 7216 (o. Anm. 16).[19] Hier dürfte die

---

18 Sie bedürften gelegentlich einer eigenen Untersuchung.
S. nur Call. *D.* 48.7.7, 4.2.13; allgemein dazu Ulp. *D.* 42.1.59.1.

19 War der Text ursprünglich lateinisch (vgl. aber die
Gohariener-Inschrift von Dmeir [Roussel-de Visscher, *Syria* 23 (1942/
43) 173ff. und Kunkel, *Festschrift Lewald* (1953) 81ff. mit weit.
Lit.]), so könnten sich die Varianten beider Texte aus verschiedenen
Übersetzungen ergeben; s. zum Problem Lewis, *Cd'E* 51 (1976) 322f.

Inskription anders gelautet haben. Nach einer Lücke am Anfang, die
mit ἐξ ὑπομνηματισμῶν oder ἐκ ἀποκριμάτων ergänzt werden kann,
folgen die (ebenfalls z.T. ergänzten) Worte: τοῦ κυρίου ἡμῶν
Σεουήρου 'Αντωνείνου Ε]ὐτυχοῦς Εὐσεβοῦς Σεβαστοῦ. Wahrscheinlich
stammt P. Berl. inv. 7216 noch aus der Lebenszeit des Caracalla.

Lewis hat es plausibel gemacht, dass die Inskription des Berliner Exemplars vertrauenswürdiger ist als die des Michigan-Papyrus.
Für sie spricht vor allem, dass im Protokoll Caracalla allein als
urteilender Richter erscheint. In die gleiche Richtung deutet das
Auftreten des "Lollianus," der auch in der Gohariener-Inschrift als
Advokat auftritt; diese wird durch die Titulatur der Praetorianer-
Praefekten auf die Zeit nach dem 27. März 216 datiert (vgl. CJ
9.51.1). Wie Kunkel vermutet, wurden die Advokaten vor dem Kaisergericht bisweilen aus dem Kreis der amici genommen. Er identifiziert Lollianus mit dem bekannten Egnatius Lollianus, der seine
lange Karriere mit der Stadtpräfektur endete und als Redner gerühmt
wurde. So spricht vieles dafür, dass unser Protokollauszug sich
nicht auf die gemeinschaftliche Regierungszeit von Septimius Severus
und Caracalla bezieht, sondern eine Verhandlung vor dem Kaisergericht im Jahre 215 (in dem sich Caracalla in Ägypten befand)
wiedergibt.

Wenn man die Inskription des Michigan-Papyrus als fehlerhaft
bezeichnet, so ist der Fehler doch nicht ohne Interesse. Man hat
bereits früher eine Eigentümlichkeit der Konstitutionen des Septimius Severus und Caracalla hervorgehoben: die häufig fehlende Über-
einstimmung der Inskriptionen mit den Konsulardaten. Fast alle
Konstitutionen aus der Alleinherrschaft des Septimius Severus
werden beiden Kaisern zugewiesen; aus der Zeit der Gesamtherrschaft
trägt eine (CJ 2.3.1 vom Nov. 200) allein den Namen des Septimius
Severus, während mehrere Konstitutionen allein dem Antoninus Caracalla zugeschrieben werden (s. etwa 5.72.1, 8.52.2, 9.1.2, 2.11.7-
10, alle aus den Jahren 205-208; allerdings schliessen sich die
Konstitutionen 2.11.8-10 durch schlichtes "idem" an die Konstitution 7 an). Bei CJ 6.28.1 ist die handschriftliche Überlieferung
widersprüchlich. Schliesslich gibt es Konstitutionen aus der Zeit

der Alleinherrschaft des Caracalla, die beiden Kaisern zugeschrieben werden.[20]

    Van Sickle hat es wahrscheinlich gemacht, dass entgegen der
Überlieferung im *Codex* die Juristen Ulpian und Modestin (vgl. nur
Ulp. *D.* 14.18.1.16 mit *CJ* 9.41.1) bei der Zuweisung der Autorschaft
die beiden Kaiser trennen. Immerhin sei erwähnt, dass Modestin
(*D.* 27.1.10.4)--inhaltlich, aber nicht formal zutreffend--eine von
ihm wörtlich zitierte Konstitution der Kaiser Septimius Severus und
Caracalla als: διάταξις τοῦ θειοτάτου Σεβήρου bezeichnen kann.
Wenn im *Codex Gregorianus* (*App. Wis.* 1.4; s. *CJ* 2.38.1) eine Konstitution vom 3. März 198 den "*Augusti*" Severus und Antoninus zugeschrieben wird, obwohl Caracalla damals noch Cäsar war, so ist das
allerdings nicht weiter auffällig. Caracalla wurde noch im Herbst
dieses Jahres "*Augustus*," woraus sich die (Rück-)Titulierung leicht
erklärt.

    Die selbst für den *Codex* Justinians einzigartige Häufung
solcher Versehen provoziert die Frage nach der Ursache--die durch
den Hinweis auf mögliche Interpolationen nicht beantwortet, sondern
allenfalls verschoben wird. Da die Konstitutionen dieser Epoche
aus dem *Codex Gregorianus* in den *Codex* Justinians übernommen wurden,
spricht vieles dafür, dass die "Fehler" bereits dem 3. Jahrhundert
angehören. Was die Quellen des *Codex Gregorianus* betrifft, so
nimmt man üblicherweise an, dass der Sammler aus den kaiserlichen
Archiven geschöpft hat. Ist das richtig, so könnte man sich überlegen, ob die archivalische Anordnung für die Zusammenstellung der
Konstitutionen des Severus und des Caracalla verantwortlich ist
(vgl. auch Anm. 20). Vielleicht sollte man aber auch an private
Sammlungen denken, in denen die Konstitutionen der beiden Kaiser
zusammengefasst waren. So muss man die Inskription von *P. Mich.* IX
529 vielleicht auch vor diesem Hintergrund sehen.

    Zu welchen Hypothesen man sich auch entschliesst, es bleibt
als störender Faktor eine inschriftlich (Heberdey, *Forsch. in*

---

20 Belege (unvollständig) bei van Sickle (o.A. 4). Sie lassen
sich im übrigen leicht aus der Appendix I der beiden Codex-Ausgaben
von P. Krüger sammeln. Möglicherweise besteht ein Zusammenhang damit, dass Caracalla seine Regierungsjahre vom Regierungsantritt
seines Vaters an datiert (s. dazu z.B. O. Montevecchi, *La Papirologia* [Turin 1973] 68).

Ephesos II [1912] 125ff.) überlieferte *epistula* des Caracalla allein, von der es Pflaum wahrscheinlich gemacht hat, dass sie aus der Zeit zwischen 200 und 205 stammt.[21] Daraus folgt, dass Caracalla--der anscheinend eine juristische Naturbegabung hatte[22]--als alleiniger Urheber von Konstitutionen aus der Zeit der gemeinsamen Herrschaft mit Septimius Severus nicht völlig auszuschliessen ist. Es darf daran erinnert werden, dass er auch im Jahre 206 eine das Schenkungsverbot unter Ehegatten einschränkende *oratio* im Senat gehalten hat (Ulp. *D.* 24.1.3; 32). Neuerdings schreibt ihm Honoré (*JRS* 69 [1979] 64; s. u. V 5) einen eigenen *a libellis* zu.

Was *P. Mich.* IX 529 betrifft, so dürften trotz dieser Überlegungen die etwas stärkeren Indizien für die Herkunft des Protokolls aus der Zeit der Alleinherrschaft Caracallas sprechen. Doch bleiben Unsicherheiten übrig. In jedem Falle wäre es gefährlich, den Begriff "apokrima" für technisch zu halten. Zwar lassen *P. Tebt.* 286 und *P. Mich.* IX 529 (wozu man noch 2 Cor 1.9 zählen kann) erkennen, dass "apokrima" im Begriffsfeld "Urteilsspruch" gebraucht werden kann. Eine schlichte Identifizierung von *apokrima* und Urteil ist mit diesen Belegen aber nicht zu beweisen.

Das zeigt auch ein weiterer--nun sogar amtlicher--Text, in dem zwar nicht der Erlass eines *apokrima*, aber immerhin die Tätigkeit des ἀποκρίνεσθαι erwähnt wird. Nach der Ermordung Getas hatte Caracalla einen Amnestie-Erlass verkündet,[23] der bald einer

---

21 *Les carrières procuratoriennes équestres*... (1960/61) II, 610ff. In der Inschrift werden Aelius Antipater als *ab epistulis* und Aelius Coeranus als *a libellis* genannt. Wenn man Honoré (*JRS* 69 [1979] 64) folgt, müsste man wohl beide ausschliesslich dem Caracalla zuweisen. Eine nicht ganz entfernte Parallele ist es, dass der freilich viel ältere Antoninus Pius als Mitregent Hadrians einen eigenen *a libellis* (Maecian) hatte; s. *CIL* XIV 5347f.; Kunkel, *Herkunft und soziale Stellung der römischen Juristen* (1967²) 174.

22 Herod. 4.7.4ff.; Birley (o.A. 5) 272. Zu den "juristischen Eigenarten" Caracallas, s. jetzt Williams, *Latomus* 38 (1979) 67ff.

23 Vgl. dazu nur Heichelheim (o.A. 17) 18ff.; er lässt den Erlass bereits mit I 60 beginnen. Nicht nur die Verwendung des Wortes "*diatagma*," sondern auch allgemeine Überlegungen sprechen für ein Edikt. Daher ist es kaum möglich, die dramatische Schilderung der Senatssitzung bei Cass. Dio *ep.* 78.3.3 mit der Bekanntgabe der Amnestie gleichsam *in transitu* (vgl. *CJ* 9.51.1 u. u. IV) zu einer anderweitigen Interpretation von ἀποκρίνεσθαι im Sinne eines mündlichen Bescheides zu verwenden. Ob man die Worte im Senat bereits als Verkündung oder als Ankündigung der Amnestie interpretiert, jedenfalls muss sich *P. Giss.* 40 II.7ff. auf einen schriftlich formulierten (Edikts-)Text beziehen.

Präzisierung und Novellierung bedurfte; sie ist in *P. Giss.* 40
II.1ff., teilweise auch in *CJ* 10.61.1 (s. auch Ulp. *D.* 50.2.3.1)
überliefert. Auf den ersten Erlass nimmt die Novelle in folgender
Weise Bezug (Z. 7ff.): ...ἐκ τῶν ῥημάτων τοῦ προτέρου διατάγματος,
ἐν ᾧ οὕτως ἀπεκρινάμην; ''Ὑποστρεφέτωσαν πάντες εἰς τὰς πατρίδας
τὰς ἰδίας.' Nach dem Text wird mit ἀποκρίνεσθαι das *"dicere"* des
Edikts (*diatagma*) umschrieben. Die Wortwahl ist sicherlich auffällig und erklärungsbedürftig. Dass im lateinischen Text *rescribere* stand, ist unwahrscheinlich. *Scribere, respondere, dicere,
decernere, constituere, iubere, statuere* kommen mit grösserer oder
kleinerer Wahrscheinlichkeit als Kandidaten für den Urtext in Betracht, drängen sich aber nicht gerade als Äquivalenzen auf.
Sollte im Original ein "untechnisches" *respondere* gestanden haben,
so hat der amtliche Übersetzer wörtlich übersetzt; andernfalls hat
er einen Begriff gewählt, der offensichtlich nur geringe technische
Dignität besass.

Zuletzt darf noch auf *SB* VI 8247 (*FIRA* III 171b; a. 63)[24] hingewiesen werden, wo--wahrscheinlich in einem privaten Protokoll--
u.a. formlose Bescheide (*interlocutiones de plano*; s.u. IV) des
Praefectus Aegypti Caecina Tuscus gegenüber Veteranen wiedergegeben
sind. Sie werden von dem Praefekten *pro tribunali* wiederholt; dabei bleibt offen, ob damit ein Urteil im förmlichen Sinne gefällt
wird. Für die Zwischenbescheide werden die Worte ἀποκρίνεσθαι und
εἰπεῖν verwendet. Die Verwendung von ἀποκρίνεσθαι wird damit zusammenhängen, dass der Praefekt auf eine Bitte der Veteranen re-
agiert.

Bereits jetzt lässt sich die Vermutung formulieren, dass man
aus der Verwendung des Wortes *"apokrima"* am Beginn des *P. Col.* 123
--das möglicherweise aus einer privaten Übersetzung stammt (s.u.
V 4)--keine Schlüsse auf das "Wesen" der *apokrimata* ziehen darf.
Das ist nicht weiter verwunderlich, wenn man bedenkt, dass auch der
amtliche und der juristische Sprachgebrauch für die Konstitutionen
weit weniger technisch sind, als es die modernen Lehrbücher vermuten lassen. Einige Belege dürften genügen (vgl. auch u. IV).

Im Edikt des Prätors werden (neben Gesetzen, Plebisziten,
Senatsbeschlüssen) nur die *edicta* und die *decreta principum* als

---

24 Dazu etwa Wenger, *SZ* 59 (1939) 380ff.

Rechtsquellen genannt.[25] Es besteht kein Anlass zu glauben, dass
damit etwa nur auf "Urteilssprüche" (decreta) hingewiesen werden
soll (s. nur Pap. Iust. D. 2.14.37; Ulp. D. 43.8.2.10,16). Gerade
das Wort "decretum" hat anscheinend die Tendenz, für alle (oder
mehrere) Konstitutionenarten einzutreten (Pap. D. 1.1.7; PS 3.4b.2
[etwas anders Cons. 4.7, 7.4f.]; Fronto ad Marc. imp. 1.6; vgl. im
übrigen auch Marcian D. 1.22.2; Ulp. D. 42.1.47, 50.5.1.1 und das
"epikrima" im 3. Edikt von Kyrene [FIRA I 68]). Gaius (inst. 1.5)
nennt als Konstitutionenarten decretum, edictum und epistula. Die--
ihm als Rechtsquelle bekannte [1.94]--subscriptio hat er entweder
der epistula (oder dem decretum) zugeordnet oder er hatte überhaupt
keine vollständige "divisio" der Konstitutionenarten im Sinne (s.
auch das Fehlen der mandata wie in Ulp. D. 1.4.1.1). Selbst das
"edictum" kann anscheinend als "Symbol" für alle Konstitutionenarten
dienen (Marcian D. 28.7.14). Weniger bedeutsam ist es, dass statt
dem üblichen "rescriptum" (vielleicht nur bis zur Severer-Zeit) auch
rescriptio verwandt wird (Iul. D. 1.18.8; Call. D. 1.8.9; Mark Aurel
in Inst. Just. 3.11.1; Verus bei Fronto ad Ver. Imp. 1.1.1; CJ
5.47.1 [itp?]). Für den Urteilsspruch werden verschiedenartige
Verben gebraucht: pronuntiare, dicere, decernere, placere, selten
respondere (s.o. bei A. 21), möglicherweise sogar rescribere (Paul.
D. 35.1.113; s. aber auch D. 49.14.48). In den constitutionum
libri des Papirius Justus sind trotz des weiten Titels möglicherweise nur Reskripte gesammelt. Die Beispiele lassen erkennen, dass
die römischen Juristen nicht geneigt sind, modernen Vollständig-
keits- und Präzisionsbedürfnissen in pedantischer Weise zu entsprechen.[26]

---

25 Ulp. D. 2.14.7.7, 3.1.1.8, 43.8.2 pr. Es kann hier dahinstehen, ob sich edicta allein auf vom Princeps erlassene Edikte bezieht (s. etwa Ankum, SZ 97 [1980] [Besprechungsaufsatz Chorus im
Druck] bei A. 95 u. 125); sicherlich werden diese aber mit einge-
schlossen. Ebenso bleibt die mögliche Entwicklung der Terminologie
für die Konstitutionen hier ausser Betracht. In Dessau 540 wird
ein Reskript als θεία ἀναγραφή bezeichnet.

26 Die Vermengung von Edikt und Reskript bei Arcadius Chari-
sius D. 50.4.18.30 ist für unsere Epoche nicht beweiskräftig. Bei
Coll. 15.2.4 und D. 5.3.25.16 ist es nicht ganz sicher, ob der die
Unterschiede von decretum und Reskript missachtende Sprachgebrauch
dem Ulpian zugeschrieben werden darf.

Unter diesen Umständen wird man auch die Präzisionsansprüche
an denjenigen, der die Sammlung in *P. Col.* 123 mit dem Titel:
antigrapha apokrimaton versehen hatte, nicht übertreiben dürfen.
Möglicherweise ist er mit der Schwierigkeit, lateinische Rechts-
terminologie ins Griechische zu übersetzen, nicht recht fertig geworden; über sie berichtet selbst ein des Griechischen durchaus
kundiger Jurist wie Modestin (*D.* 27.1.1.1). Was die lateinische
Terminologie selbst betrifft, so haben die Kolonen des *saltus
Burunitanus* anscheinend *libellus* und *epistula* durcheinander ge-
worfen (*FIRA* I 103 II.19); es wäre sicherlich verfehlt, aus diesem
Sprachgebrauch allein gewichtige Schlüsse zu ziehen.

Sieht man von all diesen Ausführungen ab, so bietet sich als
nächstliegende Erklärung für die Wahl der Überschrift des *P. Col.*
123 vielleicht eine sprachliche. Das griechische Äquivalent von
rescriptum ist bekanntlich "*antigraphe.*" Eine Überschrift: ἀντίγραφα ἀντιγραφῶν wäre gleichzeitig missverständlich und maniriert.
Was *subscriptio*/ὑπογραφή betrifft, so ist--für den Statthalter--die
Zusammenstellung: ἀντίγραφα ὑπογραφῶν überliefert (*FIRA* III 28,30);
ob sie feinerem Sprachempfinden Genüge leistet, bleibe dahinge-
stellt. Was den Kaiser betrifft, so existiert für die Übersetzung
von "*subscriptio*" durch ὑπογραφή anscheinend nur ein Beleg (Antoninus Pius in *P. Rendel Harris* 67). Dies seltene Auftreten dürfte
damit zusammenhängen, dass sich dieser Begriff anscheinend auf die
entsprechende Tätigkeit des Statthalters spezialisiert hatte (s. etwa
die ἱερὰ ὑπογραφή in *P. Oxy.* 3364, a. 208/9). Ähnliches mag für
sein lateinisches Äquivalent gelten (s. Modestin *D.* 48.10.29). Bekanntlich ist im Verhältnis zur Menge der überlieferten kaiserlichen
Reskripte das Substantiv *subscriptio* überaus selten belegt.[27] Wenn
man von Ulpian *D.* 1.4.1.1 absieht, so gehören die (wenigen) Belege
in den Juristenschriften alle dem 2. Jahrhundert an. So ist es

---

27 Dazu etwa Kübler, *RE* IV A 1 (1931) 490ff. Vgl. Gai. 1.94;
Ulp. *D.* 1.4.1.1; Paul. *D.* 4.8.32.14 (*subscribere*); *Inst. Just.* 2.12
pr; *CJ* 7.43.1 (Antoninus Pius); *FIRA* I 103 IV.10ff. Bei *CJ* 7.57
(Titel), 7.57.3 u. 5 dürfte sich *subscriptio* ebenso wie bei Modestin *D.* 48.10.29 auf den statthalterlichen Akt beziehen; in dem
Modestin-Text ist der Gegensatz zwischen dem Reskript des Kaisers
und der *subscriptio* des Statthalters auffällig. Die Abkürzung *S.*
für *subscribere* oder *scribere* wird demgegenüber weiterhin verwandt;
vgl. einstweilen Honoré, *Emperors and Lawyers*, II, 1.

vielleicht auch kein Zufall, dass das einzige Auftreten des griechischen Äquivalenz-Begriffes in den Papyri von Antoninus Pius stammt.
An die Stelle der *subscriptio* trat für den Kaiser das (allgemeine)
rescriptum (zu den Gründen s. auch u. V 2). Somit musste sich für
die kaiserlichen Bescheide des Jahres 200 die Überschrift ἀντίγραφα
ὑπογραφῶν nicht gerade aufdrängen.

Schliesslich könnte der Autor auch der Meinung gewesen sein,
dass die Sammlung zu vielfältig sei, als dass man hier sinnvoller-
weise einen exakten Titel voranstellen dürfte. Mit dieser Überlegung kommt man auf die inhaltlichen Probleme der *apokrimata*, die
hier offen gelassen werden sollen. Keinesfalls steckt hinter der
Verwendung des Wortes *apokrima* ein offizieller Sprachgebrauch. Es
ist ein schlechter Wegweiser bei der Suche nach dem "Wesen" der in
P. Col. 123 überlieferten Bescheide.

                                IV

Wie gerade der erwähnte Versuch von Lewis, eine neue Konstitutionenart "*apokrima*" zu konstruieren, zeigt, ist die Einordnung der
apokrimata in die Konstitutionentypen noch keineswegs mit Sicherheit gelungen. Auszugehen ist von dem umfassendsten Katalog der
Konstitutionenarten bei Ulp. *D.* 1.4.1.1; *Quodcumque igitur imperator per epistulam et subscriptionem statuit vel cognoscens decrevit
vel de plano interlocutus est vel edicto praecepit legem esse
constat. haec sunt quas vulgo constitutiones appellamus.*

Sicherlich wäre es voreilig, in diesem Katalog eine vollständige Klassifizierung der Konstitutionentypen zu sehen. Statt
der dann zu erwartenden Verwendung von *aut-aut* benutzt Ulpian die
lockere Anknüpfung mit *vel.* Das *vulgo* lässt erkennen, dass das
Begriffsfeld nicht vollständig technisiert ist (s. auch o. III bei
A. 25). Man muss sowohl mit hybriden Formen[28] als auch mit

---

28 Vgl. etwa den Streit über die Einordnung der umfangreichen
Konstitution Mark Aurels (vor allem zu Statusverhältnissen in Athen);
s. Oliver, *Marcus Aurelius. Aspects of Civic and Cultural Policy in
the East* (*Hesperia* Suppl. 13, 1970) 35ff.; C. P. Jones, *ZPE* 8 (1971)
161ff.; Oliver, *ZPE* 14 (1974) 265ff.; ders., *AJP* 100 (1979) 543ff.;
Williams, *ZPE* 17 (1975) 37ff.; s. auch S. Follet, *Rev. Phil.* 53
(1979) 28ff. Unter diesem Aspekt ist es ein symptomatischer Fehler
--wenn überhaupt ein Fehler--, wenn (vielleicht) ein *decretum* Domi-
tians (*FIRA* I 75) und eine *subscriptio* der Philippi (*FIRA* I 107) mit
der Briefformel *valete* bzw. *vale* schliesst. Vgl. auch Honoré a.a.O.
II 2 A. 75.

katalogfremden Konstitutionenarten rechnen. Was letzteres betrifft,
so darf an die *mandata* oder an eine *oratio* (etwa im Prätorianer-
lager; Ulp. *FV* 195, a. 168) als mögliche Rechtsquellen erinnert
werden; auch mündliche Antworten auf Anfragen von Gesandtschaften
(s.o. A. 10) kommen vielleicht als solche in Betracht. Trotz dieser Vorbehalte dürfte es sicherer sein, zuerst den Katalog Ulpians
mit den "typischen" Konstitutionenarten auszuschöpfen, bevor man
eine neue Form postuliert.

In der bisherigen Diskussion der *apokrimata* hat man sich auf
die "*subscriptiones*" konzentriert. Von dem "*interloqui de plano*,"
das bei Ulpian gleichberechtigt neben anderen Konstitutionentypen
erscheint, war bisher keine Rede--obwohl es sich vielleicht als
Surrogat für die von Lewis erwogene, aber nicht nachgewiesene Konstitutionenart des *apokrima* erweisen könnte. Das mag vor allem
damit zusammenhängen, dass das *interloqui de plano* sowohl in den
rechtshistorischen Handbüchern als auch in sonstigen Darstellungen
überhaupt nicht oder allenfalls am Rande erscheint. Eine rühmliche
Ausnahme ist Williams, der wenigstens versuchsweise für die Charak-
terisierung der in P. Berlin Inv. 7346 (*SB* IV 7366; Frisk, *Aegyptus*
9 [1928] 281ff.) überlieferten *apophasis* der Kaiser Septimius Severus und Caracalla vom 4. März 200 auf die *interlocutio de plano*
verweist.[29] Allerdings geht auch er auf die Eigenart dieses Konstitutionentypus nicht näher ein. Das ist verständlich, da wir
über die *interlocutio de plano* nur recht wenige Quellen haben und
auch diese Quellen bisher nicht ausreichend analysiert sind.[30]

---

29 *ZPE* 22 (1976) 241ff. (244). Der Text enthält eine Ausfertigung der (lückenhaft erhaltenen) Entscheidung aus dem Archiv (des
Statthalters?); beteiligt waren ein Πομπήιος Λιβελάριος und ein
Chrescentianus in offizieller Funktion (vgl. auch die Inschrift von
Banasa (Girard, *Textes*[7] VIII 16) Z. 20ff.). *Libelarios* wird gewöhnlich zu "*Liberalis*" verbessert und als Namensbestandteil ge-
lesen. Eher ist an einen Archivbeamten zu denken (*libellarius*,
oder gar *librarius*). Für *libellarius* gibt es aus der hier interessierenden Epoche zwei (etwas unsichere Belege); vgl. *BGU* 423
(Wilcken, *Chrest.* 480), *O. Bodl.* II 2358. Es bleibt offen, ob die
"*apophasis*" nicht doch die schriftliche Antwort auf eine Petition
ist.

30 Zur *interlocutio de plano* in *D.* 1.4.1.1 vgl. etwa P. Krüger, *Geschichte der Quellen und Litteratur des römischen Rechts*
(1912[2]) 103; Düll, *SZ* 52 (1932) 189f.; Berger, *ED* s.v.--alle wenig
befriedigend. Bereits Justinian hat die *interlocutio de plano* aus
hier nicht zu erörternden Gründen zusammen mit der *subscriptio* im

Selbst eine skizzenhafte Darstellung ist an dieser Stelle unange-
bracht; es muss die Formulierung einiger Thesen und Fragen genügen.
    Wenn man nach einem technischen Begriff der *interlocutio* sucht,
so trifft man auf eine--häufig in lockerer Form formulierte--
Zwischenentscheidung eines Richters in einem "normalen" Prozess;
sie erfolgt also *pro tribunali* (vgl. etwa *CJ* 7.57.4 (a. 239); *FIRA*
III 165). Ein juristischer Akt ergeht demgegenüber *de plano* (oder
in transitu), wenn er nicht in einem formellen Verfahren, sondern
"auf ebener Erde" oder "im Vorübergehen" erfolgt (vgl. etwa die
Beispiele für den Statthalter in Ulp. *D*. 1.16.9.3, 48.2.6). Wenn
der Kaiser in einem Prozess einen Zwischenbescheid erlässt, so ver-
fährt auch er *pro tribunali* oder *in auditorio* (s. etwa Paul.
40.5.38). Trotz des etwas überraschenden Terminus "*interloqui*,"
wird man als *interlocutiones de plano* solche Akte des Kaisers bezeichnen dürfen, die ausserhalb eines normalen Prozesses ergehen.
    Allzuviel ist mit dieser Festlegung nicht gewonnen. Es ist
sicherlich nicht vorstellbar, dass jede gelegentliche Willens-,
Meinungs-, Unmuts-, Beifallsäusserung des Kaisers--soweit sie nur
passenden Inhalt hatte--Gesetzeskraft (*legis vicem*) haben sollte.
Ein irgendwie gearteter "Rechtsgeltungswille" des Kaisers musste
nicht nur vorhanden gewesen, sondern auch zum Ausdruck gebracht
worden sein. Aber nicht nur im öffentlichen Interesse, sondern
auch im Interesse der Beteiligten bedurfte die *interlocutio de
plano* einer gewissen--wenn auch minimalen--"Formalisierung." Da es
keinerlei Indizien dafür gibt, dass kaiserliche *interlocutiones*--
wie Reskripte--in Schriftform erteilt wurden, so muss man wohl mit
einer "Protokollierung" des Bescheides rechnen. In diese Richtung
deutet der Umstand, dass die Amtshandlungen von Magistraten *de plano*
bisweilen die Mitwirkung eines "bürokratischen" Stabes (Ulp. *FV* 112)
oder zumindest von Zeugen erkennen lassen (so vielleicht in *FIRA* III
171b). Es wäre etwa daran zu denken, dass der Bescheid des Kaisers
einem "Sekretär" diktiert oder in eine Zeugenurkunde (*testatio*) auf-
nommen wurde.

Paralleltext *Inst. Just.* 1.2.6 beseitigt; s. auch Theophilos z. St.,
sowie *CJ* 1.14.3 (a. 426). Zur prozessualen *interlocutio* und zum
Verfahren *de plano* vgl. nur Kaser, *Das römische Zivilprozessrecht*
(1966) 145, 392 passim. Vgl. zur *interlocutio de plano* D. Nörr,
Studi Sanfilippo (im Druck).

Wie bereits Schiller vermutet hat, lassen sich solche *inter-locutiones de plano* des Kaisers möglicherweise in den *sententiae et epistulae Hadriani* finden.[31] Für unsere Zwecke mag ein Hinweis auf den "Gnadenakt" Caracallas genügen, von dem *CJ* 9.51.1 (a. 216) berichtet: *Imp. Antoninus A. cum salutatus ab Oclatinio Advento et Opellio Macrino praefectis praetorio clarissimis viris, item amicis et principalibus officiorum et utriusque ordinis viris et processisset, oblatus est ei Iulianus Licinianus ab Aelio Ulpiano tunc legato in insulam deportatus. Antoninus Augustus dixit: Restituo te in integrum provinciae tuae. Et adiecit: Ut autem scias, quid sit in integrum: honoribus et ordini tuo et omnibus ceteris.*

Mit grösster Wahrscheinlichkeit handelt es sich hier um eine--bei der *salutatio* (s. auch Suet. *Aug.* 53.2) gefällte--Entscheidung des Kaisers *de plano* (vgl. das Wortfeld *de plano, procedere, prodire* (Gai. *D.* 40.2.7), *in transitu* (Gai. *inst.* 1.20)). Weiterhin darf unterstellt werden, dass der Akt vorbereitet war; ein Deportierter wird sich kaum ohne Erlaubnis vor den--im konkreten Fall wohlunterrichteten--Kaiser gewagt haben. Obwohl es sich dort um ein Verfahren "*in auditorio*" handelt, ist die Parallele zur Gohariener-Inschrift (s.o. A. 19) auffällig. In beiden Fällen wurde anscheinend ein Protokoll aufgenommen, für das möglicherweise die mit den *cognitiones* befasste Kanzlei zuständig war.

Folgt man diesen Indizien, so stehen die *interlocutiones de plano* des Kaisers zwischen den Urteilen (*decreta*) und den Reskripten (*subscriptiones*). Auf der einen Seite sind es mündliche Bescheide, die protokolliert werden wie Gerichtsurteile; auf der anderen Seite sind sie das mündliche Gegenstück zu den Reskripten und dienen als solche der Erledigung von (mündlichen oder schriftlichen) Petitionen.

Kehrt man zu den *apokrimata* zurück, so steht inhaltlich nichts im Wege, sie als *interlocutiones de plano* zu begreifen. Doch macht die formale Seite zumindest derzeit noch Schwierigkeiten. Vor allem stört die Tatsache, dass die Entscheidungen proponiert wurden. Gerade wenn man die *interlocutiones* als mündliche Akte mit der Funktion von Reskripten bezeichnet, so wäre das *proponere* schwer verständlich. Während es bei den Reskripten primär den Zweck hat,

---

31 Vgl. *Atti II° Congr. Int. SISD* (Florenz 1971) 717ff.; Volterra, ebda 869ff.

den Petenten die kaiserliche Willensäusserung kundzutun, würde es
jetzt nur noch dazu dienen, dem Petenten die Verfertigung einer
durch Zeugen bestätigten Abschrift zu ermöglichen. Aber auch wenn
man an die urteilsmässige Protokollierung der *interlocutio* denkt,
wäre das *proponere* verwunderlich. Man müsste dann unterstellen,
dass die Kanzlei aus dem Protokoll einen Auszug herstellt, der aus-
gehängt wird. Was wir--und das ist allerdings wenig genug--von den
in Protokollen festgehaltenen Gerichtsurteilen der Kaiser wissen,
lässt an einem solchen Verfahren zweifeln. Eine "Proponierung" von
decreta dürfte nicht völlig ausgeschlossen, aber unüblich gewesen
sein.

Nach unserem Wissensstand spricht wenig dafür, die *apokrimata*
unter die *interlocutiones de plano* einzuordnen. Dass eine *interlocutio* eines Praefekten einmal auch mit dem Verbum ἀποκρίνεσθαι
eingeleitet wird (*FIRA* III 171b [a. 63]; s.o. A. 24), ist sicherlich kein ausreichendes Indiz. Doch darf nicht vergessen werden,
dass wir über die kaiserlichen *interlocutiones de plano* viel zu
wenig wissen, als dass hier mehr als nur (schwache) Wahrscheinlich-
keitsurteile möglich sind. Die Verwendung des Wortes *apokrima* ist
jedenfalls ohne Beweiswert in die eine oder andere Richtung.

                                V

Es bleibt die Frage, welche Umstände für oder gegen eine Einordnung der *apokrimata* unter die Gruppe der Reskripte (*subscriptiones*) sprechen. Die Überzeugungskraft der folgenden Ausführungen
wird darunter leiden, dass an dieser Stelle keine Auseinandersetzung mit den Thesen Wilckens möglich ist, die bis heute unsere Vorstellungen von der Reskriptenpraxis beherrschen.[32] Auch wenn man
sie in vielen, gerade auch in grundsätzlichen Punkten für durchaus
plausibel hält, so werden sich doch gewisse Einschränkungen und
Nuancierungen nicht vermeiden lassen. Sie hängen vor allem mit
zwei angreifbaren Prämissen Wilckens zusammen: Einmal glaubte er--
trotz kleinerer Vorbehalte (*Hermes* 55 [1920] 38)--

---

32 *Hermes* 55 (1920) 1ff.; *APF* 9 (1930) 15ff.; letzthin etwa
Williams, *JRS* 64 (1974) 86ff. Bestritten werden die Thesen
Wilckens in letzter Zeit nur von A. d'Ors-Martin, *AJP* 100 (1979)
111ff.; dazu jetzt W. Williams, *ZPE* 40 (1980) 283ff. Eine ein-
gehende Begründung meiner Auffassung soll in *SZ* 98 (1981) erscheinen.

die Promulgationspraxis im wesentlichen auf Grund der Inschriften und Papyri und ohne breite Benutzung der in den juristischen Texten überlieferten Konstitutionen beschreiben zu können; zum anderen übertrug er allzu unbefangen die Charakteristiken der *Hypographe*-Praxis des Statthalters Ägyptens auf die kaiserliche Reskriptenpraxis.

1. Die Veröffentlichung der *apokrimata* geschah bekanntlich durch *proponere* (προτίθεσθαι) in der Stoa des Gymnasiums in Alexandria. Zwar wurden auch andere kaiserliche Rechtsakte (vor allem Edikte, bisweilen aber auch *epistulae* und möglicherweise sogar *decreta*) proponiert. Doch ist das *proponere* der *apokrimata* sicherlich ein wichtiges Indiz dafür, dass es sich bei ihnen um Reskripte in der Form der *subscriptio* handelt. Immerhin ist nicht zu vergessen, dass es auch andere Promulgationsformen gab, die uns sogar in engster zeitlicher Nähe zu den *apokrimata* begegnen. Zwei der Belege dürften der 2. Aprilhälfte des Jahres 200 zuzuweisen sein. Der Petent von *CJ* 8.37.1 empfing (vgl. *accepta*) die Antwort auf seinen "*libellus*" anscheinend persönlich. Im zweiten Fall (*CJ* 6.2.1) spricht der Sachverhalt für ein Reskript in Form der *subscriptio*--wenn auch eine *epistula* nicht völlig ausgeschlossen werden kann; der Bescheid wurde dem Petenten mittelbar oder unmittelbar übermittelt (*dare*). Auf gleiche Weise wurde ein Reskript vom 1. Juli 200 promulgiert (*CJ* 3.31.2); da der Adressat ein *miles* ist, dürfte auch hier eine "*subscriptio*" vorliegen. Es gibt keine sicheren Indizien dafür, dass zum *accipere* oder *dare* des Reskripts noch ein *proponere* hinzutrat.

Bekanntlich wurden die 13 *apokrimata* an drei verschiedenen, nacheinanderliegenden Tagen proponiert. Wenn man an dieses Faktum Überlegungen über den täglichen Ausstoss der Kanzlei anknüpfen will, so soll man nicht vergessen, dass auch andere Promulgationsmöglichkeiten bestanden. Dass im übrigen die reskribierende Tätigkeit der Kaiser Severus und Caracalla sich über die in den *apokrimata* erwähnten Daten hinaus erstreckte, dafür spricht schon, dass Kaisernamen und - titulatur erst später eingefügt wurden. Anscheinend hat der Abschreiber nur einen Teil des Aushangs berücksichtigt. Doch kommt man damit zu den Problemen des Zweckes der Abschrift, die hier nicht erörtert werden sollen.[33]

2. In der Diskussion über die Rechtsnatur der *apokrimata* wird
immer wieder der Umstand erörtert, dass der Papyrus nur die kaiserlichen Bescheide, nicht aber die Petitionen enthält. Geht man von
der These Wilckens aus, dass die *subscriptio* zusammen mit der Petition proponiert wurde, so hat man zwei Erklärungsmöglichkeiten:
Entweder man schliesst daraus, dass die *apokrimata* eben keine *subscriptiones* sind. Oder: man begnügt sich mit der Feststellung,
dass der Schreiber sich allein für die--ohne die Petition häufig
kaum verständlichen--kaiserlichen Bescheide interessiert habe; den
libellus hätte er nur insoweit benutzt, als er aus ihm den Namen
des (der) Adressaten entnommen hätte. Dieses Verfahren wäre allenfalls mit dem Hinweis auf Bequemlichkeit oder Kostenersparnis zu
begründen--wenn man nicht unterstellen will, dass dem Abschreiber
oder seinem Auftraggeber die *libelli* anderweit bekannt waren. Das
hier skizzierte Problem ist leichter lösbar, wenn man die These
Wilckens mit den notwendigen Einschränkungen versieht.

Sowohl der Terminus "*subscriptio*" als auch die Existenz des
liber libellorum rescriptorum et propositorum (s. *FIRA* I 106) deutet darauf hin, dass einmal--möglicherweise am Beginn der Entwicklung der Reskriptenpraxis--die Reskripte in der von Wilcken beschriebenen Form promulgiert wurden: Der Kaiser (die Kanzlei) setzte
den Bescheid unter den *libellus* (*subscribere*); *libellus* und *subscriptio* wurden proponiert. Wenn auch keine plausiblen Zeugnisse
dafür vorliegen, so mag auch in der uns interessierenden Epoche
bisweilen dieser Weg noch eingeschlagen worden sein. Im übrigen
sprechen viele--hier nicht zu erörternde--Indizien dafür, dass jetzt
in der Regel allein der kaiserliche Bescheid proponiert wurde. Entgegen der "natürlichen" Praxis der *subscriptio*--wie sie bei der

---

33 Was den Zweck der Abschrift betrifft, so scheint mir die
Vermutung plausibel zu sein, dass der Abschreiber für sich oder für
einen Auftraggeber *exempla* für künftige Prozesse und Streitigkeiten
sammelte; vgl. dazu ausführlich Schiller, *BASP* 14 (1977) 75ff.;
Williams, *JRS* 64 (1974) 90ff. Eine andere Frage ist es, ob die an
drei aufeinander folgenden Tagen proponierten Bescheide unbedingt
den "Tagesausstoss" der kaiserlichen Kanzlei darstellen. Es ist
nicht ausgeschlossen, dass der Abschreiber sich von einem für uns
nicht mehr erkennbaren Auswahlkriterium hat leiten lassen; vgl. nur
die spätere Einfügung von Kaisernamen und -titulatur.

statthalterlichen *Hypographe* weiter fortlebte--wurde es jetzt notwendig, der kaiserlichen *subscriptio* den Namen des Adressaten vor-
anzustellen.   Bereits dadurch lockerte sich die Verbindung zwischen
dem *libellus* und dem Bescheid; letzterer näherte sich einer *epistula*, so dass man--streng genommen--in dieser Epoche nur mehr von
einer "unechten" *subscriptio* sprechen dürfte.   Zu dieser Entwicklung gehört auch der bereits erwähnte Umstand, dass die Bezeichnung
subscriptio für den kaiserlichen Bescheid zugunsten des Terminus
rescriptum (*rescribere*) aus dem Rechtsverkehr gezogen wird; sie
bleibt der statthalterlichen (echten) *subscriptio* vorbehalten
(s.o. III a. E.).

3. Wir haben bisher festgestellt, dass (nur) Adresse und
Tenor der Entscheidung proponiert wurden.   Insoweit entspricht die
Veröffentlichung der *apokrimata* der üblichen Praxis.   Der Abschrei-
ber konnte daher die *libelli* auch nicht in die Abschrift aufnehmen.
Auffällig ist aber eine weitere--wiederum nur scheinbare--Unvoll-
ständigkeit der *apokrimata*.

Bekanntlich geschah die "Ausfertigung" des Reskripts dadurch,
dass der Kaiser den Bescheid mit seiner Unterschrift: (*re*)*scripsi*
versah; den Bestätigungsvermerk (*recognovi*) fügte (nach herrschen-
der Auffassung) die Kanzlei hinzu.   Man muss wohl davon ausgehen,
dass dadurch der Bescheid "rechtskräftig" wurde.   Wären die Reskripte einschliesslich der Klauseln: *rescripsi*, *recognovi* proponiert worden, so müsste den Parteien--möglicherweise aber auch
Dritten, die die Reskripte als *exempla* gebrauchen wollten--unbedingt
daran gelegen sein, diese Klauseln auch in ihre Abschriften aufzu-
nehmen.   Doch fehlen sie beispielsweise in allen Reskriptenabschrif-
ten aus der Aufenthaltszeit des Septimius Severus in Ägypten.   Aber
auch sonst finden sich keine Zeugnisse dafür, dass die Ausferti-
gungsklauseln im proponierten Text des Reskripts standen.   Soweit
sie überhaupt--und das ist selten genug--in unseren Quellen erscheinen, spricht alles oder einiges dafür, dass es sich um Abschriften handelt, die nicht vom proponierten, sondern vom archi-
vierten Text genommen wurden.

Ist das Gesagte richtig, so ergibt sich das zwingende--im
übrigen auch praktisch einleuchtende--Ergebnis, dass nicht der Ori-
ginaltext der kaiserlichen *subscriptio* den Risiken der öffentlichen
Proponierung ausgesetzt wurde, sondern von vorneherein nur eine

Abschrift. Auch insoweit sind die *apokrimata* Zeugnisse für eine
Regel, nicht für eine Ausnahme.

4. Wenig Sicheres lässt sich im Moment noch zum sprachlichen
Problem der *apokrimata* sagen. Allem Anschein nach war es die
Praxis der Kanzlei *a libellis*, die *subscriptiones* in lateinischer
Sprache zu verfassen und herausgehen zu lassen.[34] Doch gibt es
immerhin Fälle, in denen die Umstände mit grösserer oder geringerer
Wahrscheinlichkeit auf eine *subscriptio* in griechischer Sprache
deuten. Das klarste Zeugnis ist das von Callistratus (*D.* 50.6.6.2)
zitierte Reskript des Pertinax; es nimmt in seinem Text ausdrücklich auf einen *libellus* (*biblion*) Bezug. Im Falle von *CJ* 4.24.1
(a. 207) spricht immerhin der lateinische Propositionsvermerk für
eine *subscriptio*; doch ist eine *epistula* nicht ausgeschlossen.
Wegen des Sachzusammenhanges zu *apokr.* 10 würde man gern auch ein
von Ulpian (*D.* 16.1.2.3) zitiertes griechisches Reskript des Severus hierherzählen; doch muss auch hier mit einer *epistula* gerechnet
werden.[35]

Unter diesen Umständen ist eine griechische "Urfassung" der
apokrimata nicht ausgeschlossen. Dass sie unwahrscheinlich ist,
liesse sich nur durch eine (auf den ersten Blick nicht schwierige)
Rückübersetzung der *apokrimata* ins Lateinische demonstrieren. Wenn
man die Existenz eines lateinischen Originals ablehnt, so muss man
zumindest konzedieren, dass der Verfasser weithin lateinisch "gedacht" hat; der lateinische Sprachduktus schimmert überall durch
den griechischen Text hindurch. In jedem Fall sind sowohl die übliche Verwaltungspraxis als auch die vielen Belege für lateinische
Reskripte aus der Zeit des Ägyptenaufenthalts der Kaiser, wie sie
sich im *CJ* finden, starke Argumente für einen lateinischen Urtext.[36]

---

34 Vgl. dazu jetzt Honoré, *Emperors and Lawyers*, II, 2 bei
Anm. 90.

35 Bei *CJ* 9.6.1, Maec. *D.* 14.2.9 und Call. *D.* 8.3.16 kann es
sich sowohl um *epistulae* als auch um *subscriptiones* handeln.

36 Vgl. auch H. J. Wolff, *SZ* 73 (1956) 406ff. S. ferner
Lewis, *BASP* 13 (1976) 170f. zu *P. Oxy.* XLII 3018.1ff. (Reskript der
Kaiser Severus und Caracalla, das auf ein [im Gymnasium in Alexandria proponiertes] Reskript derselben Kaiser vom April 200 verweist). Vgl. Th. Drew-Bear (-W. Eck-P. Herrmann), *Chiron* 7 (1977)
356ff. zu den *sacrae litterae*.

Was den Adressatenkreis betrifft, so lassen sich weder auf
Grund der *apokrimata* und der anderen in Ägypten gefundenen Belege
noch auf Grund der in den juristischen Quellen enthaltenen Reskripte
ausserägyptische Petenten und Adressaten in den *apokrimata* beweisen
oder ausschliessen. Immerhin ist die Existenz der im *CJ* überlieferten Reskripte eine deutliche Warnung vor einer vorschnellen Ein-
grenzung aller *apokrimata* auf die spezifischen Verhältnisse Ägyptens.[37]

Ob im Falle einer Übersetzung diese von der Kanzlei--sicherlich
nicht von der Kanzlei *ab epistulis Graecis*, deren Vorstand zu dieser
Zeit der Stilkünstler Aelius Antipater gewesen sein könnte (vgl. o.
Anm. 21)--oder vom Abschreiber verfertigt wurde, lässt sich nicht
feststellen. Das Fehlen eines privaten Übersetzervermerks (wie er
etwa in *FIRA* I 78 oder in *P. Harr.* 67 erscheint) ist ebensowenig
ein ausreichendes Kriterium wie die Datierung der *apokrimata* mit
ägyptischen Monatsnamen[38] oder die ungefüge sprachliche Fassung.

5. Mit den Überlegungen zur Sprache der *apokrimata* kommt man
in unmittelbaren Kontakt zu den häufiger erwähnten Studien Honorés
über den Stil der Reskripte und die Verwendung von Stilmerkmalen
zur Identifizierung der jeweiligen *a libellis*. Die *apokrimata* sind
für ihn anscheinend wenig aufschlussreich. Vielmehr veranlasst ihn
das Fehlen sicherer stilistischer Merkmale zu der Überlegung, ob
die *apokrimata*--entgegen der üblichen Praxis--nicht vom Kaiser
einem Schreiber diktiert worden sind.[39]

Die kaiserlichen Kanzleien (oder Teile von ihnen) befanden
sich sicherlich mit den Kaisern in Ägypten. So könnte das in *P.*
Oxy. XLII 3019 überlieferte Protokollfragment einer Sitzung *pro*
tribunali letztlich auf das von der Kanzlei *a cognitionibus* (oder
a memoria/a commentariis)[40] verfertigte offizielle Protokoll

---

37 Vgl. auch die Tätigkeit Mark Aurels in Pannonien, deren
Wirkungskreis sich keineswegs auf die nächste Umgebung beschränkte;
s. nochmals Oliver (o. A. 28).

38 Vgl. zu diesen etwa *P. Giss.* 40 II.1ff. und (problematisch)
P. Oxy. XII 1407 (a. 258/59).

39 *JRS* 69 (1979) 55; Honoré, *Emperors and Lawyers*, II, 3.

40 In dieser Epoche hiess die zuständige Kanzlei wohl
a memoria; vgl. zum Problem Millar (o. A. 1) 259ff.

zurückgehen. Auf diese Kanzleien musste man vielleicht auch
zurückgreifen, wenn man die *apokrimata*--gegen die erste Wahrschein-
lichkeit--als *interlocutiones de plano* auffassen möchte. Handelte
es sich dagegen bei ihnen um Reskripte (*subscriptiones*), so war die
Kanzlei *a libellis* zuständig. Wie Honoré nachgewiesen hat (s.
Tryph. *D.* 20.5.12 *pr*),[41] war der jeweilige *a libellis* am Erlass der
Bescheide in der Regel aktiv beteiligt. Als *a libellis* der Jahre
199/200, der die Kaiser nach Ägypten begleitete, kommen Aelius
Coeranus--den Honoré aber lieber als nur für Caracalla zuständigen
a libellis ansehen möchte[42]--oder der berühmte Jurist Papinian in
Betracht. Geht man mit Honoré von letzterem aus und legt man an
die *apokrimata* die stilistischen Maßstäbe an, die er für Papinian
entwickelt hat,[43] so ist die Ausbeute nicht allzu reichlich. Beispielsweise ist *apokr.* 8 anders formuliert als das (inhaltlich ver-
wandte) Reskript *CJ* 3.28.8 (a. 196), für dessen Verfasser Honoré
Papinian hält. Immerhin gibt es auch kleinere Indizien für den
Stil Papinians.

So finden sich nach Honoré in den Reskripten der Jahre 194 bis
202 häufig Antithesen oder Parallelisierungen;[44] ähnlich formuliert

---

41 Die Mitwirkung des Kaisers bei *subscriptiones* oder *epistulae*
geht etwa aus Iul. *D.* 1.18.8 hervor. Es bleibt offen, in welcher
Funktion Julian die Reskriptenpraxis des Kaisers beobachtete. Möglicherweise zeigt der Text, dass (fallweise oder in bestimmten
Epochen) das *consilium* beteiligt war.

42 *JRS* 69 (1979) 64; s. auch Pflaum (o. A. 21) 610ff. Zu
Papinian vgl. auch D. Nörr (o. A. 6) 74f.; Syme, *SZ* 97 (1980) 83ff., 94.

43 *JRS* 69 (1979) 57ff.; Honoré, *Emperors and Lawyers*, III, 1
Nr. 1.

44 Vgl. beispielsweise *CJ* 4.14.1; s. Honoré, *Emperors and
Lawyers*, II, 4 nach Anm. 249. Besonders deutlich sind *CJ* 10.41.1
und *D.* 18.2.16; beide Reskripte, die nicht präzise datiert sind,
werden von Honoré Papinian zugeschrieben (III 2 A. 579 und 620).
Wenn man die antithetische Form berücksichtigt, so entfallen auch
die Schwierigkeiten, mit denen sich der scharfsinnige Kommentar von
Westermann-Schiller (o. A. 5) 56ff. zu *apokr.* 4 herumschlägt. Es
handelt sich schlicht um verschiedene (vielleicht benachbarte)
Grundstücke desselben Schuldners/Petenten; obwohl sie nach Behaup-
tung des Petenten nur teilweise verpfändet waren, versuchte der
Gläubiger anscheinend aus allen Grundstücken Befriedigung zu erhalten. Offen bleibt das Verhältnis der *lex conventionis* hinsichtlich des Pfandes zur *vis*; vgl. dazu *CJ* 8.13.3 (a. 205); Ulp. *D.*
47.2.56. Vgl. zum Problem Kaser, *Das römische Privatrecht* I (1971^2)
471 (mit Lit. 395 A. 52, 470 A. 9); II (1975^2) 314 Anm. 13 und

ist das *apokr.* 4. Für den *a libellis* Papinian soll es weiterhin
charakteristisch sein, dass er den Petenten Hinweise über das richtige Verfahren gibt; zu vergleichen sind hier die *apokrimata* 4,8,
11,13. Der Stil Papinians gilt allgemein als schwer und gedrängt;
damit mag es zusammenhängen, dass die mögliche Rückübersetzung einzelner *apokrimata* trotz aller durchscheinenden Latinismen des
griechischen Textes zu wenig eleganten lateinischen Texten zu
führen scheint (s. etwa *apokr.* 1,4,12). Wie man auch allgemein zu
den Thesen Honorés stehen mag, jedenfalls wird es nützlich sein,
bei einem Versuch, den lateinischen Text der *apokrimata* herzustellen, besonders auf den Sprachgebrauch Papinians zu achten.

    Auch wenn man Papinian (und nicht etwa einen anderen *a libellis*
oder einen Kanzleigehilfen) hinter dem Inhalt der *apokrimata* zu
suchen unternimmt, so kommt man doch um die Feststellung nicht herum, dass besondere juristische Finessen in ihnen nicht erkennbar
sind. Das bekannte Reskript über die *longi temporis praescriptio*,[45]
das ebenfalls in die Zeit des Ägyptenaufenthalts fällt, eröffnet
hier--wenigstens auf den ersten Blick--ganz andere juristische Di-
mensionen. Nicht verwunderlich ist es, dass die *apokrimata* gerade
solchen Problemen viel Raum geben, die nicht zum Privatrecht im
engeren Sinne gehören. Der *CJ* zeigt mit aller Deutlichkeit die
Wichtigkeit des "Verwaltungsrechts" in der kaiserlichen Konstitutionenpraxis. Dass die überlieferten Konstitutionen der hohen und
späten Prinzipatszeit ein gewisses Schwergewicht im Privatrecht erkennen lassen,[46] ist nur ein Überlieferungsproblem. Im Hintergrund
steht das bekannte Phänomen der grösseren Stabilität und Kontinui-
tät des Privatrechts im Vergleich zum Verwaltungsrecht.

                              VI

    In den vorhergehenden Ausführungen konnte nur ein kleiner Teil
der Probleme angesprochen werden, die im Umkreis der *apokrimata*

---

passim; ders. *SDHI* 45 (1979) 7ff. Was den Wortlaut betrifft, so
liesse sich auch *apokr.* 12 mit Pap. *D.* 40.8.8 vergleichen.

    45 *BGU* I 267; *P. Stras.* 22 (*FIRA* I 84f.). Zum Datierungs-
problem s. Nörr (o. A. 5) 74 Anm. 2.

    46 Zum Problem vgl. auch Honoré, *Emperors and Lawyers*, I nach
Anm. 112.

auftauchen.   Folgendes ist festzuhalten: (1) Bei der Untersuchung
der *apokrimata* dürfen der *Codex* Justinians und insbesondere
diejenigen Konstitutionen nicht übersehen werden, die während des
Ägyptenaufenthalts der Kaiser Septimius Severus und Caracalla erlassen wurden.   (2) Wenn man das "Wesen" der *apokrimata* zu bestimmen
unternimmt, so ist das Wort "*apokrima*" kein zuverlässiger Wegweiser.
(3) Bei eben dieser Untersuchung trifft man auf einen in der modernen Literatur fast vergessenen Konstitutionentypus: die *interlocutio de plano*.   Gerade wegen unserer weitgehenden Unkenntnis
über diesen Typus ist es nicht ausgeschlossen--aber auch nicht be-
weisbar--, dass die *apokrimata* ihm zuzuordnen sind.   (4) Will man die
apokrimata den Reskripten (*subscriptiones*) zuweisen, so tut man
sich leichter, wenn man die Thesen Wilckens über die Reskriptenpraxis in einzelnen Punkten einer auch sonst angezeigten Revision
unterzieht.   So verstanden, sind sie zugleich ein Beleg dafür, dass
zumindest in der hier interessierenden Epoche in der Regel weder
der *libellus* noch die (*re*)*scripsi/recognovi*-Klausel proponiert
wurden.   (5) Bei der Erörterung der Sprachprobleme der *apokrimata*
sind die Untersuchungen Honorés über den Stil der kaiserlichen Reskripte zu berücksichtigen.

München   Dieter Nörr

PART 10

RELIGION AND MAGIC IN THE PAPYRI

DAS NEUE TESTAMENT AUF PAPYRUS

Die griechischen Papyri des Neuen Testaments sind eine Entdeckung des 20. Jahrhunderts. Dies ist in einem doppelten Sinn zu verstehen: bis zur Jahrhundertwende waren gerade neun der bis heute gezählten 88 Papyri bekannt bzw. ediert, nur einer, der p^{11}, das Fragment aus dem damaligen Petersburg, mit Versen aus dem 1. Korintherbrief, war in Tischendorfs *Editio octava critica maior* (1869) aufgenommen worden. Obwohl in der Folgezeit dauernd neue Papyri gefunden und auch publiziert wurden, fanden sie recht wenig Resonanz; erst die Veröffentlichung der Chester Beatty-Papyri I-III durch Kenyon ab 1933 (in der Handschriftenliste des Neuen Testaments $p^{45, 46, 47}$) und des Johannes-Fragments aus der Rylands-Library, p^{52}, durch Roberts (1935) erregte Aufmerksamkeit. Man kann aber sagen, daß eine neue und grundsätzlichere Diskussion über die Papyri insgesamt und eine Abkehr von der einseitigen Bevorzugung der großen ägyptischen Pergamenthandschriften erst durch das Bekanntwerden der Bodmer-Papyri ($p^{66, 72, 74, 75}$) ab Ende der fünfziger Jahre erfolgt ist.

Ich möchte hier jedoch nicht die Geschichte der Entdeckungen und Veröffentlichungen, aber auch keine speziellen Probleme der neutestamentlichen Papyri behandeln, sondern zu skizzieren versuchen, welche textkritische Neueinschätzung ein bestimmter Teil der Papyri in neuerer Zeit erfahren hat.

Die textkritische Forschung hat sich immer recht schwer getan, wenn es darum ging, den Charakter eines jeden einzelnen Papyrus zu bestimmen und in größere Zusammenhänge einzuordnen. Bei der Veröffentlichung eines neuen Papyrus verfuhren die Herausgeber so: entsprechend den Apparatnotierungen einer der kritischen Ausgaben des Neuen Testaments, meistens der Tischendorfs und von Sodens, wurde der Text einerseits gegen die großen "ägyptischen" Unzialen, vor allem die *Codices Sinaiticus* und *Vaticanus*, andererseits als Kontrast gegen den Vertreter des "westlichen" Textes, den *Codex Bezae Cantabrigiensis*, und auch gegen die "Koine"-Gruppe verglichen. Die Urteile waren entsprechend: man ordnete den Papyrus einer dieser Pergamenthandschriften zu, mit dem Zusatz, mehr oder weniger

Varianten seien aus den anderen Handschriften bzw. Gruppen einge-
flossen.

Exemplarisch für dieses Vorgehen ist die Papyrusliste in Bruce
Metzgers Buch *The Text of the New Testament*: vergleichbar den
Farben eines Prismas gehen die Einstufungen von "alexandrinisch"
bis "westlich" in allen möglichen Kombinationen. Dazu ist zu sagen:
es ist generell problematisch, einen Papyrus z.B. aus dem Anfang des
3. Jahrhunderts an einer Handschrift des 4. oder gar eines noch späteren Jahrhunderts zu messen: die zeitliche Reihenfolge wird auf
den Kopf gestellt, das Frühere am Späteren beurteilt. Mag jedoch
das textkritische Urteil über den betreffenden Papyrus im Einzelfall
auch zutreffen, so ist dennoch die Schwierigkeit erheblich, ja, es
ist sogar unmöglich, mit dieser Methode zu einer Systematisierung
der Papyri gelangen zu können. Denn die Maßstäbe, die von den Editoren herangezogen werden, sind ja selbst schwankend. Es ist nicht
so, daß die beiden "ägyptischen" Zeugen, die *Codices Sinaiticus* und
Vaticanus, für das gesamte Neue Testament *den* Text bieten, der nach
den Erkenntnissen heutiger Textkritik dem Original am nächsten
kommt. Andererseits aber ist der *Codex Bezae* nicht durchgehend
"westlich," sondern in der großen Anzahl der Fälle gehört er zu den
textkonstituierenden Handschriften, weil seine Vorlage, sofern sie
nicht geändert wurde, ein vorzüglicher Zeuge des frühen Textes ist.

Deshalb schien es uns geboten, alle Papyri gegen den Text des
Novum Testamentum graece / 26. Auflage bzw. des *Greek New Testament* /
3rd Edition zu kollationieren, um anhand dieses modernen Textes als
Leitlinie unter gleichbleibenden Maßstäben verbindliche textkritische Kategorien aufstellen zu können.[1]

Den Anfang der Arbeit machten die 40 frühen Papyri (hinzukämen
noch 5 Pergament-Fragmente), d.h. jene, die bis ca. 300 n. Chr. anzusetzen sind.[2] Für die Textgeschichte des Neuen Testaments sind

---

1 Die Möglichkeit, daß in ein paar Jahren nach erneuter gründlicher Überprüfung und Wertung der handschriftlichen Zeugen der Text
an nicht wenigen Stellen geändert wird, ist nicht auszuschließen;
ebenso kann jeder neue Handschriftenfund eine Revision des Textes
notwendig machen.

2 Zur Analyse des äußeren Befunds der frühen Papyri cf. E. A.
Judge und S. R. Pickering, *Prudentia* 10 (1978) 1-13.

sie von besonderer Bedeutung, weil sie vor der Bildung der großen
Texttypen geschrieben sind: erst im 4. Jahrhundert, nach Konstantin
dem Großen, haben sich in ihren festumrissenen Formen der "alex-
andrinisch-ägyptische" und der "Koine"-Text entwickeln können, als
das Christentum nicht mehr verfolgt wurde und in den Skriptorien
der Bischofssitze eine "Massenproduktion" an Handschriften ein-
setzte.

Der Text, den die frühen Papyri bieten, läßt sich in vier
Gruppen einteilen, wobei es Übergangsformen geben kann (in einigen
Fällen ist wegen zu starker Fragmentierung kein sicheres Urteil
möglich): (1) der "feste" Text, (2) der "Normaltext," (3) der
"freie" Text und (4) der Text der Papyri 29, 38 und 48.

(1) Der "feste" Text, d.h. der Text, der sich an die Vorlage
des Urtextes mit ganz geringen Abweichungen hält. Zeuge für diese
Textform ist der wohl berühmteste Papyrus, der P. *Bodmer* XIV/XV,
der p[75]. Seine Qualität erregte vor allem deshalb Aufsehen, weil
die bisher anerkannte These von einer Text*rezension* im Ägypten des
4. Jahrhunderts, wie sie z.B. im *Codex Vaticanus* Gestalt gefunden
habe, nicht mehr aufrechterhalten werden konnte: für den Bereich,
den beide Handschriften gemeinsam haben, also große Teile von Lukas
und Johannes, muß man folgern, daß der *Vaticanus* bestenfalls eine
Revision des jetzt schon um 200 n. Chr. nachgewiesenen "festen"
Textes ist. p[75] steht aber keineswegs allein: nach unseren Kolla-
tionen sind mindestens acht weitere Papyri in diese Kategorie einzuordnen, unter ihnen z.B. p[23] (P. *Oxy.* 1229) mit Versen aus dem 1.
Kapitel des Jakobusbriefes oder p[27] (P. *Oxy.* 1355) mit Teilen aus
Römer 8.

(2) Der "Normaltext," d.h. der Text, der den Urtext mit
Abweichungen wiedergibt, wie sie die neutestamentliche Texttradi-
tion im Gegensatz etwa zur nahezu buchstabengetreuen Überlieferung
des hebräischen Alten Testaments oder des Korans kennzeichnet.
Zeuge für diese Textform ist der P. *Bodmer* VII/VIII, der p[72], diese
merkwürdige Sammelhandschrift, die durch die Tatsache, daß sie die
beiden Petrusbriefe und den Judasbrief (vollständig) enthält, auch
kanonsgeschichtlich höchstes Interesse beanspruchen kann. Auch der
älteste neutestamentliche Papyrus aus dem Anfang des 2. Jahrhunderts,
der p[52], gehört in diese Gruppe, die insgesamt 10 Papyri umfaßt.
Zwischen dem "festen" und dem "Normaltext" stehen weitere 7 Papyri,

so daß man als Fazit konstatieren kann: etwa zwei Drittel der frühen
Papyri gehören den beiden ersten Gruppen an. Daher muß die bisher
herrschende Meinung, wie sie an Metzgers Liste deutlich wird, vom
Text der frühen Papyri als eines mehr oder weniger "freien" revi-
diert werden.

(3) Der "freie" Text, d.h. der Text, der seine Vorlage erheblich umgestaltet. Zeuge für diese Textform ist der *P. Chester
Beatty* I, der zusammen mit dem Wiener Fragment den p^{45} bildet. In
seiner Einleitung zur Edition charakterisiert Kenyon den Papyrus
sinngemäß so: er repräsentiere einen Texttyp im Ägypten der 1.
Hälfte des 3. Jahrhunderts, der von einem Text, wie wir ihn in B
(*Codex Vaticanus*) finden, verschieden ist, stark durchdrungen von
"westlichen" Lesarten, ohne jedoch deren typische größere Abweichungen vorzuweisen. Der Apparat des *Novum Testamentum graece*
bestätigt dieses Urteil; angemerkt muß dazu allerdings noch werden:
zu einem "freien" Text machen ihn gerade die zahlreichen Sonder-
lesarten, und "westlich" ist der p^{45} sicherlich nicht, auch wenn er
manche Lesart mit D (*Codex Bezae*) teilt. Andere berühmte Vertreter
dieser Gruppe sind: *P. Chester Beatty* II, zusammen mit dem Michigan-
Teil der p^{46}, von den Bodmer-Papyri der II., p^{66}, auch der p^{13} (*P.
Oxy.* 567 und *PSI* 1292) mit großen Teilen des Hebräerbriefes, und
vier weitere Papyri. Erwähnt werden muß hier auch der p^{69} (*P. Oxy.*
2383) mit Teilen aus Lukas 22. Von den insgesamt 13 z.T. sehr umfangreichen Abweichungen gegenüber dem *Novum Testamentum graece*
sind neun Singulärlesarten. Diese erlauben eine Einordnung unter
den "freien" Text, wenn auch die Möglichkeit, daß der Papyrus zur
nächsten Gruppe zählt, nicht auszuschließen ist.

(4) Der Text der Papyri 29, 38 und 48 (hinzukäme noch die
Majuskel 0171). Diese Papyri sind immer als Kronzeugen für die
Existenz eines griechischen "westlichen" Textes *vor* D angeführt
worden. Mit der Bezeichnung "westlich" ist früher gerade bei den
Papyri viel Konfusion geschaffen worden: "westlich" zumindest beeinflußt war ein Papyrus schon dann, wenn er ein paar Lesarten mit
D teilte; dessen große Textänderungen brauchte er gar nicht zu
haben. Kamen dann noch Itala und Vetus Syra als Zeugen hinzu, war
das Urteil "westlich" perfekt. Das läßt sich nach unseren Arbeiten
nicht mehr aufrechterhalten. Als Phänomen bleiben allerdings diese
drei Papyri. Sie bieten Verse aus dem Text der Apostelgeschichte,

einer Schrift, die offensichtlich in besonderem Maße zu theolo-
gischer Diskussion und damit auch zu textlicher Umgestaltung her-
ausgefordert hat, wie wir sie z.B. in D vor uns haben.

Bei p[29] (P. Oxy. 1597) für Apostelgeschichte 26 haben wir
keinen Text von D, der Papyrus scheint aber vor allem mit dem *Codex
Gigas*, der berühmten lateinischen Handschrift des 13. Jahrhunderts,
Gemeinsamkeiten zu haben.

p[38] (P. Mich. 138) zeigt, wenn auch mit Abweichungen, in
Apostelgeschichte 18/19 den D-Text. p[48] (*PSI* 1165) hat in Apostelgeschichte 23 teils eigenständigen, teils auch wieder mit dem Gigas
verwandten Text, der *Codex Bezae* fehlt uns auch hier.

Man kann vielleicht so zusammenfassen, unter Vermeidung des so
mißverständlichen und mißbrauchten Wortes "westlich": die drei
Papyri bearbeiten ihre Vorlage *im Stil von D*, ohne jedoch, das
zeigt immerhin p[38], mit ihm identisch zu sein; sie sind--auf die
Apostelgeschichte bezogen--Vorläufer bzw. Ableger des D-Textes wie
etwa auch die griechische Minuskelhandschrift 614 (13. Jahrhundert),
der lateinische Gigas und die Randlesarten der syrischen Harclensis
(7. Jahrhundert). Wenn die Betonung darauf liegt "im *Stil* von D,"
so ist damit schon gesagt, daß es im Gegensatz zum "ägyptischen"
und zum "Koine"-Typ keinen "D"-Typ gibt, "Typ" im Sinne von Stan-
dardisierung und Verbindlichkeit.

Die hier notgedrungen nur kurz umrissene Arbeit an den frühen
Papyri wird auch auf die späteren ausgedehnt werden; auf die Ergebnisse wird man gespannt sein dürfen, zumal jetzt, bei den Da-
tierungen ab 4. Jahrhundert, die großen Textgruppen in die Überlegungen mit einbezogen werden müssen.

Soweit zu diesem Thema.

Einem anderen schwerwiegenden Mangel versuchen wir durch ein
größeres Vorhaben abzuhelfen. Die Papyrus-Editionen sind weit ver-
streut, zudem editorisch, bezüglich des transkribierten Textes und
des Apparats, z.T. veraltet und fehlerhaft. Während wir mit dem
Repertorium der griechischen christlichen Papyri, herausgegeben von
K. Aland, dem *Catalogue des papyrus grecs juifs et chrétiens*, herausgegeben von J. van Haelst und *La Papirologia* von O. Montevecchi
immerhin neue Werke haben, wo neben Beschreibungen auch eine Bibliographie zu den einzelnen Papyri zu finden ist, fehlt ein solches
Werk zu den *Texten* der Papyri. Schofields Buch *The Papyrus Fragments*

of the Greek New Testament (1936) ist ebenfalls überholt und mußte
mit p[54] enden.

Daher wird von uns eine kritische Ausgabe *Das Neue Testament
auf Papyrus* vorbereitet, die auch von der Anlage her eine Neuheit
ist. Unter der Leitzeile des *Novum Testamentum graece* / 26. Auflage stehen untereinander die in Frage kommenden Papyrus-Texte, so
daß man auf einen Blick die jeweiligen Abweichungen zur Leitzeile
sehen kann. Unter den Transkriptionen befinden sich zwei Apparate,
ein Papyrus-Apparat, der in erster Linie der Auseinandersetzung mit
der *editio princeps* dient, und ein textkritischer Apparat zu den
Papyrus-Varianten bezogen auf die Leitzeile mit der Angabe sämt-
licher Majuskeln und des "Mehrheitstextes."

Der 1. Band dieser Ausgabe mit den Katholischen Briefen ist
bald abgeschlossen.

Das Institut für neutestamentliche Textforschung hofft, mit
diesen Projekten zum komplexen Gebiet der Papyrologie einen nicht
ganz geringen Beitrag leisten zu können.

Institut für neutestamentliche   Winfried Grunewald
Textforschung
Münster

Proceedings of the XVI Int. Congr. of Papyrology (Chico 1981) 613-620

FOURTH-CENTURY MONASTICISM IN THE PAPYRI

[*P.Oxy*. XXXIII (1968) 2665 (Rea)	*Certificate* 305/6	"Paulos from the Oxyrhynchite nome" condemned in Thebaid but cannot be traced in property register.]
1. *P.Col*. VII (1980) 171 (Lewis)	*Petition* 6(?) Jun 324	Antoninos διάκων and Isak μοναχός rescue Isidoros of Karanis from assault.
2. *P.Lond*. VI (1924) 1913 (Bell)	*Deed* 19 Mar 334	Pageus (i.e. Paieous?) πρεσβύτερος from Hipponon notifies τοῖς προεστῶσι μονῆς μονοχῶν at Hathor of locum tenens of μονή.
3. *P.Lond*. VI (1924) 1914 (Bell)	*Letter* May/Jun 335(?)	To Paieous on Athanasios maltreating τοὺς μοναχοὺς τῶν Μελιτιανῶν at Alexandria.
4. *P.Würzb*. (1934) 16 (Wilcken)	*Surety* 10 Oct 349	Written by Agathos [ἀποτα]κτικός for a διάκων who guarantees a πρεσβύτερος from Tristomos (Fayyum).
5. *P.Herm.Landl*. (1978) (Sijpesteijn-Worp)	*Register* Early-Mid-IV(?)	Makarios identified as ἀποτακτικός amongst landholders of Hermopolis.
6. *P.Lond*. VI (1924) 1925 (Bell)	*Letter* Mid-IV	Appeal for prayer to ἄπα Papnoutios ἀναχωρητής at μονή μοναχῶν(?).
7. *P.Lips*. (1906) 43 (Mitteis-Wilcken)	*Judgment* IV	Plousianos (Hermopolite) ἐπίσκοπος on Thaesis ἀειπάρθενος accused of appropriating "Christian books."
8. *CPR* V 26 (1976) (Sijpesteijn)	*Tax List* IV	[Incerta] μοναχή listed without parentage as taxpayer of Skar (Hermopolite).
9. *P.Herm*. (1964) 9 (Rees)	*Letter* IV	Appeal for prayer to Joannes (Hermopolite) ἀποτακτικός who in 10 calls himself παναχωρητής.
10. *PSI* XIII (1953) 1342 (Manfredi)	*Letter* IV	Appeal through Paesios διάκονος for ἄπα Sabinos ἀναχωρητής to influence (Hermopolite) tax debtor.
11. *P.Iand*. VI (1934) 100 (Rosenberger)	*Letter* IV	Bessemios reports trading difficulties to two "fathers" and greets τοὺς ἀδελφοὺς πάντας τοὺς ἐν τῷ μοναστηρίῳ.
12. P.Berl.inv. 11860 A/B (1975) (Wipszycka)	*Tax List* 367/8	Anoubion ἀποτακτικός τοῦ μοναστηρίου of Tabennese pays tax on its land near(?) Magdola Mire (Hermopolite).
13. *P.Lips*. (1906) 60 (Mitteis)	*Certificate* 371(?)	Son, and daughter Didyme ἀειπάρθενος, receive requisition on a prytanis of Panopolis (presumably deceased).
14. *P.Oxy*. XLVI (1978) 3311 (Rea)	*Petition* c.373/4	Ammonios ἀποτακτικός had failed to bequeath the estate he controlled.
15. *P.Lips*. (1906) 28 (Mitteis)	*Deed* 31 Dec 381	Silbanos ἀποτακτικός, trustee for brother, adopts nephew and makes him heir to his property (Hermopolis).
16. *P.Oxy*. XLIV (1976) 3203 (Haslam)	*Lease* Jun/Jul 400	Two named sisters μοναχαὶ ἀποτακτικαί lease part of house to Jose Ἰουδαῖος.
17. *SB* VIII (1965) 9683 (Zilliacus)	*Complaint* End IV	Timotheos reports anchor stolen from πολλῶν μονάζον ἀναχωριτῶν of the μονή.

Although ecclesiastical writings from the first half of the century are not scarce, they offer no clear reference to the origins of monasticism. For Reitzenstein, writing only two-thirds of a century ago, the very name μοναχός was historically suspect

(*SbHeid*. 1914.8.47,60,61). He thought it must be a retrojection of
mid-century usage by Athanasius. The archive of Apa Paieous (items
2, 3 in list above), published in 1924, demonstrated the existence
of well-established monastic communities using the term μοναχός in
the mid-330s. This settled the meaning of the solitary instance
of the term in Eusebius (*PG* 23.689B, in the commentary on the
Psalms).

Now we have the new petition of Isidoros of Karanis (no. 1),
the latest-dated document from his archive. This civil citation of
a μοναχός decisively antedates the reference in Eusebius. The μοναχός, moreover, is coupled with a διάκων, the earliest instance of
that title in the papyrus documents. The only ecclesiastical style
attested in a public document that can be dated with certainty
prior to this is the ἀναγνωστής of 5 February, 304 (*P. Oxy*. XXXIII
2673).

The matter-of-fact way in which Isidoros of Karanis cites the
deacon and the monk is striking. In both cases the title has dis-
placed the usual patronymic. We are dealing with ecclesiastics
officially designated in terms of their profession. In June, 324,
the world was awaiting the final confrontation between Licinius and
Constantine. Licinius had allegedly been curbing the activities of
the churches, and a victory by him would certainly have been taken
as the vindication of the old gods. Yet in Karanis, firmly within
his domain, the establishment of the church and of monasticism
alike are apparently taken for granted.

Since the archive of Isidoros suggests he had no personal connection with Christianity, but he can yet take deacon and monk for
granted, we may safely project the emergence of monasticism onto
the public scene back across the remaining two decades to the traditional point of impact--St. Antony's emergence from self-
imprisonment to challenge others to take up the solitary life.
It is with reference to this stage of his career (about 305?) that
Athanasius first uses the term μοναχός, an historical instinct now
implicitly justified by the new papyrus.

It is just conceivable that another recently published document could vindicate the historicity of the figure Jerome set up to
outdo the Antony of Athanasius: Paul of Thebes, the first hermit.
In a certificate of 305/6 (unnumbered item at top of list) the

property registrars report that they cannot trace either property
or wife for "Paulos from the Oxyrhynchite nome." He had been sentenced by the governor of the Thebaid, Satrius Arrianus. The con-
junction of his increasingly fashionable name with that of the notorious persecutor in a text of that year invites one to envisage
a Christian identity for Paulos, though the papyrus gives no positive hint of that. The inability of the officials to discover his
lawful name, implied by lack of reference to his father, and their
consequential inability to trace either property or wife, may then
lead the imagination on to the solitary calling which was supposedly pioneered by Paul of Thebes. Yet Jerome does not make his hero
a victim of the persecution.

The papyrus evidence proves the early establishment, in both
civil and ecclesiastical (or at any rate Meletian) usage, of the
term μοναχός. But it does not resolve for us the question of its
meaning or history (*Jahrbuch für Antike und Christentum* 20 [1977]
72-89). In spite of its early appearance, it does not become the
prevalent term for ascetics in the papyri. More surprisingly still,
in two documents published in 1976 (nos. 8,16), it has now appeared in
the feminine form (attested only once in Lampe). Otherwise in our
list μοναχός occurs only in the damaged address of a letter (no. 6).[1]

The term μοναχός seems to have been coined for the male ascetics, who had long lacked a name to distinguish them from the
female virgins and the widows in the churches. It may well have
originated not in ecclesiastical usage but in the parlance of the
general community, marking the point at which the phenomenon of
male asceticism became publicly conspicuous. Its meaning would
then have to be sought not in theology but in social convention.
It could have arisen in response to some early fourth-century innovation in the pattern of residence or dress, and need not then be
explained with reference to the ideals of singlemindedness or of
celibacy, which had long flourished amongst men in the churches
without supplying a name for those who pursued them. Cf. *SB* IV
7315, an inscription dated early IV, recording two martyrs, one

---

1 A substantial addition to the fourth-century attestation of
the term is expected from the forthcoming edition of the documents
preserved in the bindings of the Nag Hammadi codices, to be edited
by G. M. Browne and J. C. Shelton.

called ὁ μακάριος παρθένος, the other ἐγκρατής, while the latter's
son is called μαθητής παρθένων.[2]

The commonest term for ascetics in the fourth-century papyri
is ἀποτακτικός. There seems no doubt as to the origin of this
name. It is apparently derived from the command of Jesus (Luke
14:33) that those who follow him should renounce all possessions
(or should it be family connections? - Luke 14:26). Epiphanius
(*Haer.* 61.1), writing ca. 376, says that the heretical ἀποστολικοί
call themselves ἀποτακτικοί and make a practice of abandoning possessions. Julian's taunting use of ἀποτακτῖται for the Cynics (*Or.*
7.18 Bidez) proves that this form had in-group currency in the
church circles in which he was brought up, let us say in the 340s.
The papyrus usage (nos. 4,5,12,14,15) shows that by the same stage
the form ἀποτακτικός was an accepted professional identification
in civil documents. The two sisters (no. 16) who call themselves
μοναχαί ἀποτακτικαί are presumably using the broad public appela-
tion of monastics coupled with the official church term which indicates a particular category of them.

Letters from the archive of Apa Joannes (no. 9), which has
been dated both to the second and to the first half of the fourth
century, address him both as ἀποτακτικός and as ἀναχωρητής, a style
he assumes himself moreover. This term is also used in fourth-
century papyrus letters in addressing Apa Papnoutios (no. 6) and
Apa Sabinos (no. 10). In 17 it identifies one of several types of
monk itemized. Two women are described in formal documents as
ἀειπάρθενος (nos. 7,13). This could, however, be simply a legal
way of indicating that they were unmarried women.

Apart from no. 3, these technical terms are confined to formal
documents and the covering addresses of letters. They identify
monastics as having a publicly recognized station in life of an
occupational kind. It may displace their patronymic in formal
references to them (so in nos. 1,5,7 and 8, but not in 4,12,13,14,
15 or 16). Within the thirty other letters and one other petition

---

2 For the complex question of the origins of monasticism in
Egypt, and the bearing on it of the Cologne Mani Codex, see now the
discussion by L. Koenen, "Manichäische Mission und Klöster in Ägypten," *Das römisch-byzantinische Ägypten, Akten des internationalen
Symposions, 27.-30. September 1978 in Trier* (Deutsches Archäolo-
gisches Institut; Mainz, forthcoming).

(P. Amh. II 142) of the fourth century that have been held to refer
to monastic communities there is a complete absence of such terms.
The "brothers" or "sisters" simply address each other within familiar bonds that need no formal specification (as in no. 11).

The fourth-century diversity of monastic nomenclature is not
sustained in the papyrus record. In the fifth century (no. 17),
the terms μονάζων/μονάζουσα take over. Μονάζων is the dominant
term thereafter, though μοναχός (the prevalent title in the literary sources) is also prominent from the sixth century. Ἀναχωρητής
continues in use, but the commonest fourth-century term, ἀποτακτικός, disappears, except for a limited reappearance in the ninth
century, while ἀειπάρθενος is reserved for the ever-virgin Mother
of God.

Since four of the seven ἀποτακτικοί are from the Hermopolite
nome, one may ask whether that term may not have had a particular
currency there, and whether its relatively frequent appearance in
property transactions points a way forward. All but one instance
(no. 9) are in civil documents. Julian's ἀποτακτῖται made small
sacrifices with a view to getting their hands on everything else.
The ἀποστολικοί of Epiphanius called themselves ἀποτακτικοί to
celebrate their renunciation of property. The aputactitae whom
Egeria observed towards the end of the fourth century seem to have
been an order devoted to fasting and to the liturgical exercises of
the church in Jerusalem. The term is also found in both Greek and
Coptic in the Pachomian literature, where it was clearly one of the
terms accepted for those who joined the monasteries. It may have
been that apotactics were those who pooled their property in a small
community that remained closely related to church life.

Given that the technical terms for monks seem typically to
arise in formal documents, and that formal documents typically relate to property transactions of some kind, it is not surprising
that the papyrus record appears to indicate a close involvement of
monastics with property (only nos. 1 and 6 contain no such suggestion). But that hardly invalidates the general picture we have
from the literary sources of monasticism as a movement which re-
nounced property. Those who did that will have been the ones who
have left no trace in the papyrus record. Moreover it is usually
impossible to determine whether the monks who are recorded have
any direct stake in the property transactions in which they appear.

The new Berlin papyrus (no. 12) published by Wipszycka (in
Hommages Préaux, 625-36) has shown the way in which the Pachomian
monasteries stepped into the economic breach by taking up abandoned
lands, thus sharing the tax burden of the public community. This
could explain the other cases (nos. 5,8) where monastics appear in
tax connections. They too could have been acting for their monasteries. In both cases they are the sole monastics in long lists
which include a number of other people with ecclesiastical titles.
The ἀναχωρητής (no. 10) who is asked to persuade a reluctant tax-
payer may also belong in this context. The trading difficulties of
monasteries are referred to in the letter of Bessemios (no. 11),
while the archive of Apa Paieous (the subsequent *P. Lond.* letters
associated with my items 2,3) contains a good deal of evidence for
traffic in goods.

Agathos the [ἀποτα]κτικός (no. 4) describes himself as the son
of a πρύτανις of Arsinoe, but we do not know whether he had inherited the estate, or expected to. But Didyme ἀειπάρθενος (no. 13)
and her brother were apparently responsible for the estate of their
father, also a former magistrate. The two sisters μοναχαὶ ἀποτακτικαί (no. 16) are at least the managers, and one would have supposed the owners, of the house in which they let rooms. Joannes
ἀποτακτικός (no. 9) was closely involved in the debt problems of
one of his correspondents, and was himself prosecuted on charges he
considered false. The evidence falls short, however, of proving
that he held property. Silbanos ἀποτακτικός (no. 15) agrees to be-
queath his property to the nephew whom he adopts. The ownership
of personal property is clearly stated here, and one may note the
implication that there will be no other children to contest the
inheritance.

Especially tantalizing is the case of Ammonios ἀποτακτικός
(no. 14). This is the sole instance in our list where the meaning
of the technical term appears itself to be a point of substance to
the author. It is given three times in the course of an argument
about property rights. Two sisters state that their paternal cousin had allowed his estate to pass under the control of his maternal
uncle, Ammonios, although the ultimate title to the property would
apparently fall to the sisters. Ammonios, however, died still being an ἀποτακτικός, and had made no will. Whether this is meant to

explain why he had not made one is not clear. The sisters claim
that the property is rightfully theirs but that it is being forcibly retained by a certain Ammon, who is neither son nor heir. Rea
is inclined to think that this means that Ammon is indeed next of
kin, but that the sisters are relying on the insinuation that the
property had never been formally bequeathed to Ammonios by their
cousin in the first place. But another possibility is that the
cousin had permitted Ammonios the use of it for the benefit of his
community, and that Ammon is a fellow ἀποτακτικός who desires to
retain the use of it in the spirit of the cousin's intention.

The relationship of monastics to church life is also difficult
to sort out. If Antoninos (no. 1) is a διάκων of the village
church, the implication is that Isak the μοναχός is a related
figure, but monastic communities also had deacons. In no. 17 it was
the debt owed by one of the deacons of the monastery of Ankyronites
in the Herakleopolite that led to the theft of the anchor by the
creditor (a soldier), and the community consists of a large number,
including presbyters and deacons as well as μονάζοντες and ἀναχωρη-
ταί, together with a fifth, unidentified, category. In no. 10, a διάκονος is the avenue of approach to the ἀναχωρητής, while in no. 4 the
ἀποτακτικός is writing for a διάκων who guarantees a πρεσβύτερος.
Wilcken assumed that the last was a presbyter of the church, but
one should ask whether he might not have been a monastic one, or
even a secular village elder. The documents are quite capable of
specifying when a deacon or presbyter belongs "to the catholic
church," and this is done in no. 7 for the bishop. In no. 2 Pageus,
the head of the monastery, is a πρεσβύτερος, from the village of
Hipponon, and the council he summons to elect his locum tenens includes another πρεσβύτερος of Hipponon and a διάκονος from another
village, as well as an "original" or "senior" μοναχός. One may ask
whether the community itself is attached in some way to the village
church. Only in no. 3 do we have a clear picture of the relation between monks and the churches, but the dramatic struggles in Alexandria are hardly to be taken as typical.

As for the general life of the civil community, our monks do
not seem especially remote. Their various styles are taken for
granted, and they include their fair share of people in trouble in
various ways. In nos. 3, 7, 9 and 17, and perhaps 10 and 14, they are

subject to accusations, usually financial. Only in no. 6 do we meet
the archetypal anchorite, whose holiness has made him a desired
source of intercession. But even he is surrounded by brothers.
The true hermit will by definition not be documented.

The purpose of this survey is to illustrate the questions that
are raised by a systematic review of the documentary papyri bearing
on the history of Christianity in Egypt. At Macquarie University,
I and my colleagues in the School of History, A. M. Emmett, B. F.
Harris and S. R. Pickering, have undertaken to prepare a corpus of
such material. We commend ourselves to the *amicitia papyrologorum*
in the hope that our work may clarify some of the uncertainties
that beset such documents.

Macquarie University   E. A. Judge

LA VERSIONE DEI LXX E I PAPIRI: NOTE LESSICALI

Quelli che sto per presentare sono alcuni risultati di studi di carattere lessicale che si fondano sul confronto tra la versione greca dei LXX e i documenti su papiro. Queste ricerche si rifanno da una parte al testo ebraico dell'A.T. e arrivano dall'altra al N.T. e, talvolta, agli autori giudaici e ai Padri della Chiesa, e si ricollegano a quelle proposte e presentate da Orsolina Montevecchi in precedenti Congressi.

Io stessa, con il medesimo metodo, ho già tentato qualche ricerca di questo genere[1] ed altre ancora ne ho iniziate ed ho in programma. Ritengo infatti, che queste ricerche portino a risultati interessanti, sia per lo studio dello sviluppo della κοινή tra i secoli III a.C. e I d.C., sia, soprattutto, per una miglior comprensione della lingua dei LXX e, attraverso di essa, delle scelte teologiche e pratiche che hanno spinto questi traduttori a preferire alcuni termini ad altri, a formarne talvolta di nuovi, ad adattarne altri ancora, sorti in un contesto ben diverso da quello biblico ed ebraico. Si può notare che la situazione storico-sociale dell'Alessandria del III sec. a.C., in cui sono vissuti i traduttori, ha influito in modo spesso determinante sulle loro scelte, anche se a prima vista il fenomeno non appare evidente. I LXX hanno, per così dire, datato e ambientato il loro lavoro per mezzo di particolari, che noi possiamo scoprire solamente grazie all'aiuto insostituibile dei papiri, che ci testimoniano i molteplici aspetti della vita e della lingua del tempo in cui vissero. Esaminerò dunque le parole: νομός, δῆμος, ἀνδρίζομαι e παστοφόριον.

Avevo in programma l'esame di altri termini: βωμός e θυσιαστήριον e la terminologia delle colpe, ma durante la ricerca il materiale si è allargato in tal misura da costringermi a limitare la mia comunicazione.

---

1 "ΣΚΥΛΜΟΣ," *Aegyptus* 54 (1974) 197-202; "Euergetes," *Aegyptus* 56 (1976) 177-91; "La metafora biblica di Dio come roccia e la sua soppressione nelle antiche versioni," *Eph. Lit.* 91 (1977) 417-53. Altri studi saranno pubblicati sulla rivista *Aegyptus*.

NOMOΣ

E' noto il valore di νομός come "distretto, circoscrizione territoriale" nel linguaggio greco amministrativo dell'Egitto. Nella LXX esso compare in otto passi,[2] di cui solo due[3] possono essere confrontati con l'originale ebraico. Il più interessante è *Is.* 19,2, che appartiene ad un oracolo sull'Egitto, perchè, passando dal T.M. alla versione greca, scopriamo che vi è stato un adeguamento alla situazione storica. Il traduttore, cioè, ha modificato il testo rendendolo più attuale. Il passo, che nel T.M. suona così:

> Ecciterò gli Egiziani contro gli Egiziani,
> ognuno combatterà contro il proprio fratello,
> ognuno contro il suo prossimo,
> città contro città, *regno* contro *regno*

rimane invariato nel greco, tranne la seconda parte dell'ultimo stico. Al posto del regno (*mamlākā* in ebraico) troviamo νομός, quindi leggiamo: "città contro città, νομός contro νομός."

L'autore ebraico del brano può aver pensato ai due regni in cui era suddivisa la Palestina (del Nord e del Sud) o, più probabilmente, si è ispirato alla situazione egiziana, che in diversi periodi fu contraddistinta dalla coesistenza dei due regni (Alto e Basso Egitto) il cui ricordo permaneva nella doppia corona portata dal Faraone. Il traduttore, invece, ha ritenuto più preciso introdurre nel testo in luogo del termine "regno," che non trovava più riscontro nella realtà storica dell'Egitto tolemaico, il vocabolo "tecnico" relativo alla suddivisione territoriale di quel paese, formando, anche dal punto di vista letterario, un crescendo più graduale (fratello-prossimo-città-distretto).

Νομός compare anche nei libri dei Maccabei, di cui non abbiamo l'originale ebraico: i passi in cui ricorre fanno parte di documenti ufficiali inseriti e riportati nel testo: lettere tra sovrani e condottieri[4] e un decreto regio.[5] In essi troviamo il termine νομός

---

2 *Is.* 19,2; *Ger.* 10,25; I *Macc.* 10,30.38; 11,34.57; II *Macc.* 5,14; III *Macc.* 4,3.

3 *Is.* 19,2 e *Ger.* 10,25.

4 I *Macc.* 10,30.38; 11,34.57.

5 III *Macc.* 4,3.

applicato alla situazione territoriale della Palestina per indicare
alcuni territori appartenenti un tempo alla Samaria e annessi in
seguito alla Giudea.[6] La suddivisione della Palestina in distretti
(νομοί) risaliva per l'appunto alla dominazione tolemaica ed è te-
stimoniata anche da Flavio Giuseppe.[7]

ΔΗΜΟΣ

Un altro termine collegato con il linguaggio amministrativo-
politico è δῆμος. Non mi soffermo sui significati che questa parola assume nel mondo greco classico, richiamo solo il fatto che in
Alessandria, come in altre città greche le φυλαί si suddividono in
δῆμοι,[8] come ci testimoniano non solo i papiri, ma anche la versione dei LXX.

Occorre ricordare che per la struttura etnica e sociale del
popolo d'Israele, oltre che per motivi storici, la tribù vi esercitò, almeno per il periodo dell'esodo, della conquista e dell'insediamento in Canaan, fino all'età dei Giudici, un ruolo di prima-
ria importanza, come punto di riferimento per l'individuo e per la
suddivisione territoriale. Successivamente rimase vivo, come entità sociale, solo il clan, suddivisione della tribù, benché anch'esso tendesse ad identificarsi con il villaggio.

La terminologia ebraica del settore è complessa: dalla famiglia ('ohel = "tenda," poi, per metonimia, la "famiglia"), si passa
al casato (bêt 'āb), al clan (mišpāḥâ), alla tribù, che può essere
indicata con due termini equivalenti: maṭṭeh e šēbeṭ. Essi originariamente significano "ramo," poi "bastone del potere," poi
"tribù," cioè ramo in continua espansione e ramificazione a partire
dai patriarchi eponimi. Per tradurre questi vocaboli i LXX si servono dei termini φυλή e δῆμος e nello stesso rapporto che inter-
corre tra di essi in Alessandria (e in altre città greche, particolarmente in Atene di cui Alessandria tendeva a riprodurre la
struttura). I δῆμοι indicano i clan in cui si ripartisce la φυλή,

---

6 I Macc. 10,30.38; 11,34.57.

7 Ant. Jud. XIII 4,9.

8 Satiro in Theophil., Ad Autol., 2,7 (Fr. Gr. Hist. 631 F1);
P. M. Fraser, Ptolemaic Alexandria (Oxford 1972) I v. cap. 2; P.
Hib. 28 = W. Chr. 25 (265a).

come mostrano i passi in cui questi termini compaiono insieme. I
passi della LXX in cui ricorre δῆμος sono 154,[9] ma in un quarto
circa di essi il termine è ripetuto da due a sei volte,[10] per un
totale di più di 200 volte. Δῆμος è quasi sempre,[11] la traduzione
costante dell'ebraico mišpāḥā "clan," e i due termini corrispon-
dono, se consideriamo il significato che la parola greca aveva
nell'ordinamento dei cittadini di Alessandria. Troviamo δῆμος soprattutto (92 passi) nel libro dei Num. (cap. 1.3.4. e 26 in modo
speciale) in cui vengono registrati i censimenti del popolo ebraico
prima della partenza dal Sinai (cap. 1-4) e dopo la traversata del
deserto di Mô'âb (cap. 26). Nei libri deuterocanonici[12] e in Dan.,
il vocabolo è usato nelle accezioni più comuni alla lingua classica
(popolo,[13] popolazione,[14] gente,[15] folla[16]). I passi dei libri dei
Macc. (tranne due[17]) appartengono a documenti ufficiali, che riguardano i rapporti dei Giudei con i Greci e i Romani, ed è naturale che
δῆμος vi sia adoperato per indicare il popolo sovrano. Dei passi in
cui il testo ebraico e la versione greca differiscono[18] o ci sono

---

9 Cfr. E. Hatch-H. Redpath, *A Concordance to the Septuagint
and the Other Greek Versions of the Old Testament* (Graz 1975) s.v.
δῆμος.

10 2 volte: *Num.* 4,42; 26,5.6.13.16.17.21.24.40.49; *Gios.* 7,
14.17; 3 volte: *Num.* 3,21.33; 26,23.29.30.31.32.35.37.45.48; 4 volte: *Num.* 26,12.15.20.26.38.42.44.57; 5 volte: *Num.* 3,27; 6 volte:
Num. 26,58.

11 *Num.* 18,2 šēbeṭ "tribù"; *Dan.* 8,24; 9.16; 11,32 'am
"popolo" (Teodozione λαός); *Dan.* 11,23 gôy "popolo," qui = "gruppo";
Num. 23,10b roba' "quarta parte," "accampamento" (quadrato) >
esercito.

12 I-II *Macc.*; *Giudt.*, *Sap.*; I *Esdra*.

13 *Giudt.* 4,8; *Sap.* 6,24; I *Macc.* 8,29; 14,21.23.25; 15,17;
II *Macc.* 11,34.

14 I *Macc.* 12,6; 14,20.

15 I *Esdra* 9,53.

16 *Giudt.* 6,1(2).

17 I *Macc.* 14,25; II *Macc.* 4,48.

18 Omissione di termine: *Num.* 36,6.8; -inserzione di termine:
Num. 36,12; 3,24 - *Gdc.* 17,7; 18,19 -correzione *Num.* 4,18.

varianti nei codici greci, i più interessanti sono *Num.* 4,18 in cui
il greco corregge lo scambio e la confusione dei termini, che si
verifica nel T.M. (ebr.: 'et-šēbeṭ mišpᵉḥot "la tribù dei clan,"
gr.: τῆς φυλῆς τὸν δῆμον "il clan della tribù"); e II *Macc.*
4,48 che presenta un plurale (δήμων), incomprensibile se riferito a
Gerusalemme di cui si parla, ma spiegabile se si pensa a una πόλις
greca: si tratta dei demi, delle circoscrizioni rurali contrapposte
alla città. Si delinea così una netta differenza nel significato
del termine δῆμος tra i libri dei *Num.*, di *Gios.*, dei *Gdc.*, tra-
dotti dall'ebraico, e quelli dei *Macc.*, di *Giudt.*, della *Sap.*, I
Esdra, composti in greco direttamente. Nei primi è il "clan," la
suddivisione della φυλή, come nella città di Alessandria, negli
altri è ora il "popolo," ora la "gente" o la "folla," ora la "circoscrizione rurale": significati diversi, ma attestati tutti ampiamente nella lingua e nell'uso classico.

Delle altre versioni greche antiche ci restano solo 18 dei
passi corrispondenti a qualli dei LXX esaminati. Solo *Num.* 4,18
nella versione dell'anonimo ("Αλλος) ha δῆμος con il senso di
"clan," per il resto è stato scelto un termine diverso.[19] Nonostante la scarsità del materiale, la scelta differente potrebbe essere un'altra prova del fatto che i traduttori hanno modellato il
significato di δῆμος e il suo rapporto con φυλή su quello esistente
nella città in cui risiedevano.

ΑΝΔΡΙΖΟΜΑΙ

Questo verbo è attestato nella lingua greca in tutte le epoche,
ma assai scarsamente. Dal significato originario, di "diventare
uomo, comportarsi da uomo," si passa gradualmente ad una accezione
più spirituale del termine che acquista il senso di "farsi coraggio,
non perdersi d'animo." Con questo valore lo troviamo usato nei papiri e nella LXX. Nella Bibbia il verbo è spesso in binomio con un
altro, di senso affine, e in discorsi di incoraggiamento rivolti da
Dio o da un capo del popolo. Nei LXX compare in 21 passi,[20] per lo

---

19 Soprattutto συγγένεια.

20 Cfr. Hatch-Redpath, *A Concordance*, s.v. ἀνδρίζεσθαι.

più all'imperativo,[21] in una sorta di formula del tipo ἴσχυε καὶ ἀνδρίζου[22] (o viceversa[23]), oppure ἀνδρίζου καὶ κραταιούσθω.[24] Accanto al verbo ἀνδρίζομαι se ne trovano altri, sempre di significato affine a ἰσχύειν.[25]

Le formule che abbiamo appena riferito, sono rafforzate da uno o più imperativi negativi di verbi che indicano timore e paura,[26] a sottolineare la differenza tra due stati d'animo opposti. L'esortazione viene anche motivata con un σὺ γάρ[27] seguente, che enuncia e ricorda la grandezza della missione affidata[28] a colui a cui si parla, o con un ὅτι, che introduce il motivo dell'incoraggiamento,[29] che è soprattutto la vicinanza del Signore.[30] Senso ironico possiamo invece scorgere in *Sir*. 34(31),25 imperativo negativo motivato da un γάρ: ἐν οἴνῳ μὴ ἀνδρίζου, πολλοὺς γὰρ ἀπώλεσεν ὁ οἶνος "non fare lo spavaldo col vino, infatti ne ha già rovinati molti."

Le espressioni formulari viste nei LXX sono il calco di un'equivalente frase ebraica in cui i due termini del binomio sono sempre e solo i verbi 'āmaṣ e ḥāzaq, che indicano sia la forza fisica, sia (soprattutto nei passi che ci interessano) quella

---

21 *Deut*. 31,6.7.23; *Gios*. 1,6.7.9.18; 10,25; II *Re* (II *Sam*) 10,12; 13,28; I *Cron*. 19,13; 22,13; 28,20; II *Cron*. 32,7; *Sal*. 26 (27),14; 30(31),24(25); *Nah*. 2,1(2); *Mi*. 4,10; *Dan*. 10,19; 11,1; *Sir*. 34(31),25; I *Macc*. 2,64.

22 *Gios*. 1,6.7.9.18; I *Cron*. 28,20; II *Cron*. 32,7.

23 *Deut*. 31,6.7.23; *Gios*. 10,25 (al plur.); I *Cron*. 19,13; 22,13; *Dan*. 10,19; I *Macc*. 2,64.

24 *Sal*. 26(27),14; 30(31),24(25); II *Re* (II *Sam*) 10,12.

25 II *Re* (II *Sam*) 13,28; *Nah*. 2,1(2).

26 *Gios*. 1,9; 10,25; I *Cron*. 22,13; 28,28; *Deut*. 31,6; II *Cron*. 32,7; II *Re* (II *Sam*) 13,28; *Dan*. 10,19.

27 *Gios*. 1,6; *Deut*. 31,7.23.

28 *Gios*. 1,6.7.9.18; 10,25; *Deut*. 31,6.7.23; I *Cron*. 22,13 e 28,20; *Gios*. 10,25; I *Cron*. 19,13 = II *Re* (II *Sam*) 10,12; II *Cron*. 32,7; I *Macc*. 2,64; II *Re* (II *Sam*) 13,28.

29 I *Macc*. 2,64; *Nah*. 2,1(2); *Mi*. 4,10; *Ger*. 2,25.

30 I *Cron*. 28,20; *Gios*. 1,9; *Deut*. 31,6; *Gios*. 10,25.

morale. Le versioni greche diverse dai LXX non registrano ἀνδρίζομαι se non una volta come variante.[31] Pare quindi che lo abbiano
usato meno dei LXX. Nel N.T. I *Cor.* 16,13 si ispira all'A.T.:
Γρηγορεῖτε, στήκετε ἐν τῇ πίστει, ἀνδρίζεσθε, κραταιοῦσθε. Il
verbo κραταιόω, spesso combinato con ἀνδρίζομαι, è attestato solo
in ambiente biblico-giudaico; nei LXX,[32] nelle versioni di Aquila,
Simmaco e Teodozione,[33] in Filone Alessandrino[34] e nel N.T.;[35] infatti non compare nè nella lingua classica, nè in quella dei papiri.
Potrebbe essere una creazione dei LXX.

Nei papiri il verbo ἀνδρίζομαι compare solo cinque volte, tutte in documenti del III sec. a.c.: quattro lettere[36] a una petizione in forma epistolare. Nelle prime il verbo ha il senso di "farsi
coraggio, 'star su di morale.'" In *P. Petr.* II 40a c'è, come nei
LXX, un invito al coraggio preceduto da un imperativo negativo μὴ
ὀλιγοψυχήσετε e seguito da un γάρ che introduce la motivazione. La
petizione (*PSI* IV 402) è il documento più interessante: Harentotes,
il φακηψός di Filadelfia, chiede una dilazione nel pagare le imposte perchè i suoi affari, a causa della concorrenza dei venditori
di zucche, non sono più buoni come prima. Fino al presente, dice
Harentotes, ἀνδρίζομαι, cioè mi sono "comportato da uomo," "ho fatto
tutto il possibile" per pagare ogni mese le tasse. Impossibile
rendere bene in una lingua moderna la vena di umorismo che, a mio
parere, sta sotto il verbo ἀνδρίζομαι in questo contesto, quasi "mi
sono fatto coraggio" a pagare le imposte. E' notevole il fatto che
dopo i LXX e i papiri (del III sec. a.C.), Filone e il N.T., strettamente connessi tra loro, il verbo non sia più attestato nell'accezione morale vista.

---

31   Cod. 88 in *Is.* 41,6.

32   64 volte; traduce 12 termini ebraici soprattutto ḥāzaq (32
volte) e 'āmeṣ (7 v.) usato specialmente nei libri dei *Sal.* e dei *Re*.

33   In passi per lo più diversi da quelli in cui lo troviamo
nei LXX.

34   *De agricultura* 160; *De confusione linguarum* 101, 103 (L.
Cohn-P. Wendland, *Philonis Alexandrini opera quae supersunt* [Bero-
lini 1897] II).

35   *Lc.* 1,80; 2,40; I *Cor.* 16,13; *Ef.* 3,16.

36   *P. Petr.* II 40a.13; *PSI* IV 326.10 (261/0 a.); V 512.29
(253/2 a.), *P. Cair. Zen.* IV 59579.5.

ΠΑΣΤΟΦΟΡΙΟΝ

In un ambito differente dai precedenti ci porta il termine παστοφόριον che è attestato nella lingua greca solo in età ellenistica e romana. I vocaboli παστοφόρος e παστοφόριον sono stati coniati in Egitto per tradurre termini che si riferiscono al culto egiziano. Παστοφόριον compare in 28 papiri[37] e 17 passi dei LXX.[38] Lo troviamo poi in Flavio Giuseppe,[39] in due commentari biblici di Padri della Chiesa[40] e nelle *Constitutiones Apostolorum*.[41] In tutti i casi si tratta di un locale adiacente all'edificio sacro, in cui sta chi si occupa del culto e che, talvolta, serve da ripostiglio o magazzino di oggetti inerenti il culto. Παστοφόρος indica una categoria di sacerdoti egiziani. L'etimologia da παστός[42] e φέρω, sembra chiara, ma le ipotesi[43] sulla funzione principale dei παστοφόροι sono almeno tre: a) portatori di edicola o celletta con la statua della divinità; b) portatori di oggetti tessuti; c) portieri, se παστοφόρος traduce il demotico *wn* "portiere, apritore," forse di tendaggi posti davanti a qualcosa di sacro, da tener celato ai fedeli. La prima interpretazione sembra da scartare sia perchè παστός nei documenti greci non significa mai edicola, che è ναός o ναΐσκιον, sia perchè basata su un'interpretazione errata

---

37 Cfr. F. Preisigke, *Wörterbuch der Griechischen Papyrusurkunden* (Berlin 1925-1931); E. Kiessling, *Supplementum* 1940-1966 (Amsterdam 1969-71); IV (1.2.3.4.) (Berlin 1944-71); S. Daris, *Spoglio lessicale papirologico* (Milano, 1968).

38 Cfr. Hatch-Redpath, *A Concordance*, s.v. παστοφόριον.

39 *Bell. Jud.* IV 9,12.

40 Eusebius Caesariensis, *Commentaria in Isaiam*, cap. XXII; J. Ziegler, *Der Jesajakommentar*, in Eusebius Werke IX vol. (Berlin 1975) par. 82 (22,15-25) p. 147, rr. 26-30; Olympiodorus Alexandrinus, *Fragmenta in Jeremiam*, cap. XXXV, *PG* 93, 696 D.

41 X. Funk, *Didascalia et Constitutiones Apostolorum* (Paderbornae 1905) I, 159-61 (1.II,57,3); 518 (1.VIII,13,17).

42 Ptc. del verbo πάσσω "tessere una decorazione in un tessuto," fin da Omero, come sostantivo solo dall'età ellenistica (= velo o cortina ricamata del talamo).

43 H. B. Schönborn, *Die Pastophoren im Kult der ägyptischen Götter* (Meisenheim am Glan 1976) 6.

della parola παστός nelle prime traduzioni del IV mimo di Eronda.[44]
Anche la seconda e la terza ipotesi tuttavia non sono del tutto
convincenti.[45] Ritengo che sulla base appunto dell'etimologia, si
possa proporre un'altra soluzione; non potrebbero i παστοφόροι
prendere il nome da un velo o qualcosa di simile che faceva parte
del loro abbigliamento? Come è noto essi erano sacerdoti di rango
inferiore rispetto agli ἱερεῖς e nei documenti ne sono sempre distinti.[46] Il παστοφόριον era originariamente il locale destinato
alla loro abitazione, all'interno del recinto del tempio. Dai papiri però appare che esso non era riservato ai παστοφόροι e alle
loro famiglie,[47] ma poteva servire eventualmente anche per i κάτοχοι[48] o per altre persone, almeno provvisoriamente.[49] Il termine è
usato spesso al plurale, il che fa supporre l'esistenza di più ambienti del genere nello stesso recinto templare;[50] altre volte

---

44 O. Crusius, *Herondae Mimiambi* (Lipsiae 1908) IV, 55-58; G.
Puccioni, *Herodae Mimiambi* (Firenze 1950) 82: "cella," da cui *LSJ*,
s.v., n° 5 "perh. shrine"; cfr. anche W. Otto, *Priester und Tempel
in hellenistischen Ägypten* I (Leipzig 1905) 95 ss.: "Götterzelle";
H. Bonnet, *Reallexikon der ägyptischen Religionsgeschichte* (Berlin
1952) 583: "Kleiner Schrein"; H. I. Bell, *Cults and Creeds in
Graeco-Roman Egypt* (Liverpool 1954) 51 "*pastophoroi*, who carried
the little shrines in processions." Traducono rettamente O. Crusius, *Die Mimiamben des Herondas*, riv. da R. Herzog (Hildesheim
1967) 115: "der Vorhang"; I. C. Cunningham, *Herodas Mimiambi* (Oxford 1971) 139: "curtain"; pensando probabilmente ad una camera
chiusa da cortine, da una tenda (cfr. p. 197), W. Headlam-A. D.
Knox, *Herodas. The Mimes and Fragments* (Cambridge 1922) 171 rendono
"sacristy."

45 Schönborn, *Die Pastophoren im Kult.*

46 Cfr. *BGU* V 1: Gnomon dell'Idios Logos, par. 82; *P. Fouad*
I 10, pp. 18-22.

47 *BGU* VIII 1849; 1816(?).

48 *UPZ* I 5,6 (18 ott. 163 a.) 13 (158 a.).

49 *UPZ* I 12 (158 a.); *BGU* VIII 1816.

50 *P. Ryl.* II 155.11; *P. Eleph.* 20.50; *PSI* X 1145.21; *P.
Eleph.* 24.4-5,13; *SB* VI 9065.14; *BGU* IV 1061.8; *P. Grenf.* II 34.2;
UPZ I 6,5,12,13; *P. Petr.* II 1; *UPZ* I 119.18; *P. Oxy.* I 984.13;
BGU VIII 1849.5.

invece il termine al singolare sembra indicare più stanze o, addirittura, un edificio intero.[51]

Il παστοφόριον era un bene immobile soggetto a proprietà privata e ad operazioni commerciali: compra-vendita,[52] affitto,[53] divisione di proprietà,[54] cessione,[55] prestito,[56] donazione o eredità,[57] spesso frazionato,[58] come avviene in Egitto per le case di abitazione. I papiri in cui compare il termine vanno dal III sec. a.C. al III d.C.[59] Può stupire che questo vocabolo specifico della terminologia cultuale egiziana sia stato assunto dai LXX per indicare dei locali esistenti nel recinto del Tempio di Gerusalemme. Παστοφόριον nei LXX è la traduzione costante del termine ebraico liškā, che significa "stanza" sia per abitazione sia per deposito. Liškā può essere reso anche con altre parole greche (ἐξέδρα, γαζοφυλάκιον, οἶκος, αὐλή, σκηνή, κατάλυμα), ciascuna delle quali sembra

---

51 P. Tebt. II 383 δίστεγος "a due piani."

52 P. Grenf. II 35 (98 a.); P. Ryl. II 161 (71 p.); UPZ II 177 (136 p.); CPR I 131.8 (III p.).

53 P. Eleph. 20 (III a.).

54 P. Mich. V 2,322a (46 p.); P. Tebt. II 383 (46 p.).

55 PSI X 1145 (II in.p.).

56 P. Tebt. II 543 (I p.).

57 P. Tebt. II 489 (II p.); P. Mich. V 2,322a.

58 P. Tebt. II 383 (46 p.); P. Grenf. II 35 (98 a.); P. Ryl. II 161 (71 p.); P. Mich. V 2,322a; SB VI 9065 (I a.).

59 Petizioni: P. Petr. II 1 (III a.) fr.; UPZ I 5 e 6 (163 a.) 119 (rr. 1-17: cfr. P. Par. II, pp. 206-07) (156 a.) BGU VIII 1816 (60/59 a.); 1849 (48/46 a.); SB VI 9065.14 (I a.); P. Athen. (età Tol.); BGU IV 1061 (14 a.) παστοφόριον = luogo di reclusione dei κάτοχοι (v. sopra UPZ e P. Petr. II 1 (III a) o di abitazione (UPZ I 12; BGU VIII 1849; P. Oxy. VI 984; P. Grenf. II 35; BGU VIII 1816; P. Tebt. II 489; παστοφόριον + gen. di persona (possessore o abitante) UPZ I 12; P. Grenf. II 35; P. Mich. V 2,322a; P. Tebt. II 383; PSI X 1145); i documenti commerciali o giuridici o di altro genere: P. Mich. V 2,238 II-IV (46 p.); P. Oxy. VI 984.13 (I p.): rapporti giudiziari: UPZ I 119 (156 a.); P. Tebt. II 489 (II p.); P. Erl. 90.6 (II p.); lettere: UPZ I 78 (159 a.); 12 (158 a.); 13 (158 a.). (dal III a. al III p.) in cui esso è materia di possesso o comunque variamente cedibile.

indicarne un uso differente.[60] Nell'A.T. si dice che i παστοφόρια stanno attorno ai cortili[61] o danno su portici,[62] e sono nominati accanto ai posti di guardia,[63] alle porte,[64] ai vestiboli.[65] L'uso di abitazione è confermato dai brani in cui (come nei papiri) al nome παστοφόριον segue il genitivo di un nome di persona.[66] Ma nel Tempio di Gerusalemme non c'era spazio per la proprietà privata, e i παστοφόρια al suo interno non erano oggetto di transazioni commerciali come gli omonimi ambienti dei templi egiziani e potevano essere abitati solo da addetti al culto, non dai loro familiari e tanto meno da donne. Solo in I *Esdra* 8,58 (60) si attribuisce ai παστοφόρια funzione di deposito di materiali preziosi elencati nei versetti precedenti (56.57). In due altri passi questi locali sono nominati accanto ai θησαυροί[67] e alle ἀποθῆκαι,[68] per cui questo uso sembrerebbe da escludere. Il numero dei παστοφόρια del Tempio di Gerusalemme doveva essere molto alto considerando la centralizzazazione del culto e la quantità di personale che vi era votato.

Ez. nella visione del Tempio futuro conta trenta παστοφόρια. Pare tuttavia che nel Tempio ebraico con la parola παστοφόριον si indicasse un solo locale e non più stanze o un edificio come nei papiri esaminati. Le persone che usufruivano dei παστοφόρια erano

---

60 ἐξέδρα: abitazione dei sacerdoti; deposito di vittime sacrificali e paramenti sacri; (*Ez.* 40,45; 42,13; 44,19); γαζοφυλάκιον abitazione forse nè di sacerdoti, nè di Leviti (IV *Re* 23,11; *Neh.* 13,8) deposito di decime e offerte alimentari [*Neh.* 10 (II *Esdra* 20)38-40; 13(23) 5.9]; οἶκος camera di uno scriba [*Ger.* 43 (36),10.12.20.21]; αὐλή sala (per intratenere estranei) [*Ger.* 42 (35)2]; σκηνή ripostiglio di cose preziose offerte per il Tempio [(II) *Esdra* 8,29] i κατάλυμα "sala," albergo, ma connesso con cose sacre [I *Sam* (I *Re*) 9,22].

61 I *Cron.* 23,28; 28,12; *Ez.* 40,17; I *Esdra* 9,1.

62 *Ez.* 40,17.

63 I *Cron.* 26,16.18.

64 I *Macc.* 4,57; I *Macc.* 4,38; *Ez.* 40,38.

65 *Ez.* 40,38.

66 *Ger.* 42,4; I *Esdra* 9,1.

67 I *Cron.* 9,26.

68 II *Cron.* 28,12.

o Leviti,[69] o altri addetti al culto alle loro dipendenze,[70] con funzione di portieri e di custodi.[71] Anche i Leviti, come i παστο-φόροι erano di ordine inferiore rispetto ai sacerdoti, e avevano compiti di custodia nei confronti degli edifici del Tempio e di chi vi risiedeva.

Il termine παστοφόριον è passato anche nel linguaggio cristiano in due passi delle *Constitutiones Apostolorum*, da cui apprendiamo chi i παστοφόρια, volti ad oriente come la chiesa, si disponevano su entrambi i suoi lati lunghi (II 57,3) e in essi i diaconi porta-vano ciò che avanzava dalla distribuzione dell'Eucarestia ai fedeli (VIII 13,17). Questi παστοφόρια si identificano quasi con certezza con quei locali posti presso l'abside, che noi attualmente chiamia-mo "sacrestie," e con quelli che nelle chiese di rito orientale si trovano inseriti direttamente nell'abside (spesso tripartita) (πρό-τεσις a Nord; διακόνικον a Sud) in cui ancor oggi si consumano i resti del pane eucaristico.*

Università Cattolica-Milano   Anna Passoni Dell'Acqua

---

69   I *Cron.* 9,26.

70   I *Cron.* 23.28.

71   I *Cron.* 9,26; 23,28.

* La ricerca sui termini παστοφόριον e ἀνδρίζομαι comparirà in una trattazione più ampia nella rivista *Aegyptus* 61 (1981).

Proceedings of the XVI Int. Congr. of Papyrology (Chico 1981) 633-642

PATRISTIK UND PAPYROLOGIE
(GRUNDSÄTZLICHE ERWÄGUNGEN ZUM PROJEKT DES REPERTORIUMS DER GRIECHISCHEN CHRISTLICHEN PAPYRI)

I. Die Ausgangssituation

Kurz nach dem ersten Weltkrieg wird in der den literarischen Texten zugewandten Papyrologie ein ziemliches Desinteresse an Papyri christlicher Provenienz unübersehbar. Deutlich, ja provokant artikuliert wird diese Abwendung in der 1923 erscheinenden Auflistung literarischer Papyri von Oldfather,[1] in deren Einleitung es im Tone unverhohlener Geringschätzung heißt: "The christian papyri and such products as are connected with magic and divination are excluded." Diese Abwertung der christlichen Literatur blieb, wie die Zusammenstellungen von Reggers,[2] Giabbiani[3] und die erste Auflage des Packschen Repertoriums[4] zeigen, in der Papyrologie für die nächste Zeit bestimmend. Die Erfassung und Auswertung der literarischen Papyri christlicher Herkunft geriet dadurch natürlich in erheblichen Rückstand. Erst in allerjüngster Zeit ist durch die Verzeichnisse von Montevecchi, Aland und van Haelst[5] in der Sache eine Wende zum Besseren eingeleitet worden; die dahinter stehende Konzeption, d.h. der Ermöglichungsgrund für diese Entwicklung, ist dagegen kaum deutlich geworden. Und so stellt sich die Frage, ob die separate Behandlung der christlichen Papyri nur das Ergebnis

---

1 C. H. Oldfather, *The Greek Literary Texts from Greco-Roman Egypt* (Madison 1923).

2 Sr. E. Reggers, *Catalogus van de grieksche letterkundige Papyrusteksten uitgegeven in de Jaren 1922-1938* (Löwen 1942).

3 L. Giabbiani, *Testi letterari greci di provenienza egiziana* (1920-1945) (Florenz 1947).

4 R. A. Pack, *The Greek and Latin Literary Texts from Greco-Roman Egypt* (Ann Arbor 1952).

5 O. Montevecchi, *La Papirologia* (Turin 1973) 295-334; K. Aland, *Repertorium der griechischen christlichen Papyri* I: *Biblische Papyri* (Patristische Texte und Studien 18, Berlin/New York 1976); J. van Haelst, *Catalogue des papyrus littéraires juifs et chrétiens* (Paris 1976).

ihrer Vernachlässigung im Bereich der literarischen Papyrologie
ist, oder ob es dafür Gründe gibt, die in der Sache, d.h. in den
christlichen Texten selbst, liegen.

II. Theoretische Grundlagen

Daß die theoretische Aufarbeitung des Verhältnisses von
christlicher und profaner Literatur innerhalb der Papyrologie der
tatsächlichen Entwicklung nicht vorangeht, sondern nachhinkt, zeigt
schon der erste Versuch in dieser Richtung. Noch 1935, zu einer
Zeit also, als die Trennung von christlich-literarischen und
heidnisch-literarischen Papyri de facto längst durchgeführt war,
versuchte Derouau(x) in einem Aufsatz über "Littérature chrétienne
antique et papyrologie"[6] die christliche Literaturgeschichte in
Anlehnung an gebräuchliche Konzepte als Abteilung der Klassischen
Philologie zu verstehen, um ihr auf diesem Umweg die Papyrologie
als Hilfswissenschaft dienstbar zu machen. Dieses Konzept wird
allerdings nicht durchgehalten. Vor allem der Drang nach möglichst
umfassender Darstellung des vorhandenen Materials überhaupt führt
häufig zu unsachgemäßen Grenzüberschreitungen. So verdienstvoll
dieser erste Versuch als solcher auch ist, die Mängel im Verlauf
der Durchführung machen deutlich genug, daß diese Hilfskonstruk-
tion nicht ausreicht, um die Einheit der (christlichen und profanen)
literarischen Papyrologie (wieder) herzustellen. Sie zeigen aber
auch, daß selbst da, wo der Wille zu einer gemeinsamen Behandlung
beider Bereiche vorhanden ist, der Charakter des christlichen Materials selber eine solche Behandlung erschwert oder gar verhindert.

Diese Einsicht hat dann 20 Jahre später Frau Montevecchi für
ein anderes Konzept fruchtbar gemacht, das sie auf dem 8. Internationalen Papyrologenkongreß unter dem Titel "Progetto per una serie
di ricerche di papirologia cristiana"[7] vortrug. Soweit ich sehe,
ist Frau Montevecchi die erste gewesen,[8] die aus der bisherigen

---

6 *Nouvelle Revue Théologique* 62 (1935) 810-43; auf derselben
theoretischen Grundlage mit aktualisiertem Belegmaterial wiederholt
in: J. de Ghellinck, *Patristique et Moyen Age* (Brüssel/Paris 1947)
II, 298-344.

7 *Aegyptus* 36 (1956) 3-13.

8 Der Begriff als solcher ist bereits kurz vorher bei A. Bataille, *Les Papyrus* (Paris 1955) 59 nachweisbar, wird dort aber
nicht weiter reflektiert.

Entwicklung die Konsequenzen gezogen und bewußt für eine "papirologia cristiana" votiert hat. Indessen liegt das innere Schwergewicht dieses Konzepts, wie ich meinen möchte, nicht auf der theolo-
gischen Seite, sondern bei der Papyrologie, und zwar jener Papyrologie, die sich selbst als Teilgebiet der Ägyptologie oder der
ägyptischen Geschichte versteht. Das wird vor allem an ihrer pro-
grammatischen Feststellung deutlich, daß christliche Papyrologie
zwangsläufig griechisch-koptisch sein müsse (S. 6); denn ein solches
Axiom hat nur auf einem an ägyptischer Geschichte orientierten Hintergrund Sinn. Aus dem Blickwinkel des Kirchenhistorikers beispielsweise wären die Akzente sicher anders zu setzen: er würde einer Verquickung des griechischen mit dem koptischen Bereich kaum in
diesem Maße das Wort reden, weil ihn an den Ägypten betreffenden
Forschungsergebnissen in erster Linie interessieren würde, was daraus für die Geschichte des Christentums allgemein zu entnehmen
wäre.[9] Für ihn wäre die Sprachgrenze im Gegenteil eine wichtige
Demarkationslinie, an der die Entwicklung vom reichsweiten zum national geprägten Christentum deutlich ablesbar ist. Und wenn der
Rahmen des Griechischen schon verlassen werden soll, so wäre eine
Bevorzugung des Koptischen vor dem Syrischen (um vom Lateinischen
zu schweigen) für einen Kirchenhistoriker kaum zu begründen. Ähnlich reserviert würde sich der Patristiker einer solchen axiomati-
schen Forderung gegenüber verhalten, denn der koptische Anteil an
originaler patristischer Literatur ist verschwindend gering. Und
bei den Übersetzungssprachen ist die koptische eben nur eine von
mehreren. Daß die Ausrichtung auf den ägyptischen Raum im Zusammenhang mit der die geographischen, sprachlichen und ethnischen

---

9 Zur Sonderstellung Ägyptens vgl. H. I. Bell, "Papyrology
and Byzantine Studies," *Vorträge des 3. Internationalen Papyrolo-
gentages* (Münch. Beitr. 19, München 1934) 314-26 (S. 315: "In the
Roman period Egypt stood in many respects apart from the other
provinces....With the reform of Diocletian...the country was assi-
milated to the rest of the Empire") und Cl. Préaux, *Cd'E* 49 (1950)
110-23) (S. 120: "Mais plus que toutes les reformes de structure,
...le christianisme lie l'Egypte au reste du monde"). Vgl. außerdem die Beiträge von J. M. Creed und De Lacy O'Leary in *The Legacy
of Egypt*, hrsg. von S.R.K. Glanville (Oxford 1942) 300-16 (Creed)
bzw. 317-31. Ferner: C. H. Roberts, *Manuscript, Society and Belief
in Early Christian Egypt* (London 1979) 49-73, und (ohne Berücksichtigung des Christentums) N. Lewis in *Proceedings of the 12th International Congress of Papyrology* (Am. Stud. Pap. 7, Toronto 1970)
3-14.

Grenzen überschreitenden Bezeichnung "christlich" also eine gewisse
Ungereimtheit darstellt, muß daher als Schwächung der Konzeption
gelten. Dennoch gebührt Frau Montevecchi unzweifelhaft das Verdienst, die neue Entwicklung erkannt und auf den Begriff gebracht
zu haben. Ob van Haelst, der den Begriff bei der Ankündigung[10] seines
inzwischen erschienenen Katalogs (S. 216) verwendet, dabei auch
diese Konzeption von Frau Montevecchi im Sinn hatte,[11] läßt sich
nur schwer entscheiden. Ähnlichkeiten in der Auffassung (vor allem
was die Bedeutung Ägyptens angeht) wären wohl nachweisbar. Daß der
Begriff im Katalog selbst (s. Anm. 5) fehlt, verrät Gespür für den
inneren Widerspruch, der in dieser Konzeption liegt.

Daß Naldini von Frau Montevecchis Konzept beeinflußt wurde,
ist dagegen sicher; er hat sich ausdrücklich darauf berufen, als er
auf dem 12. Internationalen Papyrologenkongreß zum Thema "La letteratura cristiana e i papiri"[12] sprach. Als Begründung dafür führte
er an, daß es sich bei der christlichen Papyrologie um eine Disziplin handle, die über eine eigene Methode und ein hinreichend großes
und umfassendes Arbeitsfeld verfüge. Schon an dieser Begründung
wird aber deutlich, daß hier ein Konzept nicht nur übernommen, sondern auch fortentwickelt worden ist. Das wird noch augenfälliger,
wenn man die praktische Durchführung in die Betrachtung einbezieht:
Die ägyptische Herkunft spielt kaum eine Rolle. Das Schwergewicht
hat sich auf die christliche Literaturgeschichte verlagert. Der
Widerspruch, der der Konzeption von Frau Montevecchi noch anhaftete,
ist damit beseitigt. Diese Gewichtsverschiebung war, wenn das patristische Interesse wirklich zur Geltung kommen soll, überfällig,
denn das frühe Christentum Ägyptens hat, soviel wir aus der Kirchen-
geschichte wissen, in der Alten Kirche keine Sonderstellung gehabt.
Für die frühchristliche Literaturgeschichte gilt Entsprechendes.
Das Christentum bildet gerade in seiner Frühzeit eine eigene in

---

10 J. van Haelst in *Actes de Xe Congrès International de
Papyrologues* (Breslau/Warschau/Krakau 1964) 215-25.

11 Er zitiert hier den Aufsatz von Montevecchi zwar, aber in
anderem Zusammenhang.

12 *Proceedings of the 12th International Congress of Papyrology* (vgl. Anm. 9) 379-84.

sich geschlossene Größe, ein tertium genus. Und man wird daher
auch von den kirchen- und literaturgeschichtlichen Voraussetzungen
jener Zeit aus der Konzeption einer gesonderten Behandlung der
christlichen Papyri gern zustimmen wollen. Das ägyptische Moment
kann man dagegen als etwas rein Äußerliches in diesem Bereich beiseite lassen. Damit ist die (etwas gewaltsam eingeleitete) Ver-
selbständigung der christlichen Papyrologie zum ersten Mal auf eine
tragfähige theoretische Grundlage gestellt und (zumindest von einem
Teil der Betroffenen) akzeptiert worden. Die der Sache selbst in-
newohnenden Kräfte sind auf angemessene Weise zur Entfaltung gelangt.

Trotzdem ist das, sagen wir, ägyptologisierende Konzept keineswegs ausgestorben. Erst jüngst hat es Bingen in seinem Aufsatz über
"La papyrologie grecque et latine: Problèmes de fond et problèmes
d'organisation"[13] in sehr eingängiger Weise neu formuliert. Daß
Papyri christlicher Provenienz in diesem Grundsatzreferat keinerlei
Rolle spielen, ist allerdings eine stillschweigende Bestätigung dafür, daß solche Konzeptionen im Bereich der christlichen Papyri
nicht ausreichen. Daß der Katalog der jüdischen und christlichen
Papyri von van Haelst (s. Anm. 6) trotz seiner ebenso an der Kategorie "Ägypten" orientierten Definition seines Gegenstandes existiert, ist auch nur eine scheinbare Widerlegung dieser Feststellung:
die Einführung des Begriffs der "pays limitrophes" und die Abgren-
zungsschwierigkeiten bei der Aufnahme der aus Ägypten stammenden
Pergamenthandschriften machen das Dilemma deutlich genug.

Einem Ansatz fernab der Papirologia cristiana scheint aber
auch Kurt Treu zuzuneigen, wenn er einen 1971 gehaltenen und 1974
gedruckten Vortrag über "Papyri und Patristik"[14] mit dem Satz beginnt: "Papyrologie und Patristik sind zwei Fächer, die nicht eben
eng zusammengehören." Vom Standpunkt einer Papirologia cristiana
aus würde man so jedenfalls kaum urteilen können. Vielmehr weist
auch seine Bemerkung, die Papyrologie sei aus der praktischen Notwendigkeit erwachsen, die Textfunde aus Ägypten auszuwerten, in

---

13 *Aspects des Etudes Classiques. Actes du colloque associé à
la XVIe Assemblée Générale de la Fédération Internationale des Associations d'Etudes Classiques*, édités par Jean Bingen et Guy Cam-
bier (Brüssel 1977) 33-44.

14 *Kairos* 16 (1974) 97-114.

diese "ägyptologisierende" Richtung, obwohl Treu sich von der Ägyptologie im engeren Sinne abzusetzen versucht, indem er fortfährt,
Texte aus dem vorgriechischen Ägypten könne man der Ägyptologie
überlassen (S. 99). In Wirklichkeit wird damit zugegeben, daß die
Papyrologie als eine Spezialform der Ägypten-Kunde angesehen wird.
Dabei weiß Treu sehr wohl, daß "man nicht sagen (kann), daß die
ägyptischen (Kirchen-) Väter in den griechischen Papyri vor den
auswärtigen merkbar bevorzugt wären" (S. 108), eine Feststellung,
die das Ungenügen der Kategorie Ägypten für den christlichen Bereich deutlich genug dokumentiert. Und so ist es auch kein Wunder,
daß Treu schließlich bei der Zusammenfassung seiner Ergebnisse zu
einer gewissen mittleren Linie gelangt: "Da Ägypten durch die Papyri seinen eigenen Reichtum hat, vor allen andern Gebieten der antiken Oikumene, steht es stellvertretend für die anderen, aber doch
auch zunächst für sich selbst" (S. 114). Dies freilich, meine ich,
ist eine jener typischen Kompromißformeln, die im Grunde niemanden
mehr recht befriedigen können. Für die weitere Betrachtung sehr
förderlich ist es dagegen, wenn Treu (im Rückgriff auf Wilcken und
Schubart)[15] wieder daran erinnert, daß die Papyrologie zu den historischen Hilfs- oder Grundwissenschaften gehört und somit jeder
anderen mit historischen Kategorien arbeitenden Disziplin in dieser
Funktion zur Verfügung steht. Leider hat er daraus für die Gestal-
tung und Beurteilung des Verhältnisses von Patristik und Papyrologie nicht die notwendigen Konsequenzen gezogen. Vielmehr macht der
Titel des Vortrages, der die Patristik bezeichnenderweise an die
zweite Stelle rückt, deutlich, daß die Konzeption der Papyrologie
als Hilfswissenschaft der Patristik auch hier noch nicht ernst genug genommen worden ist.
      Versucht man nun, Bilanz zu ziehen, so scheint mir nur Naldinis
Auffassung für die Bearbeitung literarischer Papyri christlicher
Provenienz den optimalen Ertrag zu liefern, dies freilich erst dann,
wenn die von Treu erneut ins Gespräch gebrachte Position der Papyrologie als einer Hilfswissenschaft auch für die Patristik und die

---

15 L. Mitteis-U. Wilcken, *Grundzüge und Chrestomatie der Pa-
pyruskunde I 1 (Leipzig/Berlin 1912) XIV; W. Schubart, *Einführung*
in die Papyruskunde (Berlin 1918) 2; vgl. auch H. I. Bell, loc. cit.
(s. Anm. 9), 317 (Hauptaufgabe des Papyrologen gegenüber dem Byzan-
tinisten ist "to present the evidence which he collects in the form
best calculated for easy use").

frühchristliche Literatur fruchtbar gemacht wird. Folgt man dieser
Linie, dann eröffnet dieses Konzept die Möglichkeit, daß nicht nur
Papyrologen, die auch etwas von altchristlicher Literaturgeschichte
verstehen, für die Bewältigung der hier liegenden Aufgaben geeignet
erscheinen, sondern auch die Spezialisten für altchristliche Literatur, die sich in die Papyrologie hineingearbeitet haben. Dabei
sind diese den Erstgenannten vielleicht sogar darin überlegen, daß
sie existentieller und gründlicher um die Bedürfnisse des von ihnen
vertretenen Faches und dessen Wünsche an die Papyrologie wissen.

Daß solche Vorüberlegungen aber nicht bloße Theorie sind, sondern auf die praktische Arbeit erhebliche Auswirkungen haben,
möchte ich zum Schluß an zwei konkreten Beispielen aufzeigen.

III. Konkretionen

(1) Beispiel: Seit ihrem Bestehen hat die Papyrologie Schwierigkeiten mit der Bestimmung ihres Gegenstandes. Und es gibt wohl
kein Handbuch und keine wissenschafts-theoretisch reflektierende
Abhandlung, die nicht mehr oder weniger wortreich und oft sogar mit
einem Schuß Selbstironie erklärte, daß der Gegenstand der Papyrologie keineswegs nur die Papyri sind. Eine Begründung dafür wird
normalerweise nicht versucht. Es genügt die Auskunft, dieses eben
sei der Usus. Wenn dieses aber nun ein Usus ist und keine unbe-
dingte Notwendigkeit, so muß es erlaubt sein, sich von dieser Gewohnheit frei zu machen, wenn übergeordnete Gesichtspunkte dies
erforderlich machen. Solche Gesichtspunkte liegen, wie sich zeigen
wird, im Bereich der NT-Papyri vor, und so meine ich, geschieht es
mit vollem Recht, wenn in die Liste der neutestamentlichen Papyri
in der Tat nur Texte auf Papyrus aufgenommen werden, zumal die
Texte anderer Textträger in eigenen Listen geführt werden und daher
jedermann zugänglich sind. Der Papyrologe vom Fach mag das bedau-
ern und, wie Treu,[16] die "äußerliche Scheidung" beklagen und außer
Acht lassen wollen, der neutestamentlichen Textkritik ist diese
Unterscheidung aus mehreren Gründen wichtig. Zunächst wäre da der
in der neutestamentlichen Wissenschaft herrschende Usus zu nennen.
Neuerungen würden hier nur Verwirrung stiften. Nicht umsonst hat
das Münsteraner Repertorium die alteingeführte Nummerierung

---

16 *Kairos* 16 (1974) 100.

übernommen und die Herstellung der Textreihenfolge einem Register
überlassen. Die Usancen der Hilfswissenschaft müssen hinter denen
der Leitdisziplin auf jeden Fall zurückstehen. Ein weiterer Grund
ist die Zeitkomponente, d.h. die Hoffnung, auf diese Weise eine
möglichst frühe Textform herauskristallisieren zu können. Und
selbst die Tatsache, daß diese Hoffnung oft genug trügerisch ist,
weil es ja auch verhältnismäßig junge Papyri gibt, ist sehr viel
eindrücklicher an einer Zusammenstellung zu demonstrieren, die sich
auf die Papyri und damit auf den vorgegebenen Erwartungshorizont
beschränkt, als an Hand eines allumfassenden Sammelsuriums von Papyri, Pergamenten, Ostraka, Inschriften und Graffiti, das den Blick
nur verstellt. Daß wir aber beim NT jeden Grund haben, die Papyri
getrennt zu behandeln, lehrt die Geschichte seines Textes zur Genüge: Ob es einen ägyptischen Text, der sich zumindest später auch
in anderen geographischen Räumen findet, in diesem Sinne je gegeben
hat, wird sich, wenn überhaupt, nur dadurch ermitteln lassen, daß
man die Handschriften mit gesicherter ägyptischer Provenienz von
den anderen zunächst einmal getrennt hält. Handschriften von gesicherter ägyptischer Provenienz aber sind nur die Papyri, während
bei den Pergamenten Unsicherheit herrscht; sie mit einzubeziehen
bringt Chaos statt Ordnung in die Dinge. Ich glaube daher, daß den
Worten Alands im Vorwort seines Repertoriums,[17] es sei zwar "der
Beschreibstoff an sich" (d.h. ohne das qualifizierende Interesse,
das ihm -im vorliegenden Falle von der alt- und neutestamentlichen
Textforschung- aber entgegengebracht wird) "kein Selektionsprinzip,"
doch gelte diese Feststellung genauso für den Fundort, heute nur
dieses noch hinzugefügt zu werden braucht, daß auch die Traditions-
geschichte einer Handschrift, will sagen die Art und Weise, wie sie
der Nachwelt erhalten worden ist, ein solches Kriterium, jedenfalls
aus dem Blickwinkel jener Wissenschaften, für die das Repertorium
gemacht ist, nicht sein kann. Mit einem Satz: Weil die Papyrologie
eine Grund- oder Hilfswissenschaft ist, die daher nicht nur dulden,
sondern geradezu wünschen muß, daß ihre je konkreten Ziele in den
Fällen, wo sie zur Hilfeleistung herangezogen wird, von den Interes-
sen derjenigen geleitet werden, die sie zur Erfüllung eigener Aufgaben um Hilfe angehen, kann von einem Repertorium biblischer

---

17 Op. Cit. (Anm. 5), 4.

Papyri der Verzicht auf die in der neutestamentlichen Textforschung
als nützlich erkannten Unterscheidung von Papyrus- und Pergamenthandschriften sachgemäß weder verlangt noch durchgeführt werden.

(2) Beispiel: Durch die Zusammenstellungen bei Montevecchi und
durch van Haelst ist im Bereich der patristischen Papyri ohne Zweifel ein bemerkenswerter Fortschritt erzielt worden; das Optimum ist
jedoch noch nicht erreicht, und zwar deshalb nicht, weil die Inter-
essen der Leitdisziplin nicht genügend berücksichtigt sind. Das
wird einem Benutzer sofort klar, wenn er sich die noch nicht iden-
tifizierten, nur als "christlich-literarisch" oder "theologisch"
klassifizierten Papyri anschaut. Hier nutzt die bloße Auflistung
oder Beschreibung der Texte dem Patristiker wenig; zu weit ver-
streut, zu vorläufig sind hier oft die Publikationen. Wenn diese
Fragmente wirklich je die Chance erhalten sollen, vor das Auge des
vielleicht einzigen Fachmannes zu gelangen, der eines von ihnen auf
Grund seiner langjährigen Erfahrung mit einem bestimmten Autor ei-
nigermaßen sicher zuordnen könnte, so müßten sie mit vollem Text
zugänglich gemacht werden. Nur wenn dieser Aspekt berücksichtigt
ist, gewinnt ein solches Repertorium vom Blickwinkel der Patristik
aus seinen vollen Gebrauchswert. Im zweiten Band des Münsteraner
Repertoriums wird deshalb jeder Text dieser Kategorie mit Hilfe der
vorhandenen Wörterbücher und Indizes auf die Möglichkeit einer
Identifizierung überprüft und wenn eine Zuweisung auf diesem Wege
nicht gelingt, im vollen Umfang abgedruckt. Daß dieses Verfahren
auch unmittelbar bessere Ergebnisse bringt als die bloße Auflistung,
sei durch ein einziges Beispiel wenigstens belegt. So hat sich bei
den Vorarbeiten herausgestellt, daß es sich bei *P. Amh.* II 197, fr.
a um ein Stück handelt, das als *P. Amh.* 190, fr. b+c bereits identifiziert und publiziert ist; es kann also aus der Liste der "Textes
non identifiés" bei van Haelst (Nr. 1113), wo es noch als Ineditum
geführt wird, gestrichen werden.

Ich breche hier ab mit dem Hinweis, daß auch der zweite Band
unseres Repertoriums sich auf die tatsächlichen Papyrustexte beschränken wird, nicht weil dies (wie im Bereich der biblischen Papyri) durch die Sache gefordert wird (in der Patristik liegen die
Dinge anders), sondern weil die vollständige Einbeziehung aller
Handschriften (und nur dieses käme nach dem oben Gesagten in Betracht) das Erscheinen dieses Bandes ad Kalendas Graecas verschieben

würde. Andererseits kann in diesem Zusammenhang und zur Erläute-
rung der Gesamtperspektive darauf verwiesen werden, daß die Arbeitsstelle Münster ein solch umfassendes Arbeitsinstrument nicht nur
plant, sondern durch die fast abgeschlossene Sammlung der einschlä-
gigen Kataloge[18] auch schon ein Stück weit vorangetrieben hat; der
Patristica-Band des Münsteraner Papyrus-Repertoriums muß also als
Teil eines größeren Ganzen angesehen und verstanden werden. Daß
bei den weiteren Bänden, die die Liturgica sowie die Urkunden-
papyri mit Anzeichen christlicher Herkunft zur Darstellung bringen
sollen, die Grundkonzeption die gleiche bleiben wird, ist sicher.
Gerade deswegen werden sie sich in Form und Methode der Darbietung
von den bisherigen Bänden unterscheiden. Denn einerseits ist hier
ein ganz anderes Fachgebiet angesprochen, andererseits bekommen die
national-ägyptischen Komponenten in diesem Bereich ein solches Über-
gewicht, daß die Kategorie "Ägypten" hier ernsthaft respektiert
werden muß. Auch die Aufteilung nach Überlieferungsträgern kommt
dadurch natürlich in Fortfall.

Ich hoffe, daß der Rückblick in die Entwicklungsgeschichte der
dem Münsteraner Repertorium zugrundeliegenden Konzeption gezeigt
hat, daß diese Konzeption nicht willkürlich ist, sondern die fol-
gerichtige Aufnahme und Verarbeitung einer (zwar von außen in Gang
gesetzten, trotzdem aber) durch die besondere Beschaffenheit des
Materials selbst bedingten Entwicklung. Ich hoffe ferner, daß die
Beispiele für die Konkretisierung dieser Konzeption die Realisation
als folgerichtig erweisen. Daß dabei Wege beschritten werden müssen, die dem Papyrologen noch unkonventionell erscheinen, ist eine
Folge ihrer Besonderheit und Neuheit.

Patristische Arbeitsstelle   Hans-Udo Rosenbaum
Münster

---

18 Vgl. *Jahrb. Heidelb. Akad. d. Wiss.* (1976) 115; (1977)
124; (1978) 131; (1979) 154.

THE HYMN TO THE MOON, PGM IV 2242-2355

The big Paris magical papyrus is obviously a collection, but
whether the collection was made in the early fourth century by the
man who wrote the papyrus, or whether the writer merely copied,
with minor alterations, an older collection, is uncertain. Kuster[1]
thought the existence of an older collection, made in the early
second century A.D., was proved by lacunae and errors explicable
from physical damage to the archetype, and also by references to
variant readings found in different texts. However, the damage
might have occurred to the manuscripts of individual spells, or of
smaller collections, used by the final compiler of this large one,
and the variant readings might have been noticed by the final writer, as well as by some earlier collector.

That the compiler of the present large collection either used
or himself made smaller collections is obvious. At the beginning
stands a group of rites for divination (to which the "Mithras Liturgy" has been forcibly adapted); then comes a series of *agogai*
and all-purpose spells; these are succeeded by rites to get *pare-
droi*, two of which (1298ff.; 2006ff.) are also, but falsely, entitled *agogai*, probably by careless carryover from the previous
section; then comes a group of spells to control Hecate-Selene and
make her pimp, murder, and send dreams; finally comes a miscellaneous lot, which looks like an appendix, since it includes examples
of all the earlier types. This appendix may be evidence that a
previous collection has been expanded.

None of these sections, however, is tightly organized. Dis-
crepant elements occur in all. More important, I have nowhere
noticed anything like section headings or conclusions, let alone
titles, of smaller collections that have been incorporated. This
absence is the more striking because many of the individual spells
and rites do have titles, and these titles are of different sorts,
from the formal pseudoepistolary incipit, "Nephotes to Psammetichus,

---

1   B. Kuster, *De tribus carminibus papyri Parisini magicae*
(Königsberg 1911) 13f. (henceforth "Kuster").

immortal King of Egypt, greetings" (153ff.), and the trade name,
"The Sword of Dardanus" (1716), to mere identifications, "For
plucking herbs" (286), etc. Of these, the more elaborate titles
presumably came from the sources, not the compiler, since they are
not consistently introduced. Therefore the compiler copied them,
and if he had used collections with titles he would presumably have
copied those titles, too. Since he did not, he probably did not
use earlier collections. Therefore I incline to think of the text
as the work of a writer who had assembled a great many short magical texts, most of them single spells, had sorted them out, but
only roughly, by subject, and now made a single fair copy of the
whole lot, working down through his pile and taking one after another, as they came. This hypothesis would account for two facts:
First, that different spells show different degrees and kinds of
textual corruption, as well as of basic literacy; second, that
many stand by themselves, with little or no relation to the context.

That spells circulated singly and in small groups is proved
by many examples, sometimes sufficiently alike to justify a textual
stemma (cf. D. Wortmann, "Neue magische Texte, *BJ* 168 [1968] 59,
where one of the texts comes from the Paris papyrus, 335ff.). The
ancient copyist, like some modern editors, when he had several
texts of the same spell, used the one he thought best, and made
occasional notes of variants found in the others. Alternatively,
he may earlier have noted the variants in his own copy of the spell,
when comparing texts with a fellow quack.

The spell that now concerns us, lines 2242-2355, shows an un-
usually large number of undoubted errors in spelling, grammar, and
meter. The archetype evidently came from a copyist of the sort
described by Colwell[2] as a word-by-word worker, reliable as to
words and their order, but not as to inflection, initial letters
of pronouns, etc. In elements like these last, therefore, emendations are most apt to be justified.

At present this spell--the first of the hymns calling on the
moon to destroy an enemy--stands by itself. Neither the section
preceding nor that following has anything to do with it. After

---

2 E. Colwell, "The Nature of Scribal Errors in Three Early
Papyri," a paper delivered in the American Textual Criticism Seminar, New York, 1964.

the preceding section the copyist drew a horizontal stroke and
left a blank line; the following text is a fragment introducing a
protective rite evidently for some other spell now lost (lines
2355-58, beginning with a pseudepistolary formula). The other
hymns inciting Hecate to murder begin some eighty lines later.

This isolation does not prove our spell a unit, and it has
commonly been thought composite. Most editors have read as an insertion the unmetrical epithets making up lines 26-43 of the text
as revised by Heitsch (PGM^2 II, pp. 250ff.,[3] henceforth referred
to by its line numbers). Heitsch's text stops with PGM IV line
2347, after which another unmetrical invocation begins; the copyist
thought the spell continued to line 2355.

As a first step towards understanding the text, the title,
omitted by Heitsch, must be correctly translated. It reads Δέλτος
ἀποκρουστική πρὸς Σελήνην. Preisendanz translated: *Abwehrende Inschrift an Selene.* Whatever he meant by *Inschrift*,[4] its usual
sense will not do; the poem makes no pretense of being an inscription and is not apotropaic, but is an invocation culminating in
the goddess' arrival. Actually δέλτος can be used of any written
document and can mean simply "a text," and ἀποκρουστική when used
of the moon means "waning" (LSJ s.vv.). It should here be given a
final nu to agree with Σελήνην (cf. Gignac, *Grammar*, 111f.), and
the whole translated, "A text (to be said) to the waning moon."
So, already, LSJ. This fits the context perfectly.

Let me now go on through the poem, picking out misunderstood
items, mainly, but not exclusively, those important to the structure.[5]

Line 2: εἰλημμένη. Probably not *genommen* (as Preisendanz),
but "whirled" or "rolled"--perfect of εἰλῶ with an "incorrectly"
doubled mu.[6] Lucian (?) used the verb for the movements of the

---

3   From E. Heitsch, *Die griechischen Dichterfragmente der
römischen Kaiserzeit* (Göttingen[2] 1963) I, 59.9, pp. 187ff.

4   The term is ambiguous, as Prof. Koenen told me in a letter
of October 1, 1980. To this letter, and to a number of other com-
munications, the present article owes many corrections and suggestions for which I am most grateful.

5   Almost all the anapests accepted by Heitsch (n. 2) should
probably be eliminated by elision or synizesis.

6   See the variant spellings cited by E. Hatch and H. Redpath,
A Concordance to the LXX (Oxford 1897) s.v. εἰλεῖν.

stars, and Plato playfully made Socrates suggest it as a source of ἥλιος.[7] *PGM* LXXI 2 invokes "Great Ouranios" εἰλῶν τὸν κόσμον. A prayer to the planet Jupiter begins, εἰλὲ παντεργάτη--"Roll on, Omnific, ...who bring all creation into being" (*Cat. Codd. Astrol. Gr.* IX ii 160). Compare the use, for the moon's course, of the cognate ἑλίσσω/εἱλίσσω in *PGM* V 405; VII 671f. Stobaeus I iii 52 is ambiguous; see Festugière, *Corpus Hermeticum* III 45, n. 3.

Since Selene, qua Isis, is also Tyche, there is no need to marvel that she turns everything upside down by her random plans (βουλαῖς ἀστόχοις). Consequently necessity is subject to her, as line 5 says, however bad its meter. Pace Kuster (p. 89), one shoul should not object that Tyche herself is now to be subjected to compulsion. She is compelled by magic (line 75), not by *necessity*, for magic is above necessity.[8] Even had she been bound by the famous bonds of necessity[9] she is now loosed and must come to roar at the victim, for Klotho thus will spin her web. The magician controls the fates (*PGM* IV 271f.; Porphyry in Eusebius, *Prep. Ev.* VI 4).

This argument is reinforced with threats. The goddess had better consent before she is compelled to obey resentfully. The magician threatens violence: he will take hold of her sword-bearing fists. This threat is explained by the report of its fulfillment, line 84 (one of the many ties that bind together the two parts of the hymn and argue its original unity)--καὶ σφιγγανάγκη[10] ἀντίχειρά σου κρατῶ--he has her thumb in the familiar schoolboy's grip, a well-known compulsive device. When Hecate-Selene is represented in statuettes as holding her swords upright, her thumbs stick out as thumbs are apt to when tubular objects are so held.[11] To some

---

7 Lucian (?), *De astrologia* 29; Plato, *Cratylus* 409a. Cp. the hymn to the sun (*PGM* IV 436ff. and parallels) which uses ἀμφιελίσσω as Plutarch does ἐξελίσσω of the moon (*De Iside* 42).

8 Line 68. Further examples in H. Schreckenberg, *Ananke*, *Zetemata* 36 (Munich 1964) 143 (henceforth "Schreckenberg"). In his comments on our hymn (140ff.), S. was misled by Preisendanz.

9 Schreckenberg, ch. IV 1; pp. 72ff.

10 I follow Heitsch, who followed Schmidt, in emending the papyrus' σπινγι αναγκη.

11 So in the Capitoline example, no. 36, *ex coll.* Chigi; Boston MFA no. 104 (cat. Comstock-Vermeule); National Museum, Athens, no. 523, etc.

irreverent magician the statuettes suggested this practical
procedure.

In line 10, Kroll's conjecture, πρὶν ἡ <β>δελύσσῃς (*Philologus*
54 [1895] 563) should be adopted. If the goddess does not obey,
the magician warns, she will loathe the consequences. She might,
indeed, go into a frenzy (from λυσσᾶν), but for the magician's
purpose that would not be helpful. He wants to demonstrate his
control. Therefore the emendation ὑπο<υργός> in line 14 is too
humble. Kuster's ἐπόπτης τ᾽ is ideal for content and meter, but
not close to the preserved letters (υποτρ). Whatever the wording,
the sense is clear: because of his knowledge of her secrets the
goddess *must* obey; the compulsion is emphasized by the repetition
and contentual doubling of line 11 in lines 15f. as a refrain used
twice again (lines 56f. and 80) to mark the conclusions of arguments and also tie the poem together.

Next the magician conjures the goddess by the last night of
the old moon, when the powers of underworld darkness are about to
prevail over her light. The lunar side of the deity is now uppermost in thought; her role as ruler of the underworld is neglected.
The dog-(headed) Anubis with the key of the underworld is familiar.[12]
Unfamiliar are his apparent identification with Cerberus and the
conception of Anubis-Cerberus as the underworld darkness which,
during the interlunar period, gapes open and overcomes the moon.
Selene at this time can be conjured by the darkness's temporarily
superior power; at other times she keeps Cerberus enchained (IV
2861). This passage supports A. Herrmann's identification of Cerberus as a personification of the underworld[13] (following Jacoby,[14]
he found an Egyptian forerunner in the devouring, dog-faced demon
of *The Book of the Dead*, ch. 17), but it contradicts his too sharp
distinction between Cerberus and Anubis. The Anubis-Cerberus figure in turn explains Macrobius' identification of Cerberus as

---

12 S. Morenz, *Wiss. Zeitsch. Leipzig*, G. W. Reihe 3 (1953)
79ff. The figure often appears on magical gems.

13 *RAC* II (1954) esp. 979f., s.v. *Cerberus*. Cp. also K.
Meuli, "Die gefesselten Götter" in *Gesammelte Schriften* (Basel-
Stuttgart 1975) II, 1078ff. on Orcus enchained.

14 A. Jacoby, *ARW* 21 (1922) 219ff., esp. 224.

devouring Time,[15] and also the identification of Anubis with Isis'
enemy Seth, which repeatedly appears on magical gems.[16] More to
our purpose, it explains one of the main themes of our poem, in
which the magician repeatedly bullies the moon goddess by threatening to destroy her light and return the world to perpetual darkness
unless she does his will.

Here he goes on to conjure her by her nature and name (Μήνη),
and immediately reminds her that she depends on the sun and shines
by alien light (ξε<ί>νη<ν> αὐγή<ν>, as Heitsch rightly conjectured,
lines 22-24).[17] After line 25 the reader expects a conjuration,
but the one supplied--seventeen lines of unconnected and unmetrical
epithets--is so unlike the rest of the hymn that I agree with the
general opinion which takes it as an interpolation.

With line 44 we return to the former claim: the magician knows
her secrets, therefore she must obey. He "justifies" his claim to
knowledge by claiming also to be various magical and divine digni-
taries, among them Hermes (i.e., Thoth), her father. The *onomata
barbara* in lines 48f. are not to be deleted; they include three of
her secret names (Βριμω, Σαχμι--i.e., Sechmet--and Νεβουτοσουαληθ)
and an acclamation, (ηω) φορβα, elsewhere associated with Βριμω
(line 2963, where φορβεα, and *PGM* LXX 20), and they roughly fit the
meter:

> ἄκουσον ηω φορβ<ε>ᾱ Βριμω Σαχμι
> Νεβουτοσουαληθ. {του} τὸ γὰρ σὸ<ν>[18] σύμβολον
> τὸ σάνδαλόν σου ἔκρυψα

Σαχμι produces a scazon. There are two other scazontes in the
poem, in lines 72 and 89, of which I propose to eliminate that in

---

    15 *Saturnalia* I 20.13ff., on which R. Pettazzoni, "Sarapis
and his 'Kerberos,'" *Essays on the History of Religion* (Leiden
1954) 164ff.

    16 A. Barb and J. Griffiths, *Journal of the Warburg and
Courtauld Institutes* 22 (1959) 367ff.

    17 On the omission of the final nu, see above on ἀποκρουσ-
τικ ή<ν>.

    18 σὸν Koenen, on the basis of my conjecture; σου P. One
could scan Νεβουτοσοῦᾱληθ, thus metrically allowing for the following τοῦτο, but the parallel construction τὸ γὰρ...τὸ σάνδαλον argues
for reading τὸ. See further below.

72 by emendation (not because it is a scazon, but because it
doesn't make sense). It is hard to know how much weight should be
given to metrical considerations in trying to decide the original
wording of a composition like this one. By imperial times and on
this level of popular composition classical standards were often
neglected. This particular poet certainly wrote a good many rough
lines.[19] In the case of line 48 the magical name is a sufficient
excuse for the scazon, as "proper names caused special problems for
the meter[20] and made licenses necessary."[21] In the present hymn,
the τὸ δεῖνα of lines 7, 11, 16, 57, etc. would have had to be replaced by specific names and terms each time the hymn was used for
a spell. This would often have produced unmetrical lines. The
same license may be permissible here and may explain this scazon.
It presumably covered formulae, too, like the final ηη of line 59.

As Preisendanz punctuated the text, the above acclamation and
names are said to be the goddess' σύμβολον. From the rest of the
poem, however (esp. lines 60, 67 [see below] and 89ff.), and from
the related *defixio* discussed by Wortmann,[22] it is clear that her
σύμβολον is the sandal (here immediately following). Τοῦτο should
therefore be reduced to τὸ, which should begin a new sentence, "For
I have hidden your symbol, your sandal...." That the deletion of
του produces an evenly divided line adds one more item to the list
of the poet's metrical failings, but this also may be excused by
the necessity of accommodating the preceding name.

In everyday life the common word for "proof of veracity," "of
authenticity," and the like, was σημεῖον[23]--so especially in letters,

---

19 In the second iamb of line 5 as reconstructed by Kuster -ᴗ
occurs instead of ᴗ- (*anaklasis*). One might as well accept the
reading of the papyrus: φρικτῆς ἀνάγκης πάντοτέ σοι ὑπεστρωμένης
though the line most likely is corrupt. Another problem is presented by line 74, and others can readily be found.

20 Cp. R. Merkelbach, *ZPE* 12 (1973) 172; R. Kassel, *ZPE* 19
(1975) 211ff.

21 Thus Koenen, who refers, for example, to A. Dihle, *Hermes*
97 (1969) 257f.

22 D. Wortmann, *Bonner Jhb.* 168 (1968) 56ff., no. 1; cp. *ZPE*
2 (1968) 155ff.

23 H. Youtie, *ZPE* 7 (1970) 105ff. (*Scriptiunculae* II 963); J.
Rea, *ZPE* 14 (1974) 14; R. Merkelbach, *ZPE* 6 (1970) 245f.; L. Koenen,
ZPE 17 (1975) 79f.

but also in epigrams and comedy; σύμβολον in this sense was rare.[24]
PGM uses σύμβολον more often (roughly ten times, against seventeen
for σημεῖον), but usually in a different sense. The σύμβολα are
not commonly proofs of the veracity of the magician's statements,
still less of the authenticity of documents, but (as here) are secret signs of the gods which give, to those who know and can de-
clare them, power to control the gods. The two meanings, however,
are connected, and in *PGM* σημεῖον sometimes has this sense of σύμβολον (as in our text, line 90).

The magician now renews his threats to prevent the goddess'
leaving the underworld, and so to prolong indefinitely the interlunar darkness: I have hidden your sandal; I have your key (to the
doors of the underworld); I have withdrawn the bar that holds back
the power of Tartarus (again Cerberus); I have given over to darkness this night (which will be) endless. Consequently line 52 must
be emended. If the magician were to swing the rhombus he would
help frighten away the power of darkness, as he would if he shook
the cymbals. Instead, he is threatening a strike--he will not
touch the cymbals. Therefore he will not help with the rhombus
either, and ῥόμβον στρέφω σοι must be corrected, possibly by emending it to ῥομβοῦ στερῶ σε, as I proposed, but more probably, as L.
Koenen has suggested, by inserting <δ'> before οὐχ "with the nega-
tion extending its negative force to the first colon," as occasionally in poetic language.

The goddess should look at herself while yet she can; she will
soon be blind. Aristotle had shown (*De gen. animal.* 780 b f.) that
we see in part by projection from the eyes. In eclipse, the moon's
projected light will be black, as line 55 predicts. Again the refrain emphasizes the spell's compulsive power and indicates the
argument's conclusion.

With 58 we return to the magician's knowledge of the goddess'
secrets, which enables him to control her. Again her "symbols" are
revealed. A similar list in VII 780ff. concludes, "I have declared
your signs and the symbols of your name, that you should hear me."

---

24 Youtie has only one example: Plato, *Ep.* XIII, where the
beginning of the letter, εὖ πράττειν is to be the σύμβολον ὅτι παρ'
ἐμοῦ ἐστιν. None of the other writers cited in the preceding note
adduces any other example. Cf. Preisigke, s.v.

Accordingly, in lines 60 and 67 of our text μου must be changed to
σου.

68-87: more threats, again classical Egyptian, as Sauneron has
shown.[25] The bonds of necessity (line 68) are those which hold
Plato's world together.[26] Helios will hide in the south (line 69)
because that is where he goes in winter when he withdraws his light
from men and leaves them in cold and darkness. In line 70 κουφίσει
makes no sense. Tethys, the primordial waters of Egyptian and
other near eastern mythologies, should flood the world; therefore
read ἐκκλύσει. Koenen[27] observes that, since heaven and Hades are
specified separately in the context, "the inhabited world" (οἰκουμένη) that is to be flooded should be the earth's surface. However,
the goddess is Selene-Persephone; Selene's world is the heavens,
Persephone's, Hades; and Sauneron (p. 13) cites an Egyptian threat
that heaven will be flooded: "The Nile goes up into heaven and sees
the truth, while Re descends into the water and sees the fish" (*The
Book of the Dead*, 65.11f.). Perhaps, then, the primary meaning of
οἰκουμένη should not be pressed, especially since the second element of the Egyptian threat is also paralleled here--Kronos, like
Re, descends, but into Persephone's Hades. Since Re went into water, Hades will be flooded (70, 72f.). That Kronos descends from
fear of the goddess's "compelled mind" seems unlikely, so van Her-
werden's conjecture, πόλον instead of σου νοῦν, is attractive
(*Mnemosyne* N.S. 16 [1888] 316f.).

Lines 75-76 do not suit the context. In Greco-Roman magical
texts generally it is magic that compels the gods, not vice versa.
In this text, particularly, the purpose is clearly to compel the
goddess to do the will of the magician. This has repeatedly been
stated (lines 4, 7-16, 48-52, 56-57) and is stated again in the
lines immediately following (77-87). Consequently the sense of

---

25 *BSFE* (Nov. 1951) 11ff., an outstanding article.

26 *Republic* 616ff., on which see Schreckenberg, 81ff.

27 He compares the "Deliverance of Mankind from Destruction"
(*ANET*, 10f.), the Egyptian myth in which mankind plotted against
Re, the king of gods and men. Hathor would have killed all men in
a flood of blood if, at night, Re had not made beer and poured it
on the fields. The goddess drank it and forgot her intentions.
Cf. D. Wortmann, *ZPE* 2 (1968) 228f. (beer = blood = Nile flood).

lines 68-76 must be: All these cosmic catastrophes will occur "unless you are compelled by my magic (which is) a flying arrow most
swift to run to its goal": ἂν μὴ μαγείης τῆς ἐμῆς (in the sense of
μαγείῃ τῇ ἐμῇ) ἀναγκασ<θ>ῆς, | βέλος πετηνὸν ταχύτατον τέλος
δραμεῖν. The change of ἀναγκάσῃς to ἀναγκασ<θ>ῆς is not difficult
(though it produces another scazon, see above on Σαχμι line 48),
nor is the fact that βέλος does not agree in case with μαγείης;
neglect of agreement in apposition is common throughout the vulgar
Greek of this period (L. Radermacher, *Neutestamentliche Grammatik*
[Tübingen² 1925] 106-12). The change of μαγείης τῆς ἐμῆς to the
dative could be justified by the characteristics of this copyist
(see above, paragraph 5 and note 2), but perhaps may be unnecessary.
Could the genitive be understood to define the ἀνάγκη implicit in
ἀναγκασθῆς--"be subject to the ἀνάγκη of my magic" (cf. Aesch. *Agam.*
1042, ἀνάγκη...τύχης; *PGM* IV 2763, ἔρωτος; Arist. *Nubes* 1075, τῆς
φύσεως; etc.)? Or is it an early instance of the replacement of
the dative by the genitive, which will become common in the middle
ages?

        In lines 77-78 read μοῖράν μου λόγων | <ἣν> δεῖ {σε} γενέσθαι.
μὴ σ<α>υτὴν ἀναγκάσῃς (σ<α>υτὴν being Preisendanz's conjecture,
following Wünsch and Eitrem). In line 79 ἄνωθεν εἰς ἄνωθεν may be
an idiom for "over and over again."[28] Cp. ἔτος εἰς ἔτος "year after year," in Sophocles *Ant.* 340 (Jebb cited the modern Greek
parallel χρόνο σὲ χρόνο); αὖθις αὖ πάλιν in Sophocles *Phil.* 952;
Oed. Col. 1418; inverted in Arist. *Nubes* 975; πάλιν ἄνωθεν in Gal
4:9; and the parallels collected by Wettstein. In John 19:18
ἐντεῦθεν καὶ ἐντεῦθεν means "on both sides."[29] Similar uses of
prepositions with adverbs are frequent.[30] Also in line 79 συμβόλων
is Kroll's conjecture, but σύμβολον, the reading of the papyrus,
fits the sense better; the thing she would have to hear over and
over again would be the one formula.

---

        28 For single ἄνωθεν meaning "over again, anew," see LSJ and
Bauer, *Worterbuch zu den Schriften des NT*, s.v.

        29 Cf. Apoc. 22.2, where many mss. read ἐντεῦθεν καὶ ἐντεῦθεν.
For a different, though related, use of adjectives and adverbs in-
stead of the comparative degree (type ἤδη ἤδη, ταχὺ ταχύ), see A.
Henrichs, *ZPE* 39 (1980) 12 n. 9 (with references).

        30 L. Radermacher, *Neutestamentliche Grammatik* (Tübingen²
1925) 66.

Heitsch is probably right in bracketing line 85 as a prose
interpolation; the revision needed to make it verse is too drastic
for this text. In any event it concludes the list of threats. The
magician now backs them up, in lines 86f., by claiming to have the
gods on his side. He has indicated (his wishes) to the chief judge,
Hermes (again Thoth). For ἔνευσας, therefore, read ἔννευσα. Consequently, as he concludes in line 87, he has the goddess in his
power.

Next comes another exposé of the goddess's secret signs. Such
lists are normally strings of names in the nominative, so the de-
mons of line 95 should probably be in the nominative, like the others. Hell fire does not frighten the Erinyes, nor does the Erinys
(sing.) frighten her attendants; she is simply, absolutely "frigh-
tening" or "frightful," so Heitsch's accentuation should be changed,
read φοβοῦσ' Ἐρινύς, δαίμον<ε>ς τεράστιο<ι>. For the absolute use
of φοβέω, see LSJ s.v., A, end, citing Soph. Phil. 864 and Plato,
Rep. 551b.

Finally the goddess enters and is conjured to direct her wrath
against the magician's enemy who is eo ipso an enemy of the gods
"in heaven." Since Osiris is not in heaven, "the gods in heaven"
must refer to Helios and Isis. Hence Ὀσίριδος is probably to be
connected with both Ἡλίου and συνεύνου <τ'> Ἴσιδος. For such
double use of words (brachylogy), see R. Kühner and B. Gerth, Ausführliche Grammatik, Satzlehre (Leverkusen[4] 1955) II, 564. Postponed τε is not infrequent.[31] The meaning seems to be: "to NN, the
enemy of the heavenly gods, Helios, son of Osiris, and Isis, wife
of Osiris."[32] Helios is of course Harpocrates, the son of Isis and
Osiris.

The meter is abandoned in lines 2348-2355 (omitted by Heitsch),
the string of onomata barbara and vowels with which, as an ultimate
conjuration, the text closes. The initial variations on φορβα are
perhaps intended to imitate the barking of Hecate's dogs. The last

---

31 Cf., for example, J. Denniston, The Greek Particles (Oxford[2] 1954) 515ff.; E. Handley, The Dyskolos of Menander (London
1965) 131, on line 10.

32 Cf. L. Koenen, "ΘΕΟΙΣΙΝ ΕΧΘΡΟΣ," Cd'E 34 (1959) 103ff.
F. Uebel, in a letter of Jan. 20, 1965, to L.K., referred to SB VI
9259, πρὸς τὸν θεοῖσιν ἐχ<θ>ρὸν Πτέλλι<ν>.

word, however, is plain ancient Greek--indeed, pre-Greek--ἄνασσα.
Against Preisendanz, it should be separated from *Harkentechtha*,
which begins the next text. *Harkentechtha* was not a queen, but a
form of Horus; see Bonnet, *Reallexikon der ägyptischen Religionsgeschichte*, s.v. *Chentechtai*.

Columbia University   Morton Smith

PART 11

PRESERVATION AND PHOTOGRAPHY

Proceedings of the XVI Int. Congr. of Papyrology (Chico 1981) 657-663

NEUERUNGEN IN DER PAPYRUSRESTAURIERUNG

Seit den großen Papyrusfunden des ausgehenden 19. und des beginnenden 20. Jahrhunderts haben viele Papyri den Weg nach Europa und Übersee gefunden. Sie bildeten den Grundstock zahlreicher Papyrussammlungen und begründeten eine neue wissenschaftliche Spezialdisziplin.

Obwohl die rasch einsetzende wissenschaftliche Bearbeitung dieser Schriftträger in manchen Fällen ohne vorherige Restaurierung unmöglich war und in vielen Fällen unvollständig bleiben mußte, haben sich mit Restaurierung nur wenige Leute befaßt. Zumeist waren es die Textbearbeiter selbst, die ordneten, Fasern und Falten glätteten und die Aufbewahrung der Objekte organisierten. Fast völlig außer acht gelassen wurde der Umstand, daß Papyri, Pergamente, Ostraka, Leder, Holz und andere Schriftträger dem günstigen Klima Ägyptens entrissen waren, welches diese Objekte überdauern hatte lassen. An ihren neuen Aufbewahrungsorten waren die Papyri nun geänderten Luftfeuchtigkeitswerten ausgesetzt und werden neuerdings vor allem im urbanen Bereich durch erhöhte Luftverschmutzung beeinträchtigt.

Während Gemälde- und Skulpturrestaurierung schon jahrhundertelange Tradition besitzen und Graphik-, Buch- und Papierrestaurierung nun auch schon seit Jahrzehnten wissenschaftlich-methodisch betrieben werden, gibt es für die Papyrusrestaurierung noch so gut wie keine Richtlinien. Immer noch besteht seit den Tagen eines Hugo Ibscher ein fast geheimnisvolles Image des Papyrusrestaurators. Die Folge ist, daß an den meisten Papyrussammlungen keine restauratorische Betreuung der Objekte gegeben ist und man über die notwendigen Bedingungen für eine dauerhafte Aufbewahrung nicht Bescheid weiß. Aus diesem offensichtlich "weltweiten" Mangel an Papyrusrestauratoren ergeben sich meiner Meinung nach folgende Konsequenzen: entweder man überläßt die restauratorische Betreuung den Restauratoren der Papierrestaurierung für die in jeder großen Bibliothek Werkstätten eingerichtet sind--zu diesem Zweck müßten Papierrestauratoren auf die Papyrusrestaurierung umgeschult werden--oder die

Papyrologen müssen sich mit zumindest einfachen konservatorischen
Maßnahmen befassen und die sachgemäße Aufbewahrung und Verwahrung
der Objekte sowie deren Betreuung in Ausstellungen besorgen.

Aufbewahrung der Papyri

Richtige Aufbewahrung und Lagerung sind für die Erhaltung der
Objekte von größter Bedeutung; welche Maßnahmen dabei zu beachten
sind, soll hier kurz beschrieben werden.

Magazine und sonstige Aufbewahrungsräume sollen möglichst
lichtarme Räume sein, aber sich nicht in Keller- oder Dachgeschossen
befinden. Sie müssen mit einem Ventilationssystem ausgestattet
oder zumindest durch Fenster belüftbar sein. Vor allem darf sich
keine Heizung--insbesondere Zentralheizung--in diesen Räumen befinden. Regale und Schränke sollen vorwiegend aus Holz bestehen, da
Holz zur Regelung der Luftfeuchtigkeit beiträgt. Metallschränke,
in Museen während der letzten Jahre häufig zum Feuerschutz ange-
schafft, haben sich aus klimatischen Gründen als nachteilig erwiesen
und sind bei großem Feuer nicht selten der Sarg der Objekte, da sie
zusammen mit diesen schmelzen.

Die Papyri selbst legt man am besten in holz- und säurefreie
Papierumschläge und bewahrt sie in Kartons auf. Im allgemeinen ist
das übliche "Zwischen-Glasplatten-legen" zu vermeiden, da die Papyri dabei gewissermaßen nicht gut atmen können. Für größere Blätter,
Rollen oder fragmentierte Stücke verbleibt freilich nur die Montage
zwischen Glasplatten, wobei eine Unterlage von holz- und säurefreiem
Papier unbedingt erforderlich ist, da dieses im Glas überschüssige
Feuchtigkeit absorbiert und somit Schimmelbildung verhindert. Auch
bei beidseitig beschriebenen Texten muß so verfahren werden wobei
von der schwer zugänglichen Rückseite zuvor ein Photo gemacht werden
kann. Beim Zukleben der beiden Glasplatten ist darauf zu achten,
daß an den Ecken die Luft Zutritt hat.

Ganz besonders entscheidend für den Fortbestand dieser wichtigen Schriftträger ist das in den Aufbewahrungsräumen herrschende
Kleinklima. Die richtigen Werte im Zusammenhang mit der richtigen
Lagerungsweise sind die beste vorbeugende Konservierung. Jahrelange
Forschungen und jahrzehntelange Beobachtungen haben ideale Tempera-
tur--und Feuchtigkeitswerte für die Lagerung von Büchern, Graphiken
und anderen Archivalien dieser Art ergeben. Diese konnten unter

Berücksichtigung der Eigenheiten des Papyrusmaterials und der klimatischen Bedingungen in Ägypten für unsere Zwecke umgelegt werden. Die relative Luftfeuchtigkeit soll demnach in den Depots zwischen 40 und 60% liegen, während die Temperatur 17 bis 20 Grad Celsius betragen darf. Etwa einmal wöchentlich ist durch Ventilation für Frischluftzufuhr zu sorgen. Ganz wesentlich hierbei ist, daß diese Werte möglichst konstant gehalten werden--vor allem jene der Luftfeuchtigkeit. Schon kurzzeitige Abweichungen können große Schäden nach sich ziehen.

Zur Regelung der Luftfeuchtigkeit genügt in den meisten Fällen --da wir meist zu hohe Werte vorfinden--ein Luftentfeuchtungsgerät. Abschließend kann zum wichtigen Problem der Aufbewahrung festgestellt werden, daß dieses mit geringem technischen und finanziellen Aufwand gelöst werden kann--auch in kleinsten Sammlungen.

Restaurierung und Konservierung der Papyri

Viele Versuche der Regenerierung des durch Jahrhunderte brüchig gewordenen Papyrus sind unternommen worden, chemische Mittel wurden angewandt und sogar Einbetten--sandwichen--zwischen Chiffonseide oder Synthetics als endgültige Konservierung versucht. Die Ergebnisse waren zumeist unbefriedigend und ergaben oftmals eine wesentliche Beeinträchtigung der Lesbarkeit. Vor allem aber entsprachen diese Methoden nicht den Anforderungen die man heute an jede Restaurierung stellt: ein restauriertes Objekt muß solchermaßen behandelt sein, daß eine spätere Überarbeitung möglich bleibt! In Wien ist man auf ein sehr einfaches Verfahren zur Konservierung gekommen, das auf dem Studium der chemischen Zusammensetzung des Ausgangsproduktes--also der Papyruspflanze--beruht. Das Mark der Papyrusstaude bestand fast zur Gänze aus Zellulose--einem Polysaccharid. Die Papyrusblätter werden nun mit flüssiger Zellulose, die aus Baumwolle gewonnen wird und in Wasser im Verhältnis 1:3 gelöst ist, besprüht. Dies bewirkt eine Auffrischung der Zellulosesubstanz durch Einbringen neuer Zelluloselangkettenmoleküle. Diese wiederum sind Stützsubstanz für die im gealterten Papyrusblatt enthaltenen Holzstoffe--Lignin. Diesen Abbau der Zellulose zu Lignin erläutert am besten das Beispiel unseres Zeitungspapiers, das nur geringen

Zelluloseanteil hat und schon bei kurzzeitiger Bestrahlung durch
Sonnenlicht und dessen intensiven UV--Anteils braun und brüchig
wird. Die Regenerierung des Papyrusblattes durch Zellulose ergibt
eine merklich erhöhte Flexibilität des Blattes und kann leicht von
jedermann ausgeführt werden. Eine weitere wesentliche Verbesserung der Restauriermethoden
ist dadurch erreicht worden, daß nun bei der Zusammensetzung frag-
mentierter Blätter auf synthetische Klebestreifen (scotch, Tixo
u.a.) verzichtet werden kann. Diese leider so häufig und wahllos
verwendeten, auch über der Schrift befestigten Klebestreifen haben
große Zerstörung angerichtet. Der Klebestoff dieser Streifen wan-
derte vom Träger in den Papyrus und zerstörte dort die Zellulosemoleküle; dies führte zu Verhärtung (Glasigwerden) und irreversibler
Brüchigkeit. Die Folge ist Nachdunkeln des Papyrus und unleserlich
gewordene Schrift.

Man kann nun in die feuchten, mit Zellulose besprühten Frag-
mente--und zwar zwischen die Horizontal--und Vertikalfasern eine
oder mehrere Fasern einweben. Die Fragmente werden dann nach der
richtigen Plazierung gepreßt und man hat eine unsichtbare, arteigene
Verbindung hergestellt. Auch wenn diese Methode für ungeübte Hände
Schwierigkeiten bereitet, so muß unbedingt von der Verwendung von
Klebestreifen aller Art Abstand genommen werden. Man kann sich damit behelfen, die Fragmente in der richtigen Plazierung für die
Textbearbeitung unter Glasplatten zu fixieren und dies mittels Photographie festzuhalten. Hinzugefügt sei noch, daß Klebestreifen in
manchen Fällen mit einem eigens dafür entwickelten Mittel--
Isopropylalkohol--abgelöst werden können.

Mumienkartonage

Die Restaurierung von Mumienkartonage stellt in Wien seit
Jahren kein Problem mehr dar und es scheint wichtig, auf das nun
angewandte, einfache Verfahren hinzuweisen. Denn immer noch hört
man im Zusammenhang mit Kartonage und deren Auflösung Worte wie
"Kochen" oder "Waschmaschine." Die mittels Knochenleim zu Makulatur zusammengeklebten Papyrusblätter werden in ein Bad von lauwarm-
em Wasser gelegt, in welches ein Zusatz von Essig (10%ig) beigefügt
ist. Die warme Essigwasserlösung löst den Leim in kürzerer oder

längerer Zeit--je nach Kohäsionskraft des Leimes. Sodann ist es
vor allem eine Frage der Geduld des Restaurators, um die kreuz und
quer liegenden Blätter und Fragmente herauszuschälen. Das Reinigen
der abgelösten Blätter von Kalkresten und Leim erfolgt wiederum in
einem Wasserbad, aber ohne Zusatz, denn dieses dient sogleich zum
Ausschwemmen des Essiganteils.

Die Tinte, in der Zeit der Kartonage meist eine gut mit Gummi
Arabicum gebundene, übersteht diese Arbeiten meist ohne Verluste.
Am Ende der Arbeit des Ablösens werden die Blätter, wie oben be-
schrieben, mit Zellulose regeneriert und gepreßt.

Verkohlte Papyri

Ganz kurz auch zu den carbonisierten Papyri, die es ja nicht
nur in Herculaneum gibt, sondern auch in Köln, Paris, Florenz, Manchester und Wien. In den meisten Fällen liegen Rollen oder Teile
von Rollen vor, deren "Aufrollen" große Probleme macht. Darunter
gibt es zu festen Stücken gebackene Röllchen, die als hoffnungslose
Fälle bezeichnet werden müssen. Die meisten Verkohlten aber haben
gut zu unterscheidende Blattschichten, die nur mäßig aneinander
haften. Da der Text bei der aufgerollten Rolle üblicherweise innen
zu liegen kommt, liegt dem Restaurator die unbeschriftete Außenseite
vor. Dieser glückliche Umstand kann nun folgendermaßen genützt
werden: Bestreichen der unbeschriebenen Seite mit einer Lösung aus
Zellulose + Polyvenylacetat; bei besonders brüchigen Blättern wird
zusätzlich dünnes Japanpapier mit aufgeklebt. Der Effekt ist eine
Fixierung des Blattes, wodurch es möglich wird, diese manuell vom
nächsten zu trennen. Abgelöste Blätter werden, so sie nicht schon
mit Hilfe von Japanseide getrennt wurden, auf eine solche aufgeklebt und dadurch vor weiterem Verfall geschützt.

Schriftverstärkung

Für die Verbesserung der Lesbarkeit von Papyrustexten, die
wohl das größte Anliegen der Papyrologen ist, konnten in den letzten
Jahren zwei Methoden entwickelt werden, die mitunter überraschende
Ergebnisse liefern.

Neben mechanisch beschädigten Stellen, Wurmfraßlöchern und
ähnlichem sind es meist verblaßte Tinten, die dem Bearbeiter das

Lesen erschweren. Dieses Verblassen--Ausfall des Farbstoffes--
tritt meist bei mit Eisengallustinte geschriebenen Texten auf (d.i.
braune Tinte), während das Lesen der schwarzen Rußtinte oft durch
zu geringen Kontrast zwischen Tinte und Schriftträger, dem nach-
gedunkelten Papyrus, erschwert wird. Bei Rußtinte kann nun durch
Bleichen des Papyrus relativ einfach wieder ein größerer Kontrast
zwischen Tinte und Schriftträger hergestellt werden. Dies erreicht
man durch Chlordioxidgasbleiche, die für die Zellulosemoleküle
völlig ungefährlich ist, gegen deren Bleichkraft die Rußtinte aber
resistent ist. Selbstverständlich wird auch hier wie bei allen
Restaurierarbeiten vor Abschluß der Arbeit der p-H Wert gemessen,
um das chemisch-neutrale Klima des Materials festzustellen.

Eine noch effektivere Methode konnte für die Auffrischung
verblaßter Eisengallustinten entwickelt werden. Und zwar wird der
Tinte in einem vorsichtig dosierten Bad der fehlende Farbstoff
wieder zugeführt. Die Funktionsweise ist dabei folgende: Eisengallustinte besteht aus Eisenvitriol + Galläpfelextrakt mit Gummi
Arabicum als Bindemittel. Der ausgebleichte Farbstoff der Galläp-
fel kann nun in Form von sogenannter Gallapfeltinktur wieder zugeführt werden und lagert sich an den im Papyrus verbliebenen Eisen-
teilchen an. Dadurch tritt die Schrift wieder merklich besser
hervor. Unmittelbar nach der Behandlung erscheint die Tinte dunkel-
blau, nach mehereren Monaten geht dieser Farbton in ein Grauschwarz
über. Die Eisengallustinte war ursprünglich ebenfalls schwarz.

Photographie

Diesen Beispielen verbesserter Restaurierung und Konservierung
können noch einige Hinweise auf verbesserte photographische Tech-
niken folgen.

Wie allgemein bekannt, kann in manchen Fällen die Photographie
eine großen Hilfe beim Lesen der Texte sein. Störend an den Photos
sind oftmals die Schlagschatten, die durch Belichtung an Bruch-
stellen und Löchern im Papyrus entstehen. In Heidelberg ist nun
eine sehr einfache und wirksame Methode gefunden wurden, diese
Schlagschatten zu vermeiden. Man photographiert die Texte im
Gegenlicht--Licht von hinten und vorne--und erhält Bilder ohne
Schatten.

Die immer sorgfältigere Bearbeitung der Texte hat jetzt schon verbreitet dem Mikroskop Eingang in die Arbeit der Papyrologen verschafft. In Wien sind wir in diesem Zusammenhang noch einen Schritt weiter gegangen: wir photographieren mit einem speziellen Fotozusatzgerät über ein Stereomikroskop jene Textstellen, deren Bearbeitung Schwierigkeiten macht. Dies hat unter anderem den Vorteil, daß bei Anfragen betreffend Wiener Texte dem Fragesteller ein bis zu 40-fach vergrößertes Bild der unklaren Stelle zugesandt werden kann.

Weiteres ist beabsichtigt in künftigen Publikationen solche Mikroskopbilder mitabzudrucken, wenn beispielsweise die Lesung einer Textstelle unklar blieb oder eine Abkürzung mehrere interpretationen zuläßt. Mit Hilfe dieser Vergößerungen ist es dann besser als bisher vom normalen Foto möglich, solche schwierigen Stellen zu beurteilen.

Abschließend zum Kapitel Photographie soll noch auf die Sicherheitsverfilmung und den Mikrofilm und seine Anwendung bei Papyri hingewiesen werden. Es hat sich in der umfangreichen Wiener Sammlung als sehr nützlich erwiesen, daß hier alle Papyri auf Mikrofilm aufgenommen sind. Dies erleichtert die Suche nach "zusammengehörigen" Texten, wobei die Originale geschont werden. Die in Archiven und Bibliotheken immer häufiger angewandte Sicherheitsverfilmung auf hochwertigem Planfilmnegativen ist eine empfehlenswerte Vorsichtsmaßnahme hinsichtlich Verlust oder Zerstörung der Papyri in einem Katastrophenfall.

Ausstellungsgestaltung

Von oft übersehener Bedeutung ist auch der Schutz der Papyri vor schädlicher UV-Strahlung in Ausstellungen. Diese Ultraviolett-Strahlung wird sowohl vom Tageslicht als auch von künstlicher Beleuchtung bewirkt und hat rasches Bräunen des Papyrusmaterials und Verblassen der Tinten und Farben zur Folge. Folgende Schutzmaßnahmen sind möglich: Das Tageslicht kann durch Vorhänge oder Rollos leicht abgehalten werden, über Schauvitrinen legt man Lichtschutzfolien (z.B. Ultraphan). Für die Beleuchtung gibt es eigene UV-freie Leuchtstoffröhren.

Wien   Michael Fackelmann

Proceedings of the XVI Int. Congr. of Papyrology (Chico 1981) 665-676

DAS ABLOESEN DER MALEREI VON MUMIENKARTONAGEN

In letzter Zeit sind verschiedentlich wichtige Funde für die
Papyrologie aus Mumienkartonagen hervorgegangen. Damit ist das
Interesse am Inhalt dieser Objekte stark gewachsen. Beim Öffnen
der Kartonagen ist es jedoch bis vor Kurzem nicht möglich gewesen,
die Kalkbemalung auf der Vorderseite vor der Zerstörung zu bewahren.

Auch wenn die Bemalung in sehr unterschiedlicher, ja oft recht
primitiver Qualität ausgeführt wurde, so muss dem Objekt aus kunst-
und kulturgeschichtlichem Aspekt doch ein gewisser Respekt entgegengebracht werden.[1]

Die Aufgabe des Ablösens dieser Malerei stellt ein Zwitterding
zwischen Papyrus- und Wandmalerei-Restaurierung dar.[2] Die Kombina-
tion von Dr. Harrauers langjähriger Erfahrung in der Papyrus- und
meiner Kenntnisse der Wandmalerei-Restaurierung ermöglichte es, in
relativ kurzer Zeit ein grundlegendes Konzept für das Ablösen der
Malerei auszuarbeiten. Die Methode, basierend auf einen speziellen
Fall von Wandmalerei-Restaurierung[3] musste in der Freizeit ausge-
arbeitet werden, da die Beteiligten beruflich anderweitig voll en-
gagiert waren. Ich möchte deshalb speziell darauf hinweisen, dass
das Vorliegende nur eine Grundlage darstellt, welche in vielen
Teilen verbessert werden kann. Die Arbeit ist so beschrieben, dass
sie von jedem mit dem Öffnen von Kartonagen Vertrauten nachvollzo-
gen werden kann. Darin liegt auch meine Hoffnung, dass möglichst
bald von verschiedenen Seiten Verbesserungsvorschlage kommen.

---

1 Die Verdammung dieser Malereien, die sich in Aussagen wie
"Pappsärge, die aus zusammengeleimten alten Papyri hergestellt und
mit barbarisch bunten Zeichnungen wild beschmiert sind" (s. Knaurs,
Lexikon der ägyptischen Kultur [München 1959] 226 s.v. Sarg) bedarf
mehr als nur einer Revision.

2 *Maltechnik/Restauro* 4 (1979) 315-19. In dieser Zeitschrift
galt der Apell, der Zerstörung dieser Malereien Einhalt zu gebieten,
vordringlich den Restauratoren.

3 O. Emmenegger, *Pontresina Sta. Maria*, Restaurierungsbericht
beim Amt für kulturelle Angelegenheiten, Bern, und der kantonalen
Denkmalpflege Chur.

Der Arbeitsablauf erstreckt sich aus technischen Gründen über
mehrere Tage, die einzelnen Etappen erfordern aber zum grössten
Teil nur einen kleinen Zeitaufwand. Die Materialkosten halten sich
in kleinem Rahmen.

Es kommen für die Bearbeitung nur Kartonagen in Betracht, die
aus Papyrus gefertigt sind. Kartonagen aus Leinen von der Malerei
zu trennen scheidet aus, da bisher kein Beispiel bekannt ist, nach
dem beschriftetes Leinen aus Mumienkartonage herausgelöst worden
wäre.

Die Arbeitsgänge gestalten sich folgendermassen.

A. Flache Objekte

1. Dokumentation und Reinigen des Objektes

Vor dem Bearbeiten dokumentieren wir das Objekt in der denk-
malpflegerisch üblichen Weise, indem wir es schwarz/weiss photo-
grafieren und Dias anfertigen.[4]

Die meisten Objekte weisen Verschmutzungen auf (Abb. 1). Es
handelt sich dabei hauptsächlich um feinen Quarzsand, der sich im
allgemeinen mit einem feinen Pinsel leicht von der Malerei abkehren
lässt. Die am häufigsten verwendete Farbe, Rot (Eisenoxyd), hat
jedoch die Eigenschaft, dem feinen Sand besondere Haftung zu ver-
leihen. Wir benetzen diese Stellen mit Aceton und heben mit einem
Skalpell die gröbsten Verschmutzungen ab. Wasser dürfen wir dazu
nicht verwenden. Die Malerei könnte dadurch entbunden werden.
Selbstverständlich lassen wir hartnäckige Verschmutzungen lieber
stehen, als dass wir die Malerei beschädigen. Bei den grün bemalten
Stellen (Grünspan) bedarf es besonderer Vorsicht. Das Pigment ist
fein und ergibt im Anstrich eine geschlossene Oberfläche. Die Malschicht ist sehr brüchig. Grünspan greift den Papyrus an und die
darunterliegende oberste Papyrusschicht ist nach unseren Beobachtungen immer zerstört. Die Schrift ist dort unwiederbringlich
zerstört.

---

4 Farbfotos und -dias sind nicht unbeschränkt haltbare Dokumente. Früher oder später treten, je nach Material und Lagerung,
Farbveränderungen auf. Schwarz/Weiss-Aufnahmen sind in dieser
Hinsicht problemloser. Im *Test 112* (Bern 1980) der Stiftung für
Konsumentenschutz wird zu diesem Thema Bezug genommen auf Untersuchungen der englischen Consumers' Association sowie auf die
schwedische Konsumentenzeitschrift *Råd och Rön* 10 (1979).

2. Fixieren der Malerei

Zur Sicherung der Malschicht wird die bemalte Fläche mit ver-
dünntem Planatol PP[5] (4 T. Planatol, 7 T. Wasser) abgetupft. Es
sollte nicht gestrichen werden, weil die Farben oft wischen. Die
Stellen, wo die Mal- und Kalkschicht ausgebrochen ist und der Papyrus somit freiliegt, sollten nicht mit Planatol in Berührung kommen.
Auch entlang dem Rande der Kartonage ist mit Vorsicht zu arbeiten,
da hier der Leim auch zum Papyrus vordringen könnte. Sollte trotzdem einmal etwas Planatol auf den Papyrus gelangen, so lässt es
sich am besten später im warmen Wasserbad entfernen. Mit diesem
Auftrag, der nach ca. 6 Stunden trocken ist, erreichen wir, dass
sich das nun anzubringende Japanpapier nicht mit der rauhen Oberfläche der Malerei verfilzen kann. Er bildet eine verbindende
Zwischenschicht.[6] Herausgebrochene Partikel der Malschicht betup-
fen wir an der Unterseite mit etwas Zellulose-Lösung (ca. 1:1) und
plazieren sie an der richtigen Stelle. Anstelle von Zellulose kann
auch stark verdünnter Körnerleim verwendet werden.

3. Anbringen der Oberflächensicherung

Zum Aufkleben der Sicherung, eines mittelstarken Japanpapieres,[7]
brauchen wir wiederum Planatol in der Verdünnung 4:7. Wir können es
diesmal aufstreichen, da die Malerei fixiert ist. Nachdem wir das
Japanpapier aufgeklebt haben, bestreichen wir dieses wieder mit
Planatol und kleben damit das Sicherungsleinen (Schleiernessel oder
Calico) auf.

---

5 Hochelastischer Kunstharz-Kaltleim. Hersteller: Planatol-
werk W. Hesselmann, Rosenheim-Thansau (BRD).

6 Im Anfangstadium (*Maltechnik/Restauro* 4 [1979] 317) wurde
die Malerei mit einem schwachen Kaseinanstrich fixiert. Es zeigte
sich aber, dass die erforderliche Stärke dieses Fixiermittels sehr
schwer abzuschätzen war und die Gefahr einer Pellwirkung auch bei
stärkerer Verdünnung bestand. Desgleichen werden die Fehlstellen
nicht mehr mit feinem Sumpfkalk ausgefüllt. Dieser Arbeitsgang er-
übrigt sich, wenn beim Abtupfen mit Planatol sorgfältig gearbeitet
wird.

7 Japanpapier "Misumi" 65 g oder "Inshu Kocu" 70 g. Für den
neuen Träger verwenden wir das Papier der Stärke 70 g oder "Hodo-
mura" 90 g. Die Bezeichnungen entsprechen dem bei Japico in Wien
erhältlichen Fabrikat. Entgegen der ersten Praxis hat sich dünnes
Japanpapier als ungünstig für den 5. Arbeitsgang erwiesen.

Japanpapier und Leinen reichen seitlich je ca. 3 cm, oben und
unten ca. 5 cm über die Kartonage hinaus. Beim Aufkleben achten
wir darauf, dass keine Blasen entstehen. Wir beginnen im Zentrum
mit dem Andrücken und arbeiten strahlenförmig nach aussen. Das
Planatol braucht nun etwa 8 Stunden zum Trocknen.

4. Trennender Malerei vom Papyrus

Das Trennen ist der zeitintensivste Arbeitsgang. Wir legen
das Objekt mit der Malerei nach oben in ein Warmwasserbad (60° C),
in das wir etwas Cellulose (auf einen 1 Wasser ca. 1/2 Essl. Cellu-
losepulver) zur Stärkung des Papyrus mischen (Abb. 2). Die nun
folgende Einweichzeit bewegt sich zwischen 5 Minuten bis zu 1-1/2
Stunden. Die grossen zeitlichen Unterschiede für die einzelnen Objekte ergeben sich aus der Dicke und Konsistenz des Kalkes, der Anzahl der als Träger zusammengeklebten Papyrusblätter und der Mate-
rialstärke der einzelnen Papyrusblätter selbst. Wir lassen deshalb
die Kartonage 5-10 Minuten im Bad schwimmen und drücken sie nachher
leicht unter Wasser, so dass auch die Oberseite nass wird. Sobald
sich nun diese beim Druck mit dem Finger nicht mehr hart, sondern
angeweicht anfühlt, beenden wir die Wässerung. Bei besonders harter
und kompakter Kartonage kann man die Einweichzeit leicht durch Was-
serwechsel alle 10-15 Minuten abkürzen. Sie soll ja möglichst kurz
gehalten werden, damit Papyrus und Tinte nicht Schaden nehmen.

Für die Trennung legen wir die aufgeweichte Kartonage mit der
Malerei nach oben auf eine Glasplatte, bei nicht rechteckigen Stücken das breitere Ende gegen uns gerichtet. Nun klammern wir Leinen-
und Japanpapierenden zusammen auf den "Kranstab," eine selbst ge-
baute Hebevorrichtung (Abb. 2) für unsere Arbeit. Unseren Arbeits-
platz haben wir so eingerichtet, dass sich die nun folgende Arbeit
in Augenhöhe abspielt.

Während der Papyrus flach auf der Glasplatte liegen bleibt,
ziehen wir über die Drehachse die am Kranstab befestigte Sicherung
mit der daran haftenden Malerei hoch, Millimeter um Millimeter. Wir
beginnen ganz langsam und helfen mit dem Skalpell bei der Trennung
nach. Dies ist besonders bei den grün bemalten Stellen der Fall (s.
auch unter A. 1). Dabei darf der Papyrus keinesfalls verletzt werden. Das sollte--wenn genügend Konzentration und Geduld vorhanden
sind--leicht durchführbar sein. Von Zeit zu Zeit muss die

Trennungslinie nachgefeuchtet werden. Wir sprühen dazu wenig Wasser
so auf den schon freiliegenden Papyrus, dass dieses gegen die Tren-
nungsstelle läuft. Die bereits abgelöste Malschicht darf nicht besprüht werden.

Nach der Trennung steht die Makulatur dem Papyrusrestaurator
zur Verfügung (Abb. 3). Darauf gehen wir hier nicht näher ein. Es
sei jedoch gesagt, dass sich die einzelnen Lagen Papyrus zu diesem
Zeitpunkt gut voneinander trennen lassen. Es bedarf dazu keiner
weiterer Feuchtigkeit.

5. Anbringen des neuen Trägers auf der Rückseite

Wir legen die abgelöste Malerei mit der Sicherung nach unten
auf ein Stück Melinex (um das Ankleben auf der Arbeitsunterlage zu
verhindern) und bestreichen die nach oben liegende Rückseite der
Malerei sorgfältig mit Planatol, diesmal 8:7 mit Wasser verdünnt.
Dies trocknet als Fixierung der Malerei. Nach ca. 8 Stunden Trock-
enzeit wird neuerlich Planatol aufgestrichen, diesmal 4:7 verdünnt
mit Wasser, und ein mittelstarkes Japanpapier aufgelegt und ange-
drückt, dieses gleich mit derselben Planatolverdünnung bestrichen
und ein zweites Japanpapier derselben Stärke daraufgedrückt. Die
beiden Papiere bilden den neuen Träger der Malerei. Sie sollten
unten und oben ca. 5, auf beiden Seiten ca. 3 cm über die bemalte
Fläche hinausreichen.

6. Ablösen der Oberflächensicherung

Nach ca. 10 Stunden ist der neue Träger trocken. Wir legen
das Objekt mit der Sicherung nach oben auf eine Glasplatte und
decken das Leinen im Bereich der Malerei mit 2 Lagen Papiertaschen-
tüchern ab und benetzen diese ausgiebig mit Aceton.[8] Dann geben
wir über das ganze Stück eine lösungsmittelbeständige Plastikfolie
und beschweren diese an den Rändern, damit sich die Lösungsmittel-
dämpfe möglichst im engen Bereich der klebenden Sicherung konzentrieren. Schon nach 5-10 Minuten lässt sich das Sicherungsleinen
leicht abziehen. Der Zug darf dabei nicht nach oben erfolgen, sondern immer flach dem Objekt entlang. Zum Lösen der ersten Sicherung
(Japanpapier) wiederholen wir den Vorgang wie beim Abnehmen des
Leinens.

---

8 Von allen erprobten Lösungsmitteln zeigte Aceton die
schnellste und beste Lösewirkung.

Sind an der jetzt freiliegenden Oberfläche der Malerei noch
Rückstände von Planatol zu erkennen (Glanzstellen), benetzen wir
diese Stellen mit Aceton und tupfen sie mit einem Papiertaschentuch
ab. Dabei lösen sich oft gleichzeitig stehengebliebene Verschmutzungen. Für diese Arbeit sind Wattetampons nicht zu empfehlen,
weil sich die Fasern leicht in der reihen Oberfläche verfangen
(Abb. 4).

7. Abschlussarbeiten

Um dem Objekt bei der weiteren Aufbewahrung den grösstmöglichen
Schutz zu gewähren, geben wir es zwischen Glasplatten (kein Kunst-
glas). Ein schlichter, ca. 1 mm starker Passepartout verhindert,
dass die Malerei mit dem Deckglas in Berührung kommt. Das Objekt
wird nun von dem grosszügig bemessenen neuen Träger durch das An-
pressen der Umrahmung gehalten. Klammern oder Klebestreifen halten
die Glasplatten zusammen (Abb. 5).

Es könnte für spätere Forschung oder Vergleiche von grossem
Nutzen sein, wenn der Malerei ein kurzer Text mit Angaben über die
aus dieser Kartonage entnommenen Papyri beigegeben würde. Darin
sollte auch Datum und Ort der Auflösung enthalten sein sowie die
dabei verwendeten Materialien.

B. Dreidimensionale Objekte[9]

Die Arbeit wird anhand des Vorgehens bei Kartonagebüsten
erklärt.

1. Reinigen in der selben Art wie flache Kartonagen (Abb. 6)

---

9 Da mein berufliches Engagement mir nicht erlaubte, selbst
praktische Studien über das Ablösen der Malerei von dreidimension-
alen Objekten durchzuführen, besprach ich meine Vorstellungen mit
Dr. Harrauer. Er war es schliesslich, der die Ideen in die Tat
umsetzte. Das vorliegende Resultat finde ich persönlich soweit
erfreulich--die an der Malereisubstanz entstandenen Verluste zeigen
jedoch deutlich, wie schwierig es ist, nach fremden Angaben zu
arbeiten, besonders wenn Schwierigkeiten auftreten (hier speziell
durch die Verwendung eines anderen Klebstoffes). Ich lege dies
hier ganz offen dar um zu zeigen, dass bei der Arbeit nicht stur
nach Rezept vorgegangen werden kann und dass die Anforderungen--
auch für einen an Überraschungen gewohnten Restaurator--gross sind.
Auf jeden Fall sollte er Erfahrung mit zweidimensionalen Objekten
haben.

2. Fixieren der Malerei

Ausgebrochene Stellen fixieren wir mit Cellulose an der richtigen Stelle (s. auch oben unter A. 2). Wie bei den flachen Kartonagen tupfen wir zuerst die Oberfläche mit Planatolverdünnung (4:7) ab, um die Malerei zu sichern und ein Wischen zu verhindern. Ist der Sicherungsanstrich durchgetrocknet, kann man die Kartonage an den deformierten Stellen von der Innenseite her mit feuchten Tüchern anweichen und dann sorgfältig in die ursprüngliche Form bringen. Anschliessend stopft man sie mit Zeitungspapier aus und lässt sie trocknen.

3. Anbringen der Oberflächensicherung

Japanpapier mittlerer Stärke, anschliessend das Sicherungsleinen werden wie bei flachen Objekten aufgeklebt. Um die Rundungen formgetreu bekleben zu können, werden Japanpapier und Leinen in Dreiecke geschnitten (aus Quadraten 10 x 10 cm). An den Rändern des Objektes werden wiederum ca. 3-5 cm Rand zugegeben (Abb. 7). Nach dem Trocknen wird die Büste geteilt: man schneidet mit einer scharfen Schere von Schulterbogen zu Schulterbogen. Nun decken wir das Sicherungsleinen mit Seidenpapier ab. Damit es sich gut anschmiegt, benetzen wir es mit Wasser und legen es vorsichtig auf. Es soll verhindern, dass das flüssige Polyurethan (Zweikomponentenschaumstoff), welches wir nun aufgiessen, um eine Negativform von der Oberfläche zu erhalten, nicht am Sicherungsleinen kleben kann (Abb. 8).

4. Trennen der Malschicht vom Papyrus

Die Kartonage wird in der Schaumstoff-Negativform liegend ins Wasserbad gegeben (Wassertemperatur ca. 60° C). Im Gegensatz zu flachen Objekten, von welchen wir die Malschicht nach oben abschälen, müssen wir hier die Papyrusmakulatur aus der Form herausheben. Dies erfordert viel Geschick und individuelle Hilfsmittel. Es sollten sich bei dieser Arbeit zwei Personen an die Hand gehen können.

Man beginnt am besten mit dem relativ flachen Brust- bzw. Rückenansatz und arbeitet von allen Seiten her zum Gesicht bzw. Hinterkopfzentrum (Abb. 9). Gelegentlich ist das Gesicht mit einem Stück Leinen (zwischen Malschicht und Papyrus) verstärkt. Auch die

auf den Brustteil laufenden, Haarsträhnen darstellenden erhöhten
Streifen sind manchmal mit Leinen unterlegt. Das erleichtert die
Trennung ganz wesentlich. Beim Herauslösen des Papyrus belassen
wir dieses Leinen auf der Malerei und trennen es anschliessend ein-
zeln in einem neuen Arbeitsgang heraus. Dies erwies sich als notwendig weil sonst die Haftung des neuen Trägers an diesen Stellen
nicht genügend erfolgt. Bei einer bearbeiteten Büste wurde es
nicht herausgetrennt. Die Haftung der Malschicht am neuen Träger
war ungenügend und es entstanden an diesen Stellen grössere Verluste.

Nach dem Herauslösen lässt sich die Papyruskartonage gut in
die einzelnen Blätter zerlegen. Für die Zusammenführung der durch
den Schnitt zerteilten Blätter sind entsprechende Notizen hilfreich.

5. Anbringen des neuen Trägers

Sogleich nach der Trennung wird die in der Negativform liegende
Malschicht auf der Innenseite mit der Planatolverdünnung (8:7) abgetupft. Es soll wiederum nicht gestrichen werden, um ein Wischen der
Farbe zu verhindern. Das Objekt ruht, bis es völlig durchgetrocknet
ist (ca. 8 Std.). Dann wird Planatol (4:7) aufgestrichen und der
neue Träger, bestehend aus zwei Lagen zu Dreiecken geschnittenem
Japanpapier, aufgeklebt (Abb. 10). Man drückt das Japanpapier gut
an. Es ist darauf zu achten, dass keine Luftblasen entstehen. Zum
Trocknen lassen wir die nun übertragene Malschicht in der Negativform liegen (ca. 12 Std.).

6. Ablösen der Oberflächensicherung

Die Malschicht wird aus der Negativform herausgehoben. Das
vorher auf die Oberfläche gegebene Japanpapier haftet nun an der
Negativform. Wir machen nun eine Negativform von der Innenseite
oder füllen den Hohlraum mit einer Art Kissen aus, damit das Objekt
während der Arbeit an der Oberfläche gestützt ist. Wie bei den
flachen Objekten werden die Sicherungen mit Aceton gelöst und Stück
für Stück der kleinen Dreiecke aus Leinen und Japanpapier entfernt.
Es ist ratsam, eventuelle Planatolreste auch gleich abzutupfen,
befor diese wieder erhärten.

7. Abschlussarbeiten

Die beiden getrennten Hälften werden mit einem ca. 4 cm breiten Leinenstreifen auf der Innenseite wieder zusammengefügt (Klebstoff: Planatol). Je sorgfältiger die einzelnen Arbeitsgänge durchgeführt werden, desto weniger wird die Schnittlinie sichtbar sein. Es ist auch hier von Vorteil, wenn der neue Träger über die bemalte Fläche hinausreicht. Dies kann besonders das Zusammenfügen entlang der Schnittlinie erleichtern (Abb. 11).

Aufbewahrung

Am besten werden die Kartonagemalereien in Holzschränken aufbewahrt. Diese schützen vor schädigender Lichteinwirkung, Staub und regeln die Raumtemperatur und Luftfeuchtigkeit (Ideales Raumklima: 16-18° C, Feuchtigkeit 55%).

Alice Stohler-Zimmerman

Bildlegenden

Abb. 1   Kartonage vor der Reinigung
Abb. 2   Wasserbad und Hebevorrichtung
Abb. 3   Rechts: abgetrennte Malerei - Links: Rückstände auf dem Papyrus
Abb. 4   Nach dem Ablösen: Malerei auf dem neuen Träger, daneben Sicherungs-Japanpapier mit den Verlusten
Abb. 5   Zwischen Glas gelegtes Objekt
Abb. 6   Kartonagebüste vor der Reinigung
Abb. 7   Die Malerei ist mit Japanpapier und Leinen als Sicherung überklebt
Abb. 8   Mit Polyurethan wird vom Gesicht ein Negativ angefertigt
Abb. 9   Die Papyrusmakulatur wird aus der Gesichtshälfte herausgehoben
Abb. 10   Der neue Träger wird auf die Rückseite der Malerei geklebt
Abb. 11   Wieder zusammengefügte Büste nach dem Abnehmen der Oberflächensicherungen

Abb. 1

Abb. 2

Abb. 4

Abb. 3

Abb. 5

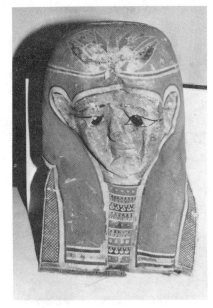

Abb. 6

Abb. 7

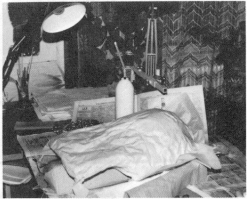

Abb. 8

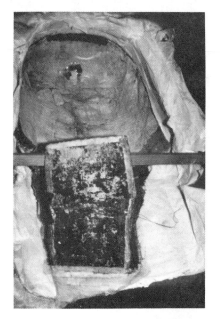

Abb. 9   Abb. 10

Abb. 11

Proceedings of the XVI Int. Congr. of Papyrology (Chico 1981) 677-680

SMALL-FORMAT PHOTOGRAPHY OF CARBONIZED PAPYRI

The American Center of the International Photographic Archive
of Papyri has found two techniques for successful photography of
fully carbonized papyri which will not respond to the usual photographic processes.[1] Both use small-format (35mm) equipment, but
the principles are applicable to medium- and large-format work.

The carbonization process generates a thin clear film on the
surface of the papyrus, but not on the ink. Light hitting this
thin film creates specular highlights, while light falling on carbon ink is absorbed by its matte finish. If the papyrus is illumi-
nated by a broad and wide light source, highlights will be produced
over most of the surface of the papyrus, giving a lighter background
against which to photograph the ink. If photo lamps are directed
toward the ceiling rather than at the papyrus, a wide bright area
is created on the ceiling, which will then function as a broad
"bounce-light" source, and the ink can be recorded on film. Contrast in the negative will probably be unsatisfactory, and steps to
increase contrast may be required.

Use of a high-contrast film is the obvious first step. Do not
use orthochromatic or blue-sensitive films, and do not use filters
on the lens. The highlights vary widely in color over the surface
of the papyrus, and use of an unfiltered panchromatic film is imperative if the entire surface is to register.[2] Careful overexposure
(about four times as long as recommended by exposure meter) will

---

1 ACIPAP is funded by a grant from the National Endowment for
the Humanities. I would like to thank Professors John F. Oates and
William H. Willis of Duke University for permitting us to work with
their carbonized papyrus. Techniques detailed here are to be found
in the standard photographic literature, but only with some effort.

2 The thin film acts as a quarter-wavelength interference
filter, cancelling those colors whose wavelength is four times the
thickness of the thin film, and reinforcing those whose wavelength
is double the thickness of the thin film.

overexpose the highlights without recording the ink, thus increasing contrast.[3]

Closing the lens down to its smallest aperture will dim the image significantly. The ink will appear so dim that the film will have great difficulty "seeing" the ink. The highlights will continue to register normally on the film. This phenomenon is known as Reciprocity Failure Effect. With this effect operating, exposure time can be doubled without recording ink, thus increasing contrast.

Most papyrological photography is done at image-to-subject ratios of 1:4 or less. That is to say, the papyrus is no more than four times as long as the negative, nor more than four times as wide. At such ratios, the lens is pulled well away from the film. The farther the lens is pulled from the film, the larger the image, and the more area to be covered by a given amount of light, and so the dimmer the image.[4] This dimming enhances Reciprocity Failure Effect.

The latent image recorded on the film fades rapidly immediately after exposure, with substantial fading occurring in the first half-hour following exposure. This fading affects the highlight areas of the film more than the ink areas. The full roll should be exposed as rapidly as possible, and development begun immediately, in order to avoid this Latent Image Regression. Ten minutes from first exposure until the developer is put into the tank is probably as fast as small-format work can proceed.[5]

---

3   Use an incident-light meter, or a grey card (18% reflectance) with a reflected-light meter. Do not try to meter off the papyrus itself. Control exposure with the shutter speed; save the aperture for contrast control.

4   Actual f-number is the ratio between the aperture diameter (measured at the front of the lens) and the distance from approximately the last glass element of the lens to the film (v). The f-numbers engraved on the lens are computed for infinity focus (f), where f=v. At 1:1 image-to-subject ratio, v=2f, and actual f-numbers are double the values engraved on the lens. Thus, at 1:1 ISR, if you set the lens to f/32, you actually get f/64, two stops dimmer.

5   Times can be shortened with sheet-film work, if the copy setup is placed next to a developing bath in the darkroom. Film can be exposed and then placed immediately into the developing bath. In this case, work will proceed one sheet at a time, for copy work must be stopped for development of each sheet as it comes from the camera.

Use of a high-contrast developer is obvious. Careful over-development (four times as long as recommended) will increase the highlight image without affecting the ink portion of the negative. This is called "developing to gamma infinity."

Once the negative has been produced, steps in the enlarging/printing process can further increase contrast. Choice of an enlarger (if used) is important. Condenser enlargers produce a more contrasty print from a given negative than do diffusion enlargers, because of the Callier Effect.[6] Use of a hard grade of printing paper ("high-contrast" paper), a more "active" than normal developer, and overdevelopment of the print all will increase contrast. Careful underexposure will avoid printing the highlights while allowing the ink to register normally on the paper.

All of these steps, if taken together, will produce an extremely contrasty print, almost devoid of greys. It will be necessary to experiment to find which combination of procedures best suits the subject. The photographer's personal techniques will also influence the outcome. For example, the manner and frequency of agitation during development affects contrast. Tailor the procedures to fit your needs.

Infrared photography is less successful in small-format, but may be suitable for some applications. Generally, the resolution of the image is poorer in infrared work than in the techniques detailed above.

-----

6 The Callier Effect results from the scattering of light within the negative. In a diffusion enlarger, light is already scattered by the diffuser before it enters the negative, and light passing through the highlight portion of the negative is scattered onto the ink portion of the print, and light passing through the ink portion of the negative is scattered onto the highlight portion of the print. In a condenser enlarger, light enters the negative in rather straight lines, and light passing through the ink portion of the negative proceeds straight through to the ink portion of the print, while light passing through the highlight portion of the negative is scattered (by the silver particles there) onto the ink portion of the print. Thus the ink portion of the print in a condenser enlarger receives its full exposure from the ink portion of the negative, plus some extra light from the highlight portion of the negative, while the highlight portion of the print loses some of the exposure from the highlight portion of the negative. The result is that the highlights are slightly underexposed, and thus lighter, while the ink is slightly overexposed, and thus darker.

Kodak's present black-and-white IR film (High-speed Infrared) is almost useless for small-format work because of its large grain structure. Better results will be had with Ektachrome Infrared, a color slide film. Best results obtain when a Wratten 87 filter is placed on the lens. The in-camera techniques for increasing contrast, given above, may be useful for IR work, particularly very slight overexposure.

Remember to test extensively under controlled lighting conditions. Light meters do not measure IR, light sources vary widely in their output of IR, and different substances have different reflectivities of IR, unrelated to their visible reflectivities. Papyrus, even when totally carbonized, reflects IR very well; carbon reflects it poorly.

We find it difficult to read the black-on-red image produced by the Ektachrome Infrared film when filtered with the Wratten 87 filter. However, the color transparency can be rendered into a black-and-white print by copying onto panchromatic black-and-white film, and then printing normally.

University of Illinois   E. W. Wall
at Urbana-Champaign

PART 12

MISCELLANEOUS

Proceedings of the XVI Int. Congr. of Papyrology (Chico 1981) 683-684

PAPYROLOGY IN CZECHOSLOVAKIA

The interest of Czechs in the monuments of Greek literature can be traced back to the beginnings of the 16th century. At Wittenberg, Jan Blahoslav, later bishop of the Unity of the Czech Brethren, learned Greek and the members of his community translated the New Testament from the Greek. The return to Catholicism in the 17th and 18th centuries reasserted the domination of Latin studies over Greek in the now Czechoslovak states. The teaching of Greek declined until the humanistic revival which accompanied the incorporation into the Hapsburg monarchy. The most important educational reforms were enacted in 1854 and, although the Reform has been changed in details, its enactments dominated Czech high schools for more than a century. The climate of interest was a favorable one in Czechoslovakia when large quantities of papyri in Greek began to come to Europe from Egypt in the 1880s.

In 1934 the Library of the University of Prague acquired its collection of papyri from Theodor Hopfner, professor at the German University of Prague. The collection had previously belonged to Carl Wessely, and Hopfner stipulated that these papyri, which are still in the library, bear the name *Papyri Wessely Pragenses* (PWP). It was also Hopfner who began the publication of these papyri; first in 1935, the so-called "magic papyrus" in *Archiv Orientální*, and the second in 1936, "Letter from Syros to Heroneinos," in a history of the Roman Empire in Czech.

After World War II almost all the other pieces of PWP were published by Ladislav Varcl; they proved to be documents of economic character illustrating the activities of an Egyptian farm in the 3rd century A.D. The texts were subsequently printed in *SB* VI 9406-9415. Jan Merell, professor of the Theological Faculty of Prague, has not only edited papyri (e.g. "Nouveaux Fragments du Papyrus 4," *Revue Biblique* 43 [1938] 5-22), but his monograph dealing with papyri and textual criticism in the New Testament has served as an introduction to papyrology to many Czech students and scholars since its appearance in 1939.

Before World War I two legal papyrologists, disciples of L.
Mitteis, Egon Weiss, a German, and Otakar Sommer, a Czech, had come
to Prague. Weiss was first Reader and then Professor of Roman Law
at the German University, while Sommer was Lecturer in Roman Law on
the Law Faculty of Prague, and later Professor at Bratislava.
Weiss' *Griechisches Privatrecht* (Leipzig 1923) made copious use of
papyri; Sommer's *Katagrafé* of 1922 had its origin in a seminar on
legal papyrology. Three of Sommer's disciples remain active: Vác-
lav Budil, who became Reader at Bratislava on the basis of his
monograph, *Hypografé* (1936); Jiří Cvetler, who was Reader at the
Prague Law School and whose monograph on *daneion* in the Ptolemaic
period appeared in 1934; and Adalbert Poláček, who has written
widely in the field of Roman law, as well as papers and reviews on
more papyrological subjects.

The Nazi occupation and the opening of World War II brought
the closing of the law schools in Czech universities. After the
war Cvetler tried to revive interest in papyrology, both in his capacity as Reader in Prague and later as Professor at Brno. Cvetler
accepted the chair at Brno because of the short distance to Vienna
with its collections of papyri; yet in 1950 even the Faculty of Law
at Brno was abolished. Despite other discouraging developments
during the 1950s, an international Congress on Graeco-Roman antiquity which took place at Brno in 1966 brought about the reintroduc-
tion of Greek into a limited number of Czech high schools. Further,
when the Faculty of Law at Brno was reestablished in 1969, Cvetler
took the chair of legal history there; a small number of students
began once again to participate in a seminar on Greek papyrology.
Of these pupils one must note in particular Lubomíra Havlíková, now
a promising Byzantinist, and Stanislav Balík, Reader in the Prague
Law School, who has recently published a paper on monopolies in
Hellenistic and Roman Egypt (1978) in Czech with English summary.

Ulrich Wilcken wrote that the best way to learn to read the
difficult hands of the papyri was to perfect one's knowledge of the
language of Greek. It is still possible to study Greek in the uni-
versites of Czechoslovakia. In addition, a section of the Czecho-
slovakian Academy, the Cabinet for Greek, Roman and Latin Studies,
not only publishes periodicals in which matters concerning papyrology are welcomed, but also organizes meetings on classical antiquity.

Brno   Jiří Cvetler

Proceedings of the XVI Int. Congr. of Papyrology (Chico 1981) 685-690

A COMPUTERISED CORPUS OF DOCUMENTARY TEXTS FROM OXYRHYNCHUS

In 1978 the Computer Committee of the British Academy undertook to sponsor afresh and independently, at the Oxford University Computing Service, the machine-readable transcription of all documentary texts published in the 46 volumes then to hand (now 47) of *The Oxyrhynchus Papyri*. In the course of this presentation, a progress report, I shall review a number of the problems encountered in transcribing one large class of texts in a series with a long publication history, and attempt to acquaint you with the measures undertaken to meet them. Not all questions will have been answered, and perhaps for a variety of reasons cannot be. At the very least, however, an attempt is being made to prepare as clean a text as possible of the *editio princeps*, in order to establish a significant block in the corpus of machine-readable papyri, the desirability of which has so often been remarked upon.

I shall also speak of a new and comprehensive computer package, the Oxford Concordance Project, developed at the Oxford University Computing Service, of potential value to those of you engaged in literary and linguistic studies. A general-purpose research tool, the OCP may be brought to bear on all natural languages, and on alphabets other than the Roman.

Technical specifications of all machinery and details concerning the respects in which this project differs from models and recommendations of others involved with similar projects may be obtained from the address provided at the end of this paper.

In view of the increasingly sophisticated editorial technique employed in the latest of the 32 (now 33) volumes containing documentary texts, it was decided to tape the series from volume 46 backwards, with a view to adjusting the conventions of the earlier volumes, insofar as it is now possible, in consultation with Messrs. Coles, Parsons, and Rea. To date, the documents of volumes 46 through 12 have been entered in transliteration on the limited, but more dependable, ICL 1906A computer. As they are completed, these tapes are transferred to the newer ICL 2980, with its more extensive

character set, for editing from the corrected printout. The texts
are so prepared that it will ultimately be possible to read them
on the screen of a terminal purpose-built at the Computing Service,
which displays the full range of Greek and Roman upper and lower
case, accents, breathings, subscripted letters, diaereses and editorial conventions. On the completion of this stage the tape will
be made generally available, as will specific elements requested
by individual scholars, prepared on microfiche or in camera-ready
copy produced by a Lasercomp Photocomposer. The remaining volumes
of the series, the earliest (10-1), are to be read so far as is
possible in view of their special difficulties, by an optical character reader, the Kurzweil Data Entry Machine, thus avoiding further prolongation of a long and tedious clerical process. By the
use of this machine, capable of learning a variety of typefaces and
subsequently reading them, the project can be maintained and expanded as new or reedited documents from Oxyrhynchus appear.

Among the questions first raised in a preliminary assessment
of the series was what constitutes a documentary text. Editorial
classification in the course of the 82 years since the inception of
the series has varied. If documentary, even if complete, what is
its form?

A few examples will serve to illustrate. Prayers, charms,
amulets, spells, horoscopes, oracles and astrological tables constitute a particularly troublesome range of texts. One magical
spell (P 2753) appears under the heading "Sub-literary," a Christian amulet (P 1077) under "Theological," in contrast to other
Christian prayers and amulets (P 1058, 1059, 1151) which are classified "Documentary," as is an astrological table (P 3299). An
astrological calendar (P 465), however, appears as a "Miscellaneous
Literary Fragment." A chronological list of Ptolemaic kings (P
2222) appears under "New Classical." Other general categories,
such as "Texts First Published Elsewhere" and "Miscellaneous" contain documentary texts. For the purposes of this project all editorial classifications of this nature must be reexamined.

Further, those of the approximately 275 documentary texts
merely described in volumes 1 through 4, and subsequently published
elsewhere, are to be included.

Various symbols, frequent in the earlier volumes, are to be resolved insofar as possible by those technically qualified to do so, and the variety of hands, printed in a salad of typefaces, will be marked in the simplified manner of the latest volumes.

The close cooperation of the Oxford papyrologists will be of great value as we approach the closing stages of the preparation of the basic text, and not least in the preparation of the referencing system, to which I now turn.

The series of references prefaced to each text are of two kinds, together fulfilling most desiderata. One is essential for the retrieval of texts under various headings and the second, not so used, supplies additional information appropriate to its retrieval category. It may be desirable at some time to include some of the latter within the body of the text. All are laid out according to the requirements of the old COCOA retrieval package, subsumed without conversion in the new Oxford Concordance Project, and are as follows.

The <V> reference, entered once only, retrieves the volume in the series, and is prefixed, as are any references requested, to the line or word in that volume. The following <P> reference, supplying the papyrus number (under unusual circumstances subdivided A + B), is accompanied, where it can be furnished, by additional information concerning the location of a published photograph, of a negative or print, of a plate in the volume itself, and by supplementary bibliographical information from subsequent volumes in the series and from the *Berichtigungsliste* and *Sammelbuch*. Much of this material, to be drawn from Dr. Coles' *Location-List of the Oxyrhynchus Papyri*, 1974, and supplemented by records in the Ashmolean, has not yet been entered, pending completion of the body of the text next winter.

The papyrus number is then followed by a <T>, a retrieval reference, to indicate the type of document where this can be ascertained. There follow a number of <S> retrieval references which may be used, if thought desirable, to indicate subjects of importance within the document. Sometimes, of course, this is no more than a new name; in other instances, in long documents, there may be very many subjects indeed, and special study may be required to determine

the relative importance of each. Both these long and delicate
tasks of classification lie ahead for the papyrologists. It remains to be seen whether the effort involved proves worthwhile in
all instances.

A <D> retrieval reference furnishes the date, whether stated
or assigned to the document by the editors of the *editio princeps*.
A <W> reference then follows stating the current whereabouts, if
known, of the original, and in addition, in (( )), an inventory
number, if assigned. Again, all to be drawn from Dr. Coles' *List*
and records in the Ashmolean.

The following <O> retrieval reference--although unlikely to be
used as such--gives in abbreviated form the subject of the "other"
side, if stated and not transcribed. If transcribed and appended,
or published elsewhere in the series, or blank, this is also noted.
If published elsewhere, the information will be provided in (( )).
The remaining retrieval references, as many as three, provide the
number or letter of the fragment, the column, and the number of the
line with which the published text begins. The enumeration proceeds
automatically. Interlinear remarks have been set off by A, B, C,
etc., and the number of the line they precede. It was not thought
necessary in our preliminary discussions to include the measurements
of the papyrus.

The text itself has been entered continuously in transliteration, as I have said, and in its original, uncorrected, orthography
with two considerations in mind: one, to reproduce as nearly as
possible the look of the text as published, and two, to suit the
exigencies of the computer. The result is an arbitrary compromise.
Ultimately, with the incorporation of the appropriate shift-charac-
ters, the transliteration will automatically be converted to Greek
and Roman typefaces. To the extent to which the conventions of
transliteration differ from those of L.A.S.L.A. or the *Thesaurus
Linguae Graecae*, they may be altered by conversion programs.

What then will it be possible to do with this quantity of text,
once this stage has been completed, and what remains to be done before it is of optimum use to papyrologists? Some of the answers
will be apparent from what has been said so far. There may well be
others we have not yet considered.

With the new Oxford Concordance Program it will be possible to
produce from this, or from any other series of texts, a cumulative
forward or reverse word index, with references, in Roman and Greek
alphabetical order (the Greek subsorted by accent) of all or a
selected range of documentary texts in both scripts; or a wordlist
in ascending or descending order of frequency; or a concordance
with numerous options.

The range of choice is perhaps best illustrated by example.
A selection of words may be made either by alphabetic range (e.g.,
Σ-Ω), or by frequency range (e.g., all those words occurring between 5 and 50x); or by length of word (e.g., 7 to 10 letters); or
by defining a list of words to be searched (e.g., orthographic
variants, known or suspected); or, finally, of collocations (e.g.,
combinations of proper names for prosopographical purposes). A
range of words may be selected (all those occurring between 2 and
10x, and 75 and 100x) in a series of texts selected by type, e.g.,
leases. There are also negative options: to search for all words
except those occurring, e.g., more than 100x, or those longer than,
or shorter than, x letters. If specific classes or patterns of
words are wished, the insertion of two extra characters expands the
options very considerably: @ = 1 letter; * = zero, or more letters;
e.g., *H (in transliteration) will yield all words ending in -η, or
η itself, while @H will yield all 2-letter words ending in -η; H@@,
all 3-letter words beginning with η-, etc. Another example of a
different nature: a request for πρ*ται will give all forms of any
length beginning with πρ- and ending -ται. The program may be
phrased to select a sample of the words requested, say, 1,000 occurrences of a form, with references, or to test a range of 1,000
words for any occurrence of the specified pattern. Fragmentary
words, or words within restorations, may be isolated by requesting
all words containing [or], or the words contained within them.

In the production of concordances, too, numerous options are
available. Key words may be sorted in Greek or Latin alphabetic
order by the beginning or ending of a word, by ascending or descending frequency, or by ascending or descending length. Contexts
may be arranged by alphabetic order to the right or the left of the
keyword, by references, or by the punctuation adjacent to the keyword. The amount of accompanying context may be defined by a number

of letters, words, or up to a specific character. The user may
specify the position of the keyword in the concordance relative to
the context, or in a word index relative to the references.

In short, the number of options available to the user of the
Oxford Concordance Project is more comprehensive at every stage
than in any other existing program of similar character, offering
the greatest degree of flexibility. It is also easy to employ, as
commands are in simple English, and may be used on any computer,
even by those with no particular knowledge of computer technology.
It will be of much help in completing the task at hand: the production of a clean text of the published *Oxyrhynchus Papyri*.

What then remains to be done? Numerals will need to be marked
off in these texts to avoid their useless incorporation in word
lists, as will words within restorations, affecting these same word
lists and statistics based on them. Personal and geographical
names, and the names of months, require distinction.

Other specialized matters remain for the future, the largest
being comprehensive lemmatization; marking off of homographs; analysis of syntactic function; and incorporation of scholarly conjectures and corrected orthography.

The Oxyrhynchus Computer Project is the result of the efforts
of many specialists. But even so many cannot foresee all questions
of importance to potential users. Those who have had experience
with similar projects, or who foresee some use in it for their own
work, or who are simply curious, are invited to comment and question. We welcome it. It is their interests which those who are
involved in this project hope to serve.

If any of you are interested in obtaining a sample of the
material nearest completion (volumes 46-44 at this writing), or in
further information concerning the availability of the Oxyrhynchus
Computer Project or the Oxford Concordance Project, or if you have
particular requests, I would ask you to write to me. I shall be
pleased to see that your inquiries reach the proper channels.

Oriental Institute   John E. Keefe
Pusey Lane, Oxford

PAPYROLOGICAL STUDIES IN GREECE

The main and only substantial collection of papyri in Greece is that of the Archaeological Society, published by George Petropoulos in 1939. Petropoulos was Professor of History of Roman Law at the University of Athens (Faculty of Law). Because of his profession and his special interests, he was in a position to pay more attention to the legal content of the papyri than to other subject matters, which were equally and even more interesting.

The papyri of this collection were partly bought by Dimitrios Papoulias for the Archaeological Society, and partly donated to the same society[1] by Dimophilos Chostevas in 1921. Both scholars had obtained the papyri from a Greek merchant residing in the Fayum. The society possessed also a small number of papyri, donated by N. Chaviaras who in collaboration with Antony Chadzis published four of them in 'Αρχαιολογικὴ 'Εφημερίς (1920) 72-75. The three of them were reprinted by Petropoulos in his edition (Nos. 31, 58 and 69), and again two of these three (Nos. 58 and 69) were published after an eyewitness inspection of the originals by George Parássoglou ('Ελληνικά 29 [1976] 56-59).

The society had also a Coptic papyrus which had been published by Chadzis, who was untutored in the Coptic language, in the same periodical in 1915 (pp. 30-31). This Coptic papyrus was reedited later by W. Crum.

Petropoulos published seventy papyri in all, but the collection contained additional items. Petropoulos chose the best preserved papyri and those with interesting content (i.e. with special attention, as I mentioned, to the legal, financial, and administrative topics in the papyrus texts).[2] The unpublished pieces of the

---

1 A preliminary paper on the papyri in possession of the Archaeological Society was presented by G. Petropoulos in the 5th International Congress of Papyrology at Brussels in 1938; see *Actes du Ve Congrès de papyrologie*, 337-43.

2 G. A. Petropoulos, *Papyri Societatis Archaeologicae Atheniensis* = Πάπυροι τῆς ἐν 'Αθήναις 'Αρχαιολογικῆς 'Εταιρείας (Athens 1939) [abbr. P. Athen.].

collection still await the attention of the papyrologists. Whoever will handle these remnants must bear in mind that their state of preservation is very bad, that decipherment will be difficult and in some cases impossible. In this, as in almost all collections of papyri, the best preserved texts were selected for publication by the fortunate scholar who undertook the "editio princeps." The rest must wait for someone else more skilful and patient, if not also wiser.

Petropoulos' edition was welcomed by papyrologists more or less with praise. Many of the papyri of this edition were corrected in reviews, and then used variously[3] because of their interesting content. All the published papyri have been photographed by J. Bingen, and the photographs are now deposited in the International Photographic Archive at Brussels.

Isolated Papyri in Greece

Apart from the above-mentioned collection of papyri there are some isolated papyri in several institutions in Greece.

1. National Library

In the Department of Manuscripts and Facsimiles of the National Library in Athens there are the following papyri:

EBE P1: A hieratic papyrus (The Book of the Dead, 0.34 x 0.28 m.) of the 3rd-2nd century B.C. Still unpublished.

EBE P3: A roll made up of four pieces of papyrus (list of daily expenses, 2.30 x 0.075 m.) of the 3rd century B.C. published by M. E. Egger in *JSav* ([1873] 30 and 93), and reedited by U. Wilcken in *UPZ* II 158A. The papyrus was first donated to the University of Athens in 1866 by Joseph Sakkakine; afterwards, it was

---

3 For particulars, see S. von Bolla, *Untersuchungen z. Tiermiete u. Viehpacht*,(Münch. Beitr. z. Pap. (1940) 77; B. A. van Groningen, *Museum* 47 (1940) 261; F. M. Heichelcheim, *JEA* 27 (1941) 177; M. Hombert, *Cd'E* 29 (1940) 163-64; S. Kapsomenos, *EEThess* 7 (1957) 357-58; H. Koskenniemi, *Studien zur Idee und Phraseologie des Griechischen Briefes bis 400 n. Chr.*, 132 and 163; S. Kougéas, ʽΕλληνικά 11 (1940) 335-50; W. Kunkel, *JSav* 61 (1941) 420; G. M. Parássoglou, "Miscellaneous Notes on Some PSA Athen.," ʽΕλληνικά 29 (1976) 47-60; C. Préaux, *Cd'E* 38 (1963) 130; W. Schubart, *Gnomon* 15 (1939) 639; P. Viereck, *Phil. Woch.* 60 (1940) 646-48; E. P. Wegener, *BL* III 219; U. Wilcken, *Archiv* 14 (1941) 158-62; H. C. Youtie, *TAPA* 71 (1940) 636 = *Scriptiunculae* I 76; H. C. Youtie-O. M. Pearl, *AJP* 63 (1942) 306-7.

given to the Archaeological Society which sent it to the National Library in 1902.[4]

EBE P4: A papyrus fragment (part of a letter, 0.11 x 0.08 m.) of the 6th century, of which only the end of the three last lines can be read.

] καλοῦμεν καὶ
]ερον ἵνα
]ν θέλετε

It was donated to the library by I. N. Svoronos in 1909.

EBE P5: A small fragment (0.055 x 0.05 m.) from a 6th century list or account which can be read:

]. Κολλουθο[
]τονουτικια
]ιος - -
]ου - - -

verso: τηϛαυτο[

It was donated to the library by I. N. Svoronos in 1909 together with the previous one.

EBE P6: A papyrus (part of a petition, 0.13 x 0.116 m.) of the 2nd century A.D. It was published by N. Chaviaras and S. Kougéas in 'Αρχαιολογικὴ 'Εφημερίς ([1913] 17-19) with a photograph at the end of the volume, and reedited by Fr. Bilabel in SB III 6002. It was donated to the Archaeological Society and subsequently in 1914 deposited in the library through the Ministry of Education.

EBE P7: A papyrus (receipt for the sale of a donkey, 0.138 x 0.89 m.) dated A.D. 179. The notice πλαστόν "forged(?)" appears in the library's register, made by the Director of this department, Dr. P. Nicolopoulos. The papyrus was published by N. Chaviaras and S. Kougéas in 'Αρχαιολογικὴ 'Εφημερίς ([1913] 17-19) with a photo-graph and reedited by Fr. Bilabel in SB III 6001.

EBE P8: A papyrus (0.165 x 0.225 m.) donated to the library by K. Kourouniotis in 1933 and characterized as Coptic(?). Again the

---

4 For details see E. Θόμψωνος-Σ. Λάμπρου, 'Εγχειρίδιον 'Ελλη-νικῆς καὶ Λατινικῆς Παλαιογραφίας (Athens 1903) 231-32 (n. 5); so also in UPZ II 158A. The papyrus was also published by E. Revillout in Rev. Eg. 3 (1885) 118ff.

indication πλαστόν "forged" occurs in the library's register; I
think that in both cases Dr. Nicolopoulos is correct.

2. National Museum in Athens

This institution possesses one papyrus which bears the date
252 B.C. and has been identified as part of Zenon's archive. It
was published by S. Kougéas in 'Ελληνικά 9 [[1937] 11-15) with a
photograph, and reedited by Fr. Bilabel and E. Kiessling in *SB* V 8244.

3. Historical Seminar Collection of the University of Athens
(Faculty of Philosophy)

Two Zenon papyri once in possession of this institution and
now lost. They were published by S. Kougéas in 'Ελληνικά 9 ([1937]
5-11) and reedited by Fr. Bilabel and E. Kiessling in *SB* V 8242,
8243 on the basis of the photographs. According to Kougéas, these
papyri were lost before he was able to undertake their publication
and he had to work from photographs. Although Kougéas stated in
'Ελληνικά 11 ([1940] 388) that "these papyri have now been found in
a drawer of the University and have already been placed, safe and
sound, in the Library of the History Department seminar," the
statement proved false. I have personally checked the records for
the collection belonging to the seminar from 1934, the point at
which the records begin, and I have found no mention of papyri.

4. Classical Seminar Collection of the Athens University (Faculty
of Philosophy)

This institution possesses two Ptolemaic papyri written on
both sides and two of the Roman period written only on the side
where the fibres run horizontally. To be precise:

(1) Inv. 2780 (A^r i)   : medical prescription by Mnason
              (A^r ii)   : medical prescription
              (A^v i)   : memorandum
              (A^v ii)   : memorandum
(2) Inv. 2781 (B^r i)   : medicines
              (B^r ii)   : medical prescription by Praxagoras
              (B^r iii) : medical prescription
              (B^r iv)   : medical prescription

	(B^V i)	: unpublished
	(B^V ii)	: unpublished
	(B^V iii)	: unpublished
	(B^V iv)	: memorandum
(3) Inv. 2782 (C)		: maxims
(4) Inv. 2783 (D)		: report

These papyri have been the subject of a doctoral dissertation
by M. Tsoucalas,[5] submitted to the University of Athens (Faculty of
Philosophy) in 1961. They had been given to him by a doctor and
friend who remained anonymous. Later Tsoucalas donated the papyri
to the Classical Seminar. Tsoucalas did not publish cols. i, ii
and iii on the verso of 2781 (B), but left them as material for
another study he hoped to do in the future. Tsoucalas' sudden
death last year put an end to his intention to edit the remaining
parts. I have assumed the task of their publication which will
appear, I hope, in the near future.

5. The Dervéni Papyrus

The Dervéni papyrus is a carbonized papyrus roll found in a
tomb during excavations conducted by the Greek Archaeological Service at Dervéni in 1962. The importance of this papyrus lies first
in the fact that it is the only papyrus to be discovered on the
Greek mainland and second in the fact that its script suggests it
is the oldest Greek manuscript now in existence. Of the whole roll
only twenty-two columns remain in a readable form, of which seven
columns[6] have been published *exempli gratia* by S. Kapsomenos in the
Ἀρχαιολογικὸν Δελτίον.[7] There are no comments in this preliminary
edition except for a few notes on palaeographical matters with an
introductory "commentary."[8] Obviously, Kapsomenos postponed the

---

5   M. Tsoucalas, Ἀνέκδοτοι φιλολογικοὶ καὶ ἰδιωτικοὶ πάπυροι
(diss.) (Athens 1962).

6   Cols. 14 (= 12 lines), 15 (= 10 lines), 17 (= 12 lines),
18 (= lines 7-11), 19 (= 10 lines), 20 (= 12 lines), 22 (= 12
lines).

7   19 (1964) 17-25 plus a two-page summary in English and
eight plates with very good photographs.

8   Basically the same text in English was presented by Kapsomenos at the Annual Meeting of 1964 of the American Society of

thorough examination of the papyrus roll, intending to prepare a
proper edition at a later date. Unfortunately neither Kapsomenos
nor his successor, Professor K. Tsantsanoglou, finished this work.
The papyrus roll has been deposited in the Archaeological Museum in
Thessaloniki in the room of the Dervéni finds.[9]

As can be seen from the data assembled above, the publication
of papyri in Greece has been the work of a very narrow circle of
scholars. That is why papyrology in Greece has taken the form of a
kind of exploitation and interpretation of the papyrus texts published outside Greece. Philologists as well as linguists have used
published papyri according to their own interests and their personal abilities. Literary papyri have been viewed with great expectations, as every classical scholar has from the start been aware
of the invaluable contribution they may make possible to classical
literature. Furthermore, papyri have been highly valued by Greek
scholars in Greece because of their lasting interest in research in
the Greek language.

Training in papyrology has been carried out in Greece under the
auspices of the chairs of classical literature: papyrology is taught
in the University of Yannina by Prof. M. Papathomopoulos, who follows the French School; in Thessaloniki by G. Parássoglou, pupil and
sometime collaborator of Prof. Naphtali Lewis; and in Athens by me.
My training in papyrology took place at Oxford under J.W.B. Barns
and Peter Parsons. I hasten to add that other scholars connected
with these universities deal with papyrology as well, though papyrology is not their main field.[10]

Papyrologists at the American Philosophical Society in Philadelphia,
Pennsylvania. The paper was published soon after the meeting in
BASP 2 (1964-65) 3-12. On pp. 15ff., the papyrus is discussed by
E. G. Turner, G. Daux, B. A. van Groningen, Cl. Préaux, C. B. Welles,
H. C. Youtie, Kurt von Fritz and others. See also P. Boyancé, "Re-
marques sur le papyrus de Dervéni," *REG* 87 (1974) 91-110; W. Burkert,
"La genèse des choses et des mots. Le papyrus de Dervéni entre Anaxa-
gore et Cratyle," *Etudes Philosophiques* (1970) 443-55; idem, "Orpheus
und die Vorsokratiker. Bemerkungen zum Dervéni-Papyrus und zur py-
thagoreischen Zahlenlehre," *Antike und Abendland* 14 (1968) 93-114.

9   In a recent visit to the Museum (August 1980), I did not
see the papyrus in its place; I was told that it had been removed
for preservation.

10   For example, M. Kokolakis and N. Livadaras in Athens,
Christina Dedoussi in Yannina, K. Tsantsanoglou in Thessaloniki,
N. Panayiotakis in Yannina and Crete and others.

There is no chair of papyrology in any of the universities in
Greece. Certain new chairs, recently founded as a result of the
educational reforms since 1975 are of limited scope and secondary
significance in general. In any case, the fact is that no further
thought has been expressed in favour of papyrology nor are there
any plans to promote this field through chairs which could combine
papyrology with palaeography and/or epigraphy and/or Hellenistic
literature. My personal efforts in this direction were met with
unjustifiably negative reaction. My proposal was finally rejected
with the ready and superficial answer: "there are no papyri in
Greece."

Fortunately for the future of this field there is a chair on
the list of chairs to be established at the newly founded University of Crete. The Organizing Committee of the University in Crete
succeeded in adding it to the list of projected needs of that university for the near future to provide for the enrichment of studies in classical literature and the ancient world in general. The
protagonist in this move has been Prof. Nikos Panayiotakis, a byzantinist, who has devoted much time and research to the field of
palaeography, and consequently is fully aware of the benefits of
papyrology.

Greek papyrologists may be classified into the following
groups: (1) Classical philologists--this is the largest group of
scholars dealing with classical and Hellenistic literature. They
work on topics provided by excavated papyri. A number of doctoral
dissertations have been written in this field by Greek scholars
either in Greece or abroad. (2) Members of the legal profession--
they deal mainly with the history of Greek and Roman law, which is
the reason why they all have some connection with the faculties of
law, especially with the chair of Roman law. Some of them are well
known abroad, and have occasionally edited papyri, as is the case
of G. Petropoulos. (3) Linguists--they are interested in the history of the Greek language, or the form and function of that language during the period of papyri. Their studies and research on
these topics have yielded results of substantial assistance to the
editors of papyri. (4) Historians--they have benefited from the
historical data found in papyri, with considerable advantage to
their research. This is a relatively small group. (5) Theologians--

they are confined to the faculty of theology, and deal with the
history and interpretation of the NT. In both Athens and Thessaloniki, the scholars of this group who are connected with papyrology are preeminently concerned with NT studies.

In conclusion, I may say that papyrological studies in Greece
consist of a sustained effort to draw information from edited papyri about classical literature, Greek language, life in antiquity,
Greek and Roman law, NT studies; we study to understand these
branches of knowledge in a fuller way than that available to previous generations.

There is a promising sign for the future of papyrology in
Greece, and I am privileged to announce it here. Professor Giuseppe
Giangrande of the University of London has provided the impetus for
the formation of a group of Greek papyrologists from all universities in Greece with the following goals: to coordinate the various
activities connected with papyrology, to inspire the study of papyri and to recruit young people to papyrology, to publish an annual
journal entitled Παπυρολογικὴ Ἐφημερίς. Giangrande's plan has already been accepted by Greek scholars with enthusiasm, and is expected to materialize soon. This development, I think, will prove
to be a substantial contribution to the future of papyrological
studies in Greece as well as outside this country.

University of Athens   Basil G. Mandilaras

Addendum: A chair of papyrology was established in the Faculty of
    Philosophy at the University of Athens in 1910, but was not
    filled for reasons of economy. Seventy years later a chair of
    papyrology was created in the new University of Crete, but it
    has not yet been advertised.

Proceedings of the XVI Int. Congr. of Papyrology (Chico 1981) 699-706

HOLOCAUST, TWO MILLENNIA AGO

The present essay may differ a little from the usual dogmatic
or descriptive discussion. This is due only to the fact that the
method employed is one which guides the researcher from the mere
surface of the phenomena to their inner essence.[1]

Aside from this, attention needs to be drawn to two books:
the first was published by Hannah Arendt in New York two decades
ago (1961) under the title *Between Past and Present*. The book received a very kind reception. In the introduction, the author
quoted two Frenchmen, Alexis de Tocqueville and René Char, to
underpin her notion that "the past ceased to throw its light on
the present and the future." As a result, the past is not in a
position to teach us anything further and, she says, we are obliged
to make an entirely new beginning, exclusively on the basis of our
own experience. The second book appeared six years ago, published
in the same city: Kurt von Fritz's *The Relevance of Ancient Social
and Political Philosophy for our Times* (1974) replied directly to
Arendt's argument. His ideas are worthy of attention and appreciation, but we must be content here with merely this modest reference
to them.

I. Let us have a brief look at the scene of the events first.

Alexandria, founded in 322 B.C. by Alexander the Great, became
under the Ptolemies not only the metropolis of Egypt, but also the
most important economic and cultural center of the Hellenistic
world. More than half a million inhabitants lived there in the
first century B.C. At her apogee, Alexandria shared all Egypt's
fate, occupation by Rome. Nonetheless, her position of importance
did not suffer. The Romans respected the privileged status of the
Greeks, as the Ptolemies had done formerly, and they likewise dis-
dained the native Egyptians. Between these two large groups of

---

1 Only some of the pertinent works and articles can be cited
here, because of the limitations of space; for more information,
cf. J. Modrzejewski, *APF* 26 (1978) 193ff. As for the question of
methodology, see A. Poláček, *Reality--A Challenge* (Kiel 1979).

inhabitants, the Greeks and the Egyptians, there was, and had been
for a long time, sufficient space for a special group within the
population, the Jews.

Their social status is debatable. Some scholars infer from
the documents preserved that rich Jews constituted only a small
stratum among their fellow-countrymen.[2] This is certainly true,
but not only in this instance: the rich have always constituted
merely a small segment of every community, regardless of size. Experience has shown that some peoples, and certain nations, had, and
have, a particular propensity and ability to make money. It is only
historical fact that both Jews and Greeks have always been successful in this respect.

Success, and particularly material success, has very often been
a source of envy as well. Other common causes of spitefulness in
human society arise, e.g., from the behavior of an individual or of
a group.

Jews have always represented (and continue to represent) a
particularly cohesive ethnic group, bound together by their religious ties. Solidarity of such a kind deserves respect, but it
sometimes happens that this cohesiveness is misconceived by out-
siders. Man often reacts in a hostile manner when someone else
dissociates himself from the larger social group, or exhibits an
air of real or assumed superiority and exclusiveness. Religion is
one of the areas which are unfortunately stigmatized by intoler-
ance, especially when the followers or the adversaries acknowledge
or defend their own religion and their own ideology to the exclu-
sion of other beliefs and points of view. The situation in Alexandria in the early Roman period was overshadowed by these and other
ominous features.[3]

---

2 Cf. V. A. Tscherikover and A. Fuks, *C. P. Jud.* II, Introduction to section VII, p. 3 and the papyri, nos. 142, 145, 152;
see also, e.g., L. Poliakov, *The History of Anti-Semitism* (London
1974) 5f.; J. N. Sevenster, *The Roots of Pagan Anti-Semitism in the
Ancient World* (Leiden 1975) 57ff. Already in 1914, J. Juster, *Les
Juifs dans l'Empire romain* (Paris 1914) II, 265ff., had presented
a large documentation about the wealth of the Alexandrian Jews.

3 Cf. also Poliakov, loc. cit., 7ff.; Sevenster, loc. cit.,
89ff., 163; O. Montevecchi, *Aspetti dell' opinione pubblica nel
mondo antico* (Milano 1978) 85ff.; *C. P. Jud.* 152.

In the so-called "Boule Papyrus," dating probably from the
years 20/19 B.C., an Alexandrian spokesman expresses the desire of
his Greek fellow-citizens to keep their ethnic community undefiled
by any foreign influence (*C. P. Jud.* 150). Jews are not explicitly
named, yet the admonition that the Greeks should guard themselves
against any destructive ideas from outside was undoubtedly directed
against the Jews. The Egyptians were far from being able to threa-
ten the cultural and ethnic integrity of the Greek community.
Further, the Romans, as occupiers, were not in a position to win
over the Greeks: on the contrary, the Greeks eventually produced a
party of "Greek," i.e. anti-Roman, nationalists. The Jews, on the
other hand, at once sided with the conquerors, and the Romans knew
how to demonstrate their appreciation for this. They respected the
privileges the Jews possessed in the past and they respected their
institutions and synagogues.

The Greeks, in possession of Alexandrian citizenship, had
further privileges: they were exempt from the provincial poll-tax
which other inhabitants, the Jews included, were required to pay.
Historical documents give evidence that the Jews, both as individuals and as a community, were worried about this discrimination.[4]

There is no superabundance of documents about the existence of
animosity against the Jews in ancient Egypt. Facts generally known
and personal feelings have seldom been the subject of daily discussion. They are, however, constantly present, and concrete expression of such assumptions and feelings appear, whenever there was,
or is, a serious impulse to it. Cato's slogan about Carthage and
Seianus' plan to extirpate all Jews are eloquent examples.[5]

II. Since 32 A.D. the prefect of Alexandria and Egypt was
Aulus Avilius Flaccus (Phil., *In Flacc.* 1 ff.). He was on good
terms with the Emperor Tiberius. The subsequent accession of Gaius
Caligula in March, 37 A.D., considerably endangered his position.
The fate of several previously influential men in Rome induced him,
according to Philo, to accept a proposal from the anti-Semitic
party in Alexandria: the Greeks suggested that if Flaccus gave them

---

4   Tscherikover-Fuks, *C. P. Jud.* I p. 61 and II pp. 29ff.

5   Cf. Philo, *In Flaccum* 1, *Legatio ad Gaium* 160. Cf. also
Euseb., *E.h.* II.5.

support, they and the city as a whole would stand by him and protect him against the hostility of the Emperor (21ff.).

This may be true, but is not an absolute necessity. It does
not explain, e.g., why Flaccus did not support the demands of the
Jews who obviously enjoyed the Emperor's favor--unless we are here
dealing with one of those irrational decisions which sometimes are
made in the course of history.

III. Something similar should be said about the Jews. For a
long time, neither Philo nor other Jewish leaders drew practical
conclusions from the ominous signs of impending disaster or took
safety measures against them.

The situation came to a head on the occasion of the visit of
Herod Agrippa to Alexandria early in summer, 38 A.D. The Alexandrian Greeks obviously resented the recent appointment to kingship
of a Jew, previously known in the city as a playboy whose pockets
were constantly empty, and they ridiculed him publicly in a defama-
tory fashion (Philo, loc. cit. 36ff.). Then, perhaps because they realized that they had insulted an imperial favorite, they were quick
to show their devotion to the Emperor and they invited Flaccus to
set up images of Caligula in the synagogues. The Jews protested,
of course. Flaccus reacted immediately: he issued an edict (πρόγραμμα) in which he designated the Jews among others as "foreigners
and aliens" (ξένους καὶ ἐπήλυδας).[6] The question should be left
open as to whether he acted of his own accord, or at the instance
of some sworn enemies of the Jews. Even so, the edict could be,
and certainly was, understood not only as an accusation that the
Jews were opposed to the Emperor and that they had assumed unjustified privileges, but also as a signal to the non-Jewish population
that the Jews stood outside the protection of the law.

The consequence of this, the disastrous pogrom, was not slow
in coming.

There were five quarters in Alexandria at that time. The Jews

---

6 In the preceding paragraph (53), the reader is told that
Flaccus had also pillaged the synagogues. In *Legatio ad Gaium*, the
events are presented in a different sequence (sections 120-131,
events of the pogrom, 132 and 134, destruction and burning of synagogues [!]). It is difficult to reconstruct the precise course of
the events, but the date of the plundering is known; see below n. 8.

were expelled by the mob from four of the quarters and were compelled to immigrate to one quarter in the Delta area which was to
be exclusively Jewish (Philo, *In Flacc.* 55). Philo describes the
events as follows:[7]

> (56) The Jews were so numerous that they poured over
> beaches, dunghills and tombs, robbed of all their belong-
> ings. Their enemies overran the houses now left empty
> and turned to pillaging them, distributing the contents
> like spoils of war, and as no one prevented them they
> broke open the workshops of the Jews which had been
> closed as a sign of mourning for Drusilla,[8] carried out
> all the articles they found, which were very numerous,
> and bore them through the middle of the market-place,
> dealing with other people's property as freely as if it
> were their own. (57) ...The tradespeople had lost their
> stocks, and no one, husband, shipman, merchant, artisan,
> was allowed to practise his usual business. Thus poverty
> was established....[9]

---

7   The translation of F. H. Colson (Cambridge, MA 1960, LCL)
has been used here.

8   Drusilla, Caligula's sister, died on June 10, 38 A.D.; cf.
also Suetonius, *Gaius* 24.1.

9   Also *Legatio* 123: "the rich became poor...."! As L. Koenen
points out, this sentence (and other statements in Philo's report)
seems to be colored by allusion to classical topoi of Egyptian descriptions of national catastrophes and chaotic times (e.g. *Prophecy of Neferyt* 50: "its [sc. Egypt's] servants are rich" [thus in
the translation of H. Goedicke, *The Protocol of Neferyt* (Johns Hopkins Near Eastern Studies, Baltimore and London 1977) 112ff.] and
55, "The poor man will make wealth" [A. Wilson in *ANET*[3] 445; W.
Helck, *Die Prophezeiung des* Nfr.tj (Kl. Ägypt. Texte, Wiesbaden
1970) 48: "Arme werden sehr Schätze erwerben"; P. G. Posener, *Littérature et politique dans l'Egypte de la XII dynastie* (Paris 1956)
143; for a different translation, see Goedicke, 120 and his note
364]; *Admonitions of Ipuwer* VII, "Behold, the owners of robes are
now in rags...," IX, "Behold, nobles' ladies are growing hungry..."
[*ANET*, 442]). Such descriptions of the reversal of the social order were still used in Ptolemaic and Roman times for the purpose
of political propaganda (cf. *The Oracle of the Potter*, as edited by
L. Koenen in *ZPE* 2 [1968] 178ff. and 13 [1974] 313ff. [see particularly P3 36ff.; cf. Koenen in *Proc. of the XII Intern. Congress of
Pap.* (Am. Stud. Pap. 7, Toronto 1970) 249ff.; F. Dunand in *L'apoca-
lyptique* (Et. d'hist. des rel. 3, Paris) 41ff.] and the anti-Jewish
prophecy of *PSI* 982 [*C.P.Jud.* III 520]). The defamation of the
Jews as ξένοι καὶ ἐπήλυδες in Philo's report (see above) points
toward the same traditions, though from the Greek point of view.
Since prophecies of this type end with the renewal of good times
under a new ruler, the allusions to the traditional descriptions
of chaos imply hope (see the following remarks above) and are of

(58) Unbearable though these things were, yet compared with subsequent actions they were tolerable....

Philo digressed at this point to depict the deeds of conquerors in war; he soon returned to his main topic by saying:

(62) Let us see what was done in peace by our friends
of yesterday. After the pillaging and eviction and violent expulsion from most parts of the city, the Jews were
like beleaguered men with their enemies round them. They
were pressed by want and dire lack of necessities; they
saw their infant children and women perishing before their
eyes through a famine artificially created.... (64) Unable any longer to endure their privation, some of them
contrary to their former habits went to the houses of
their kinsmen and friends to ask for the mere necessities
as a charity.... (65) ...They were at once seized by
those who wielded the weapon of mob rule, treacherously
stabbed, dragged through the whole city, and trampled
on.... (66) ...Any Jews who showed themselves anywhere,
they stoned or knocked about with clubs.... (68) ...Whole
families...were burnt in the heart of the city by these
...ruthless men who showed no pity for old age nor youth,
nor the innocent years of childhood....

It has been necessary to quote a part of Philo's report in
detail in order to present a vivid picture of the events. An abstract says little, by comparison, and the reader gets from it only
a superficial, hazy impression at best.

The subsequent events will be presented in condensed form: on
the orders of Flaccus, thirty-eight prominent Jews were arrested
and then flogged in public;[10] the houses of the Jews were ransacked
in a search for hidden weapons (which proved not even to exist);
Jewish women were maltreated, etc. In short: if we were not explicitly told that the story happened in ancient Egypt, nearly two
millennia ago, and if we had not mentioned the places and names of
the known participants, we would surely be at a loss about the date
and the site of these events. Times out of number, the history of
humanity has been polluted by acts of cruelty, mocking all noble
commandments about human rights.

---

political significance. On the other hand, the use of these traditional colors does not imply that Philo's description is historically false. Cf. also L. Koenen, *Gnomon* 40 (1968) 254 on *P. Lond.* 1912
(on this document, see below).

10 The Jewish Council of Alexandria numbered 71 members.
Nearly half of them obviously took the only life-saving step available to them: they absconded at the last moment.

Fortune, or favorable conjuncture, or, as the Jews themselves maintained, the special Providence of God did not abandon them (Philo, *In Flacc.* 121ff., 191). Flaccus, long suspected by the Emperor, was now charged by Herod Agrippa with improper behavior against the Emperor, for Flaccus had suppressed the congratulatory letter sent by the Jews to Caligula. He was arrested, his property confiscated; he himself was sentenced to deportation and later, to death. No wonder that the Jews welcomed Flaccus' fall with boundless joy. Instructive is the reaction of the Greeks: they did nothing on Flaccus' behalf. On the contrary, they sent a delegation to Rome to complain...about Flaccus. Two of their demagogues, Isidorus and Lampon, were members of the commission (Philo, loc. cit., 125ff.).

A Jewish delegation also appeared in Rome. The negotiations with the imperial court and the Emperor were unsuccessful, but an armistice between the two opposing parties endured until the accession of Claudius in 41 A.D.

IV. The Jews seem to have brooded on vengeance in the meantime. We possess little information about the riots which took place, but an official document, the well-known *P. Lond.* 1912, speaks for itself.[11] In the third part of his letter to the Alexandrian Greeks, the Emperor Claudius warns the parties as follows (lines 73ff.):

> With regard to the responsibility for the disturbances and rioting, or rather, to speak the truth, the war against the Jews...I have not wished to make an exact inquiry, but I harbour within me a store of immutable indignation against those who renewed the conflict. I merely say that, unless you stop this destructive and obstinate mutual enmity, I shall be forced to show what a benevolent ruler can be when he is turned to righteous indignation.

Then Claudius ordered the Alexandrian Greeks to behave gently and kindly towards the Jews, for both were inhabitants of the same city. The Jews, on the other hand, were ordered not to aim at more than they had previously possessed, since they enjoyed an abundance of all good things in a city which was not their own.

---

11   *C.P.Jud.* II 153, with literature. Vague intimation about the vengeance of the Jews: *C.P.Jud.* II 153.73f.; Josephus, *Ant. Jud.* XIX 278f.

It stands to reason that this document, as well as others
which relate to these events, are able to raise further problems,
such as the question, repeatedly discussed in the literature,
whether the Alexandrian Jews actually possessed Alexandrian citizenship or not, and the question whether the Emperor and/or the
prefect were personally the authors of these documents, or were
their letters and decrees the work of counselors or secretaries
instead.[12] These and questions of a similar nature lie outside
the focus of this paper.

V. The following conclusions may, I believe, be drawn from
the material presented above and the observations made about that
material. It is possible to regard these events as a mere chapter
in history, as an account, as a story from times long past. A more
attentive reading of this material shows, among other things, that
many a modern phenomenon has its counterpart in events of the past.
Further, these "modern" events have often come about because none
of the participants was willing or capable of responding to the
warnings offered by the past. And this statement returns us to
the warring points of view found in Arendt and von Fritz which were
aired at the beginning of this essay.

Both papyrology and ancient history, fields which seem to be
reserved for a small group of initiated specialists, can present
interesting and useful information about the past, as well as warnings to contemporary society. A more detailed analysis would, I
believe, reveal in what ways the events of the years 38 and 1938
A.D. were identical, in what ways they differed, and would suggest
reasons for the differences. Events which are separated by two
thousand years can be juxtaposed with profit, and the comparison
can highlight not only a time long past, but also the recent past
and the present.

This essay is only a modest attempt, but it was undertaken in
the hope and fervent wish that the approach used here may attract
others and may find in them more influential pioneers.

Kiel   Adalbert Poláček

---

12 Cf. e.g. Tscherikover-Fuks, loc. cit. (see n. 4) II, 38.